A Journey through the Slave States of North America

Sale of Estate, Pictures and Slaves in the Rotunda, New Orleans

A Journey through the Slave States of North America

J.S. Buckingham

Charleston   London

the
History
PRESS

First published 1842
Copyright © in this edition 2006
Nonsuch Publishing Limited

Published in the United Kingdom by:
Nonsuch Publishing Limited
The Mill, Brimscombe Port, Stroud, Gloucestershire, GL5 2QG
www.nonsuch-publishing.com

Published in the United States of America by:
The History Press
18 Percy Street, Charleston, South Carolina 29403
www.historypress.net

British Library Cataloguing in Publication Data.
A catalogue record for this book is available from the British Library.

ISBN 1-84588-045-5 (UK)
ISBN 1-59629-124-9 (USA)

Typesetting and origination by Nonsuch Publishing Limited
Printed in Great Britain by Oaklands Book Services Limited

CONTENTS

INTRODUCTION TO THE MODERN EDITION

> I have endeavoured to describe the State of Slavery in the Southern States
> ... I expect my full share of censure from a large section, at least, of the
> people of America, for daring to speak, as truth compels me to do, of
> the wretched condition of the great body of the African race throughout
> the South; and of the reckless indifference to human life and human
> obligations of every kind, which the very system of Slavery engenders in
> nearly all the white population who live beneath its influence.

By 1842, when James Silk Buckingham was writing an account of his journey through the southern states of North America, entitled *The Slave States of America*, slavery was a contentious and problematic issue for the relatively new country of the United States. After gaining its independence from the United Kingdom in 1781, debate had been growing over about the morality of slavery. By 1800 a number of the northern states had abolished slavery and, with the Northwest Ordinance of 1787, which provided the means for creating new states in the western lands for admission into the Union, the federal Congress prohibited the spread of this institution into the vast territory north of the Ohio River. However, during the same period the southern states were winning concessions from the legislators which would protect what they saw as their inherent right to own slaves, including the fugitive slave law of 1793, allowing runaway slaves to be detained for return to their owners across state lines, and the continuation of slave trading with Africa until 1808. Most importantly, perhaps, was the Three-Fifths Clause, which classified slaves as three-fifths of a person, and, since representation in government was apportioned according to numbers, led to the domination of the Electoral College and hence Congress by the slave-owning states, preventing major changes in national policy until the time of the Civil War.

By 1839, when Buckingham was beginning his tour of the southern states, slavery was as prevalent as ever in the region. One of the largest products of these states was cotton, which required a massive amount of man-power to cultivate effectively. Furthermore, in 1793 the cotton gin, invented by Eli Whitney, (a machine which removed seeds and rubbish from the short-staple cotton which up to this time was combed by hand) greatly increased the amount of cotton that could be produced daily and, as a result, the slave population which worked in the cotton fields rose dramatically, from 697,897 in 1790 to over 4 million by 1860 in the states of Alabama, Mississippi and Arkansas alone. Both Mississippi and South Carolina had a larger slave than free population.

Moreover, the laws governing the treatment of slaves were harsh and unforgiving. The slave was the property of the owner, with not even the most basic of human rights. When the importation of slaves was legally prohibited, the slave owners encouraged their existing slaves to have children, and any children born to a slave woman, whether the father was another slave or free, belonged to the owner of the mother. Disobedience was punished with brutal force, the most common punishment being whipping, but other permissible methods included branding, beating and mutilation of the body, such as clipping the ears and slitting tongues.

It is unsurprising that such harsh and unforgiving treatment of any human being was abhorrent to Buckingham, and that he chose to make it the main topic of his account of the southern states of America. Buckingham himself was noted for his espousal of social reforms whilst serving in the British Parliament as the Member for Sheffield, such as the attempt to outlaw flogging in the navy. Furthermore the United Kingdom had outlawed the slave trade in 1807 and completely abolished slavery throughout the British Empire with the passing of the Abolition of Slavery Act by both Houses of Parliament in 1833. Although the abolitionist movement was growing in the northern states in America, it was to take more than thirty years and a Civil War before the USA would follow suit. Finally, in 1865, the Thirteenth Amendment to the Constitution was ratified and proclaimed to be in effect, abolishing slavery in the 27 states of the United States.

In *A Journey through the Slave States of North America*, an abridged version of his original two-volume account published in 1842, Buckingham effectively exposes the cruelties inherent in the system of slavery in the southern states, as well as the hypocrisy of slave owners, who insist their slaves are happy, but admit to having a serious problem with runaways. However, this book is much more than simply a criticism of slavery in America. The author also provides a compelling view of the people and places he visits, and finds as much to praise as to condemn in a country made up of diverse and multifarious elements.

CHAPTER I

On Friday, the 11th of January, 1839, we embarked at New York, on board the packet-ship, Calhoun, for Charleston in South Carolina. The distance of this city from New York by land exceeds 700 miles; and as the bad state of the roads through the latter part of the route makes land-travelling disagreeable during the winter months, we were induced to prefer the sea voyage, though this also has its inconveniences at this season of the year. The ship in which we had taken our passage was 275 tons burthen, and had her cabins and dining-room under a poop-deck; two of these cabins, with double berths in each, and separate accommodation for a man-servant, were assigned to us for 90 dollars passage-money.

We hauled off from the wharf about eleven o'clock, and were towed down by a steam-vessel as far as the Narrows, (the usual charge for the hire of such steam-vessels being ten dollars an hour,) where we began to make sail. This was, however, a work of some difficulty, as the crew were all intoxicated; some, indeed, were so drunk as to be wholly unfit for duty, and all were in a state of confusion and insubordination. The captain was obliged to assume a rigorous exercise of authority to prevent a mutiny; and the greater part of the actual labour devolved upon his mates and himself. I learnt from the pilot that for years past it had been a rare case for a ship to sail from the harbour of New York, without the greater number of the crew being drunk; and he thought that this evil had increased rather than diminished of late,

The system of shipping seamen here is like that of nearly all the seaports of England and America. A set of worthless and abandoned men, who keep boarding-houses and grog-shops combined, lie in wait about the wharfs and docks for the sailors as they arrive in port; when, by various arts and insinuations, they prevail upon them to bring their chests and hammocks to their houses, where, in a very short time after landing, they are plied with liquor till they become insensible of all that is passing around them. They are then put to bed, and most probably robbed of all their hard-earned wages, the reward of a toilsome and perilous voyage: or, if not directly robbed of it by the landlord, it is soon dissipated in cards, women, and drink, the largest portion of it finding its way into the landlord's pocket. Thus destitute, they are kept by these harpies until some ship requires hands: and then, with a bill of several dollars run up against each, for maintenance and supplies, at a most extravagant rate, they are handed over, in a state of intoxication, to the ship requiring them, The advance of wages which ought to be appropriated to the purchase of clothes and other necessaries for the seaman's voyage, is then taken by the landlord for the payment of his demands, while the plundered victim of his villany and avarice goes to sea perfectly unprovided for; often, indeed, without a second shirt or jacket to shift in wet weather, and wholly without the ordinary necessaries of a seaman's life.

As we beat out through the Narrows, with a fine breeze that had just sprung up from the south-west, the harbour and city of New York appeared to us quite as beautiful as when we first entered it, upwards of a year ago, from sea. The forest of ships' masts, and the number of flags and signals waving from them, as they fringed the shores of the city, which we were fast leaving behind us, on the Hudson and the East River sides, with the Battery and Castle Gardens in the centre: the forts on Governor's Island and Bedlow's Island, the heights of Brooklyn, the town of Brighton, and the beautiful villas on Staten Island, all appeared, in the brightest sunshine, and beneath a cloudless and deep-blue sky, more beautiful than I could have thought possible at this wintry season of the year; and we enjoyed the prospect exceedingly.

The passage out through the Narrows, from the Bay of New York to the sea, is among the finest pictures of marine scenery that can be imagined. The hills on both sides are thickly studded with mansions, villas, hotels, and other buildings, many of them with porticos and pediments like Grecian temples; and these being of the purest white, they look like Parian marble from the sea: while the blue waters of the Atlantic, seen through the opening of the Narrows in the distance, affords a pleasing contrast, and makes up a picture of great beauty.

Our voyage to Charleston occupied nearly seven days, as we did not arrive there till late on the night of the 17th, though the passage is often effected in three days; and taking it altogether, it was one of the most disagreeable passages I ever remember to have experienced. The ship was unobjectionable, as she sailed well, was an excellent sea-boat, and performed all her evolutions with ease and safety. The captain, however, though a good seaman, and very vigilant and attentive to the navigation of the ship, appeared to feel no more concern for the comfort of his passengers, than if they had been so many head of cattle that he was transporting from one port to another. He never once sat at table with us, having his meals either sent on deck, or taken to him in the steward's pantry: and he never once took off his clothes, or went to bed, during the whole passage, lying on the hen-coops on the poop, or on a bench in the cabin. The mate was just as rough and unpolished a being as the captain, and quite as careless about the cleanliness of his person and apparel. The passengers had not one redeeming quality that we could discover, but were uniformly low, vulgar, ignorant, and dissipated men. Their constant occupation, from immediately after breakfast till near midnight, with the intervention of meals only, was playing at cards and dominos on the cabin table, or smoking cigars on the deck. The wind being foul for the greater part of the way, and the cold and damp atmosphere rendering the deck unattractive, these men remained in the cabin all day, sitting around the stove. This so completely destroyed all privacy, that we were never alone but when in bed, and even then we were perpetually disturbed by their gambling and vociferation; so that our only refuge, and that a most imperfect one, was to shut ourselves within our sleeping-berths, and read through the tedious and weary day, which seemed twice its ordinary length.

On passing round Cape Hatteras, which lies about midway on the coast between New York and Charleston, we experienced the usual weather commonly found off that projection, in thunder, lightning, and heavy rains. We had heard no such rains, indeed, since we were in Bengal, when the heavy setting in or breaking up of the monsoon deluges the earth; and these were to the full as violent. We approached the shoal off Cape Hatteras as near as seven fathoms, and had a most turbulent swell and long-ranging sea, with a mist arising from the water (its temperature being 64° while that of the atmosphere was only 42°) which was driven across its surface like steam from a boiling cauldron, and made it often difficult to see the water itself more than a few feet from the ship, though the air above was perfectly free from fog.

On the 6th day at noon we hauled in for Charleston, and soon obtained a pilot; but as the state of the tide was unfavourable for our crossing the bar, we had to wait on the outside, lying to, under easy sail, until four P.M. when we stood in for the entrance, with a light wind from the north-east.

The greatest depth over the bar at spring-tides is 16 feet at high-water, and 10 feet at low. As our vessel drew 12 feet, we were enabled to pass over it at half-flood; but two larger vessels, the Isabella of Greenock, and the Jesse Logan of Liverpool, were obliged to anchor in the offing all night, for want of sufficient water during daylight to take them in.

The entrance to Charleston has nothing of the grandeur that characterizes the bay and harbour of New York, though the appearance of the city is interesting.

The bar is difficult, from the channel over it being so narrow; the passage is well buoyed, however, on both sides; and, with the light-house and several landmarks near it, the navigation is easy and safe. The shores all around the entrance are low and sandy, with wood and cotton plantations, and are entirely destitute of picturesque beauty.

It was on Thursday night that we arrived in Charleston, and I devoted the two following days to the delivery of the numerous letters of introduction with which I had been furnished by friends at Boston, New York, Philadelphia, and Washington, to resident families at this place. By all parties I was received with a great degree of cordiality and kindness, and nearly all of them took the earliest opportunity to wait on us at the hotel.

We remained at Charleston for three weeks; and during that period I enjoyed frequent opportunities of friendly intercourse with many of its most distinguished and intelligent inhabitants, and obtained access through them to everything I wished to see, and to all the information I desired to obtain. My lectures on Egypt and Palestine, which were first given in the Hall of the Medical College, and then in the First Presbyterian Church, were attended with audiences exceeding a thousand in number, and our stay was rendered as agreeable and instructive as possible. Before entering, however, upon a description of Charleston, it may be well to give a brief sketch of the past history and present condition of South Carolina as a State.

Chapter II

The early history of the territory now occupied by the States of North and South Carolina, is not so accurately recorded, or so fully detailed, as the histories of the more Northern States, but sufficient is known of it, to form a narrative of some interest. It appears that so early as the year 1512, the Spaniards set up their claim to nearly all the territory south of Virginia; contending that Sebastian Cabot, the Venetian navigator in the service of the English, had never advanced farther south than the Capes of the Chesapeake; whereas, in that year, 1512, a Spanish officer, named Ponce de Leon, then governor of Porto Rico, landed on its shores. The object of his voyage was indeed a curious one, as it is described by the Spanish historians, to have been undertaken in quest of a land, which was reported to contain a brook, or fountain, endued with the miraculous power of restoring age and decrepitude to the bloom and vigour of youth. Believing that he had now attained the favoured region, he hastened to take possession, in his sovereign's name, of so rare and valuable an acquisition. He bestowed on it the name of Florida, (a name now confined to the southern portion of the whole coast,) either on account of the vernal beauty that adorned its surface, or because he discovered it on the Sunday before Easter, which the Spaniards call "Pasque de Flores;" but though he chilled his aged frame by bathing in every stream that he could find, he had the mortification of returning an older instead of a younger man to Porto Rico. No settlement was, therefore, effected in the country by this expedition.

It was in 1562 that the first two vessels containing the Protestant refugees were despatched from France; and these arriving at the mouth of the Albemarle River, or Sound, landed there, when, in honour of their sovereign, Charles the Ninth, they called the country Carolina. In 1564, these were followed by three other ships, bearing more of the unfortunate Huguenots, as the French Protestants were called, and these were speedily followed by a still larger squadron; the king of France having countenanced and assisted these emigrants to leave their native shores, as Charles had done with the Puritans in England. Their fate, however, was far more unhappy than that of the New England Pilgrims; for scarcely had they begun to realize some of the benefits of their new abode, before they were attacked by the Spaniards; and when they had surrendered as Frenchmen, they were all put to death as heretics! a placard being affixed at the place of execution, announcing that "the captives were not put to the sword as subjects of France, but as followers of Luther!" Nearly a thousand French Protestants were thus put to death; and only one of their whole number was allowed to live, in order that he might carry intelligence of the massacre to France.

The French monarch, though he had assisted the emigration of the exiles, did not feel a sufficient interest about their fate to take any steps, on this intelligence; but a French nobleman, De Gorgues, indignant at such treachery and inhumanity, fitted out three ships at his own expense, and sailed for Carolina, where he attacked the unsuspecting occupants; and obtaining the co-operation of the Indians, he overpowered and put to death all the Catholics, who offered any resistance, and hung up those whom he made prisoners, on the nearest trees, announcing, after the manner of the first murderers, the cause of the massacre, by a placard exhibited at the place of execution, which stated that "the captives were not put to death as Spaniards, but as murderers and robbers." Having thus accomplished his purpose, he razed the forts to the ground, and, destroying every habitation, he left the country, and returned to France.

In 1588, Sir Walter Raleigh established his first settlement on the Isle of Roanoak, in Albemarle Sound, and the name of the whole country was changed from Carolina to Virginia. In 1622 some English planters and their families settled here, as refugees from other parts of North America, especially from Massachusetts. At this time, Charles the First granted to his attorney-general, Sir Robert Heath, a patent of the whole region, under the new name of Carolina; but this was subsequently forfeited, by his not performing the conditions annexed to the grant.

It was not until 1663, and after many unsuccessful attempts to colonize this territory, that a charter was obtained for its possession and government, of Charles the Second, in a remarkable manner. Some of his courtiers, to whom he had been most indebted for his restoration, presented to him a memorial, representing to him "their earnest desire to promote the propagation of the gospel, and desiring for this purpose the royal grant of some part of America not yet settled or planted, and where there were only such barbarous people as had no knowledge of God." On this pretence, the whole region, from lat. 36° north, about Albemarle Sound, a little to the north of Cape Hatteras, all the way to the river St. Matheo, was erected into a province, under the name of Carolina, and granted to the following persons:—Lord Chancellor Clarendon; Monk, Duke of Albemarle; Lord Craven; Lord Berkeley; Lord Ashley (afterwards Earl of Shaftesbury); Sir George Carteret; Sir John Colleton and Sir William Berkeley. By these, a joint-stock company was formed, in shares, and a proprietary government established. As an inducement for persons to emigrate and settle in the new province, the fullest enjoyment of religious freedom was promised by the very parties who were most hostile to its exercise at home: and every freeman arriving in the country was secured the enjoyment of a hundred acres of land for himself, and fifty for his servant, at a rent of only a halfpenny per acre, for five years, with complete exemption from all taxes, customs, or other dues.

These attractions drew many settlers; so that in the course of a few years, the coast to the south had been so far surveyed as to open new sources of profit, and to induce the original patent-holders to seek for an extension of their limits and powers. Accordingly, in 1665, a second charter was obtained by them, reciting and confirming all the privileges of the first, but extending their limits southward to the 29th degree of north latitude, and making their breadth to extend from the Atlantic Ocean to the Pacific or South Sea! The powers granted to the patentees were almost equal to those of royalty itself. They were allowed to create an order of nobility, by conferring titles of honour, differing only in style from those conferred by the British monarch; and this proviso was again emphatically introduced—"The proprietors were authorized to grant indulgences to such colonists as might be prevented by conscientious scruples from conforming to the Church of England: to the end that all persons might have liberty to enjoy their own judgments and consciences in religious concerns, provided they disturbed not the civil order and peace of the province."

New energies being thus called into action, the peopling of the province went on more rapidly; and a number of planters came from Barbadoes, conducted by Sir John Yeoman, to settle themselves near Cape Fear. There appears, however, to have been great laxity in morals; and a premium was offered to dishonesty by the regulations introduced professedly to induce emigrants to flock hither. Among other things, it was enacted that no settler should be liable to be sued for any debt owing out of the province for the space of five years; and that none of the inhabitants should be at liberty to accept a power of attorney to sue their neighbours for debts contracted abroad. This colony was, therefore, for a long time considered as the peculiar asylum of fugitive debtors and criminals. As there were few clergy or other ministers of religion, during the first twenty years of the settlement, it was enacted "that in order that none might be hindered from a work so necessary as marriage for the preservation of mankind, any man and woman presenting themselves to the governor and council, along with a few of their neighbours, and declaring their mutual purpose to unite in matrimony, should be legally deemed husband and wife."

This state of things became at length so unpromising, that a new form of government was deemed necessary. Accordingly, in 1669, an instrument was drawn up by direction of the proprietaries, under the title of "The Fundamental Constitution of Carolina;" its preamble assigning as a reason for its adoption, "that the government of this province may be made more agreeable to the monarchy under which we live; and that we may avoid creating a numerous democracy." What gives a more than usual degree of interest to this instrument is the fact, that it was drawn up by the celebrated John Locke, the author of the "Essay on the Human Understanding," who was patronized and employed for this purpose by the Earl of Shaftesbury. Some points of this are too curious to be passed over without notice, especially as coming from such a pen; as it is believed that Locke had full powers to frame as well as to compose this Constitution; indeed, he himself, at a subsequent period, represented the work as his own, and became, through it, a competitor with William Penn for the honour of being the first enlightened legislator for America.

There were altogether eight proprietaries already named, to whom the grant of Charles the Second had been extended. Of these, the eldest was, by Locke's Constitution, to be palatine of the province during his life, and at his death to be succeeded by the eldest of the surviving seven. The seven other proprietaries, were to be severally invested with the chief offices of state, as admiral, chamberlain, chancellor, constable, chief-justice, high-steward and treasurer. All these great officers might reside in England, and each appoint his own deputy to act in the colony. There were to be eight supreme courts, to each of which was to be attached a college of twelve assistants: and each of such courts was to be presided over by the deputy of one of the eight great officers of state. The palatine's court was to represent the king, and through it the palatine would ratify the enactments of the legislature, and exercise all the ordinary executive powers of royalty.

Two classes of hereditary nobility, with possessions proportioned to their respective dignities, and for ever inalienable and indivisible, were to be created by the proprietaries, under the titles of landgraves and caciques; and these, together with the deputies of the proprietaries, and representatives chosen by the freemen, constituted the parliament of the province. This was appointed to be called together every two years, and, when assembled, to form one deliberative body, and occupy the same chamber; but no measure could be discussed here, that had not been previously approved by the grand council of the province, which consisted almost exclusively of the proprietaries' officers and the nobility.

Trial by jury was established in all the courts; but the office of hired or professional pleaders was disallowed, as a base and sordid occupation! and no man was admitted to plead the cause of another, without previously deposing, on oath, that he neither had received, nor would accept, the slightest remuneration for his services!

To avoid the confusion arising from a multiplicity of laws, all acts of the provincial parliament were appointed to endure only one hundred years; after which they were to cease and expire of themselves, without the formality of an express repeal; and to avoid the perplexity occasioned by a multiplicity of commentators, all written comments whatever on the Fundamental Constitution, or on any part of the statutes or common law of Carolina, were strictly prohibited.

The most remarkable part of this Fundamental Constitution, however, is that which secures to all persons the right of freely exercising their own religion. As the reasons assigned for this privilege appear to be as cogent and effective as they are simple and intelligible, they are well worthy of extensive diffusion, and of practical adoption in every code of laws or regulations for the government, not only of colonies, but of mother-countries also. The provision is expressed in these terms:—

> Since the natives of the place who are concerned in our plantation are utterly strangers to Christianity, whose idolatry, ignorance, or mistake, gives us no right to expel them, or use them ill; and those who remove from other parts to plant there, will unavoidably be of different opinions concerning matters of religion, the liberty whereof they will expect to have allowed them, and it will not be reasonable for us on this account to keep them out; that civil peace may be maintained amidst the diversity of opinions, and our agreement and compact with all men may be duly and faithfully observed, the violation whereof, upon what pretence soever, cannot be without great offence to Almighty God, and great scandal to the religion we profess; and also that Jews, heathens, and other dissenters from the purity of the Christian religion, may not be scared, and kept at a distance from it, but having an opportunity of acquainting themselves with the truth and reasonableness of its doctrines, and the peaceableness and inoffensiveness of its professors, may, by good usage and persuasion, and all those convincing methods of gentleness and meekness suitable to the rules and design of the gospel, be won over to embrace and unfeignedly to receive the truth—THEREFORE any seven or more persons agreeing in any religion, shall constitute a church or profession, to which they shall give some name to distinguish it from others.

To show, however, how possible it is for extreme liberality of sentiment on some topics, to co-exist in the same mind with illiberality on others, it should be stated, that this same Fundamental Constitution recognized the lawfulness of slavery, one of its provisions being couched in these terms:—"That every freeman of Carolina shall possess absolute power and authority over his negro slaves, of what opinion or religion soever." This provision is the more remarkable, as at this time there were few or no negro slaves in the province, excepting only a very small number who had accompanied Sir John Yeamans and his followers from Barbadoes. Locke, however, lived to have clearer ideas of the injustice of slavery before he died; for at a subsequent period, in his controversy with Sir Robert Filmer, the great apologist for tyrannical government in England, Locke thus expresses himself: "Slavery is so vile and miserable an estate of man, and so directly opposite to the generous temper and courage of our nation, that it is hardly to be conceived that an Englishman, much less a gentleman, should plead for it."

The adoption of the Fundamental Constitution for Carolina was immediately followed by the installation of the Duke of Albemarle into the office of palatine of the province; and the sum of 12,000*l.* sterling was expended on the equipment of a fleet, which sailed in 1670, with emigrants and provisions for the colony. With this expedition was sent out to the governor a letter of instructions, containing twenty-three articles, called "Temporary Agrarian Laws," relative to the distribution of the lands, together with the plan of a magnificent town, which he was desired to build with all convenient speed, and to call it Charles-Town, in honour of the king; and in 1671 the foundation of this town was laid on the banks of the Ashley river, as the metropolis of Carolina. From this time onward, additional settlers came more rapidly, but they were of very mixed character. Among them were many of the Puritans of England, who were induced to prefer this new region to that of their brethren in Massachusetts; but among them were also many of the disappointed Cavaliers, for whom no recompense could be found in England, and to whom estates were given here; as well as rakes, gamblers, and persons of profligate habits and desperate character: so that the most opposite sentiments, views, and feelings were brought into conflict with each other.

In 1679, the position of the first Charleston having been found inconvenient, a new locality was fixed upon for a second city of the same name; and the point chosen for this purpose was at the confluence of the rivers Ashley and Cooper, nearer the sea, where the modern town now stands; and in this year, 1679, its foundations were first laid.

An Indian war broke out in 1680, in which many of the Indians were taken captive. The governor encouraged their capture by offering a certain sum for every Indian brought to Charleston, and he reimbursed himself by selling these Indians to traders who frequented this port from the West Indies, where they were taken and sold for slaves. This practice of kidnapping the Indians for sale, continued long after the war had ceased; so powerful were the temptations which it offered to men who were too indolent to labour, and too unprincipled to be scrupulous as to the manner of acquiring gain. As one evil almost constantly engenders others, so this early slave-trade in the persons of the native Indians brought a new curse on the colony; for the traders from the West Indies, who were the purchasers of the slaves, imported chiefly rum in return; and the cheapness and excessive use of this led to all manner of disorders in the habits of the people; the evil indeed, became so crying as to induce the legislature, in 1683, to pass certain laws for the repression of drunkenness.

The revolution of 1688 in England made little or no change in the relationship of Carolina with the mother-country; but in 1693, the "Fundamental Constitution" of John Locke, which had lasted only twenty-three years, was abolished; and "its abolition," says the historian, "was unregretted by any party, for it had neither procured respect to the government, nor afforded happiness to the people."

It was about this period, 1694, that rice, now the staple produce of Carolina, was first introduced into the province; and this circumstance is thus recorded by Mr. Grahame:—"A vessel from Madagascar, on her homeward voyage to Britain, happening to touch at Charleston, the captain, in acknowledgment of the hospitable civilities which he had received from the governor, South, presented him with a bag of seed-rice, which he said he had seen growing in eastern countries, where it was deemed excellent food, and yielded a prodigious increase. The governor divided it between several of his friends, who agreed to attempt the experiment of its culture; and, planting their parcels in different soils, found the result to exceed their most sanguine expectations. From this casual occurrence, Carolina derived her staple commodity, the chief support of her people, and the main source of her opulence."

The first governor appointed under the new system of government meant to supersede the Fundamental Constitution, was John Archdale, a Quaker, one of the proprietaries at home, a man of excellent understanding and great command of temper. He was invested with almost absolute power, but used it with great discretion; and adhering rigidly to his Quaker principles throughout, he effected more valuable reforms in public policy and private manners, than any of his predecessors. This same individual, after his return to England in 1698, was elected a member of parliament for the borough of Chipping Wycombe, and actually entered the House of Commons as such; but refusing to take the usual oaths, and tendering his simple affirmative instead, this was rejected, and he was accordingly prevented from taking his seat. In the year of his quitting the government of Carolina (1696), which he did with all the honours that a grateful community could bestow, there arrived from Massachusetts some members of an association formed at Dorchester near Boston, "to encourage the settlement of churches and the promotion of religion in the southern plantations;" and by these the sacrament of the Lord's Supper was for the first time administered in Carolina. They founded the small town of Dorchester, about eighteen miles from Charleston, in memory of the town from which they originally came.

In 1703, an Indian war broke out, occasioned by the influence which the Spaniards exercised over the native tribes, and their desire to turn their arms against their English rivals. In this contest the British lost 800 men; but they completely subdued the Indians, burnt and destroyed all their towns; and transported 1,400 of the Apalachians to the territory now denominated Georgia, where they were compelled to live in dependence on Carolina.

It is remarkable, that though the professed object of the noble courtiers who obtained the first grant of the territory of Carolina from Charles the Second, was to "propagate the blessings of religion and civility in a barbarous land," yet for forty years no effort had been made by them to advance this "noble and pious purpose," as it was called; and so, no doubt, it would have remained for forty years more, if left to their own direction. But about this period, a few missionaries were sent out by the Society then incorporated in England for the propagation of the gospel in foreign parts. Up to this period, the only "instruction" that the native Indians had received from the Europeans, was at the hands of a French dancing-master, who settled in the county of Craven, and there acquired a large estate, by teaching the savages to dance and play upon the flute. The only places of worship existing in the colony were three—an Episcopal, a Presbyterian, and a Quaker church or meeting, all within the town of Charleston, but not one throughout all the rest of the province; and in the northern part of it there was no religious place of worship, and no religious services held, of any kind whatever. It was not until 1705 and 1706, that two religious edifices were erected in the northern province. In 1715 it was divided into nine parishes, each with a parochial vestry and minister; and the province was then erected into a separate colony, under the title of North Carolina.

At this period the whole population of Carolina amounted to about 6,000 persons. Printing had not yet been introduced into the colony; the laws were published by oral proclamation, and copies deposited at the courts in writing, which courts were then held in private houses, there being no court-house erected till 1722. Rents and debts were generally paid in hides, tallow, furs, and other productions of the country. Two persons only had suffered death upon the scaffold—one, a Turk for murder; and another, an old woman for witchcraft. At this time there were only a few negro slaves in the country; but the increasing cultivation of rice, which was thought too unhealthy for European constitutions, led to an increased demand for slave-labour, which was easily supplied. Charleston now contained a population of 3,000 inhabitants, a public library, and many handsome edifices; but it was not until 1780 that any printing-press was established in that city.

In the early period of the colony, land was sold at twenty shillings for every 100 acres, and sixpence of quit-rent; in 1694 it was raised to thirty shillings, and in 1711 to forty shillings, with one shilling of quit-rent. The disposition of the occupiers of lands was, however, generally averse to labour, and their tastes extravagant; so that debts were frequent, and insolvent debtors were treated with the utmost indulgence: while the neglect of education, the prevalence of intemperate drinking, and the existence of negro slavery, all contributed their share to retard the general prosperity. This last evil was greatly encouraged by the conduct of the mother-country; for by the treaty made at the peace of Utrecht in 1713, it was stipulated that the British should enjoy for thirty years the exclusive privilege of supplying the Spanish settlements in South America with negroes; and Queen Anne, who had before given her royal patronage to the slave-trade, engaged that her subjects should, during that period, transport to the Spanish settlements 144,000 of what were called in the language of the trade, "Indian pieces," but which meant negro slaves, in certain specified terms, at the rate of 4,800 negroes a year. This was the contract between His Most Catholic Majesty of Spain, and the Protestant Defender of the Faith, the British Queen; so that her subjects, whose professedly "noble and pious purpose" in founding the colony of Carolina was to "propagate the gospel among barbarous people," were the chief instruments of this odious traffic.

The Indian war of 1715 had greatly drained the revenues and impeded the prosperity of Carolina: and in 1717 the coast of this province was infested with pirates, composed principally of British officers and seamen who had been trained to ferocity and injustice by the legalized piracy of the slave-trade. Many of these were taken and hung at Boston, one of their vessels being captured on the coast of New England, and another wrecked off Cape Cod; while others were captured off the coast of Virginia; and some, who were detected there in the guise of merchants, were executed and hung in chains; while no less than twenty-three persons, the leader of whom was a major in the British army, were taken on the coast of Carolina, and hung at Charleston in 1718.

Among the most prominent of these naval marauders was the celebrated Blackbeard, whose real name was John Heart, and who had been considered, by the rest of his co-operators in this work of villainy, to be so superior to them all in ferocity and wickedness, that they elected him chief of their confederated body, at New Providence in the Bahama Islands;[1] but he subsequently preferred to act alone, and chose for his rendezvous the river of Pamlico in North Carolina. In addition to the ferocity of his personal appearance, with his full black beard purposely arranged so as to produce terror in the beholders, with a pair of pistols in holsters, another pair thrown over his shoulders, and lighted matches under his hat, protruding above his ears, he used to perform such fantastic tricks as often to endanger the lives of his associates. On one occasion he undertook to personify a demon, and to show his followers, by anticipation, a picture of hell! in doing which, he nearly suffocated his crew with the fumes of burning brimstone; and on another, while seated in his cabin, drunk, he took a pistol in each hand, and, cocking them under the table, blew out the lights, and, crossing his hands, fired right and left at his companions, one of whom was so severely wounded as to be maimed for life. He kept no less than fourteen women who were called his wives, and who were alternately the objects of his sport and the victims of his cruelty.

Yet with such a monster as this, the governor, Eden, and his secretary, Knight, openly communicated—bribed, as every one then believed, by the pirate's gold; so that he carried on his robberies with impunity. A royal proclamation issued by George I having offered pardon to all pirates who would surrender within twelve months, Heart availed himself of this, surrendered to the governor, and took the oath of allegiance; but squandering his ill-gotten wealth in debauchery and dissipation, he again resumed his old pursuits, and brought into Carolina a French vessel in a state of perfect soundness, but without a crew; alleged by him to have been found deserted at sea, but which every one else thought had been taken by force, and her officers and crew all put to death.

The Governor Eden, however, admitted the plea as valid, and accordingly the pirate escaped; but some of the merchants of Carolina, indignant at this indulgence towards so profligate a wretch, communicated the fact to the governor of Virginia, Colonel Spottiswoode, who offered a large reward for the apprehension of the monster; and Lieutenant Maynard, then in a ship of war in the Chesapeake, collecting a chosen crew in two small vessels, went out to hunt this lion in his den; when a most sanguinary battle ensued, in which there was great slaughter on both sides. The pirate, in apprehension of defeat, had placed one of his crew with a lighted match over the magazine of gunpowder, with instructions to blow up the ship rather than surrender; but before this could be accomplished, the leader of this desperate gang himself fell on the deck covered with wounds, and faint from loss of blood. The vessel was then taken, and all the survivors of the crew were hung. But though this action gave a great check to piracy on these coasts for a time, it did not entirely extirpate it: for five years after this, no less than twenty-six persons were executed at the same time, for piracy, at Rhode Island.

An important change now took place, in the position of South Carolina. War having been declared between England and Spain, the latter conceived the project of invading the coast of Carolina, and for that purpose fitted out an armament at the Havannah. To meet this, the governor convened the assembly, and asked for funds to put themselves into a position of defence. This the assembly refused, as they were disgusted with the proprietary government. But at the same time, they took advantage of the moment, to raise the standard of revolt against the authority of the proprietary, to elect a new governor, and to proclaim him publicly as governor "in the name of the king." They elected also twelve councillors to assist him, and thus set up an entirely new government, which was subsequently recognized at home, as the proprietaries were declared to have forfeited their charter. As the Spanish armament was defeated in its first attack on New Providence, and nearly all its vessels subsequently wrecked in the Gulf of Florida, all danger was at an end; and the change was hailed by all parties in Carolina as a great blessing.

The new governor, Sir Francis Nicholson, gave a new impetus to many undertakings of public improvement: he promoted the establishment of schools and the spread of religion; he concluded treaties of peace with the Indian tribes, the Creeks and Cherokees: and gave great and general satisfaction. Meanwhile, in 1729, the original proprietaries of Carolina, among whom were the Duke of Beaufort, Lord Craven, and the Honourable Doddington Greville, were entirely divested of all authority over the province, and a compensation of 17,000*l.* sterling was awarded to them by act of parliament. The two provinces of North and South Carolina were thus vested in the crown; and in 1730, Sir Alexander Cumming took seven of the Cherokee chiefs to England, where they affixed their marks to a treaty of amity with Britain. The account of their visit is thus recorded: "When they were presented to the king, they laid their national emblems of sovereignty at his feet, and by an authentic deed declared themselves his subjects, and acknowledged his dominion over all their countrymen, who, they averred, had fully authorized them to make this recognition. They promised especially to assist the English in the pursuit and recapture of fugitive slaves. They were amazed and confounded at the splendour of the British court; comparing the king and queen to the sun and moon, the princes to the stars of heaven, and themselves to invisible motes in the rays of a dazzling effulgence of grandeur; and being loaded with presents, both useful and ornamental, they were reconveyed to their own country."

In the following year, 1731, a valuable accession of settlers was made, in the persons of 370 Swiss, who were taken out by one of their own countrymen, named Purry, he having obtained from the British government a large grant of land, and 400*l.* sterling, for every hundred able-bodied labourers that he should land in Carolina; and with these he founded the town of Purrysburg, still known by the same name. But about the same period, misrule, corruption, and bribery in the public departments, existed to a lamentable extent; and the paper money that had been issued in both these provinces had so declined in value, that it was depreciated 700 per cent, which led to all manner of fraud, gambling, and embarrassment.

Notwithstanding all these disadvantages, the population still continued to increase. In 1700, it was not more than 6000: in 1723, it was 32,000, of whom there were 18,000 negroes to 14,000 whites. No less than 439 slaves were imported in one year, 1724. In 1730, the negroes amounted to 28,000; and, encouraged by their large numbers, they conceived a plot for massacring all the whites, but it was happily detected and defeated. Such, however, was the cupidity of the slave-merchants in Britain, and the rice-planters in the colony, that in the very face of this danger, they went on importing more negroes from Africa, there being no less than 1500 imported in one year, 1731. In 1734, the colonists themselves publicly adverted to this source of danger, when, in an address from the assembly of Carolina to the king, on the state of the province, they declared that they were "subject to many intestine dangers from the great number of negroes that are now among us." At the same time an ordinance was passed, commanding all the white inhabitants to carry arms with them when they went to the public assemblies and to church!

A strange sect of fanatics, principally among the French refugees, appeared in Carolina about this period, pretending that they were guided in every thing by the impulse of the Divine Spirit, which was superior to all law; and they lived in open incest and adultery, as they pretended, under the direct guidance of the Deity. Like the Mormons of the present day, now engaged in warfare in the settlements of the west, they defended their doctrines by arms; but were ultimately overpowered, and some of them were executed for murder. Excessive heats and droughts created almost a famine; the country was swept by a most furious hurricane, and the yellow fever raged with such malignity, as to hurry multitudes, both of the white and black population, to an early grave. But from all this the colony soon recovered; and in 1733 it experienced a great influx of capital and population, which, with the planting of the neighbouring colony of Georgia, and the encouragement afforded to their productions at home, relieved it of most of its embarrassments, and caused a great in crease of wealth, among the planters especially.

The emigrants that now repaired to Carolina were more numerous than before, and embraced parties from Ireland, Germany, and Holland; while large numbers of Scotch who had been engaged in the rebellion of 1745, were sentenced to be transported to Carolina and Georgia. The discovery of the indigo plant growing spontaneously in the wild glades of the forest, happening just at this time, furnished abundant occupation for all the newcomers; while the profit derived from its culture, and the extract of its dye, being immense, the number of persons engaging in that occupation was so considerable, that in 1767, 300,000 lbs of indigo had been shipped from Carolina to England: and at this period there were 330 ships and about 2,000 seamen engaged in the trade with Great Britain.

With all their prosperity, however, there was one danger, always inconvenient, and always increasing; namely, the large proportion of the negro population to the whites, and the constant dread of their mutiny or revolt. This fear is strikingly displayed in a memorial from the planters of South Carolina, presented to the British government, against a bill for preventing the exportation of rice from any part of the British dominions, in which they say, "If any stop be put to the exportation of rice from South Carolina, it will not only render the planters unable to pay their debts, but also reduce the government of this province to such distress for want of money, as at this present precarious time may render the whole colony an easy prey to their neighbours, the Indians and Spaniards, and also to those yet more dangerous enemies, their own negroes, who are ready to revolt on the first opportunity, and are eight times as many in number as there are white men capable of bearing arms." This expression of their alarm was perhaps quickened by the fact that the Spaniards, with a force of 32 ships and 3,000 men, had effected a landing in Georgia; and among the force was a regiment of free negroes, the black officers of which were dressed in the same uniform as their white comrades, enjoyed the same rank with the Spanish officers, and maintained exactly the same freedom of intercourse with the commander-in-chief, Don Manuel de Monteano; as such a sight, to the negroes of South Carolina, if they should reach so far, would be an irresistible incitement to the outbreak of that revolt, for which their masters knew they were ripe.

After an interval of nearly twenty years, we find South Carolina in a more prosperous condition than the once threatening aspect of affairs would have given reason to expect in consequence of large grants of money from the provincial assembly, to encourage the influx of emigrants, they had come in great numbers from all parts of England, Scotland, Ireland, and Germany: so that in 1765 the population had advanced to 130,000, of whom only 90,000 were negroes, thus materially altering the relative proportions between the slaves and the free.

But new sources of discontent began to develop themselves; and the general dissatisfaction of the American provinces with the rule of the mother-country, was felt as strongly in South Carolina as elsewhere. In 1776, when the revolution had made considerable progress in the north, the Carolinians made a noble and successful defence of the city and port of Charleston against the attack of

General Clinton and Sir Peter Parker, at the head of a force of 3,000 men, and a squadron of ships mounting 254 guns. The fort, which the people of Charleston had erected on Sullivan's Island, within their harbour, mounted only 26 guns; and the whole number of their troops amounted to no more than 375 regulars, and a few militia-men; but though the assault of the British was maintained for ten hours against this inferior force, it was wholly unavailing; and three of their ships grounding on a shoal, the expedition was abandoned, with the slight loss on the side of the besieged of only 10 men killed and 22 wounded, and the fort but little injured, though many thousand balls had been expended on it from the British squadron.

Since the period of the revolution, the most marked circumstance in the history of South Carolina has been the attitude of opposition in which it placed itself to the tariff of the general government; and the threats of separation which it made, and seemed prepared to execute, by an appeal to arms. The origin and end of this celebrated controversy may be thus briefly stated. The people of the free states, including all those of the Union north of the river Potomac, wishing to encourage domestic manufactures, and thus to render themselves independent of importations from England, were powerful enough in Congress to establish by law a scale of high duties on almost all British manufactures, ranging from 20 to 50 per cent, professedly with a view to protect the dearer manufactures of their own country. To this the people of the South very naturally objected, as they would derive no benefit whatever from the establishment of manufactures, since their States were not likely to establish any; while on the other hand, they would be injured to a considerable extent, by being obliged to pay for every manufactured article of which they stood in need, from 20 to 50 per cent more than the price at which they could be supplied from England if no such tariff existed. These high duties were, therefore, clearly founded in injustice, by taxing the consumers of the whole country, for the exclusive benefit of the few engaged in manufactures.

To this system, therefore, the Southern States generally objected and South Carolina put herself forward as the leader of the opposition, who were called Nullifiers, and their doctrine, Nullification; because they contended that, by the right of State sovereignty and independent government, which each State reserved to itself, and had not conceded to the general government, they were perfectly justified in nullifying all the acts of Congress founded in such gross injustice to their particular interests. The more violent of the Nullifiers recommended an appeal to arms, to maintain their position; for, having been threatened by the then existing president, General Jackson, with invasion and coercion by force, to adopt the new system, they had determined to resist force by force, and, if necessary, declare their separation from the Union, and form a confederation of the Southern States, to erect them into a new republic. This state of things lasted for many months, under the greatest excitement, and no less than 30,000 men were said to be under arms in South Carolina alone. At length it was happily terminated by the compromise bill of Mr. Clay, which proposed a gradual biennial reduction of the rates of the tariff till the year 1840, when the duties would be reduced to a very moderate scale, and by which time the native manufactures might be expected to be able to sustain themselves, without much fear of competition with foreign productions.

Since that period, Carolina has enjoyed a comparative calm, and is now, at least, tranquil on the subject; though there are still causes of discontent, which will be adverted to further on, after a description of the State, in its present condition, shall have been given.

1.   Having visited the Bahama Islands about 30 years ago, I remember to have been shown a large overshadowing tree, not far from the port of Nassau, under which Blackbeard and his gang used to hold their councils of war; and a cave not far from thence, where he used to conceal the spoils. The tree, I believe, has been since blown down; but the island is full of the traditions of his diabolical and ferocious exploits.

Chapter III

The State of South Carolina is 188 miles long, from north to south; and 260 broad, from east to west; lying between latitude 32 and 35° N., and between longitude 78° and 83° W., and containing an area of 33,000 square miles, or about 20,000,000 of acres. It is bounded on the north and north-east by North Carolina, on the south-east by the Atlantic, and on the west by Georgia.

The climate, as far as temperature is concerned, is more agreeable than in most other parts of the United States, having no greater heat than Maine and Massachusetts in summer, and being free from their intense colds in winter. In Charleston, for seven years, the thermometer was not known to rise above 93° or fall below 17° above zero; while in Boston it was during the last summer above 100°, and in the present winter was at 8° below zero. Frost very rarely occurs on the low lands, nor ever lasts more than a day or two; and it is mentioned as a very unusual circumstance, which alarmed many of the people of the country, that snow once remained on the ground for a period of three days. The most variable period of the year is February; the most sultry is August; and the greatest variation of temperature ever experienced in any one day was 46°. In the highlands and mountains, towards the western boundary of the State, the frosts are sometimes severe, and snow remains for weeks in succession.

Among the articles of culture, fruits abound, and pears, pomegranates, melons, oranges, and pine-apples, are produced in great perfection; while apples, peaches, nectarines, apricots, figs, olives, and almonds, are also grown in various parts of the country. Grain is not much cultivated, at least in wheat, barley, or oats, for all these are imported from the north, and their growth is neglected for the more profitable cultivation of rice and cotton, which form the staple productions of the State. The introduction of rice by a ship from the East Indies, and the discovery of the indigo plant growing wild in the woods, have been already mentioned. These constituted, with tobacco, the earliest articles of produce, until about 1795, when cotton began to be raised; and since that period rice and cotton have formed the chief articles of growth and export from the States.

Of mineral productions there are, in various parts of the State, lead and iron ore, potter's clay, fuller's earth, talc, marble, and limestone; with several ocherous earths used in the manufacture of painters' colours. Gold, also, is produced in this region; but this precious metal abounds most in North Carolina, where there are at present not less than 30,000 persons employed in the gold district, in the mines under working, and in digging for the discovery of new veins. It is found generally mixed with the soil, from the smallest particles up to pieces of one or two pounds weight, valued from 100 to 1,000 dollars; and one piece was dug up in Cabarras county, worth about 8,000 dollars, or 1,600*l*. sterling. The present product of the gold-mines is said to be about 100,000 dollars per week, or a million sterling per annum. It is worthy of remark, that in the opening of new mines, evidences are found of their having been previously worked, and that by the native Indians; as crucibles and mining instruments have from time to time been discovered under circumstances, and in situations, which make it impossible to attribute them to even the earliest of the European adventurers.

The population of South Carolina has been progressively on the increase, but with nothing like the rapidity of the Northern States, as will be seen by the following statement:—

In	1701	it was	7,000	In	1800	it was	345,591
	1749		30,000		1810		415,115
	1750		64,000		1820		502,714
	1765		130,000		1830		581,458
	1790		249,073				

The increase in the slave population was, however, more rapid than that among the white; for their numbers stand thus:—

In	1765	it was	90,000	In	1810	it was	196,365
	1790		107,094		1820		258,475
	1800		146,151		1830		315,365

So that in 1830 the whole population comprehended 581,458, of whom only 257,878 were whites, and 315,365 slaves, the remainder being 7,215 free people of colour, making the whole coloured population greatly in excess at the last census. The general impression here is, that the proportions of the excess has rather increased than diminished since that period; so that the evil of this disproportion is continually on the advance.

Some large mills, for the spinning of cotton yarn, have been established of late years in South Carolina, and these are said to yield a good profit. They are worked by machinery made at West Point, on the Hudson river, turned by water-power, and directed partly by free and partly by slave labour; the more expert of the latter being found to be the only persons fit for such employment among their race. Some of the yarn is exported to the north; and some is woven into coarse clothes adapted for negro apparel, in which it is chiefly consumed.

The internal improvements of the State are advancing, though slowly in comparison with those of the northern sections of the Union. A canal, extending 22 miles from the Santee to the Cooper river, was completed in 1802, the length of which was 22 miles, at a cost of 650,000 dollars. Several smaller canals and streams extending beyond this, continue the water navigation to Columbia, the capital of the State, a distance of about 130 miles directly inland from Charleston. A railroad from Charleston to Hamburgh, a small town immediately opposite to Augusta, on the Savannah river, has also been completed for 135 miles, at a cost of about 800,000 dollars; and a railroad from Charleston to Columbia is in progress, and a large portion of it completed.

The government of South Carolina is conducted at the capital, Columbia, which is nearly in the centre of the State, where the legislature assemble once in each year. Its executive consists of a Governor, at a salary of 3,500 dollars per annum, a Secretary of State, and seven or eight other functionaries, at salaries of from 1,500 to 2,000 dollars per annum each; and a House of Assembly and a Senate form the two legislative chambers. The State is represented in the general legislature at Washington, by nine members of Congress sent by general election of the citizens to the House of Representatives and two Senators elected by the Legislature of the State.

The Judiciary consists of four Chancellors in Equity, at 3,000 dollars per annum, who perform the duty of Circuit Judges, and hold Equity Courts at different points of the State at fixed periods; and seven Judges of the General Sessions and Common Pleas, at the same salaries, who perform similar duties in the administration of the statute and common law, for civil and criminal cases. Appeal Courts are held also at Charleston and Columbia: and a Court for the correction of errors, composed of all the Judges of Law and Equity, is held to consider all questions on which the Appeal Courts may be divided in opinion. The Judges are all appointed for life.

Education is not neglected in this State; for besides the College at Columbia, and the South Carolina College at Charleston, each containing a large number of students, schools are very numerous, and the State Legislature appropriates the sum of 40,000 dollars annually for the support of free schools, of which there were in the last year about 920, with from 9,000 to 10,000 scholars.

Of the various sects of religion in the State, the Methodists have the greatest number of church members, upwards of 30,000, though their ministers do not exceed 60. The Baptists have the greatest number of churches and ministers, 168 of the former and 142 of the latter, with about 15,000 communicants. The Presbyterians have 82 churches, 58 ministers, and about 15,000 communicants; and the Episcopalians have 28 churches, and 36 ministers; while Roman Catholics, Unitarians, and Universalists, have each a few congregations only.

Such is the present condition, as nearly as it can be ascertained, of the State of South Carolina.

CHAPTER IV

The city of Charleston is most advantageously situated for commerce with the interior, and communication with the sea; having, in this respect, a striking resemblance to the position of New York; for in the same manner as that city is seated on a peninsula, washed on the east by the East river, on the west by the Hudson, and on the south by the sea, so Charleston is seated on a projection of land, almost insular, and joined, like Boston, by a narrow isthmus, called "The Neck," to the mainland, having the Ashley river to wash its sides on the west, the Cooper river to fringe it on the east, and its southern extremity bathed by the junction of these two streams in their passage to the sea; there being, as at New York, a point at this junction, called "The Battery," forming an agreeable promenade.

The city, extending from this point inland, or upward, occupies an area of about a mile and three-quarters in length, from north to south, and an average breadth of about a mile and a quarter, from river to river, east to west. This area being a perfect level, enabled the founders of the city to lay out its plan with tolerable regularity; the streets, therefore run generally, but not exactly, north and south, and east and west, the latter crossing the peninsula from river to river; the wharfs for the shipping, like those in New York, being chiefly ranged along the eastern edge of the town. The streets are generally from 50 to 80 feet in breadth. They were, up to a very recent period; lined on each side with trees, like those of Philadelphia; but within the last two years, these have been removed; the public authorities of the city entertaining an opinion that their roots injured the pavements, so as to cause great expense for their repair, and that the decayed vegetable matter, occasioned by the falling leaves in autumn, was unfavourable to health. The centres of the streets are macadamized, and the side pavements are of brick. The streets are lighted with oil lamps, and are kept in good order.

W. H. Brooke F.S.A.

T. A. Prior

Charleston, South Carolina

A very recent and destructive fire happening in the summer of the year 1838, destroyed nearly half the town. Its ravages were confined chiefly to the upper part of the city, where the dwellings were principally of wood, though many fine brick buildings were destroyed at the same time; and the distress created by this calamity was general. A very liberal subscription was raised in the cities of the North, for the relief of the sufferers, to which the Bank of the United States at Philadelphia alone contributed 20,000 dollars; and the Legislature of the State advanced large sums by way of loan to individuals desiring to rebuild, on the security of their ground and premises, so that the work of restoration is now going on rapidly. As the State Legislature has passed a law prohibiting the future erection of wooden buildings, all the new edifices are to be built of brick, by which not only the beauty of the city will be much increased, but the safety of life and property be much greater than formerly. Here, as in the great fire at New York, most of the buildings were insured; but the excess of loss sustained, caused the bankruptcy of the Insurance offices, and, therefore, left the sufferers without remedy.[1] What added to the distress of this visitation was that it was accompanied by a most fatal sickness, occasioned, it is thought, by the exposure of so many cellars, pools, cisterns, and drains, to the burning sun, by the destruction of the buildings, and uncovering of the soil by which they were before shaded; and this sickness, far more virulent than their ordinary fevers, carried off large numbers of the native inhabitants as well as strangers.

The general aspect of the city is far inferior to that of Boston, New York, Philadelphia, or Baltimore; nor has it the solidity and thriving appearance of Albany, Utica, Rochester, or Buffalo, or the beauty and elegance of Geneva, Canandaigua, or New Bedford. It more resembles a West Indian than an American city—from the number of wooden buildings painted white, the large verandas and porticoes of the more stately mansions of brick, and the universal prevalence of broad verandas, green Venetian blinds, and other provisions to secure coolness and shade. The shops have none of the exterior elegance or display, which characterizes those of the Broadway, in New York, or Chesnut-street in Philadelphia; but are literally stores, like those in Pearl-street and Pine-street, in the first-named city.

Among the public buildings, the Exchange, the City Hall, the Court House, and the State offices, may be mentioned as the most prominent. The two first were built while Charleston was an English colony; and it is the opinion of the residents here, in which strangers would join them, that there have been no public edifices erected since the revolution, so good as those constructed before. Both the buildings named are as fine as any of the kind in the United States, and both are admirably adapted to the purposes for which they were erected. The first is of stone, the second of brick, with an ornamented front of Ionic pilasters and pediment, and the exterior and interior of each is in perfect harmony and keeping, blending, in a very happy manner, solidity, elegance, and utility. The Court House and the State offices, which are both near the City Hall, one built of stone, in a chaste style of architecture; while the latter is made fire-proof, by the exclusion of all wood, and the use of plates of copper for the roofing.

Of churches, there are not less than 23, including 6 Episcopal, 3 Presbyterian, 1 Baptist, 4 Methodist, 2 Catholic, 1 Unitarian, 4 Independent, 1 Quakers' Meeting, and 1 Synagogue. Two of the Episcopalian churches, St. Philip's and St. Michael's, were built before the revolution; the first was so much injured by the late fire, as to require to be almost entirely rebuilt. The second is the largest church, and has the tallest steeple (165 feet) in the city. In its interior it is so like an old English church in every particular, that it is difficult, when hearing the Episcopal service read in it, and looking round on the congregation, to imagine one's self anywhere but in England. The high pews, dark panelling, like well-polished oak or old mahogany, the altar with its tablets of the Commandments and the Creed in gold letters on a black ground, the antique pulpit, with its suspended sounding-board, deep-crimson velvet cushions, and the mural monuments of persons buried nearly a century ago—are all so thoroughly English, that, but for the substitution of the "President and the Congress," in the public prayers, instead of "Her Majesty and the High Court of Parliament," there was nothing here to remind one of America.

There are several excellent institutions of a benevolent and charitable nature in Charleston, of which the principal is the Orphan Asylum, supported partly by the city funds, and partly by legacies, donations, and private subscriptions. It contains frequently from 150 to 200 orphans, for whose present state and future condition it provides judiciously and liberally. There is also a good general Hospital, and an Almshouse for the sick and the needy; these last being more numerous here than in the northern sections of America, because, though wages are high, there are not so many resources of employment for those who may require it, and especially for the foreign emigrants who find their way here. The poor are supported at the expense of the inhabitants of the districts from whence they come, or in which they are found. In the last year, before the great fire already described, the number of paupers in the poor-house were 373, of whom 171 were foreigners: and the number of persons to whom rations were granted as out-door pensioners during the same year, were 180, of whom 20 were foreigners. Since the fire, the number of both classes is much greater, but this is, of course, no criterion of the general state of things.

The commerce of Charleston is greater than that of any port between New York and New Orleans, exceeding that of Philadelphia or Baltimore. The extent of its shipments in the two great staples of rice and cotton has been given in the description of the State; but it may here be added, that the ships actually belonging to the port of Charleston, including large and small, amount to nearly 20,000 tons; while not less than 180,000 tons, exclusive of coasters, enter the harbour in the course of the year. It is one of the ports of the United States that has provided a "Sailors' Home" or Temperance Boarding House, with a church attached to it; for its seamen only. It is presided over by a young minister of the gospel, who was himself once a sailor, and who evinces the most disinterested zeal in the discharge of its duties. Regular lines of packets sail from hence to the principal ports of America and the West Indies; and steam-vessels go to all the ports of the west, and up the rivers into the interior. Vessels from London, Glasgow, Liverpool, and Havre, are almost always found in the harbour of Charleston; and of late years there has been a growing desire on the part of the merchants to make the trade between Europe and South Carolina much more direct, instead of going, as at present, by the circuitous, and as they think less profitable channels, of New York, and the ports of the north.

There are eight Banks, all conducting their business on a large scale; five Insurance Companies; and a Chamber of Commerce, for guarding the interests of trade; and nowhere does there appear to be a more gentlemanly and liberal mode of conducting business of every kind than here, mixed with great civility and politeness, and a freedom from that eagerness of gain which is so characteristic of the north.

The Institutions for education are extensive in number, and excellent in character, in the city of Charleston. Besides the College for classical instruction, and the Medical college for professional education, there are no less than 80 schools, for the younger portion of the community, including boarding, day, and free schools, and the number of pupils in the whole are not less than 2,000. I learnt, from persons connected with the business of education, that it was formerly the custom for the more wealthy families to send their children to the Universities of the north, especially to Providence and Boston, for education; but that latterly this practice had decreased, and given place to the much more general one of educating them in Charleston or Columbia, within the State. On inquiring the cause of this change, the reason assigned was this: that the students returning from the north so often came home "*tainted* with Abolitionism," (that was the exact phrase used) and with such a "distaste for their *domestic institutions*," meaning slavery, (that being the term usually substituted for this disagreeable word), that it was thought dangerous to the welfare of the country any longer to continue the practice of sending their children to the north, where they imbibed such dangerous doctrines as Abolitionism, and were thus rendered averse to the "domestic institutions" of the south.

The literary productions of Charleston have been characterized by great ability, but from the want of proper support they have not been able to sustain themselves, and have accordingly, after a short existence, been discontinued. The Southern Review was one of these, and the Southern Literary Journal another: the pages of both bear witness to the talents and learning of the editors and their contributors; but neither of them had a sufficient circulation to cover their expense. At present Charleston has a weekly periodical, entitled "The Southern Rose," edited by Mrs. Caroline Gilman, and, as a work of professedly light literature, it exhibits a happy union of information and good taste. There are three daily newspapers, two morning and one evening, all advocating the democratic principles of the revolution. The leading morning paper, the Courier, is conducted with great ability, by Mr. Yeadon, a barrister of the city; and the evening paper, the Patriot, is edited by Mr. Cadoza, a Jew; but all three are characterized by a more gentlemanly and courteous tone towards each other, than rival or friendly papers are in the north; and I did not see so much of vituperation of men and measures, in all the Charleston papers for three weeks, as one may sometimes see in a single paper of Boston and New York in as many days. Besides these, there are three religious newspapers, the Methodist, the Presbyterian, and the Roman Catholic, all published weekly, each adapting its information to the peculiar views of the sect for which it is issued; and the Southern Agriculturist, a work devoted exclusively to objects connected with the cultivation of the soil.

Among all these publications, whether quarterly, monthly, weekly, or daily, there is not one that ever ventures to speak of slavery as an institution to be condemned, or even regretted. They are all either indulgent towards, or openly advocates of, this state of bondage; and the higher the rank or character of the publication, the more boldly it speaks out on this subject, and the more popular it becomes in the south by so speaking. A few examples of this from one of the ablest of the works referred to, "The Southern Literary Journal," may be offered in confirmation of this view.

In the first volume for 1835, (p.127) an extract of a letter is given from an anti-abolitionist at the north, in which he says, "I believe that facts will warrant the assertion, that the condition of the slave population in the aggregate is better than that of the free black, who assumes all the cares and responsibilities of self-support." And after denouncing, as the greatest of evils, all attempts to promote the abolition of slavery, he thus describes its inevitable consequences, if accomplished—"Your fair land, which now supports a numerous and *happy* population (it is thus he speaks of the slaves), would become the wretched abode, of the desperate and depraved." And then he exclaims—"What Christian, what philanthropist, would aid in such a work! Every step the abolitionist would take, to dissolve abruptly the relations of master and slave, would be *evil* in its progress, and *evil* in its results. Is any man called upon, on *Christian* principles, to be a minister of *evil*? Surely, no!" Puerile as such a method of arguing this question must appear to most persons, first prophesying consequences, then assuming qualities, and lastly begging the whole question; yet the editor of the Southern Journal says, of this communication—"These views reflect credit both upon the *head* and the *heart* of the writer—are philanthropic, christian, and politic." It is thus that compliments and eulogies are exchanged between those who uphold this system; and who, if the weakest and most superficial remarks in favour of slavery were to be put forth in any shape, and from any quarter, would praise them in the loftiest terms.

The concluding passage, however, of the editor's remarks on this communication, exhibits an attachment to slavery, which no purchase-money, in the shape of compensation, could lessen; for in reference to the supposed willingness of the north to give an *equivalent* to the planters of the south, for the purchase of their negroes' freedom, as was done by the British towards the proprietors of slaves in our West India islands, he says—"On the subject of an *equivalent*, however, to be offered by the citizens of the north for our slaves, we undertake to say that South Carolina, at least, would not, *for all the wealth that is garnered up in the coffers of the New England States*, become a party to a bargain so ruinous and degrading. *The citizens of the south stand upon their rights*! They are able to protect their domestic institutions (this is the mild phrase under which slavery is usually described in the Southern writings) by the shield of the constitution, and could easily show, *if they would condescend to do it*, that slavery has been not only theoretically, but practically recognized as lawful, in every country, under every government, and by every religion. Under these circumstances, *they would scorn to barter away their dearest rights for money*. There is no equivalent that *can* be offered them, which they would think it their duty to accept."

It might be thought unnecessary to go further than this, to show the tenacity with which the Southerners cling to their "domestic institutions," and at what hazards they are ready to uphold and defend them. But a few references to other authorities may be given, to show how extensively these sentiments are diffused. Dr. Cooper, the president of Columbia College, in the capital of South Carolina, says, in an article on slavery in the same volume, p.188—"I do not know a more bold, a more impudent, a more unprincipled, unblushing falsehood, than to say that *slavery is inconsistent with the laws of God*, if the Bible be assumed as the repository of those laws. I do not wish to go over the ground again, already trodden for the hundredth time; but I claim the right of appealing to your readers who read the Bible, whether, from the time of Abraham to the time of the Apostle Paul, there be not the most ample proof of domestic slavery being ordained, practised, and approved by the Jews in the Old, and by the Christians in the New Testament, without *one* contradictory or condemnatory passage or precept?" While such are the sentiments of learned heads of colleges in the south, it is not to be wondered at, that those who conceive their *interests* involved in the maintenance of such views generally, should be afraid to send their children to be educated in the north, as there at least such doctrines are not likely to be taught.

In the same volume (p.207) is a brief enumeration of the recent publications on the slave question, which the editor has received for review; and on these, including nine different works by different authors, he has the following remarks: "'The Amenability of Northern Incendiaries, as well to Northern as to Southern Laws,' is the title of a pamphlet by the senior editor of the Charleston Courier, a gentleman well known in our community as a sound constitutional lawyer, and a successful advocate. The right of South Carolina to demand of the Northern States the *persons* of the incendiaries, for the purpose of punishment, he places on the broad and recognized principles of the law of nations applicable to such cases; the only ground, in law, upon which, in our opinion, the right can be maintained." Another of the works reviewed is entitled, 'An Appeal to the *good* sense of a *great* people; the tribunal that must finally settle this vexed question;' on which the editor says, "that is, as *we* understand it, the People of the South; for an appeal to any *other*, we should esteem worse than idle." 'Remarks on Slavery, by a Citizen of Georgia,' is described as "an able and successful attempt to prove that slavery is upheld and countenanced by the writers of the Old and New Testaments;" and another work, entitled 'Two Sermons on the subject of Slavery, by Simon Dogget,' is said to "sustain ably the scriptural argument in *favour* of slavery, from the classical pen of a venerable clergyman of Massachusetts, who passed the last winter among us (in the South)."

In an article entitled 'A Visit to Sir Roger de Coverley's Plantation,' purporting to give a faithful picture of a southern estate, is found the following remarkable passage. After describing the little dwellings of the negroes, which were all whitewashed, the owner of the plantation, represented under the name of Sir Roger de Coverley, thus explains the reason of this:—he says, "I have these houses whitewashed every spring; this contributes not only to their good appearance, but to the health of their inmates. Cleanliness is indispensable to health, and *makes the slave prolific.* I have, at this time, a hundred and fifty of these people; and their *annual increase* may be estimated as *adding as much to my income* as arises from all other sources." No wonder, therefore, that Sir Roger should feel a little uneasy at the progress of Abolitionism, as being likely to disturb this *annual increase to his income* from the prolific qualities of his slaves. "This endearing relation," he continues, "with feelings of virtuous indignation apparent on his countenance," (such is the language of the narrator,) "equally *beneficial* to both bond and free, is the one which ignorant, envious, self-styled philanthropists have pronounced to be tyrannical and unjust. How little do these meddlers know of the actual state of things which they so vehemently condemn! You see around you, Sir, only healthy, laughing, contented beings, of either sex, all of them well clad, all of them engaged in wholesome and moderate labour, without which the mere name of freedom, even if they possessed it, would be a curse: you see them comfortably provided for; all their reasonable wants daily and duly supplied; they are at no expense for the support of their families; they incur no debts; they pay no fines; they fear no bailiff; they are free from corroding cares; they are not harassed by the restless desire of amassing fortunes, which a breath of wind may dissipate; they are remote from the vexatious arena of political life—the mad strife for office and honour. By day they labour cheerfully; at night their sleep is sweet, and they care not for the morrow." To all which, Mr. Addison, another of the conversational party, is made to reply as follows:—"I think that the pseudo-philanthropists to whom you refer, have done you and the cause of truth no little injustice. What more does man really require, than a sufficiency to supply all his natural wants? Society, it is true, places him in an artificial position, and extends his desires indefinitely, but is it certain that this change renders him a happier being? I doubt it. I am not certain that the slave, all things considered, is not more independent of events than his master—that he is not, in fact, a *freer* being."

The last example I shall quote will be from an article entitled 'Reflections elicited by Judge Harper's Anniversary Oration, delivered before the South Carolina Society for the Advancement of Learning, December 9, 1838.' The judge, it appears, in this address, invited the attention of the members of this Society especially to the subject of Domestic Slavery, or, in the language of the editor, one of the "cherished institutions" of the South; and the learned orator thus speaks of it himself:—"I believe that no one who has the slightest acquaintance with the subject, on whom argument would not be wasted, imagines it to be possible that slavery should cease to exist among us in our day, or for *generations* to come. Our proudest and most deeply-cherished feelings, which others, if they will, may call prejudices—our most essential interests— our humanity and consideration for the slaves themselves—nay, almost physical impossibility, forbid that this should be done by *our own act*; and, thank God! we, the slave-holding communities of the South, are too strong, and on this subject too united, to admit the thought that it can be effected by external force. As to the aid which external force may derive from insurrection, as far as relates to the final success of such an attempt, we do not admit it into our thoughts:

no—if that event is ever to be brought about, it must be by a force superior to that of all the people and potentates of the earth."

When such influential persons as editors of quarterly journals and daily newspapers, presidents of colleges, and judges on the bench, maintain and propagate such views as these, it is certainly not to be wondered at that the youths of Carolina, educated at home, and hearing scarcely any other views of slavery expressed, but such as I have quoted, should grow up in the belief that they are just and sound, and receive them as the maxims of wisdom from the lips and pens which are guided by age and experience. A stranger, not so brought up and imbued with those "proudest and most deeply-cherished feelings, which others, if they will, may call prejudices," may be forgiven, however, for saying, that as far as his senses can inform him, he does not recognize the fidelity of the picture which these writers give of the condition of the slaves of South Carolina. Instead of seeing only "healthy, laughing, contented beings of either sex," I confess I have never witnessed, in any population of the earth, less indications of laughter and content than on the countenances of the slaves met with at every hour of the day; their general expression being that of great gravity and gloomy discontent; and a pretty strong evidence of their not being quite so "happy and contented" as is described, may be found in these facts;—that every precaution is taken to prevent an insurrection, by a large military and police establishment, which exercises great vigilance by day and by night; that guard-houses, bells, and drums, warn the coloured person, whether slave or free, not to be found out of his dwelling after nine o'clock;—and that their meeting in greater numbers than a dozen, even for religious purposes, without the presence of a white man, is strictly prohibited and enforced. Instead of "all of them being well clad," a very large number have ragged, and nearly all dirty clothes; and on some plantations, a single suit of a woollen jacket and trousers, without a shirt, is the whole apparel allowed for a year! Instead of "all being well fed," the scanty measure of Indian corn is barely sufficient for subsistence; rice is in many instances thought too costly for them; salt is either stinted or withheld; and as to animal food, it is rarely given at all, except on very particular occasions. Instead of "wholesome and moderate labour," the employment of many is, in the marshy lands, so fatal to life, that no Europeans can reside there through the summer, and even the negroes suffer from agues and fevers; while their labour is often excessive, both in the length of time it endures and the toil it requires.

It is quite true, as the same writer says, that "they are at no expense to maintain their families;" but it should be added, that they give all their labour, by which alone they could do this, to their masters, and thus their families are deprived of whatever that labour, if fairly paid for, could provide them beyond bare subsistence. It is also true, that "they incur no debts;" but neither do they ever accumulate a surplus; "they pay no fines," because their penalties are taken from them in stripes; "they fear no bailiffs," but they have often reason to dread the whip of the overseer; "they are not harassed by the restless desire of amassing fortunes," which cuts them off from all the pleasures of advancement in the world by their own industry; and if "their labour is cheerful by day, and their sleep sweet by night," they are, nevertheless, continually in the habit of running away, most foolishly, of course, from all this happiness and contentment; just as sailors desert from ships of war into which they have been impressed, and as debtors and criminals escape from the prisons in which they are confined against their will. This love of freedom is *known* to be so strong, even among these "happy and contented beings," that nothing is more common than to see, in the daily newspapers, rewards offered for the apprehension of runaways, with the occasional offer of "freedom" to those who may give information of robberies and conspiracies, as the highest reward that can be offered, to tempt slaves to furnish the information required.

All these things make an impression on the mind of a stranger; and, without doubting for a moment that there are many kind masters and mistresses, who do much to make the condition of their slaves easy and tolerable, it cannot but be evident to him, that the great mass of them are not treated so well as many of the brute creation; and that the dogs and horses of their masters are better fed, have less labour, less punishment, and quite as much of intellectual culture and enjoyment as the slave: for if the one has not the capacity to learn, the other is strictly forbidden to acquire the power to read. This shutting up of all the avenues to knowledge in the slaves, is, no doubt, done with a view to keep them in a state of greater dependence and subordination; but it is defended on the ground of their utter unfitness for mental improvements, and an entire deficiency of a capacity for education. And yet, according to good authorities, several Catholic bishops have been negroes, one of whom was canonized as a saint at Rome; and a negro was ordained as a priest of the Episcopal Church of England, by Bishop Keppell, at Exeter, in 1765. Instances of hundreds of intelligent and educated free negroes are found in the north; Hayti is governed entirely by educated blacks; and even at the colony of Liberia, founded chiefly by the slaveholders of America themselves, a public newspaper is written and printed by negroes, schools are conducted, and public worship is carried on, as well as in any part of the Union. The pretence of the incapacity of the negro race to receive instruction, must, therefore, be known to many who use it, to be a false one.

The great plea for the continuance of slavery, in this quarter, is, however, that the slaves are wholly unable to maintain and protect themselves, and that it is pure humanity towards the race to keep them in this condition. And yet, so well able are the greatest number of negroes to earn their own subsistence, and conduct their own affairs, that many of them are hired out by their masters to various persons needing their labour; by which they get so much more than is necessary for their own support, that they maintain themselves out of their wages first, and then hand over the surplus, often amounting to half their earnings, to their masters, as interest or profit on the capital laid out in their purchase. One master mentioned to me his having given 1500 dollars, or 300*l.* sterling for a slave; and when I asked why he paid so large a sum for him, he answered, that the man was fully worth it, because he could earn a handsome income. But when I followed up this question by asking whether the income made by the slave's labour and skill were given to *himself* the master replied, without being apparently conscious of the wrong, "Oh, no! his earnings belong to *me*, because I bought him; and in return for this I give him maintenance, and make a handsome profit besides." It is in this way that the increase of slaves by breeding, as in Sir Roger de Coverley's plantation, adds to a planter's income; but if the slave were free, the earnings would be his own, while now they are taken from him; and if this be not a violation of the scriptural maxim that "the labourer is worthy of his hire," it is difficult to know what would be so.

On this subject, however, the prejudices of the southern people are as inveterate as those of the inhabitants of China or Hindoostan in favour of their ancient customs and superstitions; or as those of certain classes in England, on subjects in which their own personal and pecuniary interests completely blind their judgments.

1.   Charleston was burnt down in 1740, when 300 of the best houses were consumed, and £200,000 worth of property destroyed. On this occasion the British parliament granted £20,000 for relief.

Chapter V

At the season of the year in which we had the pleasure of being at Charleston, January and February, 1839, nothing could be more agreeable than the temperature, nothing more healthy than the climate. The thermometer was usually from 50° to 60° in the daytime, and rarely below 40° at the coolest part of the night. There was occasional rain, but neither frost nor snow; and the bright sun was deliciously warm and pleasurable in the open air. We enjoyed this the more, perhaps, from having, by our coming here, escaped the excessive cold of the North; for, in addition to the violent gales and floods that had committed such ravages at Boston, New York, and Philadelphia, since our arrival here, we gathered the following particulars respecting the temperature at the North since we quitted it:—

> Severe cold at the North.—The Albany Argus states, that on Wednesday last, the thermometer, at seven o'clock, A.M., stood at twenty-two degrees above zero, and in two hours and a half thereafter had fallen to zero! From that time the mercury continued to fall, but more gradually, and at eight o'clock, P.M., stood at eight degrees below zero! There was a keen and violent wind from the north-west through the whole day.

The following day appears to have been much colder, according to the annexed report of the temperature, which we find in the New York Commercial Advertiser;—

At					
	Saratoga Spa	Jan. 24,	7 A.M.	33	below zero
	Balston Spa	"	7 "	33	"
	Albany	"	6½ "	14	"
	Boston	"	7 "	14	"

Charlestown, near Boston	"	7 A.M.	10	below zero
Chelsea	"	8 "	7	"
Dorchester	"	6 "	15	"

During our stay at Charleston, we had an opportunity of learning some useful information respecting the recent introduction of the culture of silk in various parts of the country, for which the soil and climate are admirably adapted, but especially in the southern states of Carolina, Georgia, and Florida. The following article on this subject appeared in one of the Charleston papers during our stay there.

Silk Culture.—An interesting article on the silk culture will be found in this day's paper, taken from the Richmond Enquirer. If that important culture has attracted much attention in the North, certainly in the South, where the climate is better adapted to that branch of agriculture, a greater interest should be taken in its improvement. That the people of the north can raise and manufacture silk to great advantage, we had ocular proof on Tuesday last, in company with a number of our citizens, at the Eagle and Phœnix hotel. Mr. Olmsted, a gentleman from East Hartford, Connecticut, who has devoted much of his attention to the subject, and who is now on a visit to the South, was kind enough to exhibit to us a number of samples of sewing, twist, and raw silk, of various colours, which will bear a comparison with any of the same kind imported, and which was raised and manufactured on his own farm, during the past year, by Mr. J. Danforth. The samples exhibited to us were parts of the product of an eighth of an acre of ground, planted as an experiment. We were informed by Mr. Olmsted, that the trees from which the worms were fed were planted between the 15th and 20th of May last, in rows of 3½ feet, on land cultivated the preceding year, and of a sandy loam, ploughed up about the middle of September, at the rate of 20,000 an hour. He commenced gathering the leaves and feeding about the 10th of July. The quantity of leaves gathered amounted to 1194 lbs. The quantity of silk-worms fed, 32,000; and the quantity of cocoons produced nine bushels, yielding nine pounds of silk, waste silk and floss one pound. About 5000 of the worms were fed on 180 lbs. of leaves, and the product of them was two bushels of cocoons, or two pounds of silk. This establishes the fact, that 90 lbs. of leaves of the *Morus Multicaulis* are sufficient to produce one pound of silk. He commenced plucking the leaves when the trees were four and five feet high, leaving four leaves at the top of the tree. He thinks the products of an eighth of an acre would have been more than

1200 lbs. of leaves; but being short of worms, he had use for no more than 1164 lbs. If we take the estimate of 1200 lbs. of leaves to the eighth of an acre, as a basis, the product of an acre would be over 100 lbs. of silk; but allowing even 100 lbs. to the acre, the silk, manufactured in sewing-silk, being worth ten dollars per pound, the produce of one acre of land would be 1000 dollars, besides multiplying the trees for market.

The exhibition taking place at the hotel at which we were staying, I attended it; and I thought the specimens, both of raw and manufactured silk, of which there were various kinds, quite equal to any that I had seen in Europe. If this be the result in the very infancy of the undertaking, there can be very little doubt that the culture and manufacture of silk will, in a few years, become a most important branch of domestic industry in the United States; the more so, as it can be cultivated in all the States, from Maine to Louisiana, whereas the present chief staple, cotton, can only be grown in the warm region south of the Potomac. Already, it is said that nine of the States have offered premiums for encouraging the culture of silk, and others will probably soon follow.

The population of Charleston city was, by the last decennial census of 1830, returned at 30,289; the Neck, which adjoins it, though beyond the city boundary, contained 10,054; and the whole district of Charleston has 86,338. The proportions of this population are at present estimated to be about one-half white and one-half coloured, including slaves and free. This proportion applies to the city population only; as in the entire State the coloured persons exceed the whites; the whole population, in 1830, being 581,458, in the following classes:—

| White Males, | 130,590 | Slaves, Males, | 165,625 | Free Coloured Males, | 3,672 |
| White Females, | 127,273 | Slaves, Females, | 160,040 | Free Coloured Females, | 4,249 |

The white population of Charleston are chiefly engaged in trade and commerce, though there appears to be a larger proportion of professional men, clergy, lawyers, and physicians, mingled with these, than in the northern cities; and even the merchants have a more liberal education, and more gentlemanly deportment, than is general with the same classes in the north. The native Southerners are easily distinguished from the New England settlers, and from other foreigners, by their brunette complexions, black eyes, and black hair. There is a sort of dandyism, in the dress of the young men especially, which is peculiarly southern: short frock-coats, small black stocks, rounded shirt-collars, turned down outside the stock to give coolness to the neck, hair or beard under the throat, low-crowned and broad-brimmed white felt hats, and walking-sticks, are among the most striking parts of the costume. The women are, in general, handsomer, more graceful, and more ladylike, than those of the same classes in the north; and the style of living with both is on a more sumptuous and liberal scale than in the northern cities; while they continue to sustain the ancient reputation of Carolina for "the hospitality of her sons, and the intelligence and influence of her daughters."

The descriptions given of the State in 1764, by Grahame, from the best authorities of that day, would equally apply to Charleston, at least, in the present. He says, "South Carolina, which had continued to advance in growth, notwithstanding the pressure of the war, reaped an ample and immediate share of the advantages resulting from the peace of Paris. 'It has been remarked,' says the historian Hewit, at this period, 'that there are more persons possessed of between five and ten thousand pounds sterling, in South Carolina, than are to be found anywhere else among the same number of people.' In point of rank, all men regard their neighbours as their equals, and, a noble spirit of benevolence pervades the society. The planters were generally distinguished by their hospitable dispositions, their sociable manners, and the luxurious cheer of their tables. Almost every family kept a one-horse chaise, and some maintained the most splendid equipages that Britain could furnish. All the new literary publications in London were regularly transmitted to the province. Hunting and horse-racing were favourite amusements of the men—assemblies, concerts, balls, and plays, were common. 'It is acknowledged by all,' says Hewit, 'but especially by strangers, that the ladies in this province considerably outshine the men; they are not only sensible, discreet, and virtuous, but also adorned with most of those polite and elegant accomplishments becoming their sex;' a praise, which was justified in a very remarkable manner in the year 1780, when the courageous patriotism and inflexible fortitude of the women of South Carolina restored the expiring cause of liberty in the province."

At present there is the same hospitality and generosity among the men, and the same elegance and politeness of manner among the women; but balls and concerts are now very rare, and the only theatre here is not much frequented, at least by the higher classes of society, its chief supporters being strangers, and persons below the middle rank of life; which is the case, indeed, throughout the United States generally. A taste for literature is more prevalent here, however, than in most of the American cities; and there appeared to me to be a much more general acquaintance with the popular writers of Europe among the society of Charleston than in that of Boston, with less of pretension. The library of the city is much resorted to by all classes, and it contains an excellent collection of the best works of the last and present century, exceeding 15,000 volumes. Attached to the library is also a museum of natural history, in which are collected a number of interesting objects, the inspection of which afforded me several days agreeable and instructive occupation.

Among other facts communicated to me during my stay here, I learnt that there had never yet been a divorce granted, either by the judiciary, or the legislature of this State, though one of the oldest in the Union. There is no law against granting divorces, nor have there been wanting many applications for them, and some strongly supported; but the general feeling of the legislature and bench has been, that it is better for a few to be denied this release from uncongenial alliances, than that a door should be opened for the too frequent separations of those who are once united. The effect of this is said to be to produce greater care and caution, in the formation of marriage unions; and if so, society is greatly benefitted thereby.

Before the revolution there was one British governor, at least, who appeared to have taken great pains to promote intermarriages between the native Indians and British or American females. Sir William Johnson is said by Grahame, on the authority of the Annual Register for 1766, to have "cultivated the good-will of the Indian tribes by the respect which he showed for their manners and usages, and studied to promote their friendly coalition with the British colonists, by encouraging the intermarriages of the two races. His exertions appear to have been attended with some success; for we find that in the year 1766, no fewer than eighteen marriages were contracted, under his auspices, between Indian chiefs and young white women of South Carolina." This was at least a more humane mode of subjecting the Indians to British influence, than the horrid attempt made only two years before, in this quarter, when, according to the same authority, "there was despatched from England to America a pack of bloodhounds, by whose peculiar instinct it was expected that the British troops would be materially aided in discovering the tracks and retreats of their Indian foes."

CHAPTER VI

On Friday, the 8th of February, we left Charleston for Savannah. We were attended to the steam-boat "William Seabrook," by a number of friends, whose expressions of regret at our departure, and hope of our meeting again, were more than usually ardent, and, as we had every reason to believe, sincere. We quitted the wharf about 11 o'clock in the forenoon. Our voyage was to be made by the inner passage, as it is called, for the purpose of touching at several small villages and plantations on our way, this steam-vessel being so occupied for the accommodation of the planters living near the route. All along the coast of North and South Carolina, as well as of Georgia and Florida, there are a number of small low islands, separated from the continent only by narrow arms of the sea, in the shape of creeks; and these mingling with branches of rivers, bays, and lakes afford a continuous chain of water communication, within the island, at distances of from ten to fifty miles inland from the ocean. This series of islands is chiefly devoted to the cultivation of the finer kinds of cotton, called, from the place of its growth, "Sea-Island cotton;" and as the plantations are numerous and the population considerable, the inner passage, between these islands and the mainland, is more interesting to one who wishes to see the country, than the outer passage by the sea. We therefore preferred going by it, although I had been offered a passage for myself and family in the larger steam-vessel, the "Charleston," which was going round from hence, under the direction of General Hamilton on his way to Texas, to the government of which this steamer had been sold, and on her way she was to touch at the principal parts of Georgia and Florida.

In the course of the afternoon we took in tow a long boat, rowed by twelve negroes, with a covered cabin, in which were two slaves in custody of a white sheriff's officer, conveying them to one of the judicial stations for trial. It appeared that an overseer, or driver, on a plantation, had been shot dead by a negro belonging to an adjoining estate, and these two men were taken up on suspicion, one as the perpetrator, and the other as an accomplice in the act. The reason assigned by our white informants on board for the murder was this:— They alleged that the negroes were often in the habit of stealing cattle from their masters' plantations, as well as from the neighbouring estates, and their overseer being a vigilant man, had often detected them; so that to remove him, and thus carry on their depredations unmolested, they had shot him with a rifle. I inquired what they did with the stolen cattle, when they escaped detection; and was informed that they killed them in secret for food, some using the flesh themselves, others exchanging it with other negroes for rice; and some being given to runaway negroes, who were often secretly sustained in this manner by their fellow-slaves, till they could get safely out of their hiding places, and effect their escape.

I ventured to remark, that this seemed to prove two things: first, that the negroes were not sufficiently fed, as they were willing to encounter the risk of death in stealing food for their own use; and secondly, that there must be great sympathy among them with their runaway brethren, to incur the risk of death, to supply them also with the means of subsistence. But the general opinion of those with whom I conversed seemed to be, that there was something in the African race which made them naturally incapable of moral improvement, and insensible to all notions of distinction between right and wrong.

I could not help observing, however, that the testimonies of the same persons differed very much according to the turn which the conversation took. When they spoke of the coercion employed towards the negroes, and endeavoured to justify the necessity of it, they were represented as "an indolent, worthless, and ungrateful race, wholly incompetent to arouse themselves to voluntary labour by any adequate motive, and so ungrateful for favours received, that the better they were treated the worse they behaved." On the other hand, when it was lamented that they could not be elevated from their present condition, and made to feel the influence of hope for the future, and a desire to improve their circumstances, and bring up their children with some education, it was replied that "they were already as happy as persons could be, that they were perfectly contented with their condition, and on the whole a much better race without education than with, as they were now faithful, kind-hearted, and attached to their masters, whereas education would destroy all their natural virtues, and make them as vicious as the lower orders in other countries." Such were the contradictory statements which I heard, not from different persons, but from the same individuals.

About three o'clock in the afternoon, we entered one of the narrowest of the cuts communicating with the creeks and rivers between the islands, and close to the battle-ground of Stona, where a desperate conflict arose between the British and American forces during the revolutionary war. Here the steam-boat took the ground at the very top of high water, so that all hopes of getting her off again were vain, until the next return of the flood, when the night tide, being higher than that of the day, would probably float her through.

We remained here, therefore, through a tedious night; though there was much in our favour, to counterbalance this inconvenience; for the boat was furnished with excellent accommodations: the table was better supplied than in most hotels on shore, the captain was a gentlemanly and attentive man, and the passengers, to the number of nearly 100, contained many intelligent and agreeable persons, so that the time was beguiled by varied and instructive conversation. During our stay in this creek, only one alligator was seen, though they abound here in the summer; but at this season they are thought to be concealed in holes along the banks, in a state of torpidity. They are not dangerous to man, like the alligators of the tropics, but fly at the least sound or pursuit; though they will sometimes stand at bay with a dog, and instances have been known of large alligators drawing a young dog into the water, but this is rare. Musquitoes also abound here in the summer season; and the whole region being one of marshy land, and often flooded, is extremely unhealthy from August to October, when few white persons remain here, and all intercourse by the inner passage is then suspended for the more healthy route by the open sea.

At four o'clock in the morning of the 9th, the water was found to be just high enough to float the vessel off the mud, though we had not three inches of depth to spare; and we were obliged to propel the vessel to her utmost capacity of speed to get through this shallow cut while the high water continued. We continued our course through the same description of creeks and narrow passages, and with the same character of scenery on both sides; the weather was however delicious, the thermometer being at 65°, the air fresh and balmy, like a fine English day in June, though now in the early part of February, when the cold in the Chesapeake was so severe, as to close the navigation of that noble bay by the ice.

At sunrise of the second day we arrived at Edisto, a small village on the northern edge of the island of that name, one of the sea-islands devoted to the cultivation of cotton. And after receiving a supply of fire-wood, we proceeded on our way, with increasing breadth of water, and increasing interest of scenery from the greater variety and abundance of wood; until, at sun-set we reached the town of Beaufort, or Port Royal, where we remained for an hour to discharge and take in freight and passengers.

This is a small place, inhabited chiefly by wealthy planters, and families in easy circumstances, who come here to reside at certain seasons of the year, for the sake of the sea-breezes, which blow through the inlet at the head of which it is situated, and is not at all a place of trade. Its population, white and coloured, does not exceed 1,000 persons. The most healthy spots along the coast are the dry sandy ridges near the sea; and these preserve their salubrity throughout the summer and autumn; while, within a mile of such positions, where moisture and decayed vegetation exist, the miasma produces a fever that is fatal to strangers, and very dangerous even to the natives of the soil, who leave these parts to the negroes and a few overseers on their estates.

At eight o'clock we left Beaufort, and at ten arrived at a place called Hilton Head, the opening of a broader passage, where we anchored for the night; and getting under way at four in the morning, we passed at daylight, a small fort and light-house, on Cockspur Island; and at eight o'clock entered a stream called the Tybee, which led us soon into the Savannah river. After passing by a number of large ships anchored a few miles below the town, two or three only of which were American, and the greater number from London, Liverpool, Glasgow, and Cork, we reached the city of Savannah at ten o'clock, and hauling alongside the wharf, were soon furnished with conveyances to take us to the Pulaski Hotel, where we took up our abode.

We remained here a fortnight, and passed our time most agreeably. Having been favoured with many letters of introduction from Charleston, we were soon surrounded by a large circle of friends, and many of the principal families to whom we had no letters, were quite as cordial in the voluntary tender of their hospitalities. We attended several large parties, and many more small social circles, in each of which we found ourselves completely at home. We were taken to some of the pleasantest drives around the city, and to all the public institutions within it, while my two courses of lectures, which were very fully attended, that on Palestine in the Unitarian church, and that on Egypt in the Baptist church, brought us every day acquainted with new friends, not only among the residents of the city, but with persons from the interior passing through Savannah, on their way to other places, and many and urgent were the entreaties that I would visit the several towns from whence they came.

CHAPTER VII

The history of the foundation and progress of the State of Georgia may be more briefly told than that of the more northern provinces, though it is not without its incidents of public interest. It appears from Sir Walter Raleigh's Journal, corroborated by the testimony of the Indians, at the first settlement of Georgia, that long before its being taken possession of by the English, it had been visited by Sir Walter Raleigh who sailed up the Savannah river, and landed and held a conference with some Indian chiefs on the very spot on which the city of Savannah now stands. The territory now forming the State of Georgia, was first included in the patent granted to South Carolina, of which the history has been already given; and it was then under a proprietary government. In 1719, however, it became a royal territory, its limits being between the 31st and 36th degrees of latitude; and it was not until 1732 that it was granted by charter to an incorporated company by George the Second, in honour of whom its present name of Georgia was given.

The circumstances which gave rise to this grant were of a mixed character. The possession of Florida by the Spaniards was a source of continual apprehension and difficulty to the settlers of South Carolina; and it was thought desirable to interpose between these two a barrier State or province, and by peopling it with Europeans well armed and trained, to make it answer as an advanced post of defence. This was undoubtedly the first motive which led to the settling of Georgia. About the same period, however, that this was projected, a number of Englishmen, some animated by religious zeal, some by philanthropy, and some by patriotism, conceived the design of promoting the settlement of this then unoccupied region; the religionists, to open an asylum for the persecuted Protestants of various countries in Europe; the philanthropists, to secure a home for the many poor families in Britain, whose labour was inadequate to obtain them a decent subsistence; and the patriots, to strengthen the British power, and extend its dominion over these distant lands.

It was in 1728, that General Oglethorpe, who may be called the founder of Georgia, being then a member of the British House of Commons, obtained its sanction to the appointment of a committee of inquiry into the state of the prisons in England. Of this committee he was nominated chairman; and in the following year it presented a report which induced the House to adopt measures for reforming some of the most prominent evils of the prison-system of discipline then existing. The illustrious Howard, in his philanthropic labours of examining the prisons of England, and exposing their abuses, had brought to light such facts as almost staggered belief, while they touched the sympathy of many benevolent hearts, and prepared the way for a great effort of reformation. A rich and humane citizen of London, having bequeathed his ample fortune for the express purpose of liberating as many insolvent debtors from prison as its amount would allow, some members of parliament undertook to visit the jails, and select the objects that seemed most worthy to be participators of this generous bequest. The difficulty of obtaining for these released debtors suitable and profitable employment when set free, was, however, much greater than the task of selecting them; and it was partly to meet this difficulty, as well as to provide for the other objects named, that Oglethorpe and his benevolent associates conceived the plan of founding a new colony between South Carolina and Florida, and transporting to it as settlers as many of the poor and destitute thus released from their imprisonment, as could be prevailed upon to go, including as many others as their means of transport and settlement would admit.

In pursuance of this philanthropic design, application was made to the monarch, by Oglethorpe and his associates, for a charter of incorporation, which was readily granted, and the sum of 10,000*l.* sterling was also obtained by a vote of the House of Commons, to be added to the private estate left by the London merchant for the liberation of insolvent debtors. To this also was promised to be added the funds previously raised for Bishop Berkeley's college for instructing the Indians, but never appropriated. The Moravians, who in 1727 first proclaimed their intention of undertaking missionary labours on an extensive scale, hearing of this intended new colony, offered to unite a portion of their body with it; so that the foundation thus appeared to be laid of a useful and prosperous settlement. The royal charter granted in 1732 ceded all the territory between the rivers Alatamaha and Savannah, as a separate and independent province, under the title of Georgia, to twenty noblemen and gentlemen under the title of "Trustees for settling and establishing the Colony of Georgia." Among these were the celebrated Lord Shaftesbury, author of "The

Characteristics," Lords Percival, Tyrconnel, Limerick, and Carpenter, James Edward Oglethorpe, and Stephen Hales, an English clergyman, and one of the most distinguished natural philosophers of the day. These were entrusted with the powers of legislation for twenty years, after which the colony was to lapse to the crown, and be placed under such form of government as the monarch then reigning might determine.

The trustees being empowered to collect contributions from the public for assisting the first settlers, gave an example to others by their own liberality, which was imitated by many wealthy persons. The Bank of England gave a large donation; and the House of Commons voted several sums, amounting in the whole to £36,000. Some silk-workers from Piedmont, bringing with them a quantity of silk worms' eggs hatched in Italy, were engaged to accompany the first expedition; as the cultivation of silk was one of the first objects intended to be put in practice. All being prepared for their departure, General Oglethorpe, placing himself at the head of the first body of emigrants, sailed from Gravesend with 116 persons, to found the colony proposed.

In January, 1733, they reached Charleston, where they received considerable assistance from the Carolinians. After a short stay there, they proceeded to the station then called Yamacran, where they planted their first settlement, and called it, from the name of the river on which it stood, Savannah. In the preliminary operations of felling trees, clearing the ground, and erecting dwellings, Oglethorpe himself joined with cheerfulness and zeal; and in the intervals between this labour, he exercised his followers in military movements and discipline; while steps were taken to establish a friendly relation with the Indians then residing here. By the assistance of an Indian female, the wife of a trader from Carolina, who could speak both the English and the Indian tongues, an invitation was conveyed from General Oglethorpe to all the Indian chiefs of the Creek tribe, to hold a conference with him at Savannah; and they came readily, to the number of fifty warriors, at the time and place appointed. To these, the General represented the great power of the English nation, and pointed out the advantages that would result to the Indians from their friendship and alliance. He added, that as the Indians had much more land than they could occupy, he hoped they would readily grant a portion of it to the people who had come from so great a distance to settle among them; and in token of his good-will, he distributed various presents among the chiefs.

To this, the most aged warrior of the tribe, Tomochichi, replied, by giving the assent of himself and all his followers to the request made, while he in turn presented, to General Oglethorpe, a buffalo's hide, on which were delineated, an eagle to represent speed, and a buffalo to represent strength, saying, "The English are as swift as the bird, and as strong as the beast; since, like the first, they fly from the uttermost parts of the earth over the vast seas; and, like the second, they are so strong that nothing can withstand them." He added, that the feathers of the eagle were soft, and signified love; the buffalo's skin was warm, and signified protection; and he hoped that the English would exemplify those attributes in loving and protecting the families of the Indians. He acknowledged that the Great Spirit, which dwelt in heaven and all around, had endowed the English with wisdom and riches, so that they wanted nothing; while the same Power had lavished great territories on the Indians, who were still in want of everything. He added, that the Creeks would be quite willing to resign to the English, the lands that were useless to themselves, and permit the English to settle among them, so that they might be instructed in useful knowledge, and supplied with improved accommodations of life. A treaty was accordingly concluded by the Indians with the English; rules for mutual traffic, and the adjustment of mutual disputes, were established; all lands then unoccupied by the Indians were assigned to the English, under the condition that the Indians should be previously apprized of the intended formation of every new township; and they then promised, "with straight hearts, and love to their English brethren," that they would allow no other race of white men to settle among them in the country.

The trustees in England now began to frame a code of laws for Georgia, and these were some of its most prominent enactments. It was provided that each tract of land granted to a settler should be held as a military fief, obliging the possessor to appear in arms whenever called upon for the public defence; and that no original tract should exceed fifty acres. In order to keep up the military hardihood and spirit, and to prevent a plurality of tracts coming, in process of time, into the same hands, and engendering wealth and habits of luxury, it was enacted that males only should succeed to the property of deceased parents; that women should be incompetent to inherit landed estate; and that in the failure of male heirs, the lands were to revert to the trustees as a lapsed fief, to be granted to other colonists on the original terms. No inhabitant was to be allowed to quit the province without a license, to prevent fraudulent escape of traders dealing with the Indians. The importation of rum was disallowed; trade with the West Indies was declared unlawful; and negro slavery was absolutely prohibited.

The reasons assigned for this last enactment are sufficiently curious to be given in detail. They do not appear to have been founded on any notion of the injustice or inhumanity of slavery, but purely on prudential and selfish grounds. It was thought that the first cost of a negro would be at least £30, and this would exhaust so much of the capital of a poor settler, as to cripple his means in the very outset of his career. It was thought also that the white man, by having a negro slave, would be less disposed to labour himself, and that a great portion of his time would be employed in keeping the negro at work, and in watching against any danger which he or his family might apprehend from the slaves. It was believed that upon the admission of negroes, the wealthy planters would, as in other colonies, be induced to absent themselves to more pleasant places of residence, leaving the care of their plantations to negroes and overseers; and that the introduction of negroes would increase a propensity for idleness among the poor planters also, as well as their families, and thus entirely defeat the object of the settlement, which was to provide for and bring up a race of industrious and prosperous people.

These reasons, satisfactory as they may appear to some, as to the *inexpediency* of negro slavery in such a settlement, to say nothing of its *injustice* anywhere, made no impression on either the Georgians or Carolinians; the last, especially, were not slow to express their indignation and disgust at laws which indirectly cast so severe a censure on their own institutions. It was easy, of course, to find excuses for negro-slavery, as it is for any other injustice; and accordingly it was alleged "that it was indispensable to the prosperity of the settlement, because the strength of European constitutions, unaided by negro labour, could make no impression on the vast and stubborn forests by which they were surrounded." Upon this Mr. Grahame very justly and forcibly remarks, that "Europeans had now become so habituated to regard negroes as slaves, and to despise them as a servile and degraded race, that it never occurred, either to the trustees or the colonists, that, by an equitable intercourse and association between white men and negroes, the advantage of negro *labour* might be obtained, without the concomitant injustice of negro *slavery*."

In 1735, General Oglethorpe returned from England to Georgia, accompanied by a small party of Moravians, who had accepted a grant of land for cultivation, and an exemption from military service, as, like the Quakers, they refused, on religious grounds, to engage in any war; and like them, also, the preachers as well as the hearers were enjoined to obtain their own subsistence by their labours.

The celebrated John Wesley, and his brother Charles, also accompanied General Oglethorpe on this voyage, as well as several of their religious brethren; and there were no less than three hundred passengers, including one hundred and seventy Germans of the Moravian society. Their voyage out was long and stormy, as they sailed in October, 1735, and did not arrive till February, 1736; but the manner in which they passed their time, shows that no inconveniences or privations could damp the ardour of the spirit by which they had been animated to undertake this perilous enterprise. The importation of such a body of people as these into a colony originally planted by insolvent debtors, where, mingled with the poor and needy, were many desperate and reckless characters, could hardly fail to produce great benefits; and such, indeed, was the result. About the same period there arrived also in the settlement, a hundred and fifty Highlanders from Scotland. These formed a small town on the river Alatamaha, which they called New Inverness. They also built a fort, which they called Darien, the name now borne by the town itself, which has grown up to be a considerable place. Here they continued to wear the Highland dress, and to preserve their national manners, as among their native mountains, and lived in a state of great industry, independence, and contentment.

The Wesleys, meanwhile, were stationed at Frederica and Savannah, at which they preached; but the ministry of John Wesley, at the last named place, was so much more rigid than was acceptable to the colonists, that he was obliged to quit it in 1736 for England, where he soon after founded the great sect of the Wesleyan Methodists, that still bear and venerate his name.

Augusta, nearly 200 miles up the Savannah river, was now begun to be built, and it and Frederica were fortified with artillery from England; but troubles multiplied thickly. War with the Spaniards of Florida threatened the Georgians on the one hand, and the discontent of the Carolinians menaced them on the other; while the dissatisfaction of the Georgians themselves with the restrictions placed on the importation of rum, in which their neighbours traded freely, and with the prohibition of employing negro slaves, which the people of Carolina did extensively, made them impatient and desirous of change.

The only two portions of the settlers who did not share in these discontents, were the Moravian Christians, and the Scotch Highlanders, each of whom pursued their industry, quietly, prosperously and happily. The former body had already made a plantation, which was a model of neatness, comfort, and successful husbandry; they had assisted their poorer and less industrious neighbours, and established a school and mission among the Creek Indians, with the most promising appearance of success. With indefatigable industry and charity they combined the most rigid sense of justice; and before another year had passed, they repaid to the Georgian trustees the money that had been advanced in London, to enable them to emigrate to America;—so that while the more indolent and dissolute of the early settlers clamoured against the prohibition of negro slavery, and declared that without this it was impossible to cultivate their lands or provide for their posterity, the Moravians silently demonstrated, by their successful industry, that slavery was unnecessary; and the Scotch Highlanders, to their great honour, protested against it, as an *outrage on justice*.

Soon after this, in 1738, war was declared between Great Britain and Spain; and General Oglethorpe, who had in the interim revisited England, sailed for Georgia again, with a regiment of 600 men, and a commission as commander-in-chief of all the forces in South Carolina and Georgia, while the Parliament made an additional grant of £20,000 for military services, and authorized the allotment of twenty-five acres of land to every soldier of seven years' service.

Just at this period, the Spaniards had been successful in exciting the negro slaves of South Carolina to revolt, by proclaiming liberty and protection to all who should seek refuge from slavery in Florida; and the excessive cruelty with which the slaves were then treated in this colony, induced many to become fugitives, and others to take up arms against their masters. The Journal of Charles Wesley contains some striking instances of this; but one or two are selected out of many. He says, "Colonel Lynch cut off the legs of a poor negro, and he kills several of them every year by his barbarities. Mr. Hill, a dancing-master in Charleston, whipped a female slave so long that she fell down at his feet in appearance dead; but when, by the help of a physician, she was so far recovered as to show some signs of life, he repeated the whipping with equal rigour, and concluded the punishment by dropping scalding wax upon her flesh: her only crime was overfilling a tea-cup! These horrid cruelties," he adds, "are the less to be wondered at, because the law itself, in effect, countenances and allows them to kill their slaves, by the ridiculous penalty appointed for it. The penalty is about seven pounds, one-half of which is usually remitted if the criminal inform against himself."

This, it may be said, was under British rule, and in colonial times—which is perfectly true; and on Britain be the just reproach of such a state of things. But the same historian very truly adds, "Traces of the cruelty with which slaves were anciently treated in South Carolina have lingered, it must be confessed, till a very late period, both in the laws of this province, and in the manners of its inhabitants. In 1808, two negroes were actually burned alive over a slow fire in the market-place of Charleston; and in 1816, the grand jury reported, 'as a most serious evil, that instances of negro homicide were common within the city for many years; the parties exercising unlimited control, as masters and mistresses, indulging their cruel passions in the barbarous treatment of slaves, and, therefore bringing on the community, the state, and the city, the contumely and reproach of the civilized world.' Here are the facts, and this the language of the jurors of the city in which they occurred, resting on the good authority of Bristed and Warden, two writers of credit in their own country; and therefore the reproach is not confined to the age of British rule, or the days of colonial cruelty.

The dissatisfaction of the slaves in Carolina led many of them to fly to Florida, where a body of about 500 negroes was formed into a regiment, by the governor of that province, with black officers. These were all clothed in the usual Spanish uniform, placed on a footing of equality with the white troops, and employed in the same warfare—a tolerable proof that the Spaniards did not doubt their *capacity*; while the people of Carolina and Georgia gave equal proof, by their alarms, how much they dreaded the *example*, not only of freedom, but of power, to their own slaves. Soon after this, in 1740, the celebrated George Whitefield visited Georgia, after the two Wesleys had left it. The first object of his mission was to preach the gospel to the Indians. He obtained a tract of land from the trustees, on which he built an orphan asylum, a few miles from Savannah, which was erected at great expense; but it has since been burnt down, and never rebuilt. During his stay here, he interested himself deeply in the amelioration of the condition of the slaves of the adjoining provinces; and one of his first publications in the colony was a letter addressed to the planters of Virginia, Maryland, and the Carolinas, on the cruelties inflicted on their negro slaves. At subsequent periods, during his long and frequent visits to America, he invariably advocated the interests of the negroes, and so successfully as to persuade a number of the planters to emancipate their slaves.

A succession of wars and skirmishes with Florida and the Indians followed, and in 1742 Oglethorpe left Georgia for England. He never after returned, though he lived to the age of 102, dying in 1785, and beholding the colony he had founded, separated from the mother-country and declared independent by the American revolution.

Ten years after Oglethorpe's retirement, the charter of Georgia was surrendered to the crown; at which period, 1752, the whole exports from the colony did not exceed £10,000 of value annually.

A new provincial constitution was given to it by Great Britain; and negro-slavery, hitherto prohibited in Georgia, was forthwith introduced into it, under the *royal sanction*; the restrictions on the importation of rum were also removed. The habits of nearly all classes were at this time remarkably intemperate and extravagant; while hunting, racing, cock-fighting, pugilistic exercises, and gambling, were too common throughout every part of the colony; arising, no doubt, from the combined causes of, first, the number of idle and dissolute persons who were among the early settlers, including even many convicted felons; secondly, the use of slave-labour, which made the whites averse to industrious occupation; and thirdly, the free use of intoxicating drinks, and the consequences always resulting from this vicious indulgence.

A beneficial change was, however, subsequently introduced, by the infusion of a much better class of men, a large number of Quakers having emigrated to Georgia, under the conduct of Joseph Mattock, a public-spirited member of this religious body. This was under the government of Sir James Wright, whose wisdom and liberality were subjects of the highest commendation; and whose example, in the successful cultivation of his own estate, was followed by many then already settled in Georgia, and by others who were induced by this success to come out as new settlers. In 1752, as we have seen, the whole annual exports did not exceed £10,000 in value; in 1763, the exports consisted of rice, indigo, corn, silk, skins, provisions, and timber, of the value of £27,000; and in 1773, the amount of staple commodities exported was £125,000.

We now approach the period of the American revolution, and find that on the 14th of July, 1774, a public meeting of the citizens of Georgia was held in Savannah for the purpose of considering what constitutional measures might be pursued to resist the arbitrary imposition of taxes on the American people by the British government. From this time onward, the people of Georgia took an active part in all measures to promote the revolution. In 1776, Savannah was attacked by the British, who were repulsed with some loss. In 1777, the first constituted Assembly met in Savannah with a Speaker and other officers, and authorized the raising and equipping a regular land-force. In 1778, another attack was made on Savannah by the naval forces under Sir Hyde Parker, and the military under General Howe; who were then more successful, taking possession of this city, and marching on to Augusta, which they captured also.

In 1779, a French fleet, under Count d'Estaing, appeared off Savannah, containing 21 ships of the line, 8 frigates, and 5 sloops, with 5,000 men. The attack was fierce and long continued, and the defence was obstinate and successful. The number of the killed and wounded on both sides was considerable; but in the end, the French fleet, and the allied army of the Americans that had joined them, were obliged to retire, and leave the British, under General Prevost, still in possession of the fort and city of Savannah. There they continued until 1783, when the general peace between Great Britain and the United States was ratified; and Savannah being then evacuated by the British, all Georgia was given up to the American government. On this occasion there embarked from Savannah, between the 12th and 25th of July of that year, 1783, about 7,000 persons for various parts of the British possessions, among whom were 1,200 British regulars and loyalists, 500 women and children, 300 Indians, and 5,000 negroes; but a large number of persons attached to the British cause; having property and connexions in this country, continued to remain there, and became legally-constituted American citizens.

From that period up to the present time, Georgia has gone on progressively improving in the developement of her resources, the building of cities and towns, and the formation of roads, canals, and steam-boat communication, as well as establishing institutions for the promotion of education; and the advance which it has made may be seen in the progressive increase of her population, and expansion of her exports and imports.

Population at different periods

In 1749	6,000	In 1800	162,686	In 1820	348,989
1790	82,548	1810	252,433	1830	516,567

And of this last number, taken by the census of 1830, the following were the different classes and proportions:—

| White Males | 153,236 | Free Coloured Males | 1,256 | Male Slaves | 108,946 |
| White Females | 143,378 | Free Coloured Females | 1,227 | Female Slaves | 108,524 |

| Deaf and Dumb | 147 | Blind | 143 | and | Aliens | 86 |

The State of Georgia, as at present established, since the cession of the large tracts of land given up to the general government, to form the States of Alabama and Mississippi, N. of 31°, amounting to 100,000 square miles, is in length from N. to S. about 300 miles; in breadth from E. to W. about 200 miles. It contains an area of about 60,000 square miles, or nearly 40 millions of acres; its latitude being from 30° to 35° N., and its longitude from 80° to 86° W. Like the Carolinas, it has three distinct zones, or belts, of territory; that on the sea-coast being low, and full of islands and creeks; that in the centre being dry and sandy, or pine-barrens; and the westernmost belt being hilly and mountainous, increasing in salubrity as you advance from the sea into the interior.

The government of the State consists of a Governor, and two Houses of Legislature, which meet at Milledgeville, the legislative capital of the State, for a few months in the winter. The constitution of the State, and the election and term of office of its representatives and senators, differ in nothing from that of the other States generally. The governor has a salary of 3000 dollars, or 600*l.* sterling, per annum; while the secretary of state, the comptroller-general, the treasurer, and the surveyor-general, have each only 2000 dollars. The judiciary is divided into ten circuits, with a judge for each circuit; their salaries being each 2100 dollars. These judges are appointed by the legislature for life, or during good behaviour. But there is an inferior court held in each county, composed of five justices, who are elected by the people every five years, and who serve without salary. There is, however, no court of errors, or tribunal of appeal from the decisions of any of the circuit courts, so that the judgment of each is final; and though several attempts have been made to establish such a court, public opinion seems to be against it, from a conviction that increasing the number of courts and judges, only gives rise to increased litigation and increased expense to the suitors.

The maintenance of the poor is by a "poor-tax," levied on the inhabitants of each county in which any poor are found. But as the slave population perform almost all the laborious duties in agriculture, and as emigrants do not come here from Europe direct in any great numbers, the poor are so few that no returns are ever made of their numbers, or the cost of their subsistence.

Education is well provided for in Georgia. At Athens, in the interior of the State, is a college which has about 200 students. At Columbus, in the same State, is a female college, recently established, and containing an equal number of students; and in each county there is an academy for the higher branches of education. An act was passed, in January of the present year, to establish a general system of education by common schools, by which the academic and poor school funds are to be blended in one, and augmented by occasional grants from the State, to be applied to the promotion of education generally in all its branches. The whole of the schools, academies, and college, are under the superintendence of a board, called the *Senatus Academicus*, composed of the governor and senate of the State and fifteen trustees. These appoint a board of commissioners in each county, of which there are 39, to superintend the academy and common schools in each. In 1817, 200,000 dollars were appropriated by the State legislature, for the establishment of free-schools, and there are now upwards of 100 academies in the State, besides common schools, increasing in number every year.

Religion is also well supported, and wholly by the voluntary system. There are upwards of 400 Baptist churches and 40,000 communicants. The Methodists have 80 ministers and about 30,000 members. The Presbyterians have 60 churches, the Episcopalians 6; and there are places of worship also for Universalists, Unitarians, Lutherans, Quakers, and Jews; but the last five are among the fewest in number of all the sects. The aggregate, however, makes nearly 600 churches to a population of 600,000 in round numbers; thus keeping up the usual ratio throughout the United States, of a place of worship to every 1000 inhabitants; a larger proportion, it is believed, than that of any other country on the globe; and itself, no doubt, a consequence of the larger proportion of schools and people educated, to the whole community, than anywhere else exists.

The banking capital of the State is considerable, exceeding, it is believed, at the present moment, ten millions of dollars. A large proportion of this, however, is employed in promoting internal improvement in railroads and canals; the result is, that these works are carried on with great vigour, and bid fair to place Georgia on a par with any of the northern States in these respects, within a few years from the present period.

CHAPTER VIII

Savannah, the principal city and sea-port of Georgia, is agreeably and advantageously situated; it was founded, and its plan laid out, by Governor Oglethorpe in 1733; and as his own description of the locality, and the reasons which induced him to select it, are remarkable for their clearness, and interesting from their precision, I transcribe them from an original letter of his writing, dated "From the camp near Savannah, the 10th of February, 1733," and addressed to the trustees who formed the proprietary government then in London.

I gave you an account in my last of our arrival in Charleston. The governor and assembly have given us all possible encouragement. Our people arrived at Beaufort on the 20th of January, where I lodged them in some new barracks built for the soldiers, whilst I went myself to view the Savannah river. I fixed upon a healthy situation, about ten miles from the sea. The river here forms a half-moon, along the south side of which the banks are about forty feet high, and on the top a flat, which they call a bluff. The plain high ground extends into the country about five or six miles, and along the river-side about a mile. Ships that draw twelve feet water can ride within ten yards of the bank. Upon the river-side, in the centre of this plain, I have laid out the town, opposite to which is an island of very rich pasturage, which I think should be kept for the trustees' cattle. The river is pretty wide, the water fresh, and from the key (quay) of the town you see its whole course to the sea, with the island of Tybee, which forms the mouth of the river. For about six miles up the river into the country, the landscape is very agreeable, the stream being wide, and bordered with woods on both sides. The whole people arrived here on the 1st of February; at night their tents were got up. Till the 10th, we were taken up in unloading and making a crane, which I

then could not get finished, so I took off the hands; and set some to the
fortification, and began to fell the woods. I have marked out the town
and common; half of the former is already cleared, and the first house
was begun yesterday in the afternoon.

The city is laid out with the greatest regularity, the streets running in parallel
lines with the river from east to west, and these crossed by others at right angles
running north and south. Philadelphia itself is not more perfect in its symmetry
than Savannah; and the latter has this advantage over the former, that there are
no less than eighteen large squares, with grass-plats and trees, in the very heart of
the city, disposed at equal distances from each other in the greatest order; while
every principal street is lined on each side with rows of trees, and some of the
broader streets have also an avenue of trees running down their centre. These
trees are called by some, the Pride of India, and by others, the Pride of China;
they give out a beautiful lilac flower in the spring. There are others also, as the
live-oak, and the wild cherry, both evergreens, and, when in full foliage, their
aspect and their shade must be delightful. Even now, in February, when this is
written, the prospect up and down every street in the city, intersected as it is by
squares and rows of trees, is peculiarly pleasing, and gives the whole the most
rural appearance imaginable.

Along the bank of the river, and on the edge of the bluff on which the city
stands, is a long and broad street, having its front to the water, and built only
on one side. The part nearest the water is planted with rows of trees, having
seats placed between; and this street, which is called "The Bay," is the principal
resort for business. The counting-houses, warehouses, and best shops, are along
this Bay; the Exchange and Post Office, as well as the city offices, are here; and
underneath the bluff, or cliff, are the warehouses and wharfs, alongside which
the vessels load with cotton, while the tops of their masts are a little higher only
than the level of the street, the height of the cliff from the water varying from
forty to seventy feet.

The greater number of the dwelling-houses are built of wood, and painted
white; but there are many handsome and commodious brick buildings occupied
as private residences, and a few mansions, built by an English architect, Mr.
Jay—son of the celebrated divine of that name at Bath—which are of beautiful
architecture, of sumptuous interior, and combine as much of elegance and
luxury as are to be found in any private dwellings in the country. The shops
are in general small, and not well provided with goods, though some wholesale
warehouses on an extensive scale are found. Of hotels, there are three, the City
Hotel, the Mansion House, and the Pulaski; but as they all belong to the same
proprietor, there is no competition among them, and the usual consequences

follow—great indifference, and most extravagant charges. The Pulaski, at which we stopped, was the best, and the dearest;—our party of four, including my youngest son and a man-servant, costing, to board and lodge, without private sitting-rooms, ten dollars per day.

Of public buildings there are not many remarkable ones. The Exchange, Post Office, and City Offices, are all included in a large brick edifice on "The Bay," surmounted by a tower, and from this is to be had the finest and most interesting view of the city. The Court House is a chaste building, of the Doric order, with portico and colonnade, near the centre of the town. The United States' Bank, and the Bank of the State of Georgia, are two handsome edifices; and these, with the Custom House, the Academy, the Theatre, the Public Market, the Arsenal, and the Jail, with some new barracks recently built for the United States' troops, who are now employed in the Florida war, make up the sum of the public buildings of the city.

Of churches there are ten; two Presbyterian, one Episcopal, one Methodist, one Baptist, one Roman Catholic, one Unitarian, one Lutheran, and two meeting-houses for coloured people, as well as a synagogue for the Jews, who are here as numerous and wealthy as at Charleston. Of these churches, there is but one that is very conspicuous, and this is the Independent-Presbyterian church, which is really a beautiful structure. It was built by the architect of the two fine churches at Providence, but is larger than either; its spire is one of the loftiest, lightest, and most elegant that I had yet seen in the country; its portico is chaste and well proportioned; and its interior, for vastness, richness, and general beauty of effect, surpasses any place of worship that I remember to have seen in America. It cost 120,000 dollars, and is as substantial as it is elegant.

Of the public monuments there is one in the centre of Monument-square, being an obelisk of stone, on a raised pedestal, erected to the memory of Count Pulaski, a Polish noble, who, like his countryman Kosciusko, and Lafayette of France, took an active part in the war of the American revolution; and receiving his death-wound in the attack on Savannah, when the fleet of France and army of the United States combined for that purpose, while it was in possession of the British, he died at sea, and was buried in the deep with martial honours.

The population of Savannah is estimated to be at present 10,000, of whom about 5,000 are whites, and the remainder mostly slaves, though there are some free coloured people residing here. The white population are chiefly merchants, planters, bankers, and professional men; the laborious trades being all carried on by coloured persons, and nearly all the severe and menial labour is performed by slaves. Like the society of Charleston, this of Savannah is characterized by great elegance in all their deportment; the men are perfect gentlemen in their manners, and the women are accomplished ladies. A high sense of honour, and a freedom from all the little meannesses and tricks of trade, seem to prevail universally among the gentlemen, who are liberal, frank, and hospitable, without ostentation, or much pretence; while the ladies are not only well educated, but elegant in their manners, and mingle with the pleasures of the social circle, much of grace, and dignity, blended with the greatest kindness and suavity.

The social entertainments and family circles which we had the privilege of enjoying in Savannah, were extremely agreeable. As almost every family keeps a carriage, morning and evening visits are rarely interrupted by weather; and, as great cordiality appears to exist among all the residents, so strangers who become known to one family, are speedily introduced to every other. Gentlemen have their convivial meetings at each others' houses, and enjoy their athletic sports in clubs; one of which, the Quoit Club, I visited, and found a number of the members engaged in the healthy and vigorous exercise of throwing the discus, in which both strength of arm and accuracy of sight was manifested. The game was played after dinner, commencing about three in the afternoon, and lasting till sunset. The ground was about half a mile from the town, under the shade of a cluster of fine trees. Wine and cigars were provided for the members and visiters; and the use of both is so universal here, that I was the only visiter the members could remember since the club was formed, who had declined to partake of either. It should be added, however, that though wine is universally drank here, and champaigne in abundance, of which the ladies partake as freely as the gentlemen, I saw no intemperance, in the *ordinary* acceptation of that term, or, in other words, no intoxication. Spirit-drinking has been long since discontinued by the gentry, though it was once as frequent as wine-drinking is now; and when the Temperance Societies of the South shall take the high ground of entire abstinence from all intoxicating drinks, I have no doubt, that after a few years, wine-drinking will become as rare as spirit-drinking is at present.

The ladies of Savannah, though enjoying freely all the pleasures of elegant society, are not behind their countrywomen in the north, in the zeal with which they promote benevolent objects. An Orphan Asylum for the maintenance, education, and putting out to useful occupations, of orphans of both sexes, is chiefly maintained by ladies here; they have also Sewing Societies, the members of which meet once a week at each others' houses, and occupy four or five hours in needlework, the produce of which is devoted to the support of benevolent objects at home, and missionary exertions abroad; they appeared to me religious without being fanatical, and pious without being puritanical; thus blending elegant and innocent recreation, with charitable and philanthropic undertakings.

The military spirit seems to be as strong in this quarter as elsewhere, and men of all classes delight in military titles, and military displays. The principal banker and the principal bookseller of the city were both colonels; the hotel-keeper was a major; and captains abound in every class; nor do they receive their titles on parade only, but in the everyday address of business and conversation. During our stay at Savannah, the anniversary of Washington's birth-day, February 22d, was celebrated by a military display; and the companies that turned out on that occasion were well dressed, well disciplined, and had as perfectly martial an air as the National Guards of Paris, to which, both in uniform, stature, and general appearance, they bore a marked resemblance. During their exercises of the day, they fired at a target with rifles, and put in their balls with extraordinary skill. They are habituated to this practice, it is true, from their youth upward, for almost every boy of fourteen or fifteen has a horse and a rifle. Shooting matches are therefore frequent, and in deer-shooting they have almost daily opportunities of trying their aim; as the wild deer are here so abundant that they are shot in the woods within a mile or two of the town; and venison is therefore to be seen on almost every table.

The youths of both sexes appear to be brought up in less subjection to parental authority than in England. The boys are educated chiefly at day-schools: between the hours of school-attendance they are under very little restraint, and do pretty nearly what they like; many carry sticks or canes with them, and some even affect the bravo, by carrying bowie-knives, but it is more for show than use. The young ladies being also educated at day-schools, or at home, have much greater liberty allowed them in the disposal of their time, and the arrangement and control of their visits, than girls of the same age in England. The consequence is, great precocity of manners in both sexes, and often very early marriages. The following is taken from the newspapers of Savannah, and from the Augusta Sentinel, of February 20, 1839:—

MARRIED—On the 7th inst., by the Rev. S. Gibson, Mr. Hiram Dill, aged 14, to Miss Margaret Ann Langley, aged 13 years, both of Greenville District, South Carolina.

There are, however, few elopements, or seductions, and domestic infidelity is very rare; so that on the whole, married life appears to be quite as happy as in England; with this great advantage on the side of married life in America, namely, that almost all who marry are in easy circumstances as to fortune, or if not, they are sure to become so, if they exercise only ordinary prudence, because every kind of business is prosperous here, and labour of every description is handsomely rewarded; while in England, there are hundreds of newly-married persons who struggle on from month to month and year to year, with difficulties, arising from competition in the same branch of business, or the same professional career, which no amount of industry or prudence will overcome, and from which nothing but extraordinary ability, powerful patronage, or that favourable combination of circumstances, called "good luck," will extricate them. The same persons, if they could be transplanted to almost any part of the United States, would not only live at ease for the present, but, by a very slight attention to economy, would be sure of laying up provision for the future; and, above all, would be able to ensure to their children, however numerous, a good education, useful and well-paid employment, admission into good society, and every prospect of an elegant, if not an opulent retirement in old age:—prospects that are but dim and distant to the great majority of the struggling middle classes in England.

I have so often been struck with this since our residence in America, that I have thought it might be worth while to devise some plan by which the governments of the two countries might co-operate to promote the transfer, from various parts of Britain to the United States, not of the utterly destitute, as in the case of emigrants, but of people of small means, but good information, and high moral character among the middle classes. Both countries would benefit greatly by such an operation. England, by lessening the severity of that competition which makes all classes feel they are overstocked with labourers, and can only live by outbidding each other in the smallness of the remuneration they will consent to receive; and America, by the infusion into her growing population, of a much better stock and race than the present emigrants generally are.

CHAPTER IX

There are two newspapers in Savannah, the Daily Georgian, a democratic print, and the Daily Republican, a whig journal. Neither of these are so remarkable for talent or circulation as the Charleston Courier; but, like the Charleston papers, they are untainted by the vituperative language and abusive style of too many of the papers of the north. A third paper was attempted while we were here, called the Daily Telegraph; and though we were only in Savannah a fortnight altogether, we were there long enough to witness its birth and death, for it lived only eight days, and then expired.

The condition of the coloured population, slave and free, excited in me the liveliest interest, as I was anxious to see and judge for myself on this much contested point. Here, as at Charleston, the greatest anxiety seemed to be manifested on all sides as to my opinions on slavery. With some few I could safely venture to let these be known; as they were liberal enough to suppose that a man might, from conviction, be in favour of abolition, without designing any evil to the country; but with the great bulk of the white population here, the name of an abolitionist was more terrible than that of an incendiary, a rebel, or a murderer, and to such it would have been useless to make any observations on the subject.

From all I could perceive or learn, the condition of the domestic servants, or slaves of the household, was quite as comfortable as that of servants in the middle ranks of life in England. They are generally well-fed, well-dressed, attentive, orderly, respectful, and easy to be governed, but more by kindness than by severity.

If the slaves of America were confined to household attendants, I have no doubt that their condition would be very far from miserable; because the master and mistress of a family, and all the younger members of it, feel as natural a pride in having their personal attendants to look well in person and in dress, when slaves, as they do when their servants are free; for the same reason as ladies or gentlemen in England like to have their livery servants handsome and well-dressed, and their carriage-horses sleek, glossy, well-fed, and caparisoned with handsome harness. But when slaves are employed in field labour, as instruments of producing wealth, or when they are owned by one party, and hired out to another for wages to be received by the owner, then the case is very different, because the object is then, in each instance, to make as much money by them as possible, and turn them, as property, to the most profitable account; so that the least expense in food and clothing, compatible with keeping them alive and in working condition, leaves the largest amount of gain; and therefore their personal appearance is no more attended to than that of cart-horses or posthorses, as compared with the attention bestowed on the carriage-horses as a part of the family equipage.

We visited one of the rice plantations in the neighbourhood of Savannah, and saw the condition of the slaves on it with our own eyes. The estate was considered to be a valuable one, and under a fair condition of management, not among the best nor among the worst, but just such an average plantation as we wished to examine. The dwellings for the negroes were built of wood, ranged in rows of great uniformity, raised a little above the ground, each building containing two or more rooms, with a fire-place for two. We saw also the nursery for the children, and the sick-room or hospital for those who were hurt or diseased, and we had communication with the overseer, and several of the people, from both of whom we learnt the following facts, as to their routine of labour, food, and treatment.

The slaves are all up by daylight; and every one who is able to work, from eight or nine years old and upwards, repair to their several departments of field-labour. They do not return to their houses either to breakfast or dinner; but have their food cooked for them in the field, by negroes appointed to that duty. They continue thus at work till dark, and then return to their dwellings. There is no holiday on Saturday afternoon, or any other time throughout the year, except a day or two at Christmas; but from daylight to dark, every day except Sunday, they are at their labour. Their allowance of food consists of a peck, or two gallons, of Indian corn per week, half that quantity for working boys and girls, and a quarter for little children. This corn they are obliged to grind themselves, after their hours of labour are over; and it is then boiled in water, and made into hominey, but without anything to eat with it, neither bread, rice, fish, meat, potatoes, or butter; boiled corn and water only, and barely a sufficient quantity of this for subsistence.

Of clothes, the men and boys had a coarse woollen jacket and trousers once a year, without shirt or any other garment. This was their winter dress; their summer apparel consists of a similar suit of jacket and trousers of the coarsest cotton cloth. Absence from work, or neglect of duty, was punished with stinted allowance, imprisonment, and flogging. A medical man visited the plantation occasionally, and medicines were administered by a negro woman called the sick-nurse. No instruction was allowed to be given in reading or writing, no games or recreations were provided, nor was there indeed any time to enjoy them if they were. Their lot was one of continued toil, from morning to night, uncheered even by the *hope* of any change, or prospect of improvement in condition.

In appearance, all the negroes that we saw looked insufficiently fed, most wretchedly clad, and miserably accommodated in their dwellings; for though the exteriors of their cottages were neat and uniform, being all placed in regular order and whitewashed, yet nothing could be more dirty, gloomy, and wretched than their interiors; and we agreed that the criminals in all the state-prisons of the country, that we had yet seen, were much better off in food, raiment, and accommodation, and much less severely worked, than those men, whose only crime was that they were of a darker colour than the race that held them in bondage.

It is constantly alleged here, that the condition of the field slaves, though confessedly inferior to that of the domestic attendants, is not worse than that of the labouring population of England; but though this is much worse than it ought to be, it is still greatly above the condition of the slave, even in a physical point of view; while in a moral and intellectual one, the superiority is still more marked. The slave can never be instructed—the law forbids his being taught to read or write, under the severest penalties. He cannot, therefore, ever receive much of moral or intellectual culture, neither can he hope in any way to rise from his present dependent condition; but an English peasant, manufacturer, or artisan, may be taught anything he has a disposition to learn, and may rise to independence at least, if not to opulence; while the hope of better days never abandons him, but sheds a ray of light on his path, and comfort around his heart, which the very condition of a slave renders it impossible that he should ever experience.

It is usual here also to say, that supposing the slaves were made free, they would be unable to maintain themselves, and would not work even for their own benefit, as they are incapable of voluntary exertion. Yet in the face of this often-repeated assertion, I learnt here the following facts, and from the same persons that so confidently insisted on the indolence and incapacity of the slaves—

A wealthy planter said to me, "I assure you that these negroes are the laziest creatures in the world, and would never work but by compulsion. Now, I have a fellow on my plantation, who for fourteen or fifteen days past has been complaining of rheumatism, and could not be brought to work for an hour; he was so ill, as he said, as to be unable. On Sunday last, I was walking on the bay, looking down the river, when who should I see but my rheumatic rascal, pulling up in his boat with some things to sell on his own account, the fellow having rowed a distance of fourteen or fifteen miles for a market." I replied, "The reason is very plain: he was too ill to work for *you*, because he got nothing more by working than by being idle; but he was quite well enough to work for *himself*, because his labour was well rewarded." "Egad!" said the planter, "but you have hit it; that is no doubt the cause of the difference." I rejoined, "This is the whole solution of the question; no man will labour for another's profit with the same zeal that he will for his own; and the difference between the indolent apprentice toiling for his master, and the active journeyman working for himself, is just the difference between the exertions of the slave and the free." To this no reply was made.

I was further shown instances of coloured persons settled in the town, as carpenters, bricklayers, tailors, barbers, &c. who had acquired property, in materials of trade and houses, and managed their affairs with so much prudence as even to be getting rich, merely because they received the whole of the profits of their labour, instead of its being handed over to a master, who, after maintaining them, pockets the surplus as his own lawful profit.

Instances of hiring out negroes to work, not for their own benefit, but for that of their owners, are common; and I select, from among a hundred such cases that came every day before the public eye, the following, taken from a single column of a Charleston newspaper, in succession—

"To be hired, three able-bodied experienced Boatmen. Inquire at this office."

"To be hired, a Boy, a good House-servant, and capable of taking charge of horses. Apply at this office."

"To hire, a likely Mulatto Boy, fifteen years old, accustomed to House Work. Apply at this office."

"To hire, a Boy accustomed to waiting about House. Inquire at 43 Beaufain-street, opposite Coming."

"To Master Tailors.—To hire by the year, at very low wages, a young Fellow who has served six years at the Tailoring Business. Apply at 112 Queen-st."

"Nurse to hire. A young Wench, of good disposition. Also, two prime young Wenches. Apply at this office."

These were all negroes, or coloured people, belonging to owners who hired them out to others, and received a profit from their labours, as interest of the capital laid out on their purchase. In the Savannah papers the following appeared—

Negroes wanted.—The contractors upon the Brunswick and Alatamaha Canal, are desirous to hire a number of Prime Negro Men, from the 1st October next, for fifteen months, until the 1st January, 1840, or for any term within these dates, not less than twelve months. They will pay at the rate of Eighteen dollars per month for each prime hand. Payments to be made quarterly.

These negroes will be employed in the excavation of the canal. They will be provided with three and a half pounds of pork, or bacon, and ten quarts of gourd-seed corn per week, lodged in comfortable shantees, and attended constantly by a skilful physician.

As the Contractors are now making their arrangements for the work of the next year, all those who will be disposed to hire negroes for the coming season are requested to make immediate application, and obtain any further information that may be desired at the office of the contractors in Brunswick.

J.H. COUPER,
P.M. NIGHTINGALE.

It will be seen that there are two strong inducements offered here—high wages to tempt the owner to hire out his negroes, and good living to tempt the men to go readily into such service, if their masters desired them. But it cannot fail to be also seen, that if the men's labour is really worth the eighteen dollars per month, and their provisions besides, it is a positive robbery of their only natural wealth, the labour of their hands, to steal it from their pockets, and place it in that of their owners. It does not require the aid of reading and writing for the negroes to discover this: and the greater part of them are no doubt quite conscious of the injustice thus done to them, though the remedy is beyond their reach. The only thing they can do is to run away, and try to get to some place where they can work for themselves, and enjoy the profit of their own toil. The following, from a Savannah paper, as one of a hundred such announcements, abundantly proves this.

One Hundred Dollars Reward will be given for my two Fellows, Abram and Frank, who have absconded, or fifty dollars for either of them, to be put in some secure jail, so that I get them. Abram is a tall, likely black man; Frank, a yellow complected man; he stutters, and has a pleasing countenance; both likely, active men. Abram has a wife at

Colonel Stewart's in Liberty County, and a sister in Savannah at Capt. Grovenstine's. Frank has a wife at Mr. Le Cont's, Liberty County, a mother at Thunderbolt, and a sister in Savannah. They will, in all probability be at work on the wharves in Savannah, and on board of vessels. All persons are cautioned not to harbour or employ them, as no expense will be spared in prosecuting, if proof can he had.

WM. ROBARTS,
Walthourville, Liberty Co. Jan. 5, 1839.

This is an announcement, dated from "Liberty County," and the object is to arrest and punish those who thought that liberty was better than slavery, and therefore sought the change. As a proof, however, that it was not indolence, or a dislike of labour, which prompted this step, their very owner publicly asserts the probability that they would "be found *working* on the wharves or on board ships," where they would enjoy the fruits of their own labour, instead of its being appropriated to enrich another.

Here, too, as at Charleston, the most democratic papers were most violent in their denunciation of Abolitionism; and the strangest contrast was often observable in the columns of the same paper; one page teeming with proofs of the ultra-democratic or extreme republican views of the editor, and the other advocating the most uncontrolled despotism over the slave population, and deprecating any interference with the "cherished institutions" and "constitutional rights of the South." The Daily Georgian, for instance, from which some of the advertisements respecting the sale and hire of slaves, and rewards for their apprehension, were taken, has, over its leading article, an American flag unfurled, exhibiting its stripes and stars to the eye, and under it are the following lines, repeated in every day's paper, as the motto of its principles—

Flag of the Free! still bear thy sway,
    Undimmed through ages yet untold;
O'er Earth's proud realms thy stars display,
    Like morning's radiant clouds unrolled.
Flag of the Skies! still peerless shine,
    Through ether's azure vault unfurled,
Till every hand and heart entwine,
    To sweep Oppression from the world.

In the same spirit, and to keep alive, as much as possible, the democratic sentiment, all anecdotes tending to exhibit this prominent characteristic of American institutions, are highly relished and universally acceptable; such as this, taken from the Charleston Mercury, and repeated in all the papers, probably, of the Union—

> A distinguished American lady, while at Rome, was asked by a Cardinal, if he could have the pleasure of presenting her to the Pope. On her inquiring whether she would be permitted to converse with His Holiness, the Cardinal replied, that she could not; for this was an honour confined to princesses of the blood, the daughters of sovereigns. 'But, sir,' replies the lady, 'I am a princess of the blood, and a daughter of a sovereign; for in America the people are all sovereigns, and I am the daughter of one of the people.' His Holiness was so much pleased with this Spartan boldness, that an interview was granted, and the American princess admitted to an honour to which no lady of private station had ever before aspired.

When these American princesses, however, attempt to exercise even the rights of ordinary citizens in their own country, on the proscribed topic of Abolition, they are soon taught, by severe public rebuke, that they are not quite so free as they are represented to be, and that their "sovereignty" is very limited indeed. Of this, the following may be taken as proof, from the Savannah Telegraph of February, 1839—

> *Abolition in Delaware.*—The following brief, but significant report, was lately made in the Legislature of Delaware, by Mr. Jones of Wilmington, an able Democratic member.
>
> Mr. Jones on Friday presented the following report:—
>
> The Committee, to whom was referred the petition of 319 women of the city of Wilmington and county of New Castle, praying for the Abolition of Slavery throughout this State, beg leave to report—
>
> That they consider the petitioning of women, to our National and State Legislatures (which they regret to see is becoming so general a practice) as derogatory from that refinement and delicacy which should, under all circumstances, accompany the female character, and as an unwarranted interference in subjects that should more properly belong to their fathers, husbands, or brothers.
>
> Your Committee are also decidedly of opinion, that the petitioners whose names are affixed to the memorial under consideration, would confer more real benefit upon society, if they hereafter confined their attention to matters of a domestic nature, and would be more solicitous to mend the garments of their husbands and children, than to patch the breaches of the laws and Constitution.

It was during my stay in Savannah that the speech of Mr. Clay, the Whig candidate for the Presidency at the next election, was published in the newspapers, and made matter of universal comment and conversation. It was delivered in the Senate of the United States on the 7th of February; and, both from the importance of the subject, and the position of the speaker, it was made the subject of eulogy, or censure, in almost every paper of the Union. Mr. Clay is the most prominent of the Whig leaders in Congress; but of late there had been some doubt as to the part he would take on the subject of Abolition. The friends of this doctrine in the North, belonging to the Whig party, had begun to indulge hopes that he would be with them; and many sincere Abolitionists were on this ground added to the ranks of his supporters for the next presidency. But he found by experience that he lost more friends in the slave-holding States, than he gained supporters in the free States, by this temporizing conduct; and discovered, also, that General Harrison, his rival Whig candidate, was gaining on him in many quarters. It is remarkable, too, that Mr. Van Buren's only hope of re-election to the presidency, was from his retaining the support of the South, by his opposition to negro-emancipation: they like his democracy well enough, but they like his determined opposition to the Abolitionists much better. For any one to compete successfully with Mr. Van Buren for the presidency, it was indispensable that he should be as zealous an opponent of Abolition as the reigning president, or he would be deserted by the entire South, and consequently lose his election. This late movement of Mr. Clay, to proclaim his horror of Abolitionists, and their views and practices, is believed, therefore, by many to be a mere political manœuvre, and as such is denounced by most of the friends of the doctrines he espouses. As this is a very instructive lesson on the subject of American politics and politicians, I have selected for insertion here, three of the shortest and most striking comments on this speech, from the papers of the day. The first is from "The Constitutionalist," of Georgia, a very moderate and impartial journal; the editor of which says—

> We have read the speech of Mr. Clay on the Abolition question. The influence of his name will be felt, and the position he has assumed will have the salutary effect of neutralizing the efforts of the most fanatical of the Abolitionists to disturb the harmony of the Union, and the peace of the country. With pleasure then we receive the declarations of Mr. Clay on that deleterious question.
>
> We shall not question the sincerity of the declarations of Mr. Clay; but it must be permitted to us to express our surprise at the late period at which these declarations are made. Can it be possible that it is only a few weeks ago that Mr. Clay has formed an opinion on that important topic

of the day? Why were not these declarations, and the expression of his opinion, made years ago? If he had taken two years ago that position which he now has assumed, the influence of his name would have prevented the angry feelings which sprung up in the South against a portion of our Northern brethren; because many of those Northern Whigs, friends of Mr. Clay, would have paused and reflected, before connecting themselves with the Abolitionists. Silence on the part of that gentleman has, no doubt, increased the number of those deluded citizens, especially when he was charged with an indirect support of the scheme proclaimed for the abolition of slavery in the district of Columbia and in the South. This charge was never publicly denied by Mr.Clay, until recently. Why then is the charge now denied? Is it to allay the excitement, which, by his silence, he has contributed to create? Is it to verify the charge alleged against him by one of the Georgia senators? If Mr. Clay believes that he will reap in the South all the benefits which he calculates on by his recent declarations, he will find himself greatly mistaken. The people of the South will not abandon men who have stood with them in defence of Southern institutions and Southern rights, when those institutions and those rights were assailed, for a man who stood aloof when the South wanted friends, and who, now that he finds it of necessity to propitiate this section of the Union, comes at the eleventh hour, and claims the same reward, for a labour which interest, perhaps, has induced him to perform.

The official organ of the government at Washington, the "Globe," deals with the speech in less measured terms, and speaks more truly the general feeling of the democratic party. The following is the article from that journal

In the senate to-day, Mr. Clay appeared in a new part. For some years past he was one of those who saw no harm in the Abolition movements. His biographer, Mr. Prentice, of the Louisville Journal, in his sketch of his life, has taken pains to varnish up for display in the light of Northern philanthropy, Mr. Clay's early Emancipation principles. This, Mr. Clay carefully kept alive himself, by proposing to set apart, in his distribution of the public lands, a portion to carry out this scheme. In 1836 he voted against the effort made by the administration to prevent the circulation of incendiary prints in the South, tending to excite insurrection; and even as late as the last session, he voted against Mr. Rives's resolution, throwing cold water on the firebrand petitions continually sent into Congress. But, to-day what a sudden change we have had in all the senator's courtesy, kindness, and forbearance for Abolition—no sudden flaw of our variable city weather equals it. During the first part of the session Mr. Clay dodged every vote, and avoided, by a retreat behind the columns, any expression of opinion about the reception of Abolition petitions; but to-day he brought in an anti-abolition petition, and never was a party so belaboured in a set speech of some hours, as the fanatics! fanatics!! He denounced them all, and did not spare even the fair spinsters of the East. He conjured them to remember, that when with their fair hands they dipped their pens in ink to sign an Abolition petition, they dipped them in blood! He exhausted his pathos in portraying "conflagrated cities," "desolated fields," and scenes of "butchery and murder." There was not a man in the senate who did not see through this new act of the drama, the moment the curtain rose. Mr. Clay finds Harrison has the start of him with the Abolition-Antimasonic-Whigs.

The most able and influential of the southern papers, the "Charleston Courier," is so much more enamoured of Mr. Clay's anti-abolitionism than it is displeased with his Whig principles, that it is lavish in his praise; and if the "Washington Globe" speaks the probable sentiments of the great bulk of the democratic party, and the "Georgia Constitutionalist" embodies the views of the more moderate of the Southern politicians, the Charleston Courier, no doubt, represents, with greater accuracy than either, the feelings and opinions of the slave-holding States, and its language is therefore important, as the index of the policy which that party are determined to preserve. The editor, Mr. Yeadon, is a gentleman of the bar, eminent in his profession, estimable in his character, sincere in his opinions, and independent in his expression of them; and all these qualities give force and value to the productions of his pen. These, then, are the terms in which he speaks of Mr. Clay's speech—

Mr. Clay's Speech.—We have given a hurried perusal to Mr. Clay's great anti-abolition speech in the American senate: and we will lay it before our daily readers as soon as our crowded columns will permit. It crowns its author with glory, and gives him new claims to the name and fame of a true and fearless patriot, and to the warm gush of Southern gratitude. The political tenets of the South may forbid it from ever supporting Mr. Clay for the presidency, but let it not deny him the meed due to his patriotism and fidelity to the Constitution. Twice before, namely, on the Missouri question and on the Tariff compromise, has he played the noble part of pacificator of the Union, and he has now literally swept Abolition from its moorings and coverts, dissevered it from the right of petition and other adventitious aids, and held it up, in isolated odium, to the scorn and indignation of the republic, leaving its frenzied advocate, the notorious Morris of Ohio, nothing but the sneers of the august and enlightened assembly he dared to insult with his treasonable balderdash.

He divides the Abolitionists into three classes;—those who oppose slavery on grounds of humanity and philanthropy, and do not shame their profession by traitorous plottings, and conspiracies against the tranquillity of the South and the peace of the Union;—those who are misled into seeming co-operation with Abolition, by the false issue raised on the right of petition;—and those who recklessly and wickedly pursue their bad purpose, in utter disregard of the rights of property, the provisions of the Constitution, the rights of the States, and the preservation of our Union, and its glorious system of government;— and each class receives its due appreciation. An excoriating allusion is made to O'Connell, as the plunderer of his own country, and the libeller of a kindred people; and Mr. Stevenson is held pardonable for being made to swerve from his propriety by virtuous and patriotic indignation against the wretch. The mingling of Abolitionism with the politics of the country receives the just and stern rebuke, and is held up as an alarming symptom of the times. A rapid survey is taken of the three prominent eras of Abolitionism in our republic. Simultaneously with the first operation of the federal constitution, it broke ground in the halls of the national legislature, by the process of petition, and a temperate and well-reasoned report reduced the Abolitionists themselves to reason, and quieted the country. Next, the Missouri question shook the Union with fearful motion; but the spirit of compromise, which dictated the Constitution, was again invoked, and we escaped the peril. The third epoch includes the last few years and the present time.

This last excitement is the result of the stimulus given to the spirit of Abolition by British West India emancipation, an example inapplicable in all its aspects, political, social, and statistical, to this country; and the evil influence has been heightened and aggravated by those who would stake the peace and glory of their country on the hazard of the die, in the game of politics. Abolition in the district of Columbia, it is argued in a masterly and convincing manner, would be a violation of the public faith, implicitly pledged to Virginia and Maryland, when they ceded the district to the Union for a seat of government, and an unjust and dishonest perversion of the grant of exclusive legislation over the district to the national legislature. Abolition in Florida, it is insisted with equal force, would be in violation of the Spanish treaty of cession, and a trampling under foot of the Missouri compromise. The prevention of the removal of slaves from one state to another, is shown to be the result of a *destructive*, and not a *conservative* construction of the power to regulate commerce among the several States, and to be concluded by the constitutional recognition of slaves as 'property.' And the clause relating to the migration and importation of slaves, is proved to refer to the introduction and not the removal of that description of persons. Mr. Clay denounces the Abolitionists as aiming at universal emancipation; he shows that on the principles of the British example, their scheme would require, to carry it out, an indemnity of *twelve hundred millions of dollars*, which they ought to begin by raising, to pay the despoiled South. He demonstrates the malign workings of Abolitionism on the interests of the slaves themselves, by checking the efforts of benevolence for the melioration of their condition; and closes with uneloquent, touching, and heart-stirring appeal to all parties in Congress, and all classes of his fellow-citizens, to resist the evil spirit of Abolitionism, rally around the constitution, and preserve the peace and tranquillity of the country.

When Mr. Clay sat down, Mr. Calhoun, with honourable liberality, rose, and said he had heard the speech of the senator from Kentucky with the greatest pleasure. He thought it would have great effect. The work, said he, is done! Abolition is no more! The South is consolidated!

Nor do we quarrel with him, that he should have added,

'Quorum pars magna fui.'

One of the most amusing peculiarities of American politicians, is the extraordinary effects which they predict, or proclaim, of the delivery of remarkable speeches. Mr. Calhoun says, "Abolition is no more." "The work is done;" and his admirers throughout the South will reiterate this Sentiment in their several journals and meetings for a few weeks, when they will discover that Abolition is as fresh and vigorous as ever, and they will then be proposing new checks to keep the monster down. Though they exclaim, "and thrice we slew the slain," yet, after this threefold death, the demon rises again into stronger life than ever; and every subsequent death only makes his resurrection the more certain. It was during the last session of Congress only, at Washington, that Mr. Calhoun made a speech, in which he denounced Mr. Clay in such terms as induced the Washington editor of the "Chronicle" to say that Mr. Clay was "annihilated," and to predict that his name would again be mentioned but as an "object of ridicule and scorn;" yet, in twelve months afterwards, his very denouncer is the same individual who rises to do him honour; so short-sighted are political predictions, and so transient in duration are the most powerful political harangues.

Upon the whole, our stay in Savannah was as agreeable as any that we had yet made in either of the cities of the United States, and our enjoyments were unalloyed by a single drawback. Our only regret was that an intercourse so pleasurable as that which we had enjoyed with its intelligent and hospitable families, should be of such short duration, and so suddenly broken off. Every family on whom we called to take leave, evinced sincere regret at our departure, and we felt as though we were separating from friends of long standing, instead of two short weeks' acquaintance.

Chapter X

On Monday, the 25th of February, we left Savannah for Augusta, in the steam-packet, "Thorne." The morning was extremely disagreeable—a heavy rain descending in torrents, and the river being so covered with fog as to make it difficult to see the opposite bank. The temperature, however, was mild, as the wind was from the S.W. We left the hotel at nine o'clock in the morning, having previously sent on our baggage by two negro slaves from the house; but on reaching the vessel we had the mortification to find that only one portion, and that the least important, had reached its right destination, the other having been carried off, by mistake, to the "William Seabrook," another steamer just on the point of starting for Charleston, and lying at another wharf nearly a mile distant. By a great effort of speed, our servant arrived at the wharf just in time to prevent its embarkation; and we were thus saved, by a hair's-breadth only, from one of the most disagreeable incidents of a steam-boat voyage.

The first place of interest that we passed, was a spot called "Raleigh's Mound," raised, it is said, by the Indian chiefs of the olden time, to commemorate the visit of Sir Walter Raleigh, and the "talk" which they held with that distinguished navigator on this spot; and from the history of that period, there is no room to doubt the accuracy of this tradition. This is about three miles above Savannah.

Alligators frequent this river, and one or two were seen by us on our way, but almost lifeless, as they remain torpid during the winter. In the hot summer months they are seen in great numbers at every mile of the stream, and especially in the sweeps or bays occasioned by the serpentine turnings of the river, which are unusually tortuous and frequent. The alligators never attain to a greater length than twelve feet, and are not at all dangerous to man, from whose approach they invariably fly. It is said that they devour and feed upon their own offspring; and it is from this that many account for their not increasing very much; since, in their retreats, or nests, called alligator-holes, as large a brood as a hundred are seen at a time; but they do not come to maturity, as the numbers remain nearly stationary through a series of years, or diminish rather than increase. Snakes are found in the cane-brakes also; and some of these, particularly the rattle-snake, are formidable. The turkey-buzzard preys upon the carrion along the river's banks; while wild turkeys and wild ducks are in sufficient abundance to furnish game for food.

The mocking-bird, and the red bird or Virginian nightingale, are each inhabitants of these woods, and often enliven the solitude with their songs; and the little kingfisher with its pencilled and golden hues, dazzles and sparkles along the bushes which overhang the stream, perching sometimes on the same branch with a terrapin or small turtle, that has just emerged from the river to take the air, and both within a few inches of the surface of the stream. There are many animals in the woods: wild deer, wild hogs, and wild horned cattle. As these lands all belong to private individuals, though not yet cleared or appropriated, there is an annual slaughter, or *battu*, by men employed for the purpose of shooting them, and the spoil is divided among the proprietors of the woods in which they are shot.

In the extremely tortuous and winding course taken by the river, the actual distance from Savannah to Augusta is 250 miles by the stream, though not more than 120 by the land journey. In the bends and turnings thus occasioned, there are a succession of small bluffs, pointed promontories, and sweeping little curves or bays, alternating on either side; for it almost uniformly happens that when there is a bluff or cliffy bank on the one side of the stream, there is a marsh or swamp on the opposite side, and *vice versa*. There are some small islands in the middle of the stream, and the land has gained in some places and lost in others, while the whole bed of the river appears to be somewhat elevated above the surrounding country, as is the case with most streams that carry along in their course much alluvial deposit. In some of the bluffs or cliffs, there are seen horizontal strata of fossil shells, on beds of yellow clay, superimposed by sand and light loam; but these cliffs, if so they may be called, are rarely more than twenty or thirty feet high.

In our voyage up the river we met several large rafts of timber, floating down with the stream, guided by two men, one at each end, with a large rude oar; and a small hut built on the centre, for the cooking. Several of these had forty or fifty bales of cotton as freight; though by such a mode of conveyance it was very likely to get wetted. I learnt, however, that this was very little thought of, as not more than one bale in fifty of all the cotton in Georgia was under cover to protect it from rain. It frequently happens that when the raft takes the ground, the cotton bales are thrown overboard and float in the river till the raft is got off, when they are picked up and taken on board again; the water does not penetrate more than an inch beyond the surface, and this soon dries up. More than one half of the whole crop produced in Georgia, is transported down to Savannah for shipment by this river.

On the Carolina side, on our right hand, we passed a station called "The Willow Oak Spring," where a fine spring of beautifully clear water is found very near the river; but some traditional stories of ghosts being connected with this locality, the negroes, who are very superstitious, have great dread in passing it at night. Many of the negroes now in this country are of African birth. The direct importation of slaves from Africa did not cease till long after the revolution; and some, therefore, of these imported slaves still survive, retaining many of their idolatrous notions and practices, and nearly all their native superstitions.

As we approached nearer to Augusta, the signs of cultivation began to appear nearer the river's edge, and through openings in the woods we could perceive cattle grazing, and Indian corn lands lying in stubble. The soil here is peculiarly favourable for the cultivation of this grain, it requiring about a bushel and half to sow an acre, and the returns yielding sixty bushels at least, and often more.

Still nearer to Augusta, and on the Carolina side, is a stream of fine clear water, emptying itself into the river with great force. It is called Horse Creek; and some few miles upward, on its banks, are seated two cotton factories, worked by water-power, at a place called Vaucluse. They have been established about nine years, and are considered prosperous and profitable concerns. They are principally devoted to the spinning of cotton yarn, though some weaving of coarse cotton cloths is done in them also. The labourers employed are chiefly negro slaves, especially women and girls; and under the direction of a few white superintendents, or overseers, they are found to perform their duty very well.

About noon on the second day of our voyage from Savannah, we came in sight of Augusta, which, with its dwellings, spires, and bridge, presented a promising appearance on a bluff, or high land, like Savannah, and on the same side of the river, namely, the S.W. or on the left hand as you sail up the stream. At one, we reached the landing-place, having been about twenty-seven hours, or twenty-five deducting the stoppages, performing a distance of 250 miles against a current of four miles, thus making an actual rate of fourteen miles an hour all the way.

Chapter XI

We remained at Augusta for a week, and were very pleasantly accommodated at the private residence of Judge Hale, to whom we had letters of introduction from our friends at Savannah, and where we found ourselves as much at home as in our own abode. My lectures were given in the Baptist church every evening of the week without intermission, where they were very largely attended; and here, as at Savannah and at Charleston, the resident families seemed to vie with each other as to who should show us the greatest kindness and attention. We interchanged many agreeable visits, were taken by families in their carriages to several pleasant excursions in the neighbourhood, and saw all that was worthy of interest in the town itself.

Augusta was first founded in 1735, and was so called in honour of London, of which this was the ancient Roman name. It was planned by General Oglethorpe, the founder of Savannah; and though at first only intended as an interior station for collecting the peltries, or skins, with which the settlers were supplied by the Indians, yet it was laid out by him with all the regularity becoming a great city, which he, no doubt, believed it would one day become.

The population of Augusta is estimated at about 8,000, of whom there are not more than 4,000 whites, the remainder being negro slaves and coloured people. The whites are almost all engaged in trade with the interior; and from Augusta being the great centre of banking operations and exchange for a wide tract of inland country beyond it, it is thought that there is no city of the same population, more wealthy than Augusta in the United States. The planters of Georgia send their cotton in here for sale, and draw from this all their supplies for interior consumption; so that there is a very active business continually carrying on, especially in the spring and fall of the year.

There is a good Hospital in the city, supported by the municipal funds; and a Medical College, with chaste Doric portico and dome, at which there are

W. H. Brooke. F.S.A.

A. Willmore.

Court House, Medical College and Church at Augusta in Georgia from 70 to 80 students, the college being endowed by the State, and having an excellent Museum and apparatus. There is a Jail also, for debtors and criminals; but in the treatment of these last they neither adopt the Philadelphia system of solitary confinement, nor the Auburn system of labour and silence, but suffer them to congregate together and to be idle, which is a double evil, and the cost of their maintenance is a burden to the City funds. There are from forty to fifty persons in it at present, the debtors being separated from the criminals, and the white prisoners from the coloured.

There is a large Academy close to the Medical College, for the higher branches of education, supported by the County funds; a Free School on the Lancasterian plan, originally instituted by private subscription, but since maintained by the interest of a large bequest made by a benevolent individual for its support, and now therefore rendered independent of all pecuniary aid. There are also some Common Schools for boys, and an excellent Seminary for girls, under the direction of Mrs. Moise, a Jewish lady of great accomplishments, there being many wealthy merchants of the Hebrew nation settled here; and in this school every department of female education is well conducted.

There is a small theatre in Augusta; but, as in all the smaller cities of America, it is feebly supported, and indeed rarely frequented by the more respectable inhabitants, except on the occasion of some attractive performer visiting the place.

An attempt was recently made to establish a Lyceum, for regular lectures; but it failed. There is a tolerable library, which is used, however, only by a few, as business seems to leave but little leisure or inclination for study, with any class of society in this busy town.

There are two newspapers, the Daily Sentinel and Chronicle, of Whig politics; and the Constitutionalist, published three times a week, of Democratic politics, with a monthly literary journal, called the Augusta Mirror. These are, however, but feebly conducted, and seem to exercise little or no influence on public opinion. The Whigs have gained great strength here of late. Both parties, Whig and Democratic, are now favourable to the continuance of the Union, and unwilling to endanger it by pressing too closely the doctrines of State rights and Nullification, like their neighbours in South Carolina. All are Anti-abolitionists, though, as respects the inhabitants generally, they are more kind in the treatment of their slaves, and less apprehensive of danger from insurrection, than in Carolina. Though the law here, as in all the slave states, forbids the instruction of negroes, many of them learn, of their own accord, to read and write, and some are taught by masters; and this illegal practice is winked at by those who know it, because it is found that no danger arises from such instruction. The children are said to be quite as apt as the whites in acquiring knowledge, and display in general greater eagerness to attain it.

The law also forbids any man to give freedom to his slave, except he is taken out of the territory. But even this is evaded by some humane owners, who, though they cannot give their slaves legal freedom in the State, give them the entire command of their labour, and allow them to work for themselves, and enjoy without deduction all the fruits of their industry. Several such cases were mentioned to us, and in every instance, the slaves so enjoying the rewards of their own labour appropriated a portion of it to the learning of reading, writing, and arithmetic, and sometimes to the acquiring the knowledge of some trade by which their gains could be increased. This sort of emancipation is quite within the power of all slave-owners to give to their negroes; and no one pretends to say that this would be dangerous; but then it would require the sacrifice, on the part of the owner, of all the gains he now makes from the labour or wages of his slaves—and this, his selfishness will not permit him to make. It is, therefore, a mere question of pecuniary loss or gain, after all. Indeed my own conviction is, that if the slave-owners of America could but be persuaded that they would *gain* more by setting their slaves free, than by keeping them in bondage, they would all do so to-morrow; and that all their pretended alarms about insurrection, annihilation, and so on, would vanish like a dream.

There are two large cotton factories in Georgia, within eight or ten miles of Augusta, worked by water power, and chiefly engaged in spinning. In these, white labour is more used than black, there being, in the interior of the State, a number of poor white families, to whom this occupation is a great relief. Most of these are either actual emigrants from Ireland, or descendants of such emigrants; and their poverty is wholly attributable to their habits of intemperance. I was assured, by a gentleman who had paid great attention to this subject, that the average life of an Irish emigrant here, rarely exceeds three years, if he persists in drinking spirits; but that in the few instances in which men had been prevailed upon to leave off this poison, and use water only for their beverage, they were as long lived and as prosperous as the natives of the country. There has been some reform of late in this respect, by the operations of the Total Abstinence Society, recently established here, to succeed the old Temperance Society; and therefore, while in Savannah, with a population of 10,000, there are still 125 licensed spirit-shops, yielding a licensed revenue of 5,000 dollars per annum to the city-funds, there are here only about 50 licensed spirit-dealers, paying 50 dollars each for a license; and this privilege is often refused by the council to persons of bad repute.

There are two rail-roads leading from Augusta, one to Charleston in South Carolina, which begins at the village of Hamburgh, and goes for 136 miles, the distance being performed in about nine hours; and the other towards Milledgeville in Georgia, about 70 miles of which are completed, and the rest is in progress.

The steam-vessels that ply on the river, and carry cargoes of cotton, as well as passengers, from Augusta to Savannah, are mostly built of iron. We saw several of these at the wharf where we landed. It is said that the first iron steam-vessel used in America was on the Savannah river. The castings and the wrought-iron, for both are used in their construction, are made in England, and they are allowed to pass free of duty, for this specific purpose. They are found to be strong, safe, light, and durable, and are likely to supersede the use of wooden steam-boats altogether, especially as, in addition to all their other advantages, they cannot be consumed by fire.

During our stay in Augusta, we made a pleasant excursion up to the Falls of the river, about three miles above the town. We rode up on the Carolina side, and went to see a spot called Snow Hill, which overlooks the Falls, and commands an extensive and pleasing view of the country on both sides the stream. The Falls, or Rapids as they should rather be called, are occasioned by ledges of hard rock that stretch across the bed of the river, like the second cataract of the Nile above Philöe or Assouan. This is the boundary of steam-navigation up the stream; but long and narrow boats come down these rapids, and shoot through small openings known to the pilots, carrying forty or fifty bales of cotton in each boat. At present there are a large number of traps set along the ledges, for catching the shad-fish; and some of the trappers make, it is said, fifty dollars in a single night, by the fish they take in this way.

The three adjoining counties are here called Richmond, Chatham, and Burke, after the Duke of Richmond, the Earl of Chatham, and Edmund Burke—all friends of America, in her struggle for independence. These counties are devoted to agriculture and pasture; the chief products being cotton, corn, and oats, on the highlands; and pasturage, or rice, on the low. The soil, however, is said to be everywhere deteriorating, even at this early period, for want of rest and manure.

This recklessness and indifference as to the soil, has, no doubt, arisen from the facility with which land has been hitherto obtained by the planters of the country. It has been already mentioned, in the history of Georgia, that 100,000 square miles of territory were ceded by the legislature of this State to the general government, soon after the incorporation of the several States into the Union, for the purpose of forming the two new States of Alabama and Mississipi; the whole of which tract had been previously purchased by land-speculators for 100,000 dollars, or one dollar for a square mile!

The general government undertook to compensate these speculators for the loss of their bargain, and to extinguish also all the Indian titles to the Cherokee lands within the limits of the newly circumscribed state of Georgia. Several hundred thousand acres being thus left at their disposal, a lottery was formed of the whole, and they were thus distributed:—First, a survey was made of all these lands; then they were marked off into townships and sections, and numbered in consecutive order. Each section of 160 acres was designated by a particular number, and tickets corresponding to these numbers were put into a wheel, as into any ordinary lottery. Every person residing in Georgia, at the time of the drawing, who had been living six months in the State, was entitled to a draw, if a single man or single woman; and every married man had a draw for himself, his wife, and each of his children, however many, and however young; and there were sections enough for all. Accordingly, men of large families, and who were fortunate in obtaining lands in a good position, were made rich; there were no blanks, except that some sections were sandy, others marshy, and others woody, and therefore worth less than others; but as nothing was paid for the privilege of a draw, no one could lose by such a lottery. As there were known to be many, however, who if they drew good lands would have no capital to work them, but would be obliged to sell out, it was not difficult to speculate upon their shares; and accordingly, land jobbers from the north went about and bought up men's chances for a small sum, never paying more than 50 dollars, and getting many for 5 dollars, by which large fortunes were made in this way. One gentleman told me that he sold a lot which came to him through this lottery for 500 dollars, within a week after he had drawn it; others had cultivated their lots, and these were now worth 20 dollars an acre, or upwards of 3,000 dollars per lot. These fluctuations of fortune produced, as lotteries everywhere have done, a spirit of speculation and gambling, which it is easy to engender but very difficult to subdue; and the effects of this continue to the present day, in speculations, jobbing, and lotteries, of which Augusta is still full.

Another excursion that I made during my stay in Augusta was to the town of Hamburgh, on the Carolina side of the Savannah river. This town was begun and named by a German merchant now living, who has expended too liberally for his means in the promotion of his favourite object; but the town has now attained to sufficient standing to go forward without further adventitious aids. It is here that the railroad from Augusta to Charleston commences, and has its depôt; and from hence also large shipments of Carolina cotton takes place for transporting down to the port of destination by the river.

The plan of Hamburgh exhibits streets of great breadth and regularity; and there are stores, hotels, banks, and all the auxiliaries of a rising and prosperous settlement. In the rear of the town is a natural hill, from 50 to 60 feet above the general level, called Liberty Hill, where the Americans were posted at the revolutionary war, when they obliged the English forces to evacuate Augusta.

From this hill the finest views of the town of Hamburgh and the city of Augusta, on the opposite side of the river, are to be had. The top of the hill has been excavated with a ditch surrounding the upper mound; and large beams of wood have been placed, to form flights of stairs for ascending to the summit. All this I was told was the work of the German gentleman before alluded to, who became so infatuated about his pet town, that he seemed to wish to imitate the style and state of a petty German prince; for he called this his castle, and employed several Germans of the humbler classes, with muskets and bayonets, to mount guard upon the fortress, and even to warn persons off who were approaching it, a folly that has still further encroached upon his means, and left him now as much embarrassed as any of the German princes whose state he was so desirous of imitating.

In our ramble through Hamburgh I was shown two houses, to which negro slaves are brought for sale from Virginia; and being purchased here by slave-dealers, they are taken on to the South-western States for a higher market. In Virginia, the soil has been so much exhausted, by the cultivation of tobacco, that thousands of acres are now unproductive, and unsuited for any tillage. The wealth of the planter who owns such lands, consists therefore chiefly, if not entirely, in his negroes. These are regularly bred and multiplied for sale, like cattle; and as the progeny increases, the more saleable portions are selected, and brought on to the South, or sent to the slave-market at Washington, or some times sold in Virginia itself. They are thus passed on from the State where their labour is not in demand, to the rising states and territories, in which labour is in request; and accordingly, in the Augusta papers, as in the Washington journals, every day are to be seen advertisements, offering "Cash for likely negroes."

A slave-trade is thus carried on throughout the Southern States, under the gentle name of the "removal of slaves from one state to another;" and though this is not attended with all the horrors and cruelties of the "Middle Passage," which characterized the Atlantic slave-trade of former times, yet it leads to the separation of husband and wife, of parents and children, and brothers and sisters, without the most distant hope of their ever meeting again; and from all the information I could obtain on this subject, the negroes feel these separations as acutely as any whites could do, and are unhappy for years afterwards.

Here, however, as everywhere throughout the South, slavery is a topic upon which no man, and, above all, a foreigner, can open his lips without imminent personal danger, unless it is to defend and uphold the system. Then, indeed, he may speak as freely as he pleases; but if it is even to doubt whether slavery be on the whole either just or profitable, he is sure to be assailed with imputations of being an incendiary, of desiring to incite the slaves to rebellion, to bring about the massacre of the whites, and the annihilation of their property. The violence of the measures taken against the few who from time to time venture to express themselves in favour of Abolition, is such as to strike terror into others; and thus all public discussion of the question is as effectually suppressed, as if there were a censorship of the press, or a holy inquisition. I feel assured that it would not be so dangerous for a man to preach the right of resistance to despotic authority in Petersburg or Vienna, to inveigh against popery at Rome or to denounce Mohammedanism at Constantinople, as it would be for him to proclaim himself, either by his pen or by his tongue, as an Abolitionist in the slave-holding States south of the Potomacs in America; and yet, to tell the Americans that they have neither freedom of the press nor freedom of speech, to the extent to which both are enjoyed in England, would greatly offend as well as surprise them, though nothing could be more true.

To form an idea of the horror with which the very name of an Abolitionist is regarded; and to see how men who avow themselves to be opposed to slavery in the abstract, shrink from such an imputation as that of being favourable to Abolition in practice it is only necessary to read the report of any proceedings in Congress at Washington in connexion with this subject. To those of the American nation who think Mr. O'Connell "foul-mouthed," and complain of the coarseness of vituperation with which he speaks of slave-holders and slave-breeders in the United States, the language used in the debates of their own House of Representatives, may be held up as a mirror, in which they may see a portrait as revolting, to say the least, as any that Mr. O'Connell ever presented of themselves.

I am no apologist for vituperation, under any degree of injury or excitement; because I think it degrades the person using it, be he of what nation, sect, or of party he may. But if it be an offence in one man to speak strongly when he denounces a system which he believes to be cruel and unjust as well as impolitic, it is equally reprehensible in others to follow the same course. But the Americans are not the only people to whom the prayer of Burns is peculiarly applicable; for almost every nation under the sun might profit by it if such a prayer could be granted to them; when the poet says.

> O that the gods the gift would gi' us,
> To see oursels as others see us!

The subject of a direct trade between the Southern States and Europe, without the intervention of the Northern States, through which that trade is now almost entirely carried on, has been recently agitated in Augusta, as well as in Charleston, and is still indeed under discussion in most private circles, having already been the subject of a public convention. The planters and merchants of the interior, however, are not so eager on this subject as those of the sea-ports, because their interests are not so deeply involved. They dispose of their cotton to buyers here, or at the ports on the coast, and trouble themselves no further, as they find all the supplies they want in the stores of the towns at which their sales are made; but the ship-owners and merchants of the coast naturally look with jealousy on a state of things which leads to the importation of all their European supplies through the ports of the North. It is certain that three-fourths of the exports of America are from the South-western States; the cotton, rice, and tobacco of which, as well as flour, hemp, and rice, go to all the countries of Europe; yet the imports, in return for all this, come in by way of New York: so that when the imports of the whole United States amounted to 190 millions of dollars, the share of the importation that fell to the South-western States was only 20 millions. Georgia and South Carolina alone export to the value of about 24 millions, yet the united imports of both amount to only 4 millions; all the rest being imported first into New York and other northern ports, direct from Europe, and thence indirectly brought to the south, thus increasing the cost to the consumer.

On the whole, our visit to Augusta was very satisfactory. The city is handsome, the surrounding country picturesque, the resident families intelligent, hospitable, and agreeable; while everything indicates great present wealth and comfort, and promises great future opulence. It may be doubted whether there is any town in Great Britain, containing only a population of 5,000 whites, that has so much of wealth, industry, and enterprise, combined with such excellent public and private buildings, and means of education and improvement, as Augusta.

CHAPTER XII

On Monday the 4th of March we left Augusta for Macon, on our way to Mobile and New Orleans, wishing to see the interior of Georgia and Alabama, and finish our examination of the Southern States before the approach of the hot weather. We had to set out at six o'clock, and go by a railroad from hence to Warrenton, a distance of about fifty miles. The cars were much inferior in their accommodation and fittings to those on the northern railroads, and our speed did not exceed fifteen miles in the hour. On reaching the end of the railroad at Warrenton, we had to take the stage-coach, and were fortunately able to engage the whole of it for our party, or to "charter" it, as the expression is here, keeping up the maritime phraseology, by which the conductor is called "the pilot," and the sound of "all aboard" announces that the engine may move on, as all the passengers are in the cars. Our fare by the railroad, fifty miles, was 2½ dollars each, or about ten shillings sterling; and for the whole stage, large enough for nine passengers, we paid 48 dollars, or about 10*l.* sterling, for 75 miles; 45 from Warrenton to Milledgeville, and 30 from thence to Macon.

About two o'clock we reached the village of Sparta, there being also a Rome and an Athens in the same State; the former on the Etawah river in Floyd County, and the latter on the Big Sandy Creek, near Hermon, in Clark County, not far from the Land of Goshen, which is close to Edinburgh, Lincoln, Lisbon, Petersburgh, and Vienna, so strange are the juxtapositions of names on an American map. We halted at Sparta to dine; but the sight of the public table prepared for the passengers was so revolting, that, hungry as we were after our long and cold ride, early rising, and violent motion, we turned away in disgust from the table, and made our dinner in the coach on hard biscuits. There were three lines of coaches on this road, all leaving at the same hour, and arriving at the same time—the Mail line, the Telegraph line, and the People's line. The passengers from each of these took their seats at the table, and many of them appeared to dine as heartily as if they saw nothing unusual in the fare. But the dirty state of the room in which the table was laid, the filthy condition of the table-cloth, the coarse and broken plates, rusty knives and forks, and large junks of boiled pork, and various messes of corn and rancid butter, added to the coarse and vulgar appearance and manners of most of the guests, made the whole scene the most revolting we had yet witnessed in the country. The ancient Spartans themselves, with their black broth and coarse fare, could not have been farther removed from luxury than these Spartans of modern days; and one might almost be tempted, from what we saw, to suppose that the modern Spartans affected the manners of the ancient Lacedemonians, in diet at least, to justify the appropriateness of the name they had chosen for their village.

We left Sparta at three o'clock; and after a cold, dreary, and tedious drive through thick woods and over broken roads, we reached Milledgeville about eight, having been assured before setting out that we should reach there at three. As this is the legislative capital of the State of Georgia, we had hoped to find a good hotel here at least, as the legislatorial body consists of nearly 400 members, and these all reside here during the few months that the two houses are assembled in annual session. But our hopes were not realized. The inn at which the coach stopped was a wretched one; and though all we desired to have was a cup of tea and some cold meat for our party, we had the greatest difficulty in getting either. It was our wish to remain here all night, and go on to Macon in the morning; but on inquiry we found that no private or extra conveyance could be had from hence to Macon in the daytime, for love or money, though this is the seat of the State legislature, and Macon is only thirty miles off. Three stage-coaches pass through this place, between Augusta and Montgomery, at night, and these are the only conveyances to be had; so that if we did not go on to-night we could only proceed on the following, there being no conveyance whatever for day-travelling. This was a great disappointment—but we were without a remedy; and so we prepared to go forward, cold and weary as we were. The tea was tardily and reluctantly prepared for us in a bedroom; and it may give some idea of the rudeness with which this was done, to say, that the dirty negress who made the tea, brought the stinted quantity required in the hollow of her hand, without any other receptacle for it—that the milk was placed on the table in a broken tea-cup, milk-cups not being in use—and that when a slop-basin was asked for, the thing was unknown, and a large salad-bowl was brought for that purpose.

We left Milledgeville at nine, and, after a more comfortless ride than we should like to endure again, we did not reach Macon till four in the morning, having been seven hours in performing thirty miles, over roads that would be thought impassable in any part of Europe, and which would break to pieces any description of carriages except the ponderous stage-coaches of this country, which are made as heavy and as strong as the union of wood and iron can make them. One reason assigned for this entire neglect of the public roads, is, that the scantiness of the population along their borders would make any assessment on the lands or the inhabitants, sufficient for this purpose, so burdensome, as to be ruinous to those who had to pay it, and, would, consequently, drive all the population away from the very track to which it was most desirable to attract them. Another reason is, that railroads are so increasing over every part of the country, that stage-roads will soon be useless, and therefore it would be a waste of money to make or repair them. The wretched state of the ordinary roads thus operates as an additional stimulus to the construction of railroads wherever it is practicable; so that perhaps in a few years from this, there will be a connected series of railroad and steam-boat communication from Maine to Louisiana, and the journey from Portland to New Orleans may be then performed in a few days.

At Macon we found comfortable apartments prepared for us in the Central Hotel and having, through the influence of a private friend, obtained the rare luxury, in this country, of a private sitting-room, and separate table, we enjoyed our week's stay here extremely. During the week, my lectures were given in the new Presbyterian church, a very handsome building just finished, and they were well attended by the most respectable classes of the community, to whom they gave so much satisfaction as to lead to an arrangement for my returning again to give another course at a more advanced period of the spring.

The town of Macon, or city, as is should be more correctly called, it being incorporated as such, is of very recent origin, as, only fifteen years ago, the ground on which it stands was covered with primeval forest; and not a single dwelling was then erected here. At that period, there was a military station near it, called Fort Hawkins, which was then the frontier station of the whites towards the south and west; the whole of this territory being then occupied by the Creek Indians, while the Cherokees occupied the more northern parts of the State. In the survey of the lands, adverted to in the previous sketch of the history of Georgia, when the Indian titles to large tracts were extinguished by the general government paying to them a compensation or purchase for the same, and when the whole was divided in to sections and put into a lottery, in which every citizen had a right to a ticket or a draw, certain localities were reserved by the State government of Georgia, for the formation of towns, and this was one of them. Accordingly, the town of Macon, so called after a wealthy citizen of Carolina, was laid out by the state-surveyor, and the ground sold in lots to private purchasers for building. It was soon after incorporated with all the municipal privileges of a city. Since that period it has gone on increasing in wealth and population, till the present year, when it numbers upwards of 8,000 inhabitants, of whom about 5,000 are whites, and 3,000 slaves and coloured people; and though only fifteen years old, its exports of cotton amounted last year to 5,000,000 dollars, and its imports to 4,000,000 dollars—the surplus of about 2,000,000 dollars being expended in building, in railroads, and various other improvements.

The plan of Macon, like that of nearly all the towns in the United States, is remarkably regular; the streets run at right angles with each other, and are from 100 to 120 feet in breadth. The houses are mostly of wood; many of these are spacious and elegant; and some of the private dwellings are of brick, well built and in good taste. The public edifices are large, well proportioned, and indicative of a rising and prosperous city. The City Hall is among the most prominent of these; it stands in a fine open space at the end of one of the principal streets, which displays it to great advantage.

A neat market-house, with open colonnade and tower, occupies the middle of the same street, and near this is the Railroad Bank, with a fine Doric portico of fluted pillars; while the new Presbyterian Church, with its square tower, completes a very interesting architectural group.

On the west of the town is a rising ground terminating in a hill, about a hundred feet in height, over-looking the town on the east, and having behind it on the west, a pretty valley, beyond which are clusters of villas and cottages, to which the wealthy inhabitants retire in the hot season to sleep, coming into the city for business only. On this hill are several private mansions as large and as handsome as any of those which excited our admiration at New Bedford. On this elevation is now constructing, and nearly completed, an extensive pile for the Female College of Macon. This edifice, which is built of brick and stone, is sufficiently capacious to accommodate 200 boarders, and to educate 200 day-scholars besides; in addition to this, it has ample accommodation in rooms, for study, recitations, and every other requisite for pupils, with an excellent private dwelling for the master and teachers. Though the building is not yet finished, there are already 150 young ladies, from 10 to 18 years of age, receiving their education there; and the style of tuition, and range of subjects taught, are not inferior to those of any of the Female Academies of the North. I had an opportunity of conversing with the head master; and enjoyed the advantages of the services of the Latin, French, and Spanish teachers for my son; and they appeared to me to be quite as competent to the discharge of their duties as those of the best schools of Europe.

In front of the College is a space of six acres of sloping land, which, as well as the site for the building, was the gift of a Methodist minister, who is also a merchant in Macon, and which it is intended to lay out as a Botanical

Garden for the recreation and improvement of the students. Instruments are also providing, for giving them instruction in chemistry, mineralogy, and astronomy, so that the course of education will be solid and useful, while languages, music, and drawing will make it also ornamental. The whole will be extremely cheap; the English literary and scientific course, including the French language, being only 50 dollars per annum, or 10*l.* sterling. The funds for the erection of the building was raised by the Methodists, who, when the land was given for the site and garden by their minister, organized a committee, and sent agents throughout the State to collect funds by subscriptions or donations. When a considerable amount had been thus raised, so as to ensure the certainty of building a College, the resident inhabitants of Macon began to perceive that it would be to their interest to have a handsome building and an efficient establishment, and they contributed largely also; so that from these united sources, the sum of about 50,000 dollars, or 10,000*l.* sterling, was raised. The State Legislature next chartered a State Bank, on condition of its paying 25,000 dollars towards building the College; and the Methodist minister gave twelve acres of land, worth 36,000 dollars; all of which sums will be spent in its completion. The land, when given by the minister to form the site of the building, was not considered to be worth more than 100 dollars per acre, the ordinary price of cotton farming-land in the surrounding country being 10 dollars per acre. But since the erection of the College, and the increased demand for building-lots in its vicinity, the value of the land in this locality has so increased, that a gentleman wishing to erect a country mansion on the hill, surrounded by a garden, had to pay 3,000 dollars, or 600*l.* sterling per acre, which, five years ago, might have been had for 100 dollars, and fifteen years ago might have been had for 1¼ dollar; so rapid is the increase of value in land by augmented population, and increased demand for it.

Of churches there are five in Macon—Episcopalian, Presbyterian, Methodist, Baptist, and Universalist. The first three are the largest and most popular. The Baptists are of the order called here "Hard-shelled Baptists," a phrase which was new to me; and which was given to them, as I understood, from their being so impenetrable to all influences of a benevolent kind, and so hostile to all the auxiliary aids of missions, tract societies, temperance societies, peace societies, sick-visiting societies, and other charitable and philanthropic associations; against all of which they are said to set their faces, and to denounce them as interfering with the free operation of the gospel, and substituting human machinery for apostolic preaching. They are accordingly given to the pleasures of the table without restraint; and one of their veteran preachers here is said to have declared from the pulpit that he would never submit to be deprived of his "worldly comforts" by the fanatics of modern times; and among those comforts he numbered his "honey-dram before breakfast," and his "mint julap or sling, when the weather required it."

The Universalists are very few in number, though they are zealous in endeavouring to obtain converts. Of these the following anecdote is told here:—A Universalist preacher assembled a number of the citizens to preach to them a probationary sermon, in which he endeavoured to persuade them that the idea of eternal damnation was wholly unwarranted by Scripture; and that even temporary punishment after death was not to be expected, as the wicked had their sufferings before they descended to the grave; and all beyond that would be universal happiness. After this discourse, he told the congregation that he was about to make a journey farther west; but that in a short time he would return among them again, to ascertain whether they would wish to build him a church, and engage him as their preacher. He returned after a short absence, as promised, and repeated, to the same audience, all his former opinions, desiring, at the close of his discourse, that the assembly would indicate to him, by some means, the resolution they had taken as to his future stay among them. Upon this, an elderly man arose and said, that having listened with deep attention to all that had been uttered by the preacher in his two sermons, he had come to this conclusion—that if all he had stated was *true*, and there was to be no punishment for the wicked after death, he really did not see the use of churches or preachers at all, for the police and the laws were sufficient to deal with criminals while in this world; but if, on the other hand, what he had been saying was *not* true, then, certainly, he would be a very improper person for their pastor: so that whether his views were true or false, they should not be disposed to require his further services.

The lands around the town are devoted chiefly to the cultivation of cotton, and 150,000 bales were sent last year from this small town to Savannah and to Darien, for shipment to Europe. The crop was then short, and this year it is said to be still shorter, occasioned by unusual drought, though cotton bears the absence of moisture better than almost any other vegetable production. It is estimated that the crop of this year will fall short of that of last by 300,000 bales, and holders of cotton are therefore averse to sell, though the present price is eighteen cents per pound; while last year, about the same period, it was from nine to twelve cents only. Last year, up to the 1st of March, 86,209 bales had been received in Macon from the surrounding plantations. Up to the 1st of March this year, only 59,924 bales have been received; so that there is a deficiency of 26,285 bales in this town only, as compared with the same period last year; and then the supply was less than the average of many years preceding.

In the cultivation of cotton, the labourers employed are wholly negro slaves; their condition is generally better than that of the slaves employed in the cultivation of rice or sugar, the occupation being more healthy, and the profits admitting of a more liberal allowance of food; though in all other respects, as to clothing, lodging, cleanliness, and education, they are in the same dark, degraded, and hopeless state as the African race generally through out the Southern States. Here, too, as elsewhere, there is a great difference between the condition of the field-slaves on the plantations, and the domestic slaves about the houses of respectable families. These last are as well fed and as well clad as the free domestic servants of many countries of Europe, though far inferior to those of England; but still, even these are wholly uneducated, and entirely without the hope of benefiting their condition by any exertions of industry or economy, to the practice of which they have no conceivable inducement whatever. The field-slaves, being regarded as instruments of production, are maintained with as little cost as possible, compatible with the keeping them in good working condition; because, in proportion to the great quantity of work got out of them, and the small cost of their maintenance, will be the profit of the planter. He has every motive, therefore, to increase the one, and lessen the other, till he brings each to the point beyond which it is unsafe to carry them. In the domestic service of most private establishments here, there are often more slaves than are necessary for the labour required of them, many being kept for state, or ostentation; and as the coachman, footman, lady's maid, butler, cook, and other household servants, are continually passing before the eyes of the master and mistress, as well as their visitors and guests, they are almost sure of being well clad and kindly treated, because the sight of dirty and miserable-looking attendants would be painful to those by whom they are surrounded, as well as to themselves.

On this question, of the false economy of employing slave-labour in the cultivation of the land, every thing I heard and saw confirmed me in the opinion, that it was most injurious to the interests of the planters; and that none would benefit more by a system of free labour than the very landowners themselves. At present, if a planter wishes to purchase an estate for cultivation, he can get 1,000 acres of land for 10,000 dollars; and if he could obtain free labour to till his fields, hiring it by the day, and paying for such labour as he required, and no more, 5,000 dollars would be ample for a reserved capital by which to procure his seed, labour, and stock. But as he must, according to the present system, buy his slaves as well as his land, it will require at least 500 dollars, or 100*l.* sterling, for each working negro that he may need; and supposing only 100 negroes to be purchased, this would require 50,000 dollars to be laid out in the purchase of *prospective* labour, paying for it before he receives the slightest benefit, and under all the risks of sickness, desertion, and death. In this manner, according to the statement of Mr. Clay, in his recent Anti-abolition speech in Congress, there is locked up, of dead capital, in the purchase and cost of the negro slaves of the United States, the enormous sum of twelve hundred millions of dollars, or about two hundred and fifty millions sterling! Now, if slavery had never been permitted to exist here, and labour could have been hired by the day, or week, or year, as in other free countries, this enormous amount of capital would have been available to devote to other purposes; and the whole country would have been advanced at least a century beyond its present condition.

It may be quite true that the African race can alone sustain the exposure to heat and labour combined, which the cultivation of rice, sugar, and cotton, demand; but it is at the same time as true, that their labour might be hired and paid for only as it was employed, instead of the ruinously improvident system of buying up all the labour of their lives, and paying for it beforehand; thus sinking an immense capital in the very country where capital is more valuable, because more productive of wealth, than in any other country that can be named. If a large manufacturer in England, when he had built his mill and fitted his machinery, were required to buy all his working hands at £100 each, and then maintain them all their lives, sick or well, aged or infirm, with the risk of loss by desertion or death, he would be less able to work his mill with £100,000, than he now is with £20,000; and consequently not half or a fourth of the mills now in operation could be established. If a shipowner, when he had built, equipped, and provisioned his ship for her voyage, had to buy up all his seamen at £100 a head, and maintain them all their lives afterwards, it would require four times the capital that is now necessary to send a large ship to sea, and consequently fewer persons could equip vessels. Thus the manufacturing and the shipping interests would both be retarded in their progress by this improvident and heavy burden of paying for a life of labour in advance, instead of paying for it by the week or the month, as its benefits were reaped by them.

Exactly the same effects are produced in retarding the prosperity of agriculture; and thus it is that the old slave-states of Virginia and Maryland are already exhausted. The Carolinas and Georgia are ready partially so; and in process of time this will be the fate of Alabama, Mississippi, Kentucky, and the other slave-states; while those who employ the cheaper, more vigorous, and more productive element of free labour, will outstrip them in the race, from the mere advantage of a better system of industry. While I believe, therefore, that the condition of the slaves would be much improved by their being placed under the influence of those higher and better motives to labour which the enjoyment of the reward of their own toil can alone create, I also believe that the planters would all benefit by the substitution of free-labour for slave-labour, because the former is cheaper and more productive than the latter can ever be made. The slave-owners are indeed their own enemies, in opposing or retarding the emancipation of their labourers.

It is no doubt very difficult to prevail upon a man who has laid out 50,000 dollars in the purchase of 100 negroes, to set them all free, and pay them for their labour by the day; but it is often wiser to break up a bad system at almost any loss, and substitute a better one, than it is to continue the practice of the old, because of the capital sunk in it, when the new would be so much more profitable. But the competition of free labour in the free states will ultimately render this indispensable; and the parallel to this may be often seen in the case of manufactures. A manufacturer purchases, at great expense, a machine for producing a certain fabric. He has scarcely got it into full use, before a new discovery is made, of some superior machine, by which the fabric can be produced with much greater rapidity and at much less cost. If he adheres to the use of his old machine, because of his reluctance to throw away that which cost him so much money, his competitor will soon beat him, by underselling him in price, and surpassing him in quantity and quality. But if he consent to sink his former outlay as a dead loss, and adopt the improvement of his rival, he will keep pace with him at least, and thus live and make a fair share of profit, though the former course could only end in ultimate bankruptcy and ruin. It was so with the small sailing-vessels for rivers, and passage-boats from port to port, when steam-navigation was first introduced. Many of the owners of the old sailing-smacks and vessels, unwilling to throw away what cost them a large sum, continued to sail their vessels against the steamers, and sunk money every trip. The wiser owners laid aside their vessels altogether, to employ steamers in the same trade, and these soon recovered their first loss, and prospered. And so it would be with the owners of slaves, if they were to set them free even without compensation, rid themselves of all the burthen of compulsory maintenance for inefficient work, employ only the hands they wanted, pay them for their labour as they required it, and thus proceed on the same system as the free states, when they would soon equal them in production and prosperity.

Among the new objects to which public attention has been much attracted in Georgia, is the cultivation of the *morus multicaulis*, or Chinese mulberry, for the rearing of silk-worms and the production of silk. It will be remembered that a hundred years ago, in the first settlement of this tract as a British colony, the cultivation and manufacture of silk was one of the objects which was to be specially encouraged and promoted, the soil and climate having been considered peculiarly favourable for this purpose. The recent introduction of the *morus multicaulis*, with its wonderful powers of re-production and multiplication, has, however, given an entirely new stimulus to this subject. Already there are two monthly periodicals in circulation here, one published in Baltimore, and one in Philadelphia, exclusively devoted to the silk question; there may be others, but these I have seen. Several Silk Societies have been established in different States of the Union: while from Maine to Florida, the *morus multicaulis* is cultivated, advertised for sale in every paper, and hundreds of thousands, or perhaps I might safely say, millions of cuttings disposed of at high prices. One person alone, at Augusta, sold 500,000 cuttings in the course of the last and present year, and realised a profit of 30,000 dollars by his labours; and it seems to have taken the place of the late land speculation, in exciting and occupying the minds of the more active money-getters of the community.

New as Macon is, as a city, I was told that there had been already several attempts to set it on fire by incendiaries—two of which occurred in the last year only; and the general supposition was, that these attempts were made by dissatisfied slaves, who either hoped to be able to realise something by plunder, and effect their escape, or else to avenge themselves on their masters for real or fancied ill treatment. It may be numbered among the many disadvantages of slavery, that the master or owner loses one of the strongest holds that an employer has over a free domestic. If the servant in a free country behaves ill, the master can discharge him; and the servant is thus punished for his fault by want of employment, the fear of which is sufficient to keep him, generally, in a state of obedience and anxious desire to please. The slave-owner, however, has no such remedy; he cannot threaten to discharge a slave as a punishment, because this would be to give the slave that which he most desires, his freedom; and the fear of his taking this, by running away, is often so great on the part of the master, that he is prevented from inflicting punishment to the extent he might desire, lest the slave should abscond, or take a sulky fit and not work, or poison some of the family, or set fire to the dwelling, or have recourse to any other mode of avenging himself. Among domestic slaves, all this would be perfectly easy; and therefore masters are slow to irritate or offend them by much severity: but as the facilities for such modes of vengeance are fewer among the field-slaves, these are not so much dreaded, and therefore they are made to feel the full force of the owner's displeasure. That vindictiveness should seem a virtue, and not a crime, in the eyes of an uneducated and oppressed slave, who can wonder, when the higher classes among the Southern gentlemen set such examples of its practice, as in the case of the Speaker of the House of Assembly in Arkansas murdering a member on the floor of the hall of legislature during the last year. Scarcely a month passes in the south-western States without some such scenes and examples.

In the neighbourhood of Macon, on the opposite side of the river to that on which the town is built, are several mounds of different sizes, all of higher antiquity than the date of the earliest settlement here, which are believed to have been thrown up by the Creek Indians, or, as some suppose, by a race anterior even to them. They must be several hundred years old, at least, as on some of them are trees of a very large size, evidently grown there since the mounds were formed. Whether they were for purposes of fortification, or of burial, or of both, it is not easy to determine. In the midst of them is the spot originally occupied as Fort Hawkins, when this was the frontier post to the south-west of the white settlers in Georgia; and from its summit a commanding view of Macon and the surrounding country is enjoyed.

In making our excursion to this and some other places in the neighbourhood, we saw many of the country people coming into town; some on horseback, some in waggons, and some on foot. They were in general as primitive in their dress as the farmers of the remotest parts of England and Wales a century ago, as far as we can judge of these by the pictures and prints of their costume: single-breasted coats without collars, broad-brimmed and low-crowned hats, and grey hair floating in loose locks over the shoulders, were among their peculiarities; and in their conversation they were as rough as in their appearance. They are called by the town's-people, "Crackers," from the frequency with which they crack their large whips, as if they derived a peculiar pleasure from the sound; and in a local little volume, entitled "Georgia Scenes," which I had the opportunity of perusing while in Macon, and which are said to be drawn to the life, it is clear that the manners of the planters in the interior, are generally dissipated, their language coarse, and their amusements as barbarous as they were in England three or four centuries ago. The appearance, indeed, of nearly all the men we saw from the country, as well as those travelling to and fro on the road as passengers by the stages, was reckless, dirty, dissipated, and vulgar, and greatly inferior to that of the American men seen in the Atlantic cities, from Savannah to Boston —especially those of the South.

In the course of our ride to and from the Indian mounds, we passed the dwelling of a free negro, named Solomon Humphries, whose history, as related to us by persons who had known him for years, was sufficiently remarkable to be detailed. He was originally a slave to a Georgia planter; but being a person of more than usual intelligence, activity, and probity, he was entrusted with confidential employments, and had special privileges granted to him. By these means he contrived to scrape together, bit by bit, the means of placing a small sum out at interest, and by the increase of this, with some fortunate purchases and sales, he acquired money enough to buy his own freedom. This being obtained, he commenced business on his own account, as a general dealer in such commodities as could be turned to profit. Being punctually honest in fulfilling his engagements, he was readily trusted beyond his actual means, and thus soon acquired money enough to buy the freedom of such of his own family and kindred as were near to him. Every year his exertions were well rewarded, till he at length got rich; and though unable to read or write himself, the laws of the Southern States forbidding the teaching of slaves to do either, he obtained the services of two white clerks, who kept his books and wrote and replied to his letters; till, by his skill and integrity, he acquired as large a credit as any merchant in the South. One gentleman of Macon assured me that he had given him credit for 10,000 dollars' worth of goods at a time, and was never under any anxiety as to its ultimate payment, and others dealt with him on the same scale.

The merchants and traders of the North with whom he dealt and corresponded, always paid him a visit when they came South for business or pleasure; and as he kept an excellent house, with abundance of servants, and good fare, he very often entertained a large party of white persons at dinner, giving them choice dishes and excellent wines. He never ventured, however, to seat himself at the table, but waited on his guests, superintending and directing the details of the feast, which these white persons condescended to receive and enjoy at his hands, though they would have thought it an indignity offered to them if the giver of the entertainment, whose bounty they so unscrupulously enjoyed, should have dared to place himself at the head of his own board! So revolting to every sense of propriety and justice are the notions and associations engendered by this prejudice of colour and caste! This negro is still in comfortable circumstances, and still trades with the whites as before; but he is no longer opulent, as his two white clerks, for whose engagements he made himself responsible, entered into wild speculations with his funds, and squandered, in profligacy and dissipation, the profits of his concern, which he was obliged to contract in its operations, and carry on by himself, to avoid ultimate bankruptcy and ruin.

The case of this negro is constantly referred to as a proof that, after all, the African race is not so ill treated as the Abolitionists assert, and that, on the whole, their condition is better than that of the poor whites; it being forgotten, that if it were not for the benumbing influence of slavery, hundreds of instances similar to that of the negro adverted to, would be perpetually occurring; but the great difficulty being to get the first step, namely, to accumulate sufficient to purchase their freedom, they cannot get over this, and therefore cannot accomplish the rest. Here, too, as everywhere else that we had yet seen throughout the South, the state of the peasantry in Ireland, and of the children in the manufactories of England, and of the free States of the North, were continually pointed at, as worse than that of the slaves engaged in cultivation; forgetting, that supposing this to be true, one wrong can never justify another, and that all these conditions equally demanded reform. An article which appeared in one of the Georgia papers during our stay here, the "Daily Georgian," of Savannah, expresses this sentiment so fully and unequivocally, that it may be given entire, as an exact index of the general feeling here on this subject. The article is headed, "White Slavery," and proceeds thus:—

The factory system which flourishes in the Eastern States, under the very auspices of those who are most fanatical in their zeal to emancipate the African race, and give them all the rights enjoyed by the white citizens of this republic, is one fraught with abominations. Yet these zealous reformers overlook what is at their own doors, and stretch forth their organ of vision, to penetrate that which their disordered fancy pictures as existing at a distance.

We, of the South, know comparatively little of the sufferings of the countless number of poor infants who toil from year to year, in these establishments, deprived in a great measure of both the air and light of heaven. The subject, however, is better understood in England, where the heartless system of inuring weakly children to perpetual labour originated. When we reflect that these innocent babes are, by the improvidence or poverty of their parents, let out to hire, at a period of life when they should, by right, be imbibing the principles of Christianity, and receiving at least the rudiments of an English education, we may well say that this system is at once subversive of morals and religion. Is it not, then, strange, that when the *soi-disant* philanthropists of England, and of America, were searching for blemishes in the face of society, and busy in endeavouring to uproot what they considered the great evils of the social system, they should be blind (not to say culpable) enough to pass over the worse than Egyptian bondage of so large a portion of their own race and colour, and be entirely destitute of charity for the tender and youthful beings, who, for a miserable pittance, were wasting their infant strength in adding to the store of luxuries for the opulent. No—all the tears flowed for the imaginary sufferings of the well-fed and contented descendant of Ham, whose life rolls on without care or sorrow, and who works with cheerfulness his daily task, happier in many instances than his master,—is well clothed in health, well nursed in sickness, and well taken care of in old age. Could our words reach the ears of the misguided people who are so much imposed on by the arch-leaders of the abolition movement, we would beg them to free the *White Slaves* of Great Britain, and of the manufacturing States of the North, before they interfere in the domestic institutions of the South. All the evils they complain of, as existing amongst us, may be found in bold relief, by examining the state of thraldom in which the factory children are held, from the cradle to the tomb. Education is to them a dead letter—and religion can afford them little consolation. The ignorance in which they are brought up renders them almost incapable of appreciating the divine lessons of the gospel— even if their weary limbs, aching from the incessant work of a week, enables them to visit the temple of God on the Sabbath day. Ye who are Christians, and call yourselves philanthropists, look to this. Here is work for you. Commence to plough the stubble of this field, and all those who are lovers of rational freedom will cheer you on, and you will exhibit a convincing proof of your sincerity.

We were induced to make these remarks, on perusing, in an English paper, the following article. It is peculiarly acceptable at the present time, and shows the great misery of the labouring classes, as well as the pharisaical spirit that animates the Abolitionists generally.

An article is then given from an English paper, entitled "Infant Labour in English Factories;" and because this blot stains the picture of English humanity, therefore it is sought to be inferred that slavery in America is no blot at all! Such are the delusions which prejudice leads men to practice—first, on themselves, and then on each other! How much more would the true freedom and happiness of the human race be advanced, if, instead of clinging to abuses, because they are practised by our own country, and denouncing evils because they belong to some other, we followed the more catholic practice of calling evil, evil—and good, good—wherever either existed; thus placing the Inquisition of Spain, the bow-string of Constantinople, the knout of Russia, the conscription of France, the impressment of England, the white Slavery of the factory, and the black Slavery of the field—all on the same footing; condemning all, because oppressive, and seeking to remove all, as obstacles to the happiness of the great human family, without stopping to inquire by what nation they are practised, for the sake of palliation if by one, or for severer censure if by another. Instead of this, there are many who can feel the highest admiration for liberty, when they are themselves in the enjoyment of that blessing, but think nothing of the wrongs of those that are without it.

CHAPTER XIII

The inconvenient hour at which the regular stages pass through this town to the west, from 12 to 4 in the middle of the night, had induced us to seek for an extra coach in which to perform our journey from hence to Columbus; but, as none were to be had, we were obliged not only to start at this inconvenient period, but to sit up, in order to ascertain whether there was room for our party of four in the coaches running through, as no places could be secured to us beforehand. When the first arrived, which was near four o'clock, there were as many persons congregated around it, to see it come in and go out, as if it had been the first time of its passing through; so long has the curiosity to see, outlived the novelty of the object to be seen.

On this head we were told some curious anecdotes of the country people and the negroes of the town. It is not long since the first church-bell was erected in Macon; and when it rang for the hour of worship on the sabbath, crowds of persons from the country would assemble in groups to see it, and watch its upward and downward motions with all the eagerness of children witnessing for the first time the movements of a new toy. The river of Macon, the Ocmulgee, is navigable by steam-boats of light draught of water, up to the bridge; its length, by the circuitous windings of the stream, being about 600 miles. When the first steam-boat arrived here from Darien, it was in the middle of the night, so that the letting off the steam was heard with great distinctness, from the absence of all other sounds. The negroes not being informed of the expected arrival, and never having heard any similar noise before, arose in great alarm, and hurried to the spot to see what was its cause; when perceiving the intense lights from the furnace, and observing the sparks vomited forth by the wood fires from the large chimney, accompanied with the violent hissing of a column of steam, or as they called it, "white smoke," some of them thought the last day had arrived, and deemed this the summons to judgment. Their ignorance and fear soon causing this impression to spread, in a short time it became general, and created the greatest consternation among the coloured multitude, which was only allayed by the return of daylight, and the sight of the boat in a state of quiet and repose.

At 4 o'clock on the morning of Monday the 11th of March, we took our seats in the mail for Columbus, with no very pleasing anticipations of our journey; as the companion-coach, the Telegraph, which started from the same point at Augusta and had run all the way with the mail, was upset about two miles before reaching Macon. Its passengers, wounded and bruised, were brought on in the mail in which we were about to set forward; the coach being left broken to pieces on the road. Our way until daylight was over an undulating surface, the road being as rough as before, and passing directly through a dense forest of pine-trees, the aspect of which was gloomy and monotonous in the extreme.

At twelve miles from Macon, we passed an inn, kept by Mr. Lachaise; and this having the reputation of being one of the best on the road, we requested the driver to let us stop here for breakfast, it being near eight o'clock. But though there was only one passenger in the coach besides our party, and we were unanimous in our request, we could not prevail on him so far to accommodate us. We drove on, therefore, to Knoxville, a small village about thirteen miles beyond this, and there breakfasted at half-past ten. The fare was as rude as we had been taught to expect; coffee weak and cold, tea without taste, eggs scarcely warmed through, and no bread but hot cakes of Indian corn. There was so evident a desire, however, on the part of the young landlord and his "landlordee"—as here, for the first time, we heard the mistress of an inn called—to meet our wishes, that their cheerfulness rendered the rudeness of the fare less disagreeable.

Soon after leaving Knoxville, while slowly ascending a hill, we overtook a very aged negress, well mounted on a beautiful horse. She was dressed in a fantastic manner, with an old black beaver bonnet, tied down with a dirty white handkerchief, like the gipsies of Europe, a plaid mantle, rather the worse for wear, floating over her shoulders, and a large crooked-branch of a tree in her right hand, as a whip. Though her features were African, her complexion was not quite black, but a sort of reddish brown, such as characterizes the mixed offspring of the Negro and Indian races, of which class she probably was. She had not a tooth left, and her voice was loud, hoarse, and croaking; though her dark eye was full of fire and expression. As she drew up to the coach-window and accosted us, we thought we had never seen a more perfect picture of the Meg Merrilies of the Northern Wizard. On her salute of "good morning" being returned, we asked her how she did; and her reply was, "I'm a young girl yet, though over a hundred years old, and this morning I'm going a frolicking." We thought she must be crazy; but the stage-driver and our fellow-passenger, who knew her well, said she was an old slave of a planter in this neighbourhood; that she was born at Newburn in North Carolina, and that she was undoubtedly more than a century old, though vigorous enough to ride on horseback several miles a day. Her owner, ever since she had passed her hundredth year, had allowed her a fine horse, with a handsome saddle and bridle, to ride about the country. This she decorated, as well as herself, with the most fantastic ornaments, and calling herself "The Sheriff," she rode from one plantation to another, hearing and telling the news, delighting in gossip, always finding something to eat and drink, and some one to help her on her horse when she departed.

We passed also a party of German emigrants going farther west, bivouacking in the woods. A little covered cart, with tattered awning, conveyed all their moveables, but the people themselves went on foot, except an occasional ride for the women and children; and their mode of life was perfectly gipsey-like through all their journey. Being among the most sober of the emigrants from Europe, they are the most successful, and their services are always preferred to those of the intemperate Irish, whose lives are thought here to be not more than three years on the average, after their landing; the abridgment of their natural term being caused wholly by drinking to excess.

Some of the German and Swiss broom-girls find their way here also, and gain a handsome livelihood and a surplus on which to return home, after a few years. We saw a party of half-a-dozen remarkably handsome young females, in Macon, who travelled in company with their two brothers, of men's age, and a younger brother, quite a boy; and by singing, dancing, and selling brooms, they had accumulated, it was thought, a handsome little fortune, or what at least would be so considered among the peasants of Germany and Switzerland. The boy, though not more than ten years of age, was an excellent performer on the pianoforte; and one mode by which he ingratiated first himself, and then all his party, into the good graces of the American families, was by asking if there was a piano in the house, and offering to play them some German music, at his skilful execution of which they were usually astonished, and rewarded him accordingly. As there is scarcely a dwelling of the most ordinary kind containing American females, in which there is not a pianoforte, almost all the female children being taught to play a little on it—though very few indeed evince either taste or skill, or make any progress beyond the few first lessons—so the instrument itself is found everywhere; and any good performance on it by a stranger is regarded with surprise.

Along the whole of the road, for nearly all the distance from Knoxville to Talbotton, log-huts and rising settlements, hardly yet amounting to villages, were seen, the edge of the road being favourable for sending produce to market, and receiving supplies. But the soil here is not so good, as the road runs along the summits of ridges, where the ground is high, and hard or sandy, the rich lands being in the bottoms or water-courses on each side. The settlers' first dwelling, however, is usually erected near the road, and the low lands are brought into cultivation as they can be cleared afterwards.

It is difficult for any one living in England to appreciate the difficulties, toils, and privations which a settler and his family have to undergo in clearing land, and surrounding themselves with even the barest necessaries. Every member of the family must work hard, from daylight to dark, the women as well as the men, and the children as well as the grown people. We saw many boys and girls, of not more than six or seven years of age, some using small axes, others carrying wood, and others assisting in domestic duties. In general they were very dirty in their persons, the mother being too weary to wash them; ragged and ill-fitted in their clothes, there being no tailor or dressmaker to make them; and some of the boys especially reminded me of Cruikshank's ludicrous sketch of a "boy wearing out his father's garments," for many of them had the coats and hats of grown men, so that the former came down below their ankles, and the latter covered their eyes, and required constant lifting. They were all apparently unhealthy, parents and children looking pale and haggard, over-worked in body, and over-pressed with thought and anxiety in mind. What adds greatly to the disadvantage of their situation is, that there are no schools, Sundays or week days, and very few places of worship; while dram-shops, under the name of confectionaries, exist in great numbers, where sweetmeats, cordials, and spirits are to be had so cheap, that the poison is abundant and the remedy scarce; so that the border population, surrounded by such circumstances, can hardly fail to be reckless and unprincipled.

As we were journeying in the mail-stage, we had to stop at every post-office; and these are so numerous, one occurring every ten or twelve miles, that it was impossible to have a separate bag for each; so that at each office the great mail-bag had to be opened, the letters examined to see if there were any for that station or district, and then it was necessary to make up the bag again, repeating the same process at every office. As this took half an hour at least, and our rate of travelling never exceeded six miles an hour, the mail was frequently overtaken and left behind by the ordinary stage-coaches. The rate of charge for fare is the same, however, in each, being about a dollar for every ten miles as the cheapest, and a dollar for every eight miles as the dearest on the road.

The post-offices, which are very humble buildings, and often mere sheds, are more numerous, it is said, than the correspondence of the country requires; but as the appointment of the postmasters rests with the president, this forms a large branch of executive patronage. Since the days of General Jackson, it is well known that the only qualification required for such appointment, has been the advocacy of the politics of the ruling party; there is thus an army of political postmasters arrayed on the side of the Administration. The post-offices in the country and districts here are like the old barbers' shops in English villages a century ago—places for the idle and the gossiping to assemble and discuss the news. To add to the attractions of the post-offices here, many of them are also "confectionaries," at which liquors of all kinds are freely sold; and the class of persons usually assembled to hear the news on the arrival of the mail, were among the most dirty, dissipated, and reckless in their appearance.

The drivers on this road were very inferior to those of the Northern States in deportment and language; they were often insolent, always unaccommodating, and frequently most profligate in their oaths; while, having no fee to expect from the passenger, they appeared to me to be studiously disrespectful, as if they sought that mode of displaying their independence. We sometimes hoped to get a better, by their frequent change, as each driver went only the one stage with his team, usually from ten to twelve miles, but there was a great uniformity in their worthlessness. These, as well as most of the men of these parts, that we had yet seen, had tall gaunt figures, wanting firmness and compactness, though not deficient in strength. They were all ill-dressed, scarcely a garment fitting them well, being more like ready-made clothes bought at a venture, than fitted by any tailor. The greater number went without neckcloths, some without coats, and a good hat was a rarity. Instead of woollen cloths, a kind of grey, or blue-and-white cotton cloth, of domestic manufacture, was used for coats and trousers. Tobacco, was in almost universal use, and the youngest of boys were seen chewing and smoking; while the number of idlers lounging about as though they had nothing to do, could only be accounted for by the fact, that here the negro slave does the greatest part of the labour, while his white master receives the profits of it.

As we passed a spot where some negroes were cutting up the wood for rails or fences—all the divisions between different properties being made here by the zig-zag, or snake-fence—our fellow-passenger, who was himself a slave-owner, said that such negroes as these, stout healthy men, were worth in the market from 1,000 to 1,200 dollars, or from £200 to £250 each. On asking him the cause of this high price, he said it was owing to several circumstances, but especially the following: first, a demand for slaves to clear the new lands in Texas; secondly, a demand for slaves to cultivate cotton in Alabama, and sugar in Louisiana; and thirdly, a demand for slaves to work on the many new railroads now making all over the country. These new sources of demand had given, he said, great increased value to negro property; and more money, he thought, was at this time made by trading in slaves within the United States, than by almost any other occupation. Many speculators travelled over the older States of Virginia and Maryland, bought up the surplus stock found in the hands of the slave-breeders there, and brought them to the South, for a profitable market. Others purchased slaves within the State, and hired them out to work on the railroads, making, as interest on their investment, from 30 to 50 per cent, while capital invested in planting did not yield more than 20 per cent on the average.

In the course of our ride, we stopped at a log-hut, to take in a young lady as passenger. She was apparently about 14 or 15, and, like almost all the American females at that age, was remarkably pretty, with as much feminine delicacy as would be seen in the highest circles in England, though with less of polish or of grace. Though coming from so humble a dwelling, her apparel was of silk, while the gold rings on her white and taper fingers, and the green veil hanging from her Leghorn bonnet, showed that her hands had not been much inured to labour, or her complexion much exposed to the sun.

There is a great difference between the condition and appearance of young females in the humbler ranks of life in England and America. In the former, they labour to assist their parents, by which they get an air of roughness, and rude health, accompanied with a plainness of attire, such as is thought becoming in persons of inferior station. Here, except it be among the emigrants and first settlers, who are mostly foreigners, few females assist their mothers in household or any other duties. They are brought up to be waited on by a negro girl, who does all that is required; and every white woman's daughter, begins from the earliest years to think herself a lady. Fine dress and delicate appearance, with an imitation of genteel manners, are the business of her life, until she gets married, which is here often at 14 and 15; and then her utter inefficiency as a mother may be readily conceived.

On the road we passed a few cotton-gins, for separating the seed from the cotton. Each crop produces about four times as much seed as is necessary to plant the same space on which it was produced; and the residue is sold for seed-cotton, to supply new plantations. We saw also several cotton-presses, in the fields, for pressing the cotton when it is packed into bales, though the greatest number of these are under cover. Cotton and Indian corn are the chief productions of all the cleared lands here. The value of such land was estimated at from ten to twenty-five dollars an acre, according to its position, before a single tree was cleared. The whole of the land in this State being now appropriated as private property, none remaining, any longer in the hands of either the general or the State governments, large fortunes will be made by such as can afford to hold their possessions, (nearly all having bought at a dollar and a quarter per acre,) as every year adds considerably to its value, and some few patches in the bottom lands are already deemed worth fifty dollars an acre at least.

The only place of worship we passed in all our day's ride, was a new clap-board meeting-house, just erected on the edge of the woods, near the road-side, but not yet opened. It was named Mount Sinai, and might truly be called a "tabernacle in the wilderness." It was built by the Methodists, who are here, as everywhere, the pioneers of religious instruction, as their system of circuits and itinerant preaching peculiarly fit them for going into the rude and untrodden paths, to open a highway for those who are to follow after them. A fact was mentioned to us here, as of recent occurrence, which will sufficiently shew the necessity of more churches and more preachers, to correct the present state of things. In this quarter there are two descriptions of Baptists: the orthodox, or evangelical, who are practically as well as theoretically pious, and disposed to assist in all benevolent undertakings; and the Antinomians, or, as they are here called, "hard-shelled" Baptists, who preach the doctrines of unconditional election and reprobation in their severest forms, and whose practice shows how little importance they attach to good works. In the neighbourhood of the road between Knoxville and Talbotton, was a small chapel, which belonged to the latter; and one of the preachers of the former wanted to occupy it on a Sabbath evening, when the others had no service, but it was refused. There was then a great question agitating the public mind here, whether Christianity should be preached to the slaves, and missionaries be permitted to go among them for this purpose or not. The evangelical Baptists desired this; but the "hard-shelled" order opposed it. In this they were supported by the majority of the whites here, who conceived that preaching to slaves would only make them more dissatisfied with their condition, and encourage them to rebel against their masters. The "hard-shelled" minister denounced missions and missionaries, from his pulpit, and was applauded and caressed by his hearers. The evangelical minister commended missions and missionaries, from such elevated stumps as he could find among the trees to preach from, and was insulted and driven off the ground; since which the "hard-shelled" Baptists are said to have had everything their own way, in this quarter.

A competition or rivalry of a different description took place here recently, and has but just ended, among the proprietors of the three lines of coaches running on this road. The fare from Macon to Columbus, a distance of ninety miles, was twenty dollars, while the mail-stage had the monopoly. A second line was set up, and reduced it to ten dollars. A third line followed, and brought it down to five dollars. The two former reduced their rates to one dollar; and the new adventurers absolutely carried their passengers for nothing, while the hotels furnished them with dinner and champaigne at the cost of the coach-proprietors! This could of course last but a little while: all parties soon saw the folly of such a career of mutual loss, which must end in the ruin of one or more, if persisted in, and they settled a compromise of all running at the same hours, and the same rates, ten dollars per ninety miles. As, however, there are rarely more than enough passengers to fill one coach, they are all losing money, even at this rate, yet fear to raise it, lest a higher fare might tempt some new competitor into the field.

It was five o'clock when we reached Talbotton, a pretty little place, forming the principal town of the county of Talbotton, and having a good brick court house, a large inn, many shops and stores, and some very neat and tasteful private dwellings. The place was in a great commotion about a piece of scandal that had set the whole community by the ears; though, at first, the story was unintelligible to us. A young girl of the neighbourhood had been recently married, at little more than twelve years of age, and the rumour had gone abroad that the first offspring of this young mother, produced after seven months' gestation, was "a mule!" This tale, which at first shocked us by its grossness, and then became incredible from its absurdity, was rendered more intelligible by an explanation that this was a cant phrase to denote a "coloured child." The inference intended to be drawn from this slander was, not only that the child was not the husband's, but that its real parent was a coloured person; an offence which, in the language of some of those whom we heard speak of it, "all the waters of Georgia would be insufficient to wash out." It had been already ascertained that the child was no browner than many white children are known to be at birth, who get fairer afterwards; and there was nothing in its features or hair to indicate African blood, even in the second or third degree; so that public indignation was now beginning to be turned from the innocent mother, to the criminal originator of the scandal; and it was thought that if he or she could be discovered, and the proof of guilt be brought home to them, nothing short of their assassination would appease the incensed community.

Many were the exclamations uttered on this occasion against the Abolitionists, and the horrors of amalgamation; but when I endeavoured indirectly to draw from some of the speakers their opinion as to the frequent amalgamation, by African mothers having offspring by American fathers, no sort of censure was thought due to this. It was not denied that there were many instances in which white men became fathers of offspring by their own negro women, and as the children follow the fate of their mothers, such offspring would be his slaves, and might be lawfully sold by him as his property, and often were so disposed of! Such is the obliquitous morality of those who are loudest in the expression of their horror at amalgamation, when imputed to the Abolitionists!

From one of the residents of Talbotton, who was our fellow-passenger here, I learnt, what I confess surprised me, yet he assured me it was true, that though in the large towns of Georgia, and particularly those to the eastward, such as

Savannah, Augusta, and Macon, the white population and the blacks were nearly equal in numbers; yet, taking the State all through, the proportion was at least ten negroes to one white; the number of negroes employed in the cotton plantations causing this great difference. In Alabama, where I expected the disproportion would have been greater, he said it was less, being not more than four negroes to one white; but this he accounted for by stating that a great many poor white families were settled in Alabama as cultivators, and did the work there, which negroes perform here. The most startling part of all was, however, that in Mississippi, the next adjoining State, the number of negroes was at least fifty to one white person; though even here, he said, they were not in such constant apprehension of danger as they were in Charleston. This he attributed to the circumstance that in Alabama nearly all were slaves, and so scattered and employed incessantly in labour, that they had not the means of combination; whereas, in Charleston, the number of free blacks was very considerable; and as many of these had leisure and means, and communicated freely with the slaves, a union and concentration of their sympathies made them much more dangerous, though their numbers were so much fewer, and their proportion to the whites so much less, than in the State of Mississippi. The gentleman who made these statements was himself a slaveholder, an anti-missionary man, and a great hater of the Abolitionists.

On our way from Talbotton to Columbus, there were many log-huts near the road, and much ground fenced-in for clearing; but our way was through endless forests of pine, under the varied aspects already frequently described. When the sun had set, and the night was fairly closed in, the fires, still burning in many parts of the woods, glared, from various points, and exhibited a wild and romantic picture; the red glow of light in the heavens reflecting the blaze below, and adding much to the impressiveness of the scene. Every now and then we passed by a log-hut, through the open chinks of which, the light could be so well seen, as to form horizontal lines of red, alternating with the dark logs of wood between, while here and there, in the very deepest recesses of the forest, would be seen the twinkling taper of some distant cottage, dimmed by the blue haze which usually follows the close of a sultry day, as this had been. The thermometer at noon was above 70°, though on this day week, it had been down to 20°; and while the forest trees on each side presented a dark mass of foliage at their summits, and the tangled grape-vines and creepers, mixed with the smaller trees, formed impenetrable thickets below, the sky above our heads was of the brightest azure, and spangled with stars that shone out with more than ordinary lustre, making the whole scene a mixture of the solemn, the beautiful, and the sublime.

It was midnight before we reached Columbus, where we found accommodation, such as it was, at the Oglethorpe Hotel, and here we determined to remain for the night, as the roughness of the roads, the violence of the motion—which had twice broken down our coach, and obliged us to halt for its repair on the way—and the wretchedness of the fare at all the tables we had seen, made us anxious to rest and recruit for a day. The hotel was very large, and the rooms more spacious than usual; but though not built more than four or five years, it had all the defects of a much older building. The doors of the rooms were many of them shattered, hinges and locks out of repair, windows broken, and sashes and blinds out of order, without any attempt being made to remedy all this. It seems quite characteristic, indeed, of the Southern hotels to have almost everything in need of repair. When the building is once erected and finished, no one seems to take any pains to keep it in good condition; but when things get injured they are suffered so to remain till they are altogether worn out.

All the servants here being slaves, and no master or mistress of Southern hotels appearing to take the least interest in the reception or accommodation of their visitors, those who arrive are entirely dependent on these slaves for whatever they require. Though three coaches stopped at the door, no one was ready to receive them. The negroes belonging to the house were all lying huddled together on the floor, none of them being provided with more than a blanket, which they rolled round them, but without bedding or pillow. They sleep so soundly that it is a matter of the greatest difficulty to wake them; and even then, it requires a long time to make them understand what you wish. Not a single bed-room that we were shown into was ready, the beds being unmade, the rooms unprepared, and all in disorder and confusion; the reason alleged was, that it was quite time enough to get rooms ready, when they were sure they would be wanted. Everything being in disorder, therefore, it took an hour, at least, to put the room in decent condition; and even then it was most uncomfortable.

In this hotel, the out-door accommodation for gentlemen (water-closets being a luxury here unknown) was worse than I had ever before found it, bad as this is in every part of the United States; but it would seem that as the traveller goes South, where the increased warmth of the climate would require greater attention to personal comfort and purity, as well as to cleanliness of apartments and food, everything gets worse; and we thought that we had here arrived at the *ne plus ultra* of disorder, neglect, and dirtiness; though we were told, in the ordinary phrase, that we might "go farther and fare worse," and moreover be obliged to pay more and more extravagantly, as the accommodations grew less acceptable.

We remained at Columbus during the whole of Tuesday; and though much fatigued, had an opportunity of seeing something of the town, and some of its most respectable citizens, to whom I had letters of introduction. The town is only ten years old, being one of the newest places of any size in this part of the country, yet it already contains about 8,000 inhabitants, in nearly equal proportions of black and white; and both its public and private buildings are substantial, commodious, and ornamental.

In the town itself, we observed a more than usual number of the places called "Confectionaries," where sweetmeats and fruits are sold; but the great staple supplies of which are peach-brandy, whiskey, rum, and other ardent spirits, of which the consumption here, by all classes and in various forms, is said to be considerable. We observed also, what to us was a novelty, the open sale of dirks, bowie-knives, and a long kind of stiletto, called the "Arkansas toothpick." These are sold by druggists, in whose shops or stores these deadly weapons are hung up for public inspection, and sold by them as part of the legitimate wares of their calling; thus plainly indicating, that weapons to kill, as well as medicine to cure, could be had at the same shop; and placing, beside the deadly poisons of arsenic, laudanum, hemlock, and hellebore, the deadly weapons of no less fatal power.

It was a peculiar fancy of the hotel-keeper with whom we lodged, to call his children after the names of the several States, and we had accordingly a morning visit from four young ladies of the family, whose names were Georgia, Carolina, Virginia, and Louisianna. We learnt, during our stay here, a fact respecting the state of social life and morals among the slave population employed in domestic servitude, which, as it came to us in the most authentic shape, is worth noticing, as a specimen of what we were assured was of very common occurrence. A female slave, born in Georgia, had been brought up in the house of her white master, and had given birth to a child, of whom one of the white master's visiting friends was the father. When the child grew up, it was thought desirable, for the father's sake, to send both the mother and child away to some other State, and as both were the property of the white master, (for offspring in this country follow the fate of their mothers, so that the coloured child of a white father becomes the property of the master to whom the slave-mother belongs,) it was proposed to send them both into Alabama for sale. As all the slaves have a great horror of being sent to the south or the west,—for the farther they go in either of these directions, the harder they are worked, and the worse they are used—great objection was made to this, and the mother declared she would "sulk," so that nobody should buy her, and she would rather kill her brown boy than let him go to Alabama. As either of these steps would lessen the value of the master's property, and as the negroes have often resolution enough to put such threats into execution, the master began to hesitate, and the matter was compromised, by the mother being sold into the western part of the same State, and removed from Augusta to Columbia, while the child was sent farther east, to Charleston in South Carolina, and there is very little probability of their ever seeing each other again.

Such separations as these are quite common, and appear to be no more thought of, by those who enforce them, than the separation of a calf from its brute parent, or a colt from its dam. As the mother was an excellent house-servant, so large a sum as 1200 dollars, or nearly 250*l*. sterling, was given for her by her present owner; and he hired her to the master of the hotel, for a fixed sum in monthly wages, the amount of which was 20 dollars, giving the owner, therefore, an interest of 20 per cent on his investment; out of which he had no deduction to make for her maintenance, as the person hiring her undertook to feed and clothe her. For the latter, however, she was entirely dependent on any little presents received from travellers visiting the hotel; though this was very trifling, as it is not the custom to give fees to the servants in America; indeed, the charges are generally so high, as to indispose persons to add gratuities to the attendants. The condition of a large race of unfortunate dependents, among whom such instances as these are common, may therefore be better imagined than described.

CHAPTER XIV

We felt so much fatigued by our rough journeys from Augusta to Macon, and Macon to Columbus, that we were unwilling to encounter another night's travelling in the same way; and as the regular stages all pass through here at night, there was no way of escaping the evil we desired to avoid, but by taking an extra coach for our exclusive use, and giving two days to the journey of little more than ninety miles. After considerable negotiation, we were enabled to effect this, but at the extravagant charge of 120 dollars, or about 25*l*. sterling.

In this coach we left Columbus at eight o'clock on the morning of Wednesday the 13th of March; and crossing the river Chathahooche a little below the falls, by the wooden bridge described, we entered on the state of Alabama, the river being the dividing line or boundary between the two.

The change of aspect in scenery and condition was very striking. The woods, into which we were entering, seemed more wild, the road being a mere pathway through and around standing trees, the tops of which touched our heads in many places; the land was poorer in quality, but being more undulated in surface, the swamps in the bottoms were more abundant; the brooks ran with greater impetuosity, and the bridges over them were more rude than any we had yet seen. Rough corduroy roads occurred for many hundred yards at a time, and loose planks laid across horizontal beams, supported on single pillars, but neither nailed nor fastened, served for bridges; while frequently the coach would have to go through water deep enough to come close up to the coach-door, and threaten us, by the slightest false step, with immersion. The stations, where we changed horses, were mere log-huts, used as stables: and all the way, for miles in succession, we saw neither a human being, a fence, a rood of cleared land, nor anything indeed that could indicate the presence of man, or the trace of civilization, so that we felt the solitude of the woods in all its fulness.

This description applies to all the tract of land for many miles beyond the river Chathahoochee; and it was said that whoever came as far as that towards Georgia, were more disposed to go on and fix their settlement in that State, than in Alabama, which seems to have a bad name even among those who reside in it. Beyond this belt, signs of settlement began gradually to appear, but even these were of the rudest kind. A blacksmith's shop, a few log-huts, and a "confectionary," with the ever-ready poison of strong drink, constituted a village; and for forty miles of our road we saw only one instance of a store where any other goods could be procured; this being a log-house recently devoted to the purpose of a general drapery and grocery warehouse.

It was five o'clock, or nine hours after our setting out from Columbus, when we reached the little village of Tuskeegea, forty-five miles from Columbus; and here we should have halted for the night, but that there were yet two good hours of daylight, and we were desirous of making the second day's journey as short as practicable. The inn, at which we changed horses, was one of the neatest and cleanest we had seen in the South; and though very humble in its appearance and furniture, there was such an air of neatness, cleanliness, and order about it, that it excited our warm commendation. The landlady, having her sympathies touched by our praise of her management and arrangement, entered voluntarily into conversation with us, and told us the outline of her history.

She said that her husband and herself had both been brought up without having been taught the proper value of money, so that they had not been long married before they had run through all they possessed. In this extremity they had only a choice between two evils, one of which was to go to Texas, where people who were unfortunate had land given to them, and could get on fast, by industry and care; the other was to purchase a small piece of land in some rising village nearer home, and, by a little harder labour and more rigid economy, get on quite as well, though not quite so fast, as in Texas. They preferred the last, and came here about three years ago; it was then that the first tree was cut down to form the village of Tuskeegea where some Creek Indians of that name had just vacated a settlement, to go beyond the Mississippi. These Indians, she said, had been a terror to all the whites of the neighbourhood, and massacred many families in cold blood; and her statement was confirmed to us in many quarters. Among other instances of their ferocity and cruelty, we heard at Columbus, that some years ago a stage-coach had been attacked by them in the forest, and after securing the horses for their own use, the Indians broke up the coach, and burnt it in the middle of the road. They then made the passengers prisoners, and scalping them all, men, women, and children, they placed them in a small wigwam, to which they set fire, and burnt them all alive! In Florida, to the present hour, the Seminoles commit similar outrages on the whites wherever they can find them; and we heard from two ladies going to St. Augustine, that within the last two years, nearly every white family living within two or three miles of these towns, had been put to death by the Indians.

Since the settlement of this landlady and her husband, who was a general, at Tuskeegea, they had prospered exceedingly, were every year adding to their substance, and surrounding themselves with comforts and means of enjoyment. A good population had been attracted near them, comprising upwards of 300 persons; and there was now an excellent school, in which more than 100 youths of both sexes received the best education given in the country, from a male teacher from Mobile, and a female teacher from the celebrated seminary at Troy, in the State of New York. The teachers were said to be very competent, and received 1000 dollars, or about 200*l.* a year each; and music, drawing, and languages were taught, as well as the ordinary branches of an English education. No village of 300 persons in England could certainly produce the parallel of this, more especially a village only three years old.

Our next stage from hence was a distance of twelve miles, through the same description of scenery as that passed in the morning, but the soil was more clayey, and the road better, though all our drive was performed through a deluge of heavy rain, which was very acceptable to the country, as more than a month had passed since any rain had fallen.

At the end of this stage we reached a log-house, where we were to sleep for the night. The beds and interior accommodations were most uninviting; but we had no choice, so, lighting a large wood-fire, and preparing some tea, which our kind friends at Savannah had furnished us with, as none was to be had in houses of this description, we enjoyed it, and retired early. During the night, the rain poured down with great violence, and as the roof of the loghouse was not water-proof, we had streams entering at different parts of it, which made our position very uncomfortable. The partitions between the several small apartments into which the house was divided, were so thin, and the beds were placed so close to them, that the slightest noise or sound made in one room could be distinctly heard in the next; so that it was like sleeping with a dozen persons in the same apartment. The cries of some young children, the snoring of the negroes scattered about lying on the floor, the constant barking of several large dogs, saluting and answering each other in alternate volleys, and the incessant croakings of the frogs, with which every part of these woods abound, made it almost impossible to sleep. We therefore got out to trim the fire, and see the hour, several times during the night, and were extremely glad when the daylight broke on us, our first perception of this being through the chinks of the roof, as there was no window whatever in the room in which we slept.

In the morning a very rude breakfast was prepared; and happening to converse with the old woman who served us, on the state of the country, and asking whether the removal of the Indians was not considered a blessing by the settlers here, I remarked that she made no answer. We afterwards learnt, that the man by whom the house was kept was himself a half-blood Indian, and his rage was said to be so great when this question was repeated to him, that he was "perfectly mad," in the language of our informant, and declared his regret that he had missed the opportunity to shoot me for so saying. Such is the vindictive spirit that seems to flow through Indian veins, and which loses but little of its original nature, even by mingling with gentler blood than its own.

About three o'clock in the afternoon we reached Montgomery, having been seven hours performing a distance of thirty miles, with two break-downs on the way; and glad enough we were to terminate this long and tedious land-journey, in which, for a distance of more than 400 miles, we had scarcely seen anything but interminable forests on either side of our path, except in the small spaces occupied by the few towns and villages in the way, and the inconsiderable portions in which a few patches of corn or cotton cultivation bordered the mere skirts of the road.

At Montgomery we found excellent quarters in the best hotel we had seen since leaving New York, superior even, as it seemed to us at least, to the hotels of Charleston and Savannah; and, being desirous of proceeding onward without delay, we embarked in the steam-boat, "Commerce," to go down the Alabama river to Mobile, a distance of nearly 500 miles, which these fine vessels perform in about forty-eight hours, their rate of speed exceeding ten miles an hour all the way.

CHAPTER XV

The time fixed for the departure of the steam-boat was nine in the evening, as by this hour all the eastern stages were usually in; but, as often happens, one of these stages was six hours beyond its usual time, while another had broken down on the road, and was left there by the passengers, who had to walk for the remainder of the way, so that they did not reach Montgomery till near daylight; and the boat, thus delayed for their arrival, did not start till morning. The general regularity of English stage-coaches, so accustoms an Englishman to expect punctuality in the public conveyances of other countries, that he feels these irregularities the more annoying. But American travellers, accustomed to them from their youth, bear them with enviable equanimity.

The Alabama river, at the place of our embarkation, was not large, nor was the surrounding scenery interesting; but about fifty miles above this, to which the steam-navigation extends, the scenery is said to be pleasing, especially at Wetumpka, a very recent settlement forty-five miles above Montgomery, where are certain rapids or falls, the Indian name, Wetumpka, meaning, "the falling stream." Both there and at this place, a great number of fish resembling salmon are taken in traps; and as we were passing to the boat for embarkation, we met several persons coming up from the river with many fine large fish, called buffaloes, of which it was said upwards of 500 were caught, at a single haul, by a seine, or net, opposite the wharf at which we lay.

The first station at which we stopped on our way down the Alabama, was at Washington, a small settlement about sixteen miles below Montgomery, where 100 bales of cotton were taken in for Mobile. The crew were numerous, and very efficient. There were twelve white sailors, besides the engineer's department of five men, who were all whites; and twenty negroes besides. The seamen's wages were 40 dollars, or 8*l.* sterling per month, besides their provisions. The negroes, who were all hired from different masters, were paid the same sum; but these poor creatures were scantily fed by the master of the ship, and badly clothed by their owners, who received all their wages. They thus paid, probably, not more than five dollars per month to each negro for his apparel, or anything else he might need, and pocketed the 35 dollars as profit on the purchase-money invested; while the white sailors and firemen received the whole amount of their 40 dollars of wages without any deduction; such is the difference between a slave and a freeman in matters of labour and reward! Notwithstanding this, it was constantly asserted by the passengers, that of the two, the negroes were better off than the white men, because they had no *cares*; but when these individuals were asked, whether *they* would like to be "released from all cares," by some master taking from them the profits of their labour, and merely feeding and clothing them instead—they made no reply. As we proceeded down the river, the banks appeared very high, the bluffs, as they are called, being in many places more than 100 feet in elevation above the present surface of the stream; and yet even these were nearly overflowed in one of the great freshets which occurred a few years ago. The river then rose ninety feet above its ordinary level, inundating half the town of Montgomery, though it lies high upon a sloping land; but at the present moment the river was said to be from six to eight feet lower than it has been known for many years at this season. The current flowed at the rate of three miles an hour, the depth in mid-channel being not more than from six to eight feet.

As we descended the river, the bluffs became less frequent, and the low lands more abundant. The few bluffs we passed were generally occupied as cotton stations, where a low-roofed shed would be seen on the top, and a cotton-press near, with accumulated bales waiting for some conveyance to Mobile, the port of shipment for Europe. From the edge of the bluff down to the water, rails were frequently placed on an inclined plane to slide down the bales of cotton for shipment, each planter having his own landing-place at some point along the river; and these, with wood stations, occurring every five to ten miles. The chief cultivation all along the river is cotton and corn, and the labourers are all negro slaves. The average price of these at present is 500 dollars for the commonest description, and 1000 dollars for what are termed "prime hands." The number required for each plantation is, on the average, about one negro to every ten acres of cotton and ten acres of corn.

When evening came, we had time to look around a little among our fellow-passengers, as, from the darkness impeding our survey of objects without, we were of necessity driven to other objects within. During the daytime, many of the passengers were engaged at cards, and large sums of money were lost and won in this occupation. Most of the company seemed to find the time hang heavily on their hands, and though some few read, it was evidently to kill time, rather than from any pleasure that it afforded them. This, at least, we inferred from the frequent breaks, risings up, and sittings down, with occasional dozings between. Tobacco was used by almost all the men, young and old, some lads of fifteen or sixteen chewing and spitting as much as their elders, and nearly all smoking as well as chewing, so that we were the only persons on board who did neither the one nor the other.

Among the passengers was a planter from beyond the Mississippi, who evinced a great curiosity to become acquainted with us, as he stated that we were the first English persons he had ever yet seen. He seemed to be glad to find himself quite certain that he had now seen real people from the "Old Country," as he had passed his whole life in the interior, 200 miles beyond the great river, and would have something to say when he went back. Another of our passengers was a cotton planter, from the interior of Alabama, who was said to be worth 100,000 dollars, though his apparel certainly would not sell in any town of the United States for five dollars. He was about seventy years of age, had lost one eye, had only three or four teeth left, a sunburnt and wrinkled countenance, like parchment, with white locks hanging over his shoulders, a pair of scarlet cotton trousers, crossed with bars of deep blue, snuff-brown cotton stockings, shoes without buckles or strings, a short buttonless waistcoat, no braces, a nondescript coat, between a jacket and a surtout, no neckcloth, and a low-crowned and broad-brimmed brown hat. He was of a merry disposition, and communicative as well as inquisitive. He was particularly impressed with the fresh and healthy appearance of myself and family, as contrasted with the generally pale complexions of his countrymen, and asked us if all the men, women, and children in England were as robust and rosy as we were. I told him that the greater number of those who lived temperately, and took a proper portion of exercise in the open air, were so; and when he inquired into our mode of life, and found that we ate but two meals a day, breakfast and dinner, while he saw every one around him eating four—breakfast, lunch, dinner, and supper; when he learnt that we drank neither wine, beer, cider, or spirits, bathed or washed from head to foot once every day, took exercise for health, whether business required it or not, and never used tobacco in any form or shape, he said he felt less surprised than at first, at our health and vigour, but he thought it must require great resolution and perseverance to pursue so "singular a course of life," as he deemed this to be. He admitted, however, that drinking, smoking, and chewing were injurious, but thought it impossible to break the habit of either when once contracted; and when I mentioned to him successful instances of abandoning them all, he seemed incredulous, and said he had never heard so much before. He thought it a great blessing that we had no negroes in England, as he believed they were enough to destroy any country. He was going down to

Mobile, to receive money for cotton sold, and to make some purchases for his people; and when I said to him he would arrive in good time on Saturday night to go to church on the following morning, he said that he had never been in any church in all his life, and thought he was now too old to begin, though he had "heard a few preachings in the woods, but didn't much mind 'em."

About fifty miles before reaching Mobile, we passed the mouth of the large river Tumbukbee usually spelt Tombigbee, which here runs into the Alabama. From this point of junction, on to the sea, these streams lose their respective names, and their united waters are called the River of Mobile, just as in Mesopotamia, the waters of the Tigris and Euphrates, where they unite in one, lose their distinctive names, and their mingled waters, and from Korna to the Gulf of Persia, into which they discharge, are called the River of the Arabs. Along the banks of the Tumbukbee are prairies, or extensive undulating plains, without a tree for many miles. These were formerly occupied by the Choctaws and Chickasaws, tribes of Indians, who are now all gone westward to the regions beyond the Mississippi.

Not far from the junction is a military arsenal of the United States, at Mount Vernon, about three miles back from the landing-place on the right bank of the river. This arsenal and the navy-yard at Pensacola, not far to the eastward of Mobile, are the principal stations of the United States Government, for the general supply of their army and navy within and around the Gulf of Mexico.

It was past sunset before we drew near enough to Mobile to see the town, and it was then chiefly by their lights that the houses were visible. At half-past seven we reached the wharf and landed, when we made our way to the Waverley House, where apartments had been previously provided for our reception, and were glad to find ourselves once more, after our tiresome land-journey across Georgia and Alabama, in a place of cleanliness, comfort, and repose.

CHAPTER XVI

The State of Alabama, which we had now traversed, from Columbus to Mobile, is but of comparatively recent settlement and separation in its present form. It is thought, however, to have been visited, especially on its southern coast, at the same period that Florida and Louisiana were first explored. It was in 1539 that the Spanish governor of Cuba, Fernando de Soto, visited the territories named, in his way from Florida eastward to the banks of the Mississippi, where he died within three years after his leaving Cuba, when his dispirited followers soon dispersed, and became gradually scattered and extinct.

Nearly 180 years elapsed after this disastrous expedition, before any other European attempt to settle in these quarters was made. Early in the eighteenth century, 1718, the French formed the colony of Louisiana, which included not only the territory on each side the lower part of the Mississippi, but also the lands now forming the State of Alabama, at least near the coast, for the Indians still possessed the interior; it was by the French settlers of Louisiana, that Mobile was first founded, and a fort built where the present city now stands.

The original charter granted by the crown of England to Georgia, covered, however, the greater part of this territory, from lat. 31° to lat. 35° N.; and this so remained until long after the American revolution, when, in 1802, a cession was made by Georgia, to the general government of the United States, of all her Western Territory, between the Chatahoochee and the Mississippi rivers. In 1800, the whole of this tract was erected into a territorial government, under the name of the Mississippi Territory, which continued a distinct section of the Union until 1817, when, by an act of Congress passed in March of that year, it was divided into two portions, the westernmost forming Mississippi, and the easternmost Alabama; the former enjoying the distinction of a State, from its greater extent of population, while the latter still remained a Territory. Within the next year, however, 1818, the increase of population was so rapid in Alabama, as to entitle it to admission into the Union as a State; and, accordingly, an act of Congress was passed, empowering the people of Alabama to form a constitution, which being done, and ratified by the national legislature, the new State became a member of the great Federal Union.

Just previous to this period, and for a few years after it, the inhabitants suffered greatly from the hostile incursions of the Creeks and Seminoles, the two most powerful and savage tribes of Indians, by whom the territory was occupied. Their complete subjugation was only effected by long and sanguinary struggles, in which the troops of Tennessee, under General Jackson, subsequently president of the United States, took a conspicuous part. The Creeks and Seminoles dispersed chiefly into Florida, where the latter still remain in large numbers.

The State of Alabama, as at present constituted, is bounded on the north by Tennessee, on the south by part of Florida and the Gulf of Mexico, on the east by Georgia, and on the west by the State of Mississippi. Its length is 280 miles, its breadth 160, its area 46,000 square miles, or nearly 30,000,000 of acres; and nearly all this vast area is covered with productive soil.

The staple production of Alabama is cotton, but the soil and climate are favourable to the growth of wheat, rye, oats, maize, rice, and tobacco, as well as indigo. It is thought that the sugar-cane, the vine, and the olive, might all be cultivated with success here, and in time they will no doubt enter into the productions of Alabama; but so much profit is made at present from the cultivation of cotton, that it absorbs all the capital and all the attention of the people. Fruits of various kinds, from the fig to the apple, flourish abundantly; mineral coal is found in the Cahawba and Black Warrior rivers; and iron ore exists in several parts of the State; while the number of its navigable rivers affords the best means of transporting all these various products to the coast.

The seat of government for the State is at Tuscaloosa, near its centre; and the legislatorial body consists of a Governor, a Senate, and a House of Representatives. The Governor is elected for two years, and has a salary of 3,500 dollars per annum. The Senate consists of thirty members, elected for three years; and the House of Representatives consists of ninety-one members, elected annually. The pay of the members of both houses is four dollars per day, besides their mileage, or travelling expenses, to and from the seat of government to their own homes.

The judiciary consists of a supreme court, of three judges, each paid 2,250 dollars per annum, and nine circuit courts, each with a single judge, at a salary of 2,000 dollars per annum. The judges are all chosen by a joint vote of the two houses of the legislature, the circuit judges for six, and the supreme court judges for seven years. The supreme court has appellate jurisdiction only upon points of law, taken up from the circuit courts by writ of error. It sits at the seat of government. The opinions of the court are delivered in writing, and published by the official reporter. The circuit courts have original jurisdiction in all civil and criminal cases in their respective districts, and exercise chancery forms also; a circuit judge being indeed the chancellor of his district, the districts comprising about six counties each. The courts sit twice in the year, in the spring and autumn, for about eight weeks at a time; and in each circuit, there is a State attorney, who prosecutes offenders at the public expense, receiving a salary of 250 dollars per annum, in addition to his fees.

Education is amply provided for, by an appropriation of lands to raise funds for that purpose. By an act of the general Congress, passed in March, 1819, one section of the government lands, amounting to 640 acres, being the thirty-sixth part of each township, is appropriated exclusively for the support of common schools; and in addition to this, two whole townships, of thirty-six sections each, were appropriated to the support of a State university. Of these 46,000 acres, about the half have been already sold, producing, with principal and interest, the sum of about 400,000 dollars; and from the constantly increasing value of the lands, the residue will probably produce 600,000 dollars, making, therefore, a permanent fund or endowment of a million of dollars, for the support of the university alone, in addition to the ample endowment for public schools by the 640 acres of land in each township.

Provision has also been made for promoting internal improvements in the construction of roads, canals, and bridges, and for improving the navigation of rivers. By an act of Congress, passed in March 1819, it was enacted that five per cent of the proceeds of all sales of public lands, made in the State after the 1st of September following, were to be appropriated thus: three-fifths to be devoted to improvements within the State, and the other two fifths to roads and canals leading to and from the State to either of the adjoining ones; and this is in full operation, under a board of commissioners.

The whole population of Alabama is estimated at 500,000, of whom about 300,000 are whites, and 200,000 slaves. The increase has been rapid, as in 1810 there were less than 10,000 and in 1830 the numbers were 390,527, of whom 117,549 were slaves; the free people of colour being very few at either period.

Of the religious bodies in this State, the Methodists appear to be the most numerous, having about 50 preachers, and nearly 50,000 members. The Baptists have 150 ministers, but not more than 10,000 communicants. The Presbyterians have 30 ministers, and nearly 2,000 communicants. The Roman Catholics have nine ministers; and the Episcopalians only three.

The principal city and port of Alabama is Mobile. This was first settled by the French, who, in 1700, erected Fort Mobile, where the present city stands.

In 1763, this port was ceded, by the French, to England; and in 1780 the English surrendered it to Spain. During all this time it was a place of little or no importance, except as a naval and military station on the coast. In 1813 Spain surrendered it to the Americans, and from that period its progressive improvement may be dated; as it did not then possess a hundred dwellings, and these were all of the humblest kind. In 1814 it was incorporated as a town; and four years afterwards it was advanced to the dignity of a city, with a charter and full municipal privileges.

The commerce of Mobile is confined chiefly to the exportation of cotton for Europe and the northern ports, and the importation of manufactures from the same quarters. The cotton crop of Alabama, for the last year, amounted to nearly 400,000 bales; of which about 100,000 were from North Alabama; and were shipped at New Orleans; the remainder, or 300,000, were from South Alabama, and these were shipped at Mobile. Each bale weighs 450 lbs. and is worth, at the present market-price, about seventy dollars per bale, making the whole value of the cotton shipped at this one port only about twenty-one millions of dollars in a single season. The employment which this gives to capital, shipping, and labour, may be readily conceived.

The population of Mobile is estimated at 25,000, of whom about half are whites, and the remainder slaves and free-coloured people. They are chiefly engaged in commerce, though there are not wanting the full proportion of legal and medical men; but there are few persons disengaged from all active pursuits, and living a life of leisure. In their manners and style of living, the higher orders partake much of the hospitality and elegance of Charleston and Savannah; and in this rank of society great intelligence, morality, and honour are to be found. But there is a large class of inferior persons belonging to the community, some natives of the South, but many strangers and sojourners, who are among the most dissolute and unprincipled of men. Accordingly there are few weeks pass by without outrages which are shocking to persons of correct feeling; and during our short stay here the following cases occurred. I select the paragraphs from the newspapers of the day, as giving them all the requisite authenticity, having, however, other evidence of their truth, and having witnessed, indeed, the excitement and indignation occasioned by the transactions thus recorded. The following are from the Mobile papers of March 20th, and a few subsequent days:

> MURDER.—Public feeling was shocked yesterday afternoon at the commission of a most extraordinary and heart-rending murder. Mr. George Churchward, a highly respectable and esteemed commission-merchant, was instantaneously killed by the discharge of a pistol, shot

from the hands of Mr. C. B. Churchill, also a very respectable merchant. The transaction occurred at the residence of the latter, in whose family the former boarded. The parties were in an apartment by themselves, and had but a few moments prior withdrawn from the dinner-table. From various indications, it would appear that the deceased was shot from the rear, the ball having entered behind the ear, and penetrated to the brain. We forbear from any comments, the foregoing is the substance gathered from the inquest. We understand, this morning, that Mr. Churchill has been admitted to bail in the sum of 5000 dollars. On this, also, we forbear remarking.

Homicide.—An act of homicide was committed in our streets yesterday afternoon: George Churchward, a commission merchant, was shot dead through the head, by C. B. Churchill, a cotton-broker. We know nothing of the causes of the fatal act. We are pained and sickened at the repetition of these scenes, each one of which, happening with impunity, is another blow at the security of life and limb, which it is the first object of civilized laws to protect.

Another Outrage.—Attempt to Murder.—Mr. John Wylie, an old and highly respectable citizen, was yesterday shot by a Captain Taylor, who was in the employ of Mr. Wylie, as commander of a schooner. The ball entered the eye in a slanting direction outward. Mr. Wylie was living last night, but great fears are entertained that the wound will prove mortal. Captain Taylor is in custody. We are sick at heart, at recording such frequent and horrid violations of the law in our city. Cannot these brutal outrages be suppressed? Have we laws, and can they not be enforced?

Organised Band.—Great alarm and excitement have been caused in Mobile, by the settled conviction that there exists in that city an organized band of robbers, scoundrels, and incendiaries, whose determined object seems to be to riot amid ruin and distress.

The truth is, that the community want either the virtue or the courage to see the laws executed on the murderers; and thus it is, that criminals, being left to go at large on bail, make their escape for a season, and then return again. Even when they remain, the juries will not convict them; so that impunity is thus granted to the further perpetration of similar deeds. As an instance of this laxity in the administration of the law, I subjoin a short paragraph taken from the Mobile papers of about the same date, though relating to another place, but in the same Southern section of the country, in the neighbouring State of Mississippi—

> MURDER.—On the night of the 20th instant, a man named William R. Harper, was killed in a tavern, in Vicksburgh, by a person of the name of Tippo, the keeper of the tavern. They were both drunk, and in their madness they got to firing pistols at each other in their bedroom, one of the shots proved fatal. Tippo was discharged, as it was thought that he acted in self-defence.—*G. G. Advertiser.*

The habits of drinking, which are more or less the cause of the excesses here described, are more openly practised and encouraged in the cities of the South than at the North. Grog-shops of the common order abound, at every corner of almost every street. Public bars, and confectionaries, as they are called, for the gentry, are nearly as abundant; and in all of them numbers of well-dressed young men are to be seen smoking cigars, and drinking wine, spirits, and cordials, at an early hour of the day. The "Alhambra" and the "Rialto" give the aid of their classical names to establishments of this description; and there is hardly a night passes by without a riot or a fight, or without furnishing occasion for a duel or a murder at some subsequent time. More than half the fires that occur, spring from the same cause; for drunken habits among masters soon contaminate, by their example, servants and slaves; and the riot of the one furnishes a temptation and an excuse for the excesses of the other.

It is matter of astonishment, that with such elements of demoralization and destruction so constantly and actively at work, a city could ever make progress. But the resources of wealth within the reach of the community, and the eagerness of the more sober and industrious classes, to develop these with the utmost degree of speed, outstrip even the destroying elements, and produce accumulated prosperity in spite of the obstacles opposed to it. If these obstacles were removed, if intemperance were completely annihilated, and a sober, moral, and industrious population were to replace the dissipated, gambling, idle, reckless, and murdering class, the progress of prosperity would be much more rapid; and what is of much more importance, the ground gained would be attended with corresponding moral and intellectual improvement, which now lags far behind, except among the select and honourable few.

On the last day of our stay in Mobile, there was an election for the mayor of the city. The present holder of the office was a Whig; and his own party wished to secure his re-election. The opposite party being supporters of the administration, wished to displace him; the election, therefore, was entirely of a political character. We had been assured by those resident in the town, that before noon there would be 500 voters drunk at least, and before sunset 1,000. I had witnessed a Liverpool election for mayor, under the old suffrage of the freemen, and I had seen many other elections in England for members of parliament, in which drunkenness, riot, and disorder reigned; and I am bound to say that this municipal election for Mobile was just as bad as any of them, worse would, perhaps, be impossible.

Where a thousand men are drunk, under all the additional excitement of party spirit, scenes of violence are the natural fruits to be expected, and these were produced in great abundance. Let no man point to this, however, as the necessary result of republican institutions. We can match them in England, under a monarchy; and the Church and King party in English elections are often the most drunken and riotous of the two. But they are equally disgraceful in either, and deserve equally severe condemnation. It should be added, that the elections in the Northern cities are generally free from the intoxication and disorder here described; though the institutions are there as republican as here. It is the free use of strong drinks that is the source of the evil; and where these are profusely distributed, whether in monarchies or republics, the effects are the same. In England we remove the military from the scene, to preserve the free exercise of the suffrage, though they are often afterwards called in to quell riots; but it would be much wiser to remove all the sellers of strong drink, and shut up their poisonous fountains, during an election, by which moral as well as political freedom and purity would be best secured.

CHAPTER XVII

On Monday 25th of March, we left Mobile, in the steam vessel Kingston, for New Orleans, starting from the wharf soon after noon. The weather was delicious, in the happiest combination of warmth and freshness, the thermometer at 75°, a fine breeze from the sea, and a balmy softness in the atmosphere of the most agreeable kind.

Though we were sometimes ten miles from the shore, we had never more than five fathoms water; and the whole of the upper part of the Gulf of Mexico is thus shallow for a long way out to sea. When the winds blow off the shore, the waters are driven out, and return again with the winds blowing on the shore, the difference being as great as three or four feet in elevation, occasioned by the winds alone. The engines used in these steam-vessels are chiefly low-pressure, and their crews are very efficient, so that they are perfectly safe conveyances, and few accidents occur. The wages paid are very high; the engineers get 200 dollars a month; the ordinary men from 60 to 80 dollars, and the smallest boys from 30 to 40 dollars; but as in other trades, this increased rate of pay leads generally to increased recklessness and extravagance in the receivers; and there are fewer men who lay by any portion of their wages here, than among the seamen of the North, who do not receive half as much.

We continued to make progress during all the night, and at five in the morning we reached the landing-place at Pontchartrain, about five miles to the north, or at the back of the city of New Orleans. The appearance of this landing-place is very striking. A number of long wharfs or jetties, built on perpendicular piles, project out, from one common centre, like so many rays, into the water; and at the end of these, the steam boats lie. A railroad goes from the extremity of each of these landings to the centre described, for the baggage cars and goods transported; and at the centre commences the larger railroad to New Orleans.

Here we re-embarked in the first train of cars, which left at half past six; and, going for about five miles over a perfect swamp or morass, through which the railroad ran, with impervious woods and thickets on either side, we reached, in half an hour, the outskirts of New Orleans. The avenue by which we entered the city was called Les Champs Elysees; and everything that caught our attention reminded us strongly of Paris. The lamps were hung from the centre of ropes passing across the streets, as in France; women were seen walking abroad unbonneted, with gay aprons and caps; the names of all the streets and places we passed were French; the car-drivers, porters, and hackney-coachmen, spoke chiefly French; the shops, signs, gateways, pavements, and passengers moving in the streets, all seemed so perfectly Parisian, that if a person could be transported here suddenly, without knowing the locality, it would be difficult for him to persuade himself that he was not in some city of France.

After passing through the French quarter, we came to Canal Street, which divides it from the American; and crossing this fine broad avenue, lined with trees on each side, the transition was as marked as between Calais and Dover. We had now got among a new set of people; the streets had American names, the shops and stores had American signs, and everything indeed was as thoroughly American as in New York or Boston. We found excellent accommodations at the St. Charles Hotel, and here accordingly we took up our abode.

We remained at New Orleans for nearly a month, and, upon the whole, passed our time usefully and agreeably. There was one great drawback to our pleasure, in a severe attack which I suffered, of quinsied sore-throat, which was epidemical in New Orleans at the time of our visit, and from which a great number had suffered. In my own case, I was for three days unable to articulate an intelligible sound, or to swallow even a teaspoonful of water; but, by great depletion, losing twenty ounces of blood by the lancet, and about twenty more by eighty leeches, applied at two different times to the throat, I was restored; and was fortunate in having the joint attendance of a young Irish physician, Dr. Johnston, whom we had known at Highgate near London, and of Dr. Luzenberg, who had studied medicine in Germany, attended the hospitals in Paris and London, and was accounted one of the ablest physicians of the South. The former gentleman was resident as a physician at Alexandria, on the Red River, and had taken his passage for that place from New Orleans, but hearing of our arrival here, he left the steam-boat, came on shore to see us, and determined to remain a week or two for the enjoyment of our society; and mutually interesting and agreeable it was, to a high degree, to talk over old scenes and old occurrences, to recapitulate old friendships, and old social enjoyments which we had shared together. I met here, also, a gentleman who was in Smyrna in 1812, during my visit to that city; and I enjoyed a similar pleasure with him in talking of old scenes and old friends in that remote quarter; while a great number of gentlemen who had been in England, and who had known me in London, some in the House of Commons, and others in Liverpool and elsewhere, came to renew their acquaintance, and to make our stay agreeable. We became acquainted also with a most delightful circle of resident families, to whom we had letters of introduction, as well as with many who did not want for this passport to seek our acquaintance; and we found among these as many intelligent, hospitable, virtuous, and agreeable persons, as we had met with in any of the cities of the North.

With the assistance and under the guidance of the friends by whom we soon found ourselves surrounded, I had easy access to every available source of information respecting the history and statistics of the State of Louisiana. By the same means also, I was enabled to visit all the public buildings and institutions of the city, many of which interested me exceedingly, and especially those of a charitable and benevolent nature, for, after all that I had heard of New Orleans, and its dissipation and profligacy, I had hardly expected to have found so many, and such excellent institutions of this nature, and so well supported as those which I examined here.

CHAPTER XVIII

The original colony of Louisiana, of which New Orleans is the present capital, embraced what now forms the Territory of Florida, and the States of Arkansas and Missouri, as well as the lands of the Far West, beyond these, to the Rocky Mountains.

As early as the year 1512, the Spaniards first laid claim to Florida, whose shores they contended had not been visited by Sebastian Cabot, as he had never gone so far south, and therefore the pretensions of England to the possession of this territory, they held to be wholly unfounded. At this period, the Spanish governor of Porto Rico, named Ponce de Leon, arrived on its shores, in the course of a voyage he was making in quest of a land, which was reported to contain a brook, or fountain, endowed with the miraculous power of restoring the bloom and vigour of youth to age and decrepitude. "Believing," says Grahame, from whose interesting history this fact is quoted, "that he had now attained the favoured region, he hastened to take possession, in his sovereign's name, of so rare and valuable an acquisition. He bestowed on it the name of Florida, either on account of the vernal beauty that adorned its surface, or because he discovered it on the Sunday before Easter, which the Spaniards called Pasqua de Flores; but though he chilled his aged frame by bathing in every stream that he could find, he had the mortification of returning an older instead of a younger man to Porto Rico."

In 1523 the whole of this coast was surveyed with great care by the Italian navigator, Verrazzano, in the service of the French and in 1538, the celebrated Hernandez de Soto made his journey into the interior, discovering, for the first time, the Mississippi river, and passing along its banks up through the whole of the territory now forming the State of Louisiana. They encountered great difficulties from sickness, and the hostilities of the Indians; by the joint operation of which, the chief and all his followers were gradually destroyed, and found a grave in the great Father of Waters, whose mighty stream they had been the first to discover and explore.

In 1673, a French monk, named Marquette, travelled as a missionary from Canada, and after a journey of many hundred miles, full of perils, he reached the banks of the Mississippi. He was followed by others from the same quarter, and the intelligence of their journeys being conveyed to France, an expedition was fitted out from thence, with every thing necessary for the establishment of a colony here; but it was unfortunately destroyed by a storm in the Gulf of Mexico.

In 1698 a second attempt to found a colony was more successful. On this occasion, a leader named Herville, arrived with 200 colonists from France, and formed a settlement in the Bay of Beloxi, about midway between Mobile and New Orleans.

In 1700 some idea seemed to have been entertained by the English, of forming a settlement on the Mississippi; to prevent which, the French built their first fort above the Balize, as the entrance to that stream is called. Soon after this, an English ship-of-war, of eighteen guns, entered the river; but being uncertain whether it was really the Mississippi or not, the captain inquired to this effect of the governor of the fort, who appears to have answered in the negative, as the British commander is said to have turned back in his route, and gone to seek the Mississippi farther west. The memory of this anecdote is preserved in the name given to the bend of the river where this happened, it being called "The English Turn."

In 1717 a company was formed in Paris, at the head of which was the celebrated John Law, of Lauriston, the Scotch financier, and founder of the South Sea Bubble, the Mississippi Scheme, and other wild and fraudulent speculations. Although his projects brought ruin upon his own head, and on those who were involved with him, they had a beneficial effect on the interests of the colony itself; for they caused hundreds of the ruined speculators to come to the country, and thus bringing into it their labour and intelligence, they laid the foundations of its future prosperity.

After some disastrous wars with the Indians, during which a horrible massacre of the whites took place in 1729, at Natchitoches, the charter of the Mississippi Company was surrendered to the king of France in 1732, at which period the colony contained a population of 5,000 whites and 200 blacks.

In 1754 the population was greatly increased by the arrival of emigrants from Acadia, now called Nova Scotia, from whence they had been driven by the tyranny of the British government. In 1759, others, from Canada, sought a refuge in Louisiana; and these united sources added much to the strength and welfare of the colony.

Soon after this, Louisiana was ceded by France to Spain; and although the settlers at first protested against this cession, and even refused admission to the first Spanish governor, yet they ultimately yielded; though signal vengeance was taken on the leaders of the resistance, some of whom were shot, and others immured in dungeons in the Havannah.

In 1779 war was declared between England and Spain, which led to many battles and skirmishes between the ships and settlers of these two nations, when the Spaniards were successful in taking Baton Rouge from the English, and in planting themselves at Mobile and Pensacola.

In 1792 the Baron de Carondelet was appointed governor, and under his administration the first newspaper was printed in Louisiana, under the title of "Le Moniteur." The culture of sugar was now first begun here also, and superseded that of indigo, which had till this time been the staple production.

In 1795 the navigation of the Mississippi was opened by the treaty of St. Lorenzo, to the Western States of the American Union; and from this period its commercial prosperity began greatly to advance.

In 1801 the colony of Louisiana was ceded back from Spain again to France, who did not, however, take possession of it till 1803, and that merely for the purpose of transferring it to the United States, to whom it was ceded by the treaty of Paris in April of that year, for the sum of sixty millions of francs. The population of Louisiana, which then included all Florida, the towns of Mobile and Pensacola, Arkansas Territory, and Missouri, was 49,474 in the whole.

In 1804 the territory was divided into two separate governments, the upper one being above latitude 33° North, being called the Territory of Louisiana, and the lower one, the Territory of New Orleans; each governed by a legislative council.

In 1807 many thousand French emigrants from St. Domingo, driven out by the revolution of the blacks there, sought an asylum in this quarter, and largely augmented the French population.

In 1812 the united Territories were formed into the State of Louisiana, and admitted into the great American Union, with her present constitution, General Claiborne being made the first governor. In this year, too, the first steam boat seen on the Mississippi, descended the river from Pittsburg to New Orleans; and from these two events, the admission of the State into the Federal Union, and the beginning of steam navigation on the waters of the Mississippi, may be dated the rapid rise and progress of the whole region, in population and in wealth.

The State of Louisiana, as at present constituted, is bounded on the north by Arkansas, and the State of Mississippi, on the east by the same State, on the west by Texas, and on the south by the Gulf of Mexico. On the east of the Mississippi river, its boundary is the thirty-first degree of North latitude, and on the west of that river its boundary is the thirty-third degree. Its extreme eastern boundary is the Pearl River, and its western the River Sabine, while the Gulf of Mexico washes all its southern coast. Its length, therefore, is 240 miles, its breadth 210 miles; and it contains an area of 48,220 square miles, or 30,860,800 acres.

The population of Louisiana was, by the census of 1830, only 215,739 less than the population of the single city of New York; and of these at least one half were slaves, 109,631; but it is thought to have been nearly doubled during the last ten years. Those in the upper settlements, remote from the river and the sea, are chiefly French Canadians, and their descendants, from the stock of emigrants coming here a century ago. In the middle part of the State there are many Germans; in the lower part they are chiefly of French and Spanish descent; but of late years, many of the handy New Englanders, and settlers from Ohio and Kentucky, have found their way to the luxurious plains of the South, and these are fast amalgamating with the earlier population, and so far changing their habits and characters.

The great variety of condition in these several classes has struck most travellers; and it is said that in journeying from New Orleans to the Sabine River, men are met with in every stage of civilization. In New Orleans and other places on the banks of the Mississippi, the sugar and cotton planters live in splendid edifices, and enjoy all the luxury that wealth can impart. In Attakapas and Opelousas the glare of expensive luxury vanishes, and is followed by substantial independence. In the western parts of Opelousas are found herdsmen and hunters, whose cabins are rudely and hastily constructed, and the whole scenery around them recall to the imagination the very earliest stages of primeval life.

It may be readily conceived, that fruits and flowers exist in great abundance and variety. Among the former may be mentioned the peach, the fig, the orange, and the pomegranate, and among the latter, the rose, the magnolia, and the yellow jasmine. All kinds of garden vegetables also are easily produced, though horticulture is little attended to by any class of the settlers.

The predominant religion of the State has always been the Roman Catholic; the subdivision of the area being into twenty ecclesiastical parishes, each of which is supplied with priests from the old cathedral of New Orleans. Since the cession of the territory to the United States, and its incorporation into the Union, the Protestant sects have somewhat increased. They are still, however, much fewer here than in any of the older sections of the country, as may be judged from the fact, that throughout the whole of Louisiana, the Baptists have only 14 ministers, and about 1,000 communicants; the Methodists, 12 ministers, and above 2,000 members; the Presbyterians, 5 ministers, and about 300 communicants; and the Episcopalians, 3 ministers, and not more than 200 communicants.

The legislative body of Louisiana consists of a Governor, a Senate, and a House of Representatives. The Governor is elected by the people every four years. The qualifications require him to be thirty-five years of age, a citizen of the United States, and a resident of Louisiana for six years preceding his election. He must possess a landed estate of the clear value of 5,000 dollars, or 1,000*l*. sterling. No member of Congress, or person holding office under government, or minister of any religious body, can be elected; nor can any Governor be eligible to serve two successive terms. His salary is 7,500 dollars, or 1,500*l*. sterling, per annum.

The Senate consists of seventeen members, elected by the people for four years; one half being elected every two years. They must be twenty-seven years of age, have resided four years within the State, and hold landed property to the value of 1,000 dollars.

The House of Representatives consists of fifty members, elected every two years. They must be twenty-one years of age, have resided two years within the State, and be possessed of a landed estate of the value of 500 dollars.

The voters include every free white male citizen of the United States, of twenty-one years of age, who has resided one year within the parish in which he votes, and who, in the six months preceding the election, shall have paid his State taxes.

The judiciary consists of a Supreme Court, with three judges, each at 5,000 dollars a year; and eight district or circuit judges, at 3,000 dollars a year.

Louisiana sends only three members to the House of Representatives in the General Congress, (the State of New York sends forty) this being the ratio of its population; but, like all other States, it sends two members to the Senate; all the States being equally represented in that body.

CHAPTER XIX

New Orleans, the capital of Louisiana, and the only city or town of importance within the State, is a place of considerable interest, from its history, its position, and its general character, so different from that of any other city of the United States, or indeed of any other place on the American continent.

It was in 1718 that New Orleans was first founded. Previous to this period, the seat of government for Louisiana had been fixed at Biloxi, a spot between the Mississippi and Alabama rivers, on the coast; but in this year, the French governor, Bienville, selected the present site of New Orleans for his new capital, and employed men to clear the ground, and erect the necessary buildings; but, from various obstacles, the spot was not fully occupied till 1722.

In 1723, it was visited by Charlevoix, who came down from Canada, nearly all the way, by the Mississippi river, a journey of more than 3,000 miles; and he describes it as consisting then of about one hundred cabins, placed without much order, a large wooden warehouse, two or three dwelling-houses, and a miserable store-house, which had been used as a chapel; a shed being converted into the house of prayer. The population did not then exceed two hundred.

In this same year, many Germans who had come out under the delusive promises of John Law, the Mississippi schemer, augmented the numbers settled at New Orleans. They came down from the Arkansas River, where lands had been promised them, but which they were unable to obtain, and sought to find a passage back to Europe. The government, being unable to furnish this, granted them small allotments of land, on a part of the river called the German coast, where they settled, and where their descendants inhabit to this day.

In 1727, a large party of Jesuits and Ursuline Nuns arrived from France, and established themselves in a convent, on land granted to them in the city.

In 1763, the Jesuits were expelled from all the dominions of the kings of France, Spain, and Naples, by a decree of Clement XIII and were accordingly obliged to leave New Orleans.

Their property, which was seized and sold under an order in council, then produced 180,000 dollars; and it is said that the same property is now worth 15,000,000 dollars, at least, merely as land, exclusive of the buildings and improvements made on it; so great has been the increase in the value of land within the precincts of the city.

In 1764, British vessels first began to visit the Mississippi, for trade; and it is stated that they would sail up beyond the city of New Orleans, make the ships fast to a tree on the banks of the river, and there trade with the native Indians, or the citizens and planters of the neighbouring country.

In 1769, the yellow fever first visited New Orleans; and in the following year, the cold was so intense that the Mississippi was frozen over for several yards on each side of the river. In 1785, the population of the city was 4,980. In 1788, on Good Friday, a fire broke out, which destroyed 900 houses, and created great distress. In 1792, the Baron Carondelet was appointed governor, and he introduced a spirit of enterprise and improvement unknown before. He divided the city into wards, lighted it, and appointed watchmen, erected fortifications, opened a canal, raised a militia, and gave a great stimulus to commerce.

In 1794 the first newspaper was published here, under a French title, "Le Moniteur de la Louisiana," though the colony was subject to Spain. Another extensive conflagration, and a hurricane, committed great ravages, and considerably retarded the prosperity of the colony. The population of the city was then 8,056.

In 1803, the city became American, by the cession of Louisiana to the United States; and in 1805 it was incorporated by charter, and placed under the regular municipal government of a mayor, aldermen, and council. This gave so great an impetus to improvement in every way, that in 1810 the population amounted to 24,552, having trebled itself within the last seven years.

In 1812, the first steam-boat, called the New Orleans, descended the river from Pittsburg; and from that period the commerce of the city has gone on increasing with so much rapidity, that there are at present nearly 500 steam vessels plying on the waters of the Mississippi, and about 400 ships and sailing vessels in the port of New Orleans, from all quarters of the globe.

The population has increased in a still greater ratio, as will be seen from the following statement—

In	1810	24,552	In	1825	45,336
	1815	32,947		1830	49,826
	1820	41,351		1835	76,242

At present it is estimated to exceed 100,000; the proportion maintained throughout all these periods being pretty nearly the same between the black and white, their respective numbers being about equal, the former rather predominating of late, and going on increasing.

The situation of New Orleans is well chosen, and admirably adapted for a large commercial city. The Mississippi River may be said to run a general course from north to south for at least seven-eighths of its length. As it approaches the sea, however, within about 200 miles, it bends its course from west to east. Besides this general change of direction, it has several serpentine bends or curves, in which the stream actually flows from south to north. In one of these, the city of New Orleans stands; so that, though it is on the left bank of the river as you descend from its source to the sea, it is nevertheless on the west of the stream, in consequence of which, the sun rises opposite to New Orleans, and sets over the city, contrary to the impression which almost all strangers would have of its locality without seeing it.

The distance of New Orleans, from the mouths of the Mississippi at the sea, is just 105 miles, the latitude of the city being 30° N.; and it is remarkable that this line, or parallel of latitude, should cut near so many seaports, and places on great rivers, as Cairo on the Nile, Suez at the head of the Red Sea, Bussorah on the Euphrates at the head of the Persian Gulf, Mobile on the Alabama, and New Orleans on the Mississippi, at the head of the Gulf of Mexico. This city is 1,000 miles below the junction of the Ohio, 1,200 miles below the junction of the Missouri; nearly 3,000 miles from the sources of the Mississippi, and 1,200 from the seat of government at Washington—such are the distances of this extensive Union!

Everywhere along its lower section near the ocean, the Mississippi gives proof of its having, like other great rivers, gradually raised its bed above its original level, and increased its deposits near its point of contact with the sea, so as to create every day new land projecting outwards in a constantly increasing tongue or point, pushing itself southward into the Mexican Gulf. So rapid has been this increase in the elevation of the soil, that already, when New Orleans is scarcely a century old, the bed of the river has been so raised above the level of the city, as to require a high embankment on either side, under the name of a levée, to prevent the waters from bursting through, and submerging the dwellings and their inmates beneath the stream.

To prevent the waters of the Mississippi from laying all the surrounding country under the flood, it is found necessary to keep up the embankment of the high mounds constituting the levée, with great care. On the eastern side of the river, this embankment commences 125 miles above New Orleans, and extends down the river to Fort St. Philip, 60 miles below the city. On the western side, it commences at the river Atchafalaya, 140 miles above New Orleans, extending also as far down the river as the former. The levée is usually about twelve feet thick at the base, and six feet high, with a good broad footpath all along the top; but in places where the pressure of the river is greater than in others, the base is often increased to thirty feet in thickness. Notwithstanding this, however, the waters sometimes break through, forming what is called a crevasse. Mr. Brackenridge describes such a crevasse as rushing from the river with indescribable impetuosity, and a noise like the roaring of a cataract, boiling and foaming, and tearing everything before it. When such a calamity occurs, the inhabitants, for miles above and below the spot where the crevasse opens, abandon every employment, and use all their exertions to stop the breach. Their efforts are sometimes successful; but it more frequently happens that the torrent is too overwhelming to be stayed, when the destruction of crops, buildings, and even lives, often follows, while the soil is swept away and the surface left encumbered with large trees, logs, and driftwood, brought down by the current, which must all be removed before cultivation can be resumed.

The last calamity of this kind that happened, was in May, 1816, when the levée was broken through at a spot called Macartney's plantation, about nine miles above New Orleans. It spread its devastation, however, quite down to the city; and Mr. Gibson, an eye-witness of the scene, says he remembers seeing hundreds of the dwellings of New Orleans deserted by their owners and tenants, and furniture and drowned animals covering the whole of the grounds in the back part of the town. The crevasse was ultimately closed up by the sinking of a vessel in the breach, and filling up the intervening space with fascines and earth; but the injury created by it was so great, that many plantations in its neighbourhood had to be entirely abandoned, and the quality of the soil was deteriorated for miles around.

On the other hand, large tracts of soil are sometimes recovered from the river, and converted into productive lands. It is stated that the Board of Public Works for the State of Louisiana have redeemed no less than 450,000 acres of excellent land, in the clearing of Bayou Lafourche; and it is estimated that the works on the Atchafalaya river, when completed, will redeem 300,000 acres more.

On the subject of the rise of the Mississippi, and the elevation of its bed, it may be mentioned that during our stay at New Orleans, some persons were employed in digging a well, when they came, at the depth of thirteen feet below the surface, to a forest of trees, standing upright in their natural position all without leaves, and mostly without branches; or with the branches broken off and destroyed, but the trunks still fresh, and one of them was sawed through, of the diameter of eleven feet! So deep is the vegetable soil in all this quarter, that a single man can bore to the depth of fifty feet without assistance, there being nothing but soft alluvial mould all the way down to that depth; and when an experiment was made by boring to the depth of 200 feet, a bed of marine shells was found there.

The original city of New Orleans, built under the Spanish and French governments, lies in the deepest part of the curve or bend of the Mississippi. Its form is oblong, presenting a front of about 1,300 yards towards the river, and extending back about 700 yards from the stream. It is intersected by streets running at right angles to each other, the streets being twenty-two in number, and thus dividing the city into eighty-four principal, and fourteen minor blocks or squares. This portion is encompassed by three broad avenues, called Rue de l'Esplanade, Rue de Rampart, and Rue de Canal, each adorned with rows of trees, not unlike the Boulevards of Paris, and other French cities. The streets, though regular, are narrow, rarely exceeding forty feet in breadth, and the whole style of building, both in stores and private dwellings, is decidedly French, as are all the names of the streets and avenues within these limits.

Beyond the city proper, are fauxbourgs, built in nearly the same style; and beyond Canal Street, in the upper part of the city, commences what is called the American quarter, which extends along the river till you come to the adjoining city of Lafayette. This, however, may be more properly called a suburb of New Orleans, the union of the two being as unbroken as that of London and Westminster. The American quarter has more spacious streets, more substantial dwellings, and is altogether better built, better lighted, and better ventilated, than the French and Spanish sections; and there is no doubt but that all subsequent additions to the city in every direction, will partake of this improved character.

The most animated and bustling part of all the city is the Levée, or raised bank running along immediately in front of the river, and extending beyond the houses and streets, from 100 to 150 yards, for a length of at least three miles, from one end of the city to the other. Along the edge of this Levée, all the ships and vessels are anchored or moored in tiers of three or four deep. The largest and finest vessels are usually at the upper end of the city, near Lafayette, the steam-boats lie in the centre, and the smaller vessels and coasters occupy the bank at the lower end of the city. It may be doubted whether any river in the world can exhibit so magnificent a spectacle as the Mississippi in this respect. There are more ships in the Thames, but the largest and finest of these are usually in the various docks, while the smaller kind are chiefly seen without, and the Thames has not half the ample breadth and sweep of the Mississippi. There are as many vessels, perhaps, in the Mersey, but these are nearly all in dock, and the river is comparatively bare. The Tagus is a broader stream, but its shipping are neither so numerous nor so fine; and even New York, splendid as is the array of ships

presented by her wharfs, is not so striking as New Orleans, where a greater number
of large, handsome, and fine vessels seemed to me to line the magnificent curve
of the Mississippi, than I had ever before seen in any one port. The reflection
that these are all congregated here to receive and convey away to other lands the
produce of such mighty streams as the Missouri and the Mississippi, the Ohio,
the Tennessee, the Arkansas, and the Red River, including more than 20,000
miles of inland navigation, the sources of the principal streams being in the
region of perpetual snows, and their outlet in the latitude of perpetual verdure,
carries one's admiration to the verge of the sublime.

The Levée itself, on the edge of which all these ships and vessels are anchored,
is covered with bales of cotton and other merchandise; and in the busy season,
such as that in which we were at New Orleans, in March and April, it is filled
with buyers and sellers, from every part of the Union, and spectators from all
parts of the world. There are no less than 1,500 drays for the conveyance of this
merchandise licensed by the city; and they seem to be all in motion, flying to and
fro on a brisk trot, whether laden or empty—the horses never walking, and the
drivers never sitting, either on the shafts, or in the drays, as in Europe. The bales
of cotton, on their arrival in the rafts or steam-boats, from the upper country,
are carried off to the numerous establishments of steam-presses, where they are
compressed into about half their original bulk, and repacked in this reduced
shape for shipment to foreign ports. All this, with the arrival and departure every
day of many hundreds of passengers up and down the river, from Cincinnati,
Louisville, St. Louis, and Pittsburg, to the Havannah, to New York, and to
Texas, occasions such incessant bustle, that every body and everything seems to
be in perpetual motion.

Of the public buildings, the oldest and most remarkable is the Cathedral,
which is nearly in the centre of the old city. It is immediately fronting the river,
and has before it an open square, called the Place d'Armes, by which its front
view is unobstructed. This edifice was commenced in 1792, and completed in
1794, by or at the expense of Don André Almonaster, perpetual regidor, and
Alvarez Real, on condition of masses being offered for the soul of its founder
every Saturday evening, a condition which is rigidly fulfilled. The building
is in a heavy and corrupt style of architecture, a mixture of the Tuscan and
the Doric, with one tall central tower, and two shorter wing-towers, each
covered with a sort of bell-shaped cap. Nor is the interior at all more worthy
of admiration as to style of building or ornament, ranking, in these respects,
with the religious edifices of third or fourth class provincial towns in the least
frequented parts of France. The first curate of the parish that was appointed to
this cathedral was Antonio de Sedella, who filled that office for upwards of fifty
years, having come to New Orleans in 1779, and dying in 1837, at the age of

ninety years. This single individual, it is thought, during that time, celebrated and performed nearly half the marriages and funerals occurring among the Catholic inhabitants of the city for half a century. He was buried at the foot of the altar at which he served so long and faithfully, and has left behind him a reputation for virtue and benevolence, which many a Christian pastor might be proud to enjoy.

On either side of the Cathedral are two large buildings, serving as appendages, or apparent wings to the Cathedral itself, and much improving its effect as a centre. These are, the City-hall, and the Courthouse, built by the same individual, Don André Almonaster. They are in the same style of architecture, a union of the Tuscan and the Doric; but not being disfigured by towers, and having bold cornices, good pediments, and crowning balustrades, they have a much better appearance than the Cathedral; and the three edifices together make an impressive if not an elegant pile.

The other religious edifices of the Catholics comprehend the Ursuline Convent, founded in 1733, now more than a century old, and the most ancient edifice existing in the city; the Ursuline Chapel, built in 1787; and St. Antoine's, or the Mortuary Chapel, at which all the funeral services of the Catholics are now performed. A larger and more splendid building is intended to be erected, under the name of St. Patrick's Church, the design of which is to be an imitation of York Minster, on a scale of 164 feet by 93, and 190 feet for the height of its tower; the estimate of its cost being 100,000 dollars.

Of Protestant places of worship there are four. The Episcopal Church in Canal-street, with a chaste Ionic portico and pediment, and a singularly beautiful flat-domed roof; its cost being 48,000 dollars. The Presbyterian Church in Lafayette Square, of the Doric order, with a good portico, and light chaste steeple, built in 1834, and costing 55,000 dollars. The Methodist Episcopal Church in Poydras Street, of the Doric order, the details of its portico and entablature taken from the temple of Theseus at Athens, and surmounted by a singular kind of obelisk, serving as its tower, or steeple, in which is combined the massiveness of the Egyptian with the lightness of the Greek architecture. The height of the obelisk is 170 feet, and the effect produced by it is striking and pleasing. This edifice was erected in 1836, and cost 50,000 dollars. The Congregational church, the oldest of the Protestant places of worship, founded in 1819, built of brick, without the least architectural beauty, though costing more than either of the others—70,000 dollars.

The State-House, in which the Legislature of Louisiana hold their sittings, is a plain but commodious building. It was built in 1815, and used as a Charity Hospital; but it was purchased by the State in 1834, and converted into a State-House; the Senate and House of Representatives having each their chamber here, and the rest of the building being devoted to public offices, while an open space with lawn and garden in front, makes it cool, airy, and agreeable. A very splendid design has been made for a new House of Legislature, but nothing has yet been definitively settled respecting its execution.

The new Charity Hospital, which has been erected to answer the purposes of the former, was begun in 1831, and completed in 1834, at a cost of 150,000 dollars. It is about 300 feet in length of front, by 76 feet in depth, including the centre and two wings, and is three stories in height. It has wards and apartments to accommodate 500 patients. The hall and lecture-room of the medical college, the dispensary, library, and museum, are all excellent in their kind; and the grounds around it are in the neatest order. Here, too, as at Baltimore, the Sisters of Charity devote themselves, with Christian zeal and piety, to gratuitous attendance on the sick.

The Franklin Infirmary, about two miles from the town, between New Orleans and Lake Pontchartrain, is a private hospital, founded in 1835 by Dr. C.A. Luzenberg, the most eminent physician of the city (under whose skilful treatment and kind care I was restored from a most dangerous illness). It is situated in the Champs Elysées, fronting the railroad from Pontchartrain to New Orleans; is a commodious building, 65 feet by 55 feet, and two stories high, surrounded by gardens and shrubberies, and capable of accommodating, comfortably, 100 patients.

A new Mint of the United States has just been completed here, at a cost of 182,000 dollars being 282 feet in length, 108 in depth, and three stories in height. It is of the Ionic order, is in good taste, and is furnished with all the necessary machinery for coining.

It will be seen, therefore, that New Orleans is well supplied with all the necessary public edifices for legislation, the administration of justice, protection, police, health, benevolence and religion, in a greater degree, indeed, than its recent organization as an American city would warrant us to expect; and yet it is but in its infancy, compared to what it must certainly one day become.

The population of New Orleans is at present estimated to be upwards of 100,000; of which it is considered that there are about 50,000 whites, 40,000 negro slaves, and 10,000 free blacks and people of colour. Of the 50,000 whites, it is thought that there are not more than 30,000 permanent residents, 20,000 being visitors, strangers, and a transitory and floating population, constantly changing in individuals, but keeping pretty nearly to the same number in the mass, throughout the business season. This lasts from November to May; after which New Orleans is drained of a full fourth of its population, who disperse themselves through the north and west for health and pleasure, till the winter returns.

Of the resident population of the city, it is necessary to observe, that they form two very distinct bodies, Créole French, and Northern Americans, and that these are as distinct as the people of any two nations, independently of the several orders or classes into which each of these bodies is again subdivided.

The Créoles, that is, persons of pure white race, without any admixture of Indian or African blood, descended entirely from Spanish or French ancestors, but born in Louisiana, are the most numerous portion of the resident population, amounting to about 20,000 persons. They are almost entirely Roman Catholics in religion, French in language, habits, and manners, but with a mixture of the Spanish chivalry, generosity, and romance, that makes them more frank, open, warm-hearted, and impassioned than the natives of France, though not more courteous or polite.

The men are generally small, and neither robust nor active, distinguished by no particular traits of character, except it be extreme sensitiveness on points of honour, and readiness to avenge an affront by appeal to arms; duels being much more frequent with them than even with the Americans, and almost always fought with swords till one or other of the combatants fall. There being no order of nobility or privileged class, and no great wealth possessed by individuals, there is a very general equality of condition among them; and though some few of the older inhabitants live on fixed incomes derived from rents, investments in stocks and banks, and the labour of their slaves, yet by far the greatest number are engaged in business or professions, as merchants, shopkeepers, restaurateurs, and artisans, besides engaging in the liberal professions of medicine and the law. They are in general devoid of ambition, and deficient in energy, being content to live a quiet and an easy life, rather than incur the toil, anxiety, and wear and tear of body and mind, which they see the Americans endure to get rich. They are somewhat lax in their manners, which their religion and colonial origin may sufficiently account for; but they are upright in their dealings, faithful in all offices of trust, and remarkably docile and manageable with kindness in all subordinate offices as clerks, assistants, &c.

The Créole women are not so pretty as the Americans, but their manners are more interesting. They are of the most delicate and graceful forms, with a roundness and beauty of shape, figure, and tournure, which contrasts very strikingly with the straitness, and regularity of American female figures generally. Their complexions are like those of the women of Italy and the northern shores of the Mediterranean, approaching to brunette, of a rich marble-like smoothness, sometimes suffused with a glow of warmth indicative of the deepest feeling; large black eyes, full of languor and expression; jet-black hair, full, soft, and glossy; exquisite lips and teeth; and countenances beaming with amiability and tenderness. They combine, in short, the attractions of the women of Cadiz, Naples, and

Marseilles; and notwithstanding the admiration they excite in strangers, they are said to make faithful as well as fond wives and excellent mothers; except, indeed, that in this last capacity, their love for their children runs into such excess, as to cause them to be too indulgent to them, and thus to injure their future happiness by excessive kindness. French is almost the only language spoken among them; Spanish but rarely, and English still less. They are extremely polite and well-bred; and have a readiness, self-possession, intelligence, and ease and elegance of conversation, which American ladies seldom possess; bearing, in this respect, the same kind of superiority to the Americans, which the women of France do to those of England, except in the very best circles of society.

The American population of New Orleans is very mixed; so that it is difficult to give a general character that shall suit the whole. That portion of them who were among the earliest settlers in New Orleans, subsequently to the cession of Louisiana to the United States in 1803, and who have been permanent residents in the city for many years, are among the best specimens of the American people that we had yet seen. They have worn off, by contact with the Créole population, much of the stiffness, formality, and coldness, which characterizes the manners of the New England States, and of Boston especially; they have acquired much of the ease and polish of the French, and something of the chivalry and generosity of the Spanish; while a long residence in the sunny South, has both moulded their forms into more elegance and gracefulness, and expanded their ideas and feelings into greater liberality. They have lost that mixture of keenness in driving a bargain, and parsimoniousness in the expenditure of its fruits, as well as that excessive caution in opening themselves to strangers lest they should commit themselves, which is so characteristic of the people of the North. At the same time they retain, in the fullest vigour, the philanthropic spirit, which is also characteristic of the North, and cheerfully give their labour and their money to the formation and support of benevolent institutions of various kinds, of which New Orleans contains a great number, almost wholly supported by its resident American population.

The visitors or transitory population of New Orleans, amount to at least 20,000 persons at a time; but, from the changes that take place every week, embracing perhaps as many as 100,000 separate individuals during the season, they must be divided into three distinct classes. There are, first, those who come to spend the winter in New Orleans for health and pleasure; secondly, those who come from the North and the West as merchants to transact business; and thirdly, those who come to profit by the large concourse of people, in various schemes of speculation, gambling, and fraud.

Of the first class, it is almost uniformly observed, that a change of residence, even for a few months, produces a wonderful change in their habits and manners, and that for the worse. Many who are even professors of religion, and members or communicants of congregations at their own homes, seem to shake off all regard for early principles, and to become loose in their morals as well as careless in their habits here. Removed from the wholesome restraints of public opinion—which is powerfully exercised in small communities where every member is known to his neighbour—and brought here into the midst of a multitude of strangers where such opinion is scarcely exercised or felt, they gradually throw off all their former habits, and adopt those of a less favourable kind. The distinction between the Sabbath and other days of the week, is first broken through; and because the Catholic population of French and Spanish origin frequent their theatre, and have balls and masquerades on Sundays: the Protestant New Englander, of Puritan descent, forgetting all the maxims of his Pilgrim Fathers, as well as the practice of his youth, frequents the theatre, the ball, and the masquerade on Sundays also. The American theatre of St. Charles, where English plays are alone performed, and where English and American actors appear, is thronged to overflowing every Sunday night, by Northern and Western Americans; while the masquerade that follows has not a few of the soi-disant religious community of New Englanders to support it by their presence. From the first false step to the second, the descent is soon made. The bar-rooms of the hotels, next become their haunts; smoking and drinking follows; a Quadroon mistress, of the class of coloured females with the smallest mixture of African blood, called Quadroons from their being supposed to be four removes from the pure African, is next taken; and habits of betting, racing, and gambling, crown the whole. Such is the painful history of many a young New Englander coming to New Orleans for health and pleasure, and returning home a dissipated rake.

The second class are happily not so unfortunate. They are formed of those who come here, with their families, for business during the winter months, and who occupy an intermediate position between the permanent residents and the daily-changing population. Some of these take furnished houses, and have their private homes; but the greater number live at the best boarding-houses, and at the public hotels; having an office or counting-house in the business-part of the city. This class includes persons from all the sections of the Union, but the greater number come from the middle and western States. New York, Pennsylvania, Ohio, Kentucky, Indiana, Illinois, and Tennessee, furnish the largest portion. They are occupied as buyers and sellers of cotton and other produce, as well as commission merchants for the purchase and transport into the interior, of European and other manufactured goods.

Of this class it may be said, that they owe much of their virtue to being constantly occupied; as indeed it may be said of the other class, that they owe much of their vice to their having nothing to do; so true is the old adage, that "idleness is the parent of mischief," and a most prolific parent indeed. Still, even on the business-class of winter visitors to New Orleans, a visible change is made in one season of residence; for, influenced by the contagion of bad example, they relax greatly in the rigour of their principles and conduct. Many who, in their native city or native state, would not think of any open mark of disrespect to the Sabbath, fall in here readily with the practice of sight-seeing and amusements on Sunday; and the frequent visits to the theatres and other places of public amusement, added to the daily influence of a hotel life, dining every day at a table with 200 or 300 persons, beget a sort of dissipation, which, if it be not vicious in itself, undoubtedly helps to produce vicious tendencies, and to create a laxity in manners and observances that is calculated, if not carefully guarded against, to sap the foundations of morality.

Absence from home, the gaieties of the place, the sight of all sorts of costly apparel, in dresses, jewellery, and ornaments, the abundance of money, and the influence of rivalry—all beget expensive habits in the females of such families; and having no domestic duties to discharge, or household affairs to superintend, their mornings are devoted to interchange of visits, and shopping. The French and Créole shopkeepers and milliners are so winning and persuasive, and evince so much taste in the arrangement of their beautiful wares, that the largest portion of the husband's or father's gains are often expended in a single season by the ladies of his family, who carry back with them to the interior the purchases of New Orleans, to astonish and excite the envy of those who have remained at home. The single or unmarried gentlemen, having no home but the hotel, and no business occupation after sunset, resort to the theatre, the masquerade, or the ball; or sometimes frequent the billiard-room, or the bar; and not looking upon New Orleans as their homes, they are all more devoted to mere pleasure, and less scrupulous as to the shape in which it is enjoyed, than in their native cities.

The third class are the worst; and these, unhappily, have given to New Orleans the bad reputation which it possesses. These are composed of speculators, gamblers, sharpers, and ruffians, who throng here during the winter months, to prey upon the unsuspecting. When the season is at an end, they go up the river Mississippi, disperse themselves through the towns of Natchez, Vicksburg, Memphis, St. Louis, Louisville, and Cincinnati, and lead a similar fraudulent course of life during the summer and autumn, gambling, cheating, and swindling in the steamboats by the way, and playing the bully towards all who venture to take the least notice of their misconduct. This class seems to be formed of the refuse of all the States; and though they make New Orleans one of their principal haunts in the winter, they no more belong to New Orleans than they do to New York or Philadelphia. It is unjust, therefore, to the permanent inhabitants of the city, to draw the character of New Orleans from the conduct of these miscreants, who are held in the greatest abhorrence and detestation by the native residents themselves.

The negro and coloured population are here, as everywhere else throughout the United States, the proscribed class. On the whole, however, they are better off at New Orleans than in the cities of the North. The climate alone makes a large addition to their enjoyments, or saves them a great deal of suffering; and then the love of ease, which characterizes the slaves themselves, is equally characteristic of those in whose service they may be; so that as domestics and personal attendants, their labour is light, they are well fed, well clad, and do almost as they please, within the limits of reasonable service. The masters and mistresses of slaves leave much more to their management than is ever confided to the free servants of England. The slaves make purchases, as well as sales, for their owners, and by various little pilferings on each, get enough to dress very smartly, of which they are extravagantly fond. Some are let out to hire, on condition of bringing home a certain portion of wages to their masters, and these are said to accumulate property, though of course very slowly. But since the owner cannot threaten an indolent or unfaithful slave with turning him away, as a master can do with a free servant if he displeases him; and as punishing in any other way only makes the slave worse, the owner is without a remedy. The slave, knowing this, takes care to do as little as possible, and not to be very anxious about the quality any more than about the quantity of his labour.

Some of the laws of Louisiana respecting slaves are also humane and considerate. No master can sell the parents and children separately, till the latter are more than twelve years of age. A slave who is ill-treated can make a representation of his case before the local tribunal of judges; and in the event of the facts being proved on reasonable testimony—the evidence of slaves being taken in such cases—the master is compelled by law to sell the slave to another owner. Still, though there are many causes to make the situation of the domestic slave in New Orleans happier than in some other States, I could see nothing, even in their improved condition, to reconcile me to the glaring injustice towards the slave, of taking from him the fair produce of that labour, the full fruits of which every man should be allowed to reap as his own; nor any thing to change my opinion as to the injurious effects of this system towards the master as well as the slave. The system of slavery compels him to lay out a large amount of capital in the purchase of a labour which he may never realize, as sickness, death, and desertion may deprive him of all; but the labour which he thus buys, at so high an outlay, even when he gets it, is always of the most stinted kind in quantity, the most unskilful in quality, the most grudgingly bestowed, and the most unprofitable in its issue.

The free blacks are already numerous, and fast increasing, by multiplication from their own stock, as all the children of free mothers are themselves free. Add to this, there is a large number of brown or mulatto persons, of mixed European and African blood, usually called "coloured people." Of these, it may be said, that they are handsome, interesting, intelligent, and agreeable, in proportion to the distance at which they are removed from the original African stock. The first remove, formed by a white father and black mother, and called mulattoes, have dark-brown skins, and crisp, though bushy hair, with all the broadness and flatness of the African features, scarcely diminished. The next remove, formed by a white father and mulatto mother, and called brown, or yellow, as either shade predominates, begins to be good-looking, with olive complexions, like the darkest of the European Spaniards—black eyes and hair, and prominent features, small limbs, delicate hands and feet, and graceful figures. The third remove, or meztisoes, approaches still nearer to the European or American stock, in all these particulars. And the fourth remove, or the quadroons, as they are called, furnish some of the most beautiful women that can be seen, resembling, in many respects, the higher order of women among the Hindoos, with lovely countenances, full dark liquid eyes, lips of coral and teeth of pearl, long raven locks of soft and glossy hair, sylph-like figures, and such beautifully-rounded limbs, and exquisite gait and manner, that they might furnish models for a Venus or a Hebe to the chisel of the sculptor. One of the most beautiful specimens of this feminine beauty, is exhibited as a sign, in a large full-length picture in oils, over the door of a milliner's establishment at the corner of Rue de Toulouse and Rue Royale; the one view representing the lady in her "costume de promenade," the other in her "costume du bal" and inscribed, after the manner of similar signs in Paris, "A la belle Créole." I remember a very similar one, indeed, in one of the streets of the French capital, "A la belle Circassienne," under a figure of exquisite beauty, embodying the *beau-ideal* of female loveliness in the Oriental form.

I have said that the permanent residents of New Orleans are not inferior to those of any other part of the United States, in the promotion and encouragement (according to their means, and in proportion to the recent date of their annexation to the Union, and the small number of their fixed population) of works of utility, instruction, and benevolence; and this will best be proved by a brief enumeration of a few of such undertakings of each class.

For the promotion of works of utility, there was established in 1833 a Public Board of Works, authorized by a law of the State, making them a corporate body. Their funds are supplied by grants from the State, legacies and donations from individuals, and 20,000 dollars from sales of auction licenses. They had received, up to the end of 1838, nearly 400,000 dollars, and have a property on hand, amounting to about 200,000 dollars. By judicious management and expenditure, they have opened several rivers, canals, and water-courses, made and improved many roads, and reclaimed from the river's banks for cultivation, nearly 1,000,000 of acres of land, from the sale of which, future funds for improvement will be supplied.

Of improvements effected by other companies, the following may be named. The Pontchartrain railroad was the second in point of date, completed within the United States, going to and from the city and the lake; and from the date of this, to the present time, at least twenty other railroads and branches have been constructed or are in progress. One of these, the New Orleans and Nashville railroad, will be 564 miles long, and cost 10,000,000 dollars. Of canals there are also several of great utility, connecting various branches of rivers, and adding much to the facility of transporting the products of the soil to market. A large portion of the city has been also lighted with gas, though in some parts of the French quarter, they adhere to the old Parisian practice of hanging large glass lamps on a rope, suspended from pole to pole, and overhanging the centre of the street, fed with oil, and giving out a miserably dim and faint glimmer of "darkness visible" on all sides round.

In provision for education, Louisiana cannot be expected to compete with the older, more populous, and more opulent States of Massachusetts and New York; but it is advanced beyond many States older than itself, and is still advancing. In 1833, by a law of the local legislature, the Secretary of State was made "Superintendent of Education throughout the State," and the same act provided for the appropriation of funds to the support of public schools in each parish, according to the number of their inhabitants. In addition to this provision for the Common Schools of the parishes, the following institutions of education already exist, and are in full operation.

The College of Louisiana, at Jackson, incorporated in 1825, with an appropriation of 5,000 dollars annually from the State, on condition that fifteen students, to be nominated by the governor, shall be educated gratis annually; and the rest on moderate terms. Jefferson College, near the coast, in the parish of St. James's, incorporated in 1831, with a noble edifice on the banks of the Mississippi, endowed also by the State, and having many students. Franklin College, at Opelousas, incorporated in 1831, and endowed by the State, with ample appropriation. Centre and Primary Schools exist also in the city of New Orleans, which have an annual appropriation of 10,000 dollars for their support.

In addition to these institutions, which are all under the patronage of the State, there are several private establishments for education. The Ursuline Nuns, in their convent, now removed a few miles below the city—as their valuable property within the city was recently sold at a greatly increased value, for the benefit of their funds—have a boarding and day School for young ladies, which is accounted one of the best in the State. The Sisters of Charity have also a large establishment for young ladies, in the parish of St. James's, where everything required is taught with great ability. In the convent of Opelousas is another excellent Female School; and the Jesuits have an extensive establishment at the same place for the education of boys, which is conducted by ten professors and teachers from France. These are of course all Catholic schools, though many Protestants have their children taught at them, from the great attention bestowed on the pupils, and their advancement in every branch of learning.

There is, however, one Protestant Female Academy recently established in New Orleans, the history of which is peculiarly interesting. A young American gentleman, of religious disposition, married the daughter of a Scotch merchant here; and after their marriage, which was one of pure affection, the father bestowed on his daughter a handsome fortune. Soon after their marriage union, the young lady died; and as the husband had not married her for her wealth, he signified to the father that it was not his intention to use it, but caused it to be transferred back to her parents. This the father refused to accept, saying it was the husband's, by right of marriage, and should remain in his possession. The contest at length was ended by this honourable compromise. Neither would consent to accept the sum, which was considerable, amounting to 50,000 dollars. The young widower, therefore, purchased with it a piece of ground, built a Female Academy for the education of Protestant Young Ladies, endowed it with an annual income, and called it, after the maiden name of his beloved and departed wife, "The M'Ghee Female Academy." I confess that I looked on this building with feelings of peculiar pleasure, and with great veneration for its amiable and pious founder.

Among the works of benevolence, besides those enumerated under the heads of the Charity Hospital, Asylum, Franklin Hospital, and others, in a former chapter, there is an Orphan Asylum for boys, and one for girls, each containing from 150 to 200 inmates, and, as far as we could judge from our visits to each, both were admirably managed. The Boys' Asylum, is in the upper part of the city, near Lafayette, and not far from the Levée or bank of the Mississippi. The house now occupied was formerly a sugar-house, and the surrounding land a sugar-plantation, about two miles removed from the outskirts of the old city. The land was purchased a few years since for 7,000 dollars; but such has been the increased value of property, from the gradual growth of the city towards this spot, that the same land is now worth 200,000 dollars; and will, accordingly, soon be sold, for the purpose of purchasing a more eligible spot, farther removed from the city, and erecting a suitable edifice, with every requisite and every modern improvement. The institution was first commenced by the efforts of a few individuals, who struggled through many difficulties to sustain it; but it is now happily free from them all. Very recently, an old Scotch settler here, named Henderson, who was formerly a steward in the household of the Duke of Gordon, found his way to New Orleans, and in a residence of nearly forty years amassing considerable property, left, at his death, the greater part of it, amounting to 50,000*l*. sterling, to the support of the Orphan Asylum. Since that time another Scotchman, named Milne, died in New Orleans, and left 50,000 dollars to the same institution; so that with these, and the increased value of their land, they will be placed above all further need of aid, and so extend their sphere of operations, as to leave no male orphans in the State unprovided for.

There is also an Orphan Asylum for Female Children, situated nearly in the centre of the American quarter, in Poydras Street. It was founded in the year 1817, by a few ladies, who, from their private subscriptions, began the care of a few orphan girls; and, soliciting subscriptions from time to time, from others, they increased their numbers as their means augmented. A very benevolent French Créole, named Julien Poydras, made them several handsome donations during his life, and at his death left them several small properties in land, in various parts of the city, the constantly increasing value of which will furnish a large source of revenue. More recently, the same wealthy Scotchmen, Mr. Henderson and Mr. Milne, who, at their death, endowed the Male Orphan Asylum so munificently, included this Female Asylum in their bequests, and left equal sums to those bestowed on the other. At present, therefore, the wealth of the Institution is considerable, and an edifice is about to be erected, which will provide ample accommodation for all the female orphans that the State may contain. There are already about 150 children, from three to fifteen years of age, who are supported, clad, educated, and well-trained, free of all expense to themselves, and fitted to obtain their own livings in various ways. Besides these there is a New Orleans' St. Andrew's Society, for the relief of destitute natives of Scotland; an Hibernian Society for the relief of destitute natives of Ireland; an Hibernian Universal Benevolent Society, which takes a still wider range in the objects of its bounty; a Roman Catholic Association for the relief of Male Orphans, conducted by the Bishop and Clergy of that faith; and a St. Patrick's Female Orphan Asylum, conducted by the Sisters of Charity of the same Church. There are also several Masonic Lodges, Mechanics' Societies, Firemen's Charitable Associations, and other bodies founded on the principle of mutual relief in time of sickness and distress.

At New Orleans, the nights are almost always cool, and a pleasant breeze blows generally throughout the day. About two hours after midnight, the air becomes so much colder, as to require the use of a blanket; and persons who are cautious to guard against the sudden changes of climate, take care always to have one at the foot of the bed in the hottest weather, to provide against the vicissitude. The rainy season is in the winter, but New Orleans is then perfectly healthy to all parties. In the summer heats, strangers, who expose themselves, get affected with fevers; but it is not until the middle of July or August that there is danger to the stranger from remaining in the city. At that time it is prudent that he should retire, if able to do so, for a short period, but this need not be far, because, in the very hottest weather, a passage to the northern shore of Lake Pontchartrain, about 30 miles across, where many pretty villas of the merchants and others are built, or a visit to Biloxi, Mobile, or Pensacola, all healthy stations, is as good a preservative against the liability to fever, as a removal to the extremest point of the Union. The Créoles remain all the year round, and the Americans who are acclimated by one or two summers, stay without danger; while the medical men, the clergy, the public officers of government, and the great bulk of the inhabitants, are stationary throughout the year. The yellow fever sometimes comes as an epidemic, and sweeps off hundreds without distinction, and the cholera made sad havoc here a few years since; but this is not a proof of the general unhealthiness of New Orleans, any more than it is of Bombay, Madras, or Calcutta; with which, perhaps, in this respect, New Orleans may be fairly compared.

It is said that the average mortality of New Orleans, in ordinary years, is about 3,800, out of a population of upwards of 100,000, or about four per cent of the whole; and of these, one fourth, at least, die in the Charity Hospital, a large number from intemperance, and consequent disease and destitution. It is believed that about 500 strangers die every year in passing through the acclimating process; but the greatest number of these might be saved by proper precautions taken in time, and an adaptation of diet and mode of life to the changes of the season. Of pulmonary diseases, there are not more than one in fifty die in New Orleans, while to the North there are one in five or six, besides those who linger for years under this terrible affliction.

In no part of the South that we had yet visited do the whites seem to be in greater dread of the rising of the slaves, than here in Louisiana. It is said, indeed, that on the sugar-plantations they are more severely worked than anywhere else; and that the floggings of the indolent and refractory are cruel and severe, especially among the French and Créole planters. In New Orleans, as before remarked, the condition of the slaves is far from being miserable; they are upon the whole as well fed, better clad, and have much more leisure and less severe labour than the Irish peasant or the English hand-loom weaver. Many of them, too, have a great command of their time, and accumulate, by degrees, actual property, which indulgent owners allow them to enjoy; though, according to the strict letter of the law, all that a slave has or earns, or obtains by gift or any other mode, is his master's, and may be taken from him, but this is rarely done. Yet even here, under this most favourable state of things for the slave, the whites are afraid of their combinations to break the yoke of subjection under which they lie, and free themselves from their servitude.

At nine o'clock, a large cannon, fired from the centre of Lafayette Square, tells the slaves in all parts of the city that they must be in their homes, under pain of apprehension, imprisonment, and other punishment, according to the circumstances of the case. The law also enjoins that no free black shall remain in the State, though this law is not put in force; and no freedom can be given to any slave within the State, but on condition of his quitting it for ever, though this also is not rigorously enforced. Indeed, an article was published in the Commercial Bulletin, of March 20, pointing out the danger to the peace of the city in allowing any free blacks to remain in it, and calling upon the municipal authorities no longer to neglect the execution of the law which enjoined their banishment from the State for ever. The meaning of this is that they are afraid the free blacks will inoculate the slaves with a love of freedom, and excite their desire to enjoy it for themselves; and yet, in the very same breath in which they proclaim the danger of familiarizing the slave too much with freedom, lest he should become enamoured of it and seek it for himself, the newspapers and the white inhabitants tell you, with the utmost coolness, "that the slaves would not accept their freedom if it were offered; that the free blacks are more wretchedly off than the slaves; and that the instances are numerous, in which slaves, having been made free, have entreated to be allowed to return to their bondage again." I confess, however, that after the most diligent inquiry, I could never discover any well-authenticated instance of this; while, on the other hand, I saw everywhere around me proofs that freedom was anxiously desired by the slaves; that it was often given to them as a reward, and was sometimes purchased by their scraping together the hard earnings of many a long and weary year of extra toil beyond the hours exacted by the master; while the advertisements of the public prints, continually exhibit the offer of rewards for runaway slaves, on their being apprehended and lodged in jail to be restored to their owners! Such are the contradictions which facts oppose to the assertions above alluded to.

A very lively interest is felt among all classes here, in the future prospects of the neighbouring republic of Texas; and the intercourse between it and New Orleans being maintained by steam vessels, that arrive and depart almost daily, the newspapers contain repeated notices of everything that is passing in this new and rising country. I had an opportunity of seeing several persons who had recently arrived from thence; and there was great uniformity of opinion as to its speedily overcoming all its difficulties, and attaining to great importance in a comparatively short space of time. The first mode of its occupation, and the character of the first settlers by which the independence of Mexico was declared, are admitted by most candid persons to have been highly objectionable; and the fact of its having been for some time a refuge for the abandoned and profligate, as well as for the destitute, no one denies. But of late, there has been an infusion of a much better class of people; and while many of the first settlers have been killed in the wars with the Mexicans, and a large number have paid the ordinary debt of nature, their places are supplied by a very superior race, persons of capital and character, who go from all parts of the United States, to purchase land, and become citizens of the new republic. For a long time, the Texians were anxious to have their territory annexed, as a new State, to the great American Union; and this would have been easily effected, but for the fact that slavery was considered a part of its lawful and acknowledged institutions, though the Mexicans had abolished slavery in their republic; and this fact arrayed the feelings of the Free States of the North against the admission of a new Slave State into the general Confederation. The Texians, on the other hand, would not consent to prohibit slavery, as a condition of their admission; as this, they conceived, would check the tide of immigration into their territory, where planters were chiefly induced to come, because, by the labour of their slaves brought with them, they could put their purchased land under immediate cultivation, and speedily realize a handsome fortune.

At present, all desire of admission into the American Union has ceased; and the Texians have resolved to be and remain an independent republic. They have overcome all risk of subjugation by the Mexicans, who are indeed too much torn by internal struggles and civil dissensions to be able to give a thought to any exterior object. Harassed by a foreign foe from without, by whom their principal seaport of Vera Cruz has been blockaded and captured, and their chief fortress of St. Juan D'Ulloa nearly destroyed, and at the same time divided by two contending parties among themselves, the Federalists and the Centralists in arms against each other, thus working out daily their own destruction, the Texians are perfectly safe from further Mexican interference, and are wisely profiting by this circumstance to build up the republic in peace; while their finances are improving, their commerce reviving, their settlers increasing, and all the elements of prosperity are in full and active operation for good.

Chapter XX

The last day that we passed in New Orleans, was, upon the whole, one of the most interesting. Soon after breakfast, we accompanied the lady of Dr. Luzenberg, who called for us at the hotel in her carriage, to the hospital, or infirmary, established by her husband, near the Pontchartrain road, where we were met by Dr. Luzenberg himself. The spot on which this hospital stands, was originally a wet marsh, or morass—as, indeed, nearly the whole of the space between the Mississippi and the Lake Pontchartrain still is, though a railroad has been constructed across it from the city to the lake, on wooden piles for the support of the rails. The space intended for the edifice and garden was then purchased by Dr. Luzenberg out of his private means, and being filled up with earth, it was converted into dry land, on which the hospital was built and the garden laid out, and the whole establishment fitted and furnished at his individual expense in the year 1835.

The building is sixty-five feet by fifty-five, two stories in height, and being purposely constructed for a hospital, under Dr. Luzenberg's eye, it has every convenience and comfort for the accommodation of a hundred patients. A resident physician, with a competent supply of nurses and attendants, is always on the spot, and its founder visits it once and often twice a day; so that many of his private patients, knowing the great attention and comfort received, prefer coming here, when ill, to remaining in the city; and those who receive gratuitous medical attendance and care, are as well and as carefully superintended as the rest.

The surrounding garden is beautiful; and at this season of the year, April 19, when all the trees were in full foliage, and the flowers in their richest bloom, it was peculiarly so. I do not know, indeed, that I ever saw more rich, varied, and beautiful bouquets, than those that were made up in the space of a few minutes, from the flowers all around us, and presented to each. The fine air, pleasant

walks, and horticultural amusement and occupation which these grounds afford
to the convalescent, make them as useful to health as they are beautiful to the
eye.

It is worthy of remark, that though the marsh presses close up to the edge
of the garden, no injury to the health of the patients is occasioned thereby.
Dr. Luzenberg's opinion, derived from his experience of this climate, was, that
marsh lands, when well wooded, and in the neighbourhood of salt water, as
this marsh is, are not unfavourable to health; as the woods protect the vegetable
undergrowth from the operation of the sun, and no deleterious atmosphere is
engendered. But when this wood is removed, and the vegetable productions in
the water are exposed to the heat of the sun, the decomposition and decay of the
vegetable matter give out gases of a deleterious nature, and the miasma engenders
fevers among those who breathe the contaminated air. In confirmation of the
accuracy of this view, it has occurred, that while the yellow fever raged with
the greatest violence in New Orleans, no persons living at the Infirmary were
affected by it; and in an interchange of coloured servants that was made between
the Doctor's establishment in the city, and the Infirmary, it invariably happened
that those who went into the city caught the yellow fever, and those who went
to the Infirmary escaped.

The Hospital, which is called the "Franklin Infirmary," and over which is a
bust of Benjamin Franklin, another surmounting the arbour in the garden, we
accompanied Mrs. Luzenberg to the Orphan Asylum, and had an opportunity
of seeing the 130 children of which its inmates now consist, from the age of
three up to fourteen, in school. One very remarkable fact, connected with this
institution, was, that out of the whole number, at this tender age, and in this
climate, not one of the children was sick. The sick-ward, indeed, had been
empty for many months, and every one of the little orphans was in full health,
and at her post of duty. In the Boys' Orphan Asylum, which we visited with
Mr. Duncan a few days before, there was but one boy indisposed, out of all
their number, just as large as that of the girls, and he was convalescent; while
all the others were at work in the garden, or indulging in play; and when we
saw them mustered before supper, they presented the appearance of as healthy
and happy a set of little fellows as could be seen. So it was with these female
children. As they were at school when we called, we had an opportunity of
seeing them at their studies. The teacher, an elderly widow lady, appeared to
be admirably qualified for her task, and the pupils acquitted themselves in a
manner to do great credit to their tutor. They were all neatly but plainly clad,
and were all taught needlework, and made to assist in household industry, so
as to qualify them to get their own living. We were assured, that while very
many, who had left the institution, had succeeded in the various branches of

industry, to which they had since devoted themselves, a great number here married advantageously, and made excellent wives; while no one instance had yet occurred to their knowledge, in which any of them had done anything to cast a stain upon their own reputation, or bring dishonour on the institution that had protected and instructed them. Surely, if there be any charities, of unequivocal and unmixed good, they are such as provide for the fatherless and motherless, who, without such shelter as is here afforded them, would be liable either to perish for want of means of support, or become abandoned for want of protection and instruction, and if there be a sight that can cheer the heart as well as the eyes, and have no drawback to its pleasure from the intrusion of collateral considerations, it is the sight of the poor and destitute, taken from their forlorn condition of helpless misery, and sheltered and nurtured by private benevolence, till they can be placed in a situation of independent self-subsistence, to be the authors of happiness to themselves, and of comfort and assistance to others.

Among other visits we made today, was one to a most interesting Florentine lady. Mademoiselle America Vespucci, a lineal descendant of the great navigator whose name was given to the continent of America. She had just arrived here from Washington, and, besides the natural impulse of feeling, which alone would prompt an early expression of respect, and proffer of hospitality, to one of such truly illustrious descent—the convictions of duty and the calls of sympathy joined with those of more generous impulse, to induce us to pay this lady an early visit. I went, therefore, accompanied by my family, and Mrs. Luzenberg, to the Hotel St. Louis, where we enjoyed a long and agreeable interview with this accomplished and most interesting stranger. To convey to others the interest which we felt ourselves, and to state the circumstances which gave so great an additional charm to her powerful personal attractions, it may be proper to present the following particulars, from the journals of the day of the accuracy of which there is no doubt.

America Vespucci.—As this fair stranger is now in our city, perhaps some, if not all of our readers will read with interest some points in her history. The article which follows, is taken from the 'Washington Democratic Review' for February, 1839:

"After spending, like most of the young Italian ladies of rank, fourteen years of her youth in a convent for her education (the convent of *La Signora della Quiete*, in the environs of Florence) she was introduced into the midst of the brilliant society of the capital and court of the Grand Duke of Tuscany, at the age of seventeen. She was placed by her parents in the service of the Grand Duchess, as a 'demoiselle de compagne' or maid of honour. There she was of course surrounded with all the seductive influences of European aristocratic life, in the midst of the splendours and luxuries of the Pitti Palace. Her mind had, however, already—by its own self-derived impulses, as it would seem, for it was certainly entirely at variance with all the natural bias of such an education and such a position—taken a decided stand in the movement of liberal ideas which is the leading characteristic of the age, and which in no country has exercised a stronger influence upon the imagination of ardent youth than in Italy. Possessed of rare natural talents, highly accomplished by reading and cultivation, with remarkable force of character, vivacity of imagination, and energy of will, it will not be a subject of surprise, that, during the agitations that were fermenting in the north of Italy immediately after the French revolution, she was one of the few females whose social position and personal qualities gained them admission to the secret societies which were conspiring to rid Italy of the dominion of a foreign despotism, and to unite the whole of that beautiful and unhappy land under a single sovereign, who might again restore it to a rank amidst the family of nations. But we are not aware of any others whose ardour carried them beyond the private machinations of conspiracy, to the actual field of battle and blood.

"In the attempted rising of August, 1832, and in the engagement with the Austrians on the banks of the Rimini, in which, it will be remembered by our readers that young Louis Bonaparte took part, she conducted herself with great gallantry, and received a severe sabre stroke on the back of her head, from an Austrian dragoon (to whom, however, though nameless, the justice ought to be done, to state that he did not know her to be a woman,) and in her fall to the ground, her right arm was broken by the weight of her horse falling upon it. Though suspected, her disguised participation in this affair could not be proved, and after her recovery from her wounds, she spent two years at her father's house in Florence, though under a vigilant surveillance. This resulted in the interception of a letter to her, as secretary of one of the sections of the Society of 'La Jeune Italie,' which made it apparent that she could disclose its entire organization in Tuscany. She was accordingly required either to betray her associates, or to quit Florence within twenty-four hours. Her choice between these two alternatives does not need to be stated. She found a present asylum under the protection of the Queen of the French; and it is under the auspices of the French flag, and the highest guarantees of the genuineness of her title to American sympathy and friendship in all points of view—of character, conduct, family, and position—that she is now here, in the country to which she has always looked as her natural home of refuge and protection."

The object for which she had specially come to America, was to obtain, if possible, a grant of land from the Congress of the United States, as a means of honourable and independent support; and the failure of her application, as well as the grounds on which it was deemed necessary to decline compliance with the request, are fully and fairly stated in the Report made to the Senate of the United States, by Mr. Walker, of Mississippi, from which the following extract is taken:

Conceiving it to be their duty to verify the facts upon which the application was founded, they have examined a voluminous mass of documentary evidence, and find the statements of the memorial to be fully sustained. They have seen the authentic certificates of baptism, through many generations of the Vespucci family in Florence, which attest the lineage and descent of the memorialist. They have read the highly favourable and complementary letter of the Queen of the French, through her secretary, to the petitioner. They have read the letter to her of the King of the French, through the minister of the interior, subscribing for a work for the king, of which she was the author, and have also read the permission of the French minister of the marine, for her to sail in a French national vessel. The committee have also had before them her credentials from the minister of Tuscany, in France, and many other papers of high character and authenticity in her favour. They have also witnessed her own personal deportment here, and the manner in which she has been received by the French legation, which, added to other testimonials, leave not a doubt of the identity of the memorialist, and the truth of her representations.

After the lapse, then, of more than three centuries, a descendant of the celebrated Americus Vespucius is amongst us. This heroic navigator, before, and also after the close of the fifteenth century, landed upon the shores of the New World, among the most early and scientific of those who succeeded the great and pre-eminent Columbus in the discovery of this continent. A descriptive narrative of his several voyages was written and published by Americus, and Europe baptized with his name this mighty continent. This name can never now be abandoned. It is the name of our beloved country. It is associated with all the glories of the past, and the still brighter hopes of the future. It is written upon our national constitution, and engraven upon the heart of every true

American. Under this name we have succeeded in two struggles with the most formidable power in Europe, and have so wonderfully augmented in population, that should the same ratio of increase continue for the future, the close of this century will find within our limits more than one hundred millions of people, and more than five millions within the single city of New York.

In reflecting then with glory upon the name of American, can we forget the great navigator from whom we derived this proudest of earthly titles? A descendant of Americus is now here; a young, interesting, dignified, and accomplished lady, with a mind of the highest intellectual culture, and a heart beating with all our own enthusiasm in the cause of America, and of human liberty. She feels that the name she bears is a prouder title than any that earthly monarchs can bestow; and she comes here, asking us for a small corner of American soil, where she may pass the remainder of her days in this land of her adoption. She comes here as an exile, separated forever from her family and friends; a stranger, without a country and without a home, expelled from her native Italy, for the avowal and maintenance of opinions favourable to free institutions, and an ardent desire for the establishment of her country's freedom. That she indeed is worthy of the name of America— that her heart is indeed imbued with American principles, and a fervent love for human liberty, is proved in her case, by toils, and perils, and sacrifices, worthy of the proudest days of antiquity, when the Roman and the Spartan matrons were ever ready to surrender life itself in their country's service.

Such was the history of this Italian lady; and our personal interview with her, not only confirmed all our previous expectations, but went far beyond them. In person, she had the style of beauty which one sees in the finest statues of the antique—a noble head, regular and expressive features, a fair and stately neck, dark eyes, dark hair, beautiful lips and teeth, a fine expanded chest, well-rounded arms, white and delicate hands, small feet, and an exquisitely graceful figure of the middle size. She appeared in a simple yet elegant and well-made dress of black silk, trimmed with deep lace. Her head was marked by a classic grandeur, though without any kind of ornament but her rich and exuberant hair; her voice was full of music; and in her look and expression, dignity and sweetness were happily blended. Her age appeared to be about twenty-five or twenty-six, and her whole deportment presented the most agreeable combination of dignified self-respect with refinement, polish, and ease that I ever remember to have witnessed. Though opposed to royalty, and coming to seek an asylum in a republic, she looked, and spoke, and moved, as if she were "every inch a queen." She seemed to realize the idea I had often formed of the Egyptian Cleopatra; and it would not be hazarding much to say, that she was altogether the most accomplished, elegant, and interesting woman that had ever landed on this continent since the days of her great ancestor whose name it bears.

Our conversation was at first in Italian, but when a French lady arrived to join our party, it changed to French, both of which languages she spoke with an eloquence rarely equalled; and her whole discourse seemed to be composed of "thoughts that breathe and words that burn."

She spoke with great feeling, of the degraded and oppressed condition of her beloved country, Italy; and suppressed with some difficulty the emotion under which she was evidently struggling, when she said she had bidden it an eternal adieu! She expressed herself surprised and delighted at the grandeur and extent of the territory occupied by the several States of this great Republican Union; and charmed with all she had yet seen of the workings of its political system, in which freedom of sentiment and freedom of expression was enjoyed by all on topics of religion and government, and the freest exercise allowed to enterprise and industry in every branch of human undertaking. This was a state of things so new to her sight and experience, though often read of in books, dreamt of in theory, and hoped for in her aspirations after Italian liberty, but never before realized within her actual vision, that she sometimes doubted whether all she saw around her was real, or merely an allusion. Sometimes she dreaded, too, lest so fair a fabric should be prematurely undermined by some destroying principle, or some corrupting power, and thus the great example of self-government which it was exhibiting to the world, be frustrated or destroyed, before the enemies of human liberty would allow its grand experiment to be completed. Her grief, at seeing the continued existence, and hearing the continued defence of negro slavery, was the only drawback to her satisfaction; but this she condemned in terms of just indignation, and admitted, that with all their many claims to admiration, the Americans could never be recognized as a great or truly free people, until they should put away this reproach from them, by emancipating their slaves.

Since my favoured and happy residence with Lady Hester Stanhope, in the mountains of Palestine, I had never witnessed so noble a union of high birth, mental power, lofty aspirations, and generous impulses, blended with so much refinement of manners, and the whole crowned by the utmost affability and kindness, as in the person of America Vespucci. It is not too much to say of her, that there is no throne in Europe which she would not elevate by her wisdom; no court which she would not adorn by her manners; no family, that she would not delight by her conversation; and no man, however noble in birth, profound in erudition, high in station, or opulent in fortune, to whom she would not be a source of intellectual and social enjoyment, if he could but win her respect and confidence, and become the object of her esteem as well as of her affections.

CHAPTER XXI

The morning of our departure having arrived, we were busily occupied in the payment of bills; and certainly the experience thus practically afforded us, was such as to confirm the general opinion that New Orleans is one of the most expensive places in the world. Our bill at the Hotel, for three persons and a man-servant, having no private sitting-room, as this is a comfort rarely to be obtained, dining at the public table, and using no wine, was at the rate of 12 dollars or £2 10s. per day; coach-hire, a dollar for each person for the shortest ride, or 3 dollars for an hour; printing charges about four times as high as at New York; articles of apparel most exorbitantly dear, five or six times the London prices at least; and the binding of a small manuscript octavo volume was charged 5 dollars, or a guinea, which in England would have cost half-a-crown; and most other things in the same proportion of extravagance; so that we could bear testimony to the accuracy of the common saying at New Orleans, that "Economy is the greatest thief of time, as it takes longer to *save* anything than it does to *make* it."

At length, having settled our accounts, and taken leave of all our friends, with many a cordial and mutual expression of the hope that we should one day meet again, we embarked at noon on Saturday the 20th of April, on board the steam-vessel "Ambassador", for Natchez. Soon after quitting the wharf, we were underway ascending the Mississippi—again admiring, as we quitted it, the beautiful curve of this noble river, the splendid line of ships moored along the Levée, with the mingling of not less than a hundred steam vessels, and smaller craft of every rig, making altogether the finest marine picture that any river in the world could present.

As we advanced up the river the scenery, though flat, was rich, luxuriant and interesting. Among the plantations that we passed, one of the most perfect was on the estate of the late Mr. Henderson, the wealthy Scotchman, who left such munificent legacies to the Orphan Asylum, and other charitable institutions of

New Orleans. The grounds appeared to be in the highest order, the dwelling-house of the overseer or resident manager was large and commodious, and the gardens and shrubberies around it beautiful. The negro-quarters, built of wood, were placed like soldiers' barracks, in uniform rows, looking very neat, clean, and orderly. The external appearance of such establishments—and the greater number of the plantations near New Orleans partake of this character—is very apt to deceive spectators into a belief, that so much exterior neatness and symmetry, must be attended with a corresponding degree of interior comfort. Several of the passengers, knowing me to be an Englishman, and naturally inferring my disapprobation of slavery, pointed with great satisfaction, and even an air of triumph, to these beautiful plantations and their neat and orderly negro-quarters; and said, "See, sir, what comfort and happiness these slaves here enjoy. Where is the population in Europe so pleasantly quartered, and so happily provided for, as these; their food raised for them without care, medical assistance when sick, and no apprehension of starving?" I replied, that there were three classes of population in Europe who had as excellent quarters, better clothing, better living, medical attendance when sick, no care about the future, and no apprehension of starving, with extra wages besides; but who were not, for all these reasons, accounted 'happy' and these were, our soldiers in their barracks, our paupers in their new union-workhouses, and our sailors in a man-of-war. In each of these cases, the accommodations for eating, drinking, and sleeping, are far superior to those of any American plantation; the food and raiment are better and more abundant than any furnished to the slaves, and the care bestowed on them in sickness is still greater; yet, even all this, with the wages which two of these classes received, and which no slave could ever hope to enjoy, is more than counteracted, by the restraints on their personal liberty, which each of them suffer, in addition to the occasional 'floggings' for neglect of duty, disobedience of orders, or attempts to escape, and imprisonment and reduced fare in cases of indolence or obstinacy. The consequence is, a craving desire, on the part of most, to escape from their confinement; and although the captains of men-of-war defend 'impressment' as an established and safe method of keeping the sailor out of harm's way, and providing him a comfortable ship and a home; although colonels defend 'flogging,' as a wholesome discipline, good for the body and the mind, and calculated to make the soldier happy, by teaching him subordination; and although the boards of guardians and overseers of the poor think confinement to the workhouse, and spare diet, better for the health and morals of the paupers under their control, than outdoor relief; yet, these are regarded by the bulk of the community, as mere professional or interested opinions—as much so as that of a slaveholder pretending that to work from four in the morning till sunset, with slight intermissions, to be fed on the coarsest food, not sufficiently provided with garments to ensure cleanliness of apparel by change, and to be 'well-flogged' when attempting to escape, is a state of 'happiness' for the negro, which he could never attain if he were free!"

In the course of the protracted conversation to which these topics led, a gentleman from Kentucky, engaged in the growing of corn and grazing of cattle, himself a slaveholder to a considerable extent, and joining in all the denunciations of the Abolitionists, undertook to show, that after all, slavery was a much greater curse to the owners than it was to the slaves, as it absorbed their capital, ate up their profits, and proved a perpetual obstacle to their progressive prosperity. He said he had not only made the calculation, but actually tried the experiment of comparing the labour of the free white man and the negro slave, and he found the latter always the dearest of the two. It took, for instance, 2,000 dollars to purchase a good male slave. The interest of money in Kentucky being ten per cent, here was 200 dollars a year of actual cost; but to insure his life it would require at least five per cent more, which would make 300 dollars a year. Add to this the necessary expenses of maintenance while healthy, and medical attendance while sick, with wages of white overseers to every gang of men to see that they do their duty, and other incidental charges, and he did not think that a slave could cost less, in interest, insurance, subsistence, and watching, than 500 dollars or 100l. sterling a year; yet, after all, he would not do more than half the work of a white man, who could be hired at the same sum, without the outlay of any capital, or the incumbrance of maintenance while sick, and was, therefore, by far the cheapest labourer of the two.

This same gentleman told us of two instances that had happened on his own estate, of ingenious evasions of labour. One man took medicine, which he stole from the dispensary, purposely to make himself sick, to avoid work; and when examined by the doctor, he was detected in having spread powdered mustard on his tongue, to give it a foul appearance. A female slave, to avoid working for her master, produced such swellings in her arms, as to excite the compassion of those who thought it to be some dreadful disease; but the same person, who lay abed groaning with agony all day, being detected in the act of washing clothes at night, for some persons in the neighbourhood, for which she was to be paid—and to effect which in secrecy, she was found standing nearly up to her middle in a pond concealed under the trees—afterwards confessed, in order to avoid a flogging, that she had produced the swelling in her arms by thrusting them into a beehive, and keeping them there till they were thoroughly bitten and stung; and when the swelling began to subside, she repeated the same operation to revive them.

I inquired, "Why, if this were the state of things, they did not cure it by giving freedom to their slaves?" and the answer was this "that up to a very recent period, the feeling was almost universal in Kentucky, that it would be better to do so, especially as the neighbouring State of Ohio, *without* slaves, was making so much more rapid strides in prosperity than Kentucky *with* them; and that probably in a few years, their emancipation would have been agreed upon, but that the proceedings of the Abolitionists in the North wounded their pride, and they determined that they would not submit to interference or dictation in the regulation of their 'domestic institution.'" To this feeling was added another; that of 'standing by' the other Slave States of the South, and making common cause with them in a determination not to do anything by coercion or by threat, but to abide their own time, and act independently of all fear or intimidation.

The gentleman admitted, however, that this had only increased the difficulty, by putting off the evil day; for the slaves were every year increasing rapidly in numbers; and the more numerous they became, the more difficult it would be to know what to do with them. At present, no slave could be made free there, except on full provision for his leaving the State; and then they became wanderers over the North, where they were treated with more scorn and neglect than at home; the prejudices against coloured people being stronger in the Free than in the Slave States. He confessed his belief, therefore, that slavery was the greatest evil which this country now endured; that it would have been well for America if no African had ever been brought to its shores, that it would be still well, if, by any course of proceeding, they could transplant them all back to Africa in colonies; but that unless this or something else should be done, and that speedily, it was impossible to resist the conviction that a fearful conflict for emancipation would sooner or later take place; and the issue of that, no man could contemplate without trembling.

The temperature of the day had been warm, the thermometer at 85° in the shade, and not a breath of air stirring; so that when we stopped at the wood landings to take in fuel, and lost the breeze which the vessel made by her own progress through the stream, it was very sultry and oppressive, though so early in the spring (April 20); but after a rich and golden sunset of exquisite beauty, the evening was really delicious. The moon was high in the heavens, the stars shone with unusual brilliancy, and the air, though still, soft and balmy, was fresh and cool. Every one repaired to the deck; and we remained up till nearly midnight in agreeable and varied conversation.

On the following morning, April 21, we were opposite to Baton Rouge, a very old, but still small settlement on the north-eastern bank of the Mississippi, our progress having been somewhat retarded by a heavy fog, during which it was not deemed safe to run. The scenery from hence became less interesting, the villages and plantations were fewer, cane-brakes more abundant, and woods on each side continuous and unbroken.

About noon we passed beyond the eastern limits of Louisiana, which terminate here, in the latitude of 31° north; but on the western side of the stream it is continued to latitude 33°; and we had now, therefore, the State of Mississippi on the east, and Louisiana on the west, the river running here nearly north and south. So curved and sweeping are its bends, however, in some places, that where a neck of land is only a mile or two across from stream to stream, the circuit round by water is upwards of forty miles; and this was particularly the case at this part of the river. Above this, on our right, we had some high bluffs, at a place where Fort Adams was planted, the height of the yellow cliffs being from 80 to 120 feet; and opposite to this, on the left, but separated by an island from our view, was the junction of the Red River with the Mississippi.

This great stream comes from the west, flowing upwards of 1,000 miles, and its banks were originally settled by the French so that its parishes (for it had this as an ecclesiastical division) are mostly called by French names; and many of the inhabitants speak only the French tongue. Though full of marshes, and bayous, as the small streams which empty into the larger ones are called, it is accounted the most healthy part of the South; and an anecdote is told, of a medical man having gone there to seek for practice, who had not a single patient through an entire year; but when he was coming away in despair, a very old man, considerably above a hundred, was found sitting under a tree, and being observed there day after day for several weeks, the inhabitants thought he had fallen into a long sleep, death being a calamity they had altogether forgotten, from the length of time since any such event had occurred among them or their neighbours. Such is the story in the true American taste for exaggerated wit.

It was nine o'clock at night when we reached Natchez, where we ascended the steep hill from the landing-place to the top of the high bluff on which the town is built, and proceeding to the Mansion House, which is the principal hotel, we took up our quarters there.

CHAPTER XXII

The new State of Mississippi, into which we had now entered, was originally considered as belonging to the colony of Louisiana, and, as such, was under the dominion of the French, so long as that colony was possessed by it. As early as the year 1716, a small party of French colonists settled themselves among the Natchez Indians, one of the most powerful tribes of the South; and built a fort on the high bluff on which the town of Natchez now stands. The settlement continued to increase in numbers till 1729, when it was completely destroyed, the Chickasaws and Natchez tribes having united to massacre the whole of the white inhabitants, at this town and at two other small settlements, on the Washita and Yazoo rivers. They murdered no less than 700 individuals, three or four only out of the whole number escaping their arrows or their tomahawks, the weapons chiefly used by them. This event struck such terror into all white settlers, that none could be induced for many years afterwards to venture into this part of the country, and it remained, therefore, entirely in the hands of the Indians, till the territory was ceded by France to Great Britain when, as soon as possession was taken of it, several English settlers planted themselves at Natchez.

Soon after the American revolution, in 1783, England relinquished, by treaty, the whole of the Floridas to Spain; and ceded all the country north of latitude 31° to the United States; but the Americans and the Spaniards, contending for a long time afterwards as to the exact boundaries between their respective territories, the latter still kept possession of Natchez until 1798, when it was finally given up to the United States.

In 1800, the country lying between the western boundary of Georgia, and the river Mississippi, was erected into a distinct Territory, by the name of the great stream that washed its eastern border. In the following year, the Chocktaw tribe of Indians ceded a large portion of their lands to the general government; and in 1817, the Territory was thought to be sufficiently far advanced in population and wealth to be admitted into the Union, when an act of Congress was passed authorizing this step. In consequence of this, a convention of the people met in July 1817, to frame a State constitution; and the conditions prescribed by the act of Congress having been complied with, Mississippi was admitted as a new State, into the great Confederation of the North American Republic. Such is a brief outline of its history.

As the constitution of this State is one of the most recent in point of date, and may be regarded as a fair specimen of the State constitutions generally, especially those of the South, it may not be unacceptable to present a few of its most striking provisions, merely remarking, that they are all founded upon the great republican principle avowed in the opening section, and continued to be kept in view throughout. The enemies of free institutions in Europe studiously endeavour to inculcate and disseminate a belief that the Americans are already becoming dissatisfied with their republican government, and are endeavouring to retrace their steps by making their constitutions less democratic. That this is not the case with the recently formed States of the Union, the following extracts from the constitution of Mississippi will abundantly show—

Sec. 2. All political power is inherent in the people, and all free governments are founded on their authority, and established for their benefit; and therefore they have at all times an inalienable and indefeisible right to alter or abolish their form of government, in such manner as they may think expedient.

Sec. 4. No preference shall ever be given by law to any religious sect, or mode of worship.

Sec. 5. No person shall be molested for his opinions on any subject whatever, nor suffer any civil or political incapacity, or acquire any civil or political advantage, in consequence of such opinions, except in cases provided for in this constitution.

Sec. 6. Every citizen may freely speak, write, and publish his sentiments on all subjects; being responsible for the abuse of that liberty.

Sec. 7. No law shall ever be passed to curtail or restrain the liberty of speech, or of the press.

Sec. 8. In all prosecutions or indictments for libel, the truth may be given in evidence; and if it shall appear to the jury that the matter charged as libellous is true, and was published with good motives, and for justifiable ends, the party shall be acquitted; and the jury shall have the right to determine the law and the fact.

Sec. 20. No property qualification for eligibility to office, or for the right of suffrage, shall ever be required by law in this State.

Sec. 22. The citizens have a right, in a peaceable manner, to assemble together for their common good, and to apply to those vested with the powers of government for redress of grievances, or other proper purposes, by petition, address, or remonstrance.

Sec. 23. Every citizen has a right to bear arms in defence of himself and of the State.

Sec. 24. No standing army shall be kept up without the consent of the legislature; and the military shall in all cases, and at all times, be in strict subordination to the civil power.

Sec. 26. No hereditary emoluments, privileges, or honours, shall ever be granted or conferred in this State.

Sec. 28. The right of trial by jury shall remain inviolate.

Sec. 30. No person shall ever be appointed or elected to any office in this State for life; but the tenure of all offices shall be for some limited period of time, if the person appointed or elected thereto shall so long behave well.

In addition to these provisions are others respecting the formation of the legislature, and the election to office, all of which are regulated by the constitution; and among the various articles and sections, the following are worthy of notice—

Sec. 1. Every free white man, of twenty-one years of age, being a citizen of the United States, residing one year in this State, and four months in the place where he gives his vote, is deemed a legally qualified elector.

By such electors are chosen the members of the House of Representatives, the Senators, the Governor, the Judges, the Sheriffs, the Attorney-General, and Secretary of State. These are all elected by the people, for the different terms prescribed by the constitution; the Representatives for two years, the Senators for four; the Judges for two, four, and six years; the Governor for two years; the Secretary of State, Attorney-General, and Sheriffs for the same period. The only qualifications required for these respective offices, is a certain age, and certain term of residence in the State; all else is left to the discretion and judgment of the people to understand and perceive, and to elect or reject the candidates for office accordingly; there being only one general bar of exclusion, which is stated in the article of General Provisions in these terms:

Sec. 5. No person who denies the being of a God, or a future state of rewards and punishments, shall hold any office in the civil department of the State.

The Senate consists of thirty members, all above thirty years of age; and includes twenty-one planters, six lawyers, one physician, one merchant, and one fisherman.[1] The House of Representatives consists of ninety members, of whom fifty-seven are planters, twelve lawyers, five physicians, the speaker being of this number, ten merchants, one surveyor, one house carpenter, and four of professions not indicated.

The Governor has a salary of 3,000 dollars, or about 600*l.* a year; the State Treasurer and Auditor 1,000 dollars each; and the Attorney-General 1,000 dollars besides his legal practice. The Senators and Representatives have each 4 per day, and their travelling expenses. The seat of government is at Jackson City, near the centre of the State; and the session rarely lasts more than three months in the winter.

In a legislative body composed of so many planters as these two Houses contain, the question of the abolition of slavery would be likely to obtain about as much favour as the abolition of the corn-laws in the British parliament[2] and for the same reason, namely, that the legislators in both cases are more interested in upholding the value of their own property, or income, whether from slaves or land, than they are in maintaining the great principles of freedom, justice, and equal rights; and though by the constitution of both countries, power is given to legislate upon these subjects, the unwillingness to exercise this *power* will continue, so long as a depreciation in the value of property to the legislators themselves, is likely to be the result of any change. The general provisions of the constitution of Mississippi respecting slaves are sufficiently curious to deserve transcribing. They are as follow:

> Sec. 1. The legislature shall have no power to pass laws for the emancipation of slaves, without the consent of their owners, unless where the slave shall have rendered the State some distinguished service; in which case, the owner shall be paid a full equivalent for the slave so emancipated.[3] They shall have no power to prevent emigrants to this State from bringing with them such persons as are deemed slaves by the laws of any one of the United States, so long as any person of the same age or description shall be continued in slavery by the laws of this State:— *Provided*, that such person or slave be the *bona fide* property of such emigrants: *and provided also*, that laws may be passed to prohibit the introduction into this State, of slaves who may have committed high crimes in other States. They shall have power to pass laws to permit the owners of slaves to emancipate them, saving the rights of creditors, and preventing them from becoming a public charge. They shall have full power to oblige the owners of slaves to treat them with humanity, to provide for them necessary clothing and

provisions, to abstain from all injuries to them, extending to life or limb, and in case of their neglect or refusal to comply with the direction of such laws, to have such slave or slaves sold for the benefit of the owner or owners.

The Judiciary consists of a High Court of Errors and Appeals, with three judges; a Chancery; and a Circuit Court with nine judicial districts; and a judge and district attorney in each. The Criminal Court for Natchez held its sittings during our stay there; and the charge delivered to the grand jury at the opening of the Court by the judge, the Hon. Covington Rawlings was deemed of sufficient interest and importance by the jury itself, to be published under their authority. It denounced, in the strongest terms, the practice of duelling, gambling, and intoxication; and though it is the fashion in Europe to say that all these are beyond the pale of legislation, and therefore they are left to riot unchecked, the courts and public authorities of America hold a different doctrine, and deem them all fit subjects of legal punishment and prohibitory restraint.

Among the State institutions of Mississippi may be mentioned a well-organized militia, of which each county, to the number of fifty-two, furnishes a regiment, the whole directed by a general staff; and five divisions, each superintended by a major-general, inspectors, and subordinate officers. These are all armed and equipped at their own expense, reviewed from time to time, and held in readiness to be called into active service when the public exigencies may require it.

There are upwards of 200 post offices in this State, though the white population does not much exceed 150,000; but this is a branch of the patronage of the general government, which is pushed to its extreme; there being no less than 15,000 post-offices in the United States, at the commencement of the present year. The post masters at each are appointed solely by the President, and chiefly, it is believed, from persons willing to support the candidates for office in favour of the existing administration, as all of them have votes, and most of them are active partisans at all the general and local elections.

1.   Not, of course, a man who goes out with his net or line to catch fish; but one having ships or boats so engaged. The Duke of Sussex is, I believe, a "citizen and fishmonger;" and the Duke of Wellington and Sir Robert Peel are both "merchant-tailors;" by virtue of their being presented with the freedom of the City of London, as members of these corporations.

2.   This was written on the banks of the Mississippi long before the question of the
     Corn Laws led to the recent change of Administration in England.

3.   It will be here observed, that freedom is regarded as the fit *reward* for some
     distinguished service rendered to the State; and this by the parties who are continually
     declaring that the slaves do not value freedom, and would not accept it if offered to
     them!

CHAPTER XXIII

The State of Mississippi, though formed out of what originally belonged to Louisiana and Georgia, is of considerable extent, being in average length 300 miles, and breadth 160, covering therefore an area of about 48,000 square miles, or nearly 30,000,000 of acres. Its boundaries are, on the north, the State of Tennessee; on the south, the State of Louisiana and the Gulf of Mexico, on the east, the State of Alabama; and on the west, the great river from whence it derives its name, the Mississippi. This magnificent stream washes its western border, by its serpentine windings, for nearly 700 miles, though in a straight line its length is just 300.

The two most important points in the State of Mississippi for commerce are, at present, Natchez and Vicksburg, to which, perhaps, may be added Port Gibson and Grand Gulf. These owe their importance chiefly to their being seated on or near the banks of the Mississippi, from which Natchez has begun already to carry on a direct trade with Europe in the shipment of her cotton, ships sailing 300 miles up the river to load. One of the latest vessels cleared from hence, was the ship Talleyrand for Liverpool, taking a cargo of 2,160 bales of cotton, valued at 1,296,000 dollars, and the freight of which alone was 14,960 dollars. From Grand Gulf, another ship, the Franklin, cleared a few days before, taking 1,886 bales of cotton, worth 1,111,998 dollars, for Europe. But the spot of greatest promise in the future annals of this country for commercial operations, is, undoubtedly, the projected seaport of Mississippi, on the shore of the Gulf of Mexico, to which but a small portion of the State is contiguous. The following description of it, from the Register of the State, before quoted, is believed, from concurring testimonies, to be perfectly accurate:

> MISSISSIPPI CITY.—The location of this great future seaport of Mississippi, and of the south-west at large, is so commanding, that it

will ever be a matter of surprise that it was not sooner appropriated to the uses for which it was designed by the munificent hand of Nature. Neither New Orleans, Mobile, Pensacola, or Charleston, can hold competition with the vast natural advantages of Mississippi City, as a seaport of the first magnitude. The harbour-surveyors pronounce the capacity and safety of the anchorage to equal, if not surpass, that of any other harbour in the United States. Its freedom from either ice or rock bound shores—its protection from winds by the south-western neck of main land, and Cat, Ship, and other islands—its noble passes between Cat Island and the mainland, with twenty-seven feet of water, and between Cat and Ship islands, with thirty-three feet of water, and with forty to forty-three feet of water inside—its good mud bottom—all combine to render it a safe and magnificent roadstead, where ships of the largest class can ride, sheltered and safe, within a mile of the shore. Indeed, those excellent judges of naval positions, the British, anchored their fleet in this harbour during the invasion of New Orleans in the late war. The only possible approach of storms from the south-east is guarded by a chain of islands. The water in the offing gradually shallows from the Gulf to the island-passes, where there is from twenty-seven to forty-three feet to come in with.

The site presents a bold, firm, and dry front, from Pass Christian to the bay of Biloxi. There are no marshes nor low grounds in the rear, and it is far enough removed from the Pearl river swamps on the west, and those of Pascagoula on the east, to be entirely free of mosquitoes and miasmas from these sources. Instead of being under the necessity of retreating from this site to find a healthful summer residence, the reverse would be the case. This coast is now the Arcadia of the south-west—the refuge of the interior, and of the delta, from summer and autumnal fevers. The luxurious and inexhaustible oyster-beds, the almost endless variety of fish in the sea, and the abundance of wildfowl on shore, would astonish while it delighted the *gourmand*, and almost awaken life and appetite within 'the ribs of death.' The water gushes up in exhaustless profusion through the strata of sand and gravel, as pure as the rock springs of the mountains.

The entire shore is belted with fine groves of pine, towering in majestic pride, and of live oak, of which there are large reserves owned by the United States, as the future supplies of her navy yards. On such a spot, and with such resources at hand, it is really wonderful that the United States have not before this located a navy yard here, both for the facilities afforded to shipbuilding and the contiguity of the position to those seas that most require the supervision of our naval force, to prevent piracy and outrage.

This brief description, founded on undoubted authority, gives but a faint idea of the site of the future emporium of the southwest. It always holds good, that wherever Nature has furnished inexhaustible natural resources, she has also provided an outlet for the superabundance of such natural wealth. Mississippi City is destined to be the outlet of the wealth of that proud State which bears the name of the great Nile of the West.

The city of Natchez was first incorporated in 1809, but, though only thirty years old as a city, it existed as a town a full century before, having been first settled by the French, then occupied by Spaniards, and is now inhabited wholly by Americans. It has a singular situation, not unlike that of Savannah, being seated on the top of a high land, or bluff as it is here termed, at an elevation of 175 feet above the level of the river. As you ascend the Mississippi, you land first at the small collection of houses called "Natchez under the Hill," which was formerly deemed the worst point along the whole valley for the haunt of gamblers, thieves, and ruffians of every country and state; but Vicksburg has of late borne the palm of pre-eminence in this respect. From hence you ascend by a steep road cut in the side of the hill, and, after attaining the summit, and going about a quarter of a mile inward from the edge of the bluff or cliff, the upper town of Natchez commences.

Its plan of laying-out exhibits the same regularity that characterizes all American cities in comparison with those of Europe, the streets running nearly north and south, and east and west, crossing each other at right angles, from 60 to 80 feet in breadth, with good flag-pavements at the sides, and posts or rails at the edges of these pavements, for suspending awnings in front of the shops, or stores. The names of the streets are those so common in all other cities of this country, as Wall Street, Pearl Street, Pinestreet, State Street, Main Street, Canal Street, besides Washington, Franklin, Jefferson, Fulton, and others.

The private dwellings are well built, and constructed with verandas, and furnished with gardens, so as to adapt them to the climate, the latitude being 30° 34′ north, and quite as warm as New Orleans. The stores are substantial, and built after the New York fashion, with granite sub-basements, and brick superstructures. They are well furnished; but everything here is excessively dear, at least three times the price that similar articles might be had for in England. There are no less than twelve hotels, the principal of which are the Mansion House, the City Hotel, and the Mississippi Hotel; but so many of the population are in constant motion, and so many of the permanent residents live at hotels and boarding-houses, that even this large number, accommodating upon the average about 100 persons each, besides many private establishments capable of receiving fifty persons each, are insufficient to supply the demand. It is, therefore, often difficult to get a sleeping room at all, and very rarely a sitting-room; while the table is ill attended to, the slaves who act as servants are careless, and the charges are exorbitant. Yet, in all our travels through this country, we never remember to have heard or seen any person remonstrate or complain, or utter the slightest sign of dissatisfaction, or desire of amendment; not even in their conversation with each other, any more than in their intercourse with the landlord or the attendants. Whatever room the traveller is conducted to, he accepts it, without seeking for a better; and whether it be clean or dirty, ill furnished or well furnished, single or double, it is all the same; for no complaint of either seems ever to be made. So also at table, whether the meats be tough or tender, the dishes hot or cold, the tea or coffee good or bad, everyone seems to partake of whatever is set before him, to consume it rapidly and in silence, and then rise and retire. The most easy solution I have been able to offer of this to my own mind, is that the great bulk of American travellers are insensible of the distinctions between clean apartments and dirty ones, privacy or publicity, good food or bad; and like persons who have no perception of the difference of sounds in music, or who are wholly unmoved by the varied beauties of landscape or scenery, these migrating bodies seem deficient in the sense of appreciating good, or discovering evil, in the matter of accommodation, lodging, and food. If it be not this, then they must be the most patient and contented persons in the world; or their minds must be so entirely engrossed with other considerations, in the prosecution of their various pursuits after wealth, as to make all these minor matters wholly beneath their notice.

Of public buildings in Natchez, the principal are the City Hall, Court House, and Jail, a handsome Masonic Hall, (there being two Masonic Lodges, and two fraternities of the Independent Odd Fellows, in Natchez,) a Public Market, Theatre, Hospital, Orphan Asylum, Mechanic's Hall, three handsome Banks—the Planters, the Agricultural, and the Commercial; and three churches—the Episcopal, Presbyterian, and Methodist, all of which are handsome, well-furnished, and very liberally supported.

Of incorporated companies in Natchez, there are five banking establishments; the three already named, and two others; the Mississippi and Pearl River Railroad Company, and the Mississippi Shipping Company; and all of these issue notes, though some of them are at seven, others at twelve, and others at fifteen per cent discount, even in the neighbouring States of Alabama and Louisiana. In the whole State of Mississippi there are twenty-five Banking Companies, each having branches; and their nominal capital is 62,512,000 dollars, of which, however, only 18,884,340 dollars have been paid in. This is no criterion, however, of the disposable funds commanded by such banks, to meet their engagements; as this capital paid in is often represented by a very small sum turned over several times. In proof of this, the following extract from a Natchez paper may be given—

A new Way to get up a Bank.—A curious story is related by the Bank Commissioners appointed by the Legislature of Michigan, in their report, of the manner in which the Bank of Oakland was established. It appears that one W.S. Stevens, the principal owner of the concern, borrowed 5,000 dollars specie of a neighbouring bank, and sent it to the Oakland institution, to be duly credited by the cashier as capital stock paid in. He then immediately drew it out on his account, and afterwards sent his hired man with it, to be credited a second time as paid capital. This manœuvre he again repeated, thus enabling the cashier to swear that 15,000 dollars in specie had been paid in, and consequently to set the bank in operation. This accomplished, the 5,000 dollars was restored to its original owner.

This practice was very general on the establishment of banks in almost all the States of the Union, at the time when so many local banks sprang up a few years ago, after the measures of General Jackson to destroy the supremacy of the United States Bank. The facilities which this afforded to fraud, as well as to the wildest speculations, was undoubtedly the cause of much of the distress that prostrated New York, and the larger cities of the Union, a short time since, and which is now only beginning to show itself in the remoter States. This is the case in Mississippi at the present moment, where the greatest pressure for money, and the greatest depreciation of property of every kind exists, all springing from the cause adverted to.

A gentleman of great experience, who had resided in this State for many years, assured me of the following practice as quite common a few years ago: an individual would raise the sum of 625 dollars and, repairing to the Land Office at Washington, would purchase with it 100 acres of uncleared land somewhere in the States of Mississippi, Arkansas, or Missouri, at 1¼ dollars per acre. The money so paid into the Land-office, would be placed out in deposit, in one of the local banks, according to the usual practice of the government. The purchaser of the land having registered his title, and obtained the necessary certificate, would apply to this bank, and get from it an advance of the whole value of 625 dollars, on the security of the land as a mortgage, at seven or eight per cent; and with this identical money he would go a second time to the Land Office, and buy 500 acres more; in the mean while employing agents to dispose of his former purchase in small lots, and sometimes realizing a profit. He would go on repeating this operation of buying land at the government-office, and getting advances on it from the bank, for fifteen or twenty times in succession; and become thus the nominal proprietor of 10,000 acres, worth 10,250 dollars, though his original capital was only 625 dollars. Some fortunate speculators have speedily enriched themselves by subsequent sales; but, the greater part of such purchasers failed to realize while the prices were high, and are now embarrassed beyond the power of redemption.

The environs of Natchez abound with fine mansions and well-cultivated plantations; and the most wealthy and longest-settled families reside in these. My lectures, which were delivered in the Presbyterian Church, were chiefly attended by this class, and a few of the principal families in town; and though not so numerous as the audiences at New Orleans and Mobile, it was among the most elegant, both in dress, appearance, and ease and polish of manners, that I had yet seen in the United States. The frankness of the Spanish, the courtesy of the French, and the solidity and intelligence of the English character, seemed happily blended in them, and made their society very delightful.

I should have added, that among the benevolent institutions of Natchez is one called the Hibernian Society, the object of which is to afford relief to such natives of Ireland as may require it, and it is said to accomplish its purpose faithfully and generously. The Irish emigrants in America preserve most of the generous virtues of their native island—are good fathers, good husbands, good children, and good friends.

CHAPTER XXIV

We had intended proceeding from hence up the Mississippi to St. Louis; but, from the best information we could collect, the whole of the way from hence to the mouth of the Ohio river, a distance of several hundred miles, is far less interesting than the portions above; and it was considered by all whom we consulted, that it would be much better for us to return to New Orleans, and make an inland journey from Charleston through North and South Carolina, Georgia, Tennessee, and the back parts of Virginia—portions of the country but little visited by foreigners, yet full of interest—and resume our examination of the upper portion of the Mississippi, till we could visit Pittsburgh, descend the Ohio to Cincinnati and Louisville, enter the great river by that route, and then ascend to St. Louis, and as much higher up the Mississippi as we thought fit. As this arrangement seemed, therefore, in every way most worthy of adoption, we determined on pursuing this route.

Accordingly on the morning of Friday, April 26, we embarked at Natchez on board the steamer, William Robinson, from Pittsburg, for New Orleans. The weather had much increased in warmth during our short stay at Natchez, the thermometer being 85° in the shade at ten A.M. with the wind from the south. The foliage was everywhere out in rich and gorgeous fullness; the grass a bright green, and flowers in great abundance and variety in every garden. We remarked, too, for the first time, the song of birds, whose delightful warblings aroused all our agreeable recollections of an English spring; while the temperature and foliage was that of our midsummer, and parasols were acceptable shelters from the heat of the sun. Light jackets and trousers were almost universally worn by the men, and persons without neck cloths and in their shirt sleeves, were seen in every street; while the broad-brimmed straw hat so constantly surmounted the head, as to remind us of the anecdote of Mr. Elliott, in his Travels in Syria, who mentions that when some of the Arab boys saw for the first time a European traveller, with such a hat on his head, they ran after him, calling out—"Come and see the father of baskets" supposing the hat to be an article of this description; while another of the party running into the opposite extreme, by having a small black hat with a very narrow brim, they shouted after him—"Behold also the father of saucepans" the utensil which they supposed this singular head covering most to resemble.

We had quitted Natchez at twelve o'clock on Friday, and we reached the wharf, at New Orleans, at twelve o'clock on the day following, April 27th, having made the passage of 300 miles, in twenty-four hours, or nearly seventeen miles an hour, with a current of three, equal to fourteen miles an hour actual speed, and in the coolest, quietest, and most agreeable manner possible.

From New Orleans, we went by the railroad immediately to Lake Pont-chartrain, in the hope of being in time for the Mobile steamer, but were too late; and therefore remained at the Washington Hotel, on the borders of the lake, to pass the night. The weather was still beautiful, the moon bright, and the air of the lake four or five degrees cooler than that of the city. Mosquitoes, however, had begun to make their appearance, and were the only drawback to our pleasure. At the hotel was a fierce large brown bear, just brought in from the mountains of Tennessee, with whom one only of the negroes could play familiarly, and he, by feeding and caressing him, had become quite a favourite.

The morning-song of birds awoke us with the sun; and among them, the varied tones of the mockingbird were conspicuous. Parties of pleasure, bound on excursions across the lake, were arriving by every train of cars during the morning, the train starting every hour. At noon we embarked in the steamer Isabella, for Mobile.

Our passage across the Lake Pontchartrain and Borgne, was most agreeable; and the freshness of the sea-breeze, as we opened the Gulf of Mexico, most exhilarating. The night was so brilliant, with moon and stars in all their glory, that our voyage was one of uninterrupted enjoyment. We reached the outer roads of Mobile at sunrise; passed up through the large fleet of fine ships still at anchor here, loading cotton for Europe, to the number of forty or fifty sail, with an equal number at the upper anchorage; and landed at the wharf by eight o'clock, making the passage of 180 miles in twenty hours.

We remained at Mobile for three days, waiting for a vessel to ascend the Alabama river; and on Wednesday, the first of May, we embarked in the Medora steamer for this trip.

We left the wharf at Mobile at six in the evening, with a fine breeze from the southward, this being the wind that blows in from the Gulf of Mexico like the sea breezes of the East and West Indies, all the summer, and greatly tempers the heat of the atmosphere to the feelings. Our passengers were too numerous for comfort; and not of the most agreeable description, if I except indeed one family going on to the North for health and pleasure, among whom were two highly interesting young sisters, about eighteen or twenty years of age, both born deaf and dumb, but with countenances full of animation. They conversed by the fingers with each other, and with a married sister who accompanied them, and who was not subject to the same calamity; and they appeared to enjoy the incidents of the voyage, and even the anecdotes communicated to them, with great zest and earnestness.

In the course of our way up the Alabama we had abundant occasion to observe the disagreeable peculiarities by which the manners of the middle classes in America are distinguished from those of the same classes in England. Among the gentlemen, scarcely one took off his hat on entering the cabin, but nearly all sat with their hats on, during every part of the day, except at meals; and chewing and spitting was nearly universal, brass boxes being placed in rows along the floor of the cabin, to save the carpet from defilement. At meals, considerable etiquette is manifested in waiting for the ladies, who are always placed at the head of the table; the gentlemen stand behind their chairs, and no one presumes to seat himself, however long he may be kept waiting, until the ladies appear, to take their seats first. In leaving the table, however, no such punctiliousness is observed; and while in England few gentlemen would think of rising and leaving the table before the ladies were ready to do so, here every person rises as soon as he has finished, which is frequently in ten minutes or less, retiring from the table chewing his last mouthful as he goes, and then hastens to the forepart of the vessel, to light his cigar, the common accompaniment of every meal.

At the table, all persons convey their food to the mouth on the point of the knife, which practice, from its universality, attracts no notice except from a stranger. Silver forks are rarely seen, except at the best private tables; and the steel ones used have rarely more than two prongs. The knife has a very broad blade, and expanded round point, to take up a good knifeful of the food in use, and convey it to the mouth; and both knives and forks are set in large, rough, and uncouth handles of buck-horn, so irregular in shape, that it is difficult for any but a practised hand to hold and manage them pleasantly. The principal dishes are taken off the table, and carved or hacked on a sideboard by the negro stewards, who load the plates with so great a quantity of everything asked for, and so bury the whole in gravies or sauces, that it requires a very strong appetite to conquer the repugnance which it creates. No delicacy is observed in the mode of carving, serving, or helping the guests; and the gentlemen are all too busily occupied in despatching their own portion, to take this duty out of the servants' hands. Puddings are usually handed round in small white saucers, instead of plates, with a spoon in each, and nothing is refused. Every one seems to think it a duty to accept and be thankful for whatever is set before him, and appears to exercise no more power of rejection or refusal than children at school.

At breakfast and at supper—for so the evening meal at seven o'clock is usually called—coffee is more frequently used than tea; and of tea, green is almost the only kind seen. Both are made at a side table by the negroes, and handed round to the guests as they are seated. High and large cups of thick white earthenware are chiefly used; and though originally furnished with handles, three out of four will have had their handles knocked off; but neither this, nor cracks, though sufficient to make both cups and saucers leaky, is deemed disqualification for service, so that there are generally more broken vessels than whole ones on the table. The cups, too, are invariably filled to overflowing, before either sugar or milk is added; and this, with the leakiness from the cracks, is sure to make the saucer half full from the waste or surplus. On no single table did we ever see what is called a slop basin, so that there is nothing at hand into which to pour this cold surplus fluid; but the people get over the difficulty by drinking their coffee or tea out of the saucer, so that hot and cold are mingled together, and all soon disposed of.

In other matters, also, there is a great dissimilarity in the manners of the English and the Americans. In England, for instance, no person, even in the humblest ranks of life, would venture to approach a table where a gentleman was writing, to look over his papers, or take up his books for examination, without permission. But here I had been so frequently subject to the former, that I felt obliged to give up writing anywhere but in my own bedroom, and even there I was not always safe from intrusion; while as to the latter, persons in the rank of merchants and bankers would seat themselves at the table, take up any of the books which you might be using for perusal or reference, cut them open, read them, and sometimes even take them off to their own cabins, to read through, without asking permission, or seeming to think this at all necessary. On one occasion, when I said to a gentleman who was thus walking off with a volume which he had taken from under my very elbow— "I beg your pardon. Sir, but that is private, and does not belong to the ship, as perhaps you suppose," he coolly replied—"Oh, never mind, I only want to read it; and when I have done with it, you shall have it again."

In mentioning all these traits of manners, I must at the same time, in justice, observe, that however disagreeable they may be to English persons, chiefly because they differ from what they are accustomed to witness in similar classes of society at home, it is not fair to consider them as acts either of vulgarity or rudeness, as they are not essentially either, though they may be conventionally so. That cannot be *vulgar* which is almost universally practised in any nation, as, for instance, eating with the fingers instead of knives and forks, as in Turkey;

though if any man were to do this in England or America, he would excite disgust; but at Constantinople it would neither be thought indecorous nor inelegant, any more than it was among the most polished circles of Athens or Rome. And that cannot be *rude*, which does not originate either in a disregard to the feelings of others, or an intention to wound or offend them. From this I think the Americans are more free than the people of any nation I have ever travelled in. They are almost uniformly decorous, civil, obliging, willing to yield in any matter for the accommodation of others, quiet, orderly, and inoffensive; and neither at the hotels, nor in the steamboats, or on railroads, is the ear so often offended as it is in England, by oaths, vociferations, quarrels, complaints, bickerings among equals, and abuse of inferiors. These are here almost unknown; and a stranger, who himself behaves with propriety, may certainly pass from one end of the United States to the other without molestation; for those affrays, and duels, assaults, and assassinations, which are unhappily so frequent in the South, arise out of causes which do not affect the traveller who avoids the bar-rooms, gaming-houses, and places of resort for the idle and profligate.

The error which English persons commit towards Americans, is, I think, in judging them by a wrong standard. We take the manners of the best educated and most polished circles in England as the test of excellence; and if the Americans do not come up to this, in all they say or do, we set them down as vulgar, rude, and uncivilized. But we forget, that in England, a thousand years of progressive improvement have been necessary to bring the national manners to their present state; and, notwithstanding the fact that a very large portion of the population, including all the nobility, gentry, clergy, aided by colleges, schools of art, and intercourse with foreign nations, have been continually operating upon the general mass, as elements of refinement—while the wealth and leisure of large numbers even of the middle classes, give them the means of assisting in this improvement—there yet remain some ten millions of the labouring classes of England, among whom may be found as much of vulgarity, rudeness, ignorance, and intemperance, as in any classes of the lowest population of this country.

If the English nobility of the reigns of Elizabeth, James, and Charles could be raised from their graves, and transplanted to America, with no other recollections of habits or customs than of those common to the best circles in England in *their* day, they would be surprised at the comparative refinement and polish of American manners, as contrasted with these; and would award to them the palm of superiority. While it is the duty of the traveller, therefore, to note with accuracy and fidelity the real facts respecting manners as they occur, justice demands of him that he should neither impute them to motives which have no existence, nor characterize them by epithets which they do not truly deserve.

Slaves shipping cotton by torch–light, River Alabama

W. H. Brooke. F.S.A.

In the course of our voyage up the river, we made several halts at the landing-places of estates, to discharge supplies brought up as part of the cargo, and to take in wood. One of these halts was rendered peculiarly interesting, from the romantic and picturesque scene which it exhibited. The place of our halt was under a high bluff, or perpendicular cliff, of 200 feet in height, above which rose many lofty and full-foliaged trees; and at the foot of the whole was a portion of unequal and broken ground, with here and there the appearance of cavernous openings in the cliff itself. The negroes, from the plantation above, had come down to assist in landing their master's goods; and these, added to the crew, made the whole number employed, from fifty to sixty persons. The night was cloudy and dark, but myriads of fireflies spangled the air, yet not a solitary star was to be seen. Strong torchlight was therefore necessary, to enable the labourers to do their work. The pitch-pine of the woods, so full of resinous matter, was accordingly used for this purpose; and the glare of several such torches moving from spot to spot, without any visible agent—the persons of the negroes, who carried them as high as they could elevate them in the air, being hidden in the shade—the occasional waving of these torches to and fro, the bright lights on some parts of the cliff, and the deep shadows on others, with occasional flashes of forked lightning, rolling of thunder, and shouting of the men, when they hailed from the summit of the bluff above, or responded from the beach below—formed altogether a scene worthy the pen of Mrs. Radcliffe, of cave-and-bandit-loving memory, or of the pencil of Salvator Rosa, and quite worthy the terror and the grandeur of his style.

Among the passengers in the ladies' cabin, were three coloured females, going from Mobile to Montgomery, whose position was very remarkable. They were not negresses, but mulattoes of dark brown colour and strongly-marked African features, and appeared to be sisters or relatives. They were each dressed much more expensively than either of the white ladies on board—silks, lace, and feathers, with ornaments of jewellery of various kinds, being worn by them. They slept on the cabin-floor, as the coloured servants usually do, no berth or bed-place being assigned them; and they occupied a good hour at their toilette, with the white stewardess, before the ladies were moving. They remained sitting in the cabin all day, as if they were on a footing of perfect equality with the white passengers; but when meal-time came, then was seen the difference.

The order in which the meals were taken in the steam vessel was this: at the first bell, the captain and all the white passengers sat down; when these had all finished and left the table, a second bell summoned the pilot, the captain's clerk, all the white men of the engineer's department, the white stewardess, and such white servants or subordinates as might be on board; and when these had finished, the third bell summoned the black steward and all the mulattoes and coloured servants, to take their meal. So equivocal, however, was the position of these coloured ladies, that they could not be placed at either of the tables; they were not high enough in rank to be seated with the whites, and they were too high to be seated with the blacks and mulattoes; so they had to retire to the pantry, where they took their meals standing; and the contrast of their finery in dress and ornament, with the place in which they took their isolated and separate meal, was painfully striking. What rendered it more so, to me at least, was this—that however a man might yearn to break down these barriers which custom and prejudice has raised against a certain race, the exhibition of any such feeling, or the utterance of any such sentiment, would undoubtedly injure the very parties for whom his sympathy might be excited, or on whose behalf it might be expressed.

We did not reach Montgomery till the middle of the third night; and therefore remained on board till daylight, when we landed on the morning of Saturday the 4th of May, at sunrise, and found very comfortable quarters in the excellent hotel, called Montgomery Hall.

We remained at Montgomery for a few days; and I delivered a short course of lectures in the Methodist church, there being no rooms suitable for such purposes in the smaller towns of the country; and the churches of all denominations of Christians being freely granted for this purpose, whenever the subjects of the lectures are deemed useful and unobjectionable.

These were attended by audiences increasing from 250 to 300 persons, and, as usual, brought me speedily acquainted with the most intelligent and influential inhabitants of the town and neighbourhood.

CHAPTER XXV

As a town, Montgomery has few distinguishing or prominent features. It is of comparatively recent date, having been first settled in the year 1823. Its position is on a sloping declivity, on the north-eastern bank of the Alabama river, not extending quite down to the stream, but distant nearly half a mile from its borders, and elevated about 100 feet above its level. The town consists principally of one main street of ample breadth, 100 feet at least, at the bottom of which is the Court House, and lateral streets leading from this as a centre. It has but one bookseller's store, but others for the supply of goods of all kinds are numerous. It has two weekly newspapers, the Advertiser and Journal; two principal and several smaller hotels, and one of the former, Montgomery Hall, not inferior to any that we had met with out of the larger cities—spacious, clean, airy, well-conducted, and comfortable.

The present population of Montgomery is estimated at 3,000, of whom about 1,600 are whites, and 1,400 coloured people. They appeared to us more quiet, orderly, and in better condition than we had been accustomed to observe in the Southern towns, a fact to be attributed chiefly to the influence of religion, as the inhabitants are chiefly of New England stock, and there are no less than six churches, each well attended, in this small community; namely, an Episcopal, a Presbyterian, a Baptist, a Methodist, a Unitarian, and a Catholic: as many, in short, as there are in the populous, but gay and dissipated city of New Orleans. In one of these churches, the Methodist, I heard, on the Sunday after our arrival there, one of the most chastely eloquent and beautiful addresses, that it has yet been my lot to hear in this country, delivered by a gentleman of the bar, a member of the Methodist body, Mr. Hilliard, on the occasion of celebrating the anniversary of the Montgomery Sunday Schools. The audience was very large, and among them were about 200 Sabbath School pupils. The address was, however, chiefly directed to the parents and teachers, and its object was to show that merely cultivating the intellect, and adding to the stores of knowledge, without implanting moral and religious principles, and purifying and ennobling the sentiments and feelings of the heart, was not sufficient to ensure the formation of a virtuous and happy character; and this point was established, illustrated, and enforced in the most able and conclusive manner. Several negroes and coloured people were among the auditors in the gallery, where alone they are permitted to sit in this country; and the only drawback I felt to the extreme pleasure which the discourse afforded me, was the melancholy consideration, that the unhappy children of these coloured persons are excluded, like themselves, from all the benefits of intellectual cultivation, since, throughout the South, it is unlawful to teach a slave even to read!

During our stay at Montgomery, the weather was delicious, as much so indeed as it is possible to conceive. The thermometer from 65° to 70°, with a fresh bracing wind from the north-west, the sky a deep and clear blue, with small white fleecy clouds, the air balmy and odoriferous from the perfume of the surrounding woods, and the birds full of song from every tree and every bush. Nothing in the finest days in England, under the most favourable combinations, ever surpassed it in splendour or beauty.

In England, fat and corpulent men, especially above the age of forty, are frequently met with; but in America, such persons are rarely seen: the *pleasures* of the table, as they are called—though often bringing in their train the *pains* of indigestion, headache, nausea, and nightmare—not being indulged in, by any class in this country, to so great an extent as in England. The people of America are too busy, and too much engrossed with preparations for the future, to devote much of the present to the habits which make so many corpulent men in England, and which cause the tendency to corpulency to be transmitted, like the gout, hereditarily, from generation to generation. There is greater uniformity of stature, shape, feature, and expression, among both the men and the women in America, than there is in England; which is the more remarkable, because, though the English population is descended from a great variety of original stocks, Celtic, Saxon, Roman, Dane, and Norman, yet many centuries have elapsed since any large addition has been made to its population by immigration; and foreigners are not often even intermingled with us by marriage. Here, however, not only has there been great diversities in the original stock, British, Dutch, French, Spanish, Danish, Swedish, and German; but these varieties and admixtures are kept up by perpetual immigration of persons from all these distant nations. Yet the amalgamation of the whole seems to settle itself into a much greater uniformity of national stature, physiognomy, and general appearance in America than is the case in England.

The principal causes of this uniformity appear to me to be these: first, the general equality of condition in the several classes of the population, none being very rich, and none being very poor, but all provided with reasonable competency; so that the style of living, dressing, and enjoyment, is pretty nearly the same with all, except the few at either extreme of condition, which does not, however, perceptibly affect the uniformity of the mass. Second, the general equality of their lot in being all obliged to labour for subsistence; some in the higher departments of the law, medicine, tuition, and the direction of agricultural and commercial affairs; and others in the subordinate duties of handicraft and artisan occupations; but all to do something—and thus to be uniformly occupied, from morning till night, in labour of some kind or another. Hence, all persons rise early, and breakfast, dine, and sup at nearly the same hour, in the same town or district. There is no hauteur on the part of the richer, nor obsequiousness on the part of the poorer members of the community; no disputes about precedency between bankers or merchants, clergy or manufacturers, wholesale dealers and retailers; the barrister is not a greater man than the attorney, nor the physician superior to the surgeon, for these separate departments of law and medicine are united in the same individual; and the judges, the members of the legislature, and even the governor himself, mingle as freely with the humbler members of society, as if they were wholly unconnected with office. Nor does this, as some might suppose, lessen, in the slightest degree, their dignity or efficiency; and I might cite an example of a similar state of things in a part of the British dominions—the island of Guernsey, where the chief magistrate and civil governor, the venerable Daniel De Lisle Brock, may be seen in familiar conversation with some of the humblest inhabitants of the island, in their fields or in their streets, or accompanying him as he walks on foot to and from his country residence to the court-house, where he presides as judge, and as head of the legislature as well as of the executive power; and yet no man's person is more beloved, or no man's authority more revered and respected, than his, throughout all Europe.

This general uniformity of stature and appearance in the men and women of America, thus attempted to be accounted for, is accompanied with certain characteristics, which may be thus briefly described. The men are generally tall and slender in figure, more frequently above five feet ten inches than below it, and rarely exceeding three feet in circumference about the waist; the arms are long, the legs small, the chest narrow, the form not so frequently erect, as slightly stooping, arising from carelessness of gait and hurry in walking; the head is small, but the features are long, the complexion pale, the eyes small and dark, the hair straight, the cheeks generally smooth or without whiskers or beard, and the whole expression and deportment is grave and serious. The women of

America are not so tall in stature as the women of Europe generally, being oftener below five feet four inches, than above it; of slender figure, without the fulness or rotundity and flowing lines of the Medicean statue, imperfect development of bust, small hands and feet, small and pretty features, pale complexions, dark eyes, a mincing gait, delicate health, and a grave rather than a gay or animated expression. If the men seem to be marked by a general uniformity of standard in personal appearance, the women are still more alike; and it is remarkable that there is far less of diversity in the condition and occupation of females, than in that of males of the same rank and class of life in this country; for here, all the daughters, except in the very humblest ranks, are brought up as young ladies; and all the wives are so unqualified to superintend household or any other labours, that all is done for them by servants or by slaves. Thus relieved from all necessity for exercising either their physical strength or mental capacities, they soon become feeble in health, and indifferent towards society. In gay parties, they are usually neglected, because they are married; and they are not so important as the English housewife or matron at home, because they are neither active mistresses of their own household, nor active trainers or educators of their children; neither are they called upon to be such frequent entertainers of friendly guests in the evening and social circle, as married ladies and heads of families are in England. I took occasion to recommend strongly to many persons, who agreed with me as to this view of the state of female education and society in America, the perusal of Mrs. Ellis's admirable work "On the Women of England, their Social and Domestic Duties," which I purchased at New Orleans, and read with great pleasure during our voyage up the Mississippi; for, if her excellent advice was needed to change the present system of female education in the middle classes in England, it is still more required for all in this country, where the evils it desires to correct are much greater than at home.

CHAPTER XXVI

The stage-coaches of this country are not regulated by the same punctuality as those of England and France. The mail, even, will often wait for two or three hours beyond its usual time of starting, to pick up a few passengers. This morning, when we left Montgomery, May the 8th, in an opposition coach, termed the "People's Line" and professing to beat the mail especially in its punctuality, we were detained two full hours, one of which was passed by seven passengers sitting in the coach at the hotel door, waiting for a single passenger only. The cause of his detention was, that he wished to change a note at one of the banks, which did not open until nine; and though the fixed hour for departure was half past seven, we did not start till nearly ten.

The passengers by whom we were surrounded in this journey—there being eight in the whole, seven gentlemen and one lady on the inside—were not of the best kind; but as everybody travels in this country, and there are no outside places at inferior prices for the humbler classes, all meet together in this common receptacle—the stage coach. Two appeared, from their conversation, to be coach drivers, one of them chewing so abundantly, as to require a corner place, to prevent his spitting over the rest of the passengers, as his jaws were in perpetual motion, and he appeared to project his head out of the coach door, to spit once in every minute. Notwithstanding this, at every place at which we stopped he lighted a cigar, and smoked while the horses were changing; and we had the greatest difficulty in preventing him from bringing it within the coach for that purpose. He described himself as suffering the greatest torture if he was deprived for a moment of his tobacco. And I can believe it; for, like opium or brandy, it requires a larger and larger dose to satisfy the morbid cravings to which its excessive use gives rise. And yet mankind are so infatuated, that thousands in this and in other countries—for even in England we are not free from this stain—persist in the consumption of this useless and pernicious article, in snuffing, chewing, and smoking; and commit the folly of devoting thousands of acres of valuable land to the cultivation of this exhausting and poisonous weed.

The individuals spoken of as coach-drivers, had been to the Western country, beyond the Mississippi, from whence they were returning to Carolina; and among several of the new expressions in use among the Western people, from whom they professed to have borrowed them, we heard the following: speaking of the morning and evening, they use the terms "at sun-up," and "at sun-down," instead of sunrise, and sunset; as, for instance, the keeper of a log-house inn, would shake a sleeping passenger, and say, "Stranger, be stirring: it's near sun-up" and in describing the extent westward to which Ohio money would circulate, the expressions used were, "It's such good money, that it will carry you to sun-down." A handsome young girl at one of these log-hut inns had so many suitors, and rejected them so often, that it was said, "Her lovers came to visit her in *cords*—this being the measure of a pile of firewood, containing many hundred billets—and she flung 'em off by *cargoes*." A person in pecuniary difficulty, is said to be "in a tight place" or "in a bad fix" and when he runs away from his creditors, he is said to have "sloped." A soup or broth made of fowls, is called "soup with chicken fixings" and when any proposed arrangement is difficult to be settled, the phrase is, "It won't do any which-way you may fix it," or, "they can't fix it, any-how or no-how."

One of the most communicative of our fellow passengers, was a young man from Texas, who had resided there two years, and left it only a week ago; and his information respecting the actual condition of the country, was extremely interesting. I had seen the ex-president, General Houston, at Mobile. He had indeed sought an introduction to me, as we lived at the same hotel; and I learnt from him that he had attended my lectures at New Orleans, and expressed a great desire to make my acquaintance, but as our intercourse was short and interrupted, I did not learn much from him as to the state of the country. He was on his way to the Virginia springs, to recruit his health. Our fellow passenger was much more communicative, and as there was nothing to interrupt our conversation for several hours, he gave us a great deal of interesting information respecting the country of his late residence.

It appears that Texas, though originally considered but a remote and unimportant province of Mexico, is larger in area than any four of the largest States of America; and at least three times as large as England, Scotland, and Ireland combined. Its borders, on the north-east and south-west, are the two rivers, Sabine and Rio del Norte; the first separating it from Louisiana, and the second from Mexico; each of these large streams being navigable for several hundred miles above their mouths. On the southeast it has a fine range of coast, with several harbours and rivers, presented to the sea; and on the northwest, it passes, without any defined limit, into the territory occupied by the Cumanches, a powerful tribe of Indians, who are constantly receding before their more civilized neighbours. Throughout the whole of this territory, the soil is said to be as fertile as in any part of the world. There are no desert or barren tracts yet known, but all is covered with productive soil. There is more of open prairie land, with rich grass and flowers, than of wood; though these prairies are usually skirted by forests. The land is wavy in surface, and generally rising into gentle hills as you pass upward into the interior from the sea. The climate resembles that of Alabama and Georgia more than Louisiana, because, like the two former, it is dry, and without the marshes and swamps of the latter. There is no extreme cold in any part, or at any season of the year; frost being very rare, and snow almost unknown, while the heats of summer are greatly tempered by the sea-breezes from the Gulf of Mexico, which are felt to a considerable distance inland. The climate is regarded as healthy in the extreme; and everything yet known of it renders this highly probable. Owing to the richness of the soil, and the abundance of prairie land, where there are no forests to be cleared before the cultivator can begin his operation, it seems the most tempting country upon earth for a new settler; for he has only to take possession of his tract of land, and begin to plough it at once; and a few months is sufficient to give him a rich harvest to reward his toils. Two crops of Indian corn are easily grown in each year; and the return is usually about a hundred-fold; a bushel of corn being amply sufficient to plant two acres, and each acre yielding readily from fifty to sixty bushels. Cotton is also produced of as good a quality as that of Alabama and Georgia; and several vessels have already taken cargoes direct to Europe, where it is thought to be equal to the American. These will for a long time, no doubt, continue to be the chief products; though as time progressively fills the country with population, other productions for which the soil and climate are adapted, will no doubt be introduced.

Soon after the inhabitants of Texas, then very few in number, had declared themselves independent of Mexico, the Mexican government made an attempt, as the British had done before them on their American colonies, to reclaim the province by arms; but with no better success. For though their best general, Santa Anna, at the head of nearly 4,000 men, marched into the heart of the province, and had every advantage of position and supplies in his favour, the Texians, composed principally of settlers from Tennessee and Kentucky, all excellent marksmen, and familiar with the use of the rifle from their boyhood, met them at San Jacinto, under the leadership of General Houston, their late president, and, with about 800 men, completely routed the 4,000 Mexicans, took their general prisoner in the disguise of a common soldier, and left more than 800 of his followers dead on the field; while they scarcely lost a dozen men of their own. Since then, the Mexicans have been unwilling or unable to repeat their attempt; and their recent disputes with France, and civil wars among themselves, have so much enfeebled them, as to make them unable to renew their attack; so that although they have not acknowledged the independence of Texas, it seems as firmly established as that of the United States.

The policy of the Texian government being now directed to the encouragement of settlers from all parts of the world, they gave to each of the soldiers belonging to this army, a tract of 640 acres of land, allowing each person the privilege of settling and cultivating it himself, or selling it to others; and as the greater number have chosen the latter alternative, such tracts have been purchased by other settlers for very small sums, varying from five to twenty dollars only. The government gives, also, to every individual who will consent to become a citizen, a tract of 320 acres; and to every head of a family, 640 acres, free of cost; allowing them to choose it in any hitherto unappropriated spot. The only condition exacted is, that the person or persons to whom this is given, shall be in some part of Texas for a certain period of time in each year, for three years in succession; after which they may remain or not, as they choose. The country is therefore fast filling with settlers from every part of the United States, as well as from Europe; the planters coming chiefly from Georgia, Alabama, and Mississippi; and the merchants, traders, and artisans, from New York and the New England States. The present population is estimated at about half a million; but it is augmenting rapidly every day, as scarcely a week passes in which there do not arrive steam vessels from New Orleans and Mobile, bringing from 100 to 200 passengers; and these not needy and destitute emigrants, such as those who land on the shores of New York and Amboy from England and Germany, but persons of some capital, who add doubly to the wealth of the country, first by the money they bring, and next by the industry they take there, and put into immediate and active use.

There are four considerable towns in Texas—two of them of Spanish or Mexican origin, Metamoras on the coast, and Santa Fé in the interior; and two of more recent date, namely, Galveston, the chief seaport, and Houston, the seat of government in the interior. Up to the period of the Texian revolution, Metamoras had been the chief place of import for foreign goods; and the Mexicans and Indians came from the interior, and purchased these goods with specie, usually silver dollars, but sometimes gold doubloons. Santa Fé, which is about 800 miles inland, was the great depôt for the interior trade between Mexico on the one hand, and St. Louis, near the Missouri, on the other, a distance of nearly 1,000 miles, chiefly through tribes of hostile Indians, who occupy the intervening country. To secure themselves against their attacks, the Texians travelled in large bodies of several hundred mules at a time, like the great Eastern caravans of camels in Asia; the merchandise being carried in bales, slung on each side of the animals, and the owners of the goods, being well armed and provisioned, riding on a horse or mule to guard their own property. Such caravans still traverse this part of the country; but it seems probable that Galveston and New Orleans will be the future routes to St. Louis, as the steam-navigation of the Mississippi will be cheaper, safer, and more agreeable, than those long land journeys. Santa Fé is quite like an old Spanish town; it is wholly peopled by Mexicans, Indians, and native Texians, and the people speak no other languages than Indian and Spanish.

Houston, the seat of government, is on the Trinity river, which leads up from the bay of Galveston, and is navigable by steam vessels all the way to the town. It is not more than two years from the present time since the first house was built in Houston, the city being so named after the ex-president, who won the important battle of San Jacinto; and now there are said to be more than 500 substantial dwellings, with two churches, two theatres, several large hotels, and spacious stores in it. The population numbers about 8,000 individuals, and these are nearly all white; as the negroes taken into the country by new settlers are almost wholly engaged in cultivation, on the corn and cotton plantations.

Galveston, the seaport, is seated on an island, in a fine bay, the entrance into which has a passage that will admit ships drawing sixteen feet water. Though within three miles of the sea, in the Gulf of Mexico, the harbour is large, easy of access, well sheltered, with excellent holding-ground, and is distant only three miles from the continent, the space between the two being that in which the ships anchor. The island of Galveston is about thirty miles in length from N.E. to S.W., and not more than three miles in average breadth. It has a hard, sandy, compact beach all along its edge, is not much elevated above the sea, and has few or no trees upon it. It is nevertheless extremely well adapted to the foundation of a seaport town, because the whole length of its inner edge, facing the continent, is, for twenty miles at least, well adapted to building upon the very margin of the harbour, with the ships lying at the wharfs, or in the open water, a short distance off, and always commanding easy access to the shore. As a seaport, indeed, it seems to be one of the very best in all the Gulf of Mexico, from its easy passage, depth of water, amplitude of space, and perfect shelter; and it is more than probable, that before long, a great many of the ships that now frequent Vera Cruz, Tampico, and the Havannah, will prefer Galveston.

Here, as at Houston, the progress in building has been most rapid, more than 800 houses having been erected, it is said, in the course of the last year. These are run up with such rapidity, that a case was mentioned of a three-story house, with stores in the ground-floor, and dwellings above, being completed in the course of twenty-eight days from the laying of the foundation; and it was occupied within a month from its commencement. So many persons are waiting, indeed, for stores, and houses to occupy, that most exorbitant rents are given; and it has often happened that on a house being finished, the competition for its possession has been so keen, that the annual rental, settled by biddings at public auction, has been equal to the whole cost of the construction. With this, paid usually in advance, the owner has constructed another in a few weeks, and let it at the same advantageous rate. The demand for artificers is so great, and their wages so high, that five to six hundred carpenters and masons were in constant employment, and receiving generally from six to eight dollars per day, as wages. Provisions of all kinds are abundant and cheap: excellent beef, mutton, and poultry, fish of various sorts, and oysters, wild turkeys in the woods and on the river's banks; deer in great numbers, to be had for the shooting, by any one who chose to kill them; and wild horses, of a small but hardy kind, on the prairies, easily caught, easily broken in, and then pleasant for riding. All business is done on immediate payment; and it is very rare that credit is given, or books of account kept.

The public sentiment being decidedly hostile to chartered banks, every attempt to get one incorporated by the legislature has failed; so that, as yet, there is no bank in all Texas. The government have made an issue of treasury-notes, bearing interest at 10 per cent per annum, redeemable in a given period, two or three years, and these constitute the only paper currency of the country. Specie is, however, abundant, as all the trade with Mexico and the Havannah is conducted by specie payments. The ratio of value between the treasury-notes and specie is just double; every silver dollar being worth two dollars in Texian paper. General Hamilton, and Mr. Nicholas Biddle, the late president of the United States Bank, have been commissioned, it is said, to negotiate a loan of 5,000,000l. sterling, in London, on the security of the public lands and revenue of the nation; and if they succeed, the present treasury notes will all be redeemed, and a new issue take place. As there is no probability of their being engaged in a war with any foreign country, nor of their being liable to any civil contests within themselves, this loan of 5,000,000l. may be paid off in twenty years at the farthest, or in ten if it be desirable; and the country be then in full possession of all the means of self-support and future advancement.

The form of government is that of two houses of legislature and a governor, as in the several States of America; and where no statute has been passed on any subject by the legislature of Texas, the laws of the neighbouring State of Louisiana are adhered to.

The present president, General La Mar, is much esteemed, and is said to be a man of high moral principle. Many excellent laws and regulations for the suppression of gambling, intemperance, and other vicious habits and practices, have received his sanction; and the newspapers, of which there are already four, two at Galveston and two at Houston, support him with remarkable unanimity in this course. It seems admitted indeed on all hands, that not only is the population rapidly augmenting in numbers, but also greatly improving in character; and all the future prospects of the country are therefore full of hope and encouragement.

Our long ride through the deep forests of Alabama passed rapidly, and agreeably, and we all remarked that we had never before remembered any journey of the same length in which we had suffered less fatigue. When night closed in upon us, there was a new source of contemplative enjoyment opened, in the deep and shadowy gloom, and the profound and solemn stillness of the thick and apparently impervious woods which still encompassed our road on either side. For miles in succession, not a being would be visible, and no sound audible but those made by our own motion, till, every now and then, the gurgling noise of some falling or running water would indicate our approach to a stream; and myriads of frogs would announce, by their harsh croakings, the vicinity of a swamp.

It was four o'clock in the morning when we reached the banks of the Chatahoochee river, the rushing waters of which, rolling over its rocky bed, were welcome music to the ear, and, after crossing the bridge, we entered Columbus, and took up our quarters at the Oglethorpe Hotel.

Chapter XXVII

Columbus, which lies at the western extremity of the State of Georgia, is seated on the left bank of the river Chathahoochee, which divides this State from Alabama, and which, rising a great distance to the north of this, goes downward by a winding course of about 450 miles, from hence to the bay of Apalachicola, where it discharges itself into the Gulf of Mexico. It has several rapids above the town, and a very rocky bed immediately opposite to it, so as to impede navigation above this point; but from hence to the sea, it is navigable by steamboats of small burden, which are principally occupied in the transportation of goods.

It is not more than eleven years since the first house in Columbus was built, yet there is now a population of about 4,000 persons, of whom 3,000 are whites, and 1,000 blacks and coloured people; the fewness of the latter, in comparison with most of the Southern towns, arises from the fact that it is not so much an agricultural place as Montgomery, Macon, or Augusta, but chiefly commercial, and its principal residents are adventurers from the New England States.

Columbus being a county town, has, or rather had, a Court House, for the transaction of its judicial business; but it was recently burnt down, and is now ascertained to have been set on fire purposely by interested incendiaries; some of whom have been apprehended and tried, and the evidence, though not amounting to legal proof, was abundantly strong for moral conviction. It appears that some very nefarious transactions had taken place, in the fraudulent transfer and occupation of lands belonging to the Cherokee Indians, who had but recently been removed from parts of this State; and the documents necessary to give even a colourable pretext for such transfer, were deposited in the Record Office, which was in the Court House. Some disgraceful exposures being anticipated as the result of certain legal proceedings then pending on this subject, the parties implicated sought to suppress all evidence of their guilt, by burning the records, which, unhappily for the cause of justice, they succeeded in doing.

The conflagration, however, carried away with it other and important records of real and honourable transactions; and the knowledge of their destruction as evidence, led some unprincipled persons to take advantage of this fact, so that much litigation ensued in consequence. The Court was now sitting, in its fifth week, and had not got through half its business, though engaged from eight in the morning till two in the afternoon, adjourning an hour to dinner, meeting again at three, and sitting on always till sunset, and sometimes till midnight!

In the sitting-room which we occupied at Columbus, was a full-length portrait of General M'Intosh, the late chief of the Creek nation, habited in that singular mixture of European and Indian costume, which the semi-civilized chiefs delighted to wear, and being what is called a "half-breed," the son of a Scotch father and Indian mother, he had a fairer complexion and more European air than a full-blooded Indian. His character appeared to be held in the highest esteem by the American residents in Columbus, chiefly because many of them had profited by his treachery; but, as far as we could learn his history, even from the testimony of his admirers, it was base and dishonourable towards the tribe of which he was the chief and leader. The Creek nation were the occupants and admitted proprietors of a large portion of the soil of Georgia, embracing an area of 900 square miles, up to a comparatively recent period (1825), and the government of the United States, in pursuance of their long-settled policy of removing all the Indian tribes to the territories west of the Mississippi, made great efforts to prevail on the Creeks to sell their lands, and emigrate westward. As these Indians, however, like the Cherokees, had made some advances in civilization, had built houses, enclosed and cultivated farms, and were leading an agricultural and social life, they were exceedingly averse to moving, and rejected all offers made to them. Measures were then taken to bribe the chief, M'Intosh, into an acquiescence with the views of the government, and to employ his influence to bribe and seduce a few others to join him in the design. These represented themselves as the competent authorities of the whole Creek nation, which they were not. As such, they made a treaty with the United States' commissioners, agreeing, for certain considerations, to alienate their lands, and remove to the west of the Mississippi; and the government, though they know this to be unauthorized by the great body of the Creeks, proceeded in the transaction as though is were fully in accordance with the national wish. To preserve, however, as much as possible, the *forms* of legal proceeding, though its spirit was about to be violated, a council was called by the commissioners—all of whom were Georgians, and therefore personally and pecuniarily interested in the possession of the Indians' lands—and the place fixed on for the meeting was at a spot called "Indian Spring." Here the treaty of sale and cession of the Creek lands was signed. But when the rest of the nation saw that the treaty could not be abrogated, they resolved to be revenged on their chief, by whom they had been thus betrayed. About two hours before daylight, on Sunday morning, May 1st, the house of General M'Intosh was surrounded by Menaw-way, and about 100 Oakfuskee warriors. M'Intosh was within, as were also his women and children, and some white men. Menaw-way directed an interpreter to request the whites, and the women and children, to come out, as the warriors did not wish to harm them; that General M'Intosh had broken the law which he himself had long since made, and they had come to execute him accordingly. They came out of the house, leaving M'Intosh and Etomi-tustenugge, one of his adherents, therein. The warriors then set fire to the house, and as M'Intosh and his companion attempted to come out, they shot them dead.

Notwithstanding this, the treaty was acted on by the United States' government, and force was employed to compel the Indians to remove. This led, as might have been expected, to resistance; and in the war thus created, the greatest atrocities were perpetrated on either side. Columbus and its neighbourhood had its full share of the horrors of this bloody campaign; the recollection of which, indeed, is so fresh in the memory of most of the inhabitants here, that they seem to feel a renewal of the terrors inspired by the original events while describing them to others. The following copy of a letter, written from hence, at the time, May 11th, 1836, will give some idea of their nature.

I wrote you yesterday, informing you of the hostile movements of the Creek Indians, and the commencement of their murderous career. We have full information here to-day of the distressing state of things among the whites who have settled over in that territory. The Indians are killing all—men, women, and children. Vast numbers have been butchered, without doubt; and the whole country on this side of the Chattahoochee is in uproar and confusion. The population of the territory had become considerable, and they who have been fortunate enough to escape, are come over in droves on the Georgia side; some with a part of their children; some who have lost their children; some their husbands; and many children without father or mother; some are found as they were wandering about, so young, that they could give no account who their parents were. So perfect a mixture and confusion never was witnessed before. Many have seen a part of their families murdered. One gentleman saw his father shot down near him, and his mother and sisters. Some of the dead have been brought over shockingly mangled. It is thought the whole nation is in hostile array; their warriors are computed at 6,000 or 7,000 strong. The general impression is that a part of the Seminoles have come up among them. The town of Columbus is in great danger of an attack, as they have threatened it strongly. A company of forty or fifty men left Columbus yesterday morning, and went over. On their return at night they brought in seven children, which they had found scattered about.

The following additional narratives of these horrible transactions, taken from authentic records of the same period, will complete the picture.

On Monday we received information that hostilities had commenced on the road between Columbus and Montgomery, at the Uchee bridge, and further on, and in the evening, the bridge at this place, and the streets leading from it, were thronged with the unfortunate refugees, who were fleeing before their savage neighbours. The pitiable condition of many of them was past the power of description. Wives severed from their husbands, and parents from their children—all dismayed, all terror-stricken—presented a scene which we never again desire to see. An interesting-looking girl, just blooming into womanhood, was brought in on horseback, behind a benevolent stranger, who had found her in the nation, making her way, unattended, to this place. She started with her parents, but before they had proceeded far, they were brutally shot down before her eyes. She fled to the woods, and escaped from her savage pursuers, and was found and brought to Columbus as above stated.

A young man arrived at this place also witnessed the savage murder of his parents. Another young man, in the act of fleeing, perceived the Indians dragging away his sister. He returned, declaring he would rescue her or die in the attempt, and he has not been heard of. From this time their deeds of savage barbarity have been too numerous to particularize. A woman was brought in on Tuesday, wounded in the hand, whose husband had been shot the preceding evening at the Uchee bridge. Colonel A.B. Dawson's negroes, who were taken by the Indians, and made their escape, state that they saw three corpses on the road near the Uchee bridge; a man, woman, and child, who had all been murdered. We learn that about 150 friendly Indians have reported themselves at Fort Mitchell, and are ready to assist the whites. Accounts to the 17th of May further state that the Indians had entered the house of one family, and murdered the whole—including husband, wife, and six children. All were scalped, and the children beheaded. The house of a Mr. Colton had been attacked, and himself killed.

About the end of June, a party of whites, who were scouting on Flint river, accidentally found a young woman about three miles from

Cambridge, who had been wounded by a shot in the breast. She stated, that, on the 26th of June, about 300 Indians killed all the family to which she belonged, thirteen in number, except herself and her father, who made his escape. After being shot, she feigned death, and as the murdered were not scalped, she made her escape after the Indians left the scene of butchery.

These events happened about three years ago only, but though the greater part of the Creek Indians have been actually removed, and their lands are now held by American purchasers, yet the Creek war can hardly yet be said to be at an end; for a number of fugitive Indians, who would not join the removing party, still continue in the territory, and pursue a sort of guerrilla warfare against the whites, whenever an opportunity offers for revenge. Even now, in May 1839, during our actual stay at Columbus, the following events occurred, and were made public in the Columbus papers.

MORE INDIAN MURDERS.—The following letter, giving an account of the murder of several persons on the Apalachicola river, by the Indians, was received by our postmaster yesterday morning, and politely handed us for publication.

The steamer Siren, arrived this evening from Apalachicola, brings information of a horrid massacre committed by a party of Indians, on Friday night last, on the Apalachicola river, about fifty miles below the junction of the Chattahoochee and Flint rivers. Seven or eight individuals of both sexes were murdered, and their bodies burned. The Siren stopped at the spot on Sunday, and the crew and passengers interred the remains of the murdered.

Since the above was in type, we have received the Apalachicola Gazette of the 11th inst., which gives the following additional particulars.

A party of fifteen or twenty Indians, recognized to be Creeks, simultaneously attacked the settlement of Roberts, at Stefanulgee, and John and Nathan Smith's, Rico's Bluff. They burned Roberts' houses, killed a little boy, and wounded Roberts himself, who, with his wife, a man named Aldrich, and four children, escaped.

At Smith's settlement, it is supposed that Nathan Smith's three children, a Mrs. Richards and her five children, and a man named White, were murdered. N. Smith, with his wife, another woman, and two men, escaped. John Lamb was severely wounded; he recognized the Indians to be Creeks. Sixteen of the fugitives, men, women, and children, came down on the mail boat, and are completely destitute. Several of the

Indians were seen on the banks of the river, as the boat came through the narrows, miles above Fort Gadsden.

After all, it is hardly to be wondered at, that the Indians should thus act and feel towards their betrayers and oppressors; especially as the sentiment of vindictiveness, and the duty of revenge, forms so important a feature of their training and education from infancy to old age. According to the testimony of persons with whom we conversed on this subject at Columbus, it was a common practice with the whites, who had congregated here as land speculators, at the conclusion of M'Intosh's treaty before mentioned, to act thus. They would first decoy one of the Indians of the Creek tribe, by prevailing on him to drink whiskey; and when they had got him thus completely under their control, they would procure two other Indians, and two unprincipled whites as witnesses, get the Indian to swear in their presence to a document describing the boundaries of certain plots of land, as being his property, and assigning it over to the white purchaser, for a large consideration, in money, and in goods. They would then take him before a district court, or magistrate, who would publicly ratify this sale; and after paying the Indian, perhaps, a twentieth of the sum set forth in the document of sale, they would get the white witnesses to swear that he had been paid the whole amount in their presence, and had afterwards squandered or lost it. The whites then shared with each other the fruits of this atrocious system of robbery and plunder. I was assured that there were American land-owners in various parts of Georgia, who were now men of immense fortunes, acquired chiefly by this mode; and that nearly all the Indian purchases were conducted more or less after this fashion. No wonder, therefore, when the Indians became sober, and saw how they had been duped by the superior craft and cunning of their white plunderers, that they should vow eternal enmity against the whole race, and feel a savage satisfaction in perpetrating all the atrocities of war against them in its most brutal and bloody shape.

The influence of such transactions as these fraudulent land-purchases, on the general state of society at Columbus, is felt very powerfully at present, and will continue to be felt, no doubt, for years to come. That there are some excellent, honourable families living there, and in its neighbourhood, is undoubtedly true; but the great bulk of the community furnish some of the worst specimens of character, and the reputation of Columbus stands at a low estimate.

CHAPTER XXVIII

After being detained longer than we wished, from the difficulty of getting conveyances for Macon, we considered ourselves fortunate in being at length released from our confinement at Columbus. On our first passing this way to the South, there were three lines of public stages in competition with each other; and then, every facility was afforded to the traveller. Since then, one had been given up; and the other had been bought off, so that there was now only one line running, and it made the most of its monopoly. The proprietors being the only persons having horses or coaches, would not let an extra or private conveyance to any one, but preferred keeping them at the hotel till their regular stage coach should have vacancies, and then they were taken up to fill them. This was our case; we could get no extra or private conveyance of any kind, and were kept at the hotel for several days, while the coach went through full. The first vacancy that offered was, when there were places for two; and our party, consisting of four, were crammed into the coach against the will of the others occupying it; as there was but barely room for nine, yet we were obliged to ride with eleven inside; but there was no remedy, the monopolists having all power in their hands. Besides this excess of numbers, we were overladen with baggage; and an arbitrary charge was made of forty dollars for our fare, and thirty dollars for our baggage; to which, for the same reason, we were obliged to submit.

We left Columbus on the morning of Monday May 13, and though we were crowded most inconveniently, and had not a single interesting fellow passenger in all the group, we were heartily glad to escape. The day was unusually hot, and the roads so dusty as to keep us continually enveloped in a thick cloud, with every now and then some accident to the coach from its being so overladen, which obliged us to get out, and assist to repair the injury. The rails or fences of the roads were liberally used for this purpose and it was fortunate that a supply of props, levers, and posts, was thus so near at hand.

It was about four o'clock when we reached Talbotton, where the whole community were agitated by a recent occurrence, which is strikingly characteristic of the state of society in these parts, and of the manner in which the people take the law into their own hands. It appears that there was a lady who had been settled for a few months as a teacher of music at Talbotton, but not having obtained many pupils, she had contracted more debts than she could pay, and went on to Columbus to seek better fortune there. At this place, she wished to hire or rent a house, but the owner would not let it without some guarantee for the payment of the rent; and some resident of Talbotton became her security for this. As it was not paid, however, in due time, and as other debts were also unliquidated, the lady was arrested at Columbus by process of law. This, the inhabitants of Talbotton chose to interpret as an insult to their town, from whence she had come; and accordingly, a large number of the young men of Talbotton mounted their horses, armed themselves with weapons, and rode off to Columbus, where they effected her release, and assumed such an attitude that it was thought at one time, nothing short of a civil war between the two towns must follow. It had gradually cooled down, however, into a state of peace; but no legal authorities interfered to stay the proceedings of these young cavaliers, who carried their point, and made what they called "public opinion" completely triumph over the laws.

The night was as disagreeably cold, as the day was inconveniently hot; and from the impossibility of keeping out the drafts and currents of air, which rushed in at all the many openings that an American stage presents, we suffered much during the twenty-six hours, which it took to perform the distance of ninety miles to Macon.

There were two subjects, on which my opinions were sufficiently well known to make me obnoxious to two large classes of American citizens, and especially those of the South. The part I had taken in the British Parliament, in favour of the Abolition of Slavery in our West India possessions, was well known to every one who read the public journals; and this was enough to occasion me to be classed with the hated yet dreaded class of the Abolitionists. The part I had taken both in England and in this country, in the war against Intemperance, was equally well known to all classes; and this made me particularly obnoxious to all tavern-keepers, gamblers, frequenters of bar-rooms and grog-shops, and to cause me to be denounced as a Temperance Fanatic. And as in all these newly settled towns, like Columbus, Macon, and others of recent date, there are large numbers of reckless men ready for any riot or outrage, it is quite probable that if the least opportunity had been offered to them, they would have had great pleasure in making me their victim.

My servant indeed, overheard some half-drunken men around the door of one of the bar-rooms exulting in the idea of a probable "tarring and feathering" and recounting with great glee a feat lately performed on some stranger suspected by them of being an Abolitionist, whom they dragged from his bedroom, placed astride on a rail, carried him in mock-triumph through the town in this plight, and ended the penance by ducking him in a neighbouring swamp! This story was afterwards confirmed to us by some of the most respectable inhabitants of the town, who assured us, that though they felt indignant at such conduct, and would willingly have prevented its occurrence, or secured the injured party redress, they could do neither without endangering their own lives and properties, so entirely could these reckless ruffians get and keep command of the town. As it was the season when the low gamblers and pickpockets come up from New Orleans and the South, for the spring and summer months, the town was thought to be more than usually full of them, and it was therefore deemed best to remain quiet, and do nothing to provoke an outbreak, which if once roused, could not be so easily resisted or subdued.

It is worthy of remark, that when these parties were asked, as several of them were, what was the ground of their objection to me, not one stated the true cause, namely, my being hostile to Slavery, and friendly to Temperance, but one urged the fact of my "being an Englishman;" another said, I had "offered an insult to the country by saying that the Broadway of New York, though a noble street, was not so grand an avenue as the principal street of the ancient city of Alexandria;" and a third added, that I had "insulted the national character, by saying that the Bunker Hill monument at Boston, was not to be compared for size with the great pyramid of Egypt!" Such were the various pretexts which were alleged, instead of the real causes of offence; but the vindictiveness of the complainers, if once put into action, would not have been the less summary or less severe on that account.

Happily all was avoided, as on the morning of Thursday the 16th of May, we obtained an extra coach for our journey forward to Milledgeville; and being provided by our kind friends with many comforts for the way, we left Macon about ten o'clock, agreeing to pay fifty dollars for the journey of thirty miles, the regular stage fare being only twelve dollars for four persons, of which our party consisted. But the coach-monopoly continued in the same hands all along the road, and we were, therefore, obliged to submit to any terms.

As we approached Milledgeville, we met great numbers of persons on horseback and in gigs, from fifty to sixty at least, returning homeward from a convention that had been holding in that town, and which had adjourned this morning. When within five or six miles of Milledgeville, we approached the ridge of a hill, from whence a fine prospect of the town, and the rich valley in which it lies, is to be had. Being prepared for this by our driver, we halted to enjoy it, and were amply rewarded. We had seen nothing in the South, indeed, so beautiful, as a landscape; for while the valley itself was broad, deep, and most luxuriant in wood and foliage, the town in its centre appeared to add greatly to its richness the State House or Capitol, the governor's residence, some few churches with spires, and a pretty cluster of white dwellings, surrounded by gardens, made up a charming picture.

We reached Milledgeville about eight o'clock, having been ten hours going thirty miles, though we were only four persons in the coach, had four horses all the way, and did not stop either to lunch or dine on the road; so that this may be regarded as the minimum of coach speed—three miles an hour! We found the town in a complete bustle by the breaking up of the convention, and preparations for departure. The streets were full of vehicles of every description, horses, and people; and all the verandas of the hotels and boarding-houses were crowded with persons lounging about on chairs in the open air. This is a habit common to all Americans, but universal in the South, where from 50 to 100 persons may be seen from sunset till bedtime, sitting in front of every hotel, and from ten to twenty persons in front of almost every private house, in all varieties of attitudes, except the natural and erect one; the chairs are poised on one or both of their hind-posts, while the legs of the sitters are thrown into as great a variety of forms as ingenuity can devise, but they are rarely ever seen in the ordinary mode of sitting in use with us.

The members of the convention consisted of about 300 persons only; but they had brought more than twice that number of visitors in their train. Its object was to consider the propriety of reducing the number of members in both houses of the State legislature, to one-half their present amount. It had been found, by experience, that though in the multitude of counsellors there may be sometimes wisdom, yet that there is always too much talking; and as there are but two ways of correcting this evil, one by limiting the time to be occupied by each speaker, and the other to lessen their number, the convention, authorized by the legislature to propose the remedy they thought best, chose the latter. After a week's debate, they proposed, and carried by a large majority, a series of resolutions for reducing the senators from 96 to 42; and the members of the house of representatives from 276 to 138. Most persons anticipate great benefit from this; first in lessening the length of time consumed in each session; secondly, in causing greater attention to the nature of the laws passed; and, thirdly, in saving considerable expense to all parties. I have always thought that a similar reduction in the number of our legislators, or some restraint on the length of their speeches, or some better division of labour in the discharge of their duties, would be productive of corresponding benefits in England; and if a convention of delegates from the people could be legitimately formed, as in America, I have no doubt that such a reduction would be approved by a large majority. But, unhappily, this simple, yet efficient, mode of submitting all such questions to the real test of popular opinion, is unknown to our constitution. Therefore every great change, in the nature of a reform, can only be carried by years of agitation; nor even then until it approaches the very brink of a revolution. These conventions, on the contrary, are admirable and easy safety-valves, by which political pressure is let off, like surplus steam, and all fearful explosions thereby avoided.

On the following morning, May 17, we were enabled to secure another extra coach to take us from Milledgeville to Warrenton, a distance of forty-six miles, for seventy-five dollars, or at the rate of about six shillings and ninepence sterling per mile. We were still, however, in the hands of the monopolists, and this accounted for all.

We left Milledgeville about eight o'clock, and as we passed through the town outward, we admired the good taste of the governor's official residence, a beautiful building, in the purest style of the Ionic order. But the Capitol, or State House, seemed to us less perfect in a near view than at a distance; it being a large white Gothic structure, in bad taste and heavy proportions, though forming a very striking object in the remote picture of Milledgeville. There was a large penitentiary also in the town, and from 300 to 400 dwellings; but though its situation struck me as peculiarly interesting in the general picture of the valley, the town itself had no particular object of interest beyond those already enumerated.

Our journey to Warrenton was through a beautiful country, with great varieties of wood, rich soil, and abundant productions in corn, oats, rye, and cotton, all giving promise of an abundant harvest. We changed horses every ten or twelve miles, and halted at Sparta for half an hour, yet we did not reach Warrenton till eight at night, having been twelve hours in performing forty-eight miles. As it began to rain heavily about an hour before we halted, and the coaches are so loosely covered in as to afford very little protection, either from wet or cold, I suffered much from the change, and was glad enough to reach a resting place.

In this obscure village, containing only a few houses, and deriving all its attraction from being the present terminus of the railroad from Augusta, I had thought we should be wholly unknown, and counted therefore upon an undisturbed and early retirement to rest. I was surprised, however, to find that there were two individuals, one a Scotchman and the other an Englishman, to whom I was well known, though under different circumstances. The first had been a resident at Sheffield, employed in the establishment of Messrs Rodgers and Co. there; and had voted as one of my constituents in my first election to Parliament as member for that borough. The second was a glazier in London, at the time of the passing the Reform Bill; and had been employed to repair some of the windows of our residence in Piccadilly, broken by the mob in their indiscriminate attack on the houses of all those who did not illuminate on that occasion. Both of them had subsequently come to America to improve their condition; and both had succeeded in so doing; the first being now in business as a general merchant or trader, and the second being established as a master builder, and each prospering in his new vocation. They appeared to be as glad to see us and talk with us as if we had been old friends or relatives. They added, that the sight of any one from "the old country" was the most agreeable that could meet their view and the sound of their words, perfect music to their ears. We left Warrenton at eight o'clock, going about four miles on the railroad, drawn by mules. These are in very general use in Georgia, and come mostly from Kentucky and Tennessee where they are bred in large numbers for exportation and sale.

From hence we took the cars drawn by steam engine, and reached Augusta at one o'clock, going fifty-five miles in five hours, at a cost of four and a half cents, or about two pence per mile, instead of six shillings and nine pence, the rate of the preceding journey. This great increase of speed and reduction of expense make railroads even more advantageous here than in England; and from the zeal and vigour with which they are projecting and carrying forward all over the country, there is little doubt but that in a few years hence, all the high-roads will be traversed by them from Maine to Louisiana. Among our passengers was a sorrowing mother going to Augusta in search of a son of nine years old, whom the jockeys or horse-racers had decoyed away from his home, to train him as a rider. As she had never before seen a steam engine, she was greatly alarmed at its appearance and between her apprehensions of danger, and grief for her lost child, she seemed miserable in the extreme.

We remained a few days at Augusta and during the cool of the evenings, enjoyed some very pleasant drives in the neighbourhood of the town, especially at the little suburb called Summerville, or the Sand Hills. This is a village about three miles to the westward of Augusta, seated on a sandy elevation, about 150 feet above the level of the town, or 200 feet above the level of the river. The roads to it are pleasantly sheltered by wood, though the soil is very sandy. On the summit of the hill is a military barrack and arsenal, built at the expense of the United States' government, as a depôt for troops, though there are rarely more than a small staff of officers here, who have a pleasant residence, and form an agreeable addition to the society of the place. The dwellings on the hills are all detached summer residences of merchants and traders in easy circumstances, whose families live here during the hot months, instead of removing to more remote places. They are constructed after the fashion of bungalows in the East Indies, are frequently of one story only, and rarely more than two, with verandas or balconies all around, and embosomed in deep groves and gardens, so as to secure to them a perpetual shade, and make them very cool and agreeable abodes.

During our stay at Augusta, we learnt, from resident families there, some curious facts respecting the state of society, and peculiarities of opinion. It appears, that almost all the married persons resident here, become members or communicants of some church; and it is hardly thought reputable not to be associated with some religious body or other. Up to the period of marriage however, it is not deemed so necessary; and few or none of the unmarried persons are therefore members. To all who are members, dancing is strictly prohibited; and it is thought highly improper even to mix in large parties where dancing is practised by others, though the members should not join in the exercise.

It is deemed their duty not to countenance this amusement, even by their presence. No members of churches, as heads of families, therefore, ever give a party for dancing; and if any such exercise is enjoyed, it can only be by the unmarried. But of late, a curious evasion of this prohibition has been practised with success in this manner: the family give what is called "a social party" to which a large number are invited to take tea, and spend the evening. When tea is over, some young lady places herself at the piano, and strikes up a quadrille. Presently couples rise, and speedily a "spontaneous and unpremeditated dance" is got up, and continued with great spirit till midnight. This point has been submitted, it is said, to the judgment of the clergy who have decided, that if the carpets were taken up, and violins employed, and ball-dresses used, then it would be unequivocally "a dance" and, as such, clearly sinful. But the carpets being down, no music used but that of a pianoforte, and the ladies not in ball costume, it could not be considered anything more than a "social party" and in this all might innocently join.

On the subject of religious revivals, also, we heard some curious particulars. There are fixed periods of the year in which these are regularly got up, in Georgia and the Carolinas, as in a prescribed circuit. The periods chosen are those in which there is the least business doing in the towns or on the plantations. The ministers, among whom those of the Methodist and Baptist persuasions take the lead, then organize the proceedings in such a manner as to produce considerable effect; and thus add every year to the number of their communicants. It is said that this is sometimes done in schools and colleges, where youths of nine to fifteen are so wrought upon as to proclaim themselves converts, and make public profession of a new birth; but it is doubted by the less zealous and enthusiastic, whether the instances in which these conversions arise are so numerous as those in which the parties fall off, and, by a reaction, oscillate to the opposite extreme of indifference, or something worse.

CHAPTER XXIX

On Saturday 25th of May, we left Augusta at five in the morning, and crossing over the Savannah river by the bridge, we got into the railroad cars at the village of Hamburgh, and started on our journey to Charleston at six o'clock. This railroad was originally laid across all the hollow and swampy parts of the way on the ends of perpendicular posts; and in many places these rose to a height of twenty feet above the lower level; so that a turn off the road by the engine and cars would have been fatal to all embarked in them and even the looking over on each side affected the passengers disagreeably. It was found, indeed, to be so objectionable, that for the last year a number of men have been employed filling up these hollows, and the work is now nearly complete. This has occasioned, however, so much outlay of expense, that the State Legislature has passed an act authorizing the directors of the railroad to raise the fare from six to ten dollars, and to keep it at this rate till the outlay is repaid. The whole length of the road is 126 miles. In the early part of the journey we were drawn up an inclined plane by a stationary engine—the length of the plane being 3,800 feet, and the elevation 180 feet; the whole ascent for the first sixteen miles being 360 feet, and the descent from thence to Charleston, 510 feet.

We reached Charleston about three o'clock, having been nine hours on the road, and, allowing for stoppages, completed the journey at the rate of about fifteen miles in the hour all the way. We took up our quarters at the Planters' Hotel, and remained there a fortnight, during which we were much more comfortably accommodated than on our first visit; and under the new management introduced into it, since our former stay here, we found improvement in every department; the table especially being made equal to any in the United States.

On the day of our arrival in Charleston, May 25, there was a duel fought in the public street, and in the presence of many people, none of whom interfered to prevent it. Two young men from the country were in attendance at the Court of Law then sitting in Charleston, and some angry words having passed between them, there was an immediate challenge given and accepted; when the parties, either having pistols with them, or procuring them very speedily, repaired to the public street, and there, in the middle of the day, and in the presence of several spectators and passers-by, measured off twelve paces and exchanged fire. One of the combatants was shot through the cheek, and disfigured for life, and the other was slightly wounded in the thigh. The parties then withdrew from the combat, but no notice was taken of the affair by the public authorities, and with the community it excited no sensation beyond the passing hour!

In the State of Mississippi, all law, civil and criminal, seemed to be at a stand. Public meetings had been recently held, at which the speakers had proposed, and the hearers passed resolutions, to the effect that they would offer resistance in a body, to the execution of all writs or other civil processes for the seizure and sale of goods; and judges administering the criminal law, had been insulted, and even struck, on the bench. This frenzy and disorder is no doubt chiefly the offspring of extreme distress; that distress, the result of recklessness and undue indulgence of the passions; and this recklessness, to a great extent the offspring of the system of Slavery.

During my stay in this country, all I have yet seen has tended to confirm me in the opinion that Slavery, as a system, by its influence on those brought up surrounded by it, produces several effects—1st. It indisposes men who are free to use any kind of labour which can be done by slaves; and leads them to devise means of avoiding regular and laborious occupations, by entering into reckless and extravagant speculations. 2ndly. It furnishes constant temptation and opportunity for the indulgence of the passions; it begets a taste for extravagance and a love of display, as the means of assuming and exhibiting a superiority of condition, and exacting the homage paid to supposed wealth. 3rdly. It trains the free child in the constant exercise of arbitrary power over his little slave companions; it makes him impatient of contradiction from any source, as he is always accustomed to command; and it engenders such a habit of quick resentment and instant retaliation for any injury, real or supposed, by the frequent opportunities of its indulgence on unresisting and helpless slaves, that at length it forms a part of the individual's nature, and can neither be conquered nor restrained.

On the subject of that aversion to labour which is felt by all white people where slaves exist, it is hardly necessary to say a word, or to offer proof beyond assertion, as this effect is well known to all, and to none better than to slaveholders themselves. But on the subject of love of display, as engendered by this system, I may state, that in conversation with persons engaged in business, and practically acquainted with the habits of the South, I was assured that the instances in which men lived within their income were extremely rare; while those in which they lived beyond it, were so common as almost to merit the term universal. Of the merchants and traders in Mississippi especially, it had been the general custom for them to make a visit to New York in the autumn, and, after visiting the fashionable watering places, to lay in a large stock of goods on credit in New York, for sale in Mississippi. And the eagerness of the New York importer to force his sales, for the sake of appearing to do an extensive business, and thus bolstering up his own credit, is scarcely less than that of the Mississippi buyer to invest largely without payment, and go back with an immense supply. This supply was readily sold, either on credit, or for local bank-notes, which were freely advanced, on almost any security, to persons wishing to speculate. The proceeds were then invested by the Mississippi trader in lands, negroes, and houses. He forthwith became an extensive planter; and in this capacity he could raise money on his lands and slaves by mortgage, and get advances from New York merchants on his crops of cotton before they were grown. In this manner many an adventurer from the State of Mississippi, not worth 100 dollars, would obtain credit for 50,000 dollars, become nominally possessed of plantations worth 100,000 dollars and setting up carriages, building villas, and surrounding himself with all kinds of luxuries, would live at the rate of a man worth 1,000,000. The ladies of such a family would of course have their share of expenditure in ornament and fashion; and it is thought that more gold watches and jewellery of every description had been sold and worn in the State of Mississippi, within the last three years, than in any of the oldest States of the Union. When the time came round for payments, that which had been expended in thoughtless extravagance and display, could not of course be recalled; and the result may be seen by the following picture, drawn by a Mississippi editor, in the midst of the scene itself—

DISTRESSING TIMES IN MISSISSIPPI.—Never in the history of Mississippi has there been such a pressure in monetary affairs as at the present moment; and never, we imagine, has the *future* been shrouded in a deeper and more portentous gloom than at this time. Here in the city of Vicksburg, and the county of Warren, the darkest days of 1837 presented but a faint picture to what is now exhibited, and from every town and county in the State we have the same melancholy prospect. The whole community is literally upon the *rack*, and the best men in the country find it impossible to raise any amount of money, except at the most ruinous sacrifices. We are entirely destitute of a circulating medium, while thousands upon thousands are pressing for the collection of their claims—suit after suit is instituted until the docket is becoming swelled beyond any former precedent. Property is sold daily in our streets for one-fourth its value.—Men give up all they possess to satisfy their creditors, see their property knocked down under the hammer of the sheriff or the marshal, at one-fourth at least of its value, and find themselves beggars, so far as present means can make them so, and still hopelessly involved. A gentleman informs us that a lot of ground in this city, which one year ago brought 5,000 dollars was sold last week for less than 500; and yet, horrible as affairs are here, they are trifling to what we hear from Yazoo, Holmes, Hinds, &c. We are informed that land and negroes are selling under execution for a fifth of their real value. Negroes, first-rate hands, that will generally command 1,000 dollars, have sold for less than 200, while some of the best plantations in the State are being sacrificed for one-tenth their value. When or where this is to stop, God only knows.

When, or from whence relief is to come, we know not; but unless relief does come, and come speedily, this country will present a scene of wide-spread ruin and desolation, such as has never been witnessed before. The prospect is frightful to contemplate.—*Vicksburg Whig*[1]

The effect of the Slave system to engender the vindictive passions, and to present continual opportunities for their exercise, was clearly perceived by one of the most sagacious minds of this country. Jefferson, the principal framer of the Declaration of American Independence, who, himself a slave-owner, thus expresses himself in his "Notes on Virginia":—

There must doubtless be an unhappy influence on the manners of our people, produced by the existence of slavery among us. The whole commerce between master and slave is a perpetual exercise of the most boisterous passions, the most unremitting despotism on the one part, and degrading submissions on the other. Our children see this, and learn to imitate it, for man is an imitative animal. This quality is the germ of all education in him. From his cradle to his grave, he is learning to do what he sees others do. If a parent could find no motive, either in his philanthropy or his self-love, for restraining the intemperance of passion toward his slave, it should always be a sufficient one, that his child is present. But generally it is not sufficient. The parent storms; the child looks on, and catches the lineaments of wrath, puts on the same airs in the circle of smaller slaves, gives a loose to his worst of passions, and, thus nursed, educated, and daily exercised in tyranny, cannot but be stamped by it with odious peculiarities. The man must be a prodigy, who can retain his manners and morals undepraved by such circumstances.

Hence the universal irritability of temper, impatience of contradiction, and constant readiness to avenge every imaginary insult with instant and deadly punishment of the offender. Hence the frequent affrays, duels, street fights, shootings, stabbings, and assassinations, of which every part of the South, but more especially the newer States, is so full—producing, it is believed, five times as large a proportion of these crimes to population, as is witnessed in the North, and ten times as large a proportion as is seen in any of the free countries of Europe. So long, indeed, as the slaves continue to increase in numbers beyond their masters, and coercive measures towards them may seem to be more necessary, because of such increase augmenting the danger of their revolt, so long the state of things will get worse; and as fear is a prolific source of cruelty, the very fears of the whites, which are continually increasing every year, will cause a greater exercise of tyranny than ever. How these fears ooze out in almost everything they say or do, may be seen by the following circumstance. The most religious and moral of the Southern population, have been long awakened to the cause of Temperance, and are very desirous of promoting it in this State, but as almost all the Temperance publications are issued in the North, they are literally afraid of their encouraging their circulation here, lest, by any oversight on the part of the editor, some paragraph favourable to Abolition should appear: for it could only be by oversight, as all these publications professedly steer clear of every debatable subject in religion and politics, purposely to obtain a greater number of readers. The dread, however, of even an occasional line against Slavery, is sufficient to induce them to project the establishment of a Southern Temperance Advocate, which it is purposed to publish in Columbia, the capital of South Carolina; and as evidence of this dread, I copy from the printed circular of the State Temperance Society, issued during my stay in Charleston, the following paragraph—

> While it is not denied that the valuable Temperance papers published at Philadelphia and elsewhere, might be usefully circulated in this State, the committee are still fully persuaded that no foreign publication can meet the exigencies of the case, or supercede the urgent demand for a Temperance Periodical at home. For even if Northern Papers were *free from all* TAINT *or* SUSPICION *of Abolition* TENDENCIES, and if it were practical by any conceivable means to bring them into general circulation, there would still be an utter failure in effecting the great object. These Northern Journals would be wholly destitute of local information, that

adaptation of facts and details, of appeals and illustrations, to the peculiar *taste* and *feelings* of Carolinians, which will constitute the high value and efficiency of our own Temperance Journal. The impulse which can alone give energy and success to our labours, and a triumphant extension to our principles, must come from the press, and that press must be our own, managed and controlled by ourselves.

During our stay in Charleston, the weather was delightful; and though it was the last week in May, and the first week in June, the temperature was not nearly so high as it was in Philadelphia and New York about the same time last year.

The favourite evening promenade at this season is the Battery, a fine walk along the water's edge, at the confluence of the two rivers, Ashley and Cooper, which flow down on the east and west of the town, and by their union form the harbour of Charleston, as the East river and the North river form by their union the harbour of New York. The Battery at Charleston has recently undergone great improvement, and is now one of the pleasantest walks imaginable. The greater number of the visitors come in carriages, and while some alight to enjoy the walk, others prefer the slow drive around the road called the South Bay. The ladies are without caps or bonnets, in dinner-dress, and the carriages are all open, so that it strikingly reminded me of "The Course," at Calcutta. There were not less, we thought, than 200 carriages out on one of the fine evenings that we visited the Battery; there being more families who keep carriages in Charleston than in any city of the United States, more than even in Boston, Philadelphia, or New York, though its population, including the suburbs, does not exceed 30,000, while the three other cities have 100,000, 200,000, and 300,000 inhabitants respectively: indeed, the practice of riding and driving is so general in this city, that a family is hardly deemed within the circle of genteel society, if they do not keep their own carriage.

During our absence, great progress had been made in the erection of the new buildings, to replace those destroyed by the late fire; and these being all built of brick, were calculated to add much to the beauty as well as the security of the town. Persons had been allowed to put up temporary wooden buildings for their immediate necessities; but the term of this permission having expired on the first of June, these were all taken down, to give place to more substantial structures in their stead. What added much to the desolate appearance of the ruined masses on which the work of removal and restoration had not yet been begun, was the great number of vultures that were seen seated on the fallen heaps, as if brooding over the solitude and ruin around them. In other parts of the city these birds were as numerous as the large storks called Adjutants, in Calcutta; and they answer the same useful purpose, in devouring the animal substances of the streets, and preventing putrescent effluvia from engendering disease. To secure them in the constant discharge of this duty, a penalty of twenty-five dollars each, is imposed on all persons who may shoot or kill any of these scavenger-birds, so that they multiply rapidly. The refuse carrion of the streets and yards not being sufficient to satisfy their hunger, they congregate about the markets so thickly, and watch their opportunities so narrowly, that if the keeper of a meat stall turns his back or leaves his post for a minute, he is sure to have whatever portable piece of meat may be on the stall carried off by the beak and talons of the rapacious turkey-buzzard, whom, however, he dare not kill, though caught in the act of the theft, without incurring the penalty of twenty-five dollars for the destruction of this useful public servant.

On the last Sunday of our stay in Charleston, I assisted at a public meeting convened for the advocacy of the Temperance cause, and for the purpose of aiding the establishment of a State Temperance journal at Columbia. The meeting was held in the Circular Church of the Presbyterians, and the audience was at least 2,000 in number. The Honourable Mr. Pinckney, formerly member of Congress from this State, and now mayor of Charleston, took the chair; and after an anthem by the choir, and prayer from the clergyman, the usual way in which all Temperance Meetings are opened in this country, Mr. Pinckney delivered an admirable speech, quite worthy of the high reputation he so deservedly enjoys. The venerable Judge Lee followed, in a less eloquent, but equally useful appeal, embodying many important facts, and offering very solid reasons in support of his views.[2] The rest of the evening was occupied by myself; and the joint influence of the three addresses was such as to bring a large addition of numbers to the avowed and enlisted friends of the Temperance cause, and to ensure ample support for the paper about to be established. The committee was instructed to divide their body into several parties, and personally to canvass each of the wards for subscribers, this being the efficient and business-like manner in which they conduct affairs of this description in America. At the close of the meeting, a second anthem was sung by the choir, to the British national air of "God save the King," which I was afterwards told was done in compliment to the nation to which I belonged. I had been announced, indeed, to the meeting, by the judge, as "the distinguished *foreigner*;" which sounded strangely in my ears, when all around me—the place, the people, the language, and even the object of our meeting—seemed so thoroughly English, that I could scarcely think I was in a foreign land, more especially, as the members of my own family, who accompanied me in this tour, were near me at the time. This was the second occasion on which the national air had been selected by the choir in compliment to the nation from whence I came, at public meetings in which I had taken a part. There is, indeed, a sincere respect for England and English people, felt by all the more intelligent and opulent classes, and a high veneration entertained for "the land of their fathers" by most of the learned and eminent lawyers and statesmen of America; while there is a great readiness on the part of all classes, to give expression to this feeling, wherever occasions present themselves in which this can be safely done without any compromise of the republican principle, or any derogation to the national sentiment of superiority as well as independence.

In the course of the mayor's speech, advertence was made to the late commercial convention which had held its sittings in Charleston, and the great object of which was to throw off as much as possible the dependence of the South on the States of the North for the commerce with Europe now conducted through that circuitous channel. The idea of restoring a direct trade between this port and the various countries of Europe, is indeed one of the most popular of the present moment. My own conviction is, however, that were it not for a feeling of intense hatred towards the Abolitionists, and the great reluctance felt by all classes here to contribute in any way to their profit, which by the present mode of doing business all classes here are assisting to augment, this effort to restore a direct trade would not be so strenuously sustained. At the same time, it must be admitted, that there is abundant reason, independently of such feeling, in the people of the South, to desire to render themselves independent of all other sections of the Union; but this feeling greatly quickens the zeal of many, who but for this would be at least indifferent. Their objections to the tariff of the North to protect northern manufactures, is also very strong, and justly so, because it undoubtedly taxes the Southern States, who are the chief producers, for the benefit of the Northern States, who are the chief manufacturers: and, therefore, they are all advocates for a free and unrestricted trade. Mr. Jefferson agreed with them in this last view, though he thought every extension of foreign commerce beyond selling freely to all who came to buy, and buying freely of all who came to sell—an evil: but there is so much good sense in his admirable observations on this subject that they are worth transcribing. This is the passage—

> Young as we are, and with such a country before us, to fill with people and with happiness, we should point in that direction the whole generative force of Nature, wasting none of it in efforts of mutual destruction. It should be our endeavour to cultivate the peace and friendship of every nation, even of that which has injured us most, when we shall have carried our point against her. Our interest will be to throw open the doors of commerce, and to knock off all its shackles, giving perfect freedom to all persons for the vent of whatever they may choose to bring into our ports, and asking the same in theirs. Never was so much false arithmetic employed on any subject, as that which has been employed to persuade

nations that it is their interest to go to war. Were the money which it has cost to gain, at the close of a long war, a little town, or a little territory, the right to cut wood here, or to catch fish there, expended in improving what they already possess, in making roads, opening rivers, building ports, improving the arts, and finding employment for their idle poor, it would render them much stronger, much wealthier, much happier. This, I hope, will be our wisdom. And, perhaps, to remove as much as possible all occasions of making war, it might be better for us to abandon the ocean altogether, that being the element whereon we shall be exposed to jostle with other nations; to leave to others to bring what we shall want, and to carry what we can spare. This would make us invulnerable to Europe, by offering none of our property to prize; and would turn all our citizens to the cultivation of the earth: and I repeat it again, cultivators of the earth are the most virtuous and independent citizens.

This wise counsel, offered fifty years ago, when the future was buried in the womb of time, has not been followed. If it had been, the last war with England, growing out of the right of searching ships and the impressment of seamen, would not have taken place; all the disputes about the tariff of the Northern states and the nullification of the Southern states, would have been avoided: the conflict about the custody of the "surplus revenue," would never have taken place, and all the recent troubles about the Maine boundary would also have been avoided. If Mr. Jefferson's views on the subject of slavery, which were to give freedom to every child born after a certain date, had been also adopted, there would not by this time have been a single slave in the United States, and all the difficulties of that grave question would have been overcome; though now it threatens more fearful consequences in its issue than any other impending cause.

In connection with this subject it may be mentioned, that a new and stately guard house for the military has recently been erected at the corner of Meeting and Broad streets, nearly in the centre of the city. The four great public edifices that occupy the four respective corners of the point of intersection between the streets named, are the following, placed in the order of the dates of their erection. The oldest and first built is St. Michael's Church, established to preach the gospel of *freedom* and *peace*: the next in order was the City Hall, built to form the seat of municipal government for the protection of the *rights* of the citizens: the third was the Court House, for the administration of the *laws* of the state: and the fourth, built in 1839, is the Guard House for the military, the chief use of which is to watch and crush any attempt at insurrection by the *slaves*! These four edifices, occupying the four corners of two intersecting streets, are within fifty or sixty feet of each other, but the first and the last seemed to me to stand in painful contrast as to objects; especially when, every evening, the bell of the Christian church is tolled at nine o'clock, to warn all slaves and coloured people to repair to their homes, as it is not permitted to them, without a pass, to be in the streets after a fixed hour at night. When the church bell has ceased its office of warning, the drums of the military guard house take up the strain, and continue the admonition for a quarter of an hour longer. The last time I passed the guard house, and saw the negroes hurrying to their masters' houses, from the different quarters of the town, the drums and fifes were playing an air of—

Scots! wha hae wi' Wallace bled!

But the band being wholly formed of negroes, were no doubt unconscious of the import of the song attached to this air, as they are not permitted by law to be taught to read; and therefore were probably unacquainted with the stirring lines of that noble appeal:

Who would be a traitor knave?
Who would fill a coward's grave?
Who so *base* as be a *slave*?

for the musicians were themselves slaves, and the sound of their music was to warn their fellow-slaves to hasten from wherever they might then be, to the dwellings of their masters.

A resident gentleman of Charleston, himself possessing several slaves, described to me the alarm created, about fifteen years ago, by the discovery of an extended plot and conspiracy for an insurrection of the blacks, on which occasion, some twenty of the ringleaders were seized, tried by a jury of white freeholders, and sentenced to death. To strike the greater terror into the rest, these twenty were drawn through the streets to the place of execution, in carts, each seated on the coffin that was to contain his body, with his grave-clothes already on; and they were then all hung up in a row, and kept there some time, as a warning to the survivors of what would be their fate, if they dared to follow their example. Since then, the slave-population has been comparatively quiet, though their numbers have greatly increased. It is alleged, and I believe with truth, that since then, also, they have been much better treated, so that instances of extreme cruelty are very rare, especially in the city, where public opinion would manifest itself in severe censures on any master exercising it; but on the plantations in the country, scenes still occur which the better disposed of the slaveholders themselves condemn as altogether indefensible.

The most painful view of this subject is, the hopelessness of any relief, except by a crisis or convulsion, which every one must dread and deplore. The prejudices of the whites over all the South, appear to me to be so rooted and so strong against even entertaining any proposition on the subject of emancipation, that one might as well attempt to still the tempest by reason, as to move them even to discuss the question. Hence all their presses are silent on the subject. Hence, even from their pulpits, not the most distant allusion is ever made to the matter. And hence, in private conversation, but one strain is ever heard—denunciation of the Abolitionists as fanatics, incendiaries, and plunderers. All support each other in the assurance that "the slaves are far better off than the working population of Europe," and all contend "that they are so happy that they would not *have* their freedom, if offered to them." Nevertheless the slaves constantly *take* this liberty without its being offered to them, by running away from their masters; and in the Charleston Mercury of the 6th of June, the day on which these lines are written, I perceive a long string of advertised runaway slaves, each preceded by the well-known little black figure of a negro running off as fast as he can, with a bundle of his few miserable garments packed in a handkerchief, and carried at the end of a stick; from which I select only one example.

FIFTY DOLLARS REWARD

Run away on the 26th of December last, a negro man, named CÆSAR, about 40 years old, jet-black complexion, round forehead, a little bald, slight made, and about 5 feet 6 inches high. He was raised in the family of Bennett, of Christ Church, and was some time since owned by Mr. Chisolm, who owns a Rice Mill, and by Mr. Greer, of St. Andrew's Parish, from both of whom he ran away. He has a wife on the plantation of Dr. Baily, and a daughter belonging to Mr. Yenning, of Christ Church parish, *where he has been recently seen.* He has followed the occupation of a fisherman, and been seen to go out in the boats from South Bay. The above reward will be paid on his delivery at the Work House.

May 29.
ALEX. M'DONALD.

It is confessed, by this announcement, that till Cæsar had thus tried to escape from no less than three successive masters; that he had a wife and daughter, but that they were sold as slaves to other owners; and that he had been recently seen with them—the most natural thing in the world for a being who possessed any domestic affections, but which, in him, was a crime, to be punished with apprehension, imprisonment, and possibly flogging besides. Such instances are of daily occurrence all over the South; and prove, that although the domestic slaves, used merely as personal attendants on ladies and gentlemen, are well fed, well clad, and kindly treated, which is almost uniformly the case with this class; yet that the great bulk of the slave population, on the plantations, in gangs as labourers, and hired out to work for their masters, are nearly all anxious to escape from their bondage, and avail themselves of every safe opportunity of so doing, when not deterred by the fear of detection, and the terror of the punishment which they know will then await them.

In this condition they will probably remain for some years yet to come. The experiment of emancipation in the British West Indies seems, for the present, at least, to have acted in the very opposite way to that which might have been expected, though before long it will impress them very differently. The planters of the South, misled by the false reports of their own newspapers, see in it only the ruin of the estates of Jamaica and the other islands; so that they are more alarmed than ever for the fate of their own plantations. Moreover, the example of the British government, in having given full pecuniary compensation to the owners for every slave made free, makes them quote this as a precedent, and as a *sine qua non* of any project of American emancipation. The Abolitionists of the North will not listen to such a proposition and the very amount at which the slaves are estimated, namely, 1,200 millions of dollars, or nearly 300 millions sterling, puts full compensation out of the question.

By the general interpretation of the Constitution of the United States, the Congress of the whole Union is considered to have no power to abolish slavery in any of the separate States; to each of which, the full sovereignty of domestic legislation is guaranteed and secured. They cannot, therefore, while this is held to be the law and constitution of the country, interfere in the matter, as a Congress, any more than England could constitutionally or legally violate a compact or treaty by which he might be bound to any independent States uniting with her for common protection, or interfere with their domestic legislation. Whatever is done, therefore, in the way of legal emancipation, must be done by the legislatures of the States themselves. Now, these will not suffer the question of Abolition to be even discussed; nor is there a single member, perhaps, of all the Southern legislatures, who really thinks it would be well to abolish slavery; or if such a solitary individual could be found, he would know that it would be utterly useless for him to open his lips on the subject.

With the whole press, the whole public opinion, and the whole legislative authority, therefore, united against even the bare proposition of any plan of emancipation, it cannot be even broached in the Slave States themselves; and in Congress they cannot lawfully deal with the matter, beyond receiving petitions, and debating on them. Even this—the only thing they can do, as the law and constitution now stand—they decline, and will continue to decline, so long as the Slave States maintain their full representation in Congress. There thus seems no present hope of any speedy and peaceful means by which slavery can be abolished by the legislatures of America; while the feebleness, ignorance, disunion, poverty, and utter deficiency in intelligence, leaders, and means, must make any attempt on the part of the slaves themselves, just as hopeless; because an insurrection could never rise to any height, with the existing vigilance of the masters, without being instantly crushed; and if it proceeded to an actual war, the whites, few as they are, from their intelligence, union, discipline, and wealth, would subdue the blacks in a single campaign, and their fate would then be ten times worse than before. Emigration to Africa, or colonization as it is here termed, of all the adult population; and a prevention of an increase in the young—seem to me the only means that could effectually cure the evil, in the existing temper of the public mind; but this would require to be conducted on a most extensive scale at once, to be efficient; and would demand such sacrifices of property, and advances of money, for the carrying it out, that there is no more hope of this, than of any other remedy yet proposed. Every year, however, by adding to the number of the coloured population, only increases both the danger of insurrection, and the difficulty of averting it; so that the prospect is gloomy and fearful in every point of view.

The only ground of hope that I can perceive is this—that the real facts respecting the beneficial effects of emancipation in the West Indies, must sooner or later become known to all the slave owners in America; and when they can be thoroughly convinced by these facts, that the freedom of the negroes is not only perfectly compatible with the safety of the whites, but that their estates will yield them more profit under free labour than under slaves, and that their incomes will be increased, and their property rendered at once more productive and more secure; from that moment its speedy accomplishment will be secure.[3]

1. This is the State, Mississippi, which has since been the first to advocate the dishonest doctrine of "repudiation," or refusal to acknowledge the obligation of paying its public debt.

2. This venerable judge has since deceased.

3. Since this was written, the admirable work of that distinguished and benevolent philanthropist, Joseph John Gurney, describing the State of the West Indies from a Winter's Tour, in Letters addressed to Henry Clay, of Kentucky, has appeared; and will do more to enlist the attention of the Southern planters of America, to the pecuniary advantages of Freedom over Slavery, than all the Abolition Tracts that have ever been printed.

CHAPTER XXX

After a very agreeable fortnight passed at Charleston, where I delivered a fourth course of lectures on Arabia, Persia, and Hindoostan, in the theatre of the Medical College, and in the French Protestant church of the Huguenots, and after enjoying the delightful weather and cordial hospitalities of several friendly families among the residents there, we left the city on the morning of Saturday the 8th of June, for Columbia, the legislative capital of South Carolina. The whole distance of our journey was about 120 miles; and the first half of it was performed on the Augusta railroad, as far as a place called Branchville. We left Charleston at seven; breakfasted at Woodstock, a distance of fifteen miles, at eight o'clock; and arrived at Branchville at eleven, going, therefore, at the rate of from fifteen to twenty miles an hour, the fare being four and a half dollars for sixty-two miles. On our way we saw many alligators in the ditches and swamps; and at one of the halting places, while the boilers were filling with water, an active young sportsman among the passengers caught one of these creatures alive, dexterously seizing it by the throat, and pressing it so hard in his grasp, that it opened its jaws from the pain, and was unable to close them again. Its strength, however, was considerable, it being about five feet in length, and its twistings and writhings such as could scarcely be overcome by all the efforts of the person holding him with both hands by the throat and by the tail. At length a rope was fastened round its neck by a noose, and the end of it tied to a stake driven in the ground, when the alligator then afforded a painful sport to those who had a taste for these exhibitions, by darting towards all who approached it, and being suddenly checked by the rope around its neck, until, by the united effects of the exertion, the heat, and the dust, it appeared quite exhausted. A few pails of water poured over it, seemed soon, however, to revive all its drooping energies, when the cars drove off, leaving the creature pinioned to the ground.

Our fellow-passengers were chiefly Virginians and Carolinians, with only one young female among the number. The whole of the men smoked and chewed tobacco, and expressed their astonishment to learn, that in England and France the great majority of the community did neither. We heard from them such pictures of the prevailing immorality and dishonesty of the mercantile classes, as, if told of them by any foreigner, would have roused their indignation and such confessions of the recklessness and blood-thirstiness of the white inhabitants of the South and West, as we were hardly prepared to hear thus openly avowed. Many individuals were named by them as living in a style of great luxury and expense, who had failed three or four times over, maintaining themselves by defrauding others, and who yet, because they were believed to be wealthy, not only retained their station in society without reproach, but were even courted and sought after by those living in their neighbourhood. Other individuals were also named, as known by them to have killed more than one friend in a duel or an affray, and who had not on that account lost the slightest consideration in general society, but, in their opinion, were thought rather better of for these "manifestations of manly spirit."

The passengers dined at a small village called Orangeburgh, about four o'clock, three hours later than the usual dining-hour in the country; but there was no house between Branchville and this, at which a meal could be had. The fare at those halting places is so coarse, and the whole service so dirty and disgusting, that wherever we could avoid taking our food at them, we did, and usually provided ourselves with a few sandwiches and hard-boiled eggs for the journey, before setting out; so that water was all we needed to be supplied with. Even this, however, could rarely be had pure and clean, as it was generally brought in a dirty pitcher, or a still dirtier glass, and often so highly tinctured with the odour of rum, from the unwashed vessel in which it was presented, that we preferred taking our own clean drinking cup, and supplying ourselves, wherever it was practicable, from some bubbling spring.

About midnight we halted at a solitary house, eighteen miles before reaching Columbia; and had the unusual good fortune to obtain there, the welcome refreshment of tea, and half an hour's freedom for our cramped limbs, after which we set out with renewed vigour. The rate at which we travelled was so slow, however, as not to exceed on the average three miles an hour, though we had four horses, and these changed every ten or twelve miles. The alleged reason of this tardiness was the heavy nature of the sandy roads; but the real reason, no doubt, was, that this stage, which carried the mailbags, had the entire monopoly of the road, not by any exclusive legal privileges, but by the absence of all competition; and, therefore, they travelled at the rate they thought most easy to their cattle, while the passengers were without remedy.

At the earliest dawn of day, soon after four o'clock, we met many of the field-negroes going to their work. All of them were wretchedly clad, in tattered and ragged fragments of garments hanging in shreds around their bodies; and when, at the sight of their miserable condition, Mrs. Buckingham involuntarily sighed, and said in a scarcely audible whisper, "Poor creatures!" three or four voices immediately and impatiently exclaimed, "Ah! Madam, they are among the happiest of human beings; for when their work is over, they have no cares, as every thing they need is provided for them." It has been often remarked, that the constant representation of a falsehood ultimately occasions even its utterers to believe it to be true. This often-repeated falsehood of "the negroes having every thing they need provided for them," must be of this class; for it really seems if its utterers were, in many instances at least, so deluded as to believe it to be true. I replied, that if to be relieved from all care about food and clothing when their work was over, constituted the claim of any class to be considered among "the happiest of human beings," then all the convicts of our penal colonies—all the inmates of the State prisons and Penitentiaries—all the criminals confined for life in the dungeons of Europe, or cells of America, might put in the same claim; for they too are relieved from all care as to food and raiment; the only difference of their lot from that of the rest of mankind, being, that they have to work harder, to suffer the loss of their personal liberty, and to be liable to be whipped if they murmured, imprisoned if they absconded, and shot if they offered the least resistance! But persons brought up in slave-countries, and accustomed from their cradles to regard the institution of slavery as one of mercy instead of injustice, and to repeat every day of their lives, that "slaves are the happiest of human beings," are as impervious to reason on this subject, as the various classes of persons in Europe are to matters in which their interest blinds their judgment, and their love of gain deadens every other feeling. Such classes are unhappily too abundant in every country of the earth, and in England, perhaps, as numerous as in any other.

It was not ten minutes after the observation was made, that "the slaves were among the happiest of human beings, having all their wants amply provided for;" that the very same individual who gave it utterance, said, "I think the very devil's got into the niggers of late; for I've heard of more running away, and seen more rewards offered for their apprehension, within the last month, than I ever remember to have seen in the same space of time." Yet no one appeared to be struck with the singular contrast presented between this confession and the previous assertion; and if we had remarked their inconsistency, instead of its making the least impression on their minds, the only answer we should have had, perhaps, would have been this—"Oh! but you are English abolitionists, who have abolished slavery in the West Indies, for the sake of encouraging a negro revolt in the Southern States, and thus revenging yourselves on America."—This belief, monstrous as it is, was more than once expressed in my hearing, though not addressed to me, by persons who apparently believed to be true; and having said enough to show my own dissent from their views, I did not wish to risk the explosion which such a spark as this might have occasioned, by lighting on the combustible materials by which we were surrounded.

When the sun rose above the horizon, a thin sheet of blue mist was seen suspended a few feet only from the ground, which gradually ascended as the sun grew higher, and ultimately disappeared. It is this low mist which, in the opinion of most of our passengers, natives of the country, contains the poison that occasions the fevers of the low-grounds; and as it is carried off in vapour during the day, but returns and settles near the surface of the earth at night, when it receives the vegetable miasma of the swamps and thickets, this explained why it was perfectly safe to travel, or to visit the plantations of the low-grounds, while the sun was above the horizon, but dangerous to do either after nightfall and before sunrise. About three miles before we reached Columbia, we passed through what is very rarely seen in America—a deserted village. This is called Granby, and was the predecessor of Columbia. It was first begun to be built in the year 1800, and was occupied for more than ten years, when it was thought that the opposite side of the river Congaree, near which it was situated, was a better situation for a town, and Columbia was accordingly commenced, to which the small population of Granby gradually united itself. As the houses of the first settlers are always built of wood, and as the material is too easily procured to render it worth while to pull down a wooden house for the sake of its rafters or planks when once abandoned, these dwellings of the deserted village remain just as they were when first forsaken, and present a singular and melancholy appearance.

About two miles beyond Granby, we crossed the river Congaree by one of those closed wooden bridges so frequently seen over American streams. The whole covering is exactly like that of a long warehouse, with perpendicular sides and sloping roof, all of wood, with square windows at long intervals apart, to afford light sufficient for the passage, and no more. The interior is divided into two separate avenues, with a partition of diagonal rafters between, one passage being used by the comers and the other by the goers so that no vehicles can ever meet or come in contact with each other, nor can even a horse pass through the rafter-partition from the one side to the other—an arrangement very conducive to safety. The river was very low, large patches of its rocky bed being visible above its surface, and its waters were yellow with soil. The river is of considerable length, rising in the mountains of North Carolina, in what is called the Blue Ridge, nearly 200 miles above Columbia, northward: it is there called the Broad

River. Near Columbia it is joined by a river called the Saluda, which comes from the north-west. The united stream is called the Congaree, and is about a third of a mile broad where we crossed it. It then joins another river called the Santee, and this flowing south-eastward, discharges itself into the Atlantic near Georgetown, a little to the north-east of Charleston, on the coast.

A mile beyond the river, gradually ascending all the way, brought us at length to Columbia about six o'clock, having been thus nineteen hours performing a distance of sixty miles, scarcely more than three miles an hour. We found comfortable accommodations at the United States Hotel.

Among the inmates of the inn during our stay here, was a lady and her family from Charleston, on their way to Kentucky by land, to spend the summer. They had come in two private carriages with their own horses, with which they intended to perform the journey in easy stages of twenty-five or thirty miles a day; but by the time they had reached this, having taken three days to come from Charleston, their four horses were so knocked-up by the heat of the weather and the heaviness of the roads, that they were unfit to proceed farther, and the lady was obliged to purchase four new ones, and sell the old at a great sacrifice, there being no arrangements for posthorses, as in England, so that none can be had on the road. We had been advised to take private carriages and our own horses, for our intended journey to the Virginia mountains, and had some disposition to adopt this advice. But the example before us was sufficient to make us pause.

There was another family from the sea-coast halting here on the way to the mountains, that of a rich planter from the sea-islands on the borders of the Atlantic. He was said to be worth half a million of dollars, but he was as unpolished and uninformed as any man might be supposed to be, who had passed the greater portion of his life, as he told us he had, among his negroes, with few books, and no disposition to consider any subject but the growth of cotton; or opportunities of cultivating the acquaintance of any other society than that of planters like himself. There are very many such wealthy men in the oldest settled States; of which, this is one; and it is remarked, that the greater number of them are childless, which is, perhaps, one of the reasons why their wealth accumulates, as they have no daughters to apportion in marriage, or sons to set up in the world. There are always, however, plenty of nephews, nieces, and cousins, to come in for their share of the property after the death of the possessor; so that it ultimately gets sufficiently diffused. The men, from their more active life, bear the climate much better than the women, who being of very feeble stamina, taking little exercise, and using very ill-prepared and innutritious diet, are unable to bear up against any powerful attack of disease. There are consequently a much greater number of husbands who survive their wives, than wives who survive their husbands. We saw at Charleston a gentleman, not yet forty, who had been married to a fourth wife; and we saw here at Columbia, a lady who was the fifth wife of her present husband; and as he had had no children by either of his five wives, he deemed it an acquisition that the lady he last espoused, being a widow, had brought him not only a fortune, but three children by her first husband, to share with her the wealth of the second.

From all the observations I have been enabled to make on this subject, and from the facts I heard from others, I should think that the wealth of the respective parties about to form a matrimonial alliance, was much more frequently an object of consideration in the Southern States of America, at least, than in England. This is the more remarkable, inasmuch as there is much less necessity for such consideration here than with us. In England, the difficulty of earning in almost any pursuit of life more than sufficient to supply a bachelor's wants, at least, up to the age of thirty, makes it imperative on all prudent persons to secure, before they form a matrimonial alliance, additional means to meet the additional expense of a family establishment. But in this country, the gains of every profession, even in its earliest stages, are so much greater, and the expenses of maintenance are so much less, than in England, that no one need be deterred from marriage from a fear of being able to support themselves.

There are two causes, which appear to me to lead to this state of pecuniary consideration in the marriages of the South. The first is that in this country, the chief, if not the only certain method, of ensuring homage or consideration from the mass of the community, is by the acquisition of wealth. To this, therefore, all attention is directed, and in this almost every other passion is swallowed up and absorbed. Marriage is one of the modes by which this object of universal desire may be most easily achieved; and it is therefore planned and pursued as an affair of business: and a fortunate alliance of this description is talked of as a matter of skill and good management on the part of the husband, just as a successful issue of some well-planned speculation in a commercial undertaking. Many are the instances in which a man marries two sisters, in succession, each of them very wealthy, and sometimes even a third, so rapidly do they give place to each other. A second cause of pecuniary marriages, I think, is this—that the passion of love is not felt with the same intensity by either sex in this country as even in France; still less so than in England: and with nothing approaching to the ardour with which this passion burns in Portugal, in Spain, and in Italy. We never knew, or even heard, thus far at least, of any romantic attachment, accompanied by acts of such self-devotion as is often seen in England: and neither in the social intercourse which we have enjoyed among the young, nor in the domestic conversations of the middle-aged, have we ever witnessed that ardent attachment, and reciprocal sacrifice of all selfish considerations, which characterize the communion of passionate lovers everywhere else. All is decorous, orderly, and irreproachable: but everything is also formal, indifferent, and cold.

Both physical and mental causes may contribute to this. The youth of America have not that vigorous and robust health, and that full flow of blood, which characterize the youth of England, and which forms a large element in the capacity to feel intense and passionate love. They have less leisure for those rural walks and pleasant country excursions, and less taste for this class of pleasures, in wooded parks, green lanes, secluded orchards, verdant lawns, flower gardens, grassy dales, and by babbling brooks, than the English—and what auxiliaries to youthful attachments these are, it is unnecessary to say. The young men of America are all so busily engaged, from morning till night, in affairs of commerce or professional occupations, and so engrossed with the one great aim of getting on in business, and acquiring wealth, that they have neither time nor inclination for those romantic dreams of love, which absorb so large a portion of the time and thoughts of English youths between fifteen and twenty. When they meet the other sex, it is either at a public dinner-table, with fifty or a hundred other guests, where none remain more than a quarter of an hour, and where there is no time for conversation; or at balls and crowded parties, where the opportunities of indulging an interchange of sentiment and feeling are too broken and interrupted, to feed the passion of fervent feeling, or to suit the gravity of sentimental love. Social evening-visits, without invitation or preparation, are rare indeed in any part of America; and to morning visits to ladies, gentlemen are rarely admitted, as the ladies are then "particularly engaged," so that the thousand opportunities which these morning and evening calls offer in England, for love-making, are seldom met with, and rarely improved in America. Add to all this, that the knowledge of, and taste for the fine arts, is greatly inferior here; and that the beauties of sculpture, painting, and poetry,—all so favourable to passion—are less understood, less appreciated, and less talked of among American than among English youths; and that the exquisite and entrancing strains of music, the very "food of love," are rarely heard blending in sweet harmony from male and female voices, and binding hands, and eyes, and hearts, in one, as they often do in England; and it will be seen that there are abundant causes for that deficiency of romantic feeling, and passionate affection, the absence of which appears so characteristic of the youths of America.

Columbia derives all its importance from being the legislative capital of the State of South Carolina, and the seat of the college supported by the State. In the early period of the republic, the seat of legislation was at Charleston; and this section of country was then an unexplored and untrodden wilderness, at least to the whites—the Catawba tribe of Indians, now nearly extinct, being then its sole occupants. Like the other tribes of Indians, the great body of these have been purchased out, till they have receded farther west. A small remnant of them only is left in the interior of the State, on a piece of ground called the Indian Reservation, about three miles square, where, by the aid of a small annual stipend from the general government, they eke out a miserable existence. They are averse to industry of every kind, and are so given to intoxicating drinks, that their numbers are every year lessening from this cause, so that in a very short period it is thought that their race will become extinct.

When the State legislatures were first organized, and the States incorporated into one Federal Union, the principle of centrality in situation for the several legislative capitals, was generally adopted. The distances were so great, the roads so imperfect, and the means of conveyance so confined to that of riding on horseback, as to render it desirable that the burden and fatigue of attending the legislature should be as equally divided as possible. On this principle it was, that about the year 1800 it was resolved to remove the seat of legislation for South Carolina from Charleston to some central position and the spot where Columbia now stands having been thought the most eligible for this purpose, was accordingly determined on. The State House was then erected—hotels and boarding-houses for the accommodation of the members soon followed. The State College was next built. A Court House, Jail, Lunatic Asylum, and Academy, followed; and the usual addition of stores or shops, traders, artisans, professional men, and places of worship for the several denominations of Christians of which these were composed, came in due course of time.

The site of Columbia is on elevated ground, commanding an extensive prospect all around, though the eye reposes on little else than dense forests, as yet untouched by the woodman's axe, with a few partial clearings only, near the town. The river Congaree being within a mile of the town, and navigable by steamboats up to the bridge for the greater part of the year, affords facilities of water communication, first to the river Santee, and then by it to the Atlantic. The soil is extremely sandy, but this contributes much to the healthiness of the place, while it is sufficiently fertile to produce good crops of corn and cotton. There had recently been a tremendous hailstorm here, the stones of which were as large as hen's eggs; and the fall of which had cut to pieces all the young plants; but though considerable damage had been occasioned by this icy tempest, large crops were confidently expected.

The plan of Columbia is as rectangular as that of American cities generally. Its size is about two miles in length from east to west, and one mile in breadth from north to south. The streets cross each other at right angles, and are from sixty to eighty feet in breadth, lined, in many instances, with rows of locust and pride-of-india trees on either side, unpaved in the centre, and sandy, with partial side pavements of brick or stone.

Of public buildings, the State House is the oldest but not the handsomest. It is built of wood, without any remarkable feature in its architecture; but it is spacious, and well adapted to the purposes for which it was erected. A new edifice of stone is about to be erected, to supersede it; but this is not yet commenced. The session of the legislature is very short, rarely or ever exceeding four weeks— the two houses meeting for business in the last week in November, and always adjourning a few days before Christmas. There is, of course, but little legislative business to transact; for, beginning with a well-defined written constitution, and a republican frame of government, there are few or no reforms to make; and all the prolific sources of dispute which furnish such occupation for the British legislature, in debates on the reform of the church, adjustment of tithes, purification of municipal corporations, amendment of corn-laws, reduction of taxation, revision of the pension and civil list, and provision for paupers of a humbler degree, are here unknown; so that their sessions pass away tranquilly and briefly, and leave nothing undone to accumulate in arrear. The House of Representatives consists of 120, and the Senate of 42 members; and these, with the Governor, constitute the legislative body. The Governor has the power to reject any measure after it has passed both houses; when it is sent back, and can only become law by the concurrence of two-thirds of each house respectively. The representatives are elected by general suffrage for one year, and the senators by the counties for two years, receiving a fixed allowance of mileage for their respective journeys to and from the seat of legislation, and three dollars per day for the single month they are in session. The Governor, who is elected by general suffrage for two years, receives a salary of 3,500 dollars, or about 700*l.* a year; and these, with the judges, the seven professors of the State College, and a few other public officers, are all the individuals paid out of the funds of the State; so that the taxation is so light as to be scarcely perceptible.

The College is an assemblage of buildings occupying an area of about 600 feet by 300 within the walls, with a central space, having a double row of elms running up the centre, and the buildings enclosing the quadrangle. At the farther extremity of this from the entrance gate, is the President's House. Leading from it are two good piles of building, which will accommodate fifty students each. Beyond these are newer piles, erected for the accommodation of a hundred students more—then dwellings for the professors—and last of all, a new library, about half finished, to which the existing collection of books will soon be transferred.

This College is one of the very few institutions of learning in America, that are wholly supported by the State. Funds for building it were at first supplied by a grant from the legislature; and the salaries of its professors, and the annual augmentation of its library are all appropriated annually by the same body. The

Faculty consists of the president and seven professors; and the Board of Trustees is composed of the governor, the judges, and certain others elected to that office by the legislature; and the management is now said to be very efficient. About three years since, the college was at a low ebb in general estimation, in consequence of the laxity of discipline, and immorality and disorder, which then prevailed; so that parents became unwilling to send their children there. This is ascribed to the neglect of the late principal, who was removed from his office by the act of the trustees; and the whole establishment has been recently reorganized. Public confidence being restored, it has already recovered its former reputation, and has now a greater number of students, nearly 200, than at any antecedent period.

The general course of study embraces Greek and Roman literature, logic and belles-lettres, history, and political economy, mathematics, chemistry, sacred literature and evidences of Christianity, and intellectual and moral philosophy, there being a professor of each. A chaplain presides over the religious worship, which is according to the Episcopalian form; though the students are allowed, if the wish be expressed by their parents, to attend worship in any other church of Columbia. The youngest age for admission is fifteen; but many enter after they are twenty-one; and few leave before they are twenty-three or twenty-four.

One characteristic difference between the manners and customs of the Northern and Southern States, is the early period at which the youths of the former quit education for active business, and the later period to which studies are prosecuted by the youth of the latter. The cause of this difference is, that in the North, almost every young man is destined to be a merchant, a lawyer, a physician, or to pursue some active walk in life. In the South, the greater number of the young men who receive college education, are sons of planters, that is, of landed proprietors; gentlemen who live, not on the rental of their estates, as in England, but on the profits of the large plantations tilled by their slaves, and superintended by their overseers. Most of these are not brought up to any business; but are allowed fixed incomes by their fathers, or live with them—and assist in the management of the estates, to the whole or part of which they look for their future support. These, therefore, continue at college till twenty-four or twenty-five, and often go to Europe on a tour for two or three years afterwards, which sufficiently explains why the gentlemen of the South are in general so much more thoroughly educated in the classics and polite literature, and so much more polished in their manners, than those of the North. The whole expense of the education received, in addition to the cost of board and clothing, is only fifty dollars, or ten pounds sterling a year. The students have a common hall for their meals; but they do not study together. Each has a separate study, and separate bed-room; and while they pursue their studies alone, they have three periods of recitation in classes before the several professors, at sunrise, eleven, and four o'clock, when they have a recess for two hours, and repairing to their rooms in the evening, they there prepare themselves for the recitations of the following day.

There is one great difficulty with which the Faculty have to contend, which is, to maintain the requisite discipline of the college without risk of resistance or rebellion. The nature of the training which these Southern youths undergo before they enter college, is such, owing to the institution of slavery, that they rarely learn the lesson, either of self-control, or of patient submission to restraint placed on them by others. At home they are so accustomed to have their own way, to have every passion gratified, and no wish denied, that they become impatient of the least contradiction, and exhibit extreme reluctance to yield to authority; they require, therefore, peculiar management and great tact, to govern efficiently and tranquilly at the same time.

There are six churches in Columbia, the Episcopal, the Methodist, the Presbyterian, the Baptist, the Unitarian, and the Roman Catholic, neither of which are remarkable for size or beauty. The Court House is a substantial structure, in the centre of Richardson Street, the principal thoroughfare of the town. Here, too, are no less than five hotels, three of which are very large, and the one at which we lived, the United States, well kept, and agreeably furnished, both in bed and board. There is nothing peculiar in the stores or private dwellings of the town worthy of remark. Some are substantial edifices of brick, with granite pillars and foundation, but the greater number are of wood, though these are gradually giving way to buildings of a more durable nature. There are two excellent book-stores, at which all the recent publications of England can be had at a fourth of their London prices, in American reprints. Lady Lytton Bulwer's novel of "Cheveley, or the Man of Honour," was scattered in profusion all over the United States, within a few weeks after its publication in London, and we learnt that a great many copies had been sold here. This sort of "fashionable novel," especially when it is thought to contain a great deal of personal scandal, and an exposure of private vices to public view, is as eagerly read by the youths of both sexes, as by the devourers of this sort of highly-seasoned literature at home. On the other hand, the graver and more substantial productions of the English press, are rarely reprinted here; and thus the best English books are seldom seen out of those collegiate and public collections to which they find their way, but from which they make little or no impression on the mass of the public.

The population of Columbia is estimated to be 4,500, of whom 2,500 are whites, and 2,000 blacks; the latter being mostly slaves, as few free people of colour are found among their number. Of the white population, all appear to be engaged in trade, with the exception of a few professional men connected with the college and the law-courts; but their trading operations are on a much smaller scale than at Charleston or Augusta. In the black population I observed no peculiarities worthy of remark. As in other towns, the slaves engaged in domestic service appeared to be well treated, and generally content; but those belonging to the neighbouring plantations, and engaged in out-door occupations, were as ill-clad, dirty, and miserable in appearance, as over-worked and under-fed labourers were likely to be. We saw here, more than elsewhere as I thought, a number of children, from the ages of four to seven, playing about the streets under the care of negro boys and girls but little older than themselves. This seems to be a mode by which parents get rid of the trouble of looking after their children at home. They are sent out to walk, with a negro boy or girl to play with them and bring them back safely. But the little whites soon learn their own superiority, and make great progress in the art of tormenting and abusing their black guardians; laying, thus, in their very first steps in life, the foundation of that irascible temper, and ungovernable self-will, which characterizes nearly all the white inhabitants of Slave States. This is no doubt the true cause of all these outrages of the Southern and Western States, of which the records are so painfully abundant. One of the most recent of these is the destruction, on the 31st of May last, of nearly a whole town by fire, Port Gibson, in Mississippi. No one doubts it was the work of incendiaries, whose reckless speculations had involved them deeply in the general embarrassment which prevails over all that State; and as one of the shortest methods of disentangling themselves from their obligations, would be the destruction of all the records of their various mortgages, bonds, &c., the burning down the Court House, after the example of Columbus in Georgia, was resorted to, it is believed, for this purpose. Not to make this too evident as the ultimate design, the fire was kindled elsewhere, and publicly proclaimed to have been the result of accident; but so well was the "accident" contrived, that the Court House perished with the rest; and but a few of its records were rescued from the flames. As it is not so easy, however, to arrest the progress of fire, as it is to kindle it, the devouring element, in this instance, raged to such an extent, as to burn down all the business streets, and reduce the town to a heap of ruins; the property destroyed being estimated at upwards of half a million of dollars.

Negroes are continually exposed to sale here, passing from hand to hand, like other "cattle," for so they are chiefly considered. The men are usually called "boys," whatever may be their age; and very often "fellows." The terms "gang," as describing a number working in company; "hands," as describing a smaller number; and "force," as describing a whole body of slaves on an estate, are in frequent use. A female negro is called "a wench," or a "woman;" and it is this, perhaps, which makes the term "woman" so offensive to American ears, when applied to white females, who must all be called "ladies." Besides sales and transfers of negroes, there are frequent committals to prison of persons apprehended under suspicion of being runaway slaves, and kept in custody till they are redeemed. Some of these are of pure African birth, that is, born in Africa, imported from thence by the slave-ships trading to the island of Cuba, and brought by illicit importation into the United States. These are even more impatient of restraint than those born in slavery here; and, therefore, they more frequently attempt to escape. The following are a few notices of each class taken from the "South Carolinian" of June 14, published during our stay here.

> Valuable Negroes for Sale.—By permission of James Guignard, Esq., ordinary, will be sold, before the Market-house in the town of Columbia, on the first Monday in July next, eight valuable negroes, belonging to the estate of Mrs. Mary Clifton, deceased, on a credit of one, two, three, and four years, with interest from the sale, on the whole, payable annually. One is a carpenter, two are first-rate cooks, one a carriage-driver, one a smart waiting-boy, two girls were brought up as house-servants, and the other is a little boy. The purchaser will be required to give good personal security, and also a mortgage of the property.
>
> Andrew Wallace, Ex'r.

> Committed to the jail of Laurens District, a negro woman, named Peggy, who says she belongs to Adam Zimmerman, of Orangeburgh District, near Judge Bay's plantation. Peggy is an African[1] woman, about middle size, speaks quick, and appears rather insane, and fifty or sixty years old.
>
> A.C. Jones, s.l.d.

> Committed to the jail of Lancaster District on the 29th inst. as a runaway, a negro man, who calls his name Bob, alias Paris. He is an African,[1] about forty-five years of age, five feet three or four inches high, speaks very broken, and says that he was set free by Reuben Bozzel, of Mecklenberg County, N.C. The owner is requested to come forward, prove property, pay charges, and take him away.
>
> L. Secrest, J.L.D.

In the same newspaper from which these notices are taken, are short reports of two cases carried up from the inferior courts of the district to the court of appeal at Charleston, which are remarkable illustrations of the law and custom as it regards property in slaves. The first exhibits the care that is taken of the slaves in contracts for hire, so as not to expose their lives to hazard, and the liability of such as hire them to make compensation to the owner in case of death, or loss by any exposure provided against in the contract. The following is the report of the case.

> *Walther et al.* ads. *Sampson H. Butler.*—O'NEALL, Justice.— Defendant employed plaintiff's slaves to work on the railroad, and covenanted 'not to *expose* the slaves to rain or other bad weather, or *dangers of any kind.*' After knocking off work, one evening, the overseer of defendants suffered the slaves to get into a hand-car of the Railroad Company, which came by at the time, in order to ride over a pond, covered with thick ice, through which the road passed, at an elevation of fourteen feet, and to avoid which, the slaves had to make a considerable circuit on the way to their encampment. When over the middle of the pond, a locomotive made its appearance, and to escape it, those in the hand-car had to jump out, and some safely descended to the pond by the posts of the road, but one of the slaves, in attempting to descend, fell, and was so much injured as to die in a few days. Held that the defendants were liable on their covenant, for the injury sustained, as well from the omission of their overseer to prevent the slave from exposing himself to the danger, as if from placing him in danger by their command.

The second is still more remarkable. It frequently happens, that wealthy persons dying in the South, begin to feel, as they approach their deathbed, some stings of conscience as to the injustice of holding men in forced bondage, and depriving them, both of their personal freedom and the just reward of their labour. Such persons frequently try to soothe these stings, by making a will bequeathing freedom to their slaves, after they themselves shall die, and the slaves be of course no longer of any use to them. Even this cheap method of restitution is not allowed, however, by the laws of the Southern States, which prohibit any person from giving freedom to their slaves, unless they remove them at the same time from the territory. To evade this law, they are sometimes bequeathed in trust to an executor, who stands in the place of a nominal master, allowing the slaves to work for themselves, and receive the benefit of their own labours. But this again has been declared illegal; and such persons thus apparently set free, may be seized by *any one* who may choose to take them, and made slaves to such seizer, as their owner! This will seem incredible, no doubt, without proof. Here then is the report of such a case, and its decision—

> *Rebecca Rhame* v. *James Ferguson and John Dangerfield.* BUTLER, Justice.—A will, bequeathing slaves to an Ex'or, in trust, to suffer them to appropriate

their time and labour to their own use and to govern themselves, is an attempt to evade the law of the State against emancipation of slaves, and, if attempted to be carried into effect by the Ex'or, will subject the slaves to seizure and ownership by any one, under the act of 1800. The Ex'or of such a will may lawfully take possession of the slaves, to administer the estate; but whether the trust be void, or a court of equity will enforce it (in which event they might be escheatable, according to the case of Fable v. Brown) are questions for another tribunal. Under this exposition of the law, the jury having found against the plaintiff, the alleged captor, motion for a new trial dismissed.

Seizure under the act of 1800 may be:—1. By an actual tangible possession of the slaves. 2. By such a subjugation of them as to make them virtually prisoners. 3. By voluntary surrender of the slaves, as captives.

I have mentioned the avidity with which English novels are sought after in America, and particularly the eagerness with which all the copies of Lady Lytton Bulwer's novel was sought after in Columbia. The following notice of it from the South Carolinian of June, after the remarks adverted to were written, will corroborate this. After announcing, in a leading article, that a fresh supply of this novel had been received at the principal bookstore of the town, the editor says—

We have not yet had time to read this work, and consequently can say nothing of it from our own knowledge; but, from the extensive notice it has attracted, and the sensation it has created both in Europe and this country, be it what it may, it will be sought after and read with more avidity than any book that has appeared for years. Most of our readers are already aware, that it is a novel from the pen of the lady of the celebrated author, Sir Edward Lytton Bulwer, from whom she has been some time separated and is designed as a satire on him, and the leading members of his family, as also, on several of his friends. It is said to be remarkable, alike for talent, and, for bitter caustic, and unfeminine severity. A key to the characters is given as follows, by a late London paper.

Nearly half a column of the paper is then devoted to the "Key," in which all the several characters of the novel are appropriated to the different personages they are supposed to represent. But when Miss Martineau's new novel of "Deerbrook" comes to be noticed as imported also at the bookstore, it is as briefly as uncourteously despatched. Miss Martineau's Strictures on American Society are more unpopular in every part of America, north and south, that we have yet visited, than even Mrs. Trollope's or Captain Basil Hall's works; but in the Slave States especially, her bold and uncompromising denunciation of this plague-spot on the national escutcheon, and exposure of its evils, has made her name hateful to the great majority of the people. After barely naming the fact, that the new novel of "Deerbrook," by Harriet Martineau, may also be found at the same bookstore with "Richelieu," by Sir Edward Lytton Bulwer, and "Cheveley, or the Man of Honour," by his Lady, the Southern editor thus despatches Miss Martineau—

> Having no very high opinion of the *Great unsexed*, or anything published by her heretofore, we have *not* only not read this, but have no inclination to do so.

1.   This means born in Africa, and recently imported from thence.

Chapter XXXI

On Saturday the 15th of June, we left Columbia for Augusta, and having taken the whole of the stage for ourselves, we had the advantage of room and comfort, which, in this hot weather, was especially agreeable.

Leaving Columbia about four o'clock, we crossed the Congaree river by the bridge over which we entered the town from Charleston, and soon got into the woods, which continued all the way, with little intermission, till we reached the village of Lexington, about thirteen miles from Columbia.

Lexington is a very favourite name in the United States, there being not less than eighteen towns already so called—after Lexington in Massachusetts, about eleven miles from Boston, where the first blood was shed in the revolutionary war. That, however, is still a small place, having not more than 1,500 inhabitants. There is a Lexington in New York State, with 2,500 inhabitants. But the largest town of this name is in Kentucky, containing 7,000 inhabitants. There are no less than three Lexingtons in Pennsylvania, and three in Ohio; the others are in Virginia, North and South Carolina, Georgia, Tennessee, Indiana, Illinois, and Missouri, so that they are widely scattered. Three miles beyond Lexington we arrived at a single post-house, called, as is the custom here, after the name of the man who kept it, Rawles's, where we were to sleep for a few hours, having reached this at eight o'clock, intending to start again in the morning at two.

The house, though humble, was one of the neatest and cleanest of its kind. In the piazza or balcony in front, it had water, with a tin wash-basin, soap, and a rolling towel, provided for the passengers; and in the interior it had clean beds and wholesome fare, which we enjoyed greatly. The old host, nearly eighty years of age, was courteous, intelligent, and communicative; and his sons and daughters were affable and obliging. He had taken a part in the revolutionary war, being then a young man about twenty; he fought in several of the battles and skirmishes that took place in South Carolina, with the British troops, who came up thus far from Charleston. He was a native of this State, and had never been out of it. His principal occupation had been farming, and to this his chief attention was still directed; though, in conjunction with this, he had kept this post-house, for it could hardly be called an inn, for twenty-six years. Our road for the greater part of the way from Columbia thus far had been sandy, and the pine-forests on each side dry, of the description of land usually called "pine-barren;" and it may give some idea of the healthiness of this region, to mention a fact stated to us by Mr. Rawles, namely, that during all the twenty-six years he had resided here, no single case of fever or any other sickness had occurred among any of his household, though in the low country of the same State, the climate was so unhealthy in summer and autumn, that even the white natives were unable to remain on their plantations in July and August.

Cotton-planting is the chief occupation of the farmers in this region; and we heard here of a new species of cotton, said to have been recently brought from a field of the Petit-Gulf-Cotton, in Alabama, which has these peculiarities. It grows much taller than the ordinary plant, reaching eight or nine feet, instead of four or five. It has lateral branches unusually short, being not more than four or five inches from the main stem; and these bear clusters of six or seven pods on each branch. It has leaves like the ordinary cotton-plant, but in other respects it resembles the okra, or, as it is called in the East, the barmeah. It ripens much earlier than other cotton; and is, therefore, likely to escape the worm, which commits great havoc on the late crops of the South. The cotton is much finer than any other of the short-staple kinds, and commands a price of four or five cents more per pound; at the same time, the produce of the plant is much more abundant. It is but new at present, and the seed is accordingly scarce and dear; but littler doubt is entertained that it will soon be very generally cultivated; and, like the new introduction of the *morus multicaulis*, 100,000 trees of which were advertised for sale on one farm alone while we were at Columbia, it will add greatly to the wealth of the country.

After a quiet and refreshing sleep, we arose at two o'clock in the morning, and resumed our journey in the same conveyance. The road lay still through the thick forest, with only here and there an open patch of cultivation on either side. The coolness of the night was a most agreeable relief to us after the burning days we had recently experienced; and as the road was still sandy, and our coach passed noiselessly through its deep mass, we enjoyed the full chorus of the feathered throng, as they began their early matins at the first peep of dawn, and made the woods ring with their vocal melody. The opening of the day was also beautiful, from the many gorgeously tinted clouds and richly varied hues of the eastern sky, that preceded the rising of the sun; while the freshness of the morning breeze, and the balmy odours of the many wild flowers which rose among the undergrowth of the forest, added greatly to our pleasure.

It was sunset as we entered Hamburgh, the town recently built on the Carolina side of the Savannah river, and right opposite to Augusta. We saw here, a number of waggons and carts, in which negroes had been brought from the north, on their way from Virginia, where they are extensively bred for this purpose, down towards Georgia and Alabama, where they are in great demand for the increasing cultivation of cotton, though many of them, we learnt, were likely to be bought up here. The price of a common field-negro we ascertained to be from 800 to 1,000 dollars; of an artisan, a carpenter, or smith, 1,500 dollars; and of a smart active boy of fourteen, about 500 dollars; women of an age to begin the bearing of children, from 600 to 800 dollars, according to their good appearance and strength of constitution. The manner in which they were huddled together for conveyance, was greatly inferior in comfort to that in which sheep, calves, and hogs are carried to market; and the consciousness of the hard fate awaiting them, which was visible on the countenances of most, made them look much more wretched than "sheep led to the slaughter."

A glaring instance of the attempt to keep back the truth on this subject was pointed out in a paper which I met with at the hotel where we changed our coaches, the "National Gazette," of Philadelphia, of the 11th of June, and which had just arrived by the last post from thence. It was so apposite, and is at the same time so truly illustrative of the influence of party-feeling in this country on the subject of slavery, that it deserves to be transcribed. Mr. Paulding, the present Secretary of the United States' Navy, was for a long while a popular writer of books, and being of the democratic side in politics, he was recently appointed to his present office. The Democrats, in violation of the first principles of their political creed, are in general the most zealous supporters of slavery, and the fiercest denouncers of the Abolitionists, though there are many Whigs who are hardly less zealous than they. Mr. Van Buren is supported by nearly the whole South, because of his hostility to Abolitionism, and it is thus that his adherents commend themselves to his patronage. Here is the article from the Gazette, in proof—

> The 'Louisville Journal' exposes an instance of truckling to party opinion, in the conduct of Mr. Paulding, which is not unworthy of the great moral Janus himself. Several years ago, ere the Secretary of the Navy indulged the hope of a cabinet post; and before the mystical Kinderhook confession of faith was given to the world, he wrote a series of 'Letters from the South,' well known to the reading public. He was, then, if we may form an opinion from the following paragraph, which is found in

the first editions of those 'Letters,' an opponent of slavery, or at least of certain practices under the system.

'The sun was shining out very hot, and in turning an angle of the road, we encountered the following group: first, a little cart drawn by one horse, in which *five or six half-naked black children were tumbled like pigs together*. The cart had no covering, and they seemed to have been actually broiled to sleep. Behind the cart marched three black women, with head, neck, and breasts uncovered, and without shoes or stockings; next came three men, bareheaded, half-naked, and *chained together with an ox-chain*. Last of all came a white man—a white man, Frank!—on horseback, carrying pistols in his belt; and who, as we passed him, had the impudence to look us in the face without blushing. *I should like to have seen him hunted by bloodhounds*. At a house where we stopped a little further on, we learnt that he had bought these miserable beings in Maryland, and was marching them in this manner to some of the more Southern States. Shame on the State of Maryland! I say—and shame on the State of Virginia! and every State through which this wretched cavalcade was permitted to pass. Do they expect that such exhibitions will not dishonour them in the eyes of strangers, however they may be reconciled to them by education and habit?'

Recently the 'complete works' of the Secretary of the Navy have been published, but the reader will look in vain for the passage quoted above. True to his patron, Mr. Paulding now ranks among the 'Northern men with Southern principles,' and his 'complete works' exhibit, instead of the anti-slavery picture which he formerly drew, an essay in *defence* of the institution, of which the annexed extract is a specimen—

'The second cause of disunion will be found in the slave population of the South, *whenever* the misguided, or wilfully malignant, zeal of the advocates of emancipation, shall institute, *as it one day doubtless will*, a crusade against the constitutional rights of the slave-owners, by sending among them fanatical agents and fanatical tracts, calculated to render the slave disaffected, and the situation of the master and his family dangerous; when appeals shall be made, under the sanction of religion, to the passions of these ignorant and excited blacks, calculated and intended to rouse their worst and most dangerous passions, and to place the very lives of their masters, their wives, and their children, in the deepest peril; *when societies are formed* in the sister States for the avowed purpose of virtually destroying the value of this principal item in the property of a Southern planter, when it becomes a question mooted in the legislatures of the States, or of the General Government, whether the rights of the master over his slave shall be any longer recognized or maintained, and when it is at last evident that nothing will preserve them but secession, then will certain of the States of our beautiful constellation "start madly from their spheres, and jostle the others in their wild career."

This is a melancholy proof of the influence of position and party-spirit, not in changing men's opinions (for it probably does not effect that) but in inducing them to profess opposite ones, in the truth or soundness of which they do not themselves believe, for the sake of office and of gain. But, alas! this abandonment of truth, and propagation of falsehood for political and party-purposes, is not confined to the functionaries of the United States; for England could furnish examples equally numerous and disgraceful. But, in whatever country such abandonment of principle is shown, public odium should cover the names of the renegades with shame.

We crossed the Savannah river, and reached Augusta at eight o'clock, and after our long, hot, and sandy ride, were glad to find good quarters in the Planter's Hotel. The tranquil and agreeable rest which we enjoyed there, however, on the first day after our arrival, was like the calm which precedes a storm; for in the middle of the night that succeeded it, namely, on Monday the 17th of June, we had to experience all the horrors of a raging fire, and to be burnt out from this hotel with such suddenness and rapidity, as to require instant flight to save our lives.

It was about two hours past midnight, when the first alarm of fire was given, the discovery being accidentally made by a gentleman returning home late through the streets; and he, perceiving no sign of movement in the hotel itself, though one end of it was in flames, ran to the door, and roused up some of the slaves sleeping in the passages. These, as soon as they had recovered from their stupor, awoke others, and these again assisted to awaken the inmates; but from the common practice of locking the bed-room doors, to prevent the night-pilfering of the slaves, who are the only servants, it was with the greatest difficulty that some could be awakened at all, so that the fire had passed through nearly half the building, before any one had been roused from their beds; and two-thirds of the hotel was in flames, before those in the remoter parts of the house were up and in motion. At the time of our being called, the appearance was so alarming, that we thought it most prudent not to remain a moment, but, throwing over us the few loose garments at hand, we rushed into the street, where from fifty to sixty persons, lodging in the hotel, had already assembled in a similar condition; many, indeed, had only the night clothes in which they retired to rest; and the greater number of them had abandoned everything to the flames, considering themselves sufficiently fortunate to escape with their lives. Our faithful man-servant, James Wright, a native of Belfast, in Ireland, whom we had had with us during all our Travels in America, though especially enjoined to withdraw from the house, and not incur the least risk of danger by attempting to save anything, thought fit, in his zeal, to disregard this injunction; and having gained access to our bed-room by one of the galleries or passages, he made a rope of bed-sheets by knotting their ends together, and in less than five minutes lowered down all the trunks that were accessible, and then throwing out the bed-mattresses to soften his fall, he leaped from the window on them, a height of upwards of twenty feet, as by this time the passages were all wrapt in flames, and the very rafters of the bed-room from which he leaped, had begun to fall on the floor, so that escape by any other channel was impossible. Happily he sustained only a slight injury by the fall, from which he soon recovered. Our own loss was not so great as that of many, but a thousand dollars would not cover the value of the articles lost by us in this conflagration, while no money could replace the drawings, sketches, minerals, herbarium and flora, of *many months'* collection, which there was not time to gather up and collect together, in the darkness, smoke, and confusion that prevailed, so that these were all consumed by the flames.

The hotel was one of the oldest and largest in Augusta; it was four stories in height, and contained 104 bed-rooms. Excepting the basement walls, the whole building was constructed of wood, chiefly pitch-pine; and the bar-room and cellars, as usual, were filled with spirituous liquors. The recent hot and dry weather had also increased the combustibility of all wood-work; and these combinations of causes will account for the amazing rapidity with which the flames spread. It was certainly not more than an hour from the first alarm being given of the fire, before the whole edifice was level with the ground, and entirely reduced to ashes. The conflagration, when at its height, resembled a vast pyramid of solid flame, of about 300 feet at the base, and 200 feet in perpendicular height. The heat given out by this mass was so intense, that persons could not approach nearer than within 100 feet, without being scorched. Fortunately, there was not a breath of air stirring, and the hotel was an isolated building, surrounded by a large open space on all sides. If it had not been so disconnected, the fire would, no doubt, have so extended itself on all sides, as to burn down half the city, as was the case at New York in 1835, Charleston in 1838, and Port Gibson in the present year. The establishment of fire-companies and engines here, is so imperfect as to render them almost useless in arresting conflagrations after they have made any progress; and from the combustible nature of the materials used in building, the flames spread so rapidly as to baffle all attempts to subdue them when they have attained their height. Here there were but two engines, and neither of these arrived till the building was destroyed. Of one of them, the hose was so short as not to reach to the river, where alone water could be procured; and of the other, the condition was so rusty and stiff, as to make it difficult to work; all which seemed the more surprising to me, when I learnt that so recently as 1829, a great fire destroyed 930 houses in Augusta in the short space of three hours, leaving indeed but very few buildings of all the city unconsumed!

The inhabitants came in great numbers to look at the fire as a sight, but few of them did anything towards its suppression. As to the negro slaves who were among the crowd, it may well be supposed that they would not be likely to volunteer their services in any dangerous enterprise, as it is not the custom to reward them liberally, and all motive to such exertion is therefore destroyed. In the investigation which took place subsequently, as to the cause of this fire, there was reason to believe that it was not accidental, but the work of some of the slaves belonging to the establishment. The proprietor, Judge Hale, was a humane and kind master; but he resided in another house, nearly a mile from the hotel, and confided the management of it to others; moreover, he had lately been ill, and had not visited the hotel for several days. The manager and his assistants, being less just and considerate than the master, exercised, it was said, undue severity on the slaves, or at least on some of them, and imprisonments and whippings were matters of frequent occurrence. In such cases, it is a very usual mode of revenge with the slaves, to burn down the houses of their oppressors; for by this means they often succeed in breaking up an establishment in such a manner as to lead to a sale of their own persons; and then they have a chance of release from existing tyranny, by being transferred to a new master, with a hope at least of better treatment. Such are the effects of the slave-system on the feelings and conduct of those on whom the lives and properties of their masters are so constantly dependent; and yet, all who seek to relieve the owners as well as the slaves from the thousand evil consequences of which this system is the prolific source, by abolishing compulsory service, and substituting free labour in its stead, are branded as the enemies of the slaveowner and the slave, and denounced as the accursed of the earth!

The most recent instance that has been made public, of the fierceness with which the spirit of Southerners breaks out against Abolition and Abolitionists, wherever they may be, is in the following paragraph taken from the New York Observer of June 8, just received at Augusta:—

Two young men, one of them a law-student, and the other a member of the senior class of Yale College, have been fined six dollars each, for breaking up an Abolition meeting at New Haven, on the 13th inst., by throwing eggs at the speaker (Gerritt Smith,) making a noise, &c.

Mr. Gerritt Smith is the son of a wealthy citizen of New England, who, at his death, left the munificent sum of 100,000 dollars, or 20,000*l*. sterling, to be devoted to philanthropic and benevolent purposes; and the son following in the footsteps of his revered parent, subscribes yearly large sums for the promotion of education, religion, and other objects of the greatest public good. Among other donations, he lately gave 10,000 dollars to the fund raising in the North, for the promotion of negro emancipation; and this may account for the especial hatred of all the slaveholders of the South, and their connections, which this act has drawn upon him. The young students here named, as throwing eggs at the speaker, and otherwise disturbing the Abolition meeting at Newhaven, are mentioned in another paper, as being from the South, which will account for their active zeal. But when two young men in such a rank of society as these, students at the principal university of the country, and intended for the bar and the bench of the South, can commit outrages of this description, for the small penalty of six dollars each they will, no doubt, procure this cheap gratification of their vindictive feelings whenever the opportunity offers.

After remaining a sufficient time in Augusta, to repair, as well as we could, the most important part of our losses in the apparel, and other travelling necessaries, burnt at the Planter's Hotel, we were glad to quit a scene of such painful associations; the more especially, as the boarding-house in which we had taken up our quarters after the fire, was right opposite to the ruined pile, so that we could not look out of our window without having the wreck from which we had so recently escaped, constantly before us.

CHAPTER XXXII

At six o'clock on the morning of Friday, the 21st of June, we left Augusta for Athens, in the northern part of the same State of Georgia, intending to go from thence through the mountains into North Carolina, Tennessee, and Virginia, on to the mineral springs among the ranges of the Alleghanies, which are greatly resorted to by the opulent families of the Southern and Western States, during the hot summer months.

Our route from Augusta to Greensborough, was by railroad, for a distance of eighty-four miles, and being through an almost continuous forest of pines, it offered nothing new to our observation. The rate of speed was about fifteen miles an hour while in motion, or twelve miles including stoppages, as we were seven hours going the eighty-four miles, stopping to breakfast, and several times to replenish fire-wood and water during the way; and the rate of charge was five cents a mile.

At Greensborough, which is an old, though still a very small place, not containing more than fifty houses, we dined at one o'clock, and here the railroad terminating for the present—though it is intended to carry it all the way to Athens—there were stage-coaches in waiting to convey passengers from the north, west, and south, to their respective destinations. Among the buildings pointed out to us at Greensborough by a gentleman of our party who was born there, and was now nearly sixty years of age—which makes Greensborough a very old settlement for this part of America—was the Methodist church, a rude building of rough planks, suited to a sect, who have the undoubted precedency of all other denominations, in pioneering the way for the Gospel in the wilds and woods of this continent. The class of preachers whom they send forth to "cry in the wilderness," are often as rough and rude as their churches, but not the less zealous or self-denying, because of their want of polish or refinement, though sometimes giving utterance to sentiments and expressions, which they would themselves find it perhaps difficult to explain. One of these pioneers of the forest, was preaching in the Methodist church at a period when the country not far from this was possessed by the Cherokee Indians; and in the attempt made to eject them from their lands, they had recourse to arms for resistance. The white settlers, accordingly, often felt the edge of the tomahawk and the scalping-knife, as they continue to do in Florida at the present moment. In addition to the usual means of defence adopted by the whites, prayers were put up in the different congregations for delivery from this scourge; and at the end of an appeal of great fervour to the Almighty for protection, the preacher in this church exclaimed, "Spare us, good Lord, and deliver us from this evil; but if it be thy will to scourge us with thine afflictions, and chasten us with thy wrath—if, in short, it be thy pleasure to let us fall into the hands of savages, O let it be into thine, O Lord!" To which the congregation, of which our informant represented himself as being one, responded in the fervent manner which characterizes the devotion of the Methodists, "Amen, Lord, amen,"—their feelings being, no doubt, too completely absorbed in the consideration of the perils that surrounded them, to admit of any rigid criticism of their pastor's language or meaning.

From Greensborough we proceeded in a four horse stage-coach, well appointed, and with an excellent driver; and having only six passengers inside, we had abundant room. Our journey to Athens was forty miles, and the fare ten cents per mile, just double the rate by the railroad, while our speed on the average was five miles an hour. The road became hilly within a few miles after our leaving Greensborough, and all the way onward we appeared to be ascending. The soil changed from sandy to a red indurated clay, and we soon lost the pineforests, and came into woods of red and white oak, which furnished better shade, and afforded an agreeable relief to the eye.

In our way, about twelve miles from Greensborough, we passed over the Oconee river, which descends from hence till it joins the Ocmulgee, below Macon, and these together form the Altamaha, discharging itself into the Atlantic at Darien, below Savannah. The river was very low, in consequence of the scanty supply of water from above, no rain having fallen in this quarter since the month of March. The stream was here about fifty yards broad, and we crossed it in a flat ferryboat drawn by a chain. We learnt that on the banks of the river, rattlesnakes abounded, and one of our fellow passengers stated that he had seen one caught or killed near this stream, which measured upwards of nine feet in length.

We were joined here by a communicative and intelligent planter, just from his plantation, from whom we learnt that the excessive drought had been already fatal to a large portion of the crop of cotton now in the ground. Indeed, this was sufficiently visible to the eye, many fields exhibiting stunted plants, their colour being hardly distinguishable from the dust of the earth that covered them. Some crops of oats were in a similar condition; but many fields of wheat had been reaped, and the sheaves were now gathering in, the wheat harvest being generally over in the middle of June; and the maize or Indian corn was in a very flourishing condition. We learnt from this gentleman that there had been lately introduced into this State, a new description of grain, called Baden corn, from its successful cultivator, a Mr. Baden, of Maryland, who had taken the pains to select the best ears or cobs of corn from his own fields, and plant them in the most favourable position; going on from year to year in this manner, in the belief that he should thus greatly improve its quality, and increase its productiveness. For the first five years, there was no very perceptible difference; but in the sixth it became visibly improved; and this process being continued for twenty-five years in succession, had produced a corn of such additional productiveness, that it now yields about 250-fold, while the ordinary rate of increase in the common corn, is not more than 100-fold, or 120 in the best years. The buckwheat is also cultivated here, and yields two crops of grain in the year. It was stated, that in the cultivation of the white and the brown cotton, in parallel ridges, which is sometimes done, it will often happen that from the mingling of the blossom-flowers, or the fine powder blown from them, a sort of mulatto-cotton, or mixed kind, will be produced by the amalgamation; and the same thing has been observed of the red corn and the yellow, each of which will give, by mingling, a portion of its tinge of colour to the other. Of the brown or nankeen cotton very little is exported, as it is wrought up into nankeen cloth here, and is largely consumed in the apparel of the country-people for summer wear; none of it, we were told, had ever been sent to England, as far at least as our informant knew. It is somewhat dearer than the white cotton, and makes most durable cloth; but by repeated washing, the colour gradually grows lighter and lighter, and if washed and bleached often, it will fade away entirely, and become quite white.

About ten miles beyond the river Oconee, we came to a village called Salem, a very favourite name in the United States, of which there are not less than thirty-eight places so called in the different States of the Union. The oldest and largest of these is the Salem of Massachusetts, near Boston; but in addition to this there is one in New Hampshire, one in Vermont, one in Connecticut, one in North Carolina, one in Tennessee, one in Kentucky, one in Indiana, and one in Illinois; two in New Jersey, two in Georgia, three in New York, three in Virginia, five in Pennsylvania, and fourteen in Ohio! Little did the ancient founders of the Salem of Melchizedek, on Mount Zion, in Judea, anticipate so extensive a multiplication of the name of their City of Peace, in a world to them entirely unknown!

We had scarcely arrived at Salem before the sky began to be overcast, and in less than a quarter of an hour the heavens were of an inky blackness, threatening an immediate and violent storm. The driver persisted, against our wish, in going forward, instead of our taking shelter at Salem till the storm should be over, as it was likely to be of short duration; and we accordingly encountered it in all its force. The gusts of wind which first came, were so powerful as to prevent the horses advancing, and the dust and sand were blown up in such thick clouds, as to render it impossible to see the edges of the road from the centre. We were obliged to close the curtains and windows of the coach, and remain in perfect darkness, while the horses stood still, with their heads lowered to the ground, and the driver placed his back to the gale. This darkness was first penetrated by the most vivid lightning and peals of thunder, succeeded by torrents of rain, which almost deluged the road; and notwithstanding all our exertions to exclude the water from the coach, it penetrated at every crevice, and soon wetted it in every part. The storm did not last more than half an hour; yet such was its violence, that large trees were uprooted and thrown across the road, obliging us to turn in to the adjoining woods, and go round them; and in the hollows of the fields between the ridges of the cotton and corn plants, the water lay on the surface apparently five or six inches in depth, while in every declivity, torrents were formed, some of which were difficult and even dangerous to traverse.

Eleven miles from Salem, we came to Watkinsville, a still smaller village, where we took tea, or supper, about eight o'clock; and though this was the longest day in the year, and the thermometer had been above 90° at noon, it was now so cold as to make a blazing wood-fire agreeable. Continuing on from this place by a more steeply ascending road, for about eight miles further, we reached Athens soon after ten, and alighted at the Planter's Hotel.

As the elevation of this town is at least 1,000 feet above the level of the sea, we had a much cooler atmosphere than we had experienced for many months. Our first night, after the thunderstorm, was especially agreeable; and for the first time for many weeks past, we were free from the annoyance of mosquitos, which abound in all the low country from April to November.

CHAPTER XXXIII

On the morning of the first Sunday after our arrival at Athens, we attended the public funeral of the venerable Judge Clayton, one of the most distinguished members of the community here. The service was solemn and impressive. The judge, though a man of great integrity, and unexceptionable morality, was throughout life an avowed unbeliever in Christianity. He was one of the first graduates of the University of Athens, and its most zealous friend and patron: he was learned, intelligent, virtuous, and universally honoured and esteemed, both for his public and private character; yet he made no scruple to avow himself openly a deist; and this, too, it would seem, without in any degree lessening his standing in society. About twelve months since, he was struck with paralysis—being then fifty-five years of age; and feeling that death could not but be near at hand, his mind and heart became subdued. He expressed a desire to see the minister of the Methodist church; and the result of the interview was, that the judge, as soon as he had sufficiently recovered from the first shock of his paralysis, publicly joined this church, by going up to the altar, in the face of the whole congregation, on a Sabbath morning, when the church was full, and there giving in his public adhesion as a communicant and member. From this time onward, he continued in close fellowship with the Methodist body; and died in the fullest and most unreserved communication of his steadfastness in the faith, accompanied with deep regrets that he had lived a life of unbelief, by which he had lost "oceans of happiness"—this was his expression—to himself, and set a dangerous example to others.

These circumstances gave unusual interest to his funeral, as it was to be made the occasion of a public address over the body of the deceased, by his own pastor, who had attended him in his last moments. The time chosen for the service was the forenoon of the Sabbath; and each of the three churches of Athens suspended their regular morning worship, for the purpose of uniting their respective congregations in one. The place of assembling was the chapel of the University, the largest of the public buildings here; and at nine o'clock, the hour appointed, it was filled in every part, the lower floor being occupied by the white population, the females in the centre, and the males at the sides, and the galleries being filled by negroes, one side by the men, and the other by the women; this separation of the sexes being usual among the Methodists, in all their assemblies for public worship. On the platform were seated the whole of the clergymen of the town, including Presbyterian, Baptist, and Methodist. Immediately before them, and elevated so as to be seen by the whole audience, was placed the coffin containing the corpse. This was borne into the chapel by six gentlemen, personal friends of the deceased, who carried it on two longitudinal poles; they wore white scarfs or sashes, thrown over the right shoulder, and fastened in a knot on the left side, with crape ribbons hanging or floating from the right arm. The coffin was made of oak, and quite plain, there being neither handles, escutcheon, gilt or silver nails, covering or pall of any description, but everything was characterized by the extremest simplicity.

The Methodist pastor, Mr. Smith, of Charleston, conducted the funeral service, which differed in nothing from the ordinary routine of public worship, in the succession of prayer, singing, and preaching, except in the sermon being one especially adapted to the occasion. It was marked by great solemnity, powerful argument, and forcible appeal, and sufficiently imbued with sorrowful feeling, to make it at once devotional and affectionate. The bereaved family of the deceased occupied the pew immediately in front of the corpse, while the numerous personal friends of the late judge, surrounded these mourning survivors; and the united effect of the scene, and the address of the speaker, was such as to fill the assembly with tears. Excepting the Quaker funeral which we witnessed at Saratoga in the summer of the last year, I never remember to have seen or heard anything more impressive, or better adapted to awaken the most indifferent to the duty of preparing for death, than the scene before us on this occasion.

Mr. Smith was followed in his address by Mr. Hoyt, the Presbyterian clergyman, who had also had opportunities of personal communication with the deceased, between the period of his first paralysis and his death, and who, therefore, thought it his duty to corroborate much that had been said by the previous speaker, as to the openly avowed scepticism and infidelity of the late judge up to that period, and his sincere conversion to a belief in the truth of Christianity, in which faith he died. In the course of his address, however, he stated, that though he had been a minister of the gospel for upwards of twenty years in this country, this was the only well-authenticated instance that he had met with, during all that time, of a man who, like the judge, had been thirty years an unbeliever, and had afterwards avowed his conversion to the truth. He had generally found that men died as they lived, and that real conversion from long-established and openly-avowed infidelity was very rare. He, moreover, asserted his conscientious conviction, that the great majority of the men whom he saw before him, were in the same condition of unbelief, as that in which the deceased had passed nearly the whole of his life; and though many of them, perhaps, attended religious ordinances for the sake of standing well with their neighbours, yet he feared very few of them had any active belief in the truth of Christianity, but were infidels and sceptics, living without God and without hope in the world: all which seemed to be silently received as matter of course, and, as far as I could judge, excited neither surprise, nor any symptom of dissent, from any portion of the congregation.

At the close, the corpse was borne to the grave by the same personal friends of the deceased who brought it to the chapel, and was followed there by his sorrowing family, and a large concourse of his fellow citizens, the greater number in carriages, and many also on foot.

On the Monday after our arrival, we witnessed a grotesque exhibition of the militia muster, similar to that seen at Rochester in the summer of the last year. By the law of the State, every male citizen between the ages of eighteen and forty-five, not legally exempted, must be enrolled as a militia-man, and attend the stated musters throughout the year, under penalties for noncompliance. As this is felt here, as elsewhere, to be a duty as irksome as it is thought useless, and one from which the great majority of the community would gladly relieve themselves if they could, there seems an universal determination to bring these musters into contempt. Accordingly, while the commanding officer, under whose review they were to pass, was dressed in a field-officer's full uniform of blue and silver, and mounted on a fine charger richly caparisoned; the battalion that marched before him was as grotesque as the most ingenious caricaturist could make it. About a dozen of the whole number had muskets, some with bayonets and some without; and these were carried in as many different ways as there were pieces. The rest of the troop, about one hundred in number, carried sticks, umbrellas, waggoners' whips, and large planks or rails. Their dresses, too, were as varied as their arms; some wore cloth coats, others white cotton jackets, and many were in their shirt sleeves; while hats of all kinds, black, white, and straw, broad-brimmed and narrow, made up the motley dress of this strange company; and in marching, the aim seemed to be to make the line as irregular as possible, and cause every man to step out of time. In short, they seemed to labour under the influence of a *symmetrophobia*, and to do everything in the opposite way to that in which it should be done. The students of the university, about 120 in number, were also summoned to this muster; and as they formed a corps by themselves, they endeavoured to outvie the militia-men of the town in the grotesqueness of their appearance, and the irregularity of their movements. The band of the townsmen were composed of two black drummers, two fifers, and a long drummer; but that of the students was composed of three of their own number, playing on flutes, one of the D, or regular concert size, one of E flat, and one of B flat; and as these all played the same strain in different keys, the discord may be well imagined.

On the following day, June 25, I received from the Phi-Kappa Society of the University of Athens, a communication stating that I had been unanimously elected an honorary member of that association, and soliciting my attendance at a meeting of its members, for the purpose of being initiated in due form. In compliance with this wish, I was escorted in the evening, by some members deputed to this duty, to the hall of the society, and there, with more formality of ceremony than I had at first expected, I was introduced to about forty of the students assembled in conclave, with a president, two vice-presidents, two censors, and other officers, seated in due form. After hearing the constitution and rules of the society read by the clerk, and an address made to me by the president, I was welcomed by the simultaneous rising and bowing of the whole assembly, as an initiated member. The compliment had to be acknowledged, of course, by a speech in reply to the president's address; and at the close of this, another simultaneous rising and salutation took place, when the meeting was closed.

There are two societies of this description attached to the University, the regular members of which are all students; and the distinction of honorary membership is conferred on those strangers visiting Athens, whose name and reputation are calculated, in the opinion of its officers, to do honour to the institution. The oldest of these societies is the Demosthenian, which is cœval with the University, being about thirty-five years old. The youngest is the Phi-Kappa Society, which is about twenty years of age. The former numbers fifty-five members, and the latter forty-five.—The object of both is the same—to afford a field for exercise in debate on all topics except theological; and, by a generous rivalry and emulation in intellectual displays of composition, declamation, and written and oral efforts, to develop and mature the respective powers of the members, so as to fit them for the active duties of life, and prepare them for the bar or the senate, to which the greater number of them aspire. On the Saturday of each week, the studies of the University are suspended, and this day is devoted by the two rival societies, to the prosecution of their respective labours, their recitations and debates often occupying the entire day. At the period of "Commencement," as it is termed, which occurs in the first week in August of every year, when the degrees and prizes are awarded, after a public examination of the students, a day is set apart for the meeting of the rival societies in conjunction, and an oration is delivered by some distinguished person specially invited and appointed for this purpose.

The appearance of the town is very pretty, especially at this, the summer season of the year. The mansions are almost all detached buildings, constructed of wood, with porticos, pediments, and piazzas, surrounded with spacious and well-planted gardens; and as all the houses are painted white, with green Venetian blinds, they afford a striking relief to the deep-green foliage in which they are embosomed. There is but one regular street of business, in which the houses are continuous; and this is as yet built on one side only, the rest of the dwellings are scattered like separate villas, and the surface being greatly undulated, and the wood or forest-trees approaching close to their borders, the whole appearance of the village is picturesque and romantic.

The University Buildings form a quadrangle, covering about three acres of ground; and comprehending the rooms for the students, a large chapel, with Doric portico in good taste, the halls of the Demosthenian and Phi-Kappa Societies, and the residences of the professors. The only other public buildings are three churches, all built of wood, and very plain, the largest of which is the Methodist, the next the Presbyterian, and the smallest the Baptist.

The population of Athens is estimated at about 2,500, of whom not more than half are white, including the students, the remainder being slaves engaged in domestic service. Of the white inhabitants, the greater number are families who have come here to reside from the low country, on account of the superior healthiness of this spot, or for the education of their children, or both. There are consequently more persons of education, taste, and good manners, than is generally found in so small a community; and this, with the presence of the professors and students, makes the society unusually good, which forms a powerful attraction, and brings people in from the plantations of the interior, to make this their permanent home. Such is the general competency and comfort of all classes, that every house seemed well furnished, and every family kept a carriage, while fine saddle-horses were also abundant.

The inhabitants of Athens seem very proud of the name of their village, and call themselves Athenians. There is also a village, called Rome, in the adjoining county, and the inhabitants of this are, of course, called Romans. In the state of Ohio, however, they are so extra-classical, that they have three places called Rome, and three called Athens; and in one instance the township of Rome is in the county of Athens; while in other States there are no less than fourteen places bearing this classical name.

This subject of American names, which has long engaged the attention of foreigners, is at length beginning to attract the notice of native writers also; and I do not think that their singularity could be made more apparent than it has been by one of the Northern papers, from whence the following is transcribed—

> AMERICAN NAMES.—The editor of the 'Boston Mercantile Journal' has commenced a vigorous attack upon what he calls the bad taste of American people, in giving names to places. Among the most obnoxious which he has selected from 'Mitchell's Map of the United States,' he enumerates, among others, the following:—Bean Blossom, Bloody Run, Boggs, Bono, Bon Pas, Funkstown, Paint, Pumpkin Town, Scuffle Town, Trap, Whisky Run, Beepec Bobble, Oil, Olive Green, One Leg, Moon, Modestown, Metal, Mary Ann, Mary Ellen, Logtown, Long-a-Coming, Frogtown.
>
> Our neighbour of the 'New York Gazette,' says he can find from memory fifty other names quite as pretty and poetical. By way of specimen he enumerates—Slingtail, Shirt-Tail Bend, Hog's Calamity, Burst-up, Blatherskite, Tumbleburgh, Bumble Bee, Snakehampton, Blarneyville, &c.
>
> As the above lists are interesting, we must 'take the responsibility' of making a further addition of several poetic names. These names may not be found upon any map, but the places are, nevertheless, well known to the people inhabiting them and their neighbourhood. Without going beyond the limits of Duchess County, we may enumerate Bang All, Hard Scrabble, North Star, Kidneykill, Eel Pot, Skunk's Misery, Tinkertown, Pond Gut, Nigger Squeeze, Ass's Bridge, Bull Hill, Mutton Hollow, Canoe Hill, Scabby Valley Square, Longtown, Nine Partners, Hell Hollow, Rum Tub, &c. In other parts of the State there are places called Poke Eye, Satan's Kingdom, Poke Weed, Break Neck Hill, Monkey Town, Sodom, Thieves' Refuge, Devil's Half-Acre, Cow Bay, Skunny Munk, Smoky Hollow, Sleepy Hollow, Anthony's Nose, Spite the Devil, &c.
>
> But these names, whatever we may think of their sound, were doubtless given by the original settlers, after the manner of the Hebrews of old, to signify the early events connected with their history. They are truly rural and American, therefore, and may be put down as exhibiting about as good taste as those literary places sprinkled everywhere, called Homer, Hector, Virgil, Pompey, Cicero, Cato, Scipio, Hannibal, Camillus, Romulus, Fabius, Sallust, Ovid, Seneca, Brutus, Babylon, Jerusalem, Nineveh, Jericho, Sweden, Norway, Denmark, Russia, Poland, Italy, Venice, Persia, Chili, Peru, Jamaica, Rome, Moscow, Paris, Liverpool, Naples, Madrid, Lyons, Cairo, Batavia, &c. all of which, if we mistake not, may be found within the limits of the State of New York.—*Poughkeepsie Eagle.*

The literary taste of the South, whether evinced in its newspapers, magazines, or larger works, may be called of the florid composite order, with a singular admixture of the most opposite principles; especially of the most unbridled democracy, and an earnest defence of the institution of slavery. One of the most amusing specimens of this taste that fell under my observation during our stay here, was the prospectus of a new weekly journal, to be called "The Pioneer," announced to be published in Augusta on the 1st of October in the present year. It was intended to be "devoted to the literature, institutions, and amusements of the South;" and to form another means of excluding the productions of the North, founded on the same principle of fear of Abolition, which has led to the multiplication of seminaries of education for Southern youth; the establishment of Southern Temperance journals for Southern readers, and the employment of Southern agents for Southern Bible Societies. Mr. Charles Wyatt Rice is named as the editor of this new literary journal; and the following extracts from its prospectus will exhibit the exuberant and high-flown style of Southern composition. The editor thus opens his address.

The South is the natural home of literature. She has ever been so. Homer strolled and sung under the rays of the fervid sun; Italy and Greece have, from their first wakening into being as civilized nations, afforded their poets and orators. The literary pilgrim ever bends his step to the South of Europe, as his most favoured shrine; while there, fond memories throng to his mind, of the epic strains of Homer, the soothing measures of the Mantuan Swan, the exulting odes of Horace, and the biting sarcasms of Juvenal. While in later times he reclings to the memory of the tearful strains of Dante, the epic measures of the madman Tasso, the soft strains of Petrarch, and the pleasing images of Boccacio. And while thus fondly recalling to memory all these, he remembers that they drew their inspiration from the fervid sun of Italy and Greece. He feels in the balmy air he breathes, in the brilliant heavens that form the canopy above him, in the brilliancy of the sunset that glows in the horizon, and in the tints that the air and clime spread over the earth, the inspiration that formed and developed the genius of those whom he now so fondly regrets.

Such food for inspiration does the literary pilgrim find on the classic shores of Italy and Greece, and under the fervid sun of the South. And is it possible that a kindred clime in the Western Hemisphere presents no parallel to this? Do the same sun, the same brilliancy of the canopy of the clouds, the same glorious sunsets, the same rich tints upon the landscape, afford no inspiration here? A wilder, a more abrupt scenery than Italy or Greece can boast, speak in living tones to their beholders. While with these an Italian softness of landscape upon the Ashley, the Savannah, and other favourite streams, glorious waterfalls and streaming cascades, are everywhere claiming their worshippers in those who dwell among them.

But, more than all these, do the leisure and opportunities for mental cultivation that her *domestic institutions* afford her citizens, present strong grounds of belief that the South is destined to become the centre of literary interest. As this leisure and this opportunity for mental cultivation *find no parallel in any other country*, it is natural to believe that the South is destined to become to the world, in a new era, what Greece was to the world in the old.

This delicate phrase, "domestic institutions," as has been before observed, is the one in common use all through the South, to designate slavery; and here, it is lauded as affording to the white race a "leisure and opportunity for mental cultivation, which finds no parallel in any other country." But as this is not eulogy enough, the editor follows it up by a more open and undisguised defence of these cherished "domestic institutions," and pledges himself to defend them against every attack, and to make this one chief feature of his paper. This is his language on this subject—

> We believe that the institutions of the South are founded in the *immutable laws* of the God of nature. We believe that on them will be built a fabric of glory and greatness to the South. We believe especially that they afford to the Southern States the means of outstripping the rest of the world in their literary career. And we know that these are times of peculiar danger to these institutions; we know that they are now attacked by the insidious foe, as well as by the open enemy. We shall, therefore, place our Journal as a sentinel on the watchtower of Southern institutions, ever watchful for attacks, and ever ready to repel them.

While on the subject of Southern literature, I cannot omit adverting to a most extraordinary production that I met with at Athens, published during the last year, 1838, by a citizen of Georgia, John J. Flourroy, from whom I received a long visit during my stay here. This writer advocates the singular notion, that the negro race are the accursed of God, and designated as the "great beast" in the Apocalypse of St. John, and that as such there is no hope for America while the black race remain in it. He is, therefore, an advocate of "colonization" in the broadest sense of the term, and will be content with nothing short of the complete expulsion of the whole race, and their settlement in their original country, Africa. He greatly blames the Catholics and Protestants for deeming each other respectively "the beast" spoken of in the Revelation; and calls on them to correct this error. But the whole work is so curious, that such portions of it as may be necessary to give an idea of its style of thought and composition, should be placed before the reader in the author's own language, preserving the use of the italics and capitals of the original. Here is the opening of his work—

> This volume was designed to do away certain misconceptions which exist between the Roman Catholic and the Protestant Churches, regarding the Beast and Babylon of the Apocalypse. The two white Churches, through their authorities or Priests, have unhappily applied to each other, the persons and meaning of all these monsters. And growing fierce over the idea, that it is sinful and *unpardonable to love each other!!* the Catholics have almost always hated the Protestants, and have in turn received as free and hearty draughts of the like animosity from Protestant zealots!! Thus *Christians* have *abhorred*, where they had better have LOVED EACH OTHER; and from misunderstandings, I think, too obvious to a plain comprehension of the Bible, and certainly unwarranted by its spirit: nor is any cause seen of a nature sufficiently vast to authorize so much overt variance in Christianity, at least, to the view of the CHRISTIAN PHILOSOPHER. And, I do not believe either church, the Beast 'issuing from the bottomless pit,' and 'going into perdition;' nor that to love either sanctuary with pure devotion as houses of Christ, will affix on any forehead the 'mark of the beast,' and render any person liable to perdition. My reasons for thus believing, I shall proceed now to state at length.

An examination is then made of the Apocalypse of St. John, commencing with the passage, "A star fell from heaven, and to him was given the key of the bottomless pit;" and from these it is deduced that Ham, the father of the African race, was the "beast of great authority, with seven heads and ten horns." After this the author thus proceeds—

> Greater authority is given us from the Bible to suppose Ham and his progeny the evil monsters, than to suppose the not cursed Catholic children of Japhet, the same. And why? Because it is impossible that Christ would designate Japhet's posterity, who have benefited the world so much, and who are the only men (white men) alive, who carry the Gospel abroad to the most distant regions (the Apostles, and the Saviour himself were white,) as the vilest of creatures next to Satan; and have overslipped entirely the children of Ham, who are, and have been from

the days of Noah, *corrupt and corrupting*, and *Africa always a land of savage murderers, and abominable whoremongers, difficult to reclaim, and obstinately anti-christian*; though to them the Gospel was preached in Apostolic times, simultaneously with Europe; and which black race refused, or neglected to profit by the good seed there sown; while the Europeans took and profited most happily by the heavenly sowing.

In conclusion he contends that even where Papal tyranny and corruption seem to warrant the Protestant notion of Rome being "the great beast" of the Apocalypse, it was owing to indirect influence, flowing from *African* sources that these evils were engendered; for he says—

> That the Babylon of the Revelation, sitting on a scarlet-coloured beast, was only the influences of the Negro race, supported by the Dragon and Devil, in all those refinements of fashion, money, harlots, wine, kings, and idols, which are abominations growing out of the systems of Government and Paganism introduced by Ham. And this Babylon does not mean Rome. For the utmost violence of the Romish Inquisition, or Church Tyranny, was felt in Spain, and advised by the Spanish Cardinals, and the Cardinals from and contiguous to, Africa. And it was from Spain, by a Spanish husband of Mary's of England, Philip, that the Inquisition was introduced into England, at which Archbishop Cranmer, and other eminent and most pious men, were executed. And now an examination into the Spanish pedigree, or the ancestors of Spain, will show that much Moorish and African blood yet remains in the people, and the great majority of them are part negro—Philip himself had a woolly head, though brown skin.

What, however, will astonish Christian readers more than any of the preceding passages, startling as they are, is the use made by this Southern writer, of the authority of Christ himself for the denunciation of the negro race! This is the passage in which the author makes this extravagant assertion—

> That the Saviour himself showed something, plain enough, of the above truth, or at least a very strong suspicion that way—by alluding to dogs, as not fit to throw our bread unto; and when a woman of Canaan, a Syro-Phœnician, asked him to heal her daughter, he hesitated to notice her, and at last said, though he afterwards granted her request, 'It is not meet to cast the children's bread to dogs;' thus designating her black race as *dogs*, to whom we must not cast bread; or in other words, must

scrupulously avoid; and when the Apocalypse says 'Dogs' are without with 'whoremongers' in the lake of fire—and not admitted into the New Jerusalem—we have the finale of the picture, in mighty corroboration of my opinions of the Real Babylon.

The newspapers of Athens contain their full share of notices of runaway slaves, who appear to be just as anxious to escape from the power of the whites, as this "Expulsionist" is to rid his country of the blacks. Among the signs or tokens by which these slaves are to be recognized or known, one of the notices states, of a negro supposed to have gone off after his wife, who was living in another part of the country—"He is much marked with the whip."

In no place during our stay in the United States, did we hear so much of the immorality and depravity of the slave population as here. According to the testimony of all parties, the negroes were so addicted to lying and stealing, that they were not to be trusted out of sight or hearing; and instances were related to us, in which poisonings and secret murders had been committed by them on their own relatives, to prevent disclosures. Some had revenged themselves for offences committed by brothers and sisters, by stealing articles, and placing them secretly in the pockets of those they wished to injure, then accusing them, and becoming witnesses to convict them of the crime, for which they suffered stripes, imprisonment, and death; the accusers often subsequently confessing their wickedness, and boasting in the success of their plots. In short, it would seem impossible, according to the account of those who are surrounded by it, that any state of society can be more depraved than this. And yet, the Christian churches here, with one accord, maintain a general silence on the subject of slavery, unless provoked by some peculiar circumstances to make a public declaration on the subject; and then, it is in palliation of this "domestic institution," as it is called, and in denunciation of Abolitionism. The following is taken from the "Southern Christian Advocate," the Methodist Journal of the South, and needs no comment—

> The Georgia Conference, a year ago, declared that slavery, as it exists in the Southern States, is not a moral evil; and the South Carolina Conference, at its session shortly afterwards, had the following proceedings on the subject.
>
> *Resolved* 1st. That it is the sense of this Conference, that slavery, as it exists in these United States, is not a moral evil.
>
> *Resolved* 2nd. That we view slavery as a civil and domestic institution, with which, as ministers of Jesus Christ, we have nothing to do, further than to ameliorate the condition of the slave, by endeavouring to bring both him and his master under the benign influence of Christianity.

During our stay at Athens, I attended, on Thursday, the 27th of June, a debating club, formed of the resident gentlemen of the town, not connected with the University. It was held in a spacious room over the Post-office, which served also for the reading-room of the club, and was amply supplied with newspapers from all parts of the Union. The meeting commenced at three o'clock, and continued till seven. The members in attendance were few, but they were all above forty years of age, and nearly all had titles, as general, colonel, major, &c. The appearance of the room when we entered it, was more like some of the scenes described by Mrs. Trollope in the West, than I had ever before seen. The floor was of newly-planed pine-wood, without mat or carpet, and it was covered with saliva and tobacco juice, from the chewers of the club, for whom no spitting-boxes appeared to have been provided, and, therefore, every minute at least, some member was seen and heard to project his contribution to the floor, which was spotted over like the leopard's skin.

The chair was taken by the President, a general, and the Secretary called the meeting to order, but this did not produce the least alteration in the aspect of the meeting. The few members who were scattered about the room, sat each after his own fashion. One gentleman placed his legs on the table, and exhibited the soles of his boots to the President. Another hung back in his chair, while it stood on its two hind legs only, with his feet placed on the upper front bar of the chair, in which attitude he rocked himself to and fro like a nurse hushing a baby to sleep, and everything was marked by the greatest indifference to decorum.

The question for debate was "Ought the State to have the right to educate the children of its citizens?" The first speaker was, by the rules of the club, the gentleman who placed the question on the books for discussion. He spoke for about an hour, in support of the affirmative of this question; and argued the case closely and well; but being a more than usually copious chewer of tobacco, he spit on the floor at the end of almost every sentence, rolling his quid from side to side in his mouth during the interval. Once, during his speech, he asked for a tumbler of water, which one of the members brought him from a wooden bucket, placed in the centre of the room, with a wooden ladle to drink and fill the glass with; and he then threw away his quid, stopped to rinse out his mouth four or five times with the water, which he projected out of the window, near which he was speaking; he then took a fresh quid from a large black square mass of compactly pressed tobacco, which he carried in his waistcoat pocket, and resumed his discourse, spitting on the floor until a large pool had been formed before him; and at the close of his address, the rinsing of the mouth, and the renewal of the quid, was repeated.

This gentleman, who we understood was a man of fortune and leisure, not engaged in any business or profession, was followed by three speakers in succession, who maintained the negative of the question; and, very much to my surprise, nearly the same arguments that are used against the adoption of any measures by the State for the promotion of general education in England, were repeated here. Each of these gentlemen spoke about half an hour, and delivered their sentiments with great force and in accurate language. They all copiously loaded the floor with tobacco-juice, so that the odour began to be extremely disagreeable, especially as the afternoon was warm; the thermometer being at 90° in the shade. The fifth speaker at length took up the affirmative of the proposition, as to the right and duty of the State to educate the children of its citizens, or, in other words, to provide funds, and establish a system of National Education, by which the children of all those who were either unable or unwilling to confer on them the advantage of primary instruction, at the expense of the State.

At the close of this speech, the hour for adjournment drawing near, the chairman expressed a desire to hear my sentiments on this subject. To this I at first demurred, expressing my reluctance to offer opinions on a question which some might think not properly within my sphere of action, as a foreigner; and I was therefore desirous of leaving it in the hands of the native citizens, who were, no doubt, the best judges of what system would be most acceptable to themselves. But this objection being overruled, and a general expression being uttered of a wish to hear my sentiments on the question, I at length complied, and spoke for about half an hour, maintaining the affirmative of the subject, replying to the objections urged by the three opposing speakers; and citing the successful example of the Prussian system, as the most perfect, and that of New England as the next best and nearest example, both of the wisdom, justice, policy, and practicability of the State educating the children of its citizens. After this, the chairman summed up the arguments on each side, and gave his decision in favour of the affirmative view of the question, and thus terminated the debate.

The climate of Athens is peculiarly healthy; and in the spring and autumn of the year, is as agreeable as it is salubrious; the atmosphere being dry, and the thermometer ranging between 40 and 80 degrees. But in the summer it sometimes rises to 100 degrees, and is often at 95 degrees; while in winter it goes below zero; and in the winter before last was at 10 degrees below that point. The inconvenience of sudden changes in the same day is also often felt here; and 40 degrees difference in the range of the thermometer in the twenty-four hours has often been experienced. Still, pulmonary complaints are not nearly so frequent as in the North; and the yellow fever, which has already appeared at New Orleans and Charleston, is unknown here, nor in the hottest season of the year do the residents think it necessary to remove for their health.

CHAPTER XXXIV

Having become acquainted with a legal gentleman at Athens, who had been formerly attorney and counsel for the Cherokee Indians, the tribe that was removed, during the last year only, from the territory which they occupied in this State, to their new region west of the Mississippi, I had an opportunity of learning, partly from himself, and partly from documentary and other accurate sources, many interesting particulars respecting this tribe. Nearly the whole of the north-western section of this State was, until very recently, in the occupation of the Cherokees, who numbered about 16,000 persons, and were much more advanced in civilization than any other of the aborigines of this continent. They had well-cultivated farms, pleasant villages, and some of their more opulent chiefs lived in well-built houses, excellently furnished with tables, sofas, carpets, mirrors, beds, and table-services of china, glass, and plate. Both males and females adopted the European dress; the latter were well instructed, and some of them had pianofortes, on which they were able to play. One of their tribe, an Indian, named George Guess, invented a syllabic alphabet—though he knew no other language than Cherokee—containing fifty-two characters: the Mohawk or Iroquois had only fifteen. Such was its success, that young Cherokees learnt by it to write letters to their friends in the short space of three days, and a newspaper was published in this character in 1826, called the "Cherokee Phœnix," half in English and half in Cherokee, each part being a translation of the other. Their principal chief, John Ross, though a perfect Indian in complexion and physiognomy, (whom I had seen at Washington,) dressed well in the European mode, and wrote accurately-expressed letters, of which I saw several, both in the original and in copies. After many difficulties and great reluctance on their part, the general government of the United States succeeded in obtaining their unwilling assent to a treaty for their removal to other lands beyond the Mississippi. But so unpopular was this treaty with the bulk of the tribe, the chiefs alone being the negotiating parties, that previous to 1837, not more than 6,000 had removed, and the larger portion of 16,000 for a long time persisted in their determination not to do so. At length, however, the pressure on them by the general government, who appointed one of its most distinguished generals, with an adequate force, to execute the treaty, and compel their removal, if they still hesitated, was such as they could no longer resist, and accordingly the whole number, during the summer of the last year, left this country, and went to join their red brethren in the West.

The territory set apart for the whole of the Indian tribes thus transplanted from the east to the west of the Mississippi, is greater in area than all England and Scotland combined, being about 600 miles in length by 200 in breadth, and containing 80,000,000 of acres of land. The number of Indians among whom this territory is divided, do not exceed 95,000 persons in twenty-two tribes; about 20,000 being natives of the western lands, and 75,000 transferred from the eastern side of the Mississippi. The whole of the tract is said to be well watered, sufficiently wooded, healthy, and extremely fertile—equally well adapted to agriculture and pasture, and possessing iron and lead ore, and saltsprings, with a considerable extent of prairie land, especially on its western border.

Some well-informed persons entertain a belief that these tribes, thus placed in juxtaposition and communication with each other, will form a Federal Union, and become exceedingly formidable, especially as the Choctaws, the Chickasaws, and the Cherokees, have each a knowledge of reading and writing, and have written laws for their own government, and regular forms of legislation. These Indians are therefore desirous of having some code of international law for their adoption and use, to be passed by the United States' government, and made binding on them by their ratification of it. Others, however, conceive that anything which can tend to cement their union, will make them too formidable for the white settlers near their territory; and therefore think it is best to let them continue a divided people; so that, by wars and dissensions among themselves, they may be weakened, and ultimately destroyed. According to the most recent and accurate accounts, the following is the condition of the principal tribes in that territory.

The Choctaws, who exceed 15,000, have a tract near the Red River, and on the borders of Texas, about 200 miles long and 150 miles broad. They have nearly 200 white men married to Indian females, living among them as part of their tribe, and about 600 negro slaves. They have houses and cattle, waggons and ploughs, and cultivate corn and cotton, having raised 600 bales of the latter from their fields in the last year. They have also 1,000 spinning-wheels, 1,000 cards, and 400 looms, supplied them by the United States' government—besides mills for grinding flour and sawing timber, all worked by water-power. There are eight native merchants among them, who imported in the past year about 80,000 dollars' worth of goods.

For their government, they have adopted a written constitution, upon republican principles, with slight exceptions. It provides for a general council, or legislative body, to consist of the three principal chiefs, and thirty counsellors chosen annually by the people; that is, ten in each district. The legislative council meets once a year. It is supplied with a speaker and clerk. Two of their chiefs have the veto prerogative, but when an act is passed by two thirds of the legislative council, it becomes a law. Eighteen *light horsemen* are kept always ready to enforce the laws of the nation.

They have enacted some wholesome laws relative to the crimes of murder, theft, lost property, fences, widows and orphans, witchcraft, &c. Legal counsel and trial by jury are allowed to all. Severe enactments have been made against the introduction of ardent spirits; and these are enforced with becoming zeal, so that the evil of intemperance, which is so fearfully destructive to Indians generally, is now little known in the Choctaw country.

The English mode of dress has been adopted to a considerable extent, especially among the females, and is daily becoming more common. Many of the Choctaws may properly be classed with civilized men, while a large portion of the residue are little inferior to them in point of improvement.

They have nine schools supported by the United States' government, the teachers receiving 500 dollars each annually; and in these, 210 youths of the Indians are educated, besides 67 at the Choctaw Academy in Kentucky. There is a Presbyterian, a Methodist, and a Baptist Mission among them, with Churches and Sunday Schools belonging to it, and supported by each; the tuition to the natives being in all cases gratuitous.

The Cherokees, who exceed 20,000 in all, have a tract of still greater extent than the Choctaws, between the rivers Arkansas and Missouri, embracing about 2,500,000 acres. They are chiefly agriculturists, but have several lead mines and salt works, 8,000 horses, 20,000 horned cattle, 25,000 hogs, 200 waggons, several ploughs to every farm, many hundred spinning wheels, and 200 looms, besides saw and grist mills in abundance.

Their form of civil government resembles that of one of the American States, with an upper and lower House of Representatives, each having a President and Secretary, meeting yearly in autumn, but convened specially at other times by the principal chiefs, of whom there are three. Each district has two judges, and two sheriffs (who are called "light-horsemen," because their long journeys require them to be well mounted,) to see the laws executed. They have several merchants of their own tribe, with capitals of from 5,000 to 15,000 dollars each, and a native physician who received a medical education in the United States. They have also a Presbyterian, a Methodist, and a Baptist Mission, with Churches and Sunday Schools belonging to each.

The Creeks, who are about 20,000 in number, have a large tract which adjoins that of the Choctaws on the south, the Cherokees on the north and east, and the great prairies on the west. There is no wooded country, it is said, between them and the Rocky Mountains, a distance of nearly 500 miles, the whole of that space being occupied by level prairies of good soil, but without forests, and generally uninhabited by any Indian tribes, from the want of wood and water. The Creeks are almost wholly agriculturists, and have their fields enclosed with rail-fences. They cultivate corn so extensively, that they have sometimes had 50,000 or 60,000 bushels above their own consumption, for sale and exportation. They spin, weave, sew, knit, and follow other pursuits of industry; have permanent dwellings, mills, and looms. They are governed by written laws, resembling in spirit those of the United States, enacted by a council of the nation, convened as often as circumstances may require, and sheriffs or light-horsemen to execute their decisions, and that of the judges. They have also three missions residing among them, with Churches and Sunday Schools.

These are the three principal tribes. The others who have gone from this side of the Mississippi have neither of them more than 1,000 persons each; the Delawares and Shawanees having about this number; and the others, including the Senecas, Kickapoos, and Pottawotomies, with some smaller tribes, numbering only from 200 to 500 each. All these are less civilized, and some of them are wretched as well as barbarous, from poverty and want.

Of the indigenous tribes within this Indian territory, the Pawnees are the most numerous, having upwards of 10,000 men. In their habits and condition they are farther removed from those of civilized man, than any tribe which we have noticed. In some instances, they continue to cultivate the earth with the shoulder-bone of the buffalo. This being tied to a stick for a handle, serves the purpose of a spade or shovel. All live in villages, where their huts are crowded closely, without order in their arrangement. Besides their houses of bark, and of flags, they have a few of earth. These are circular and in form of a cone, the wall of which is about two feet in thickness, and is sustained by wooden pillars within. Like their other huts, they have no floor except the earth. The fire is in the centre, and the smoke escapes directly above. The door is low and narrow, so that in entering, a person must half crawl. The door, as in their other huts, is closed by a skin of some animal suspended therein.

The Kickapoos are one of the smallest of the tribes, but they are remarkable for having a native prophet, called Kenekuk, among them, who has established a religion of his own; and of which the following are the chief features.

He professes to receive all that he teaches, immediately from the Great Spirit, by a supernatural agency. He teaches abstinence from the use of ardent spirits, the observation of the Sabbath, and some other good things. He appears to have little knowledge of the doctrines of Christianity, only as his dogmas happen to agree with them. By some, however, it is thought that he and his party are improving in Christian knowledge and morals.

Besides the speeches of the prophet, their religious exercises consist of a kind of prayer, expressed in broken sentences, often repeated, in a monotonous sing-song tone, equalling about two measures of a common psalm-tune. All the people engage in this; and in order to preserve unison in the words, each holds in his or her hand, a small board, about an inch and a half broad, and eight or ten inches long, upon which is engraved arbitrary characters, which they follow up with the finger, until the last character admonishes them that they have completed the prayer.

These characters are five in number: the first represents the heart; the second, the heart and flesh; the third, the life; the fourth, their names; the fifth, their kindred. During the service, these characters are gone over several times: the first time the person supposes himself to be on earth; next, to be approaching the door of the house of God, in heaven; then at the door, and so onward to heaven.

Certain men are appointed to use the rod on occasions of worship, for the purpose of maintaining order. The rod, also, is applied by these men as a kind of church-discipline in cases of transgression. The offender, whose crime may be known only to himself, applies to one of the four or five persons who are authorized to use the rod, and states that he has committed an offence, for which he desires the whipper to inflict a given number of stripes upon his bare back. Having received the flagellation, which frequently brings blood, the penitent immediately shakes hands with the executioner and others near, returning thanks for the favour conferred upon him, and declaring that he feels himself relieved from a heavy burden. The prophet indulges in the privilege of a plurality of wives.

The provision made by the United States' government for the education of children in the Indian tribes removed beyond the Mississippi, is not inconsiderable. There is first an annual money-grant of 10,000 dollars from the Congress. Added to this, there have been various annuities in money and grants in land to the several tribes, in aid of this object; for instance—to the Kauzaus, 23,040 acres of good land for education, and 600 dollars per annum to aid them in agriculture; to the Osages, 34,560 acres of land for the support of schools, and 1,200 dollars a year for agriculture; to the Delawares, 23,040 acres of land for education; to the Pottowatamies, 70,000 dollars for the purposes of education and the domestic arts; 150,000 dollars for mills, farm-houses, and agricultural improvements; to the Kickapoos, 500 dollars a year for ten successive years, for the support of a school and books; and 4,000 dollars for fencing, ploughing, and agriculture: to the Pawnees, 2,000 dollars a year for ten years for agricultural implements, and 1,000 dollars for oxen and live-stock; 2,000 dollars per annum for ten years for smitheries and blacksmiths, and 1,000 dollars a year for ten years for schools. These are the grants and allowances to the smaller tribes. To the larger it will be seen to be proportionate.

To the Cherokees, 2,000 dollars annually for ten years, for the education of their children in their own country, in letters and the mechanical arts, and 1,000 dollars for the purchase of a printing-press and types. By the treaty of 1835, which stipulated for the removal of the whole tribe, a small portion only having gone beyond the Mississippi before this, the large sum of 150,000 dollars, in addition to 50,000 dollars granted before, making 200,000 dollars in all, is appropriated to the support of common schools, and such a literary institution of a higher order, as may be established in the Indian country, the interest of this permanent fund to be expended by direction of the Cherokee council, under the supervision of the President of the United States. The Creeks have a yearly annuity of 4,000 dollars for schools, and the Choctaws have a provision of 25,000 dollars permanent fund, an annuity of 2,500 dollars for twenty years, and the education of twenty youths of the nation, free of cost, in the Choctaw Academy, in Kentucky.

In addition to the means thus provided for the education and general improvement of the Indian tribes removed from their lands on this side of the Mississippi, the American Board of Society for Foreign Missions has sent among them a number of pious and devoted men as ministers of the gospel, and these are generally accompanied by their wives, who assist in the business of religious education. These are all supported by the Missionary Societies by whom they are ordained; and on very small salaries, just barely sufficient to give them subsistence. The amount allowed, varies according to the expensiveness of living at each station, and is fixed by the Missionary Societies, so as barely to cover the necessary current expenditures of the several Missions. None of them, therefore, receive any compensation which they can lay up as their own personal property. By this means, the voluntary surrender of the Missionary to labours of benevolence for the benefit of the Indians, places him beyond the influence of temptation to acquire property. He does not receive even a promise of support for his family, should they outlive him; but he trusts all to Providence. By the United States' government, Missionaries are recognized as being in its service, and, like agents, subagents, and others authorized to reside in the Indian country, they enjoy its protection. Should a Missionary be convicted of a violation of the laws regulating intercourse with the Indian tribes, the government would expel him; but this circumstance would not prevent the occupying of the station by an approved Missionary as his successor.

There has been, however, either a falling off in zeal, or a deficiency in means among the Christian community, who have these Missions in charge; for according to an official statement laid before the Board in the last year, it appears that while for two years past, the only addition made to the Missionaries for the three denominations of Presbyterian, Methodist, and Baptist, had been two males and eleven females, the increase of the Indian population within the territory had been 19,730—the Indians, therefore, increasing at the rate of 43 per cent on their previous numbers, and the Missionaries less than 1 per cent on theirs.

The several tribes have each an agent appointed by the United States' government to reside among or near them, and to be the channel of their communication with the government on all matters of business: the salary of such agents, who are usually officers of the army or militia, is about 1,500 dollars a year; and the superintendence of the whole is confided to a Chief Commissioner and Board for Indian Affairs, the former appointed by the President, and the latter composed of the members of the Congress at Washington.

The whole number of the Indians of all kinds is estimated to be as follows:—

1.	Tribes removed West of the Mississippi	68,669
2.	Tribes originally dwelling there	101,000
3.	Indians living East of the Rocky Mountains	20,000
4.	Tribes West of the Rocky Mountains	80,000
5.	Tribes within British and Russian Territories	1,520,431
6.	Indians of various tribes in Texas and Mexico	3,600,000
	Total	5,390,100

CHAPTER XXXV

The environs of Athens furnish many agreeable drives and rides, and among other spots may be named that of the Springs of Helicon, about four miles from the town: though the Athenians of Georgia have not yet realized in them the properties of the Grecian Helicon. The waters are chalybeate, and used by invalids for giving tone to the stomach, and strengthening the digestive powers. There are many ordinary springs of pure water in the neighbourhood of the town, but they had many of them failed in consequence of the severe and long-continued drought. A gentleman residing in the country to the west of this, was, indeed, obliged to send every day ten miles for the supply of water for his household, every spring within that distance having dried up. Before we left Athens, however, three days of heavy and incessant rain had refreshed the thirsty earth, replenished the exhausted springs, and rejoiced all the planters' hearts.

On the banks of the Oconee river—one fork of which runs close by the town of Athens, in a deep valley, the town itself being on a hill, and the other forks at a distance for a few miles only—are three cotton factories, all worked by water-power, and used for spinning yarn, and weaving cloth of coarse qualities for local consumption only. I visited one of these, and ascertained that the other two were very similar to it in size and operations. In each of them there are employed from 80 to 100 persons, and about an equal number of white and black. In one of them, the blacks are the property of the millowner, but in the other two they are the slaves of planters, hired out at monthly wages to work in the factory. There is no difficulty among them on account of colour, the white girls working in the same room and at the same loom with the black girls; and boys of each colour, as well as men and women, working together without apparent repugnance or objection. This is only one among the many proofs I had witnessed of the fact, that the prejudice of colour is not nearly so strong in the South as in the North. Here, it is not at all uncommon to see the black slaves of both sexes, shake hands with white people when they meet, and interchange friendly personal inquiries; but at the North I do not remember to have witnessed this once; and neither in Boston, New York, or Philadelphia would white persons generally like to be seen shaking hands and talking familiarly with blacks in the streets.

The negroes here are found to be quite as easily taught to perform all the required duties of spinners and weavers as the whites, and are just as tractable when taught; but their labour is dearer than that of the whites, for whilst the free boys and girls employed receive about 700 dollars per month, out of which they find themselves, the slaves are paid the same wages (which is handed over to their owners,) and the mill-owner has to feed them all in addition; so that the free labour is much cheaper to him than the slave; and the hope expressed by the proprietor to me was, that the progressive increase of white population by immigration, would enable him to employ wholly their free labour, which, to him would be more advantageous. The white families engaged in these factories, live in log huts clustered about the establishment on the river's bank, and the negroes repair to the huts allowed them by their owners when they are near, or stay at the mill, when their master's plantation is far off.

The whites looked miserably pale and unhealthy; and they are said to be very short-lived, the first symptoms of fevers and dysenteries in the autumn appearing chiefly among them at the factories, and sweeping numbers of them off by death. Under the most favourable circumstances, I think the Factory system detrimental to health, morals, and social happiness; but in its infant state, as it is here, with unavoidable confinement in a heated temperature, and with unwholesome associations, it is much worse, and I do not wonder that the most humane members of the community deplore the introduction of factories in the South, and wish that the labours of the people should be confined to agriculture, leaving manufactures to Europe or to the States of the North. The machinery of these establishments is made at Frankford in New Jersey, the cotton is grown here, and the wool, of which they use large quantities in the production of a coarse cloth of cotton and wool mixed, for negro clothing, is imported from Africa to New York, being coarser but much cheaper than wool from any part of Europe, and answering their purpose equally well.

The municipal government of Athens is in the hands of a body of Town Commissioners, sometimes called Aldermen, but there is no Mayor nor other office corresponding to this. The Board of Commissioners, who serve gratuitously, are seven in number, and they are elected annually, by universal suffrage and vote by ballot, every white male of twenty-one years of age, residing in the town, having a voice in their election. These Commissioners are empowered by an act of the State Legislature, to tax the inhabitants of the town for the general expenses of public works, such as the making and repairing bridges, roads. &c. and the payment of the only salaried officer employed, who is called the Town Marshall, and who has 500 dollars a year. It is his duty to maintain the peace of the town; and after nine o'clock at night he is empowered to apprehend all coloured people found out of their dwellings without a pass, and to imprison or flog them at his discretion. This power is, as may be supposed, often abused; and the last Marshall of the Town resigned his office, because he flogged a coloured girl so severely that she died of the punishment, and he refused to make compensation to the owner. Such was the most current version of the transaction among the residents; though on this, as on every other local question, there are sure to be different accounts of everything that transpires. There is no doubt, however, that great severity was exercised, and that the death of the culprit ensued.

The mode of assessing both the State and town taxes here is much complained of. Instead of its being on property or income, the most equitable of all modes of assessment, it is made chiefly on merchandize and stock in trade. The legislators, being mostly landowners, have contrived to exempt landed property and its produce, as well as negroes and cattle, which are *their* instruments of production, and stock in trade, from taxation; while the traders and storekeepers, who have stocks of goods, pay heavily. As the assessment takes place at different seasons of the year, it has been ascertained, that the goods forming the stock of an importer, have been taxed at Savannah in the early part of the year, and when sent up to Augusta, to have been taxed again in the warehouse of the merchant there; and, lastly, in the latter part of the same year, to have been taxed a third time in the store of the retailer at Athens. All attempts to alter this have hitherto been in vain; as the prejudice of the country people against those living in towns is very strong; and the planters and farmers continually assert that as they are the only people who rise early and work hard, they ought to be exempt from taxation, while the townspeople, whom they consider as a class of mere idlers, ought to pay the public burthens, however heavy they may be.

This unwillingness to pay even that which is justly due, is however a very general feature of the American community; and I have not yet discovered any difference between the Northerners and the Southerners in this respect. They mutually reciprocate the charge that they are each taxed unjustly for the benefit of the other; and in this the Southerners say truly; because the tariff-laws of the North undoubtedly impose heavy taxes on the South for the protection of Northern manufactures; while the people of the North are doing all they can to force on the abolition of slavery, which, say the Southerners, would rob us of our property, and means of conducting agriculture. That the South, however, is as unwilling as the North to pay its just debts, whenever it can evade them, the following fact sufficiently proves. The inventor of the cotton-gin, most generally in use here, Mr. Whitney, was a native of America, and when his invention was completed he took out a patent for it at Washington. This patent was continually infringed upon by dishonest men in his own State, who used it without his permission, or without paying him for the privilege, though he sold this to all applicants for a very moderate sum. Many, however, made a show of intending to be just, by purchasing the privilege to use this patent-right, and gave an acceptance of a bill under their own hand for the amount at a short date. When such bills became due they were almost uniformly refused payment, or renewed for a longer time on various pretences; and when at length their number became so considerable as to make it necessary to take legal process for their recovery, whenever it was ascertained that the consideration for which the bill was given, was the purchased privilege of using this patent cotton-gin, no jury would find a verdict for the plaintiff, because they wanted that all the planters throughout the whole State should use these cotton-gins without paying for the privilege! By making it impossible to recover damages in such cases, the machine could be used with impunity; and in point of fact the patent ceased to be productive of the least benefit to the inventor, at least in this State, though all his fellow-citizens here were so much benefited by his labours, Georgia being then the largest cotton-growing State in the Union. In South Carolina, however, where much less benefit was received, the State voted him a grant of 50,000 dollars for his invention.

We passed the great national anniversary of the 4th of July, at Athens; and after an agreeable morning ride to the Helicon spring, and drinking of its fresh and pure chalybeate waters, I attended the chapel of the University, at which the oration suitable to the day was to be delivered. The assembly was large and respectable, and contained quite as many ladies as gentlemen. It is usual for the two literary societies attached to the University, the Phi-Kappa and the Demosthenian, to elect alternately the orator from their body; and on this year, the Demosthenians furnished the speaker. The minister of the Methodist church presided, he being one of the Board of Trustees of the University, and after the reading of the Declaration of Independence, which is always done on this occasion, the young orator, a student of eighteen or twenty, advanced to the platform, wearing the badge of the Demosthenian Society, and delivered his address. The matter of this was better than the manner, at least, according to the taste which usually prevails in Europe, where the vehemence of voice, frequency of emphasis, and continued action of the arms and body, would have been thought too theatrical for the place and the occasion. But the taste of the Americans, as regards oratory, inclines them to admire the turgid, the florid, and the bombastic, rather than the subdued and unimpassioned. I was seriously asked, indeed, by one of the auditors, after the close of the oration, whether America did not produce more eloquent orators than England. It was conceded that the English were more profound and more learned; but the opinion of at least a dozen of our party was, that she could not equal the United States in the production of brilliant public speakers. It is certain that oratory is much more studied as an art in this country, than it is at home; and that public speaking and debating is more frequent, and superiority in both more eagerly sought after, and more esteemed, than in England; but with all this, I have not yet heard any of their most distinguished men, such as Clay, Webster, Calhoun, Wise, Hoffman, or any others, make such eloquent and impressive speeches as are heard every session in England, from Lord Lyndhurst, Lord Brougham, Sir Robert Peel, Lord Palmerston, Lord Stanley, Mr. Gladstone, Mr. Daniel O'Connell, Mr. Shiel, and others among the peers and commoners of England. The difference is still more marked in the students of the Universities and public institutions of the two countries; for the speeches and recitations of the students at Oxford, Cambridge, Eton, Westminster, Winchester, and Harrow, are, in general, greatly superior, in extent of learning, accuracy of composition, beauty of diction, and, above all, in elegance of action, purity of elocution, and grace of delivery, to those of Harvard, Providence, and Athens, which I had an opportunity of hearing, and with which, therefore, I was enabled to compare them.

One most disgusting feature of all the oratory that I have yet heard in the Southern States, is the constant interruption to the flow of their discourses, by the almost equally copious flow of their saliva, from their excessive use of tobacco. In the churches, at public lectures, in private parties, or in public assemblies, you hear every minute the sound of the labial ejection, and its fall upon the floor; while the chewers roll about the offensive and blackened mass in their mouths, as though it was all that was worth living for. Each young man carries in his waistcoat pocket, not in a box, but open, a flattened square mass of black compressed tobacco, like a piece of Indian rubber. From this he cuts off, from time to time, whether in the company of ladies or not, a large piece, and, taking the expended quid from his mouth, he flings it out of the window, or in any near corner, and replaces it by the new one, which he forthwith begins to roll about like any ruminating animal. Their practice is literally that of "chewing the cud," though they want the "dividing the hoof," to take them out of the class of "unclean beasts." With some this practice produces the effect of giving an unhealthy paleness to the countenance, and hollowness to the eyes; while the corners of the lips are always defiled, and the mouth, when opened, realizes the image of the "whited sepulchre, without all fair, but within, only dead men's bones and rottenness." With others, the effect produced seemed to be an extreme degree of wildness and ferocity in the eye and countenance. From what I observed here, as well as elsewhere, I do not doubt but that the extensive use of tobacco by chewing, has a tendency to make men dissipated, reckless, violent, impatient, and sensual. It has some of the evil effects of ardent spirits and opium, and, like both of these poisons, it is not productive of the slightest benefit, to counteract the many evils which they produce. How it is that the ladies of America, married and unmarried, do not with one voice and one accord, refuse the approach of lips so filthily defiled, and turn with disgust from the offensive spitting in their presence and at their very feet, does, I confess, surprise me as much as anything I have ever seen in this country. It shews that habit will reconcile people to almost anything, though this is one of the practices to which I think no degree of familiarity, and no extent of time, would ever reconcile any one who thought fresh lips, sweet breath, and personal purity, essential to the enjoyment of intimate and friendly, not to say familiar and fond intercourse.

By the way, it is remarkable that the native Indians never chew tobacco; they only use it in the pipe; and though snuffing, smoking, and chewing are all dirty practices, and detract much from the personal cleanliness, sweetness, and general acceptability of all who practise either; yet chewing seems to be the most offensive of all, and in every part of Europe has long since been confined to the lowest and most vulgar classes of society, with gin-drinking and beer-drinking, the natural allies of tobacco in all its varieties of uncleanness. It is singular, however, that of the three forms in which this poisonous weed is used, smoking is the only one publicly prohibited in certain places. It would not be tolerated for men to smoke in a ball-room, or concert-room; nor is it ever done in a place of worship; but the floors of all three are covered, after every time of occupation, by the stains of those who chew. In steamboats, railroad cars, and other places of great public resort, it is very common to see the placard, "Gentlemen are requested not to smoke here;" but the still more offensive practice of chewing and spitting is allowed with impunity. I have never yet heard a single American female speak of the practice without regretting it; and when asked their opinion on the subject, they have always confessed that they disliked it, and wished it could be altered. But they do not possess nearly so much influence in directing the manners and practices of society in this country, as women do in England or in France; and, therefore, their wishes are less regarded. The external marks of deference shown to them by men giving them the best places in steamboats and stage-coaches, and rising to give them seats in public assemblies, is not accompanied by a similar deference for their opinion and authority in literature, taste, or manners, as is so often seen in France or England.

Our stay at the Planter's Hotel was peculiarly agreeable, for though there were no less than five public hotels, and a great number of private boarding-houses in that town, we had the good fortune to be in the best, and to have the most agreeable circle of society, including several professors of the College, and students of the University, as well as one of the clergy, and several wealthy planters, on a visit here from neighbouring States. There was only one drawback to our comfort, which, it is true, was a large one, and that was the incessant and uninterrupted chorus kept up every night by the dogs, cows, and hogs, that seemed to divide among them the undisputed possession of the streets at night. Not less than a hundred of each of these seemed to be at large, as though they belonged to no one, each doing its best in foraging for provender, and each endeavouring to maintain the superiority of its class, in the barking, lowing, and grunting of their respective members. If half as many negroes had made a tenth part of the disturbance to the public peace, the Town Marshall would have had them all apprehended, imprisoned, and flogged for their audacity; but hogs, dogs, and cows were privileged creatures, and though every one complained that they could get no sleep for their noises, yet every one thought it would be unsafe and unpopular to take any steps to confine or remove the animals, to prevent it. In addition to this ordinary and regular nightly concert of the brute creation, we had two or three extra nights of performance in another line, by negroes. A wooden house had to be moved from its original position to one more distant, according to a process common in the North, by being dragged along on rollers. As there are few or no labourers here but negroes, and these are all busily employed for their owners during the day, the only period at which their assistance could be had in any numbers, was at night; and a gang of men having been borrowed from their masters for this purpose, and furnished with passes, they assembled to perform their labour. The darkness of the night, the absence of their usual restraint, the distribution of whisky, and the general hilarity of the occasion, made them for a moment as joyous and as boisterous as a set of bacchanals; so that their shouts of merriment, mingled with the yelpings, meanings, and squealings of the dogs, cows, and pigs, made up a medley that banished sleep from the eyelids of the most weary.

The white labourers here are very few; but farther in the interior they are more numerous, though the greater number of them are not native Americans, but Irish, German, or Swiss emigrants. One of the former class was employed by the proprietor of the hotel, on some labour connected with the erection of a new building, and he was said to be a fair specimen of his class; yet we had from his own lips the confession that he drank a full quart of raw whisky every day without dilution, and that he had done so for the last twelve months, with an extra gill for Sunday! Yet he assured us that he did not drink nearly so much as many of his Irish fellow-labourers!

One of the novelties we observed here, was the use of negro girls to stand behind private carriages, holding the straps like a footman; and they performed the same office by stepping down to open the carriage door, and assist the riders to get in and out, after which they resumed their station, and stood as steadily as if long habit had rendered their position familiar to them.

There were some peculiarities of pronunciation that I heard at Athens, which I had not met with elsewhere. The word prepared, was generally pronounced "preparred," the last syllable sounding like tarred. Where, was also pronounced "wharr," to rhyme with far or star. The writ of habeas corpus was called the writ of "hab-beas;" and these were not the peculiarities of an individual, but were frequently repeated by different persons. Notwithstanding such exceptions as these, it is undoubtedly true that the differences in the pronunciation of English words, is not nearly so great between America and the best part of England, as it is between the different counties of England themselves; and on the whole, the English language is spoken in greater purity and with greater accuracy over the United States of America, than it is over Great Britain, while there is more homogeneity of character, as well as of speech, in this single nation, made up of twenty-three united provinces, than there is in the single nation of England, made up of only four separate people, the English, Scotch, Irish, and Welsh.

Among the peculiar application of terms, the following may be mentioned. The word balance is constantly used to signify the remainder of anything, as, "I shall spend the summer in the mountains, and the balance of the year on the sea-coast,"—or, "I shall be at my office in the morning, and the balance of the day in the country."—"I have only read the first volume of Cheveley, but I shall finish the balance by to-morrow;"—and at dinner, it is not uncommon to be asked "What will you take for the balance of your dinner?" The beautiful firefly which abounds here, and fills the air with sparkling gems at night, is called by the uninviting name of "the lightning bug!" If a person has taken a sail or a row in a boat or canoe, this is called "riding on the water." If one has been hospitable to another, this is expressed by the phrase "he shewed him a heap of kindness." If one is advised to be very courteous and attentive to any particular person, this is expressed by saying "Now do your prettiest." A lady who had six children, the eldest of whom was about twelve years old, wishing to express the fact that their respective ages were in very close succession, said, "You see my children are all well and healthy, but they are considerable of a huddle."

Sometimes there is extreme reluctance to use particular words, because they are supposed to convey associations that ought to be avoided. For instance, I heard that on the night of the party given at the University, the president. Dr. Church, had received a slight injury in the head, by a stone being thrown in the direction where he stood, by one of the younger class of students who were dissatisfied with their not being included in the invitation, though it was never usual to extend it beyond the seniors. But the lady who mentioned this incident to me, said, "The little boy threw a *rock* at the president;" on which I expressed my surprise, thinking he must be an infant Hercules to hurl a rock; when she replied, "Oh! no, it was a very small rock, and therefore the injury was very slight." I found afterwards that it is thought indelicate to use the word stone; and that they say a house is built of rock, the streets are paved with rock, and the boys throw rocks at sparrows, and break windows by throwing rocks. To speak of the tail of a horse, or any other animal, is deemed most indelicate, and the words hip and thigh must not be mentioned. This fastidiousness is carried to such a length, as to lead to alterations in the prayers of the Episcopalian service, and even in the language of the Bible. The passage in the Litany, "When thou tookest upon thee to deliver man, thou didst not abhor the virgin's womb," is thought too shocking for the public ear; and the passage in which prayer is offered for "all women labouring with child," is also thought too gross to be uttered. In the mutilations of Scripture, these two cases were mentioned to me by a clergyman who had himself heard them. In the passage of Genesis, in which the curse is pronounced on the serpent, "On thy belly shalt thou go," the preacher read it "On thy stomach shalt thou go;" and in the passage of the Evangelist, where the Saviour says to Peter, "Verily, before the cock shall crow, thou shalt deny me thrice," another preacher read it thus, "Before a certain fowl shall crow, thou shalt deny me thrice." Some instances of this nature were mentioned to me, which I cannot commit to writing; but they were all of a nature to show that the avoidance of the supposed indecent word, was sure to suggest the very associations which these fastidious manglers of the liturgy and the scriptures professedly wished to avoid; and made persons ask themselves, why the original terms were omitted, and other phrases substituted in their places; so that instead of accomplishing the end proposed, of preserving a greater purity of thought, it produced the very opposite effect.

I had thought that here, in the heart of Georgia, I should be quite beyond the chance of meeting any old friends or acquaintances, from England especially; but we had not yet got far enough into the interior for this, for during our stay at Athens, we were visited by a literary gentleman, who had been one of the earliest writers in the "Athenæum," when first published in London, under my editorship, and who had since come to this country as a teacher, and was now at the head of a large establishment for education in Gainsville, about forty miles distant; and hearing of my being here, he had come up thus far purposely to pay me a visit, and remained here several days. We were visited also by persons who had met me at Newcastle and at Hull in England, and several who had known me in Scotland.

On the whole, the scenery, the climate, and the society of Athens, with the large attendance on three successive Courses of my Lectures, and the private hospitalities enjoyed there, made our stay at this place more than usually agreeable.

Chapter XXXVI

Having heard that the northern portion of Georgia, in the territory lately occupied by the Cherokee Indians, contained some beautiful mountain-scenery, amidst which were two splendid Falls, but little visited by foreigners, yet equal in beauty and interest to any thing of the kind in the South; we determined to visit this section of country, and instead of returning to the North by the beaten track, to go up through this region, pass over into South Carolina, and thence go onward to the mountains of Virginia. As no public stages went by this route, it was necessary to engage private conveyances, which we effected on the following terms. An open barouche and pair was provided for our party of four; and a single-horse spring waggon was furnished for our baggage, and for these we were to pay at the rate of 12 dollars per day; estimating each day's journey at about 30 miles, making the cost, therefore, equal to about 1s. 8d. sterling per mile, as cheap as posting in England, as there are here no turnpikes or post-boys' fees.

After an early dinner, and the interchange of many farewell visits with the numerous friends we had made during our stay in Athens, we left them on Tuesday the 9th of July, at two o'clock, accompanied by the assurance of more general regrets, and warmer expressions of a hope that we might one day meet again, than so brief an acquaintance could have led us to expect. Our last view of Athens, after we had crossed the bridge over the river Oconee, and gained the heights of the opposite bank, was a pleasing one, and we left it, most probably for ever, with feelings strongly tinged with a melancholy, which we were not unwilling to indulge.

It was about eight o'clock in the evening when we reached the hotel at the Madison Springs, where we found comfortable accommodation and good fare, and where we accordingly passed the night. It was too early in the season for company to be assembled here, though in August and September the establishment is very full of persons who come up from the sea-coast, to drink the waters, which are slightly chalybeate, and enjoy the delicious shady walks and quiet retreats by which the house is so agreeably surrounded.

After an early breakfast, we left the Madison Springs at eight o'clock on the morning of Wednesday, the 10th of July, and proceeding over a rough road, with descending hills, we crossed a small river called the Hudson, by a wooden bridge, at which a toll of fifty cents had to be paid for our two vehicles, the first impost of this description we had met with on the road. This stream empties itself into the Savannah river above Augusta, and is only navigable for fishing-rafts and canoes.

Soon after noon we arrived at the small settlement of Carnesville, which presented a very perfect specimen of a gradually forming American village, rising into the dignity of a country-town. In its centre was the Court House of the district, and within a few yards of this were the sign-posts of three hotels. Not far off was seen the symbol of a doctor of medicine, with his name and title at full length, under a rudely delineated pestle-and-mortar, as the emblem of his profession. Right opposite to him, in a small wooden cabin of a single room, was the office of another professional man, the attorney-at-law; and within a few doors of these, were the shops of a blacksmith, a carpenter, and a saddler, with one large grocery store, at which everything sold by grocers, ironmongers, drapers, stationers, and haberdashers, in larger places, were to be found. The whole population did not exceed 250, including black and white; but as the proportion of the former grows less and less as you leave the coast and approach the mountains, there were not probably more than fifty coloured persons among the whole. At the hotel where we stopped to dine, were two fine brown bears, that had been just caught in the hills close to the town, where they are very numerous. In addition to these, we learnt that the woods and mountains around this place were abundantly tenanted by squirrels, racoons, minxes, and wolves; the hunting of which afforded good diversion to the young men of the place.

From Carnesville our road lay through a deeper and thicker forest than any we had yet passed, the solitude of which was awful and depressing; and though some parts of the way were extremely rugged, and the path continually interrupted by huge fallen trees rooted up by tornadoes, and lying with all their branches right across the road, so as to require continual windings through the brakes and underwood, to pass around them, yet other portions of the way were rendered agreeable by the fine views of the distant mountains which opened upon us in the north, to which our course was bending.

At sunset we arrived at a farm-house kept by a Mr. Holkham, to which we had been strongly recommended by the keeper of the hotel at Carnesville, as being the best house on the road, where we should receive every attention, and find a comfortable place to rest for the night. There was something in the sounds of "Holkham," and "fine farm"—from the associations which these words would be sure to awaken in the mind of any one who had ever heard of the Holkham of Mr. Coke of Norfolk—which, unreasonably, no doubt, made us expect more than usual hospitality and accommodation. Our disappointment was, therefore, the more severe, when we reached the spot, to find great unwillingness on the part of the proprietor to receive us at all. He urged no personal objections, but merely said that "he had no room for strangers," that "his people were all too busy to attend to them," and that "he had nothing to give either ourselves or our horses." We would have turned from his gate, and proceeded farther on, but that the driver was wholly unacquainted with the road, and our long parley had taken up so much time that it was now quite dark. We asked, therefore, to be admitted for the night, if it were only for shelter, without food or refreshment; and even this was most reluctantly and surlily yielded to. On taking out the horses, however, and entering, ourselves, into his dwelling, we found everything so dirty, repulsive, and disagreeable, that we resolved on re-harnessing our steeds, and going forward, after all. We therefore begged Mr. Holkham to let one of his farm-boys go with us a part of the way, to get us into the direct road, for which we would readily pay him; but even this he refused, on pretence that his boy might be snake-bitten if he came back on foot, and that he had no horse to spare for his riding. This was so inhospitable and unfeeling, that even the driver, his own countryman, could not help telling Mr. Holkham that he did not think such inhospitable treatment could be met with in any other part of America; to which the former sullenly replied, that he did not want to be troubled with strangers, and did not care about receiving their money; though the practice is nearly universal in these roads for such houses to receive and entertain travellers at the usual hotel rates, as an additional source of income to that yielded by their farming labours. We proceeded onward, therefore, without a guide; and after some difficulty amidst the many crossing and intersecting paths which we met with in the forest, we at length descried a light in the distance; and driving on towards it, found it to be a public inn, called the Curraghee Hotel, from being seated at the foot of the Curraghee mountain. Here we alighted for the night about ten o'clock; but found only the most miserable fare, with dirty beds, filthy servants, and only two enclosed rooms in the house for sleeping, the greatest number of beds being placed in one large room, where the male passengers, at least, all slept in common, and, when pressed by numbers, oftentimes two in a bed, and sometimes even three! Of the two enclosed sleeping-rooms, neither was more than seven feet square; one of them had no aperture for light or air but the door, and the other had a small opening which let out on the public veranda, so that it could not be kept open without exposing ourselves to the gaze of every passer-by. The choice lay, therefore, between complete publicity or suffocation. There was no glass window in all the house, the open spaces, or window-frames, being furnished only with solid wooden doors, or shutters. It was with the greatest difficulty that we could procure even a candle, the business of the house being carried on after dark by the light of wooden torches. A servant took a piece of pitch-pine in his hand, lighted it at the kitchen fire, and carrying it in one hand as a candle, he did his work, whatever it was, with the other. If some operation required the use of both hands, his lighted torch was deposited erect in some part of the room where he could fix it, and his hand relieved. As an especial favour to us, who were declared to be "mighty particular," a candle was *made* while we waited for it, some threads of cotton serving for a wick, and this being enveloped in a mass of bees' wax, was brought to us quite hot from the melting. Washstands and looking-glasses were luxuries here unknown; and the travellers whom we saw in the house appeared neither to undress, shave, or wash, but simply to lie down just as they alighted from their horses or carriages, and rise up in the same manner. In our confined cell, there was not room for a single trunk, and the smallest cabin of a ship at sea, was more comfortable than this for sleeping.

We rested but little, therefore, during the night, and were stirring with the earliest dawn; there was a common wash-basin of tin-plate placed in the veranda, with a piece of coarse yellow soap, and a rough rolling-towel hung on a roller, for general use. To this some of the inmates repaired in succession for washing, but the greater number came to the breakfast-table, as early as six o'clock, as dirty as they went to bed, and the whole scene and establishment seemed hardly a single remove beyond the rudest condition of the Indians which these settlers had displaced.

The Curraghee mountain, rising just before the hotel, is an isolated, circular, and conical hill, springing up from the plain, by which it is on all sides surrounded, to a height of about 1000 feet, terminating in a sharp point, and being thickly clothed with wood from base to summit. Its name is Indian, and it forms a striking and prominent object in the picture, from every point of view.

We left this place soon after six, on the morning of Thursday, the 11th of July, and proceeded onward to the Tukoa Falls, a distance of five miles, which we reached about eight o'clock. After crossing a running brook, and arriving at the foot of an extremely steep hill, we had to alight from the carriage, and pursue our way in a narrow path, that led off from the right of the road, through a thickly wooded and romantic dell, for about a quarter of a mile or less, when we arrived at the deep valley into which the falls descend. The scene was impressive and interesting. The valley itself is about 300 feet in breadth, each of its sides being steep, but thickly clothed with trees and shrubs. The descent of the cataract is over a perpendicular cliff of solid rock, in a single fall of 180 feet. The water was not sufficiently abundant to give it the character of grandeur, but it was, nevertheless, an object of great beauty. The breadth of the stream, as it fell, appeared to be about 50 feet, but though it rolled over the edge of the cliff in a tolerably full and compact volume, before it reached the bottom it had become like a thin transparent veil of the finest gauze or muslin, through which could be dimly seen the moss and vegetation that had collected on the surface of the rock. From the base, gradually ascending upwards, were several layers or ranges of full foliaged trees, growing apparently out of the crevices of the rock, which appeared to be of micaceous limestone and schist; and on the very edge of the precipice above, were some trees having their roots on the upper platform, enabling the spectator from below to form, from their apparent height and proportion to the altitude of the cliff, some idea of the elevation of the whole. On looking steadily upward with a fixed gaze, the swift sailing white fleecy clouds, passed in rapid succession over the edge of the precipice, and the rushing of the waters in their downward motion, seen at the same time, produced a very pleasing effect; while the noise of the cataract, and the deep solitude of the dell in which we stood, assisted to complete a scene of romantic beauty and secluded grandeur.

On returning to our carriage from the Falls, we had to ascend the steep hill before us; and for this it required a greater effort than our horses had yet made; while to us, who had to make the ascent on foot, the labour was excessive under the broiling heat of the sun, with the thermometer above 90°. The angle of ascent must have been 30° at least from the base to the summit of this hill, with the additional difficulty of large ridges of rock projecting up above the road, and ruts worn by the mountain torrents to a depth of two feet below the general surface, so as to require the utmost care to avoid them both, and either would be sufficient to upset the firmest and steadiest carriage made. We were all so exhausted indeed, when we reached the top, as to require half an hour's rest before we could proceed further.

In our way beyond this, we passed some log-huts, inhabited by poor white settlers. The number of their children appeared to be excessive, ten or twelve in each hut at least, and all of them with hair as white as flax, and light blue eyes. We found, on inquiry, that this was generally characteristic of the mountain-born children, even though their parents come up from the low country, where dark hair and dark eyes are almost universal; plainly showing that climate, and elevation above the sea, have some effect on the complexions of the Caucasian race, however little it may be supposed to have had on the African and Indian tribes.

In the woods here we saw, for the first time, the exquisitely beautiful bird called the tanager. It is about the size of our English thrush, of the most brilliant

Falls of Tuloola, Mountains of Georgia

scarlet over all its head, neck, and body, with two jet-black broad stripes or patches on its wings; and as it happened to be seated on a branch of extremely thick foliage and in the full blaze of the sun, its sparkling radiance was like that of a ruby hung amidst the boughs.

Ascending the lofty eminence which still lay beyond the steep hill by which we had come up thus far, we enjoyed some splendid and extensive views of the hills and plains below us, the latter looking in the distance, as level as the surface of the sea, and the range extending to an horizon of 60 or 70 miles in a straight line, or probably 100 miles including the elevations and depressions of the roads over which we had travelled. Near the summit of the hill we came to a place where the road divided, or, as it is appropriately expressed here, "where the road forks," but though there was a post erected at the forking point, and signs of directing-boards having once been placed there, they were now gone, so that we were left to conjecture our way, there being no house in sight, and no person within reach, of whom we could make inquiries. As it happened, we chose the wrong road, but being the ascending one, it took us to the very top of the mountain, from whence we enjoyed a view that was deemed a sufficient reward for our labour. It might be truly called magnificent, from the vast extent of country it embraced, and was at the same time soft and beautiful from the variety of surfaces and shadows, foliage and tints of colouring, it displayed. From hence we retraced our steps, and, taking the descending road from the fork, we crossed a deep valley, and, ascending on the other side, reached the mountain-house nearest to the Tuloola Falls, at which, we had been informed, travellers usually halted when they came here.

The house and its accommodations were not better than that from which we were so inhospitably turned away by Mr. Holkham; but here, at least, there was no unwillingness to receive us; and though the fare was "rough," as the country phrase is, and everything of the rudest kind, yet, as there was good-will and an evident desire to please, we made the best of everything, and thus inspired those around us with a wish to do their best also. The master of the house, Mr. Taylor, was not yet returned from "the plantation," as all farms are called here; but his wife, the mother of thirteen children, though not more than thirty-five years of age, set about preparing all we required, as far as her store would furnish it. The only bread we could procure, was that made of maize, or Indian corn; tea and sugar were articles never used by them, but fortunately we were provided with both; though in making the tea, a jug or pitcher had to be used instead of a tea-pot, by which leaves and water were poured out into the cup together. We made a hearty supper, nevertheless, though, according to the custom of the country, our party was made to include the driver of the barouche, the driver of the waggon, and our own white servant, all sitting with us at the same table and at the same time. It was the only place at which we saw no negroes or coloured people employed; and we were told that there were two causes for this; one that the farmers here were too poor in money, though rich in produce, to *buy* negroes; the other, that the climate of the mountains was too severely cold for them in winter; so that whites alone were used for every description of labour.

The rudeness of manners among these dwellers in the woods, is unpleasant to those accustomed to receive courtesy and respect from their attendants. The master of the house, as well as his farming men and boys, come in and out without making any sign of respect or recognition, take a chair close by your side, sit down with their hats on, their legs thrown up in the most careless position, spit their tobacco at your feet, and accost you in the roughest way imaginable. The mistress and her grown-up daughters will do the same, wearing their cotton-quilted bonnets, with a deep curtain hanging down over the neck behind, and covering the ears and shoulders, never taking them off when they enter the room, or take their seat at the table. Another disagreeable feature of their manners is, that whatever they do for the guest or visitor, is done by them as though it were a favour; and not a service for which a fair equivalent was to be given in money paid; for though their own charges are made, and no abatement asked or wished for, they not only think, but generally contrive to say, or make you understand, that they consider you much more under an obligation to them for the accommodation they afford you, than they can possibly be to you for the money you pay to them.

We slept as well as we could on a straw mattrass, placed above the soft down-beds used here by the poorest persons; but the interruption to our rest arose from the numbers of bugs with which we found all these country houses to abound. These were of the largest, blackest, and most voracious kind, so that we had often to get out of bed, and commence a hunt, before we could obtain even the respite of a short and broken repose. Add to this, the combined noises of the numerous dogs which are everywhere kept in town and country, swelled by those of the hogs, goats, sheep, and poultry, which all occupied the common yard immediately outside the aperture in our bed-room called the "window," but which had neither frame, glass, or shutter, and it may well be conceived that our sleep was neither sweet nor refreshing.

We arose at daylight, and set out before breakfast on our excursion to the Falls of Tuloola, on the morning of Friday the 12th of July. Our way was entirely through the woods, the distance being about two miles, and the path lying chiefly over the ridge or crest of the mountain. The trees were very varied, oaks of different kinds being the most abundant; the underwood was rich in the profusion of flowering shrubs that everywhere covered the surface as far as the eye could reach, among which rhododendrons and kalmias were the most abundant, there being many hundred beautiful bushes or trees of each. In our passage along this mountain-crest, we enjoyed another of those extensive views which carried the eye over a range of country embracing a distance of from eighty to a hundred miles, gradually descending, by various steps, or stages, from these lofty eminences, about 3,000 feet above the level of the sea, to others of 2,500, of 2,000, of 1,500, and of 1,000, which was the height of the Curraghee mountain above its own base, though that base would be at least 1,500 feet above the ocean. This conical hill formed a very conspicuous object in the picture as seen from hence, rising, like the great pyramid of Cheops at Memphis, from a level plain, and, by its steep angle of ascent on either side, resembling that pyramid, at this distance, very much in shape; while beyond it, in the direction of the plains, the vast blue level mass looked like the far-off sea.

After a ride of about half an hour we arrived at the spot where a bar has been placed across between two trees at the end of the path, to indicate that it is unsafe for horses or carriages to proceed further. Here we accordingly alighted, and went the rest of the way on foot, reaching, after a few yards, the immediate edge of a precipice, over which we looked down into a deep glen or valley, from 800 to 1,000 feet below us, making the head dizzy to dwell on it with a steady gaze. On the opposite side of this valley, which is about 400 feet broad, we caught the first glimpse of the Falls, though the roar of their waters had been audible for the last mile before we saw them; but it was not until much perambulation and shifting of positions that we ascertained the three best points of view, which are at least a quarter of a mile from each other. From all of them the views are indescribably grand; not so much from the volume of the water in motion, for in this it is greatly inferior to Niagara, but from the height of the fall—600 feet at least, broken into three or four separate leaps, and these partially hidden by foliage—and from the sublime masses of huge mountains that hem in the deep and awe-inspiring valley into which the waters descend. The greatest breadth of the stream did not appear to be more than 50 feet in its fullest part, and it was often not more than half that width, which contrasted with the great depth of its descent, made it appear still smaller. But the wildness and sublimity of the surrounding scenery gave a grandeur and majesty to the whole, which was most imposing. The solitude of this spot, too, is greater than even that at Tukoa, there being no dwelling nearer to the Falls than the one at which we slept, and the savage wildness of the rocks, glens, ravines, and torrents, all combining to make up a picture of the most romantic kind.

We returned to the house about ten o'clock, to partake of a late breakfast; and had hoped, that as sheep were so abundant, a mutton-chop might have been easily procured, but we were surprised to learn that none of the people here would eat mutton, which they thought greatly inferior to bacon or pork; and, therefore, the sheep were kept only for their wool, and were never killed for their flesh. From the conversation we had with the family at and after our meal, we could gather, that they held the "low-country people," as they called them, in great contempt, thought them an indolent, luxurious, and useless race, and regarded themselves as the most important class of the productive community. The "towns-people," in their estimation enjoyed privileges and monopolies at the expense of the farmers and planters; and though they could give no explanation of the manner in which these privileges were confined to any one class to the prejudice of the others, yet they were firmly impressed with a belief that the towns-people were treated with partiality by the government, and themselves with injustice. I saw few books about the house, and those of the least useful or instructive kind, being tales and romances of the commonest order. This implied, however, that some education had been received, to the extent of reading, at least. Some of the family could also write, as the copy-book of the elder son lay exposed on one of the chairs, and in it was written, in the first page, in the worst scrawl imaginable, an entry, which showed that the propensity to boasting is not confined to the sea-coast, but has found its way into the Interior also. The entry was this:—

> William Taylor, his hand and pen,
> As good a scribe as one in ten.

We left the mountain-house of Tuloola about eleven o'clock, and retraced our steps towards the Tukoa Falls, from whence our road was to branch off to the Tugaloo river, onward to South Carolina. On arriving at the steep hill, which it had cost us so much difficulty to ascend, it looked more full of danger than when we came up. Some idea may be formed of the ruggedness of the road from this fact, that the coaches which drove this way were usually upset once in every three times passing it, though all the passengers were on foot, the wheels locked with the drags, and every care taken to prevent such accidents.[1]

On reaching the foot of the hill, about five o'clock, we halted at a house not far from the Tukoa Falls, where we had taken refreshments on coming out. There was only a little girl of ten years old at home in charge of the dwelling, the mother having gone a distance of sixteen miles, to pay a visit to a near neighbour! The brother was gone to the nearest mill, which was eight miles off, with corn to grind; and the other children, one of whom was called "Andrew Jackson," in honour of the ex-president, had gone off into the woods to play. This little girl—with whom we had a long chat while our horses were feeding, and the carriages under repair, from the shocks it had received on coming down the hill—was born in a solitary dwelling in the country, and had never seen a larger town than one containing about a dozen houses, which she thought a very large one—though she had heard that Augusta was much larger. She was, however, more full of curiosity than we had observed to be the case with the children generally, and asked a number of questions concerning the country we came from, and the sea we had to cross in coming here. She appeared to be filled with astonishment and terror at the description of the sea, and had great difficulty in understanding how a ship could be made as commodious as a house, and yet float upon the water; the originality of her observations on these and many other topics made our short halt there extremely entertaining and agreeable.

Leaving Tukoa, we proceeded by an excellent road—which seemed, indeed, by contrast with the one we had just passed over, to be perfection—and after a smooth and luxurious drive of eight miles, we arrived before sunset at a large farm-house and inn united, kept by a Mr. Jerritt: the directions by which we were enabled to distinguish it from other houses in the neighbourhood was this—that it was "the only house with glass windows in it on the road." While our luggage was unloading from the carriage, one of the white men assisting in this labour could not comprehend what our leather hatboxes were; and when, in answer to his inquiry, he was told they contained hats, he asked whether we were carrying them about for sale, as he could not comprehend why a person should take with him any more than the hat he wore on his head. When he learnt, however, that my son and myself used cloth caps for travelling, and kept our hats in these two boxes to wear when we halted, he expressed himself surprised at such a piece of folly and extravagance as that of having more than one covering for the head at a time!

We found a larger and more commodious house than we had slept in since we left the Madison Springs, and much better fare than the rude mountaineers could furnish. We had also, for our entertainment, the society of a middle-aged lady, who boarded in the house, and who joined us at table when we supped. She gave us a narrative of her success in raising the silkworm on the leaves of the *morus multicaulis*, of which she had several plants in her garden; and having purchased a quart of the eggs of the silkworm, she hoped to produce, from these, a million of workers, by whose labour she would be soon made rich. She showed us some of the cocoons, the silk thread she had spun from her wheel, and the cloth she had woven at her own loom, which, though coarse, was strong and even in texture. She added, that she could find a ready sale for as much as she could weave of this, at five dollars, or twenty shillings a yard, while English and French silks could be had for half the price. When asked the grounds of this extravagant expectation, she said that the people of South Carolina were all for living on their own resources, and having no dependence on other countries; they, therefore, readily paid double prices for silks grown and manufactured at home, because it shut out the foreign trader, and kept all the money in the country! I could not, of course, dispute the fact about the relative rates, though I ventured to doubt the accuracy of her supposition as to the willingness of the Carolinians to pay such high prices from pure patriotism. She persisted in this, however, as beyond dispute; and thought that all true friends of their country would rejoice to see the Americans using none other than domestic manufactures, and rendering themselves "wholly independent of foreigners." I could not feel wonder at such sentiments as these, uttered by a country lady in the interior of South Carolina, when I remembered the expression of similar sentiments in the British House of Commons, by the advocates of the prohibitory and restrictive systems, in opposition to the doctrines of free trade. But when I asked the lady, what the cultivators of these Southern States would do with their cotton, sugar, indigo, rice, and tobacco, were it not for the "foreigners," who were such excellent customers for them all, she was at a loss for a reply, and seemed, for the first time, to have the idea brought home to her mind, that foreign trade was at least as essential to the prosperity of America as of any other country; for her previous conviction was, as she herself confessed, that America would be far better off, if she lived by and within herself, without intercourse with any other nation whatever! Here, as in many other places of the interior, a great desire was manifested to examine the various articles of our dress, but especially those of Mrs. Buckingham. The ladies were constantly desirous of getting permission to take patterns of her gowns and caps, which was granted whenever our stay would admit of it, and always highly valued. The lady here, however, was astonished to find that they were not made in New York, but in London, for she had supposed that they were the latest New York modes; and said she had always understood that the French and English ladies invariably sent to New York for the fashions, and had their dresses made up in London and Paris, from the patterns sent there from the United States!

On retiring to rest, we were put into a large room with four beds, but fortunately we had no companions to share the room with us. When passengers on this road are more numerous, it is quite common to have all the beds occupied at the same time in the same apartment. This is a custom of the country, which is very ill associated with the excessive prudishness and affectation of its inhabitants, in avoiding all ambiguous expressions. There were no drawers or trunks for clothes; so that the garments of all the family were ranged around the room, hanging on wooden pegs, to the number of forty or fifty different articles of dress, including gowns, petticoats, and inner garments, of all sizes and materials, exposed to public view. The beds, as usual, were of three kinds; one of the softest down, another of cotton, and another of straw; the former being usually preferred by the people of this country, but the latter by strangers, as more nearly resembling moss or hair, which is too expensive to be found in any but the very best houses.

At daylight we were awakened by the sound of a common horn, with which it is the custom in the country districts to summon everybody to rise, instead of ringing a large bell, which is the custom in the towns; and as we did not intend to leave till nine o'clock, I took a walk around the farm, and conversed with the farmers before breakfast.

We left our station at nine o'clock, on the morning of July 13th, and after less than a quarter of a mile, we crossed the Tugaloo river by a wooden bridge. We thus passed from the State of Georgia into that of South Carolina, this river being the dividing boundary between the two. The roads now began to wear an improved appearance, the population were not so thinly scattered, and coloured people were more frequently met with, all arising from the greater length of time during which Carolina had been a settled country, while Georgia was of much more recent origin, and its interior not long since left by the Indians, its original inhabitants.

At the distance of a few miles only beyond the river, we were overtaken by a man on horseback, of very common manners and appearance, riding without coat or waistcoat, a dirty trousers and shirt, both of Georgia nankeen, a beard of at least a week's growth, and a hat in a state of great dilapidation, but who, nevertheless, was the Sheriff of the County in which we were travelling. This fact we learnt from himself, as he pointed out to us, while he rode along by our carriage, a rude gallows, formed by a horizontal beam, resting on the branches of two large adjoining trees, close by the road-side, on which, but a few months since, he had hung, with his own hands, a negro convicted of the murder of three white persons, at a bridge in the neighbourhood of the place of execution. The history of the case was this. A planter from Carolina, travelling with his son and daughter, had purchased a negro from another white man, and employed him as the driver of his carriage. The person selling the negro, happened to know that the gentleman purchasing him had a large sum of money with him, to the amount, it is said, of 8,000 dollars, and he conceived the diabolical plan of hiring the slave to murder his new master, and seize his wealth, on condition that the negro should have a share of the plunder, and receive his freedom besides! The slave readily assented to this, and watching his opportunity while all three of the party were asleep on a sultry afternoon, he took a small axe, with which he had provided himself, and beat out the brains, first of the father, and then of the son and daughter. In these lonely roads, there being no one near, he had time to drag the bodies separately into a neighbouring ditch, and there leave them, while he went off with the empty carriage in another direction. He was soon, however, arrested; the traces of blood on the road having led to the discovery of the bodies and the detection of the murder. When brought to trial, he confessed his guilt, and stated the facts already mentioned, as to the instigation to this act being given by his former master, and the conditions of reward promised him for its commission. But, by the laws of this and other Slave States, the testimony of a negro cannot be received in any case against a white man; and therefore, though the general opinion was that the negro was speaking truth—as the bad character of his former master rendered it more probable that he should be the instigator of the murder for the sake of the plunder, than that the negro should have committed such a deed on a whole family, in whose service he had been but a few days,—yet a negro's evidence against a white man cannot be legally taken; so that the instigator escaped all punishment, while the negro was hanged for executing his former master's wishes.

In the afternoon we crossed the river Seneca, by a wooden bridge, the stream being about 100 feet broad, but the water low, as it is in all the streams of the country at this season of the year; and after a short ride beyond this, of four or five miles through a more open and cultivated country, we reached the village of Pendleton at sunset, and halted for the night.

This is a small town, containing about 500 inhabitants, with a court-house and two hotels. The district of Pendleton, of which this was formerly the centre, having been subsequently divided into two judicial circuits, with a new court-house in each, this has been abandoned, and the building being put up to sale, was purchased by the Farmers' Society of this section, who hold their meetings here for discussions and communications connected with the improvement of agriculture and farming, which is here attended to with great zeal. The village supports a weekly newspaper, the Pendleton Messenger, and has a library and a debating-club. The hotel at which we slept, Mr. Hubbard's, was one of the best on the road, and we enjoyed our improved accommodations and improved fare. In the garden of this hotel we first saw the beautiful little humming-bird on the wing—its delicate form, small size, and exquisite colours, making it an object of peculiar interest. In the extreme South, in Louisiana and Florida, this bird is found all the year, as it is in the West India islands; but in all the other States it is a bird of passage, seen only in the summer, and retreating to its more southern home, as the cold of the winter approaches. The tubular and trumpet-shaped flowers are those from whence it most delights to draw its food; and just before it descends to plunge its long and slender bill into these storehouses, it suspends itself in the air a little above it, quivering its wings with such rapidity as to make them appear almost stationary, while the rich green and golden hues of its plumage, seen in the light of the sun, make it look like a suspended gem hung in the air.

The morning of July 14 was ushered in with heavy rain, and it was thought likely to last for several days; as it had been brought in by a northeasterly wind, which, coming over the broad Atlantic, like our south-westerly wind in England, is usually charged with clouds, that take three or four days to discharge their moisture. We, therefore, proceeded on our way with our barouche well closed in, and left Pendleton about ten o'clock.

In the few intervals between the heavy showers of rain that fell, the carriage was opened, but there were no novelties in the scenery or productions, beyond that of our seeing several fields planted with tobacco, now in large full leaf, in shape and colour not much unlike a large wide-spreading cabbage; and a fine plantation of cotton, now in full blossom, the flowers being quite white, a colour which they are said to retain all the day, but to become of a reddish hue at night.

In the course of the afternoon, we passed another river, called the Saluda, by a good wooden bridge, at which a toll of 50 cents, or 2s., was paid, this being the second or third instance only of our meeting with a turnpike at which tolls were required to be paid during our travels in the country; and continuing our way for a few hours beyond this, over an improving and more thickly-peopled country, we arrived at sunset at the river Beedy. We forded this on the shallows, a few yards above the edge of the precipice, over which it flows in a fall of thirty or forty feet, and ascending on the opposite bank about a quarter of a mile, we entered the village of Greenville, and found comfortable quarters at the Planter's Hotel.

1.   On dining, some time after this was written, with the Governor of Virginia, and a party of friends at Abingdon in that State, and describing this spot, which was known among them by name of Break-neck-Hill, we were assured by a lady of the party, that on descending it on one occasion, while her husband walked, and she alone was left in the carriage, it received such a jolt, as to throw her completely topsy-turvy, and place her head in the bottom of the carriage, and her heels to the roof. She remained in this state for some minutes, thinking, as she told us, that it was the carriage that had been upset, and not herself; and it was only when her husband came to help the driver to get it out of the pit into which it had been thrown, that she discovered her mistake! The story was told with such *naiveté*, and unconsciousness of its drollery, by the fair narrator, that it set the whole party of her auditors in a roar of laughter. The husband, nevertheless, confirmed its truth.

Chapter XXXVII

Having completed all our arrangements for the journey from hence to the Virginia Mountains, we left Greenville on the morning of Friday the 19th of July, in a stage-and-four, about nine o'clock, and pursued our way towards Flatrock, a distance of thirty-six miles, which it was thought a good day's journey to be able to reach by sunset.

Our road from hence to the commencement of the hills was through a fine and fertile country, well cultivated with corn and other grain, and the noble range of mountains called the Blue Ridge, which we were to ascend, improved in majesty and beauty as we drew nearer to it.

It was at a distance of twenty-four miles from Greenville, that we reached the house of Colonel Hodges, half inn and half farm-house, according to the custom of these parts; the keepers of such houses being almost all dignified with military titles, as captain, major, colonel, and even general, and in some instances, they are also judges. The former are purely militia titles, which when once enjoyed by ever so short a service, are continued through life. The latter is a title given to those who sit in the inferior as well as superior courts, who resemble our county and borough magistrates, and who are not necessarily members of the legal profession. Some of these hotel-keepers are, indeed, also practising physicians, as well as planters, and in this threefold capacity they make speedy fortunes. As they give most of their attention to that which is most profitable, they occupy the greatest portion of their time in attending to the business of their plantation, and the increase of their live-stock—little negroes included—while their patients have but a very partial attendance; and the business of the inn is left mostly to the black servants to manage as they see fit, unless superintended, as they sometimes are, by a white mistress, the wife or sister of the planter; but in either case, the accommodations are dirty and comfortless, and the fare coarse in the extreme. Add to this, the manners of the whites and blacks are equally rude; and among all, there seems to be a determination to do just as much, or as little, as they see fit, and no more; so that they are generally the worse for urging, and, however unsatisfactory their provender may be to the guest, they both present it to him, and receive payment for it, with the air of persons who are conferring upon you a great favour, and laying you under strong obligation.

From this house, which occupies a romantically beautiful situation in one of the most lovely dells imaginable, we began the ascent of a very steep mountain, the road winding in a serpentine form up its sides, and being extremely difficult for the horses. All the way over this hill, the road wound through thick forests, with deep hollows or glens, occasional water-falls, and splendid forest-trees; besides innumerable bushes of the rhododendron and kalmia, to the extent of hundreds in view at one time, and both agreeably diversified with the weeping willow, the oleander, and the wild vine, with large and promising clusters of forest-grapes advancing towards perfection, covering some of the smaller trees entirely, and hanging in many tresses from branch to branch of others.

Near the top of the mountain, we came to the third turnpike we had met with in the South, where the toll was one dollar and fifty cents, or six shillings English, for a four-horse coach; and about five miles further on, we met a second turnpike, where the toll was one dollar. The former of these was in the State of South Carolina, the second in the State of North Carolina, the immediate crest of this mountain dividing the two, at a distance of twenty-seven miles from Greenville in the former, and thirty-three miles from Asheville in the latter. A small erect slab of stone, standing on the crest of the mountain, marked the division; and from this point the mountain view was extensive, varied, and beautiful in a high degree.

From a little beyond the second turnpike, the road descended gradually, and was everywhere good; it wound most agreeably through lofty hedges of trees and shrubs, with frequent openings of cleared and cultivated land, and at sunset it brought us to a pretty valley, in which a large new hotel was nearly completed, about two miles beyond which, we reached Flatrock, a single house, without a village, kept by Colonel Young, and here we alighted for the night.

There were about fifty persons staying at this house, some for health, and some for pleasure, and these were said to include members of the first families in Carolina. Yet the place appeared to us to possess no one attraction, but that of climate; which could be enjoyed in as great perfection any where throughout this range, at an equal elevation, the height being about 2,000 feet above the level of the sea, and the thermometer not usually ascending beyond 85°. The bed-rooms were dark and dingy, the bedding coarse and dirty; no wash-stands, dressing-tables, mats, or carpets; broken looking-glasses, tallow candles, brass and tin candlesticks, and filthy negro servants; these were the accommodations that awaited the traveller. The dining-room was not more than eight feet high, with a whitewashed wooden ceiling, blackened with the ascending smoke of candles; it was like a badly built soldiers' barracks; and the fare was like that of nearly all the country inns, coarse, greasy, tough, badly dressed, and cold. In short, the whole establishment was forbidding and comfortless in an unusual degree; yet here many families of opulence, and especially ladies, passed several months in the summer; were anxious to get here, and always sorry when the time came to go away.

I had often been at a loss to account for the eagerness with which such places are visited year after year by the same persons, when all the charms of novelty are gone; but I had heard, lately, from native authority, a solution which seemed more probable than any I could offer to my own mind. It was this: that as marriages in the South are contracted so early in life as to lead to frequent subsequent regret in one or both of the parties, and as they are not so often contracted from love as from considerations of fortune and connections, home becomes wearisome, tedious, and monotonous; and anything which offers the relief of change is acceptable to both, but especially to the ladies. The husbands have business to occupy and divert them. The wives have neither the superintendence of household duties, which engage so much of an English lady's time; nor the training of their children, which, like household affairs, is chiefly confined to negroes here; and having little or no enthusiasm of character, or passion for any intellectual pursuit, such as literature, science, music, or drawing, their resources of entertainment soon dry up, and they are happy to go abroad in quest of the novelty and excitement which they fail to find at home. Thus they visit these springs and watering-places, where, as a gentleman truly observed to me, they do not "kill time," for that implies a battle with the enemy, or at least an active struggle, by energetic and lively amusement of some kind or other—but where they rather "lose time" in so complete a manner, by listlessness and trifling, that they are unable to give any account to themselves or others what has become of this, to them the most worthless of all possessions—since their great aim is to devise new modes to get rid of it.

After a disagreeable night, partly passed in hunting those enemies to sleep, which infest nearly all the wooden houses of the South, and which seem to be as great a torment to the people of the up-country, as the mosquitos are to those of the low, we left Flatrock at nine in the morning of the 20th of July. About a mile beyond it, we passed a very pretty country-seat, the summer residence of Mr. Charles Baring, a cousin, as I understood, of the present Lord Ashburton, and whose lady is sister, as I was also told, of the Countess of Berkeley. Mr. Baring has large plantations of cotton and rice, near the sea-coast, not far from Charleston; and while he passes his winters on these, he spends his summers here; the county of Buncombe in North Carolina, in which his seat is placed, being esteemed the most healthy and beautiful portion of all the Southern country, which I can readily believe, from all that I have yet seen of it. The house and grounds have a pleasing appearance from the road, and the parkpaling and shrubbery, the little lake and sloping lawn, the white sheep, and winding pathway from the gates to the dwelling, reminded us more of England than anything we had seen in America; and those who have visited the interior of Mr. Baring's establishment, speak of it as perfect and beautiful in all its details.

The Americans, while they admire, do not, however, imitate him; and although, at first sight, one would think that the splendid and truly English mansion and grounds of Mr. Greig, at Canandaigua in the State of New York, and the equally admired house and park of Mr. Baring here, would lead to the imitation of both, by at least the more opulent of their neighbours, no such results have followed yet; from which one is compelled to infer, either that the Americans have not a sufficiently strong perception of architectural and rural beauty, to become really enamoured of it, or that they love their money too well to spend it in such unproductive outlays.

We found a much better hotel at Asheville than the one we had left at Flatrock; and were comfortably accommodated with good rooms and good fare. We passed the evening with some very agreeable company, who had come here from the sea-coast for health and pleasure; these were chiefly ladies, there being about fifty persons in the house, of whom not more than ten were gentlemen. Our pleasure was somewhat marred, however, by a disagreeable discovery, just as we were about to retire to rest. An alarm of fire was given; and on going up stairs into the part of the house from whence the smoke came, a bed was found to be in flames, which, by grasping and pressing, and throwing such water as was at hand upon it, was happily extinguished. The most painful part of the discovery, was the evident proof of its being kindled intentionally; for, on the bed which had taken fire, was a large piece of brown paper saturated with melted grease, by which the fire had been evidently kindled; and under the bed, on the floor, was a small pool of the same material, apparently intended to give fresh fuel to the flame when once ignited. It was an unoccupied room, no candle had been known to be placed there, and the opinion seemed to be, that it was the work of some dissatisfied or vindictive negro, but it was not deemed safe to push the inquiry further; such is the restraint placed on the punishment of crime by the fearful system of slavery.

Asheville is a small village, containing a brick Court-house, a wood-built Methodist Church, in which there is only occasional services, two hotels, and about twenty stores and dwelling-houses, with a population of 200 persons, of whom not more than 120 are whites. The situation of the village is beautiful;

and from a rising at the back of the hotel, and beyond the garden of the house, is one of the most exquisite panoramic views imaginable; encircled by ranges of mountains of varied heights and distances, with swelling slopes and delicious valleys, such as one might travel a thousand miles without finding surpassed in beauty.

We left Asheville about eight o'clock on the morning of July 21, in a fine roomy stage, designed for nine inside passengers, and occupied only by five. About a mile after quitting the village, we came on the banks of a river called "The French Broad," the etymology of which no one here seemed to know. It lay on the left-hand of our road, which ran close along its edge; it was full of rocks, and so extremely shallow that it resembled a continued series of rapids, with here and there a deeper and more tranquil part for a few yards only; and this again speedily succeeded by rocks and rapids, as before. The breadth of the stream was from 200 to 300 feet; the water was beautifully clear, and in many parts it reminded me of the rapids of the Nile, at what is called the Second Cataract, the first great interruption to the full and unbroken flow of the stream, south of the island of Philöe, or the Cataracts of Syene. As we passed along its banks, we observed a ferry, at which persons drew themselves across by a cord, in a slender canoe, and horses and carriages forded the stream a little below. The wood that lined the upland slopes on either bank, was beautifully rich and varied; and all along our path, the way was fringed with the azalia, the rhododendron, and the kalmia, in countless numbers, intermingled occasionally with the wild rose and other flowering shrubs.

As we drew near the end of our journey, the river appeared to divide its stream more frequently, and to wind round several large and well-wooded islands in its way, when, about five o'clock, we reached the hotel at the Warm Springs, and halted for the night.

We were detained here for three days, as no private conveyances could be had, and the public stage passes only three times a week. We did not regret our detention, however, as we were all sufficiently fatigued to make rest extremely agreeable. The warm spring, which gives its name to this spot, rises on the left bank of the river, within a few yards of its edge, bubbling up through the rocky and gravelly bed, and preserving a uniform temperature of about 95°. A building has been erected over it, so as to enclose the water in two swimming-baths, of about twenty feet square, and four feet in depth. These are divided from each other by a wooden partition, and each has a separate entrance, one being devoted to the use of the gentlemen, and the other to the ladies. The water is beautifully clear, but very slightly mineral, and is altogether most agreeable to bathe in; but nothing can be conceived more rude and inconvenient than all the auxiliaries of the bath. The dressing-rooms, so called, have neither mat, couch, nor table;

nothing, in short, but the bare wooden walls and floor, and one straw-bottom chair. The negro attendant brings the bather a single towel on his leaving the water, but nothing else; so that those accustomed to the well-furnished baths of London and Paris, but especially those who had ever enjoyed the luxurious baths of Cairo, Aleppo, Damascus, or Bagdad, would think this the lowest in the scale of comfort. Yet, the visitors here, the greater number of whom have never seen anything better, think this excellent; and except for the purpose of stimulating them to improvement, it might be thought a pity to disturb them in their present contentment; for in this sense, if in any, the language of the poet may be true—

Where ignorance is bliss, 'tis folly to be wise.

One principal cause of the imperfect accommodation and bad fare met with in this country, is the absence of complaint on the part of those who partake of it. The keepers of such public establishments rarely or ever hear any one speak at all either in praise or censure of what is presented to them, but seeing that all is received with composure and every appearance of content, they infer that all is perfect, and that there is either no room for improvement, or at least no necessity to incur expense for that purpose, as everybody is satisfied with things as they are.

The establishment here, is most romantically situated, though it has not the climate of the Flatrock, or the accommodations of the Asheville hotel. Being only 1,200 feet above the level of the sea, while Flatrock is 2,000—and being, moreover, hemmed in a close valley, and heated by the constantly ascending vapour of the warm spring—the thermometer is usually 8° or 10° higher here than at Flatrock on the same days. The first hotel built here was consumed by fire, at the close of the last season, when about fifty guests were in it, the greater number of whom lost all their baggage, as the fire was not discovered till some time after it had broken out, and, like the Planters' Hotel at Augusta, being wholly built of wood, it was in a few hours entirely destroyed. The owner had not insured either his house or furniture, so that his loss was very severe. The actual cause of the fire was never distinctly ascertained; but either the carelessness, or intentional malevolence of the negroes, was the cause suspected and assigned.

The present building has a front of 220 feet, with a portico of thirteen plain columns, about three feet in diameter and thirty feet in height, making a noble piazza of sixteen feet in breadth, and nearly the same size, therefore, as the portico of the Congress-Hall Hotel at Saratoga, but not of so imposing an aspect. It has a lofty hall, capable of dining 500 persons, and a number of bed-rooms of all sizes; but there is the usual deficiency in those interior comforts which constitute the excellence of our English inns.

In addition to the hotel, there are a number of small brick cabins, with rooms not more than eight or ten feet square, for invalids, requiring easy access to the Warm Spring, and these are more comfortless than the large house; so much so, indeed, as to render it probable that all the benefit of bathing in the waters must be more than counteracted by the privations and discomfort of the lodgings.

While at the hotel here, we were much struck with the appearance of a little girl of ten years of age, who was sweeping the rooms; her features were African, her complexion yellowish brown, and her hair almost flaxen, in long locks, though curly. We asked her where she was born. She answered—in Virginia. We inquired where her mother was. She pointed to a negress in the passage, perfectly black. We asked this woman, who was the child's father? She replied— her former master, now living in Virginia. We inquired why she had left him. She answered, that her master had sold both herself and her child (his own offspring) to her present owner, the keeper of the hotel; for all children born of slave mothers, though begotten by free fathers, are slaves also. By so much, therefore, as a white slaveowner can increase the number of his own progeny, by the black females, with whom he may lawfully cohabit as his slaves, since "he may do what he will with his own;" by so much he increases his own wealth by selling his own children! This is constantly denied by those who are ashamed of this blot upon their country's honour: but the instances we have met with, in which the direct, unpremeditated, and disinterested testimony of the mothers, could leave no doubt on the subject—and the many other instances, in which we have seen the strongest resemblance in the mulatto-children running about the house, and rearing for the market, to the white master and father to whom they owed their being—convinced me that the practice, instead of being rare, is unhappily very general!

CHAPTER XXXVIII

We had now traversed a portion of North Carolina, which comprehended nearly the whole breadth of its south-western angle, between South Carolina and Tennessee; and certainly, a more beautiful portion of the earth's surface, it had rarely fallen to our lot to examine and admire. As it was the first, and will probably be the last occasion of our visiting this State, some account of its general extent and peculiarities may here be fitly introduced.

It was in North Carolina that the first attempt to colonize on the continent of North America was made by the English; though at that period the whole of the territory was called Florida by the French, and Virginia by the English; and it was therefore included in the first patent granted by Queen Elizabeth to Sir Walter Raleigh in 1584. About two years after this, a small number of settlers came out from England, under the auspices of Raleigh; but they were thought to have been destroyed by the Indians, as they left no trace of themselves or their descendants. It was not until 1650 that some emigrants from the Chesapeake came down here, and formed the first permanent settlement of the whites. In 1661, these were joined by a small body of colonists from Massachusetts, who settled themselves near the river of Cape Fear; being mostly Quakers, who had been expelled by the intolerant Puritans from the New England States. In 1663, Sir William Berkley, then Governor of Virginia, granted a tract of land, including 3,350 acres, on the north side of Roanoake, now Albemarle, to George Cathmaid, for the transportation of sixty-seven persons to settle there; and this is said to be the oldest land-title in the State. In the same year, Charles the Second granted to Lord Clarendon, the Duke of Albemarle, the Earl of Craven, Lord Berkeley, Lord Ashley, Sir George Carteret, Sir John Colleton, and Sir William Berkeley, all the country lying between the parallels of 31° and 36° of north latitude, from the Atlantic to the Pacific Ocean! The territory was to be called Carolina, in honour of the King, and the persons named above were to be the called Lords Proprietors. Sir William Berkeley, then in Virginia, was ordered to visit the settlement at Albemarle, and organize a regular government; which he did, appointing George Drummond as the first governor, and a council of six to assist him.

In 1665 a second charter was granted by Charles, enlarging the powers of the Lords Proprietors, and extending the southern boundary of the province from 36° 30′ N., the edge of Virginia, to 29° N., the extremity of Florida; so that the area of Carolina, within these boundaries, extending from the Atlantic to the Pacific, embraced more than a million of square miles, equal to one-half of all the territory now forming the whole of the United States!— including all the space at present occupied by North and South Carolina, Georgia, Tennessee, Arkansas, Alabama, Mississippi, and Louisiana, all Texas, and a large portion of Mexico, as well as the lands west of the Rocky Mountains! Such was the power assumed and exercised by the sovereigns of Europe, to give away the territories of other nations to a few of their own favourites!

In 1666 the first legislative body of Carolina was convened. This was composed of twelve delegates chosen by the freeholders, as a house of representatives; twelve councillors, six chosen by the delegates, and six by the governor; and the governor himself, who was appointed by the Lords Proprietors. This was called "The Grand Assembly of Albemarle."

It was in 1669 that the famous Code drawn up by Locke, the author of the "Essay on the Human Understanding," was introduced for the government of this province; but of this a full account is given in the historical sketch of South Carolina. The division between the two Carolinas into North and South, was made in 1697; and in 1729 the Lords Proprietors surrendered their government to the crown, when it became a royal colony.

Of the principal historical events, the following are worthy of mention in chronological order. We find that in 1672 the celebrated George Fox visited this colony, and organized the first religious association here. In 1700 the first Episcopal missionary arrived; and in 1704 the Church of England was established by law, as the State religion of the province. In 1711 there was a great massacre of the whites by the Indians. In 1713, the first issue of paper-money, or bills of credit, took place. In 1715, the first revision of the statute-law was made; and its publication was by means of twelve manuscript copies circulated, there being no printing-press then in the colony. In 1723, the first court-houses were erected. In 1728, the first road was made from Newbern to Bath. In 1745, the first post-route was established, from Suffolk in Virginia to Wilmington in North Carolina, the post to go once in every two weeks! In 1742, the first printing-office was introduced by James Davis of Newbern. In 1752, the first book was printed, being "Swan's Revisal of the Laws." In 1764, the first newspaper was issued, called "The North Carolina Magazine, or Universal Intelligencer." In 1775, the Royal Government was abdicated by Governor Martin, in consequence of the Revolution; and in 1776, the Declaration of Independence was made.

About the same period as that of the revolutionary war against the mother-country, an insurrection took place in the western counties of the province among some persons who called themselves "Regulators" and who professed to be aggrieved by the oppressions of the lawyers, and abuses in the administration of justice. The only remedy for this they declared to be the "complete destruction of the whole race of legal functionaries and practitioners!" They organized a body of 1,500 men, with this avowed view; but the Governor, Tryon, with 1,000 militia, marched against them, and a battle ensuing, the "Regulators" were entirely defeated, 300 of them being killed, and the rest sueing for mercy.

Since the termination of the revolutionary war, and the incorporation of North Carolina as one of the thirteen original States of the Union, its history has been barren of interesting events; and having no great sea-port, neither its population nor commerce has increased in the same ratio with many other of the States. Still, the increase of the former has been considerable, as will be seen by the following table—

In	1701	it was	5,000	In	1800	it was	478,103
	1729		10,000		1810		555,500
	1749		45,000		1820		638,829
	1763		95,000		1830		738,470
	1790		393,951	Present estimate			850,000

Since 1790, the slaves have increased from 100,571, to 245,601, which was the number given by the census of 1830; and they are not believed to be in greater numbers now than then; as the surplus occasioned by natural increase of numbers is fully balanced by the sales which take place of negroes for the south-western States, which furnishes a profitable market.

In size, the State of North Carolina is about one third larger than that of South Carolina. In length from east to west it is 362 miles; and in breadth from north to south 121 miles; it has therefore an area of 43,800 square miles, or 28,032,000 of acres, while South Carolina has only 30,000 square miles or 19,251,200 of acres. Both taken together are quite as large as all England and Scotland united, being collectively 73,800 square miles in area; while Great Britain and Ireland are only 88,357 square miles.

Its boundaries are: on the north, Virginia; on the south, South Carolina; on the east, the Atlantic Ocean; and on the west, Tennessee. There are great diversities of soil and climate within these boundaries. From the sea-coast to about 60 miles inland, the country is level, and the climate warm, and there cotton is grown in great abundance. There are many inlets and swamps near the sea, which make those parts unhealthy in summer and autumn, but the climate is delightful in winter. In the middle section of the State, the surface is hilly, but fertile; and grain of all kinds, with flax, tobacco, and fruits, find a congenial soil and clime. The western portion is mountainous, and, as has been seen by our journey across the Blue Ridge, presents beautiful scenery, a delightful temperature, and a rich variety of productions. This portion of the country was, however, but of comparatively recent discovery; as it was in 1767, not long before the independence of the United States was proclaimed, that a person named Finlay went from the banks of the Yadkin river, west of the Blue Ridge, and after a long absence from his family, by whom he was given up as lost, he came back, and gave so glowing an account of the richness and beauty of the country beyond the mountains, that others were induced to join him in a second excursion there. Among these was the celebrated prince "of backwoods-men," Daniel Boone, whose exploits are as much matter of popular tradition in this country as those of Robin Hood and his foresters in England. From this time onward, the more restless and adventurous among the settlers followed the example of Finlay and Boone, and with a few blankets for tents and bedding, rifles and ammunition for defence, and dogs to assist them in hunting for deer, they went off beyond the mountains, and wandered farther and farther west, as new temptations presented themselves.

The mineral wealth of North Carolina is considerable. Iron ore is found in the mountains in great abundance; and several large establishments for smelting and working iron exist. The gold region, however, attracts the greatest attention. It embraces the river Yadkin and its branches, and extends over a territory of about 1,000 square miles. The gold is sometimes found in the state of ore, near the surface. This is purified and smelted; quicksilver being used for separating the pure gold from the dross. It is sometimes also found in minute particles of pure gold, among the sands and soil in the beds of streams, and is then obtained by washing it. In some instances it is found in large lumps, from one to two pounds weight. Lumps worth from 200 dollars to 1,000 dollars are often found; and on one occasion a mass of pure gold, worth 8,000 dollars, was dug up in Carrabas country. The number of men employed in searching for gold, and the quantity procured, are continually on the increase. The first supply of gold to the United States Mint was, in 1814, to the extent of 11,000 dollars' worth. At present there are nearly 20,000 men employed in procuring gold in this State alone; and upwards of 5,000,000 dollars' worth of the precious metal is now obtained in the course of a year. A single company, or firm, employs nearly 1,000 hands; and these include Americans, English, Scotch, Irish, Welsh, Spaniards, Swedes, and Swiss; and it is said there are no less than thirteen languages spoken among the various people employed. The best veins of gold are neither horizontal, nor vertical; but with a dip of 45° to the horizon; these are found in the low-lands, as well as in the hills; they occur of all sizes, from a few inches to several feet in width; and of depths not yet ascertained. No shafts have yet been sunk deeper than 120 feet; and great numbers of the owners and renters of land work their several lots without the use of any machinery, merely digging, raking, and washing the earth; though others of large capital have mills worked by stream, with water-power for grinding the ore, and crucibles for fining it. What is especially remarkable is this, that in excavating the earth, old shafts are sometimes opened, and machinery and tools used by some former race, who worked these mines before the Europeans had a footing on this continent, are discovered. Among these have been crucibles, which are so superior to any now made, that the Messrs. Bissell's, who are at the head of a large mining establishment there, assert that they have tried them, and found them to last twice or three times as long as even the Hessian crucibles, the best of modern use and manufacture. It is said that the miners, who come from the mines of Europe and South America, to work in these, give it as their opinion, that this region is richer in gold than any other of similar extent on the surface of the globe. If so, North Carolina will, before many years are over, become a second Mexico, or Peru.

The commerce of this State is confined chiefly to the export of cotton, tobacco, lumber—that is, timber in various forms—tar, pitch, and turpentine, of which considerable quantities are made from the pines, growing here in extensive forests. The gold of North Carolina is sent not only to the United States Mint, but to France and other countries of Europe. There is a great obstacle to extensive commerce in this State, however, from its want of good harbours; those of Wilmington, Newbern, and Edenton, the only tolerable ones, being ill adapted to large ships; and nearly all their rivers are choked at the entrance by shoals and bars. The principal rivers are the Roanoke, the Tar, the Neuse, the Cape Fear, the Yadkin, and the Catawba. There are, however, fine canals uniting several of these streams, and improving the inland navigation; while five railroads are in progress, two of which will require a capital of 2,000,000 dollars each, and both will cover a distance of nearly 400 miles; so that, when these are completed, the commerce of North Carolina will, no doubt, be greatly improved.

The present capital of the State is Raleigh, and the State-House, now nearly finished, is described as one of the most beautiful buildings in the country. Its length is 160 feet, its breadth 140: height from the base to the top of the dome 100 feet, and of the walls of the edifice 60. The columns of the portico are 5 feet 2½ inches in diameter, standing on a basement of 16 feet high; the proportions and entablature are copied from the Temple of the Parthenon at Athens. The entire building is of hewn granite, and its cost is estimated at 500,000 dollars, or 100,000*l.* sterling.

The State has a Literary Fund for the support of Common Schools, consisting of 1,500,000 acres of land, with bank-stock and cash amounting to more than a million of dollars; and an Internal Improvement Fund of 1,000,000 dollars, both under the administration of their respective Boards.

The Legislature consists of a House of Representatives, called in this State, the "House of Commons," a Senate, or Upper House, and a Governor, who is assisted in his executive capacity by a Secretary of State, a Treasurer, and a Comptroller; the legislators being all elected for short periods, and the salaries of all the State officers moderate, the Governor receiving only 2,000 dollars, or 400*l.* sterling a year.

The Judiciary consists of a Supreme Court, with three Judges at 2,500 dollars per annum each, and two official Reporters at 300 dollars each, and seven Judges of Circuit Courts, with an Attorney and a Solicitor-General.

There is an University at Chapel Hill, near Raleigh; and 80 Academies in the State. Of the religious bodies, the Baptists have about 18,000; the Methodists 14,000; the Presbyterians, 8,000; the Lutherans, 3,000; the Moravians, 2,000; the Quakers, 1,500; and the Episcopalians about 1,200.

CHAPTER XXXIX

We left the Warm Springs of North Carolina at two o'clock in the afternoon, by the mail-stage, which passes this way, and after crossing the French Broad River, by the bridge in front of the hotel, we ascended an exceedingly steep hill, from the summit of which, looking down over a precipitous cliff, the view of the valley and the stream was strikingly beautiful. Descending from this height, the road wound along again by the margin of the river, which was here smooth and tranquil, compared with its rocky and turbulent state above. On both sides, the vines were more than usually luxuriant. In some places they encircled bare trunks of trees, that had been stripped of bark and branches, and left to stand erect till required to be removed. Clasping these near the root, they wound up spirally, like the line of sculptured figures on the column of Trajan at Rome, or the bronze pillar of Napoleon in the Place Vendôme at Paris, making a vine-clad triumphal monument of Nature, strikingly contrasting with the trees decked in their own rich foliage, and spreading their numerous boughs to the winds. In others, the vines had spread themselves over a dozen trees in succession, and made of them a complete mass of close foliage on the top and sides, with fine open spaces within, furnishing delightful shady arbours; while the roof and walls of this natural palace, or mansion, were, by the thick overlaying of the leaves, quite impervious to the rays of the sun.

About two miles beyond the Warm Springs, we came to an excellent inn, at a spot called "The Pleasant Bank," and never was a more appropriate name given. The house stood on the right bank of the river, close to the water's edge; and immediately before it were several noble trees, one of which, a weeping-willow, which had been planted by the keeper of the hotel only seven years ago, had now attained to the height of more than sixty feet; while a still larger one, planted before his arrival, towered to the height of eighty feet at least! The opposite bank was steep, lofty, and thickly-wooded; and the river ran by with great rapidity, giving life and animation to the scene. The heat of the atmosphere was at this moment, about three P.M., greater than we had felt it since leaving Columbia, the thermometer exceeding 96°; yet, in winter, the cold is described as intense here, the river being frequently frozen over for weeks in succession; and last year a high-road for waggons and carts existed across the river for some time. The changes of temperature in the spring and autumn are very sudden, and reach to great extremes, often 50° in the course of twenty-four hours. I thought this excessive; but when I expressed this opinion, I was shown the following paragraph, to prove that the differences of temperature was much greater in England. It was in a copy of the London Examiner, for the 12th of May, which had come out by the "Great Western" steamer, and had been forwarded after me here, from the Virginia Springs.

> FLUCTUATION IN THE TEMPERATURE.—A very extraordinary difference in the temperature occurred on Sunday. The thermometer, placed in direct opposition to the rays of the sun, rose to 112 degrees of Fahrenheit, the perpendicular thermometer was at 105, the one in the shade 69, and the night index sank to 46; making the very great difference, within fifteen hours, of 66 degrees. Barometer 29.85.

This subject led, by a very natural transition, to a long talk about England. The innkeeper and his wife had both been "raised in Virginia," as they termed it, close to Monticello, where Mr. Jefferson planted his University; but they had never seen or conversed with any one from England before, nor ever remembered any English person, known to them as such, to have passed this way. Their conceptions of Europe generally, were very crude, and sometimes ludicrous; but not more so than those which many people in a similar rank of life in England, entertain of France and America. There appeared, however, to be much respect for England, and great good feeling towards her people, with these unsophisticated mountaineers; though on the coast, this respect and good feeling are confined chiefly to the wealthy and well-educated classes; the prejudices of the vulgar and the ignorant being still very strong against what was once the mother-country, and which only ceased to be so because she unwisely and unjustly oppressed her colonial children.

We left "The Pleasant Bank" after a short but agreeable stay, with a new driver and a new team, and still found the road along the river more and more beautiful as we advanced. The trees on the river's banks became larger in size, and among them were now seen noble spruce-firs, blending their deep-green and feathery foliage advantageously with the lighter tints of other trees; while the dark and glossy holly, with small smooth leaf and prickly edge, afforded another pleasing variety. The river was said to abound with fish of various kinds—among others, with trout and shad; and several weirs and traps were set for catching them in different parts of the stream. Deer abounded so thickly in the neighbourhood, that three or four fine animals would often be brought home by a small shooting-party after a few hours' stroll in the woods.

About four miles from the Pleasant Bank, we came to some lofty cliffs of rock, overhanging the river to the height of 120 or 130 feet. This spot is called "The Painted Mountain," from the circumstance of there being found on the surface of the cliffs, in places thirty and forty feet from the base, and wholly inaccessible without ladders, certain devices painted in different colours, of which no one knows the history, and of the origin of which there is not the least tradition. The two places which I saw, exhibited nothing like written characters, but rather a fanciful device, like a frieze or border, and resembling some of the patterns of wavy lines seen on the vases dug up from the ruined temples of the Mexicans, and like that seen on the vase taken up from the supposed Mexican mound at Natchez. There is as much obscurity, however, about these painted signs on the rocks here, as about the written signs on the rocks near Mount Horeb and Sinai, which were at one time thought to be inscriptions made by the Israelites in their desert-wanderings—as these are thought to be signs left by some extinct races of Indians. Nor is there the least reasonable ground of hope that we shall ever know more about either of their memorials of the past, than we know at present.

Near these painted cliffs, the road divides; that on the left continuing along the edge of the river towards Knoxville; and about half a mile from this point are still loftier cliffs, rising to the height of 300 feet above the stream, and having the road overhung by a portion of them. At this spot there were formerly several narrow shafts, or square pillars of rock, that rose 100 feet above the cliff, and gave to the place the name of "The Chimnies." But limestone being wanted for the repair of the road, and the protruding masses being more easily knocked off than the more solid portions of the mass below, these picturesque objects were destroyed for that purpose. The place is still called by its former name, however, and is still numbered among the natural curiosities of the neighbourhood.

At the point where the road divides, we left the State of North Carolina and entered that of Tennessee, taking the road to the right, and leaving the French Broad River entirely, that stream flowing on westerly till it reaches the river Tennessee, which gives its name to the State, and thence going on to join the great Mississippi.

About seven o'clock we reached a clean and comfortable inn, at a station called Cave Hill, from a large cavern in the neighbourhood; and as the coach was to halt here for some time, we availed ourselves of the assistance of the usual guides for such excursions, and went to visit the cave by the bright light of a nearly full moon. Ascending to the top of a small rounded hill, we came at first to a shelving pit; we descended into this by means of two trunks of trees, placed for the visitor to slide down between them, and soon came to the overhanging rock which forms the opening of the cave. This had an aperture of about four feet in depth, so that by a little stooping it was easy to pass it, and the vast cavern beyond irresistibly tempted one to go further; but every step taken became more difficult and more unpleasant, from the deadly chill of the atmosphere. The thermometer stood here at 40°, while outside it was at 80°, so that the breath was as visible as in a frosty morning; while dripping water, and large masses of rock covered with wet clay, made it slippery to the hands and feet, and difficult to hold firmly with either. Instead of torches, we had only three small candles, and the gloom was, therefore, considerable; while the bats, the only permanent abiders in this cavernous retreat, were several times near extinguishing these by flying directly at the flame. Our party succeeded, however, in going for about a quarter of a mile into the cave, and we were all amply rewarded for our pains.

Besides the grandeur of any large subterraneous cavity like this, which extends upwards of a mile in length, and is in some places thirty or forty feet high, there were here a number of beautiful stalactytes, and petrifactions of the most grotesque forms. In-the part where our excursion terminated, there was a singular projection of rock called "the pulpit," the ascent to it being by steps, and there being a slope in its front like a reading-desk. Near the same place also is a long range of stalactytes in columns, or rather semi-columns, projecting from the rocky wall in full relief, the central ones of which are the largest; and as these gradually diminish on each side towards the end, the whole resemble the pipes of a large organ. Like these also, the upper and lower extremities of the pillars are small, and the largest parts of their diameters are in the centre. This is appropriately enough called "the organ," for in addition to this general resemblance to the exterior front of such an instrument, the pipes give forth each a different sound when struck by the hammer, from the deepest tones of the bass, by the largest pipes of the centre, to the shriller and shriller notes of the treble, as the hammer goes on striking the successive pillars, which grow smaller and smaller towards the sides. Beyond this is a fine spring of deliciously sweet, clear, and cold water; and still further on, other pillars and stalactytes, the whole cave extending for a mile, no one having yet, as our guides said, quite reached the end. As it was admitted that we had seen the most interesting portion, and as our time was limited and our candles growing short, it was thought best to be content and refrain from going further. We therefore retraced our steps, and saw rather more of the danger of a false step in coming back, than in first going in. In some places there were deep hollows of thirty or forty feet, with water in them, the depth of which was not known, and a person falling into one of these would have little hope of recovery. Even close to the entrance, where the descent made into the cave is by a ladder of ten or twelve steps, there is also a deep and yawning gulf, into which one false step would precipitate the visitor; and his destruction would be inevitable. We were all heartily glad therefore to reach the open air in safety, though, when we got there, the change from a temperature of 40° to about 80° produced a sense of suffocation, and made us perspire most copiously, as well as to feel intense thirst.

We left the inn at Cave Hill about eleven at night, for Greenville; but had scarcely got a mile from thence, before the driver bade us roll all the curtains of the coach up, and keep a good look-out, as an attempt had been made to rob the mail in this road only a few nights ago; and the parties having been then unsuccessful, he feared that they would seek for some accession to their numbers, and make another attempt on the first favourable opportunity. This was not very agreeable intelligence; but we put ourselves in a state of vigilance, at least, so as to prepare for the worst; and though we had not yet met with an instance of such an attack since we had been in the country, we thought the time might now have arrived, and that we must brave it as well as we could, for we had never carried arms of defence of any kind whatever.

On reaching the inn at which the stage usually stopped, no one was up, but, by hard knocking, we aroused someone; and in a few minutes a man appeared just as he had risen from his bed, with white cotton trousers and shirt, but without stockings, shoes, jacket, or waistcoat. As he began to assist the coachman in taking down our baggage, I supposed he was the clerk or book-keeper of the inn; for these are the only white servants they usually have, the porters and attendants being almost always negroes; but I soon heard him addressed by the title of Major Molony, and found that he was the master of the inn. We asked for bed-rooms, and were shown first to one in which were four beds, some already occupied by men; then to a smaller room, with three beds, partly occupied also in the same manner. The greatest astonishment was expressed at our objection to sleep in the same room with other persons, particularly as they often put strangers together in the same bed, two or three at a time, they said, and no one made any objections to it! At length, for the lady's accommodation, we were shown what was called the "reserved room for families;" where, in a space not much larger than enough to contain the two beds within it, we had to accommodate ourselves as well as we could. There had been smoking and brandy-drinking in it the night before, as we judged from the fragments of unfinished cigars, and a tumbler containing some unconsumed brandy; but we were assured that the room was perfectly clean, as no one had been in it but Governor Polk, and he had merely lain down on the bed without taking his clothes off.

It appeared, on inquiry, that the little town of Greenville had been the scene of great excitement on the previous day. The period was approaching for the election of Governor of the State; and the present occupant of that office, Governor Connor, a Whig, was to be opposed by his rival candidate, Mr. Polk, the present Speaker of the House of Representatives in the General Congress at Washington, a Democrat. As in England, the candidates here patronize different houses, the Whigs made the other hotel their head-quarters; and this was the camp of the Democrats. The candidates were on an electioneering tour; and both appeared in the same town at the same time, to address the people at large; but as no room could be found spacious enough to hold the auditors, this was done in the open air. They generally chose some spot in the fields, near the town; had a temporary erection there, where the auditors, ladies as well as gentlemen, gathered round them; and they spoke alternately, in attack and defence, on the measures of the administration, and on such topics as were most likely to win adherents to their respective parties. From all I could learn, the contest was likely to be very severe, though Mr. Polk was admitted on all sides to be the best orator; and this weighs much more with the people of America, than higher and more important qualifications.

Greenville itself is a very small village, containing a court-house, two churches, Methodist and Presbyterian, about one hundred dwellings and stores, two hotels, and a population of about eight hundred persons, of whom not more than two hundred are negroes, or coloured people.

We left it at eleven, by a stage from Knoxville to Blountsville—the only one in the country on which I had ever seen a picture painted on the door-panel; and this, moreover, was grossly indecent, such as no English or even French proprietor would have permitted for a moment to remain on his vehicle. The panels of both doors contained a painting, executed at the same time that the coach was built, and painted and varnished like the rest of the panelling. The picture on the one side represented a hussar warrior taking leave of his wife or lover, while his horse and his military companions awaited him at the garden-gate of his dwelling; and in this there was nothing objectionable. The picture on the other side represented a fashionably-dressed beau, embracing a lady on a sofa; and the offensively-amorous manner in which the figures were placed, seemed to attract the vulgar jests of the surrounding crowd, and to elicit from them expressions which showed how palpable was the indecency of the exhibition even to the commonest apprehensions. Yet abundant as the jests and obscenities were which passed from mouth to mouth, I heard no one speak in terms of censure. This was only another instance, added to many that I had seen before, which convinced me, that though the Americans affect to be much more delicate in their horror of certain associations than the people of any other nation, and scrupulously avoid the utterance of certain words in common use in England in the best society, without the slightest idea of impurity being attached to them by us; yet that, in reality, the men, of the South especially, are more indelicate in their thoughts and tastes than any European people; and exhibit a disgusting mixture of prudery and licentiousness combined, which may be regarded as one of the effects of the system of Slavery, and the early familiarity with vicious intercourse to which it invariably leads.

At ten miles from Greenville we came to a village called Raystown; and as the political excitement of the approaching election had spread thus far, the conversation between the postmaster, the driver, and a store-keeper who joined them, was on the state of party-strength and tactics. As the postmasters are appointed by the President, these, and the mail contractors and mail-stage drivers, are usually, though not always, supporters of the existing administration, under whom they may be said to be placemen; and such were those we saw here. The storekeeper, however, was on the other side, and he boldly denounced Mr. Van Buren as a tyrant. When asked for his reasons, he said, "Because he squandered the people's money in extravagant expenditure." He was reminded that the expenses of government were all voted by the House of Representatives; and that the President did no more than sanction their acts. "But," replied the storekeeper, "he paid 20,000 dollars for Mr. Speaker Polk's chair, which I call a pretty smart item of expenditure; and more shame to Mr. Speaker Polk to sit in such a piece of extravagance, paid for out of the people's money." This was declared to be altogether an error, the sum being 200 dollars, or about 40l. sterling; but the storekeeper persisted in his statement. He added "Van Buren is a tyrant, because he wishes to make all his sons Presidents after him, like the despots in Europe; for hasn't he sent over his son John to court Queen Victoria? and then, I suppose, we shall have Dick Johnson's nigger boys to be Vice-presidents, after their father, also." Now Mr. Van Buren is not only a thorough republican, but is complained of by his opponents as being too democratic; and, therefore, this alarm about his wishing to adopt the principle of hereditary monarchy, is as absurd as it would be for the politicians of England to accuse Queen Victoria of designing to make her kingdom a republic. But the allusion to "Dick Johnson's nigger boys," I did not understand, till it was explained to me. Mr. Richard M. Johnson, one of the senators from this State, Tennessee, to the General Congress at Washington—elected, therefore, by the legislature of this State, to represent them in the Upper House of the American parliament—is also Speaker of that House, and Vice-president of the Union, the second man in rank, therefore, in the country; and his rank as senator, and as vice-president, is conferred by popular election. His progeny, it seems, are chiefly coloured children, by mulatto mothers; and this amalgamation—which is extensively practised by the white men of the South, though such horror is expressed at it, when the Abolitionists are falsely accused of encouraging it—is made, in Mr. Johnson's case, a great crime, to serve a party-purpose; though the same thing done by a Whig, would, in the judgment of his party-supporters, be thought nothing of. The great crime of Mr. Johnson, however, is not in having coloured children, for that is a common occurrence among the planters of the South, but he has *married* the mother of these children, which is an indignity that the American people resent as an insult to their blood and race!

Beyond Raystown we came, after another ten miles, to a small village called Leesburgh; and in our way, before and after passing this station, we had some of the most rocky patches of road we had yet passed over, reminding me indeed of that stony region of the ancient Auranites, or Modern Havuran, called the district of Ledjah, in Syria. The soil appeared to become richer, and the cultivation to be conducted in a more careful manner, the fields were more free of stumps of trees and weeds, the fences in higher order, and the farm-houses were neater, and in better condition. The haymakers were in many of the fields, mowing and heaping up their second crop; the wheat-harvest had been gathered in; the oats were now reaping and storing; and the maize or Indian corn, which is not gathered till October, seemed very promising.

Five miles from Leesburgh brought us to Jonesborough, which is a larger village than either of the three preceding. We found the streets full of horses, saddled and bridled, belonging to the farmers of the neighbourhood, who had come in to attend "the speaking" as it is called, which was going on here to-day, the rival candidates for the governorship being both here literally "in the field." The place of meeting was in a field above the town, near the skirts of a wood. The audience was said to exceed 3,000 persons; and ladies and children were as numerous as gentlemen. They had been "at it" as our informant said, since breakfast-time; and as it was now nearly five in the afternoon, he thought they would soon "give over;" which we found to be the case, as we saw the crowd winding down the hill into the town just as our coach reached the post-office, where the mail was first delivered, and then we repaired to the hotel to change horses. It had been our intention to halt here for the night; but every bed in the town was engaged, and the excitement was excessive; we therefore thought it best to proceed onward. The town is prettily situated in a deep hollow, and consists chiefly of one long street, with more brick houses than wooden ones, which is unusual in the country. Its court-house was lately burnt down, fires being as frequent here as elsewhere in America. It has two churches, Methodist and Presbyterian, and a population of about 1,200 persons, including from 300 to 400 negroes.

CHAPTER XL

We left Jonesborough and all its political bustle about six o'clock, and, pursuing our way towards Blountsville, we passed through some beautiful thick forests, with immense trees and deep shadows; and here and there saw the changing leaves of the sumach as red as if they had been just dipped in blood. There were also some fine tall Lombardy poplars, exceeding 100 feet in height, and a great variety of rich and beautiful foliage. Sawmills, and flour-mills, moved by water-power, were more thickly seen than before. Brick-fields and kilns, providing materials for building, were also met with: and the signs of increasing population and increasing comfort were everywhere abundant. Neat cottages, good farmhouses, and pleasant gardens, gave indication of progressive improvement, and the whole aspect of the country was as fine as that of the best parts of Yorkshire in England, to many agricultural portions of which it bore a striking resemblance. We witnessed to-night, in the forests, one of the most gorgeously splendid and exquisitely beautiful sunsets it was ever my good fortune to behold—and yet I had seen many, in the East Indies, in the West Indies, in the Persian Gulf, in the Red Sea, in the Mediterranean, and in the Indian Ocean. Its glory was so surpassing, that no language could describe it. Its ever-changing beauty was so evanescent, that no painter could portray it; and neither the glowing pen of Milton, nor the lucid pencil of Claude, though dipped in the colours of the rainbow, would be equal to its delineation. There are some things that baffle the powers of description in proportion to the intensity of the admiration they excite, and this was one of them.

At eight o'clock we reached one of the usual stations for changing the horses of the mail-stage, just midway between Jonesborough and Blountsville, about ten miles from each. The situation was inviting, a neat brick dwelling, with double portico, seated in a valley on the banks of the Watauga river, and the keeper of it, a widow of 75, with a mother still living at 108, in the same house. We were much tempted to stop and pass the night here; but as the moon was near the full, we resolved upon going on another stage at least. While seated at the tea-table, however, an accident defeated all our plans, and compelled us to stay. The new driver, on bringing out his team of four horses, wished to teach them to follow him, as well-trained horses often do in England; but the animals were not disposed to yield to his invitation, and took it into their heads to play truant, by going off, all harnessed, at a full canter, faster than any one could pursue them. Owing to this mishap, we were kept at the Widow Hall's farmhouse, for two days and nights, in complete embargo. The mail-stage ran only every other day; and no extra coach or chaise could be had from Jonesborough or Blountsville. Here we remained, therefore, unable to move forward or backward, and subject to gross insolence from the driver, who had conceived a strong antipathy to our whole party, for no other reason than that we were English; and this he had no scruple to assign as the reason why he would not even fulfil his own engagements when asked so to do; because, he said, "he was an American, and he would never suffer an Englishman to *crow* over him, which he thought he should do, if he did anything at our bidding."[1]

In this dilemma, I happened to hear that there was an Irishman, named William Deery, who lived in Blountsville, and had a carriage and pair, which he sometimes used for carrying his family, though his horses were most frequently working at the farm. My servant being also an Irishman, I sent him over to make a statement of our case, and solicit the use of his carriage, to get us on as far as Blountsville, at least, where we should be in the line of the Virginia stages. The mission was successful, as the servant returned bringing with him the carriage and horses, by which we were happily rescued from our tedious and disagreeable detention.

In our journey from hence to Blountsville, we passed the river Watauga by fording it; and soon after crossed another small stream, the Holston, in the same manner. There was nothing peculiar in the road, it being as hilly and rocky as most that we had passed over of late; but there was a greater proportion of the blood-red leaves of the sumach and dogwood in the forests; and extensive tracts of what appeared to us at a distance to be fine green grass, but which we afterwards ascertained to be the herb or weed called pennyroyal, with a powerfully aromatic smell, and used here, as in England, medicinally, in the form of herb-tea. We found also a party of about twenty white men, farmers, repairing the road, which we remarked the more, as it was the first instance of our witnessing such an application of labour in any part of our journey, though so much needed in every district of the country.

On arriving at Blountsville, we were most kindly received by Mr. Deery, who had ordered his servant to take us to his house, and not to the hotel, and he had provided an excellent dinner for our refreshment. He wished us, indeed, to stay some time with him, and expressed his extreme delight to meet with any one from "the old country," and do them all the honour in his power. His wife, son, and daughter were as warm and cordial as himself; and their house was among the neatest and most comfortable we had seen for many a day, while everything about the table-service and the beds were remarkable for that cleanliness and neatness in all their minutiæ, which American housekeepers in the country seemed to us never to attain, either because they did not perceive the advantage, or enjoy the pleasure, of such arrangements; or because they would not give themselves that trouble, without which, neither these nor any other comforts can be provided and preserved.

Mr. Deery unfolded himself to us with a degree of frankness which was at once natural and delightful; and his history was as honourable to himself as it is encouraging to those of his countrymen who come to this country, as he did, to obtain a competency. He left the neighbourhood of Londonderry, where he was born, at the age of nineteen, and having some little money, he laid in a stock of such goods as the back-settlers needed, and came as far as Tennessee at once, it being then, in 1804, a frontier country, with Indian tribes living close to the white settlements. He was successful in his first adventure, and repeated it on a little larger scale; until, after two or three trips of this kind, he fixed himself in a store at Blountsville, where he had now been stationary for forty-two years. As his means increased, he sent home for his father, mother, brothers, and sisters. The parents lived with him to a good old age, and both were buried in adjoining graves. The brothers and sisters all prospered; and Mr. Deery has now a large store, filled with everything required by the farmer for miles round. His surplus capital he had invested in land when it was cheap; and having improved it by farming, he is now one of the wealthiest men in the town or neighbourhood; and, as we could see, by the universal respect paid to him by all we met in the streets and houses, honoured and beloved by his fellow-citizens.

His wife was a fine specimen of a hearty and hospitable matron, anxious to do everything that could afford pleasure to her guests. The eldest son was a fine-grown and gentlemanly young man, of twenty; the daughter about seventeen, well educated by two Scotch ladies, Miss Melville and Miss Gibson, who keep a Female Academy in Jonesborough; another son was at college, aged fifteen; and an interesting little daughter, of seven, was at school in the village. Add to all this, the family were temperate and religious; the father having never tasted spirits or wine for forty years—the son, never; and family-worship being their habitual practice. It was impossible to conceive a more pleasing picture of honest prosperity and innocent happiness than the history of this family afforded; and yet, it may be said that such success is within the reach of nearly all those who emigrate to this country from Great Britain, if they would only pursue it by the same steps. Industry, prudence, economy, perseverance, honesty, sobriety, filial affection, and piety. These are within the reach of the humblest; and their rewards are sure. But, blind and infatuated, the great mass of those who leave their homes in Europe, for a competency in America, are carried by the torrent of intemperance, vice, and impiety, to an early and dishonoured grave.

After dinner, we went to take a walk through the village, which is very small, containing not more than 50 houses and about 400 persons; with less than 50 negroes, the proportion of these having greatly diminished of late years, as the high prices given for them in the south and west, leads to their being sold off to slave-dealers coming up from thence; and white labourers take their places here. There is a small court-house, two churches, Methodist and Presbyterian, and two hotels. Although the village is small, it was to-day filled with people, not less than 500 farmers having come in from the surrounding country to hear "the speaking" of the several candidates for Governor, Senator, and Representatives, now canvassing the State. This took place in the Methodist church, and not in the open air, as at Jonesborough, so that the crowd was excessive, and the heat intolerable. I suffered from this inconvenience, however, much less than others, as, on being taken into the building by Mr. Deery, a way was made for us through the throng, and we took our seats on the platform, which in this country is generally substituted for the pulpit, and is capable of holding five or six persons comfortably; and here we remained behind the orators, to each of whom I was subsequently introduced. The speaking was sensible, moderate, free from bombast, and much calmer and more argumentative than election-speeches usually are in England. The rival candidates were spoken of with the greatest respect, and not a sentence of declamation, or a word of vituperation, either of parties or individuals, took place, at which I was agreeably surprised; because the excessively violent tone of the newspapers would lead one to expect a corresponding degree of severity in the candidates whose cause they espoused; but here, at least, this was not the case. The audience, like that of all political assemblies I had yet seen in America, were the most quiet and orderly that could be imagined; as much so, indeed, as a congregation hearing a sermon. There was no clapping of hands, no stamping of feet, no motion even of the head, or smile upon the countenance to indicate approbation; no cry of "hear, hear," so cheering to the speaker, and so animating to the auditors, as in England; nor, in short, any indication whatever by which anyone could ascertain whether the sentiments of the orators were in unison with those whom he addressed, or otherwise. Even at the close of the meeting, there was no resolution proposed, or vote taken, but the people silently dispersed, apparently without even exchanging opinions between themselves, as to what had been addressed to them. On the desk of the pulpit, just before the speakers, was a huge brown earthenware pitcher of water, holding from two to three quarts, which, at almost every pause, the speakers lifted to their mouths with both hands, and took a copious draught; and one of the orators, Colonel Aiken, a candidate for a seat in the Legislature of the State as Senator, had a silk handkerchief folded like a neckcloth, and hung across the pulpit-desk, with one end dangling over towards the audience, and this he drew across his mouth, from side to side, holding both ends tight as a rope, after every time of drinking.

Respecting the practice of canvassing, by candidates for office, and especially for such as that of Governor, the highest in the State, I was glad to find that the general opinion of the more intelligent classes here, was unfavourable to it; they thought such candidates should be solicited to serve, by their constituents, and not be themselves the solicitors for the appointment. I have always thought that in England it was degrading to the character and dignity of a representative of the people, to go the rounds of a political and personal canvass, soliciting men, who should be left to their own free choice, to vote for them; and, therefore, I never submitted to this practice myself, in the two elections for Sheffield, as member of parliament, and always censured it in others. But the political canvassing in America does not descend to the English practice of personally waiting on the poorest voters in their houses, shaking hands with them as perfect equals, flattering their wives, and kissing their little children, and then *soliciting* the *favour* of the individual's vote. The practice here, is confined to the visiting certain towns and districts, by appointment, throughout the State, there making a public statement of principles and opinions on the great political topics of the day, and then leaving the voters to decide for themselves. The labour and expense of such a canvass is, however, very great; as in this State of Tennessee, which is nearly as large in area as England, the candidates for the governorship, had already travelled over upwards of 2,000 miles; and it was thought that it would require a journey of at least 1,000 miles more, before they would have traversed the length and breadth of the land. It is in a few of the States only that the governors are elected by the whole body of voters. In most of them, the legislature, in joint ballot, elect the governor; and then, no such extensive canvass is thought necessary. Even in this State, the representatives and senators are sent from particular districts, and to the limits of these districts only are their canvassing labours confined; but the governors, being dependent for their election on the votes of *all* the electoral body in every part of the State, must visit every district in it, and address the people in each, if they hope to succeed, though the State is more than 400 miles in length from east to west, and more than 100 miles broad from north to south.

The shape of this State is remarkable for its regularity, being a lengthened oblong, stretching east and west from the Iron Mountains of North Carolina, to the Mississippi river, a distance of 420 miles, and having its northern and southern boundaries accurately defined by two straight parallels of latitude, namely 35° for its southern edge, and 36° 30′ for its northern; being thus a degree and half of latitude in breadth, or 104 miles. It has an area, therefore, of upwards of 40,000 square miles, or 25,600,000 acres of land, without heaths or deserts, and the greater portion of it fine fertile soil, abundantly watered with rivers. Its name is derived from its principal stream, the Tennassee, so pronounced by the Indians, and meaning, in their language, "a curved spoon," from some supposed resemblance between this, and their winding river.

The lands now forming this State, were included in the second charter of North Carolina, granted in 1664, by Charles the Second; but it was not until 1754, that a few white families ventured as far west as the Cumberland river, where they were attacked, and driven off by the Indians. A fort, called Fort London, was built here by the British in 1757; but a war breaking out between the British and the Cherokees in 1759, this fort was taken by the Indians, and all the whites in it were tomahawked. In 1761, the Indians submitted to a treaty of peace; and in 1765, emigration began towards the river Holston, and progressively increased. From this period, the white population penetrated farther and farther to the west, and planted their log-cabins amidst hitherto untrodden forests. In 1776, at the period of the Declaration of Independence, they had grown to be very numerous; and espousing as they did, heartily, the revolutionary war, they were attacked by the British from the coast, and by the Cherokees, who were in the service of the English; but a brilliant victory being obtained over both, by the riflemen of Tennessee, the power of the British was destroyed in this quarter. The territory still, however, belonged to the colony or province of North Carolina.

In 1790, the whole of the area of what now forms the State of Tennessee, was ceded by North Carolina, to the general government of the United States; and it was then erected into what is called a "Territory," such as Florida and Iowa now are, and such as nearly all the new States have been for a short period before they were regularly incorporated into the Federal Union. The Territorial government continued until 1795, when the inhabitants being found to amount to 77,262 persons, a Convention was held at Knoxville, in January 1796, and reported to the general government a form of Constitution, on which they had agreed for their new State. It was accordingly admitted into the Union, in June of the same year; since when, its increase in towns and population has been equal to that of any of the south-western States.

The seat of government is at Nashville, nearly in the centre of the State; and the Legislature consists of a House of Representatives of seventy-five members; and a Senate of twenty-five members; with a Governor; all of whom are elected, by universal suffrage and vote by ballot, for two years. The pay of the members of both houses is four dollars per day while in session, which rarely exceeds two months in the year. The salary of the Governor is 2,000 dollars, or about 400*l.* sterling per annum; and the only executive officers of his government are a Secretary of State, and a Treasurer, at salaries of 1,000 dollars a year each.

The Judiciary consists of three Judges of the Supreme Court, with salaries of 1,800 dollars a year each, and three Judges of the Court of Chancery, at 1,500 dollars a year each; there being one for each of the three districts into which the State is divided, called the Eastern, Western, and Middle Division. In addition to these, there are eleven Circuit Judges at 1,300 dollars a year each, who preside in the eleven Circuit Courts to which they are severally appointed. The Judges of the Supreme Court are elected by a joint vote of the two Houses of Legislature, for a term of twelve years; and those of the inferior Courts, in the same manner for a term of eight years. Thus, every office in the State is elective; and all power is literally derived from the people, with short periods of service, and frequent opportunities of accountability. The whole annual expense of the government of this State, as large in area as England, is less than 50,000 dollars; or 10,000*l.* per annum; which is just the salary of a single member of Council in the East India Company's Government in Bengal; and less than the emoluments of a single Bishop, or even of some sinecurists, under the government of England. The expenses of the whole government of Tennessee are these: for the Governor and his Executive, 4,000 dollars; for the two Houses of the Legislature, 20,000 dollars; for the whole of the Judiciary, comprising the Supreme and Circuit Courts, 24,200 dollars; the whole sum being less than the single sinecure enjoyed by Lord Ellenborough, in the Patent Office, of Clerk of the Writs in the King's Bench, though the duty is performed by deputy. These are comparisons which force themselves on the mind, by the power of contrast; and in giving them utterance as they occur, it is done with a hope that they may draw attention to the duty of lessening the public burdens, by simplifying the forms and diminishing the expenses of government, which experience, in other countries, has shown to be as practicable as it is desirable, and which it would be as easy, as it would be found advantageous, to introduce gradually into our own country, if it were set about with an honesty of intention and earnestness of purpose, free from party motives, and without violence or injustice.

1. Though this prejudice against the English is very strong among the ignorant classes of America, we subsequently learnt that there were peculiar circumstances in the history of this individual, which still further embittered him against the whole English nation. He was a native of Georgetown, close to the City of Washington, in the District of Columbia: and was present when the English, under Sir George Cockburn, landed at Washington, burnt the Capitol, destroyed the Public Records in their Patent Office, and the Library of Congress. He partook, therefore, as well he might, in the common feeling of indignation, which these outrages excited in every American bosom. Such is the effect of War, not only to estrange nations while engaged in actual hostilities; but to engender feelings in the people of the countries engaged in warfare, which require a lifetime of peace entirely to obliterate!

CHAPTER XLI

As our journey from Tennessee into Virginia was to be made by night—the mail-stage being the only conveyance, and that passing through here about midnight—we left our kind and hospitable entertainers in Blountsville, with a hope that we might some day or other meet again; and in an hour after we had set out, we passed the boundaries of the State, and entered on what is called "The Old Dominion." This is the name by which the Virginians still delight to call their home, with reference to its more ancient settlement than that of any other part of the North American Continent, and of its forming part of the dominion of the virgin Queen Elizabeth, in honour of whom its present name was given.

We rode all night over a rocky and hilly road; and after a journey of twenty-three miles we reached the first town in the southern part of Virginia, Abingdon, about seven o'clock, on the morning of Saturday the 27th of July. We felt so much fatigued after the rough roads we had traversed during the last fortnight, that we determined to rest here for a few days, to recruit our strength, and found tolerably comfortable accommodations at the principal hotel.

Abingdon is pleasantly situated, in an undulated part of the country, the town literally covering an extensive cave, containing a lake. A fine range, called the Iron Mountains, is seen on the east, being one of the many ridges that run southward from the Alleghanies. The town consists chiefly of one main street, and has about 200 houses, and from 1,600 to 1,800 inhabitants, including not more than 200 blacks employed chiefly as domestic servants in the town, though negro slaves are abundantly used in the cultivation of the surrounding country. There is a Court House at Abingdon, and three Churches, one Presbyterian of the old school, one Methodist of the old, and one of the new school. The Swedenborgians have a congregation, but no church. There are two hotels, several stores, and many pretty villa-residences in the neighbourhood. The

Governor of the State, Mr. Campbell, resides at Abingdon, when the Legislature is not in session, but his official residence is at Richmond, the capital of the State. There is a newspaper published here weekly, of Whig politics, called "The Virginia Statesman," but there is no bookseller in the place.

We remained at Abingdon for five days, and during that period I delivered a short course of lectures in the Presbyterian church, which were more largely attended than we had expected, from the small population of the town. Among the auditors were Colonel Campbell, the governor of Virginia, and his family, and Colonel Preston, the senator from South Carolina, whom we had heard in the great debate on the Sub-Treasury Bill, in the Congress at Washington, and who was here on a visit with his family; while many persons came from a considerable distance in the country, to attend the course.

Our stay at Abingdon was rendered peculiarly agreeable by the hospitable attentions which we received from Mr. Smith, an Englishman by birth, but who had been in this country since the year 1804; though he still retained all his attachment to his native land. We passed many agreeable hours with his interesting family, and met at his table many of the principal residents of the town and neighbourhood, many of whom were well educated and intelligent.

The system of manual-labour schools has lately been introduced into this part of Virginia, and a school of this description has been established within about ten miles of Abingdon. It is called the "Amory and Henry College," the former being the name of a celebrated and popular bishop of Virginia, and the latter the name of their great revolutionary orator, Patrick Henry. There are at present upwards of 100 pupils in the establishment, which is conducted as nearly as practicable on the plan of Mr. Fellenberg's institution at Hoffwyl, in Switzerland. The boys have two hours' study before breakfast, four hours between breakfast and dinner, three hours labour in the field, garden, or workshop after dinner, and the evening is devoted to preparing the lessons for the ensuing day. The sum paid for board and tuition is a dollar and half per week, about a shilling per day, and they are allowed five cents, or about two-pence half-penny an hour, for all labour performed, as a set-off against these charges, so that the cost of educating a boy, who performs his three hours' labour per day regularly, is not more than fifty dollars, or about 10l. sterling a year, for board and tuition in every branch of useful learning. The Superintendent is Professor Collins, from the State of Maine, whom I had the pleasure to see, and who appears to feel the deepest interest in the success of the institution, and to be well qualified for presiding over it.

I had often had occasion to observe the national vanity of the people of this country, who, with the exception of the few that have travelled or resided in Europe, seem almost universally to believe that their countrymen are superior in arts, in arms, in literature, in science—but, above all, in *oratory*—to any people in the world; and they avail themselves of every occasion that presents itself, to make this boast. One of the most amusing specimens of this feeling was presented to us at Abingdon, A gentleman, having in the reading-room the "Richmond Inquirer," of July 5, read aloud from it the following paragraph—

> We have seen in the 'London Observer' a very brief sketch of the debate upon the Earl of Winchelsea's motion in the House of Peers, of the 31st May, calling upon Lord Melbourne to afford some explanation as to the principles on which he intended to conduct the government. The 'New York Commercial' promises to give the speeches of Lords Melbourne and Brougham in full. The former frankly admitted the difficulties with which he was surrounded, but declared that the Government could be conducted on none other than the principles of progress and reform. He was followed by Lord Brougham, who ridiculed the Ministers for the attempt to gain popularity for the Queen, upon the strength of Peel's demand to dismiss the ladies of the bedchamber.—An American, who heard this speech, pronounces it one of the finest he ever heard, and Lord Brougham the most powerful debater he ever saw, and in 'senatorial gladiation' unequalled. This was regarded as one of his greatest efforts— and one of the most distinguished auditors declared that he had heard nothing like it for the last twenty or thirty years.

On this, one of the hearers exclaimed, "Well, then, I expect that this Lord Brougham comes the nearest to our Daniel Webster, of any man the English can produce." To which the others signified their assent; but no one seemed to think that he did more than approach him "at a considerable distance." One of the party, and in his general conversation an intelligent man, said that Henry Clay had electrified the English Members of Parliament when he spoke before them in the House of Commons; and that Daniel Webster, who was now gone to England, would astonish them still more, and give them a sample of what true American oratory really was. I asked when Mr. Clay had spoken in the English House of Commons, and was told that it was when he was resident as American minister in London. I assured them that on no occasion did foreign ministers or ambassadors appear in either House of Parliament in England as speakers; but the gentleman who made this assertion really believed that in his diplomatic capacity he had appeared before the House, and excited the astonishment and admiration he described! He still thought that an opportunity would be afforded to Daniel Webster to do the same. When they were informed, that among the Tory peers, Lord Lyndhurst was the most equal match for Lord Brougham, they felt this to be a confirmation of their confidence in their national superiority, as they claimed Lord Lyndhurst as an American, though they would rather have had him to be a Virginian than a Bostonian, as then he would have ranked with Patrick Henry, Washington, and Jefferson.

CHAPTER XLII

We left Abingdon on the morning of Thursday, the 1st of August, for the Virginia Springs, at 8 A.M., by the public stage. For several miles beyond the town, our route lay along the great north-eastern road, and the country presented a succession of beautiful landscapes, with an improved style of cultivation. We found, too, signs of increasing comfort, in the substitution of brick buildings for wooden tenements in many places, while fine cornfields and fruitful orchards generally lined the road.

At half-past two we reached an inn, at a place called Seven-Mile Ford, the situation of which was beautifully romantic, but both the hotel and its keeper, a fat colonel, were dirty in the extreme. We were asked here, for the first time on the road, to drink ardent spirits before dinner, this being the practice of the colonel himself, and one which he recommended to all his guests. I was happy to perceive, however, that every one declined it, and I was assured by some of our fellow-passengers, that in this there has been a manifest and extensive reform, within the last few years, which they attributed chiefly to the change in public opinion, brought about by the efforts of the Temperance Societies. It was now thought disreputable to drink spirits, whereas a few years ago it was almost a universal practice among the men, and was looked upon as no more improper than the use of tobacco.

By the way, I had remarked that since our entrance into Virginia, the original seat of the tobacco plant, there were fewer persons who chewed this stimulating weed, than in any of the Southern States through which we had lately travelled. Smoking was, however, very general; but instead of the cigar, so common everywhere else, the pipe was here more frequent; and this was constructed of a clay bowl of the ordinary shape and size, with a long thin hollow tube of cane for its stem. We saw many women using such pipes, as openly and freely as the men, a practice we had nowhere else observed among the sex, but which we were told was not at all uncommon here. Among the peculiarities of expression, we observed that baggage is very generally called "plunder," and it sounded oddly enough to hear the innkeeping colonel say to us—"Why, you and your family seem to require a pretty considerable deal of *plunder* to carry with you." Horses are called "critturs," and we several times heard the expression—"There is no getting a *crittur* for love or money; they are all employed *hauling* oats." The word "tote" is used to signify carry; and you hear the driver say—"Here, you nigger-fellow, *tote* this lady's *plunder* to her room." Up-stairs is pronounced "up-starrs;" the words bear and fear, are pronounced "barr" and "farr," and one passenger was told "The room *up-starrs* is quite *preparred*, so that your *plunder* may be *toted* there whenever *you've a mind*."

After a better meal than we had expected to get in so dirty a house, and from such filthy attendants, we resumed our journey at four, and, proceeding through an equally fine country to that passed in our morning's drive, we reached Smith's Court House at six; went on from thence to a spot called "The Pleasant Bank," which we reached at nine, the darkness of the night scarcely enabling us to see whether its scenery, or what other cause, gave it its prepossessing name; and passing, soon after, the station of Mount Airy, we reached, at two in the morning, the village of Wythe Court House. We had been thus eighteen hours in coming a distance of fifty-four miles, so that the public mail, for the conveyance of which the contractors receive forty dollars per mile per annum, was here conveyed at the rate of three miles an hour! We found but wretched accommodations, and passed a most uncomfortable night.

Previously to our retiring to rest, we had contracted with the stage-coach proprietor to furnish us an extra coach with four horses, for our journey to Newbern, twenty-eight miles distant, where the line of stages for the Virginia Springs commences its progress, and it was agreed that we should give him twelve dollars to carry us these twenty-eight miles, and twelve dollars for the coach to return; as it was contended that with the same pair of horses it would require a day to go, and a day to come back. To this we assented, and having the whole day before us for our short journey, and not having gone to bed till three in the morning, we slept till eight, and were not ready for breakfast till nine. Here we witnessed the characteristic operation of a large house-dog being sent in chase of a chicken, which he caught in his mouth and brought to the cook, who forthwith killed, plucked, dissected, and fried the same for our use; the whole operation, from the catching to the serving up, occupying less than half an hour of time. This delayed our breakfast till half-past nine, the usual hour of this meal in the country being six o'clock. The delay was now made a reason, on the part of the coach-contractor, for declining to carry us farther than twenty miles, because, as he said, we were setting out in the middle of the day, and his horses could never reach Newbern by sunset, and it would knock them up to travel after. We appealed to his contract, and argued, that whether horses set out at six and halted at six, or began their journey at ten and ended it at ten, it was but twelve hours in either case, and twelve hours was abundantly sufficient to go twenty-eight miles. But we were in his power; there was no other person who had a coach but himself, and the public stage had gone by. He said, therefore, he could only do this;—take us twenty miles with this team of four horses, then engage a new team to take us the other eight miles, and so charge us another half-day, or six dollars, for the extra team. We had no alternative; though, when we stated this to be an extortion, wholly unwarranted, and practised on us because we had no remedy, he frankly replied, "I go for making money, and nothing else, and every time I find a good opportunity of doing so, I shan't let it slip;" at which, all the by-standers laughed approbation; and some few said, "That's right," and "So would I:" but no one uttered a word of disapprobation.

The truth is, this passion for the acquisition of money is much stronger and more universal in this country than in any other under the sun, at least that I have visited; and in proportion to the strength of the passion, so is the weakness of conscientiousness, or the sense of justice, among all ranks. If money can be made honestly, it is well; but if it cannot be made without breaking down some of the barriers which conscience opposes to its acquisition in the minds of honourable men, these must be demolished, and the money acquired; till, at length, the perpetual indulgence of the passion, at all hazards, causes it to increase, like the propensity of gambling, of dram-drinking, or any other vice, till it becomes ungovernable, and sweeps all before it!

The crowning piece of duplicity in this transaction was reserved for disclosure at the end of our journey. We had agreed to pay 24 dollars to be driven 20 miles, and an extra 6 dollars was demanded, because at the end of these 20 miles it would be necessary, according to the statement of the stage-contractor, to get a new team, from the impossibility of the first team going further. It was for this alone that the extra 6 dollars were demanded and paid. Yet when we reached the end of our 20 miles, we found there was no new team there; that the stage-contractor himself knew this; and that he had, secretly and unknown to us, told the driver, when he arrived at the end of the 20 miles, to give his team a feed of corn and an hour's rest, and drive them the remaining eight miles of the way, as it must be no difference to the passengers, whether they were taken on by the old team or a new one! Wherever this was known along the road, or told by us afterwards, it was regarded only as a clever stroke of business; and Mr. Robertson, the perpetrator of this fraud and extortion, for so every just mind would consider it, was called "a smart man," who "knew what he was about," and was "very well fitted for his business." Such is the low state of morality, and the low standard of honour and fair-dealing, when money is to be made.

We left Wythe Court House at 10 o'clock, and proceeded by a hilly and rocky road to the northeast. Soon after our setting out, we observed in the fields a large sycamore-tree, with wide-spreading branches, enclosed with a neat palisade, and was told that this was a very usual way of forming a rustic cemetery, which was confirmed by our seeing several graves within the enclosure. In one of the valleys that we crossed, several terrapins, or fresh-water turtles, were seen, and water-snakes also, of a small size. The tree called the buck-eye, the *æsculus glabra*, was here first seen by us, growing to a height of about thirty feet, and having a fine foliage. It is so abundant in the neighbouring State of Kentucky, (once included as the western part of Virginia,) that the Kentuckians are often called "buck-eyes." In a few of the fields, also, we saw the buckwheat growing, from the grain of which are made the buckwheat cakes, so well known in all parts of America, as a favourite appendage to the breakfast table, both in the northern, southern, and western States. It is the *polygonum fagopyrum* of the botanists, so called from the three-cornered seed which it produces. It is not cultivated in very large quantities, nor is it ever exported; but it is a very favourite grain in the country, for the purpose described. It has a broad green leaf, and a small whitish flower; and looks rather like a shrub or plant than any description of corn. We saw here, also, a number of the small birds, called partridges by some, and quails by others; but more nearly resembling the quails of Arabia than the partridges of England, in size, form, and colour. They appeared very tame, and are said to form excellent food; but the people of the country are so satisfied with their daily fare of coarse fat bacon and beans, (called here, "snaps,") that few give themselves the trouble to shoot birds for their table.

We reached Newbern about eight o'clock; having been, therefore, ten hours in performing the twenty-eight miles; of which, however, we had less reason to complain than of the wretched beds and swarms of bugs which we had to encounter at the inn there, and which rendered it impossible to procure the refreshment of sleep.

It was with more than usual pleasure, therefore, that we received the early summons of the stage-driver at three o'clock in the morning; to which we promptly responded, as a relief from an imprisonment; and by daylight, about four o'clock, we were fairly on our way. The road still continued rocky and hilly, so that our progress was never more than three miles an hour, with four good horses, and a comparatively light coach. Not far from Newbern, we saw for the first time in this quarter an extensive grazing-farm, the rich green grass of which, so unusual to the eye, was particularly refreshing and agreeable, and reminded us more of home than any thing we had seen for some time. Vast herds of cattle are driven up here from the southern and western parts of the State—we saw as many as 600 at least in one drove—to be pastured and fattened for the eastern markets; and it is thought to be more profitable even than planting, though capital invested in that yields from 25 to 30 per cent; but in grazing it is said to realize 50 to 60 per cent, on the average of many years running.

At a distance of twenty-two miles from Newbern, we reached Giles Court House, a substantial brick building, with a tower, executed in good taste; but the other buildings were among the poorest we had lately seen. We made no stay here, except to change horses, but went up from the village over a very steep hill, from the top of which we looked down on the stream of the New River and its picturesque valley. In the rich bottom land, to which we afterwards descended from hence, the trees were of prodigious growth; some American poplars—a very different tree from the Lombardy poplar—being fifteen feet in girth.

On reaching the banks of the New River, we had to enter a flat-bottomed boat, which took the coach and horses across without unharnessing. The stream was here about 200 feet across, but the river was lower by 20 feet than usual, from the long drought. Its banks were lined with large and beautiful sycamore trees, which flourish best on the margin of streams, and whose wide-spreading roots form an excellent barrier for the embankments. This is the head-water of the Western river called the Great Kenhawa, which runs into the Ohio. In the winter it is so frozen over, that waggons of great weight pass across it daily. On the opposite bank, at a distance of some fifty yards from the stream, was one of the largest and most beautiful weeping-willows I had ever seen; but it hung its drooping branches over a wretchedly dilapidated and dirty dwelling, disgraceful to its occupant. Some of our party feeling hungry here, were desirous of procuring bread, but none was to be had. The country-people use little or no wheaten flour; the meal of Indian corn is substituted for it; and "corn-bread," as this is called, is always eaten hot. No more, therefore, is baked at any time than is thought to be necessary for a meal; and if any is left after the meal is over, it is not reserved for future use, but a fresh supply is had for each meal. Neither is it the custom to keep cold-dressed meats or poultry of any kind; so that on arriving at an inn, or a private house, nothing can be had on the sudden; everything has to be prepared; and we never yet had the slightest meal got up, even in the greatest haste, in less than an hour. Orchards, however, were abundant, and the permission of the owner of those near the house was asked, to gather of their produce; a permission which was freely given, with an expression of surprise that it should be thought necessary to ask it, as every one here takes what he pleases for his own eating, from any orchard or garden in his way, and custom attaches to this no idea of wrong.

We went from hence for some time along the banks of the river, which strikingly resembled the French Broad, in North Carolina, especially in the views we obtained of it from elevated points. A few miles brought us to a wretched assemblage of log-houses, called Peterstown, the name of the first innkeeper, whose sign was still up: "Private Entertainment for Travellers, by I. Peters," I asked the distinction between this, and public entertainment, and was told there was none, except that by calling it private, he evaded the payment of the usual fee for a license, which all public houses required. It was here, we saw the following Inscription, copied *verbatim et literatim* from a *red* directing board for the road

To The RedsuLPhe[r]
SPring—8 M ½

meaning, To the Red Sulphur Spring, 8½ miles.

The dwellings and the people we saw, from this onward for several miles, were among the dirtiest we had yet met with. The men seemed as if they did not shave more than once a month, or wash more than once a year; the women looked as though a comb never went through their hair, or soap and water over their skins; and the children, though they were all clothed, never had their garments mended, and were as ragged as they were dirty. Yet they were all of the white race; and no negroes, Indians, or savages among the wildest tribes of Africa or Australia, could possibly be dirtier, or apparently more indolent, than they were. It is indeed to this latter vice, that all their defects are to be traced. With a fine soil, a fine climate, good health, and sufficient means to cultivate their grounds, they could hardly fail, if they were industrious, to lay by a surplus every year and progressively get rich; but having negro slaves to do their work, they seem to think labour an evil to be studiously avoided; so that their dwellings and persons are dirty, and comfortless in the extreme.

After a few hours' ride over the roughest roads imaginable, we passed the Grey Sulphur Springs, and nine miles beyond these arrived at the Red Sulphur about seven o'clock.

Chapter XLIII

We remained at the Red Sulphur Springs for two days, and enjoyed the repose of body, serenity of mind, and delightful social intercourse with the visitors, as sailors do their first day in port after a long and stormy passage, or as pilgrims and caravan-travellers enjoy their first halt in green fields, shade, and water. For though we had experienced much of pleasure in our late tour through Georgia, North and South Carolina, and Tennessee, from the grandeur and beauty of Nature in her mountain-majesty, yet this had been purchased at an unexpectedly great sacrifice of personal comfort in almost every form. We had practically felt all the sufferings (for inconveniences is too slight a term) that bad vehicles, bad roads, bad beds, bad fare, and dirty and uncivil attendants could inflict; so that the contrast which the pleasures of this delightful watering-place presented to us was literally delicious, and we enjoyed it to the full. Our first day's stay here being Sunday, we attended public worship, which was held in the ball-room of the hotel. The service was conducted after the English Episcopalian ritual, by a clergyman of South Carolina, whose sermon was excellent. It embodied the more cheering view of the doctrines of Christianity, so as to lead the minds of his hearers rather by hope than by fear, to believe in the doctrines, and practise the precepts of the gospel. Nearly all the visitors of the place attended. Service was repeated, in the afternoon, with an equally full audience; and the evening was spent in walks, social visits, and conversation. Altogether it appeared to be a very happy day to all parties; and to us it was peculiarly so, from our meeting here with friends from New York and Albany on the one hand, and from New Orleans, Savannah, and Charleston on the other—embracing, therefore, the northern and southern extremes of the country; while from the intermediate cities of Philadelphia and Baltimore we met several others, whose renewed intercourse was peculiarly agreeable.

On the second day we made a more minute examination of the valley and its contents, as well as its neighbourhood; and learnt from others more conversant with the surrounding country many interesting particulars. We slept well, breakfasted heartily, and passed the day agreeably, talking with persons from various States, and of different professions, on a great diversity of topics, the politics and prospects of England included; for English newspapers by the Great Western and the British Queen had found their way even to this remote spot, and the evening was closed by an agreeable social ball, in which all the younger portion of the company joined, commencing at eight and ending at ten o'clock, so that every one had retired early, and all were steeped in profound repose before midnight.

This hotel at the Red Sulphur Springs is not more than seven years old. The mineral water here was known before that period, and resorted to by invalids; but there was merely a rude house with very inferior accommodation. About the period named, the present proprietor, Mr. Burke, a Scotsman, we were told, purchased the place and began the work of providing the requisite accommodation, since which he has from year to year expended large sums, amounting in the whole to more than 100,000 dollars, and is amply rewarded for his enterprise by the possession of an extremely beautiful and commodious establishment, a large and yearly increasing number of visitors, and a handsome profit on his outlay.

The valley in which the Springs are situated is very small, running nearly north and south, being in length not more than half a mile, and in breadth from hill to hill not more than 1,000 feet in any part, and in some not more than 500. The platform of the valley is elevated about 2,500 feet above the level of the ocean, and the hills on either side rise from 300 to 400 feet above this, being steep and rocky. They are sufficiently wooded to be agreeable to the eye; but by their precipitous rise, and close proximity, they prevent either the morning or the evening sun from being seen, and this makes the valley very favourable to the coolness and freshness so much sought for in the summer.

In this valley the two springs rise out of solid masses of rock within ten feet of each other. Over the orifice of each has been constructed a sort of square well, above ground, enclosed with four upright white marble slabs. Around these is built a platform, and the whole is enclosed within an octagonal building of wood, open on all sides, with a dome-like roof, supported by pillars; the interior being fitted with commodious seats for visitors. It is called the Red Sulphur Spring, because a reddish deposit is observed on the rock at the bottom of the well; but the water itself is quite transparent, delightfully cold, and only slightly sulphureous in taste or smell. The nature of this deposit is not yet accurately ascertained; by some it has been thought to be an oxide of iron; others have observed that it is only precipitated, when the beams of the sun play for some time on the water; and one distinguished chemist has pronounced it to be a very minute cryptogamous plant. It is, however, quite inconsiderable in quantity, and is never taken in the water that is drank, this being perfectly clear. As the water rises from the springs, the surplus is carried off by pipes to the baths, where hot or cold sulphur water may be had at any hour. The water is also bottled, and sent to a great distance; and by retaining the sulphuretted hydrogen gas, if bottled at the Spring, it preserves its medicinal virtues, and is therefore in great repute. It contains some small portion of neutral salts, is both diuretic and aperient, and has a uniform temperature of 54° of Fahrenheit's scale.

One of the most singular springs recently discovered, and which would be a great accession to any watering-place in the hot summers of America, is thus described in the public journals:—

> NATURAL SODA FOUNTAIN.—Mr. Spalding, an American missionary, writing from Fort Vancouver, beyond the Rocky Mountains, describes this phenomenon, which he passed three days' journey from Fort Hall. The fountain has several openings, one of which is about fifteen feet in diameter, with no discovered bottom. About twelve feet below the surface are two large globes on either side of this opening, whence the effervescence seems to rise. A stone cast in, after a few minutes, violently agitates the whole fountain. Another of the openings, about four inches in diameter, is through an elevated rock, from which the water spouts at intervals of about forty seconds. The water, in all its properties, is equal to any artificial fountain, and is constantly foaming and sparkling. It is stated to be very salubrious.

The most remarkable natural curiosity, however, in the neighbourhood, is a recently formed lake, on the summit of one of the ridges of the Alleghany mountains, made within the memory of man. It was formerly what is called a Salt Deer-lick; that is, a place where salt exuding from the earth, deer and wild animals resorted to lick it, this being known to be grateful to their palates. A stream of water ran through the valley, coming in by a narrow entrance at one end, and going out by a still narrower at the other. This last, either by some convulsion of nature, or the gradual accumulation of falling rock and earth from the sides of the hill, became blocked up, so that the water being deprived of its natural outlet, continually accumulated, and formed the lake as it is now seen. It is upwards of a mile in length, and somewhat less in breadth; the water is perfectly fresh, but it has risen to such a height as entirely to fill up the valley through which the stream formerly ran, and to bury all the trees on either side

of the hill. It is now indeed so deep as not to admit a sounding-line of 100 feet
to reach the bottom. Its elevation above the sea is estimated to be 3,000 feet at
least.

At a distance of nine miles only, is the establishment of the Grey Sulphur
Springs, the property of Mr. Legaré, a South Carolinian gentleman. It is chiefly
occupied by permanent visitors from that State. Being the first that is reached in
coming from the South, almost all Southern people halt at it in their way to the
North for a day or two, and visits are frequently made from hence by parties for
the day, who drive over after breakfast, dine there, and return in sufficient time
for the enjoyment of the pleasures of the evening here.

The visitors at this and at the Red Sulphur are much less numerous than
those at the White; the greatest number at the Grey Springs being about 50, and
the greatest number at the Red 200, while at the White Sulphur, 700 and 800
congregate, in full seasons. The visitors at the two former, if less numerous, are
generally more select, and are composed chiefly of persons from the South and
West, the distance and the expense operating as a restraint upon the visits of
persons from the North. We had here, for instance, at the Red Sulphur Springs,
families from New Orleans and Mobile, from Texas and the Havannah, officers
of the navy from Pensacola, and of the army from Key West in Florida, several
from Red River, Arkansas, and Mississippi, a few from St. Louis in Missouri,
many from Alabama, Georgia, and North and South Carolina, some from Ohio
and Kentucky, and the largest number, of course, from Virginia.

The contrast between this watering-place and Saratoga, at which we passed
a portion of the hot months of July and August last year, is very striking. At
Saratoga, there is a large sandy or dusty town, with about 2,000 permanent
residents, and from being little elevated above the sea, perhaps not more than
250 feet, the heat is as great as at New York, Philadelphia, or Baltimore. Here, on
the contrary, is a quiet secluded green valley, with not a particle of dust or sand,
no permanent inhabitants, and an elevation of 2,500 feet above the sea, which
gives a delightfully cool temperature, rarely exceeding 75°, while at Saratoga 95°
is not at all uncommon. The nights here, especially, are so cool, as to require
blankets for the beds, while at Saratoga a single sheet seems too heavy. At these
Springs there is but one establishment, and there is ample room in it for more
visitors than usually attend. At Saratoga there are five or six hotels, and they are
generally all crowded to excess. The bed-rooms are larger here, and the tables
better supplied; the mountain-mutton is as good as that of the South-Down
or Welsh breed in England, and the game and poultry is excellent. The milk
and butter is sweet and abundant, the water is deliciously fresh and cool, and
the attendance and discipline of the domestics is unexceptionable. Each guest
is assigned a place at table in the order of his arrival, all taking their seats at

the bottom as they first come, and being moved upwards in regular gradation as others go away and leave vacancies to be filled, so that they who remain longest always occupy the best places at the head of the table. On the plate of each person is placed a card with his name, so that there can be no mistake, and the waiters are stationed to wait in sections, one attending to about half a dozen guests. There is, therefore, none of that indecent rushing and pressure to secure good places, which is seen at Saratoga, everyone here being sure of his place, whether coming early or late to the table; and there is also none of that racing and chasing of waiters, from one end of the table to another, as at Saratoga, where each waiter seems to think it his duty to attend to everybody, as he is not specially limited to a few, and, consequently, in his attempt to answer everybody's call, he can pay no steady or continuous attention to any.

The company at the Virginia Springs is more exclusively confined to the well-bred classes, for the distance and the expense of the journey here, make it impracticable to all but those who are in opulent, or at least in easy circumstances; while at Saratoga, which is within a single day's journey from New York, and can be reached, therefore, at a very trifling cost, the humblest mechanics and most untutored individuals, as small shopkeepers, clerks, and even white servants, may go and join the crowd for a few days, and sit at table beside the highest and best in the land.

On the morning of Tuesday, the 6th of August, we left the Red Sulphur Springs in the public stage, which runs daily between this and the White Sulphur, stopping at the Salt Sulphur in the way. We started at six o'clock, at an hour when, though the sun had been up since five, its rays were not visible in any part of this deep and secluded valley.

We reached the Salt Sulphur Springs; at eleven o'clock, the distance being eighteen miles, and the time occupied four hours. We halted here, to pass the remainder of the day and night.

The general appearance of this establishment is less interesting than that at the Red Sulphur Springs. Like it, however, it is situated in a deep and narrow valley; but the same taste has not been displayed in arranging the buildings and embellishing the spot with lawn and trees, and the result of the whole is therefore inferior. The hotel is placed in the lower part of the valley, and several small cottages or cabins are built near it. The principal bed-rooms are, however, in a fine large range of stone buildings, about 200 feet in length, and three stories in height, with a wide veranda or piazza running along in front of each story. This is half way up the northern hill, with a fine view of the valley below in front, and the green grass of the brow of the hill close to the windows of the lower story behind. The rooms are of good size, well ventilated and clean, and the beds were unusually comfortable. In the middle of the valley are two mineral springs, each under its separate portico and dome, being strongly impregnated with sulphur and salts, and differing only in their respective degrees of strength and temperature, one being at 50° and the other at 56°. For the exercise of the Invalids, there is a ten-pin alley, under a shed, at which ladies exercise themselves as well as gentlemen; and as the ball is rolled along a wooden platform, and not as with us on the grass, it is less laborious, and many of the ladies whom we saw engaged, threw the ball with skill and grace. Such exercises cannot be too strongly commended for both sexes, as it is the great fault of the age, and of this country more than any other, not to educate the body as well as the mind, and not to train the limbs, muscles, tendons, and lungs to that command of power and freedom of play which frequent and varied exercise alone can give. For the evening entertainment there is a band of coloured musicians, and a ball is given every night. The grounds and garden, which might be made as beautiful as they would be interesting, are in a state of the greatest neglect, and seem rather like the wreck of some deserted village, than as belonging to a watering-place in full vigour and popularity.

On the following morning, August 7th, we left the Salt Sulphur Springs at ten o'clock, in an extra stage, engaged for the purpose of conveying us to the White Sulphur; the distance being twenty-four miles, and the sum paid, ten dollars. The first part of our way was by a steeply-ascending road, and through a country of poor soil and scanty cultivation. In the course of our drive, there was blown in through the open sides of the coach, what appeared, when it first alighted on Mrs. Buckingham's dress, a piece of greenish-yellow silk thread, or cord, about an inch and half in length, and of the thickness of the finest kind of twine. On attempting to brush it off, however, with the hand, one end of it was erected in the air, and waved from side to side, while the other stuck fast to the silk of the gown. This singular movement attracting our attention, we watched it with the greater care, and soon perceived it was a very small and delicate, but beautiful caterpillar. On putting itself in motion, it did not crawl, by many undulations of the body, and by slow degrees, as creatures of this species usually do; but instead of this, it first erected its whole body perpendicularly in the air, holding firmly by the part on which it rested, and after waving to and fro several times, it stretched its full length in the direction it intended to proceed, and then took as firm hold of the substance beneath it with its upper end, or head as we supposed it; its position was then perfectly prostrate, and as straight as if it were in a state of tension. It then let go the hold of its nether or hinder extremity, and brought it forward quite close to its head, taking firm hold by it, the whole body then forming a lofty and narrow arch in the air; when it let go the hold it had with its head, stood again erect on its tail, waved its body to and fro several times, and then repeated the same operation as before. It thus measured its way, by repeated lengths of its own body, precisely as the Hindoo pilgrims do, when they vow to measure the ground, by the prostrations of their bodies, from the holy city of Benares to the sacred shrine of Juggernaut, of which, indeed, this little creature's movements strongly reminded us at the time.

At a distance of three miles from the Springs, we reached a neat and pretty village, called Union Court-House, where, in addition to the building from whence it derives its name, were from fifty to sixty dwelling-houses, several new stores, two churches, one Methodist, and one Presbyterian, a large school, and about five hundred inhabitants. Nothing could exceed the beauty of its situation as a country village, with a rich soil, well-tilled fields, and noble mountains around it; its distance from the top of the Alleghanies, which lie directly west of it not being more than fifteen miles. There were abundance of cattle in the neighbourhood, many new houses were building, and the whole place had an air of activity and rising prosperity. Close by this little town is a large oak, which, from its size, is called The Mammoth Oak, it being the custom of this country to call every thing very large by the epithet of "mammoth;" so that one hears of a mammoth cake, a mammoth pie, a mammoth oyster—terms the most incongruous. This mammoth oak, however, is not more than twenty-two feet in circumference, which, though large as compared with oaks in general, is little in comparison with some of the cedars of Lebanon, thirty-six feet in girth, and still more so in comparison with the baobab-tree mentioned by Adanson, found by him in Africa, measuring thirteen fathoms, or seventy-eight feet, round. The celebrated Arab traveller, Ibn Batuta, mentions having seen trees of such a size in Africa, that in the hollow trunk of one of ordinary dimensions he saw a weaver working at his loom; and in this country, Hinton mentions that Judge Tucker of Missouri cut off a section of the hollow trunk of a sycamore tree, applied a roof to it, and furnished it for a study. It was perfectly circular, and when fitted up with a stove and other arrangements, it made an ample and convenient apartment. Near the Natural Bridge in Scott-county, Virginia, is the hollow trunk of a sycamore, in which fifteen persons have taken shelter at once, and had plenty of room.

Beyond this we came to the first turnpike we had passed in Virginia, and certainly the tax was well repaid by the improved state of the roads near it. In the fields on either side of the way, buckwheat was chiefly cultivated, and it was now in full flower.

At twelve miles beyond Union Court-House, we crossed a stream called Second Creek, which goes into the Green-briar river, and this empties into the Ohio. Near to tills was a hotel by the roadside, on the sign of which was inscribed "The Sugar Grove Inn, by J. Burdett." I asked here, whether the people made much maple-sugar in this neighbourhood; when the gentleman to whom my question was addressed, a planter of the neighbourhood, then on horseback at the inn-door, answered, "Yes, they do, I reckon, right smart," meaning in great quantities. A little beyond this place, we passed over a large cave, which lay immediately beneath the road, the rounded hill over which we drove being hollow nearly all the way under us; and some children, occupying a stall beneath a tree, had a large collection of stalactytes and mineral specimens, to sell to passengers as they stopped.

Not far from this, we came to a second turnpike, with a fine spring of water near it; and just beyond was the first beer-shop we had ever seen in America. Our attention was attracted to it by the singularity of its sign. On a dull lead-coloured ground, there were portrayed, in the simplest forms, a round and a square mass, with a jug or pitcher emptying its contents by a stream into a tumbler. All the figures were painted of a deep-brown, without the least attempt at shading, so that they looked like Egyptian hieroglyphics, as they are often delineated in dead colours on their wooden tablets and sarcophagi, recognizable only by their shapes. As the driver of the stage halted here, we learnt from the keeper of the beer-shop, that while the pitcher and glass would explain themselves, the circular and square forms were meant to indicate that bread might be had as well as beer. The beverage, to which he had given this name, did not much resemble the beer of England, being made only of hop-water and molasses, without fermentation, so that it would not keep more than three days in draught, or a week in bottle, and it possessed no power of intoxication, however great the quantity that might be drank. It was, therefore, merely a sweet and bitter drink, which a vitiated taste might by habit be brought to prefer to pure water, just as men bring themselves to like tobacco or any other nauseous drug. It had the advantage over English beer, of not intoxicating those who drank it, while it was quite as wholesome.

One of the most pleasing features of the rural population of this country is their universal sobriety, and decorum both of manners and speech, to strangers and to each other. In the thousands of miles we had travelled through the interior, we had scarcely seen a drunken man, and never a drunken group or party; nor had we witnessed half the quarreling, abuse, and profane swearing, that is to be seen and heard between almost any two post-towns in England. At the public tables, neither wine, spirits, or beer are placed; simple water or milk is the beverage of all; and although occasional instances occur of spirits being offered by the landlord of the hotel, this is very rare, and it is still rarer that they are accepted. In this absence of wines at the hotels, and of spirits and beer at both these and the farmhouses of the country, is to be found the cause of the general sobriety. If gin-shops and beer-shops were as multiplied in the villages and roads of this country as they are in England, many drunkards would be thereby created even here; and if they were reduced or abolished in England, just as many persons would be prevented from becoming drunkards there. The supply in this article of mischief, almost always precedes the demand; and persons are tempted to drink by the sight, smell, and offer of the liquor, who would neither need it, nor care about it, if it were not obtruded upon them by those whose love of gain is greater than their regard for the public health, or public morals.

CHAPTER XLIV

The establishment at the White Sulphur is on a much larger scale than that of either of the Mineral Springs in the mountains, and is much more frequented, having at the present time upwards of 600 visitors, while neither of the others have 200. The situation is exceedingly beautiful; the valley being broad enough to admit of a large plain between the hills, on which plain herds of cattle and sheep were grazing; and these, with the fine trees scattered over it at distant intervals, gave it the appearance of an extensive park. The hills, though not lofty, are gentle, and finely undulated, and the views of the distant mountains are at once grand and beautiful. The spring, called the White Sulphur, from the whiteness of its deposit, is under a heavy and tasteless portico, with a cumbrous dome, supported by twelve plain and ill-proportioned pillars. The whole enclosure was small, gloomy, and dirty, compared with those of the other Springs we had visited. The dome was surmounted, however, by a graceful and classic statue of Hygeia, presented by S. Henderson, and the water was as clear as crystal.

The lawns, walks, and trees around the establishment were all beautiful and in excellent order, and the drives are varied and interesting also. The number of carriages and horses here, belonging to the visitors, were very numerous, and many of them were in use. The greater number of the guests seemed, however, to be at a loss how to pass their time. It was really melancholy to see the numerous groups of both sexes who were lounging idly about, too indolent of body for active exercise, too indolent of mind for animated conversation, and evincing an appearance of the greatest lassitude and weariness in every look and tone. The fare at the table we thought worse than at any of the other Springs, and the servants, almost all negroes, were both dirty and ill-disciplined. The only beds we could procure were mattresses stuffed with straw, and these hard and uneven. We had the same difficulty as usual in procuring any of the proper accompaniments of a bed-room, such as wash-stand, dressing-table, looking-glass, tumblers, &c., all of which are considered to be superfluities, and must be literally wrung from the attendants, who think it a great and unnecessary trouble to procure such articles, especially as they see so many of their richest guests quietly and contentedly do without them.

In the evening we attended the ball, where, in a small and crowded room, about 200 persons were literally packed. In addition to the animal heat from such a number in a small space, (the room moreover being very low, and greatly heated by the number of lights,) the orchestra was filled by negro musicians; the bands being almost always formed of coloured people. Every door and window, at which, if unoccupied, fresh air might have come in, was crowded by the negro servants of the visitors, so that the heat and effluvia from such sources were far from agreeable. There was a great admixture of company also, more than I had thought likely to assemble at such a place. The majority were genteel in dress, appearance, and manners; but there were many coarse and vulgar persons, among the men especially, and some few among the women.

We saw here some of the most extravagant specimens of American dandies, of both sexes, that we had yet met with in the United States; and I doubt much whether London or Paris, productive as they are of each, could furnish anything more extravagantly ridiculous than the specimens in this place. One of the males seemed to be ambitious of rendering his appearance as much like a savage as possible; and had, therefore, suffered his hair, beard, and moustaches to grow uncut in wild luxuriance, and to all appearance uncombed; while his face, either from some artificial stain, or by more than usual exposure to the sun, had a reddish bronze copper colour, scarcely distinguishable from the complexion of an Indian. With all this, his attire was of the most fashionable cut, excepting an old battered broad-brimmed straw hat, which no one would pick up if they saw it on the road; and which he carried underneath his left arm, like an opera hat, lest he should disturb his uncombed locks by wearing it. Another of these caricatures of humanity seemed to wish to be taken for an hermaphrodite, as his dress and appearance left you in doubt to which of the sexes he belonged. His garments were all of the most ladylike tightness and delicacy of material, and his waist was evidently compressed with tight-laced stays. His beard, if he had ever had any, must have been plucked out, for there was no sign of the use of the razor; and his hair, which he put up at night, as we were told, in curl papers, hung down around his face in the most feminine ringlets; while a white seam marked the place of its parting on the top of his head; and his affected lisp and mincing gait were precisely those of a conceited young boarding-school miss. The third was a perfect nondescript; but appeared to be an attempt to embody the most incongruous characteristics of the two sexes in one; he was a tall thin man, about thirty, with a sportsman's dress, frock hunting-coat of light velvet, white corduroys, and yellow top-boots, with a huge knotted walkingstick, white-kid gloves, and full-bosomed frilled-shirt, with a fancy-printed muslin cravat. His face was long and narrow, his eyes large and protruding, and his complexion of deathlike paleness. His cheeks were hollow and sunken, so that they too visibly displayed the large rolling quid of the Virginian weed, which he thrust alternately, like an interior tumour, first against one cheek, and then against another, while the liquid of the tobacco was ejected once in every minute at the least, and sometimes oftener, on the floor of the ball-room, or on the dresses of the ladies, as it might happen. With all this, his long black glossy hair was placed in a flattened curve down each cheek, and turned up behind each ear, as ladies usually wear it; while a third portion was made to come down over his forehead in a sort of crescent, forming altogether the most fantastic figure imaginable. The few female dandies we saw were not quite so ridiculous as the males; their peculiarities consisting chiefly in the extravagant excess to which they pushed the prevailing style of dress beyond its usual limits; extremely compressed waists, very low bodies, greatly exposed back, and perfectly naked shoulders, hugely protruding bustles, and artificially projecting busts, added to the most beseeching coquetry of attitude and manner.

It should be remarked that these were only excrescences on the general surface of the society here; I know indeed that their extravagances appeared as revolting to the greater portion of their own countrymen and countrywomen, as they did to us. In general there is not so much of dandyism in either sex in America, as there is in England or in France. The men are more grave, and not so polished; the women are more reserved, and neither so elegant nor so animated as in the fashionable circles of Europe; but when they break out beyond their natural or accustomed bounds, and set up for decided "Exclusives," they run into greater extravagances than the beaux and belles of England or France; and being without the refinement of manners which these last generally possess, they become more complete caricatures in the eyes of their own nation as well as of strangers.

Immense sums have been laid out on this establishment; so that it is now thought by many to be worth a million of dollars. Certain it is that during the season, which lasts from three to four months, from June to September, the receipts are from 1,000 to 1,500 dollars a day at the hotel alone; and for stabling, carriage room, and purchase of articles at the store, 500 dollars a day more may be added; making the receipts 150,000 dollars for a season of 100 days, at 1,500 dollars a day. At the least one half of this, or 75,000 dollars, would be clear profit; making, therefore, 13 per cent per annum interest, on a million of dollars, though probably not more than half that sum has been actually expended by the proprietor himself.

On Thursday, the 8th of August, we left the White Sulphur Springs, in an extra coach engaged for the trip, and proceeded to the Sweet Springs, distant seventeen miles from hence. We set out at ten o'clock, and for the first two hours we were occupied in ascending the steep western part of the Alleghany ridge, which rises on the east of the White Sulphur Springs, and forms the dividing-line between the waters that run west to the Mississippi, and those that flow east to the Atlantic, just as the Blue Ridge divides the waters in North Carolina. We reached the summit of the Alleghany ridge about noon, and the prospect from thence was extensive and beautiful, our elevation above the level of the sea being now about 4,000 feet, the valley of the White Sulphur Springs, from which we had ascended, being about 2,700. The change that has taken place in the state of the country beyond this barrier, in less than a century, is very remarkable. The valleys west of the Alleghanies are now filled with hundreds of the gay and fashionable during the summer months; and planters and farmers reside in or near them in great numbers all the year round. Yet when in 1749 a wandering lunatic, who, though deranged, was harmless in his conduct, and therefore suffered to be at large, crossed these mountains from the east, and came back to tell of his having found the waters there all flowing to the west, instead of coursing their way to the Atlantic—he was not believed; and for many years no public or general confidence was placed in this discovery. In 1751 a small reconnoitring party crossing the mountains in the same direction, came to the waters of what is now the Green-briar river, which discharge themselves into the Kenhawa, thence into the Ohio, and by this into the Mississippi. They found here two white men, both natives of New England, living on the banks of the stream. Though these men were not many hundred yards distant from each other, and were the only white persons known to be in this region at all, it is remarkable that jealousy or fear should have prevented them, in this lonely exile, from becoming friends. They lived as much apart from each other, as both did from the world in general; and no intercourse took place between them beyond the morning salutation, when the one came out from the hollow trunk of the tree, and the other emerged from the log-hut, in which they respectively took their shelter at night. Soon after this, the Virginians attempted a settlement here, but it was entirely cut off by the Indian tribes in 1763; and it was not until after the close of the revolutionary war, and the establishment of the independence of the country, that the region was again approached; since which it has been making a steady progress in settlement and cultivation.

In descending the eastern slope of the Alleghany range, we had before us a succession of rich and beautiful valleys, through which, and over gently intervening hills, the remainder of our road chiefly lay, when, about two o'clock, we reached the Sweet Springs, where we halted to remain for the day.

This is the oldest of all the mineral springs of Virginia, having been frequented for medicinal purposes as long as sixty years ago,—a long period in American history. Its situation is the most beautiful of all, and its capacity for improvement is the greatest; so that if a judicious use be made of these advantages, it is likely to become the most attractive of all the Springs. The water has no sulphur in it; but a very small admixture of magnesia, soda, and iron. It contains a large portion of carbonic acid gas, which, in its escape, gives the brisk and sparkling appearance of soda-water. It is very agreeable to the palate, and its effects are so gentle, that persons in health drink of it as freely as invalids. The temperature being uniformly 74°, it forms a delicious element for bathing; and as the spring is copious, two spacious and comfortably enclosed swimming and plunging baths have been provided, the ladies' bath being roofed over as well as enclosed on every side, and the gentlemen's having a part of the roof open, which is pleasingly shaded by the branches of a lofty tree. The baths are sufficiently spacious, about fifty feet by forty, and four feet deep. The bottom is good, the water is as clear as crystal, and is seen bubbling up from twenty different places, instead of being supplied by a single spring. The bathing-rooms are comfortable, and the attendance good; and with a buoyant and sparkling fluid, at the temperature of 74°, the bath is the most delicious to the feelings that can well be conceived, leaving a glow of health and vigour over the whole frame. The superintendant of the bath, was an old Frenchman, who left Paris in 1789, after having been present at the destruction of the Bastile. He landed at Alexandria near Washington in that year, and has never been out of the State of Virginia since; though now eighty years of age, he is as healthy and vivacious as any Parisian who had never quitted the capital.

We had intended to have gone from hence to the warm and hot springs to the north, but the multiplicity of travellers moving in every direction, made it difficult to obtain either public or private conveyances for the direction wished; we were, therefore, obliged to move, in many cases, as the stream flowed, and as the opportunities of making progress presented themselves. These baths are more frequented by invalids, however, than by persons seeking only pleasure; as the warm bath is not so highly relished as a mere enjoyment by the people of this country, as it was by the ancient Greeks and Romans, and as it still continues to be by the Oriental nations. I had enjoyed the hot mineral springs of Tiberias in Palestine, as well as the artificially-heated baths of Aleppo, Damascus, Cairo, Bagdad, and Ispahan, the very remembrance of which is more pleasurable than the actual enjoyment of the imperfect warm baths of this country, though they have the materials here for forming the most luxurious baths in the world, had they but the taste to appreciate and design appropriate edifices and suitable accompaniments. But this, it may be presumed, will come in time.

The variety of the waters may be judged of from the fact, that almost every range of hills produces a different kind. There are said to be no less than fifty, all within a small compass, though there are but three yet enclosed—the hot, the warm, and the temperate. The former has a temperature of 106°, which is less than that of most of the hot springs of Europe: those of Bath in England being 116°, those of Aix la Chapelle in France 143°, and those of Wiesbaden and Carlsbad in Germany 151° and 165° respectively. The warm springs of Virginia have a temperature of 98°, and this is the one most frequently used for bathing.

The invalids who visit these Springs are very few, compared with the persons who come here because it is the fashion, and whose only object is the pursuit of pleasure. Hence the greater number of the visitors are satisfied with a very short stay at each, finding it very dull and wearisome to go through the same stupid round every day. They all drink the waters, and that without the advice of any medical man; though there is generally a physician at each place, but he has little practice. Many it is believed really injure themselves by the quantity of the water they drink, though all benefit by the rough journey, the mountain air, and the unavoidable exercise, as well as the temperance which all practise; for we did not see a single glass of wine, spirits, or beer drank by any of the visitors, at either of the Springs, during all our stay in the mountains. The newspapers, which arrive regularly by the mail, help to pass a portion of the time; and one occupation of great interest to all parties appears to be the endeavour to find out, by inquiring from all comers and goers, how many visitors there were at the latest date, at each of the Springs. Many take as much interest in the augmentation and diminution of numbers at their own and other establishments, as speculators do in the price of stocks, or the rise and fall of cotton; and others, who are fond of everything that is popular, regulate their movements very much by the intelligence they get as to whether visitors are increasing or decreasing at other Springs, and bend their way to them accordingly.

CHAPTER XLV

On the morning of the 9th of August, we left the Sweet Springs at ten o'clock, by the mail-stage for Fincastle, on our way to the Natural Bridge, and had the agreeable society of a family from Baltimore through the journey. Our way lay across three of the mountain-ridges belonging to the general chain of the Alleghanies, so that we were prepared for a slow and tedious journey, which we hoped would be amply compensated by rich and picturesque views; and we were not disappointed.

Our ascent of the first ridge, called Sweet Spring Mountain, occupied us about four hours; but it was four hours of continuous delight. The views grew richer and more romantic as we ascended; and from the summit the prospect was surpassingly grand. The hour's descent of the mountain on the other side was also one of similar enjoyment, for the valleys below us to the eastward were even more fertile and beautiful than those we had left. But the crowning triumph, of the romantic and sublime, was reserved for our ascent of the second ridge, called Prince's Mountain, which took us about four hours more to wind slowly up, halting at short intervals to give rest to our horses, and to drink in the splendid beauties of which the surrounding scene was so full. The grandeur of the prospect, and the depth and solemnity of its effect upon the feelings, were indescribable. I had crossed many loftier mountains than these—Lebanon in Palestine, and Zagros and Louristan in Persia, especially—but even in the former, rich and beautiful as it is in scenes of the greatest loveliness, they seemed to me all inferior to the unrivalled splendour revealed to our delighted vision, by the progressive winding ascent of the western slope of Prince's Mountain. As the road went zig-zag up the steep slope of this magnificent barrier, it was almost always overhanging a deep glen, and in some places seemed to be on the very edge of a perpendicular precipice. Dark valleys and towering trees appeared, therefore, constantly beneath us, in perpetually descending terraces, every variety of tint being communicated to their wavy surfaces by varieties in distance alone. As we ascended higher and higher up the mountain, every elevation of a few hundred feet, opened new ranges of hills, rising one above the other to the north and west, on the left and behind us; until, as we drew near the summit, a boundless view to the north-west opened to us, not less than fifty separate ridges of hills, rising one behind the other in irregular succession, each characterized by some distinct feature in outline and colour, and the whole gradually receding into the blue distance, till land and sky were blended into one. The visible horizon was thought to extend 100 miles in that direction at least, and the vista comprehended every element of grandeur and beauty. It reminded me forcibly of some of the landscape illustrations of Milton's Paradise Lost, from the pencil of Martin, where mountain, piled on mountain, goes on with accumulated grandeur, rising above and yet receding beyond each other, till they are lost in the immensity of space; while the valley of the foreground has all the softest features of rural beauty, that could be expected to adorn the Garden of Eden! Magnificent as are many portions of these United States in their scenery, Virginia carries off the palm; and the territory of "The Old Dominion" not only forms the largest of all the States, but must, I think, be pronounced, by all impartial witnesses, to be the most grand and the most beautiful.

The descent of Prince's Mountain led us again into a rich and fertile valley, after which we crossed the third ridge, called Caldwell's Mountain, which, though not so lofty as either of the others, was yet full of interesting scenery; and at nine o'clock at night we reached Fincastle, having been just eleven hours performing thirty-three miles.

We left Fincastle at nine A.M., on the 10th of August, the mail-stage waiting here all night for the accommodation of the passengers; and when we had got a few miles beyond the town, the driver handed in to the passengers a number of newspapers, addressed to various individuals in and around Fincastle. These had been sent by the mail for deposit in the post-office there; but having been overlooked, he thought it would not be worth while to return them; and, therefore, he opened them all for the use of the passengers. So lightly, indeed, are newspapers thought of, as matters of personal property, that it is very common for the idlers of a village to go to the post-office on the arrival of the mail, and appropriate to themselves newspapers addressed to others; and this is no more thought of, than the act of stopping a stage-coach near an orchard, to supply all the passengers with fruit; the indifference in both cases arising apparently from the cheapness and abundance of the articles thus misappropriated.

Our newspaper reading, as may be conceived, led us insensibly into political conversation; and I found here, as elsewhere, that the rich and the mercantile classes were nearly all Whigs; and the people of moderate fortunes, and the agriculturalists, nearly all Democrats. The difference between them, however, is not so much on the principles of general politics, as on the question of banks; the Whigs being for a national bank, a credit system, and paper currency; the Democrats being for the custody of the public money by a national treasury, ready money transactions, and a metallic currency; while both, as usual in political controversies, carry out their doctrines to extremes. A new party is rising up, however, called by themselves Conservatives, who will not ally themselves to either. By both the old parties, however, these Conservatives are called "Impracticables." Mr. Rives, a distinguished senator from Virginia, has seceded from the Democrats, but not gone over to the Whigs, nor joined the Conservatives; and as he will not yet declare the exact position which he either now occupies or means to take, it is proposed to make him the founder of a new party to be called the "Inexpressibles."

About eleven miles after leaving Fincastle, we came to the banks of a stream, which formed the head waters of the celebrated James River, on which the first English settlement was founded by Sir Walter Raleigh, under the name of Jamestown. Close by this were some of the largest and most beautiful weeping-willows we had yet seen, from sixty to seventy feet in height, and forty to fifty feet spread, and of the most graceful form. From hence there rose up, on the opposite side of the stream, an exceedingly steep and conical hill, called "Purgatory Mountain." Two miles beyond this we came to the small but increasing town of Buchanan. This is seated on the banks of the James River, and is at the head of its navigation. The river is crossed by a good bridge; and several boats laden with supplies, for Richmond, lay at the bank. The town has about 100 houses and 600 inhabitants. There was a militia muster as we passed through; but this body being highly popular here, we did not remark any of the extravagancies we had seen in New York and in Georgia, where the object of all was to bring it into contempt. On the contrary, the young men here appeared proud of their military display; and as, from the abundance of deer in the mountains, they have good opportunities of practising with the rifle, they could muster a company of 100 good marksmen, which would furnish an excellent quota to a provincial army, if foreign aggression or internal insurrection should render their services necessary. In every point of view this seems a better force for a free country to keep ready for its defence, than the standing armies of Europe.

The road from hence was sufficiently rough and rocky to account to us for the name of Purgatory Mountain, along the foot of which it ran, as our progress never exceeded two miles in the hour; but after escaping from it, and passing through a rich and beautiful country, we arrived, about three o'clock, at the Natural Bridge, the whole distance from Fincastle being twenty-four miles. We halted here, for the purpose of examining this remarkable object; and having sufficient leisure, and a competent guide, we had an opportunity of seeing it from the most advantageous points of view. Two steep and lofty hills approach each other, leaving a narrow but deep ravine between them; and about half-way up their height, these hills are connected by the mass of rock forming the Natural Bridge. The breadth across from hill to hill is nowhere more than 80 feet; and in some places less than 50; so that the length of the bridge is not more than 100 feet, and its breadth is about 60. Its grandeur consists chiefly in its height, which is 220 feet from the top of the bridge to the centre of the valley below; where a small stream, called Cedar Creek, runs along among the rocks. Its beauty consists in the lightness and gracefulness of its arch, which is about 180 feet high and from 60 to 90 feet broad in different parts, the narrowest dimensions being at the bottom, and the broadest at the top. The thickness of the Bridge, therefore, from the upper level of the road, to the topmost curve of the arch, is about 40 feet.

As you pass over the Bridge in the coach you perceive nothing of the deep chasm on each side, unless your attention should be particularly called to it; and even then you get but a momentary glance; as you are driven across the 100 feet, which constitutes the whole length of the Bridge, in a few seconds. When you alight from the carriage, however, and approach the edges on either side, the yawning gulf below excites terror in some, astonishment in others, and admiration in all: the height being 220 feet, and the sides of the cliffs perfectly perpendicular, with here and there a tree of considerable size growing to all appearances out of the solid rock, projecting its trunk and spreading branches upwards towards the Bridge, but not reaching within 50 feet of its summit. The very fear, indeed, which, in most of the spectators, this scene inspires, contributes to increase its sublimity.

The full effect of the grandeur which characterizes this remarkable object cannot be enjoyed, however, without descending into the valley, and viewing it from below. A winding but rocky path leads down from just beyond the hotel, by which, in a short time, you reach the depth of the ravine, and stand on the border of the running stream, on the south side of the Bridge. The view of it, as you look upward, is beautiful beyond description; and as its great charm is in the combination of vastness in scale, gracefulness in form, and lightness and airiness in proportion, no drawing, however accurate, can make the same impression on the beholder as the original. In this respect it resembles the pyramids of Egypt, which always look mean and insignificant on canvass or paper, but which have a sublimity, arising from their stupendous size, and a beauty arising from the simple severity of their form, that inspire one with admiration on the spot, but which cannot be conveyed by any transcript, however perfect. The view on the northern side of the Bridge, though different in some of its features, is equally beautiful with that on the south; and both may be gazed upon for hours, not only without fatigue or weariness, but with increased pleasure, as it seemed to me, from dwelling on them.

We lingered around the Bridge as long as it was possible, and tore ourselves away with the greatest reluctance; for I would willingly have passed a week in examining and enjoying it, if possible; but we were compelled to proceed, and accordingly left it about six o'clock for Lexington. In our way onward, we had a commanding view of the Peaks of Otter on the Blue Ridge, which are considered to be the highest points of all the Virginia mountains, being 4,600 feet above the level of the sea; the principal peak rising to so sharp a point, that it is said not more than twelve persons can stand on it at once. It is, however, well wooded nearly up to the highest point, and is often visited by travellers, for the fine view to be obtained from the summit, there being a good horse-road to within about a mile of the top, but the rest of the way has to be performed on foot. We continued to have delightful scenery of hills and glens through the remainder of our way, and passed over the first canal we had seen in the South, this being constructed to navigate boats round the rapids of James River. At nine we reached Lexington, and there halted for the night.

This town was first laid out by an Act of Assembly in 1778, two years after the Declaration of Independence, and was called after the famous Lexington of Massachusetts, where the first blood was shed in the revolutionary war. It was built originally of wood, and in 1794 it was almost wholly destroyed by fire. Since then, the buildings have been chiefly of brick; and it has now the appearance of a well-built and thriving town. It is elevated 902 feet above the level of the sea, and is seated near the bank of the North river, a tributary of the James River. There are about 200 houses, and 800 inhabitants, with three churches—Methodist, Presbyterian, and Baptist. There is a State Arsenal here, containing 30,000 stand of arms, under the care of a captain and a company of thirty men. In 1782, a male academy was incorporated in Lexington, under the title of Liberty-Hall Academy; but in 1812 it was chartered as a college, and called Washington College. To assist it with funds. General Washington made a donation to it of 100 shares in the James River Canal, which produced an annual income of 2,400 dollars; the value of these shares is now 25,000 dollars. A private citizen of Lexington bestowed another donation of 50,000 dollars; and the Cincinnati Society of Virginia presented it with 15,000 more, making in total 90,000 dollars. It has three neat brick buildings, with accommodation for about 100 students, a library, and philosophical apparatus; and the education obtained there is good and cheap, under a president, two professors, and a tutor. There is a female academy also in the town, called the Ann-Smith Academy, which has a handsome edifice, competent teachers in the usual branches of female education, and nearly 100 pupils. There are three public libraries in the town; and everything wears an air of comfort and prosperity.

We left Lexington on the following morning, August 11, with nine inside and three outside passengers, so that we were sufficiently crowded. Soon after leaving the town, we crossed the James River by a good bridge; and beyond this, we had a fine road and a beautiful country. The Cherry Valley, in which we were still travelling, gave evidence of its having been long since cleared and settled; the fields on all sides were without the stumps of felled trees, which so disfigure the newly cleared lands, and all the fences, gates, and by-roads were in much better condition than they are ever seen in newly settled districts. By far the greater portion of the land was under cultivation, while in the less populous parts of the country the forest still covers nine tenths of the soil. Towns and villages occur here every ten or twelve miles, instead of being whole days' journeys apart, as they are in the remoter parts of the South and West.

At a distance of twelve miles from Lexington, we changed horses at Fairfield, a small village of about 500 inhabitants. We found it, however, almost deserted, as a large camp-meeting was holding within two miles of the town, and nearly all the inhabitants had gone there; the meeting being likely to last three or four days, as we were informed. From hence the road became again rough and rocky; but the splendid views of scenery repaid us for all our inconvenience from this cause. Noble ranges of mountains still bounded our horizon, right and left; while the rich open valley, growing gradually wider and wider as we proceeded, seemed to stretch away for fifty miles ahead of us in the distance. In our road, we had the usual variety of trees, principally oak, as well as the locust, the persimmon, and the papaw tree. This last is sometimes called the Indian fig-tree. The fruit is something like a cucumber; but its form is more regular, and its skin smoother. It grows in clusters of four or five, and when ripe, it is of a rich yellow colour. The fruit was a great favourite with the Indians, and their taste, in this respect at least, was good; for while the pulp is really nutritious, being of the consistence of custard, and having the same creamy smoothness, its flavour is rendered delicious by an mixture of sweetness and spice, so as to be too rich and luscious for many palates, though generally considered exquisite by all. We passed also many fields of broom-corn, so called from the upper part of the stalk being crowned with long and full fibres forming an excellent broom, but resembling in other respects the maize; and after a journey of twelve miles from Fairfield, we reached Greenville.

At this village, which contains a population of about 400 person we halted to dine, and were much better entertained than in many of the larger towns. Instead of the constant dish of boiled bacon and beans, which stands at the head of every country table, we had excellent roast beef and roast veal, good vegetables, and light bread. The landlady indeed seemed to take a personal interest and pride in her table, which few American mistresses of hotels do; and the result was, greater excellence in everything upon it, and greater satisfaction in the visitors. Not far from Greenville are some natural curiosities called the Cyclopean Towers, said to be well worth examination, but which our engagements would not permit us to visit. We pursued our way therefore still over a rocky road, bounded on all sides by splendid scenery; and after another twelve miles we reached Staunton, where we halted for the night.

Staunton, which is 1,152 feet above the level of the sea, is one of the oldest as well as largest of the country towns of Virginia west of the mountains. It was founded by the British long before the revolution; and as early as 1745, a Court of Justice held its sittings in the Court House here, under the Colonial jurisdiction. Its streets are regular, being placed chiefly at right angles with each other; but they are narrower than is usual in the towns on the coast. This is attributed here to the desire that the original inhabitants felt to protect themselves more easily from the Indians, who at that period occupied the greater part of this valley, as well as the mountains, and who took every opportunity to attack the settlements of the whites. Staunton has now about 300 houses, and upwards of 2,000 inhabitants, with very few negroes, or people of colour. There are two Court Houses, one for common and statute-law cases, and one for chancery cases; a public market house, and four hotels; four churches, Methodist, Presbyterian, Baptist, and Episcopalian; one male academy, two female seminaries, and a primary school. A spacious and beautiful edifice standing near the entrance to the town, forms a lunatic asylum for Western Virginia; and an asylum for the deaf and dumb is also about to be erected. There is a weekly paper issued here, the "Staunton Spectator" and the stores appeared to be all well supplied. In the hotel at which we slept, our bedroom was carpeted and papered, two things which we had not seen together in any hotel since we left England, as far as I remember; the bedrooms of the hotels being rarely carpeted, and never both carpeted and papered too, that I can recollect, the walls being almost always whitewashed, and the carpeting being mere strips by the bed-side.

We were desirous of proceeding from Staunton to Wyer's Cave, it being only seventeen miles distant from this; but the number of persons travelling at this season, made it impossible for us to get extra coaches for the journey. We were, therefore, obliged to proceed on to Waynesborough, a distance of eleven miles to the eastward, on the mail-stage route, and trust to our getting private conveyances from thence to the Cave. We, accordingly, left Staunton at one o'clock, and, after a pleasant ride of three hours, we reached Waynesborough at four. Here we were fortunate in being able to procure two carriages and horses, which conveyed our party and baggage to Wyer's Cave, a distance of fourteen miles in about three hours.

Waynesborough is a small and scattered village, containing about 500 inhabitants. It has three churches—Methodist, Presbyterian, and Baptist; and there are several Dunkers in the town and neighbourhood, but these have no stated place of worship. On the road from it to the Cave, there are some rich and solemn woods; and on emerging from one of these we had a commanding view of an extensive and highly-cultivated plain, embracing, perhaps, 100,000 acres of the most fertile land, slightly dotted with clustered trees, like the finest parks in England, and presenting altogether the richest agricultural landscape that we had yet seen in the country. It struck us as more like the best parts of the Vale of Taunton, by the ruins of Glastonbury Abbey, than anything to which we could compare it at home; but being much more extensive in area, and bounded by much more lofty mountains; I thought it still more resembled the beautiful plain of Damascus, though it wanted the meanderings of

Abana and Pharpar—lucid streams,

as Milton appositely calls them, to make the resemblance complete. But as a rich and fertile plain, nothing could surpass it in beauty. A portion of it I understood was called the Long Meadows, for it is both pastoral and agricultural, being equally well adapted for both. We passed through the small villages of New Hope and Mount Meridian, on our way, reached the house at Wyer's Cave about eight o'clock, and found shelter there for the night.

CHAPTER XLVI

We remained at the hotel here for three days, during which we examined every part of Wyer's Cave at our leisure, going in on the first occasion with the regular guide, a son of the proprietor of the land, who conducted us through all its halls and passages, explaining and describing the several most remarkable objects as he went along, and affording us ample time for the most deliberate investigation. Altogether, this Cave may be regarded as one of the most extraordinary productions of this or any other country; and it is alone well worth a voyage across the Atlantic to visit. There are many other caves in Virginia—for the ridges of the Alleghannies formed, as they are, of cavernous limestone, are full of them, but none are thought so grand or beautiful as this.

We left the hotel at Wyer's Cave at nine A.M., on the 16th of August, for Waynesborough, where we arrived at one o'clock, and dining there, we left at three for Charlottesville, by the mail. Our road lay over a comparatively low portion of the Blue Ridge, in a part called the Rockfish Gap, the elevation of which was not more than 300 feet above the level of the valley. We wound our way up this amidst a heavy storm of thunder, lightening, and rain, which, while it occasioned us some inconvenience from the imperfect protection which all American coaches afford against the elements, added something to the grandeur of the mountain scenery. The storm abated, however, before we reached the highest part of the Gap, and the atmosphere becoming clear, we had a splendid and extensive view from the summit; the mountain ridges of the west being visible in succession, to a distance of seventy or eighty miles, and the broad plains below us to the east, extending the horizon to an equal distance in that direction: the latter resembling the beautiful view from the summit of Catskill Mountain on the Hudson river, from the great abundance of cleared land intermingled with the forest patches of the surface. We lingered to enjoy this splendid view, as it was the last opportunity we should probably ever possess of dwelling with delight upon the mountain landscapes of this noble State; and when we turned the brow of the Blue Ridge, to wind down its eastern face, we took our last gaze with a feeling of admiration, mingled with regret.

The descent of this mountain barrier brought us, by several smaller ridges, at length, to the lower plain; and as the point of our passage through the Rockfish Gap was not elevated more than 300 feet above the upper or western valley, while it was 1,200 feet, at least, above the lower or eastern plain, it followed that this first valley, west of the Blue Ridge, in which Waynesborough, Staunton, and Wyer's Cave are situated, is at least 1,000 feet above the level of the plain, and probably from 1,400 to 1,500 feet above the level of the sea. The difference of temperature was very perceptible to our feelings when we reached the plain, the air being not only warmer, but heavier, and more humid, so that we experienced a very disagreeable change by the transition. This Blue Ridge is the first great mountain barrier met when coming up from the seacoast on the east; and it is the geographical boundary between the two great divisions of the State into Eastern and Western Virginia. We found here, besides the marked change of temperature, two other corresponding changes;—one, the more frequent cultivation of the tobacco plant; and the other, the greater abundance of negroes.

After a pleasant ride of five hours from Waynesborough, going a distance of twenty six miles, we reached Charlottesville at eight in the evening, and took up our quarters at the Eagle Hotel.

On the following day, August 17, we made a pleasant party with our Baltimore friends, to visit Monticello, the residence of the late Mr. Jefferson, and the site of his tomb, as well as to see the University of Virginia, of which he was the founder, both being within a short distance of Charlottesville.

Winding our way to the southeast from Charlottesville, we crossed a deep valley, and ascended a steep hill, about 500 feet in height, near the summit of which we first came to the tomb of Jefferson; the neglected and wretched condition of which ought to make every American, who values the Declaration of his country's Independence, blush with shame. If the illustrious ex-President had been the contriver of a treasonable plot for the subjugation or enslavement of his country, instead of one of its most distinguished patriots and deliverers, his sepulchre could not be more entirely abandoned. It was at his own desire that his interment should be simple, and his monument plain, and this was in perfect accordance with his republican principles and practice; but this is no excuse whatever for the shameful indifference or neglect of his survivors, in permitting it to be what it now is, a perfect wreck, though little more than ten years have elapsed since his death. As at present seen, the small enclosure, not more than from forty to fifty feet square, had its stonewall half-dilapidated, its wooden gate of entrance broken and unhung, its interior grown over with rank straggled weeds: the simple granite obelisk standing over Mr. Jefferson's remains, chipped at all the angles by persons carrying off relics; the marble slab that contained the inscription, directed by himself to be placed there, taken away, and the hollow space which contained it left void in the front of the obelisk; the marble slab which covered the tomb of his wife close beside the obelisk broken in two, and large portions of one of the broken halves carried away; in short, the whole place in a state of complete abandonment and disorder.

We had some difficulty in obtaining an entrance into the house, as it was in the occupation of a family very little disposed to encourage the visits of strangers. The present proprietor is a Captain Levy, of the United States Navy, now absent on duty in the West Indies. He is by birth and religion a Jew, was a common sailor before the mast in the merchant service, rose to be a mate, was admitted from the merchant service into the Navy, and is now a captain.

He is reputed to be very rich, but the present condition of Monticello would not lead the visitor to suppose that it was the property of a person either of taste or munificence. It appears that at the period of his buying it, the house and grounds had become as dilapidated as the tomb, and the roads broken up and destroyed, in which state indeed, they all still remain, for nothing has been done apparently to improve either; but in this condition he purchased the house, the grounds, and 200 acres of farming land, for 2,500 dollars or 500*l.* sterling—a sum which any English person would think moderate for a single year's rental of the whole. He is aware, however, that this was a great bargain; for he has since refused 12,000 dollars for the purchase, and fixes 20,000 dollars as its value.

Having obtained admission to the house, we found its interior in a better condition than we had expected. The plan is more showy than convenient, everything being sacrificed to the hall, the drawing room, and the library; the taste is rather French than English, Mr. Jefferson having resided for a long time in Paris, but it is decidedly good taste; and we thought we had not seen any interior of an American residence in the South, better finished or in more harmonious proportions than this. Inlaid diagonal oak floors, lofty rooms, deep recesses, and appropriate fixtures and furniture, all harmonised well together, and left nothing incongruous among what belonged to the mansion in Mr. Jefferson's time. The present proprietor, however, had made some additions, which were not in the same good keeping. For instance, on first entering the hall, we saw on the right, affixed to the wall like a picture, the identical marble tablet which was taken from Jefferson's tomb; and which, here, in the hall of his abode while living, contained this inscription, "Here lies buried, Thomas Jefferson, Author of the Declaration of Independence, and of the Statute for Religious Freedom, and Founder of the University of Virginia". Not far from this was an oil painting, containing a full length portrait of Captain Levy, in his naval uniform, on the quarter deck of his ship; and in the same room a small lithograph of the same individual, as boatswain's mate, with his boatswain's call in his hand, leaning on a quarterdeck gun, and with full trousers and flowing cravat, in true boatswain's mate's style. Not far from this was a lithograph portrait of the celebrated rich banker of Philadelphia, Stephen Girard; and both these prints were without frame or glass and merely pinned up against the wall. Other incongruities of evidently recent introduction, were strewed around; but among the relics of its better days, were some good paintings, as well as a full length statue of Mr. Jefferson, and a good bust of Voltaire.

On retiring from the house, we sat for some time in the Doric portico, which is in excellent taste, and has the very useful additions of a compass inserted in the ceiling above, and a clock in the pediment in front, so that the bearing of every object in the horizon may be easily known. We enjoyed the view from hence greatly, and still more so the extensive and beautiful panorama which is seen from the lawn that surrounds the dwelling, and in which are several beautiful oaks and weeping willows, planted by Mr. Jefferson's own hands. To the southeast, the plain is level, and boundless as the sea. To the northwest, the town of Charlottesville, and the University of Virginia at a little distance from it are each full in sight. At the foot of the hill, which is 500 feet elevated above the plain, flows the Ravenna river, leading on to its navigable point, called the Piræus, within about a mile of Charlottesville, and ultimately going into the James river, on which Richmond is seated. A noble barrier of mountains forms the background of the extensive plain, stretching out in this direction from north to west; and the happy admixture of cultivated openings, with the woodlands intervening, make it as beautiful as it is grand.

We returned to Charlottesville by the same road; and though much fatigued by the hills and the hot sun, we went after dinner to see the University, which lies at a short distance from the town. We had been told that it was half a mile only; but our morning's experience had made us lose all confidence in the accuracy of Virginian measurements of distance; we found, indeed, upon experiment, that it was at least a mile and half.

The University was not at present in session; the vacation commencing on the 4th of July, and continuing to the end of August; so that we saw only a few of the students, who remain here, owing to the great distance of their homes. The space occupied by the buildings is an oblong quadrangle, about 500 feet in length, and 150 in breadth. At the upper end of this open space is the principal edifice. This is a substantial structure of brick, circular in form, crowned with a flattened dome, which wants a terminating lantern, statue, or other elevation, to give it the proper finish. It has a fine Corinthian portico of ten pillars, with a marble pavement, and chaste pediment; and from this portico the view of the side ranges of buildings is very imposing. These ranges, occupying the opposite sides of the quadrangle, contain the residences of the professors, connected by pillared avenues, and smaller chambers for the students; and in the former of these there are several excellent specimens of architecture, of the Corinthian, Ionic, and Doric orders. The lower stories of the principal edifice are occupied by the lecture room and museum of the University; and the whole of the upper story is devoted to the library, which contains upwards of 17,000 volumes. In front of the principal edifice is a fine lawn; continued all the way down to the end of the side ranges; while the lower part of the quadrangle is left open, which affords an extensive prospect of the country, and adds to the beauty of the scene.

This University was founded by Mr. Jefferson in 1819, and was completed in 1825, in which year it contained 120 students, the number having since progressively increased to upwards of 200. The requisite age for admission is sixteen. On entering, the student undergoes an examination, is required to read the laws, and sign a written declaration that he will observe them; he is also obliged to deposit all funds in his possession into the keeping of the patron, and to declare that he will continue to do so as he receives others, so as to place them entirely under the patron's control.

The course of instruction embraces Hebrew, Greek, and Latin; with the literature as well as languages of each. Among the modern tongues, French, Spanish, Italian, German, Danish, Swedish, Dutch, and Portuguese, are all taught. Mathematics, Natural Philosophy, Chemistry, and Materia Medica, Anatomy and Surgery, Moral Philosophy, and Law, are all taught by separate professors, of which there are nine, besides tutors or assistants.

The University has the power to grant degrees of Master of Arts, and Doctor of Medicine. The entire expense of education, board, and subsistence, for the year of ten months, during which the University is in session, varies between 200 dollars and 250 dollars or from 40*l.* sterling to 50*l.* sterling. Music, fencing, and dancing, are taught by separate masters, to those who desire it. A military corps has been formed of the students, and an officer appointed to instruct them in military exercises and tactics, to which one day in each week is devoted. But the same complaint is made here, that is made at almost all the public seminaries of education in America, of the disorderly conduct of the students, and the difficulty of keeping them under any rigid system of discipline.

Charlottesville, as a town, has nothing of peculiar interest, beyond its beautiful situation, its fine landscape views, the vicinity of Monticello, and the University of Virginia. It has a population of 1,000 persons, of whom about 400 are slaves, and 100 free blacks. Among the public buildings, erected chiefly of brick, of the deepest red colour, are a Court House; four Churches—Methodist, Presbyterian, Baptist, and Episcopalian; a Female Academy; and a preparatory school for boys destined for the University. The inhabitants are chiefly engaged in agricultural pursuits; and an Agricultural Society, well supported by the surrounding country, holds its periodical meetings in the town. It has also an annual exhibition of livestock and domestic manufactures, at which premiums are awarded for the best productions in each. The elevation of the town is ascertained to be 700 feet above the level of the sea.

We had to be roused at the early hour of three o'clock in the morning, for the stage, which did not leave Charlottesville, however, until four; and it was seven o'clock before we had performed a distance of eight miles to the first station, where we breakfasted. About five miles beyond this we passed the house and farm of Mr. W.C. Rives, the Virginia senator. Nothing could be more slovenly than the state of the husbandry all along this road, and the neglected state of the farms gave evidence of great inferiority in their mode of management. We had with us in the coach, a senator from Pennsylvania, who expatiated on the contrast presented by the appearance of the farms in his State; and I ventured to ask him what he considered to be the cause of so remarkable a difference in two districts or countries so nearly adjoining, with so great an equality of advantages in soil and climate. He replied, "There is no other intelligible cause for this difference, than that Pennsylvania is cultivated by freemen, and Virginia by slaves: the freemen have every motive to labour, because they enrich themselves by their toil, and enjoy what they produce; the slaves have every motive to be idle, because no toil enriches them, and nothing beyond bare subsistence ever rewards their exertions; therefore, the freemen do as much as possible, and the slaves do as little". He further expressed his belief, that there was many a farmer owning 500 acres in Pennsylvania, without a single slave, who was rich; while there were many planters in Virginia who were poor with 5,000 acres, and as many slaves as were requisite to cultivate the whole; because the farmer of Pennsylvania, with such an estate, would lay by money every year, while the planter of Virginia, with so much ampler means, would get every year deeper and deeper into debt! Such is the difference in the results of freedom and slavery, according to the sober judgment of a native of the country. When I asked him, whether the Virginia planters were themselves aware of this difference, he replied "The greater number of them undoubtedly are; but a spirit of false pride prevents them from acting on it." Many years ago, the Legislature of Virginia entertained the proposition of emancipating the slaves; and the public opinion of the majority of the State was in favour of such a step. Every one here, indeed, believes that if nothing had occurred to interrupt the progress of this sentiment, the abolition of slavery, in this, and the adjoining State of Maryland, would have happened long ago. But they allege, that because the Abolitionists of the North wished to force them on faster than they chose to go, they would not move at all; and since these Abolitionists have increased their pressure, the slave holders have actually receded backward, out of a sheer spirit of opposition, because they would not be driven even into the adoption of a measure which they approved. They seem, therefore, to be now in the position of a forward child, who takes delight in doing just the contrary of what he is desired to do—show his independence; for the planters of these two States say, in effect, by their conduct, "We believe slavery to be an evil to ourselves and to our slaves, and that under a system of free labour we should both be much better off. In this conviction, we were beginning to prepare measures to effect the change from the one to the other; and should have done so by this time, if no one had attempted to hurry us. But, though the abolition of slavery would be an acknowledged and undoubted good to ourselves, we will not adopt it, merely because other persons tell us we ought to do so; and therefore we will not only defer the matter altogether, but we will wholly forego the benefit we were about to confer upon ourselves, rather than permit even the appearance of our being dictated to by others!" This is not an unusual course for a forward and spoiled child, or for a wayward and capricious tyrant; but whether it is a course becoming a grave and free community, pretending to be among the most enlightened people of the world, let the reader judge.

As we proceeded on our way, we came to lower and lower levels, and more and more inferior lands; though, in one of the fields that we passed, we saw cotton, corn, and tobacco, in small patches of each, all growing within the limits of a few acres. After a journey of twenty six miles by the mail stage, which we did not accomplish till twelve o'clock, having been, therefore, eight hours performing this distance, we reached the first railroad on which we had travelled for some time. The change to this mode of conveyance was very agreeable, though its rate of speed did not exceed fifteen miles an hour when in motion, and was reduced to twelve by the frequent stoppages for firewood, water, and passengers; besides being rendered disagreeable by the frequent entry into the car of the flying sparks of wood, burning the faces of some, entering the eyes of others, and making small holes in the garments of all. We were glad, therefore, when we reached Richmond, and halted for the night.

CHAPTER XLVII

Richmond, though not one of the oldest towns in Virginia, is of British or Colonial origin, having been first established by an act of the Colonial Assembly in 1742; so that it is now nearly a century old. It did not become the seat of government, however, till after the Declaration of American Independence, when the system of fixing on some central point in the State for the place of legislation, was first acted on. It was then, in 1779, that Richmond was appointed to be the site of the Capitol. The situation of the town is peculiarly striking and beautiful; and from almost every point of view it forms a magnificent picture. The three finest views, perhaps, are from the river's bank above the Falls; from the library windows in the upper story of the State House, or Capitol; and from Gamble's Hall, where the panorama is most extensive. The town stands on the north bank of James river, at a distance of 130 miles from the entrance to the Chesapeake at the Capes of Virginia; 116 from Norfolk; 74 from the old site of James-Town; and 12 from City Point, the head of the navigation for large ships—the river admitting only small vessels above that limit, where they find a port of entry within a mile of Richmond, at a small village called Rocketts. The city itself is built on the ascending slope of the northern bank, opposite to a cluster of rocks and verdant islets in the middle of the stream, called The Falls of the James River. The Rapids would, however, be a better term, for though the navigation is entirely interrupted at this point by the shallowness of the water and the innumerable ledges and masses of rock breaking the even surface of the stream—there are no cataracts or falls more than a few inches in any one spot—though the aggregate descent in the course of a mile, is sufficient to furnish waterpower for many mills and factories now in use, and continually increasing.

On the opposite or southern bank of the James river is a small town called Manchester, and this is connected with Richmond by a bridge, over which runs the railroad between Richmond and Petersburg.

Richmond, on the James River in Virginia

Though the town of Richmond has one general ascent upward from the river's bank on the north, it has within its area several small hills and valleys, running at right angles with the stream, and consequently giving great inequalities to the surface, which, however inconvenient to pedestrians in their perambulations of the streets, adds greatly to the variety and beauty of the picture, throwing out the most prominent buildings in bold relief, elevating the spires of the churches, and domes of the Academy and Court House, and, above all, exhibiting the noble form and proportions of the Capitol, which, like the Temple of the Parthenon on the Acropolis at Athens, stands proudly elevated on the brow of the hill, to the greatest advantage.

The plan of the city, like that of most in America, is remarkably regular. The principal streets run parallel to the river along the side of the hill, partaking of its smaller elevations and depressions; and these are called by the letters, of the alphabet, from A to Z in succession, though some of them have distinctive names in addition;—such as Main Street, the great public place of business, like the Broadway of New York; Carey Street, the chief mart of the tobacco merchants; and Broad Street, which has the entry of the railroad from the north. The lateral streets, running up from the river to the top of the hill, cross these longitudinal streets at right angles, dividing the whole area into a certain number of squares. The lateral streets are named numerically, as, First Street, Second Street, and so on. If a street is called by the name of a letter in the alphabet, then it is certain that it runs parallel to the river, and by the letter of its name you can guess pretty accurately how near to or how remote from the stream it is; and so of the numerical streets, which, to a stranger, is a great assistance. They are nearly all broad and airy; but they are wretchedly paved, imperfectly drained, and never lighted, as I believe there is not a single street-lamp in the city. They are therefore the most dirty, rough, and disagreeable streets to walk in, that are to be found, perhaps, in the Union; presenting a continual obstacle to walking or visiting, as they are filled with dirt and dust all through the dry weather, and dirt and mud all the wet. Of all the reforms needed for Richmond, I should say that "Street Reform" was the most urgent and pressing.

I understood that the chief difficulty in remedying this evil, was the already heavy debt of the city, which amounted to more than 700,000 dollars. This alone requires a city revenue of 40,000 dollars annually, to pay the interest. Besides this, there are the following items of expenditure to be defrayed by the city—

For the support of the Poor	5,000	dollars
For the Free School and Orphan Asylum	2,000	"
For the support of a Night-Watch	9,000	"
For repairing the Streets	4,000	"

Markets, Fire Companies, & Contingencies   5,000   dollars
Salaries of Public Officers   20,000   "
                                                  45,000   "

So that the whole expenditure is little short of 100,000 dollars a year. This is raised by a tax assessed on the real property of persons living within the city, which, in 1833, was valued at nearly 7,000,000 million dollars, and is now thought to be worth 10,000,000 dollars. Besides this most legitimate of all sources of taxation, there is one which falls much more unequally; namely, a license tax, all trades and professions here being required to take out a license, for which they have to pay a certain sum to the city funds. By the returns of the State Commissioner for 1833, it appears there were 20 wholesale merchants in Richmond paying for licenses, 326 retail traders, 7 lottery-ticket sellers, 43 hotel-keepers, and 9 boarding-house keepers, 157 coaches, 54 gigs, and 739 horses and mules, all contributing to the city revenue.

One large item of the city debt was for the construction of the Water-works, commenced in 1830, under the direction of Mr. Albert Steen, a celebrated Dutch engineer, the cost of which has been 100,000 dollars and more. There are several reservoirs, each capable of containing 1,000,000 of gallons; and into these, the pumps force from the river, to a distance of 800 yards, and at a considerable elevation, 400,000 gallons of water in 24 hours. Fireplugs are placed in the principal streets, fed by pipes leading from these reservoirs, and these have force enough to send the water, by a hose, to the tops of the buildings, without the use of engines, so that it is an invaluable aid in case of fire. Houses are also supplied with water for domestic purposes from the same source, at a very moderate expense.

Of the public buildings, the most imposing, and in every respect the most beautiful, is the State House, or Capitol. Nothing can be more advantageous than its position, in the middle of a fine lawn, on the brow of the hill that overtops the town. Its foundation is much higher than the tops of the houses in the streets below, thus commanding a fine elevation, and ample surrounding space, to show its form and proportions to the best advantage. It is said to be formed after the celebrated Maison Carré, at Nismes, a plan and model of which was brought from France by Mr. Jefferson; but there are quite as many points of difference as of resemblance between them. It is an oblong building, of about 150 feet by 70, judging by the eye, and from 70 to 80 feet in height. Its principal front is towards the river, from which it is distant a third of a mile, overlooking the town. This front has a fine Ionic portico, rising from a platform on a level with the second story, but without an ascending flight of steps, these being supplied by heavy masses of stairs on each side, to the great injury of the edifice, the chasteness and simplicity of which, when you are near to the building, they quite destroy. They might have been placed at either end, where they would have given beauty and dignity to the structure; but standing where they are, they seem to be an excrescence, as if the architect had forgotten to provide for an entrance into his building at the proper place, and threw up these cumbrous additions, to supply the omission afterwards. The sides have Ionic pilasters to correspond with the portico, and the general effect of the whole is chaste and noble, whenever you are at a sufficient distance to lose sight of the deformity of the side steps, which ought to be removed.

The interior of the Capitol is not arranged to the best advantage, either for convenience or beauty. The ground floor is occupied by various offices. On the first story above this, is a central hall or lobby, in the middle of which is a full length statue of General Washington, executed in marble, by a French artist, named Houdon, taken while the General was alive, and said to be the most striking resemblance ever made of the great original. As this was his native State, it is improbable that this reputation for strict resemblance should be enjoyed by this statue, unless it were true, as there are still so many Virginians living to whom Washington was familiarly known. But it is certainly not like the other representations of Washington in countenance, and differs much from the celebrated picture of Mr. Stuart, which has formed the model for many thousand copies in every size, and of every price, from the excellence of the original as a picture. On this floor is the House of Delegates, as the representatives are here called, and a room occupied by the judges of the Supreme Court. The Senate Chamber is on the floor above, and the Library occupies the upper story. In all these rooms there is nothing remarkable, but each is well adapted to its purpose; and the Library, which is well arranged, and has a good collection of 10,000 volumes, is a very agreeable apartment, from its light, air, and fine prospects. In the Hall below is a bust of General Lafayette, when a young man, on his first campaign with Washington. The leading traits of his features were then the same as they appeared in his old age; and any one to whom his countenance was familiar at sixty five, might know him by his bust at twenty-five. Lafayette is everywhere associated with Washington in America; and two purer or better men were, perhaps, never united in fame than these. If the examples of their lives, public and private, could but be made to have an influence on the conduct of the American people, in proportion to the degree of estimation in which they profess to hold their names, it would be well for this country and for mankind; but that, I fear, is too much to hope for.

Near the Capitol, is the official residence of the Governor, during the session of the Legislature; it is a substantial brick mansion. Behind it is the City Hall, used for the sittings of the Law Courts, as well as for municipal purposes, with a chaste Doric portico, and circular flattened dome. A large Armoury belonging to the State was built on the lower part of the town, and the edifice still exists; but it was found that the manufactory of arms here was more expensive than the purchase of them elsewhere; and it has, accordingly, been abandoned, and converted into a barrack; being now occupied by a small number of troops.

The State Penitentiary occupies a rising ground on the west of the city, and is built and conducted on the Auburn plan, under what is called the Silent System, in contradistinction to the Philadelphia plan, which is called the Solitary System. Here the convicts all work in company, but are forbidden to speak or communicate with each other, even by signs; a prohibition, however, which they constantly evade; and the effect of their association is, in the opinion of most persons here, to make them worse. The system, however, is still continued, chiefly because the workmen, by their labours, pay the cost of their own subsistence, and leave a profit for the State, and this is more thought of than their reformation. There are about 200 convicts in it, one half being free blacks, and a large portion of the other half, foreigners: there are rarely or ever any white females in this prison, though they are frequently found in those of the North. Of charitable institutions there is a Poorhouse, and a Female Orphan Asylum, partly supported by private liberality, partly by municipal taxes, and partly by the funds of the State; and there is a small Lancasterian School, for the education of children of both sexes. One good academy now exists in Richmond, and a few small private schools. But in this respect it is singularly deficient; and though the population is estimated at 30,000, there is no literary or scientific association, such as is to be found in nearly all the smaller towns of the Northern States.

In the general aspect of Richmond, as you walk through its streets, there is nothing very striking. The private dwellings of the more opulent are chiefly on the hill, where the air is cooler and fresher, and the tranquillity greater, than below. The houses are chiefly of brick, well built, handsomely furnished, and many of them with good gardens. In one of these, belonging to the chief proprietor of the White Sulphur Faquier Springs, the garden was well laid out in the Italian style, with several fine statues of the Seasons, and one of Venus rising from the Sea, with fountains, dolphins, etc., executed in Florence, and brought out here for this express purpose. The house, with its noble portico, spacious veranda, elegant furniture, and beautiful pictures, marked a union of good taste with opulence, not very usual, except in the establishments of those who have travelled in Europe, and there acquired a good taste, by an examination of the finest models. The shops have none of the show and beauty of those in the Broadway of Boston, or Chestnut Street in Philadelphia, though the stores are substantial, and appeared to be all well supplied.

The government of the city is formed of a council of twenty-seven, who are elected annually by the inhabitants, nine from each of the three wards into which the city is divided. These again elect out of their own body, a recorder, and eleven aldermen, who form the judiciary of the city. The council also elect from the citizens at large, a mayor, who is both a judicial and an executive officer; and the remaining fifteen of the twenty-seven constitute the legislative council, by whom all acts for the city government are made.

Richmond is already, to some extent, a manufacturing city; but seems destined to become much more so, from her possession of all the necessary elements. The water-power of her Falls is almost inexhaustible, and lies along a great extent of both banks of the stream just above the city. Within a few miles of this are immense beds of coal, on which several mines are actively at work. Already there are many large flour mills, which collectively grind about 1 million bushels of wheat annually; and the brand of the Gallego Mills, on the barrels of flour exported from hence, is esteemed above every other in the South American markets. A Richmond Cotton Manufacturing Company has been established and incorporated by the legislature, which consumes 2,000 lbs. of raw cotton per day, and employs 100 whites and 150 blacks as spinners and weavers. A second, or rival body, called The Gallego Manufacturing Company, has recently started; and private factories are springing up all around; machinery and workmen being procured from England.

The population, in 1830, the last census taken, was 16,060; of whom the whites were 7,755, the slaves 6,349, and the free coloured persons 1,965; making the united black population rather more than the white. The increase since that period, is thought by some to have made the whole population 20,000; and including the opposite town of Manchester, 30,000 at least. In walking the streets, however, you appear to see and meet ten times as many blacks as whites.

On Sundays, when the slaves and servants are all at liberty after dinner, they move about in every public thoroughfare, and are generally more gaily dressed than the whites. The females wear white muslin and light silk gowns, with caps, bonnets, ribbons, and feathers; some carry reticules on the arm, and many are seen with parasols, while nearly all of them carry a white pocket handkerchief before them in the most fashionable style. The young men, among the slaves, wear white trousers, black stocks, broad brimmed hats, and carry walking sticks; and from the bowing, curtseying, and greetings, in the highway, one might almost imagine one's self to be at Hayti, and think that the coloured people had got possession of the town, and held sway, while the whites were living among them by sufferance. This is only the Sunday aspect, however, but to me it was a very agreeable sight while it lasted; the negroes, of both sexes, seemed so happy in the enjoyment of their holiday and finery, that I wished from my heart I could secure them two Sundays a week instead of one, or, still better, have them thus happy all the week through. On working days, however, the case is altered, for then they return back to their labour and dirty clothes again; though it must be confessed, that in no part of the country, in the towns, do the slaves appear to be overworked, or to do, indeed, so much as a white labourer would be expected, and indeed made to do, in the same situation of life. The truth is, that while they are naturally indolent under their bondage—for who would work hard when another is to reap the reward—their masters or owners are indolent too; and it takes so much time and trouble for a white man to be constantly overlooking and tasking a negro, to keep him to his work, that he soon gives it up. The slaves in towns, therefore, and especially domestic servants, do just as little as they like, and their masters and mistresses will not take the trouble to make them do more; so that they live an easier life than many an English mechanic, farm labourer, or servant, as far as actual labour is concerned. In the plantations under overseers, where a stricter discipline can be kept up, it is no doubt different; but in general, you see no stripes inflicted, or blows struck, or even harsh language used to the slaves in towns, by any one; nor does their own sense of their condition seem to be generally one of pain, or a strong desire to change it, though occasionally they run away, and perhaps would do so oftener were it not for the great risk of detection, and certainty of having punishment afterwards. Still, I believe, the only chance of their general improvement is to be found in their freedom. With that, they *may* ameliorate their condition, improve their minds, and become a more intellectual and moral race; without that, as a first step, it seems to me impossible.

I had forgotten to mention an anecdote on this subject, which occurred at Monticello, but which, like a hundred other things that I see and hear, was not recorded at the time, because no degree of labour would be sufficient to preserve, in writing, the half of what passes around one every day, though it would be useful if it could be noted down for future reference, if not for publication; but I will mention it now. We had reached the summit of the hill at Monticello on foot, when a family coming after us from Charlottesville, arrived in a carriage. One of our party, when the persons in the carriage had got out, addressed the driver, a negro slave, and said, "Pompey, what is the name of that hill there away in the distance?" The man replied, "I don't know, Sir". The gentleman rejoined, "But you ought to know; you who are a driver, and bring parties up here. Why don't you learn the names of all the places, so as to be able to tell them to your company?" "I should be very glad" replied the negro, "If I could learn 'em; but master knows it's more than I *dare* do, to learn anything, 'cause it's 'gainst the law". The gentleman was silent; for he had the sense to see to what this would lead, if followed up. I continued the conversation, however, by asking the negro, who was what is called here "a right smart fellow" and spoke as good English as any driver in London, having been born in Charlottesville, and always lived with a white master, whether he really had any desire to learn to read and write; and whether it was true that he was deterred from doing so because the law prohibited it. He said there was nothing he desired more; that he would give half his earnings, if he could, to accomplish this object. He was hired out by his master as a driver, and had to carry home to him a good portion of his earnings, and live upon the rest; but he declared he would give a part of that rest, to learn to read and write, if he could; for though some masters allowed their slaves sometimes to do this, it was not publicly permitted, and *his* master was not willing, because it was against the law.

There is great fear, it would seem, among the whites, that if the negroes were educated, they would turn their knowledge to good account, in corresponding, organizing plans of rebellion, forging passports for each other, and so on. Their owners have no objection to their becoming religious, as they think that safe; but they are afraid of their becoming intelligent! This fact alone is a volume against slavery, and must seal its condemnation as an unjust thing, in the mind of every man who regards the negro as a portion of the human race.

Notwithstanding this, it cannot be denied, that everywhere in the South there are abundant evidences of a retrograde movement in the state of public opinion, as to the desirableness and practicability of emancipation. Whenever the subject is talked of, the conversation is almost always sure to wind up with the assertion, that, but for the Abolitionists of the North, something would, by this time, have been accomplished; but that, by reason of their intemperate zeal, the accomplishment of negro freedom has been thrown back for an indefinite period. The people of the South use this as the strongest ground of their objection to abolition movements; though the true reason of their hostility, no doubt, is an unwillingness to part with what is to them productive property, and to some, indeed, their whole fortune, especially in Virginia, where the slaves being more numerous than they can find occupation for on their own plantations, they train them as artificers of various kinds, and hire them out to others for wages, a small portion of which subsists the slave, and the rest is gain to his master or mistress; for widows and maiden ladies owning slaves, let them out in this way for gain. The rising progeny of these slaves are regarded as so much stock, to be fed, raised, and prepared for a market, to which they are all sent in due time, so that the surplus number is a constant source of addition to the regular gains from their labour. Still the very persons who do this, and live wholly by the income so obtained, profess to be very desirous of seeing something done, towards a safe plan of gradual emancipation, and say that, but for the hasty and intemperate zeal of the Abolitionists, this would have been done long ago.

In these sentiments they are continually fortified by the testimonies of eminent men in the North; and when any of these, either in speeches or letters, give utterance to such testimony, it is, of course, eagerly caught up, and recited in every paper of the South, as strengthening the cause of the Slaveholder by weakening that of the Abolitionist.

Some might imagine that additional cruelties were practised on the negroes in consequence of the efforts of the Abolitionists, or that increase of suffering, and loss of life were produced by it. So far, however, is this from being true, that there never was a period in the history of America, when the negroes were treated with so much kindness and consideration as at present. Floggings, which were once so frequent, are now certainly very rare; and neither subordinate punishments, harsh language, or heavy labour, are inflicted on the slaves to half the extent that they were before the Abolition movements began. This change, I believe to have been brought about by the influence of public opinion. It is now necessary that the slaveholders of the South should be able to repel the charges of cruel treatment, by more kindness than ever to their slaves; to lessen the inducements to absconding, by making their labour lighter; and to prevent the disgust and indignation of Northern visitors, by being more liberal in their supplies of food and clothing, and less frequent in the use of the whip. All this is the result of the Abolition agitation; and though it may perhaps have suspended or retained all legislative measures for the emancipation of the slaves for some years, it has made it more certain that this emancipation *will* be effected, and that the progress towards it will be smoothened, if not hastened, by the gradually milder treatment of the negroes, so as to make them better able to bear the transition, and prevent the intoxication of a more violent oscillation from one extreme to another.

I feel persuaded, that the awakening the public mind to the danger that awaits the much longer continuance of slavery, is the only method of averting the catastrophe, in which, without some steps taken to avoid it, the question would make an issue for itself, by a general and successful insurrection. It is known, that the slaves increase at the rate of nearly 80,000 in each year; and that with all the pains taken to prevent their being instructed, they are nevertheless becoming more and more informed, by constant residence with the whites, and by what they hear and see around them. The example of Hayti, with a free government of blacks, is before them—the emancipation of all slaves in Mexico, is known to them—the example of England in the West India Islands, is fresh and recent—and the exertions making for their abolition in their own Northern States, are, of course, familiar to them all. It is impossible but that all this must every year increase the general *desire* to be free; and equally increase their physical and mental power, by augmented numbers, and improved information, to make themselves so. Should it ever come to that, the struggle would be dreadful, for it would be one of life or death to both parties; and neither would be willing to lay down their arms, till the other were exterminated. To avert this calamity, to which things are naturally tending every year, the humane, the patriotic, and the pious, ought to redouble their energies in favour of speedy emancipation, and the cause of "peace on earth and good will towards men" will be ultimately promoted by their success.

CHAPTER XLVIII

Having a great desire to revisit Norfolk—the only part of the United States that I had ever visited before my present tour, and this so long as thirty years ago, I availed myself of the present opportunity, though the weather was oppressively hot for such an excursion, the thermometer being from 90° to 98° daily. We accordingly left Richmond on the 26th of August, for Petersburgh, by the railroad, which carried us the twenty two miles of distance over a level and uninteresting country in an hour and a half; and here we remained for a few days, previous to our embarking on the James river for Norfolk.

I had supposed, from the name of this place, that it was of comparatively recent origin, at least, posterior to the revolution, as I could hardly think that a town of British origin would have been called after the name of one of the European capitals, and particularly that of Russia. I learnt, however, from one of the oldest residents, that it was even older than Richmond; but its original name was Peterstown, from the circumstance of the first man setting himself down here to settle, and keeping a house of entertainment, being called Peters, a very frequent origin for the names of towns in America. When it rose to be a tolerably large place, subsequent to the revolution, its name was changed to Petersburgh, from its being thought more important than its old appellation.

It is seated on the southern bank of the river Appotomax, which is navigable for small vessels from hence to the James river, close by City Point, where large vessels come up from the sea to load their cargoes. As at Richmond, there are certain rapids or falls above the town on the Appotomax, the waters of which are used for manufacturing power. A canal runs along, side by side with the river, so as to connect the navigation above and below the Falls. The town was originally built of wood; but in 1815 a great fire burnt nearly the whole of it down. Since then, the buildings have been constructed of brick, but, though sufficiently substantial, there is a heaviness and gloom about them, very different from the lightness and brightness which characterise American cities in general. The town is regular in its plan, and has several public buildings in it, including a City Hall, a Masonic Hall, and a Female Orphan Asylum, seven Churches, belonging to Episcopalians, Methodists, Baptists, and Presbyterians; and the Anderson Seminary, established as a Lancasterian School, by a legacy from a Mr. David Anderson. It has but one newspaper, published three times a week, the Petersburgh Intelligence, of Whig politics, though the population is about 10,000; a smaller proportion of newspaper force, if I may use such a term, than towns of such an extent usually exhibit.

Manufactures and commerce are here the chief pursuits, and each is said to be augmenting every year. There are eight tobacco factories, seven flour mills, two mills for expressing oil from the cotton seed, two potteries for earthenware, and one cast iron and brass foundry in the town. The cotton factories are, however, more important still, and are every year increasing. There are two Manufacturing Companies, the Petersburgh and the Merchants. One of these produces yarn, and the other weaves cotton cloth to a considerable extent; both employing about 500 operatives, a large portion of whom are women and young girls. The exports from hence embrace about 50,000 bales of cotton, this being the northern limit of the cotton growing region, 5,000 hogs heads of tobacco, and 100,000 bushels of wheat in each year.

Petersburgh, like Richmond, has its streets in a wretched condition, from want of cleansing and repair, and there are no lamps of any kind, gas or oil, used in them; so that the going out at night is inconvenient, and even dangerous, to a stranger unacquainted with the localities, unless the moon should be up to light him on his way. As a contrast to this state of neglect and disorder in the streets, and total absence of the ordinary convenience of lamps for lighting them, we remarked that this was the only place in America, in which we had seen anything like livery among the servants. It is true that this was of a humble kind, but it was remarkable from its singularity. The coloured servants of the Bollingbrook Hotel, at which we stopped, wore a uniform, a light dress, white, with green binding, and a small green military cloth cap, with two smart tassels, hanging over the right ear, which gave the wearers a very neat and disciplined appearance.

On the morning of August 29, we left Petersburgh for Norfolk, going by the railroad to the banks of the James-river, instead of by the stream of the Appotomax, as the latter, in its winding and circuitous course, makes the distance three times as great as by the former. We left the town about nine o'clock, at which time it was cloudy and cold; but before we reached the end of the railroad, a distance of only twelve miles, which was performed in about three quarters of an hour, a north east gale had gathered up, with heavy rain;

so that our embarkation in the steam boat Thomas Jefferson, which touched here to receive us, on her way down from Richmond, was most uncomfortable. We found her, however, a large and commodious vessel, and there were some agreeable companions and old acquaintances on board as fellow passengers, whom we were glad to meet.

It was about one o'clock, after being five hours under way from the place where we started, and going at the rate of twelve miles an hour, that we came in sight of the position occupied by the first English settlement ever made permanent on the continent of America, namely, James-Town, founded by Captain John Smith in 1607. The first legislative assembly of freemen, as the germ of a representative government, ever met together on this continent, was also held here in 1621. We touched at it to land some passengers for Williamsburgh, which is distant about seven miles from this, inland—this being the nearest point of navigation to it by the James-river, as it is an inland town, lying midway between this and the York-river. It was anciently the legislative capital of the province, but it is now a small and declining town, having not more than 1,000 inhabitants. It is one of the very few places in America that have any antiquities in them, and is thus interesting from that circumstance. The remains of the old palace, or Colonial governor's residence, as well as of the old Capitol, or legislative hall, are still shown; and the old Raleigh tavern, at which the Revolutionary Committees met in the War of Independence, is still kept as a public house, with the bust of Sir Walter Raleigh over the porch of entrance.

The most important building, however, at Williamsburgh, is the college of William and Mary, founded in 1693, by the sovereigns whose names it bears, they having made a royal grant of 20,000 acres of land for its support. This was subsequently augmented by grants from the Colonial Assembly, of certain duties on all tobacco, spirituous liquors, and furs, exported from the province—strange sources of revenue for the support of learning and piety, for the promotion of which this college was endowed! By its charter of 1693, it was to have five Professors, one of Greek, one of Latin, one of Mathematics, and two of Divinity, to which was added a sixth Professor, for instructing the native Indians in Christianity. The funds for this last Professorship were furnished by the celebrated philosopher, Robert Boyle, of England, who gave an estate, called the Brafferton estate, from his own property, to support this benevolent object; and like the Universities of Oxford and Cambridge at home, this college had its representative in the General Legislative Assembly of the Colony.

Of James-Town, where we stopped, although it was once a large place, there is not now a single dwelling remaining. The only relic of its ancient buildings is a small portion of brick work belonging to the first Christian church ever erected on this continent, and this is fast going to decay! By any other people than the Americans, such a relic as this would be taken the greatest care of, enclosed, and preserved, as a precious memorial of the days of their forefathers. But though there is much talk in the New England States of veneration for the character of the Pilgrim Fathers, and loud professions in the Southern States, of great veneration for their revolutionary heroes and statesmen, such as Washington, Jefferson, Franklin, Patrick Henry, Richard Lee, and others—both the Northeners and Southerners seem unwilling to testify their admiration by anything more than words, which cost nothing; for when any expense is to be incurred, whether to enclose the Rock of Plymouth, or erect the Monument of Bunker's Hill, to honour the Tomb of Washington, to preserve that of Jefferson, or to save this relic of the times of Smith, Powhatān, and Pocahontas, from destruction—no one seems willing to put their hands in their purses; but all is suffered to crumble into decay.

The Island on which James-Town stood, is united at its north-western end to the mainland by a long low bridge on perpendicular piles; and the bay or harbour formed between its south eastern end and the shore is still used as a place of shelter for the small craft of the river; while a solitary farm house, of modern erection, is the only building now seen over all the space. Near the fragment of the old church are several trees prettily grouped, and among them, overhanging the few tombs that still remain, is a fine weeping willow, an appropriate accompaniment of the scene! James-Town was the chief seat of the Colonial Government from 1607 to 1698, when a great fire occurred, and destroyed most of the public records; the capital was then transferred to Williamsburgh, where it continued till 1779. It was then removed by the first American State Government to Richmond, which has retained that pre-eminence ever since. The property of the Island of James-Town, has frequently changed hands. It was last in the possession of the family of the Amblers, but it is now the property of a person bearing the same name as its founder, Smith.

In one of the recent papers here, I met with a paragraph, which I could not help reading to some of those who boasted most of the superior morality of America to all the countries of Europe, and the superior protection of person and property which men enjoyed in this country, to that afforded them in England, as well as the greater freedom of religious opinions. The paragraph showed that all these were set at defiance, very recently, in a State that boasts peculiarly of her New England population, the greatest number of her citizens being natives of Massachusetts and Connecticut, so productive of excellence in men and women. The paragraph is this, from the Norfolk Beacon—

We learn from the 'Cincinnati Republican' that two persons, one named Mead, a Perfectionist priest, and the other Foot, were *tarred* and *feathered* by the inhabitants of the village of Batavia, Geauge county, Ohio, and after having been ridden on a rail for about five miles, were set at liberty. Outrages of this character, perpetrated against the rights of individuals, under whatever pretext they may, are wrong and unjustifiable, and cannot but disgrace the community in which they occur.

My companions admitted that this was wrong; but then, they added the almost constant remark, "You do not make sufficient allowance for us as a *young* country" and this, too, in the face of their acquiescence in the justice of those boasts, which claimed for America and the Americans, superiority over all the *old* countries of the world! So inconsistent are those who thus see their virtues through the magnifying, and their faults through the diminishing medium, and turn everything to the indulgence of their national vanity. To show, however, that if in years America is a young country, she is not so in extravagance of personal expenditure, the following extract from a New York paper, taken from the prolific columns of the same file which furnished the former ones, may be cited—

> *From the New York Dispatch.*—Who says the Times are Hard?— Walk in Broadway at the promenade hours, and see *the wealth of the Indies* carried on the backs of the ladies; notice the tasteful and elegant establishments that roll along the carriage paths; see the doors of the fashionable shopkeepers, with as many carriages drawn up before them as if a *great man's levee* were held at each—who says, in the face of these facts, that the times are hard?
>
> Look at the elegant fabrics, which Cleopatra might have desired! By the way, of Cleopatra: had Egypt offered a Broadway to go a shopping in, she could have melted the *revenue of a province* there faster than by dissolving pearls in vinegar. Look into the interior of the splendid stores which line the principal thoroughfares in our city—turn into the furniture and furnishing warehouses—and see the means of gratification for republican luxury. For all these things, *which in elegance surpass any thing which Xerxes knew*, there is apparently no lack of purchasers—and yet the times are hard!

But, amidst all this luxury of the older countries, there is, indeed, a sad mixture of the barbarity and violence of a new one. Even in Cincinnati, as we have seen, the Queen City, as she is called, the tarring and feathering a

"Perfectionist Priest" is executed by mob violence, as in the worst days of Puritanical persecution; but in addition to this instance of religious intolerance in that quarter, here is another, of outrages against men merely for their religious opinions, in the West.

THE MORMONS have excited a good deal of interest in Cincinnati, where one of the sect has been giving a history of that people and of the persecutions to which they have been recently exposed in Missouri.—It is stated in the report given in the Cincinnati News, that they were ruthlessly driven from their homes, their property destroyed, the women and children forced into the woods, without shelter from the inclemency of the weather, where they roamed about till their feet became so sore, that their enemies *tracked them by their foot-prints of blood.* The Mormons stated that there were instances where men were murdered in cold blood, and boys, who had taken shelter from the fury of the mob, were dragged from their hiding places, and after being cruelly maltreated, deliberately shot. In one case, an old man, *a soldier of the revolution*, was pursued by a mob, but finding he could not escape, turned and *supplicated their mercy.* The reply he received was a shot from a rifle, which wounded him mortally; he still besought them to spare him, when one of the party picked up a scythe, or sickle, and *literally hacked him to pieces* as he lay on the ground.

Thomas Morris, formerly U.S. Senator, addressed the meeting.—He said he had been in the vicinity of these transactions, and had taken some pains to acquaint himself with the facts; and from all he could learn, the Mormons were an industrious and harmless people; that no specific charges had been brought against them by the Executive of Missouri; but that their persecution was for no other reason than that their *religion* gave offence to a mob—for causes which may at any time induce the same persecution of any religious sect in our land. He said he believed the statements made to be true, and that they were corroborated by those who resided in the vicinity of their occurrence.

But these mobs not only take upon themselves to decide what religion a man shall believe; they determine also what degree of punishment a culprit shall receive; and though they more frequently set the law at defiance by punishing their victims previous to a trial, in some cases they do it afterwards. Here is an instance from a recent paper.

Lynching in a Court House,—At Copiah in Mississippi, shortly after a prisoner, named Alvin Carpenter, charged with murdering the late Judge Keller, had been acquitted of the crime, and convicted of manslaughter only, a mob rushed into the room, put out the lights, stabbed Carpenter in several places, and cut off his head, leaving him dead on the floor!

One other trait of American feelings I cannot omit to mention, as suggested by another extract from the file of three days papers before referred to; and in which they are as inconsistent as in all things else. There is not, I think, a nation upon the earth, more prone to make distinctions among men, from their birth and wealth, than the Americans. The talk about "old families" and being "highly connected" and "moving in the first circles of society" and the looking down with contempt upon "people whom nobody knows" or who are "not in society" is nowhere carried to a greater extent than here; and the very children are found making these distinctions. This will account for the amazing eagerness with which the greater number of Americans who go to England and France, seek to be introduced at Court, and affect to be patronized and received by the nobility and fashionable world there. This has been carried to such an extent of late, as to have become the subject of just ridicule among themselves; and especially since the "Victoria fever" as it is popularly called, has prevailed so extensively in this country, where the name of Victoria has been appended to almost every thing, from Mr. Sully's portrait of the Queen, down to the last new oyster shop opened in New York. Yet, amidst all these, this they instil in their school books and lessons to children, and by various modes among adults, the most virulent hostility to royalty. The term of the greatest opprobrium which they think can apply to a man, is to call him "an aristocrat" and to a politician, to call him "a royalist."

In conversation and discussions on all these points, sometimes waxing warm, but happily terminating in peace and harmony, we were occupied during the storm of wind and rain which prevented our going on deck, from James-Town to Norfolk, into the harbour of which we entered about five o'clock, passing close under the stern of the Brandywine frigate, lying abreast of the Naval Hospital, and threading our way up through the forest of schooners and other small craft that had run in here to take shelter from the gale, we reached the wharf in safety. The rain, however, still fell in torrents, the wharves were mostly overflowing, and the streets were filled with water; so that we had to wade our way through ponds of water to French's Hotel, where we found excellent quarters and agreeable company.

CHAPTER XLIX

Norfolk is an old Colonial town, having received its charter of incorporation from the British government, and stands next to Williamsburgh in point of date, that being the oldest existing town in all Virginia. The excellence of its port and harbour must have recommended it as an early place of settlement, as soon as it was sufficiently well known; as it is superior to that of James-Town, or indeed any other spot within the whole extent of the Virginia coast. It is so far in from the sea, so winding in its passage of entrance, and so entirely land-locked, that it affords the most complete shelter from all winds; while it has depth of water for the largest vessels that float, with shallow anchorages for the smallest craft, and excellent holding-ground for all. The points of projecting land on both sides of the channel, from the Capes of Virginia up to the town, are also well fortified, so as to make it as secure from the ravages of an enemy as it is from the fury of the storm; nor is the navigation of entrance or exit ever interrupted by adverse winds, by ice, or by any other cause, at any season of the year.

The town is built on a level but projecting plain, about eight miles within or above Hampton Roads, on the north bank of the Elizabeth river, where the junction of its southern and eastern branches just meet the tide waters of the sea. Its present area covers nearly 800 acres of ground; and buildings are every year extending themselves beyond this. The plan of the town is not marked by that extreme regularity which is so characteristic of American cities generally; but even in this respect it is much improved of late years, the streets being now more regular, and the houses larger and more substantially built, than they were formerly.

There are few public buildings of great beauty or interest in the town of Norfolk. Neither the Court House, Custom House, Alms House, Academy, or Mason's Lodge, have anything remarkable in their architecture; and even the Churches, of which there are eight in number, though neat and commodious within, have less commanding exteriors than these edifices in general possess; so that they add little or nothing to the beauty of the town. Of these last, there are two Episcopalian—one of them, St. Paul's, being a hundred years old, built in 1839, of bricks brought from England—two Methodist, one Baptist, one Catholic, and one for coloured persons, slaves and free. A Lyceum and Infant School House have lately been erected, and a Theatre, to be called "The Avon" is nearly complete, to be under the direction of Mr. George Jones, the American tragedian, who was in England, and who is endeavouring to effect the same reform in the drama in this country that Mr. Macready has done at home, by restoring the legitimate plays of the old school, especially those of Shakespeare, and performing only the most approved and classical productions of modern pens. There are two newspapers, the Herald, and Beacon, the former, whig—the latter, moderate democrat; with a larger proportion of hotels and taverns, than an inland town of the same size would require. There are several societies of a benevolent kind, one called "The Hannah More Society" for the education of poor children, of which we saw seventeen baptized in one afternoon at the Episcopalian church of St. Michael's. In the neighbourhood of the town, a large piece of ground has been recently laid out as a public Cemetery, and this is tastefully adorned with trees and shrubs.

The population of Norfolk is estimated at 12,000 persons; and Portsmouth and Gosport united, about 3,000. Of these, the proportions are thought to be 8,000 whites, 6,000 black slaves, and 1,000 free people of colour.

There are some who are very sanguine as to the benefits which will be conferred on this State of Virginia in general, and on the country around Norfolk in particular, by the new, or rather revived, culture of silk. As long ago as 1650, a pamphlet was published in London, by a writer named Edward Williams, recommending the cultivation of silk in Virginia. Even before this, as we learn from Cox's "Description of Carolina" the English colonists of Raleigh's expedition, sent home some silk, of which Queen Elizabeth had a gown made, and wore it at Court; and ten years after Williams's pamphlet was written, when Sir William Berkeley, the loyal governor of Virginia, who, in 1660, went to England from hence to congratulate Charles the Second on his restoration to the English throne, it is stated by the historian Oldmixon, that he was graciously received by Charles, "who, in honour of his loyal Virginians, wore, at his coronation, a robe manufactured of Virginian silk". From that time to this, the culture of this article appears to have been entirely neglected in this State; but it is on the eve of being revived with more than its pristine vigour. Nearly all the States of the Union, from Maine to Florida, and from New York to Missouri, appear to have entered into the cultivation of the *morus multicaulis* tree, for the purpose of rearing silkworms, and producing silk.

With the results already obtained, and with the well-founded prospects held out for the future, it is hardly to be wondered at, that all classes of persons in this country should be looking to the culture of silk as a branch of enterprise and industry, which is likely to rival even that of cotton itself, especially as the latter is confined of necessity to those Southern States in which a certain heat of climate is essential for its production; whereas, the silkworm can be reared, and silk produced and manufactured in the northern as well as in the southern States, and westward of the Mississippi as well as on the borders of the Atlantic. But the central Atlantic States, from New Jersey and Pennsylvania to the Carolinas and Georgia, are, no doubt, the best adapted to the culture, and in these it is probable that it will flourish most. Indeed, in these, and in Maryland and Virginia, the soil and climate are so favourable to production of all kinds, that it is more difficult to say what they will not yield than what they will. This is beginning at length to be more generally understood than formerly; and but for the Slave system, which hangs like a curse upon these fertile regions, the inhabitants would have availed themselves of their resources long ago.

The truth is, that agriculture and mining are occupations which are too laborious, too dull, and too steady for the general taste of the Americans, who cannot live happily but in an atmosphere of excitement; and therefore commerce, speculation, lotteries, stockjobbing, and banking, are much more to their taste. They will bustle through the streets, and in their stores, from sunrise to sunset, in the *hope* of turning a hundred dollars profit, and meet on 'Change, buy and sell, speculate and barter, with zeal and activity, dreaming of making their thousands by every large operation. But the sober labour of agriculture is too plodding and too slow for them; unless it be in the way of some speculating adventure. Thus, when the wheat cultivation was so neglected a few years ago, as to require the importation of grain for food from Europe, the production of cotton was stimulated to its greatest excess, because it was a more gambling kind of commerce. And even now, the *rage* for cultivating the *morus multicaulis*, for such it may be called, arises chiefly from the love of speculation, and delight in excitement, which the enterprise affords.

Political agitation is another powerful cause that draws off the attention of the masses in the interior from the proper cultivation of the soil; and the time wasted in reading the angry party discussions in the newspapers, in assembling at the country post-offices to know the result of the elections, which are going on nearly all the year round in some part of the country or other, as well as the habit of idle gossiping and lounging in the piazzas of the hotels and at the bars of taverns, with the chewing, smoking, and drinking to which all this leads, are serious drawbacks to the rural industry of America, especially in the Southern States, where slavery comes in to add its influence to all the other causes of retardation.

Our first excursion, while at Norfolk, was to the Navy Yard of Gosport, the suburb of Portsmouth, on the opposite side of the harbour. Having letters of introduction to Commodore Warrington, who commanded there, we were most cordially received, and the Commodore's son, himself a young officer in the navy, accompanied us in our investigations. This yard is one of the oldest, though not one of the largest, in the United States, containing an area of about twenty acres; and though its original plan is yet far from being filled up, it is, even at present, very complete in all the requisites of a building and repairing establishment. Its shiphouses, or huge sheds, under which are lines-of-battle ships and frigates building on the stocks, are equal in size, and superior in construction and finish, to any of those in the best dock-yards of England. Its mast-houses, boat houses, sail lofts, smith's forge, and other workshops, are also very efficient, and inferior to none in the world. Its dry dock is a magnificent structure of New England granite; its solidity and massiveness of material, exquisite closeness of masonry, and its perfect finish of workmanship, would do honour to any country; while its size is sufficient to admit a larger ship than has ever yet been built, even by the Americans, who have, at present, lying alongside the wharf of this navy yard, the largest vessel of war that has ever yet been launched.

We went to visit this colossal ship, the Pennsylvania, built at Philadelphia, and now lying here ready for equipment when needed. In order that we might see her from every point of view, we first rowed up and down the Elizabeth-river, on the south bank of which the navy yard is placed, and by advancing and receding, we had the opportunity of seeing her hull in every variety of position. Nothing can be conceived more graceful and beautiful than the form of this immense structure, as she reposed on the tranquil stream. Her model is perfect, and so skilfully are her mouldings and lines rounded off, so gracefully do they ascend towards the bow, and so softly are they bent towards the sternpost, that the whole fabric does not strike one so much by its magnitude, after all, as by its beauty. In this respect it resembles, in the effect produced, a colossal temple of Greece or Egypt, where the magnitude of size is lost in the symmetry of the design, and where the whole is dwelt upon with that feeling of pleasure produced by the consciousness of stability and repose, and by the sense of a perfection with which no fault can be found—so exquisitely blended, and so harmonious, are all her proportions. From having no poop deck, the cumbrous appearance of our English line of-battle ships in that quarter is avoided; and her stern having, for this reason, one tier of cabin windows less, is as light as that of an English 74, though the Pennsylvania has four tiers of batteries or decks, and carries 150 guns. On her cutwater at the head, is placed a colossal bust of the Grecian Hercules, with naked shoulders and breast, the lower part of the waist enveloped with the skin, head, and paws of the Nemean lion, while the head and beard are of the thick curly hair that denotes strength, and the countenance is as majestic as that of Jove himself. It is the rule of the Naval Service of America, to call their line-of-battle ships after the names of the States, their frigates after their rivers, and their sloops-of-war after their towns; a most appropriate and convenient nomenclature, as the name of every vessel at once indicates the class to which she belongs, and each State, river, and town in the Union, is thus likely in time to be represented by some ship of the Navy. The Pennsylvania having been built at Philadelphia, it was intended at first to place on her prow the bust of William Penn. But this was soon abandoned, as nothing could be more inappropriate than the figure of the Advocate of Peace, and founder of the City of Brotherly Love, especially as an Englishman, standing on the bow of this floating citadel, and leading its occupants, with their death inflicting artillery in an onslaught of blood upon some ship of his native country; for to such a purpose, in the event of another war would she be destined. In abandoning this intention, therefore, they adopted the idea of substituting the figure of Hercules, as emblematic of the strength of the great bulwark crowned by his bust; and as a work of art, it forms the most beautiful "figure-head" that I have ever seen in any ship in any service, having strength, simplicity, lightness, and grace, all beautifully united in one.

After examining and admiring the exterior of the hull, we went on board; and it was here that the immensity of her size became for the first time apparent. Her main-deck battery presented 18 long 42-pounders on each side; and each of her decks were splendid examples of length, breadth, height, solidity, and space. On the upper or fourth deck, where the view, in consequence of the absence of a poop, extended in one unbroken line, from taffrel to bowsprit, the vista was magnificent in the extreme. Her length is 237 feet; her breadth of beam 59 feet; her depth amidships 51 feet; and her burden 3,366 tons; her sheet-anchor weighs 11,660 lbs; the canvass required for one suit of sails, hammocks, awnings, for ship and boats, is about 33,000 yards. But while the vastness of the scale, and the massiveness of the materials, the solidity of the timbers, knees, beams, decks, cable-bitts, capstans, masts, and bulwarks, first rivet the attention; the careful and critical observer cannot fail to be subsequently struck with the minute accuracy and perfection of the interior workmanship; the shipwright's knees being as well fitted as the joiner's or cabinet-maker's bulkheads and cabin ceilings: thus uniting the excellence of greatness in size and minuteness of finish, which was observed by the Arabic historian, Abulfeda, to be characteristic of the Egyptian Sphinx, near the Great Pyramid of Cheops at Memphis, when he said, that "while its gigantic scale placed it among the most colossal monuments of the world, its minuter parts would bear to be examined with a microscope".

On our return to Norfolk, we enjoyed the pleasurable conveyance of one of the man-of-war boats, then at the Navy Yard on duty, Captain Payne of the Grampus schooner politely accompanying us. On our way we passed the noble ship of the line, Delaware, mounting ninety guns, with a fine full-length figure of a Delaware Indian Chief for her figurehead; and at the same time we saw two frigates, bearing the names of the English ships taken by the Americans; the Guerriere, the first capture made in the last war by the American frigate Constitution; and the Java, another English frigate taken soon after by the same American ship and the same captain, now Commodore Hull, commanding the Ohio of eighty guns on the Mediterranean station. These British frigates were so crippled in action, that the first was unfit for repair when taken into port, and the second was sunk in the fight. But it was thought politic to keep constantly alive in the memory of American seamen these conquests from the British on their own element, and thus to stimulate them with the hope of new victories, by having always before them the triumphs of old ones. Two frigates were therefore built by the Americans, and called respectively, the Guerriere and the Java. The first is now lying up in ordinary, and the second is in commission as the guardship of the port; but their names will, no doubt, be perpetuated in other ships that may be built to replace them; a policy of which we, at least, have no right to complain, as it was our constant practice, long before the Americans had a navy at all, to retain the names of the vessels captured from the French, both in our line-of-battle ships and frigates, as trophies of our prowess by sea, and as examples to our seamen, of what their predecessors had done, and what *they* were expected to achieve also, wherever the opportunity of so doing was presented to them.

The second excursion we made from Norfolk was to see the Naval Asylum, built on a projecting piece of land, just opposite the usual anchorage of the ships of war in the harbour, and forming a very pleasing as well as appropriate object in the marine picture. This Asylum has been erected out of a Hospital Fund, contributed by the officers and seamen of the United States' Navy, at the rate of 20 cents, or ten pence sterling per month from their pay, without asking or receiving any aid either from the general or the State government. It is intended to answer the double purpose of a hospital for the sick belonging to the ships of the navy on service and in the port, and an asylum for the aged and the disabled, when no longer fit for active duty. It is a large quadrangular building, composed of a front, a rear, and two side-wings; forming a square of about 200 feet on each side. The front pile of this quadrangle has a noble Doric portico of ten massive columns, with an ascending flight of steps, an entablature, frieze, and pediment, all in excellent taste. Before it is a fine lawn, formed by the projecting point of the little promontory on which it stands, with gravel-walks, trees, and shrubs, and surrounded by the sea on three of its sides. In this range are contained the residences of the director, surgeons, and officers, with the boardroom and other offices. The two side-wings are devoted to the sick-wards and the sleeping-rooms, for the inmates; the healthy and the sick being kept, of course, apart. These are three stories in height, with a spacious balcony or veranda to each story, both on the outer front, and on the inner one, presented to the central internal square. Every practicable arrangement seems to have been made in these, for durability, cleanliness, ventilation, and comfort. The rear range is devoted to baths, of which there are all varieties, of hot, cold, and shower baths, of fresh-water or seawater, as required; and in this range are also other offices conducive to the comfort and efficiency of the establishment.

On our way from the Hospital we visited the schooner Grampus, and the frigate Brandywine, both lying here ready for sea, the first waiting for orders, and the second about to proceed to the Mediterranean. The schooner was about 200 tons, mounted 12 guns, 18-pound carronades, and carried a crew of seventy men. She was most efficient in every requisite, and was in beautiful order. The frigate was a superb ship of her class. She was originally built to bring over General Lafayette, in his friendly visit to America, about the year 1806; and was called the Brandywine, in compliment to him, this being the name of one of the American rivers, near Wilmington, in Delaware, on the banks of which Lafayette was engaged, in the war of the Revolution, and contributed to the successful issue of the battle of the Brandywine. The name, however, is not a happy one, and many of the officers of the ship desire that it should be changed to the Lafayette. The ship is one of the finest frigates I ever remember to have seen. Her exterior form is the perfection of nautical beauty; she sits on the water with the lightness and grace of a bird; and, as in the Pennsylvania, the harmony of her proportions, and the faultless beauty of her model, take away from the impression of her size. But when you stand upon her deck, her dimensions then display themselves. She is 197 feet long, within a few feet, therefore, of the length of the usual run of English line-of-battle ships, which in two deckers rarely exceeds 200 feet; her breadth and height are in full proportion to her length; and she measures about 2,000 tons. She mounts 60 guns, long 32-pounders, and has a crew of 470 men.

In all her internal arrangements, in efficiency of stores, and completeness of equipment in every respect, no English frigate that I have ever seen, could surpass her; and her crew was the finest set of men I ever saw assembled on a ship's deck. I was present at their muster, saw them at their work, and was on board while they took their dinner, so that I had ample opportunity to observe them under various aspects. The odious and detestable practice of impressment never being resorted to, in order to man the American ships of war, the officer in command, while the ship is fitting out, has it in his power to select the best men that offer, and thus to have a picked crew. In addition to the excellent wages of twelve dollars, or about 2*l.* 10*s.* sterling per month, and full rations of the best provisions, a bounty of thirty-six dollars, or about 7*l.* 10*s.* sterling, equal to three months' pay, is given to every able seaman entering for three years, which is the utmost limit of the term required, with power of renewal or of liberty at its termination.

In the Brandywine there were forty able seamen, who were free negroes. I was much struck with the fine, and even noble appearance of these men; their erect and muscular forms no longer crouching under the influence of forced servitude, nor their heads hung down under a consciousness of inferiority, but leading a free, bold, independent, and active life, their appearance partook of these new influences, and they were among the finest-looking men in the ship. In answer to my inquiries of the first lieutenant, who had been upwards of thirty years in the service, I learnt that they received exactly the same bounty, the same wages, the same rations, and the same privileges as the whites; and that in their arrangements and classification for duty, as forecastle-men, top-men, waisters, and after guard, no distinction was made between black and white, but each were mingled indiscriminately, and classed only by their relative degrees of seamanship. In this, he said, the blacks were not at all inferior to the whites, either in their skill, readiness, or courage. Nor did the white seamen evince the slightest reluctance to be associated with them on terms of the most perfect equality in the discharge of their duties, or make their colour a subject of antipathy or reproach. The cooks and stewards were chiefly coloured men, because they stand the heat better, and fall into these occupations more readily; and from the negro sea men, the launch for wooding and watering, and for anchor duty, was generally manned, because the African constitution could stand the heat of the sun, and the atmosphere of swamps and marshes, better than the American. In point of health, however, they were quite equal; and while the service was rendered more efficient by this arrangement, neither party objected to the classification. It was really to me a most agreeable sight to see forty or fifty of these fine athletic Africans holding up their heads like men, and looking as if conscious of their independence and equality, though at the same time respectful, obedient, and less frequently subjected to punishment for neglect of duty, than their white brethren.

The officers of the ships we had visited to-day, and, indeed, all those of the naval service of America that I had yet seen, either now, or at any former time—and I have seen them in many parts of the world, and under a great variety of circumstances—appeared to me in no degree inferior to the officers of the British navy, in knowledge of their profession, gentlemanly manners, or general information: in one respect, indeed, they seemed to me superior to the officers of our own service, generally; namely, in the entire absence of hauteur, and overbearing self-importance; and in the exhibition of great mildness, and respect towards those out of their profession. Here there is no young officer, who dares presume on his high connections, to play the tyrant over his men; no sons of wealthy parents, who can afford to give them large annual allowances beyond their pay; nor are there any of the numerous class of persons possessing parliamentary interest in their families, and thereby counting on promotions and appointments, which their shipmates of longer service, and greater merits, cannot obtain for want of such connections.

In the absence of all these exciting causes of dissatisfaction, which are so prolific of discontent among the officers in the British Navy; the American Naval Service is a dignified, quiet, friendly, and gentlemanly school; where there are no high-born to look down upon the low; no very rich, to annoy, and vex by contrast, the humbler poor; and no favourites of fortune to be run up from midshipmen to post captains in a few years, while grey headed lieutenants look on with silent disgust and secret indignation. The promotions in the American Navy are by seniority, as in our Royal Marines and Artillery; and as in the East India Company's Navy and Army: and though in all such cases, the promotion will be slow, yet it being equitable, and equally rapid for all; the sense of its justice reconciles men to wait for their advancement, if all are obliged to do the same. The pay, too, is more liberal than ours. An American midshipman, besides being treated much more like a gentleman by his superior officers, than is too frequently the case in the British Navy, is four times as well paid while in active service, and receives for this half-pay, when not employed, nearly three times as much as the English midshipman on full pay: the latter, when not employed, getting no half-pay at all. Lieutenants, masters, pursers, surgeons, captains, and commodores, all receive from twice to three times the amount of pay allowed to similar ranks in the British Navy. The consequence is, that, whether promoted or not, American Naval officers can all live like gentlemen on their pay, whether on home or foreign service; whereas English Naval officers, with nothing but their pay, experience the greatest difficulty to keep out of debt; and many, from despair of obtaining promotion, abandon themselves to habits, which bring both themselves and the service into disrepute.

CHAPTER L

The third excursion we made from Norfolk, was to Old Point Comfort, the fort erected to guard the outer entrance from the Chesapeake Bay to Hampton Roads, James-river and the harbour of Norfolk. We embarked, for this purpose, on board the steamer called "The Old Dominion"—a very favourite name with the Virginians, one of the newspapers published at the opposite town of Portsmouth bearing the same title—and leaving Norfolk at ten in the forenoon, we proceeded down the harbour, passing the beautiful schooner and magnificent frigate lying off the Naval Hospital, and a number of dismasted and disabled vessels, that had taken shelter here after the late destructive gale. Continuing our way past Craney Island, the mouth of the James-river, and through Hampton Roads, we reached Old Point Comfort about half past eleven, the distance being sixteen miles; and landing at a convenient wharf there, we repaired to the hotel near the beach.

As this is one of the largest and most important forts of the country, I had naturally supposed that there would be a governor, an officer of the guard, sentries at the gates, and the usual military rules by which such places are regulated; and being anxious to conform to these, I directed my inquiries accordingly. I was surprised to learn, however, that I should find neither sentries, guards, nor officers of any kind, as there were no troops in the fort, its only occupants being a few artificers, and that, therefore, we might walk through every part of it at our leisure.

The Fort is advantageously placed on a projecting point of land, at the confluence of the James River with the Chesapeake, lying east of the former and west of the latter, and guarding the entrance to the anchorage called Hampton Roads, which must be passed through by all ships approaching Richmond or Norfolk from the sea. The area covered by the fort requires a circuit of about a mile to compass it, as you walk round the ramparts. The walls, the salient angles, and the batteries, are constructed of solid stone, and are of excellent workmanship. A regular ditch surrounds the outer wall, and is filled with water. In the interior of the fort are the usual arrangements of barracks for the troops, officers' quarters, spacious parade ground, forges, armoury, ordnance depôt, magazine, and workshops of every kind.

The works were commenced about eighteen years ago, and are not yet quite completed. It is intended to mount 400 pieces of cannon here; and it would require, to garrison the place completely, 4,000 men; but at present there are not more than 20 guns mounted, though there are many more in the fort. Of soldiers now here there are literally none, the only persons, these being the artificers, of whom we saw about fifty in the different workshops, making gun carriages, and other requisites for the completion of the establishment. The cause of the entire absence of troops, as we were told by the superintendent of the works, was the constant drain of men from all the forts of the country for the Florida war, where the rifles and arrows of the Indians, and the swamps and marshes of the ever-glades, carry off more victims annually, than any war in which the United States has ever been engaged. Yet though every fort in the country is now weakened by drafts of men to go to Florida, and some of the forts, like this, are entirely stripped of their occupants, the Indian war seems, in the opinion of most persons, to be as far from its termination as ever.

Opposite to this fort, at a distance of less than a mile to the south, and almost in mid-channel of the entrance from the sea, stands an artificial island, made after the same process as that of the Breakwater at Plymouth in England. There existed there a bar, or shoal, called the Rip-Raps, with only fourteen feet water on it at high tide, and being covered even at low water, it proved a dangerous impediment to navigation. It was therefore determined to effect the double object of first covering the shoal with a mass of large stones, heaped on it, so as to rise above the water's edge, and thus present a visible object to ships sailing by it; and, secondly, to make this the basis of a fort, to strengthen the defences of the entrance. The only deep channel lies between Old Point Comfort and the Rip Raps, and as it is not more than a mile wide, all vessels passing in or out must go within half a mile at least of these forts, and be within point blank range of their guns. The first of these objects is already accomplished, as the sandy shoal has been converted into an island of rocks rising at least twenty feet above high water; but the second object, of strongly fortifying it, remains yet to be achieved. The only difficulty in the way of this, is the appropriation of the necessary funds; but this the Government is for the present unwilling to grant. The two works, at Old Point Comfort and the Rip Raps have already cost about a million and half dollars, and it would require perhaps another half million to make them complete. But instead of new appropriations for naval and military works, the Government is at this moment curtailing even the current and usual allowances.

During our stay at Norfolk, we attended the Episcopal and the Presbyterian churches; and observed the usual characteristics of American places of worship in each. The churches are neater in all their interior arrangements, better fitted and furnished, and far more comfortable, than the average condition of churches in England. All the aisles, as well as the pews, are carpeted as perfectly as any drawing room; the cushions, footstools, and every other auxiliary of comfort and ease, are in perfect repair; the books nicely bound, and in the best condition; while ample means exist for warming the interior in winter, and cooling it in summer. The music and singing is much superior to ours in general; and the ear is never offended by those discordant sounds which are so often heard in the country churches and small dissenting chapels of England; while the quiet decorum, deep attention, and almost universal practice of kneeling during the periods of prayer, certainly give an impression of more devout feeling, than the variety and carelessness of the attitudes too often observed in the English churches. There is another feature of our places of worship which is not seen here; I mean, the number of poor persons for whom there are no pews provided, and who, by their dress and general appearance, remind you that they are the children of want—in the midst of the luxuries and superfluities of a land of opulence and plenty. No such class is seen in American churches; and from the general aspect of the congregation, you can hardly fail to be convinced that want of food, raiment, or comfortable dwellings, is unknown among them; and that competency and comfort is the lot of nearly all. It is true that there is one blot, which, in every American church that I have yet visited, I could wish to see removed; and that is, the practice of appropriating the side galleries exclusively to the use of the coloured people; the central gallery being occupied by the organ and the choir. But it should not be forgotten, that while colour is the ground of separation from the rest of the congregation here, poverty is in England as frequent a ground of separation also; for while the rich and the middle classes have their comfortable cushioned pews with lock and key, for their sole use, the poor have wooden benches marked "free seats" assigned to them in the cold stone paved aisles, and are as much separated by their poverty from their richer fellow sinners, as the coloured people are in America from their white brethren. For my own part, I think these distinctions equally inconsistent with the Christian maxim, that "in the sight of God, all his creatures are equal" and that the open and unappropriated seats of the Catholic cathedral, the Methodist conventicle, and the Quaker's meeting-house—like the unpewed equality of the Mohammedan mosque—are all preferable; for if there be one place on earth in which, more than in another, man ought to be made to feel humility, and be taught to regard his brother as his equal, being children of one great Father, who is equally the Creator and Preserver of all, it is a place of public worship, where "all that dwell upon the face of the earth" are equally invited to "come into the presence" of Him who is so truly designated as—

Father of all! in every age,
  In every clime adored,
By saint, by savage, and by sage,
  Jehovah, Jove, or Lord!

and where, if any distinctions were observed, and the example and precepts of Jesus of Nazareth, were to be made the rule of guidance, "the poor and needy" ought to have especial preference; for to them are the consolations of religion most necessary.

The transition from this subject, to that of the condition of the slaves here, is not so unnatural as it might at first seem. It is impossible, indeed, to think of religion, without being reminded, by the association of contrast, of the utter irreconcilability of slavery with the benevolence, purity, and equality of the Christian scheme of redemption. In justice to the Virginians generally, I must say, that among all the well informed classes with whom we have mingled, and in Norfolk as much as anywhere, there is little or no hesitation on their part, in admitting slavery to be a double evil, equally injurious to the best interests of master and slave, and the chief, if not the only cause of the backwardness of this noble State, in the general career of improvement; while all speak of the slave trade with horror, and express a desire to see it made piracy by all nations, and treated accordingly.

A recent occurrence has brought out the more free expression of public sentiment upon this subject than usual. A Spanish planter went up from his estate in Cuba to the port of Havannah, to purchase goods and slaves. This he effected, and was proceeding homeward by sea in a vessel containing a valuable cargo, and fifty slaves purchased by him out of a slave trader just arrived from Africa. On their voyage, the slaves sought an opportunity to regain their liberty, rose on their white oppressors, who were carrying them into forced captivity, and murdered all but three:—their purchaser or master, an old sea captain, and a cabin boy. The first they kept, with intention to shoot him at liberty; the second they retained, to navigate the vessel; and the third they spared, because of his youth and innocence. When they thus obtained the mastery of the vessel, they made the captain steer always towards the rising sun, as they knew that to be the direction of the land of their home, from whence they had been torn; but when night came on, or when it was cloudy, the captain contrived, by imperceptible degrees, to veer the vessel's head round to the west by compass, of which the Africans knew nothing, always managing, however, about daylight to bring her head again round to the place of the sun's rising; so that by this method, whatever progress they made eastward during the day, they retraced back again to the westward during night. Thus, for the amazingly long period of sixty-three days, they continued going to and fro, without falling in with any ship to board them; the hope of meeting with which, was the chief inducement for the captain's steering her backward every night, and edging also constantly to the northward. At length, by the force of the Gulf Stream, contrary winds, and counter courses, she was driven on the coast of America, and after being seen and reported by different vessels as a very suspicious craft, she was captured by a Government Surveying vessel, the Washington, Captain Gedney, and taken in as prize to the port of New London, in Connecticut. The negroes were all apprehended, and confined in jail for trial.

This event gave rise to very opposite opinions, maintained by opposite parties. The Abolitionists contended that the slaves did only what was perfectly justifiable, in endeavouring to regain their liberty, even at the sacrifice of the lives of those who unjustly held them in bondage; and that as the crew of any American ship, captured in war, would be called heroes, if they rose on their English captors, massacred them, retook the vessel and regained their liberty, so was it commendable in these African negroes to do the same; they, therefore, considered them to be entitled to sympathy and support, rather than to punishment. The apologists of Slavery, contended, on the other hand, that the Africans, being lawfully purchased at Havannah, were the lawful property of their white masters; that the crime of rising against them, and killing them, to regain their liberty, was mutiny, piracy, and murder, and should be dealt with as such. In Norfolk, opinions seemed pretty nearly equally divided; though the actual Slaveholders, of which there are many here, were very tender and sensitive on the subject, and thought it best not to make it too much a matter of public discussion, lest it should become too familiar to their own slaves. All, however, tried, if possible, to draw a clear distinction between slavery and the slave trade; and many, who saw nothing wrong in the former, affected to be greatly shocked at the latter. This, however, is to be understood with some limitation. The slave trade at which they express so much horror, is that which consists in taking the Africans from their native country, and carrying them to the West Indies and South America for sale; though it is known that large numbers are smuggled into the United States from Havannah, and through Texas; and though it is certain, also, that were it not for slavery in this country and others, there would be no slave trade, as the demand creates the supply. But to the slave trade, which consists in buying up the African negroes of the central States, such as

Maryland and Virginia, and selling them to slave dealers from the South, to be taken to Georgia, Alabama, Mississippi, and Arkansas, no such indignation is expressed.

Here, as everywhere else in the South, the negroes are all obliged to be in their houses at a given hour, eight in the winter and nine in the summer; and a warning bell is rung every night at those periods. Should any person of colour be found in the streets after this time, by the night watch, they are taken to prison, and there kept for the night, and then discharged. For the second offence, however, they are whipped, as well as imprisoned, unless their masters will pay a fine of a dollar to save them from its infliction, which is not often done.

The society of Norfolk is characterised by more of leisure, frankness, refinement of manners, and less of nationality, than that of the Northern cities. The number of persons in easy circumstances, living on fixed incomes, arising from landed property rather than trade, is considerable. The public officers of the government, attached to the naval and military department, are also numerous, and the professions of the law, medicine, and the church, furnish their full proportion; while the merchants and traders are not so entirely engrossed with the accumulation of money, as to have no time for other thoughts. The tone of conversation among the men is, therefore, more elevated, and their manners more gentlemanly, than those of the mercantile society generally of the North. Among the ladies, we saw many very beautiful women, and exquisitely lovely youths; and while the same superiority of manners is observable in the females as in the males—arising no doubt from the same causes—the lives they lead are less hurried and excited, either by business or pleasure, than in the North, and there is more leisure for cultivation and polish. As there are few large fortunes rapidly acquired here, there is no absurd competition for display, or straining everything to the utmost in dress and parties, to outrival each other. Society not being cut up into sets, and castes, and circles, as in Boston and New York, there is no jealousy about particular grades, or coldness with some and cordiality with others. All appear to feel themselves sufficiently on a footing of social equality, to be frank, open, cheerful, and unaffected in their behaviour and intercourse with each other. Norfolk, I should think, resembles much more the old Colonial state of society, in feelings and manners, than any place in the North, and may fairly rank with Charleston and Savannah, which resemble it in this respect.

CHAPTER LI

Having now traversed the greater part of the noble State of Virginia, and examined the Old Dominion through the length and breadth of the land, it may be useful to cast a retrospective glance over the rise and progress of this earliest portion of the British colonies on this extensive continent, before giving a general view of its present extent in area, productions, resources, wealth, and population.

It was by the enterprise of the Venetian navigator, Sebastian Cabot, under the patronage of Henry the Seventh of England, that the continent of North America was first discovered—the voyage of Columbus, a few years before, having brought him acquainted only with the islands of the West Indies. This was in 1498, the year in which the first British ship that ever reached the coast of this continent, sailed from Bristol; and it is remarkable, that the first vessel sent to navigate to this country across the Atlantic by steam, the Great Western 340 years afterwards, should sail from the same port of Bristol, leaving both London and Liverpool in the rear. It has been remarked by Grahame, in his excellent History, that in the first expeditions of navigators from Europe to the New World, the enterprising men who conducted them were all foreigners to the States deriving the honour and benefit of their discoveries. Columbus, a Genoese, sailed for the crown of Spain; Cabot, a Venetian, for the crown of England; and Verazzan, a Florentine, for the crown of France.

It was not, however, till the reign of Elizabeth, nearly a century after Cabot's discovery, or in 1578, that any attempt was made by the English to form a permanent settlement on this coast; and the person who first projected such settlement was the illustrious navigator, Sir Walter Raleigh, who obtained for his half brother, Sir Humphrey Gilbert, a patent from the queen, authorizing him to explore and occupy, or appropriate, all barbarous lands which he might find unoccupied by Christian powers, and hold them as fiefs of the crown, on condition of his paying, as revenue, one fifth of all gold and silver found therein. It empowered Gilbert to exercise civil and criminal jurisdiction over those who might accompany him, and made the term of the patent six years, prohibiting all persons, during that time, from occupying any land within 200 leagues of any spot discovered and appropriated by him.

In 1585, the first actual Colony was formed by the landing of 108 workmen at Roanoak, brought out in seven ships, under the command of Sir Richard Grenville. They were left here under the command of Captain Lane, assisted by Amadas, one of the commanders on a former voyage, and Heriot, a mathematician and astronomer, who excited the admiration of the natives by his telescopes and other instruments; but unfortunately, the thirst for gold was so intense, that in pursuit of it they neglected all other objects, consumed their provisions, quarrelled with the Indians, and were reduced to the last extremity, when Sir Francis Drake touched at the Colony from the West Indies, took them all on board, and conveyed them back to England.

The next expedition was sent out in 1587, when a charter of incorporation was given to Captain White and twelve assistants, to found the city of Raleigh in Virginia; but the only issue of this voyage was some better acquaintance with the country and people, and the introduction, for the first time, of the potato root and plant into England—as great an accession of good to the European community, as the importation of tobacco has proved an evil.

This was the last of the expeditions despatched by Raleigh, who, becoming engrossed with other objects, connected with Ireland, Portugal, and Guiana, transferred his interest in the American settlement to a London Company of Merchants; but these conducted their affairs so badly, that at the period of Queen Elizabeth's death, not a single Englishman was known to be anywhere settled in America; and for a while all hopes of colonization in this quarter seemed to be extinct.

At length, in 1603, James the First ascended the English throne, and the voyages of Gosnold to the northern shores of Massachusetts having revived attention to Virginia, the King was induced to grant a patent to Sir Thomas Gates, Lord Somers, Richard Hakluyt, and others, authorising them to take and hold all the lands lying between the 34th and 45th degrees of latitude, with all islands lying within 100 miles of the shore—including all the coast from Virginia up to Maine, embracing also all the new Western States, within this parallel, and comprehending, indeed, an area equal to four fifths of the whole of the present Union. The object of granting this patent was no doubt to enrich the patentees and their friends, and extend the power and resources of the King. But, as real motives are rarely avowed in political instruments, the pretence set forth in this case was a desire "to make habitation and plantation, and to deduce a Colony of sundry of our people into that part of America commonly called Virginia, that so noble a work may, by the providence of Almighty God, hereafter tend to the glory of his Divine Majesty, in the propagation of the Christian religion, to such people as yet live in darkness and miserable ignorance of the true knowledge and worship of God, and may in time bring the infidels and savages living in those parts, to human civility, and to a settled and quiet government".

The occupation of the territory was assigned to two separate companies; the southern portion being given to the London Company, including the coast from the Capes of Virginia to the present site of New York; and the northern portion, comprehending all beyond this, being assigned to the Plymouth and Bristol Company. They were authorised to transport as many English subjects as they saw fit, to their new settlements, to furnish them with arms and ammunition, and to guarantee them exemption from all custom-house dues for seven years, with a retention of all the rights and privileges they enjoyed in England.

The first body of colonists embarked by the London Company sailed from England in three small vessels, the largest of which did not exceed 100 tons; and in these were embarked, besides the crew, 105 men destined to remain in America. The command devolved on Captain Newport, and among his passengers were George Percy, brother of the Earl of Northumberland, Gosnold the navigator, and the intrepid Captain John Smith. They sailed from England in December 1606, and did not reach the Chesapeake till April 1607, as long a period as is now taken to sail from London to China. They named the southern promontory of the Chesapeake, Cape Henry, in honour of the then Prince of Wales; and the northern, Cape Charles, after another of the King's sons; and sailing up the river, then called Powhatān, they were so impressed with its excellence as a stream, and the eligibility of its banks for a settlement, that they gave the river the name of their monarch, instead of that of the Indian chief or king, which it then bore, and founded their infant settlement about forty miles from its mouth, calling it also James-Town.

It is not intended to follow up the history of this settlement in detail, or narrate the romantic adventures of Captain John Smith, tempting as the subject is, but rather to trace the broad outlines of the rise and progress of Virginia generally. It will be sufficient, therefore, to state that Smith, by his superior talents, courage, and other qualities which fitted him admirably for the post of a leader, soon obtained that distinction by consent of his companions, though they were at first jealous of his abilities. He was of a respectable family in Lincolnshire, and born to a competent fortune, but had served in the army; and being of an enterprising disposition, had embarked in this adventure with great zeal. He speedily fortified James-Town; and by his kind conduct to such of the Indians, as were friendly, and his prompt retribution on those who were hostile, he soon acquired a great reputation and influence. There is one romantic incident, however, so remarkable in the career of this truly great man, that it cannot with propriety be omitted.

In the course of an excursion, made for the purpose of surveying the interior of the country, he fell into the hands of a hostile tribe of Indians, but having resisted them by arms, though unsuccessfully, he was about, after his capture, to be put to death. With great presence of mind, he expressed a desire to speak to the sachem or chief, before his life was taken, which request was granted to him; and he then showed the astonished Indians a mariner's compass, of which he described the properties and use, and related how many new countries had been discovered by its instrumentality; as well as the form of the earth, its motion round its own axis, and its revolutions round the sun; the position of the antipodes, and the cause of summer and winter. To all, they, the Indians, listened with wonder and delight; and the fact that they could see the tremulations of the needle, while in every attempt to touch it, they found the hand arrested by the transparent glass, a substance they had never before seen, gave them an idea of its being something superhuman! For a while, therefore, they remained in doubt and suspense, whether they should put their prisoner to death, or not; but, at length, their attachment to their old customs prevailing, he was bound to a stake, to be shot through with arrows, in the ordinary way. The chief, however, Opechancanough, had been more deeply impressed than his colleagues with the superiority of Smith above the common race of mortals; and being either ashamed or afraid to put him to death, he held up the mariner's compass to his people, and ordered his reprieve; after which he was conducted, still as a prisoner, surrounded with guards, to a dwelling, and there hospitably entertained. The Indians then attempted to prevail on Smith to betray the English settlement into their hands; but his virtue remaining firm amidst all his dangers, his case was referred to the Indian king, Powhatān, before whom he was led with much ceremony; but here, after a sumptuous repast, according to their rude fashion, had been set before him, he was adjudged by Powhatān to be put to death; and the mode determined on was, to beat out his brains by their war clubs, while his head was laid on a stone. At this fearful crisis, the Angel of Mercy again overshadowed him with her wings; for the favourite, and, from all contemporary accounts, superior-minded daughter of the king, Pocahontas, ventured to intercede with her father for his life; but her entreaties failing to soften their stern and cruel purpose, she threw her arms around the body of the victim, and standing between him and his executioners, declared her determination either to save him, or to perish in the attempt. The Indians, who have a great admiration for courage and heroism in either sex, spared their captive for Pocahontas' sake; and he was not only released, but sent back in safety to James-Town, where his beneficent deliverer sent to him those supplies of provisions, of which the little Colony stood so much in need.

Soon after this, a reinforcement of 120 men from England, with provisions, seeds, and implements of husbandry, arrived, to join the settlement; but among them were so few labourers, and so many gentlemen, and jewellers, and refiners of gold, all adventurers in search of the precious metal, which they hoped to find as abundant here as in Mexico or Peru, that they were of little value; and the discovery of a shining sandy sediment, found in the James-river waters, fostered their delusion, and indisposed every one to agriculture or the industrial arts. A cargo of this sand, or dust, which was ultimately proved to be of no value, with some cedar wood from the neighbouring forests, formed the first cargo ever sent from Virginia to England; and in return, by the same ships, were sent out a supply of various officers, as if the little Colony were to become at once a great kingdom, among which were admirals, recorders, judges, and chronologists for whom there was no suitable employment.

In the mean while, Smith undertook to explore the Bay of the Chesapeake, whose Indian name, "The Mother of Waters" is beautifully expressive of the number of rivers that are poured into its bosom,—and passing up the York, the Rappahannock, the Potomac, and even the Susquehannah, he surveyed a great extent of country, and made a map of the whole, so minutely accurate, that all authorities admit it to have required scarcely any alteration or improvement, except by the addition of such places as have been subsequently visited, but were not then known.

On the return of Smith to the Colony, he found it in a wretched condition; but being elected president of the council, by the settlers, whose confidence in him was unbounded, he soon succeeded, by the admirable talents which he possessed for government, in restoring plenty, order, industry, and content, in the midst of difficulties which would have broken the spirits and destroyed the faculties of any ordinary man. A strong sense of religion pervaded his character, and governed his conduct throughout; and it was remarked of him, as it had before been said of Columbus, that though accustomed to naval and military life, and surrounded by dissolute and licentious men, he had never been known to utter an oath.

The directors of the Virginia Company at home, however, not realizing those absurd dreams of golden treasures, which they expected to receive by every ship from hence, formed themselves into a new association, by the title of "The Treasurer and Company of Adventurers of the City of London, for the first Colony in Virginia" and obtaining new associates among persons of high rank and wealth, and being incorporated by a new charter, they sent out, in 1609, a squadron of nine ships and 500 emigrants. In one of these was Lord Delaware, the new governor and captain-general of the Colony, with Sir Thomas Gates and Sir George Simons, all entrusted with large and co-equal powers. This ship, containing the chief functionaries, was wrecked on the island of Bermuda, but the remainder of the squadron reached James-Town in safety. Among the emigrants, however, were so few men of industrious habits, and so many of indolent and profligate character, broken-down gentlemen, insolvent traders, licentious youths, and corrupt and hoary villains, that their influx was the greatest curse to the infant settlement, and threw everything into confusion.

Smith, however, again assumed the command, and was proceeding with those vigorous measures necessary for the order and peace of the Colony, when an unfortunate accident occurred, which nearly deprived him of his life. A bag of gunpowder, which he carried with him for his ammunition, exploded while he was asleep, and "tore the flesh from his body and thighs in a horrible manner". The pain was so acute, that he threw himself into the river to cool the burning sensation, and was near drowning before he could be recovered: yet he had to go nearly a hundred miles in this situation, before he could reach a surgeon, or have any soothing application applied to his wound. In the midst of all this suffering, he had the additional mortification to find, on his reaching James-Town, an attempt to usurp his authority, and a plot to destroy his life. But his energies never failed him, and he defeated both, by his courage and promptitude.

At length, however, the pain of his wound depriving him sometimes of his reason, and no surgical skill in the Colony being sufficient to effect his cure, he resolved to go to England, and resigned his Presidency to Mr. Percy. The testimony paid to his virtues by those who were the companions of his misfortunes, is couched in this emphatic language—"What shall we say of him, but this:—that in all his proceedings made justice his first guide, and experience his second—ever hating baseness, sloth, pride, and indignity, more than any danger;—that never allowed more for himself than his soldiers with him; —that upon no danger would send them, where he would not lead them himself;—that would never see us want what he either had, or could by any means get us;—that would rather want than borrow, or starve than not pay;—that loved action more than words, and hated falsehood and covetousness worse than death."

The interesting heroine, Pocahontas, it appears, never came to James-Town after Smith's departure, but she was subsequently entrapped by treachery into the hands of an English captain, named Argal, and kept on board his ship as a hostage, to prevent the hostility of her father Powhatān. This was in 1611, and after a series of negotiations for her ransom, she had in the interim formed an attachment to a young Englishman, named John Rolfe, with whom, by consent of her father and brothers, as well as of the governor of the settlement at James-Town, Sir Thomas Dale, she was legally united in marriage, in April, 1613, according to the English law.

The remainder of her short history is as romantic as its commencement. When Sir Thomas Dale returned to England, the young Pocahontas accompanied her husband to his native land, and arrived at Plymouth in June 1616. Being a king's daughter, she was called The Lady Rebecca, was introduced at court by Lord and Lady Delaware, and treated with the greatest distinction. Captain Smith, whose life she had saved, having recovered from his wound, was still living, and the meeting of Pocahontas with her former friend was remarkable. She called him her Father; which Smith, under a notion that it might be thought arrogant in him to permit himself to be called by so endearing a title by a King's daughter, requested her not to do; and Pocahontas, not being able to comprehend the meaning of this scruple, was at first unhappy at what she interpreted as coldness. Her address to him, which is preserved, is full of the naïveté and frankness of her noble character.

> "You promised my father" said Pocahontas, "that what was yours should be his: and that you and he would be all as one. Being a stranger in our country, you called Powhatān 'Father' and I, for the same reason, will call you so. You were not afraid to come into my father's country, and strike fear into every body but myself; and are you here afraid to let me call you 'Father?' I tell you, then, I will call you 'Father,' and you shall call me 'Child' and so I will for ever be of your kindred and country. They always told us that you were dead, and I knew not otherwise till I came to Plymouth. But Powhatān commanded Tomocomo to seek you out, and know the truth, because your countrymen are much given to lying."[1]

In 1617, she was about to embark for her native country, but was taken ill at Gravesend, and there died, at the early age of twenty-two years. There is neither grave nor tablet, I believe, now remaining to mark the spot where her remains were deposited; but her blood nevertheless continues to flow in the veins of some existing American families, who are very proud of their descent. She left a son, then of course very young, named Thomas Rolfe, who was educated by his uncle in London, but afterwards came to America, where he acquired an ample fortune; he left an only daughter, who was married to Colonel Bolling, and left an only son; but the son had several daughters, and one of these marrying Colonel Randolph, gave birth to the celebrated Virginian senator, John Randolph of Roanoak, who, with all the other Randolphs of Virginia, was as proud of his ancestry, as any peer of England who could trace his descent from some Norman baron brought over in the train of William the Conqueror.

The pride of ancestry, from an Indian stock, is much stronger in the few Americans who have so descended, than it appears to be in any possessing unmixed European blood, as far as my opportunities have brought me acquainted with either. This is the more remarkable, when it is contrasted with the cruel treatment which the Indians have generally received from the American nation and people; and still more remarkable when we consider that there is nothing so repulsive to American feeling, as an intermarriage with persons having the least taint of colour from an African stock. The celebrated Dr. Hawkes, one of the leading Episcopal clergy men of New York, who would have shrunk with horror at the imputation of having any "coloured blood" of the *black* race mingled with his own, expressed his pride of ancestry, and descent from the *red* race, by boasting that some of the blood of Pocahontas flowed in his veins.[2]

1.   Drake's Book of the Indians, 8vo. b. iv. 18.
2.   See "America." First Series. Vol. i. p. 92.

Chapter LII

After Smith had quitted the Colony at James-Town, in 1609, a series of disasters occurred, which led to its ultimate abandonment; but Lord Delaware and his companions, who, though wrecked on the island of Bermuda, were not lost, having procured another ship, and added two others to their squadron, came, in 1610, with supplies of men, provisions, and implements; and meeting the fugitives at the mouth of the James River on their way out to sea, they arrested their progress, and restored the settlement to a habitable condition. But neither his administration, nor those of his successors, did much for the Colony until 1613, when the right of private property in lands being admitted, instead of the sole proprietorship of the incorporated Company in England, which had hitherto preceded it, a new stimulus to industry was given, and the Colony began to improve. The attention of the cultivators was first directed to what they deemed the most profitable and immediate return; and this was not provisions for subsistence, but tobacco for sale; for the use of this vile weed had so extended itself in Europe, and especially in England, that the demand for it was excessive; and to supply this demand, the whole of the surrounding lands, as well as the public squares, and even the public streets of James-Town, were planted with it in 1615: while, to obtain the supplies of provisions which they had neglected to raise for their own consumption, the planters made reprisals on the natives, and thus provoked their hostility; so that there was a constant succession of difficulties.

It was in 1619, that the first foundation of Virginian liberty was laid, by the introduction, under the administration of Sir John Yeardly, of a representative assembly, which was convened at James-Town, and was composed of the burgesses elected by the settlers, who met the governor and his council, in the same apartment, and there discussed together, in great harmony, the first acts of an American legislature, which were subsequently sent home, and received the sanction of the authorities there. It was further agreed by the respective parties, that no laws passed in the Colony should be in full force until ratified at home, and no orders or enactments made in England should have the force of law in the Colony till they were ratified by the assembly there. "Thus early" says Grahame, "was planted in America, that representative system, which forms the soundest political frame wherein the spirit of liberty was ever embodied, and at once the safest and most efficient organ by which its energies are exercised and developed. So strongly imbued were the minds of Englishmen in this age with those generous principles which were rapidly advancing to a first manhood in their native country, that wherever they settled themselves, the institutions of freedom took root and grew up along with them."

In the same year, however—so closely are good and evil blended in the mingled web of life—the fatal seeds were sown of that, which constitutes at once the greatest blot on the reputation, and the greatest hindrance to the safety and prosperity, of America: namely, Negro Slavery. A Dutch ship, from the coast of Guinea, arrived in James-river, with a cargo of negro slaves. These were sold to the English planters for the cultivation of their lands; and found to be so much more steady, obedient, industrious, and profitable, as labourers, than the idle and dissolute criminals, which had been sent out from the jails of England, as servants to the planters for limited terms, that the importation of slaves from Africa became a regular traffic. To England, therefore, belongs the disgrace of first originating the slave trade, by Sir John Hawkins, in Elizabeth's reign; and to Englishmen, the disgrace of first employing them in Virginia in the reign of James. But let it be added—for justice demands the addition—that to America belongs the disgrace of retaining the African race in bondage, after England has broken their chains throughout all her extensive dominions; and this, when it would have been so safe, so easy, so consistent, and so honourable, for the first signers of the Declaration of Independence, while freeing themselves from the tyranny of that other country, to have given freedom to the Africans in their own. It was thus they should have proved the sincerity with which they asserted their belief, that "all men were born free and equal" and that "to all belonged the inalienable right of life, liberty, and property" instead of "turning into a scene of bondage for others, that territory which had proved a seat of liberty and happiness to themselves".

In the year 1620, the difficulty seems first to have been publicly avowed, though perhaps long before felt, of attaching the men as permanent settlers to the colony, without an adequate supply of women, to furnish the comforts of domestic life; and to overcome this difficulty, "a hundred young women, of agreeable persons and respectable characters" were selected in England, and sent out, at the expense of the Company, as wives for the settlers. They were very speedily appropriated by the young men of the Colony, who paid for the privilege of choice considerable sums as purchase money, which went to replenish the treasury of the Company, from whence the cost of their outfit and passage had been defrayed. This speculation proved so advantageous to that body, in a pecuniary sense, that it was soon followed up by sending out sixty more, for whom larger prices were paid than for the first consignment; the amount paid on the average for the first 100 being 120 lbs. of tobacco, then valued at 3s. per lb.; and for the second supply of 60, the average price paid was 150 lbs. of tobacco, this being the legal currency of the Colony, and the standard of value by which all contracts, salaries, and prices were paid. This accession to the Colony was productive of the greatest advantage, as substituting the lawful and honourable enjoyments of marriage, and the holy and chaste feeling of connubial affection, for the lawless licentiousness, and dissolute and unbridled passion which preceded it; and Burk, the historian of Virginia, says, that such was the careful attention bestowed on the moral characters of those who were sent out to become the matrons of Virginia, that in the year 1632, two young women having been seduced on their passage from England, were sent back, by an order of the provisional council, as "unworthy to propagate the race of Virginians". Another excellent result followed this practice, of sending out from home those who were to become the mothers of the future colonists, which was the making some provision for the education of their offspring. For this purpose, a sum of money was collected by the bishops in their respective dioceses, by order of the King, for the education of the colonial children; and the Company aiding this benevolent project, began the foundation of the first Colonial college, which was not completed till the reign of William and Mary, by whose name it was called, and which it retains, all royal as it is, to this day. So also do Cape Henry, Cape Charles, James-river, James-Town, Williamsburgh, York River, Norfolk, and Richmond, all of which are of royal origin, but all of which are still retained as "The Old Dominion" has always cherished her British origin with more pride, and still clings to its recollection with greater fondness, than any other State of the Union to the present day.

Disputes between the King and the Colonists, on the subject of the trade in tobacco, its import duties, etc., soon arose, and in 1621, were at their height, but were happily adjusted by a compromise; until, in the following year, a new source of grievance and of danger was disclosed. The native Indians, after the alliance formed by the marriage of the young princess Pocahontas, with Rolfe, were anxious to promote more such unions between the English and their daughters. But the fairer daughters of the mother country had lessened the necessity, and abated the inclination, of the Englishmen, to seek wives among the red tribes of the forest. This was deemed an insult or disdain by the Indians, who treasured up the affront for resentment at the fitting time; and they ultimately formed a conspiracy to cut off all the English, by a general massacre of man, woman, and child.

Powhatān, the father of Pocahontas, and their former friend, was no more; and his place and power, were held by Opekankanough. The plot being matured, on the 22nd of March, 1622, at "mid-day, the period they had fixed for this execrable deed, the Indians, raising a universal yell, rushed at once on the English, in all their scattered settlements, and butchered men, women, and children, with indiscriminating fury, and every aggravation of brutal outrage and enormous cruelty. In one hour 347 persons were cut off, without knowing almost by whose hands they fell". Six of the members of council, and several of the wealthiest and most respectable of the inhabitants were among the slain: at some of the settlements, the whole of their population had been exterminated; at others, a remnant had escaped the general destruction, by the efforts of despair; and the survivors were impoverished, terrified, and confounded, by a stroke that at once bereaved them of friends and fortune, and showed that they were surrounded by legions of foes, whose enmity was equally furious and unaccountable, and whose, treachery and ferocity seemed to proclaim them a race of fiends rather than men.

After this fearful catastrophe, the dissensions between the members of the Company at home, and their quarrels with the King, led him at length to take the bold step of dissolving the Company itself, by abrogating its charter; and thus, in 1624, the possession of the Colony, and the direction of its government, was assumed by the crown. James soon after died, but his son, Charles the First, adopted all his father's views with respect to Virginia, and his arbitrary principles were acted upon to the full extent by the Governor, Sir John Harvey, who, from 1629 to 1635, exercised a continued series of insults, exactions, and oppressions on the colonists, till "he inflamed the wise with madness, and drove the patient to despair" when at length, he was suspended by the Colonial assembly, and sent home a prisoner to England, accompanied by deputies from their body to represent their grievances, and appealing to the justice of the King for redress. But this arbitrary monarch reinstated the suspended governor with additional powers, and these powers he soon used on his return, to retaliate on those who had the courage to oppose him.

In 1639, by the influence of the British parliament, to whom the Virginians had now appealed, Harvey was recalled; and the upright and excellent Sir William Berkeley appointed in his stead, with power to restore to the colonists all the privileges they had enjoyed before the dissolution of the Company by the crown; so that Charles the First was compelled to become the restorer of those Virginian liberties which he had been the first to violate. So grateful were the

Virginians for this, that in all the contests between the King and the parliament at home, they espoused the royal cause, declaring, by an enactment, issued in the fervour of their loyalty, "that they were born under a monarchy, and would never degenerate from the condition of their births, by being subject to any other government" a resolution to which their posterity have not deemed it wise to adhere. Even after Charles was beheaded, and his son driven out of the kingdom, they conducted the Colonial government under a commission from the exiled royal family, dispatched to Sir William Berkeley from Breda, on the continent; and would not acknowledge the authority of the republic, or commonwealth.

The long parliament, however, sent a squadron under Sir George Ayscue, to the Chesapeake, and the Virginians were obliged to yield, but not without stipulating for the retention of their own provisional assembly, and the privilege of perfect freedom of trade.

It was at this period, 1652, that the Navigation Laws were introduced, forbidding the importation of any productions of Asia, Africa, or America, in any but English vessels, navigated by English officers and crews; though the same principle was recognised as early as 1381, when an act of Richard the Second, enacted "that to increase the navy of England, no goods or merchandises shall be either exported or imported but only in ships belonging to the king's subjects". Yet, as this was in some degree an infringement on the stipulated free trade of the Virginians, they had the monopoly of the growth of tobacco confirmed to them, by its cultivation being prohibited in Ireland, where large quantities had heretofore been grown. About this period Virginia became the place of refuge for immense numbers of destitute cavaliers, who, following the fortunes of their sovereign, had been forced into poverty and exile; and though this brought a large infusion of chivalrous sentiment, high breeding, and polished manners into the Colony—the traces of which are visible in the well known spirit, frankness, and generosity of the old Virginia families at the present day—yet little or no industry, or useful and practical knowledge, accompanied their train, while, on the other hand, dissolute manners and intrigues were very general.

Cromwell's measures towards the Colony appear, from all authorities, to have been far more just and liberal than those of his predecessors: but with the previous attachments and pledges of the old settlers, and the opinions and feelings brought into the Colony by the new ones, it was natural that they should be averse to his usurped authority, and there was one feature of his administration which was peculiarly offensive to them—

"The Puritan colonists of New England" says Graham, "had always been the objects of suspicion and dislike to the great bulk of the inhabitants of Virginia: and the manifest partiality which Cromwell entertained for them, now increased the aversion with which they had been heretofore regarded. New England was generally considered by the Cavaliers, as the centre and focus of Puritan sentiment and republican principle, and, actuated partly by religious and partly by political feelings, the Virginian Cavaliers entertained a violent antipathy against all the doctrines, sentiments, and practices that were reckoned peculiar to the Puritans, and rejected all communication of the knowledge that flourished in New England, from hatred of the authority under whose shelter it grew, and of the principles to whose support it seemed to administer."

The traces of this feeling are still strong among the descendants of these Cavaliers; for in no State of the Union is the dislike to the Puritanical sentiments and cold and cautious manners of the people of the North, stronger than it is in Virginia; where, I believe, there are fewer persons from New England settled, than there are in any State besides. The hereditary indifference to, and disregard of popular education for the mass of the community, which characterised the best men of those times, seems also to have travelled down, through Virginian veins, to the present day. Sir William Berkeley, one of the most justly popular of their governors, for his general integrity and highly honourable character, says, according to Chalmers, in a letter written by him in the State of Virginia, soon after the Restoration—"I thank God there are no free schools nor printing, and I hope we shall not have them these hundred years; for learning has brought heresy, and disobedience, and sects into the world; and printing has divulged them, and libels against the best government—God keep us from both."

In one respect Sir William's prayer seems to have been realised; for to this day, no system of Common Schools, such as exist in New England and many of the Western States, exists in Virginia; though there are some free schools for the education of indigent children spread over the State. But in this respect it is avowedly inferior to all the older States of the Union, and to many even of the new ones; and a Virginian writer, Martin, in speaking of the capital of his own State, says, "Whilst the Northern cities can boast their literary and scientific societies, the capital of 'The Ancient Dominion' scarcely contains one which deserves the name". As to printing, and libels against the government, these have indeed increased to such a degree, that if Sir William Berkeley could be raised from the dead, and have a pile of the Virginian papers for a single week placed before him, his astonishment would know no bounds.

Under the influence of the sentiments by which Virginia was actuated at the period before spoken of (1653) and the continued increase of dissatisfaction with the doctrines and practices of the Puritans and republicans in New England as well as in Old, they availed themselves of the opportunity presented by the death of the Governor Matthews, before any steps were taken at home to name his successor, to raise the standard of revolt against Cromwell's power, and to proclaim Charles the Second as their lawful King. The more timid apprehended from this a long and disastrous conflict with the mother country, and ultimate subjugation to her superior power; but in the midst of these fears, intelligence arrived of Cromwell's death, and soon after of Charles's Restoration; "which" says the historian, "enabled the Virginians safely to exult in the singularity which they long and proudly commemorated, that they had been the last of the British subjects who had renounced, and the first who had resumed their allegiance to the crown".

Sir William Berkeley, who had been summoned by the colonists to take the reins of government from the moment they had raised the royal standard, received, after the restoration of Charles, a commission in 1660, confirming him in his power; and some good and some bad laws characterised his administration. Among the first, was the restoration of the trial by jury; among the last, was a law against the importation or harbouring of Quakers, under a penalty of 5,000 lbs. of tobacco! The Parliament of England, however, now chiefly legislated for the Colonies generally; and some of its measures were deemed so injurious to their interest by the Virginians, particularly some of the new provisions of the Navigation Laws, that they first remonstrated, and finding that useless, plotted a revolt; and though this was checked before it could be expected, in 1663, yet some years afterwards, in 1671, the popular discontent had reached its height; and in 1675 two other plots of insurrection were discovered and crushed in the bud.

In the following year, however, the Colony broke out into open rebellion, under a bold and adventurous leader, named Bacon, who, at the head of the insurgents, attacked James-Town and reduced it to ashes, permitting his followers to pillage the houses and plantations of the loyalists, and to carry off their persons as hostages; in short, the whole Colony was involved in all the horrors of a civil war.

As soon as intelligence of this reached England, the King sent out an armament under Sir John Berry, declared Bacon a traitor, tendering free pardon to all who should forsake him, and freedom to all slaves who should assist in suppressing the revolt. Bacon was prepared to resist to the death, and his followers increased rather than diminished, as his popularity and influence were unbounded. Before the forces arrived, however Bacon was seized with sickness, and died; and, at the loss of their leader, the rebel army grew dispirited, and soon became disbanded and dispersed, to the great joy of the loyalists.

In 1677 when the expected succours arrived, the rebellion was entirely suppressed; and Colonel Jeffreys, the new governor, succeeded to Sir William Berkeley, who was now grown old, having served through an administration of nearly forty years, soon after which he died, greatly and deservedly respected. Jeffrey's short career was marked by much of injustice and disaster, and that of his successor. Lord Culpepper, was arbitrary and vexatious in the extreme; so that after the short space of five years, another insurrection occurred, in 1682. The details of this period are full of the grossest outrages and oppressions practised by the Colonial governors, and sanctioned by the Monarch; and when, in 1683, Lord Effingham was appointed to govern the Colony, "The King expressly commanded him to suffer no person within the Colony to make use of a printing press, on any occasion or pretence whatsoever!"

At length, Charles the Second was succeeded by the Second James, in 1685, and the colonists then hoped the change would bring them some relief; but instead of this, their burdens were augmented: while the conduct of Lord Effingham was worse than that of any of his predecessors. Graham, on the authority of Beverley, Oldmixon, and Chalmers, says—"Lord Effingham, like his predecessor, engrafted the baseness of a sordid disposition on the severity of an arbitrary and tyrannical administration. He refused to convoke the Provincial Assembly; he instituted a Court of Chancery, in which he himself presided as judge; and besides multiplying and enhancing the fees attached to his own peculiar functions, he condescended to share with clerks the meaner perquisites of subordinate offices. For some time he contrived to stifle the remonstrances which his extortions produced, by the infliction of arbitrary imprisonment and other tyrannical severities; but at length, the public displeasure became so general and uncontrollable, that he found it impossible to prevent the complaints of the Colony from being carried to England; for which country, he, in consequence, resolved to embark himself, in order to be present at his own arraignment". But before he reached home, the Revolution of 1688 had hurled the greater tyrant of the mother country from the throne; so that the lesser tyrants found their safety in the general absorption of the public mind by changes nearer at hand. But William the Third, instead of dismissing Lord Effingham, continued him in the commission as Governor, though he never dared to return to the Colony, but enjoyed the salary of his office at home, while a deputy performed his duties abroad; and when his death created a vacancy, it was filled by the royal appointment of another Colonial tyrant, Sir Edmund Andros, previously expelled by the indignant citizens of Massachusetts for his misdeeds there. Such have been the royal patrons, who took our early Colonies under their protection!

At this period, 1692, the whole population of Virginia did not exceed 50,000, of whom it was thought that fully one half consisted of negro slaves. The only domestic tribute, or impost, was a poll tax, paid by rich and poor alike; but this ensured the political right of suffrage to all who paid it, and therefore, placed both rich and poor on the footing of the most perfect political equality. The divisions of the settled part of the country embraced about 50 parishes, with 200,000 acres of appropriated land; and in each parish was a house and glebe for the minister, whose stipend was fixed by law at 16,000 pounds weight of tobacco, the presentations to the livings being made by the Governor, and the Bishop of London being the diocesan of the colony.

Some of the laws passed at this period were remarkable. Penal enactments were made against travelling on Sundays, against profane swearing, and getting drunk. Persons riotously assembling to the number of more than eight, for the purpose of destroying tobacco, were held to be guilty of treason! Every person, not being a servant or slave, if convicted of adultery, was fined 1,000 pounds of tobacco; and if convicted of fornication, had to pay 500 pounds of the same commodity; this being, in short, the legal currency of the country in lieu of money. Women convicted of slander were, by law, to be ducked in water, unless their husbands chose to save them from this punishment by the payment of a fine. There were then no inns in the country, but travellers were entertained at private houses; the owners of these sometimes charging so exorbitantly for their hospitality, that a law was passed, declaring that unless the entertainer entered beforehand into a contract as to the rate at which he intended to charge his guest, it should be taken for granted that he intended to entertain him from pure hospitality, and without fee or reward!

If a slave were convicted of felony, and executed, his marketable value was paid to his owner out of the public treasury; but the death of a slave from excessive punishment, at the hand of his master, or by his order, was not accounted felony; as it could not be presumed, in the eye of the law, that any man really intended to destroy so valuable an article of his own property! If any person, having Christian white servants indentured for a given period, married an infidel, or a negro, or a mulatto, or an Indian, all such indentured servants became immediately free; and any free white person so marrying, as well as the minister celebrating the marriage, was punished with fine and imprisonment. Indians coming into the province were liable to be made slaves, and this was countenanced and upheld by the provisional statute law of the Colony.

At this period, there was but little attention paid to literature in Virginia. In this respect New England took the lead of all the States south of her, for while in Boston, about the year 1700, there were five printing offices, and many bookstores, there was only one of the latter in New York, and not one in either Virginia, Maryland, or Carolina. The cheapness and abundance of land ensured to every one who would use only a moderate share of industry, an ample competence; and so general was this condition, even among the humblest settlers, that it is stated by Beverley, one of the historians of the country about this time, that he had known a sum of 5*l.* left by a benevolent testator to the poor of the parish in which he lived, remain for nine years in the hands of the executors, before any poor person really in want of money could be found; and at last it was given to one old woman, whose only claim to it was, that she had not quite so comfortable a competency as her neighbours!

In 1704, the government of Virginia was conferred by Queen Anne on the Earl of Orkney, who enjoyed all its emoluments for thirty-six years, without ever once leaving England even to see the country he was paid for governing; so that he received in the whole 42,000*l.* of salary alone, besides patronage and emoluments, drawn from the pockets of a people whom he never even condescended to visit. Such acts as these might well prepare the colonists for dissatisfaction with the mother country but during this period, events were happening in the Colony itself, calculated to hasten the period when its resources and its strength should enable it to sustain the great struggle by which it was to achieve its own independence. Among these events was the exploration of the rich country beyond the Alleghanny or Apalachian mountains, which was undertaken in 1714, and crowned with complete success, opening to the view of the colonists, for the first time, immense tracts of beautiful and fertile lands, to be the future seat of wealth and population.

From this period onward, a general tranquillity and steadily increasing prosperity marked the history of Virginia. In 1722, the population was nearly double that of 1700; it having advanced, from 50,000 at the former period, to upwards of 100,000 at the latter; though these were still a mere handful, compared to the vast expanse of territory within this single State. At Williamsburgh, which was then the capital, there existed the College of William and Mary, the Statehouse, and the Capitol. There was also a theatre, the first ever erected in the Colonies. Printing was first introduced here in 1729; and the first newspaper ever published in Virginia was issued at Williamsburgh, in 1736. The produce of tobacco was at this time considerable; not less than 100,000 hogsheads being shipped annually from Maryland and Virginia, valued at 8 shillings sterling per hogshead, which gave employment to about 200 ships, and produced a gain to the mother country from this trade alone of about half a million sterling. In addition to this staple article, however, iron ore and copper ore, beeswax, hemp, and raw silk, were exported from Virginia to England, the last article of which seems likely to be revived as a commodity of trade.

The war between Great Britain and France, which broke out in 1744, involved the Colonies in the contest; and in 1751, Washington, then a youth of nineteen years of age, appears for the first time on the public stage, he having been sent as a commissioner from the governor of his native State, Virginia, to the commander of a French fort in the Ohio. The answer of the French officer being evasive, an expedition was soon after despatched to that quarter, the command of which devolved on Washington, after the death of its leader, Colonel Fry. He was at first successful in an affair with a detachment under Jumonville, who was killed; but on following this up by an attack on Fort Duquesne, the place which the expedition was sent to reduce, he found the reinforcements of the French troops such as to oblige him to retreat. After sustaining the fire of the enemy for a whole day, the French demanded a parley; and Washington surrendered on honourable terms, being allowed to pass with his troops and baggage back to the settled parts of the State from whence he had come. Washington, after this, accompanied the expedition of General Bradock as a volunteer against the French, on the Ohio, in 1755, and was a witness of his defeat; but in 1759, he was entrusted with the command of the scattered and re-collected troops of Grant, who had failed as signally as Bradock in the same quarter. At the head of these troops he took the fort which had defied all the attacks of his predecessors, and called it Pittsburgh, in honour of England's then foreign minister, the Earl of Chatham; for Washington was then fighting under the British flag.

At the termination of this war by the treaty of Fontainbleau, in 1762, the delicate and difficult question arose, of how and in what proportion the colonies of North America should be made to bear their share of its expense, as they had enjoyed the benefit of its protection; and as the Virginians had, so early as 1624, asserted "that she only had the undoubted right to lay taxes and impositions, and none other" and repeated the same doctrine, in still stronger language in 1676, it was not likely that she would now acquiesce in the propositions made by England in 1764, to raise a revenue on stamps in America, to be paid into the King's exchequer in England, as their contribution towards the expenses of the war. The proposition was resisted by memorial, petition, remonstrance, and appeal; and when all these had failed to move the British government, and the act was really passed in 1765, it excited universal indignation, which was accompanied by the cessation of all business, by persons putting on public mourning, by the courts refusing to sanction the act in any of their sittings, and by all classes of people refusing to use the stamps.

From this moment the Revolution might be said to be begun; and its first step in Virginia, was the passing, by the Legislature of that Colony, the following declaratory resolution, proposed by the celebrated orator, Patrick Henry:—

Resolved, that the General Assembly of this Colony, together with his Majesty, or substitute, have, in their representative capacity, the only exclusive right and power to lay taxes and impositions upon the inhabitants of this Colony; and that every attempt to vest such power in any person or persons whatsoever, other than the General Assembly aforesaid, is illegal, unconstitutional, and unjust, and has a manifest tendency to destroy British as well as American freedom.

The Governor of Virginia, Lord Botetourt, as representing his Majesty, no sooner heard of the passing of this resolution by the General Assembly, than he dissolved it forthwith; but the constituencies, in the election of the succeeding House, sent up only those who would sustain the resolutions, and rejected all who would not. The example of Virginia fixed the other Colonies, who passed similar resolutions, and proposed a General Congress, which met at New York, where deputies from nine of the Colonies drafted the first Declaration of Rights in 1766.

In 1774, when the draft of the Boston-port Bill, for the exclusion of the duty-charged tea, sent from England, reached Virginia, the new Governor, Lord Dunmore, dissolved the Assembly; but the members met on the following day in the Raleigh Tavern (still existing) at Williamsburgh, and drew up an able and manly paper, in which they recommended cessation of trade with the East India Company, from whom this obnoxious tea was sent out, taxed by the mother country. They also advised the assembling of deputies in a Congress from all the Colonies, declaring their opinion that an attack upon the liberties of one should be equally resisted by all. Such a General Congress was accordingly assembled in Philadelphia on the 4th of September, in the same year.

The first overt act of resistance by arms, that marked the outbreak of the Revolution in Virginia, was on the 19th of April, 1775; when the Governor, Lord Dunmore, removed the gunpowder from the magazine at Williamsburgh, on board his Majesty's ship Magdalene, then lying in the Chesapeake, which was done under cover of the night. This act becoming known, excited the indignation of the citizens, who demanded its instant restitution; but an evasive answer was given to the demand. Patrick Henry then marched with a company of volunteers, from Hanover county, and forced the King's treasurer to make compensation for the powder thus removed. Meanwhile, the Governor, feeling himself no longer safe on shore, embarked on board the Montague, which threatened to open her guns on York-Town, if any attempt were made at resistance. The Assembly invited the Governor to return on shore, to transact the necessary business of the Legislature, and sign many bills waiting this act to give them validity. This he refused to do, unless the Assembly would meet him under the guns of the ship of war, which, of course, they declined. The Governor was, therefore, declared to have abdicated his power; and the Assembly, appointing the president of the council to act in his place, joined the General Association of the original Thirteen Colonies, in their hostility to British power, till they achieved their independence.

From this period, the progress of Virginia has been steadily onward, but not with such rapidity as the more northern States. If extent of area, fertility of soil, beauty of scenery, and salubrity of climate, could have attracted population in a degree proportioned to its superiority in all these features, over all the other States, then ought Virginia to have been by this time, the most thickly peopled State in the Union; for in all these enumerated qualities she excels every other with which she can be compared. And if the production of great men could have carried her forward in a more rapid career of improvement than other States not so prolific in this respect, then ought she also to stand at the head of all the States in the Union; for none other can present such a galaxy of talent and greatness, as Virginia has produced, among which, the names of Washington, Jefferson, Henry, Lee, Monroe, Marshall, Madison, Randolph, and Clay, form but a small portion, though these are enough to stamp the State with the highest character for the production of statesmen, warriors, lawyers, and orators. But, despite these unquestionable advantages of superior resources and superior men, Virginia has not advanced with the same rapidity as other States of far inferior promise; and in looking about for the causes of this, there appear to be only the two that so long ago as 1786 struck Mr. Jefferson as the two great drawbacks to Virginian prosperity, namely the excessive cultivation of tobacco, which exhausts the soil, and is ruinous to the interests and comforts of those engaged in its culture; and the system of Slavery, which produces the smallest amount of unskilful labour, in return for the largest outlay of capital in its purchase and subsistence. Were these two causes removed, Virginia would soon overtake all her competitors in the race; but while they continue, her progress, must be comparatively slow. Still, under these two great disadvantages, she presents the aspect of a magnificent country with immense resources, as the following description of her existing condition will show.

Chapter LIII

Virginia, or "The Old Dominion" as its inhabitants still delight to call it, is not only the oldest but the largest State in the Union. Its dimensions are variously stated, but the most accurate, as I have tested it by careful examination, is that of Mitchell, an authority, in all that relates to the geography of this country, quite equal to that of Arrowsmith for the geography of Europe; his measurement of its area, makes its extent from North to South about 220 miles, and from East to West about 370 miles, its whole surface, therefore, covering about 64,000 square miles, or 40,960,000 acres. Hinton, a very good authority in most cases, is singularly inaccurate in respect to the size of Virginia, which he makes to be 430 by 150 miles, instead of 370 by 220, and on this he deduces its area to be 700,000 square miles which must be an error of the pen or the press. Even by the smaller measurement of Mitchell, it will be found that this single State of Virginia is larger than all England, Scotland, and Wales, or the whole Island of Britain, the entire area of which is estimated at 62,236 square miles, while that of Virginia, in its present limits, is 64,000 square miles. When Mr. Jefferson wrote his "Notes on Virginia" in 1786, the adjoining States of Kentucky and Ohio formed part of Virginia; its area was then 121,525 square miles, or one third larger than Great Britain and Ireland, the united area of which was estimated at 88,357 square miles. Such is the colossal extent of this great Union, made up of twenty-six States and three Territories, each large enough, with very few exceptions, to form a splendid kingdom in itself.

The literary institutions of Virginia comprehend the most ancient College of William and Mary at Williamsburgh, founded in 1693; Hampden and Sydney College in Prince Edward county, incorporated in 1783; Washington College at Lexington established in 1796; and the University of Virginia, founded by Jefferson at Charlottesville in 1819. A Literary Fund, supported by the State Legislature, for the support of academies and schools, gives some assistance to the cause of Education, its annual expenditure being, on the average, 60,000 dollars, but no general and comprehensive system of Common Schools exists in Virginia, on the plan of Massachusetts, New York, and the Northern States generally; though the soundness of the principle which makes the State the guardian and supporter of public education, being now admitted by the formation of this Literary Fund, its extension will naturally follow. The Fund was first established by the Legislature of Virginia in 1809, by devoting the proceeds of all escheats, forfeitures, and fines, to the encouragement of learning. In 1816, this was augmented by the appropriation of the amount due from the general Government of the United States to the State of Virginia, on account of advances made by this State in support of the last war with Great Britain. From these united sources, the Fund is now upwards of 1,500,000 dollars, its revenue being 78,000 dollars annually. Of this, 45,000 dollars are expended every year in the support of primary schools in the various counties of the State, for the education of white children of indigent parents. The number of such schools, in 100 counties and towns were, by the last report, 2,872; the whole number of children receiving education, on this system, upwards of 50,000 and the average expense of education for each child, was about two dollars and fifty cents, or ten shillings and sixpence only per annum, including cost of books, teachers, and all contingent expenses!

The manufactures of Virginia have been lately on the increase, those of cotton alone employing a capital of 5,000,000 dollars. The commerce exceeds 5,000,000 dollars in annual exports of native products, in addition to articles of foreign trade; but the imports are almost all obtained through New York, though great efforts are making to bring back, if possible, the import trade to Norfolk, as the most appropriate port of entry for the State.

The Legislature of Virginia is composed of a House of Delegates, consisting of 134 members, chosen annually by the people; a Senate, composed of 32 members, chosen, for four years, by the counties, one fourth being renewed every year; and a Governor, chosen for three years, and elected by the joint vote of the two Houses, or General Assembly; and in all cases the voting is open, or *viva voce*, and not by secret ballot.

The Executive is composed of the Governor, who has a salary of 3,000 dollars per annum; a Lieutenant-Governor, and two other Counsellors of State, at 1,000 dollars a year each; a Treasurer, two Auditors, a Registrar of the Land Office, an Attorney-General, and several Secretaries, with salaries varying from 2,000 to 1,000 dollars each.

The Judiciary consists of a Court of Appeal, formed of five Judges, at salaries of 2,500 dollars each; and a General Court, of twenty-one Judges, one for each of the Circuits of the State, at salaries of 1,500 dollars each. Besides these, there are County Courts held for criminal as well as civil offences, by Justices of the Peace; and on the whole, justice is cheaply, speedily, and impartially administered.

The number of paupers in Virginia is probably greater than in any other State in the Union; being in the last year upwards of 2,500; and involving an annual expense of 100,000 dollars for their support. The causes which most powerfully contribute to this state of things appear to be—First, the system of Slavery, which makes menial labour degrading, and therefore disagreeable to the whites, and indisposes them to that degree of manual exertion and industry which they would use where slave labour was unknown. Secondly, the excessive use of tobacco, which, in either of its forms of chewing or smoking, disposes men to indolence, and leads to an immense loss of time; but besides this, it too frequently, among the poor especially, brings habits of drinking in its train, and thus doubly disqualifies the subject of it from being either industrious or economical. For the support of such paupers, a tax or poor rate is raised by the overseers of the poor, and is thus appropriated:—In the greater number of the counties, the poor are boarded out in private families, frequently among their relatives, at a stipulated rate per annum; or the pauper sometimes receives the annual sum agreed on, which varies from 50 to 100 dollars for a single person, and he then maintains himself. In a few of the counties, however, but not more than a fourth of the whole number, a poorhouse is erected, by consent of the County Court. To this is attached a farm, on which, all paupers who receive relief are obliged to work, as well as to live; and their cost of maintenance by this mode is only from 30 to 40 dollars each per annum. This system, which is of comparatively recent introduction, has wrought the same reform here as the New Poor Law in England. Idle vagabonds, who forced themselves on the pauper fund by the former system, and lived in laziness upon their annual stipend, shrink from this test of working on the farm, and earning their bread before they eat it. Counties, which under the former system, had from 75 to 100 paupers each, at a cost of from 50 to 100 dollars per head, have now only from 20 to 30, at a cost of 30 to 40 dollars each; and those who are really in want have more comfortable homes in these houses than they could otherwise procure; while the lazy are made industrious by the change.

On the whole, therefore, Virginia, or "The Old Dominion", though having two powerful drawbacks to her advancing career of prosperity, in the cultivation of tobacco and the existence of Slavery, is nevertheless a magnificent State; larger in area than any other in the Union, and more diversified and beautiful in its scenery; with one of the noblest bays, and one of the finest harbours in the world, as well as some of the most beautiful rivers on the globe; as the Chesapeake, and its tributary streams of the Susquehannah, Shenandoah, Patapsco, Potomac, Rappahannock, the James, York, and Elizabeth rivers on the coast—with the Mononghahela, the Great Kenhàwa, the Cumberland, and the Ohio in the interior—sufficiently prove.

CHAPTER LIV

We left Norfolk at six A.M. on the morning of Wednesday the 11th of September, in the steamer Patrick Henry, for Richmond, intending to visit the New White Sulphur Springs, in Faquier county, east of the Blue Ridge, by way of Fredericksburg, and to go from thence to Alexandria, for the purpose of visiting the mansion and tomb of General Washington at Mount Vernon, as it would have been painful to us to quit Virginia without paying our humble homage at the shrine of one of the most illustrious of her sons.

On reaching the landing place for Petersburg, on the southern banks of the river, where some passengers were put on shore, we found lying there and at the spot called City Point, just above it, twelve large ships loading with tobacco and cotton for Europe. Among them were three fine vessels of from 500 to 600 tons, belonging to Petersburg, the others were from Boston and New York. The navigation for large vessels ends here; as above this, the river grows narrower and shallower all the way to Richmond, a distance of thirty-five miles, though the water continues to be deep enough for schooners, sloops, and steamboats. The approach to Richmond in ascending the river is very fine, the rising city on its many hills, and the prominent position of the, Capitol giving it a most imposing appearance. We reached the wharf about five o'clock, having been eleven hours performing a distance of 130 miles, or about twelve miles an hour all the way, against the current, and including all stoppages, making it therefore equal to about fifteen miles an hour without these hindrances.

Having slept at the Powhatān House, we left Richmond on the following morning (September 12) at eight o'clock, by the railroad cars for Fredericksburg. The morning was as bright and beautiful as on the preceding day, and the thermometer about 65°. Richmond itself seemed to us even more picturesque than on our first visit; but the country along which the railroad lay, between it and Petersburg, was tame and uninteresting; and the few patches cultivated

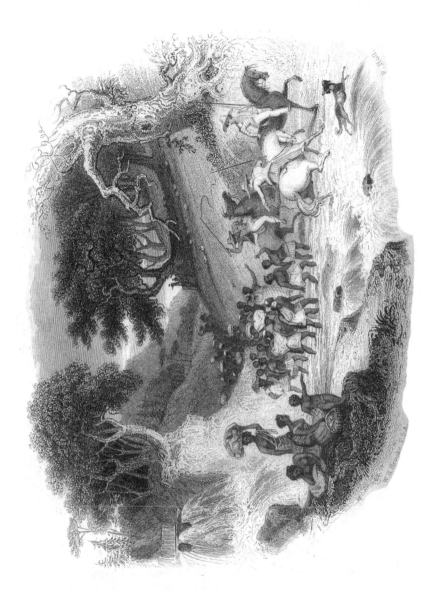

Gang of slaves journeying to be sold in a Southern market

with Indian corn, had been all destroyed by the recent violent storms. We did not reach Fredericksburg till four o'clock, having been therefore eight hours in going seventy-five miles, the fare being three dollars each. We found good accommodations for the night at the Farmers Hotel; and enjoyed the evening in an agreeable walk, through and around the town.

Fredericksburg is a regularly planned and well built town, with straight and wide streets, substantial brick houses, and all the appearances of rising prosperity. It contains a population of 4,000 persons, of whom it is thought not more than 1,000 are people of colour, the proportion of these to the whites continually diminishing as you travel northward. It contains a good Court House, and four Churches, Episcopalian, Methodist, Presbyterian, and Baptist. It lies in the county of Spotsylvania, and near the banks of the Rappahannock river. Its stores are large, and well supplied. In the neighbourhood of the town are several cotton factories for spinning and weaving, worked chiefly by white labourers, and increasing every year in the extent of their operations, which continually draws a largely increasing population to settle around them.

The early hours at which the stages leave, and the constant habit of their setting out *before* the time appointed, obliged us to be up at four; although we did not actually leave till five o'clock. The weather was now so excessively cold, as to require all the cloaks we could wrap around us, and to have the curtains and windows of the coach closed at the same time; which, as we had a slow ride of fourteen miles, at the rate of three and a half miles the hour, before breakfast, was sufficiently disagreeable, especially after the excessively hot weather we had experienced within the last two weeks only, at Richmond, Petersburg, and Norfolk.

Two miles beyond Fredericksburg, we passed through the village of the cotton factories, which, at that early hour, was crowded with wagons, of which there could not be less than a hundred in the streets. Beyond this, we saw the corn fields in the least interesting aspect which they present, with all the leaves of the corn pulled off, and piled up in heaps for fodder, the cornstalk and the naked heads of corn alone remaining. In this state they continue for a month, the grain ripening all the while, till, in the early part of October, they are gathered in and housed. In some of the fields we saw tobacco and buckwheat growing, the latter in full flower. The country was generally level; but the sight of the Blue Ridge in the northwest, gave a fine background to the picture.

It was in a valley near this, that we met a gang of slaves, including men, women, and children, the men chained together in pairs, and the women carrying the children and bundles, in their march to the South. The gang was under several white drivers, who rode near them on horseback, with large whips, while the slaves marched on foot beside them; and there was one driver behind, to bring up the rear. It did not appear that the slaves had committed any offence. They were chained together for precaution rather than for punishment; because, when accompanied only by one or two white men—and the economy of traffic would, of course, confine the expense of their escort within as narrow bounds as possible—they might be tempted to rise against them in any solitary part of the road, or, at the least, to escape from them if they could; both of which, this chaining them together renders impossible. That they do escape, not when thus chained, but when released from their fetters, every newspaper in the Southern States bears testimony, in the rewards offered for runaway negroes.

As we passed through Richmond, indeed, we learnt that three of the best waiters at one of the hotels there had gone off; and 600 dollars reward was publicly offered for their apprehension. These men belonged to different owners, who had no employment for them in their own houses, or on their own estates, and therefore let them out on hire, at high wages, to the proprietor of the hotel. As not more than half the wages earned by these men was paid to themselves, the other half going to their owners as profit, nothing was more natural than that they should desire to become free, as in such case they would receive the whole of their wages instead of a portion only. Yet, with the most natural of all motives to seek an escape to the free States of the North, where, whatever they may be able to earn, they are permitted fully to enjoy, without abatement or deduction, the Southern slaveholders affect to be very indignant at their absconding, and persist in it that the slaves are better treated than the free negroes, and always repent their running away! It is rare, indeed, however, that any of them evince this repentance by desiring to be taken back again, notwithstanding the stories to this affect, that are every now and then repeated by the Southern papers. Nor is there one slaveholder out of a thousand who would be willing to place the whole of his slaves upon the footing of giving freedom to those who desired it, and keeping only those in his possession who preferred his service to being free. Instances of individual kindness, to favourite slaves and personal attendants, are no doubt sufficiently numerous, to warrant the belief that some of these would prefer remaining the property of their masters, with all the certainty of protection and comfortable subsistence which they enjoy, to the risk of being in want, if set free to rely upon their own resources only. Even to these, however, the option is rarely offered, of choosing for themselves; and with respect to the mass of the slaves in the South, it is never placed within their reach; so that the constantly repeated assertion of the apologists of slavery, that "the slaves would not accept their freedom even if it were tendered to them, and would be worse off if they did" is never put to the test, by an actual tender of their liberty, because they know too well, that it would be cheerfully accepted.

CHAPTER LV

We reached the Faquier White Sulphur Springs at four o'clock, having been eleven hours in coming a distance of thirty five miles, and the fare being four dollars each, so that the travelling was both slow and dear. We found here a very small number of visitors remaining, though about a fortnight since there were upwards of 600 guests at the establishment. But the suddenness with which the cold weather had set in, had dispersed them all to their homes, so that there were not more than twenty remaining; and most of these were detained for conveyances, the only single stage between this and Washington being engaged for three days ahead. Among the small party left, was the widow and five children, three daughters and two sons, of the celebrated Mexican chief, Yturbide, who, about fifteen years ago, had usurped the government of Mexico, and had caused himself to be proclaimed emperor; but was soon afterwards shot, in the presence of his wife, who was at that moment near him. The widowed lady had great dignity and sorrow mingled in her countenance, and her whole demeanour was becomingly composed. The daughters were between seventeen and twenty one; and the younger son, who was born after the father's death, about fourteen. These were among the gayest of the gay; they spoke Spanish and English equally well, having resided ever since their expatriation in Philadelphia and Washington, on a pension of 10,000 dollars a year allowed to the widow, from the Mexican government, but, like all the pecuniary engagements of that distracted and embarrassed country, very irregularly paid.

We had to remain at the Springs for a few days, until a conveyance could be ensured for our proceeding; and that which made it dull to others, namely, the absence of the crowd, made it peculiarly charming and acceptable to us, as we enjoyed our garden walks, with the waters and the warm baths, in all that uninterrupted quiet, which is the rarest luxury to be procured in America.

We left the Faquier Springs on the afternoon of the 15th of September, at three o'clock, having engaged an extra stage to take us to Alexandria, and paying thirty dollars for the journey of fifty miles. In this, as in many other instances throughout the South, we found that we had been deceived and imposed upon by the false representations of the stage office keepers, as to matters of fact; indeed, we heard afterwards that they boasted of their skill and tact in having taken us in, by persuading us to believe that which was not true, and imposing on us accordingly. The laxity of morals in all dealings for money, is certainly very great in every part of the world, but it seems greater here than in any other nation in which I have travelled; and it is remarkable that here, as everywhere else, it seems to be greater among dealers in horses and carriages for public conveyance, than among any other class; at least it has fallen to our lot to discover more instances of cunning, deceit, and fraud, among the people of this class, than of any other; though I have never yet heard a satisfactory reason given for dealers in horses and suppliers of carriages being more dishonest than dealers in any other requisites for the public use.

Though we had taken the extra stage for our exclusive use, we gave a seat to a Virginia gentleman, who wished to proceed as far as Warrenton; and were agreeably entertained by his conversation during the way. In contrasting the backward condition of his native State, with the more advanced prosperity of nearly all the Northern States, he frankly admitted, as most of the candid and well informed Virginians readily do, that the great barrier to Southern improvement was the institution of slavery; which, causing all labour to be performed by the blacks made it disreputable in public opinion for a white man to labour at all. The consequence is, that all the males, except the very lowest, are brought up to the liberal professions, or to live upon the incomes of their plantations; and few enter into any kind of business by which their fortunes can be much improved. Habits of indolence, recklessness, and extravagance, result from this: so that from the want of any steady occupation or pursuit, the Virginian gentlemen pass their time in travelling from south to north, and east to west, during the migratory season, and in hunting, shooting, fishing, racing, and play of various kinds, in the stationary season. Nearly all of them use tobacco, both in chewing and smoking, most of them are fond of their wine, and many drink cordials, juleps, and brandy. They read but little, and that chiefly in books of mere entertainment. They are hot and irascible, though generous to a fault; but at the same time too regardless of the future, and too careless or indifferent about the claims of others upon them; so that a very large number are in debt, and very indifferent as to whether they are ever able to escape from it or not, living this year on advances made on the income of the next, and spending just as much in years of bad crops and low prices, as in years of good crops and high prices; so that most persons leave, at their death, embarrassments to be cleared off by their successors.

The ladies of Virginia, though free from many of the habits of the gentlemen, were described as partaking of much of their character for aversion to labour, love of amusement and pleasure, and recklessness as to expense. A prudent manager of an estate, or a thrifty housewife, would hardly be esteemed in Virginia, and there are few who ever aim at such distinction; but, a desire for equipage and servants, love of dress, fondness for balls and parties, love of watering places and gay assemblages, with rather more than a feminine share of taste for juleps, cordials, and champagne, there being few who do not take one or the other of these more freely than is usual at the North, are prominent traits of character in the upper classes, according to the testimony of a native, who expressed his desire to give as favourable a character of both sexes as he could.

Our road from the Faquier Springs to Warrenton, was an agreeable one, with hilly outlines of background, and gently undulated surface; and after leaving this small but unusually pretty village, which is eight miles from the Springs, we reached, in seven miles more, the village of Buckland, where we found a house of private entertainment, at which everything was clean and inviting; and here we halted.

On the morning of the 16th, we left Bucklands at eight A.M. in a thicker fog than we had yet seen in this country; but it was of short duration, as in less than an hour we had all the warmth and brightness of the Southern autumn, so delicious to the feelings, as well as to the sight. The road was rougher than usual, though the face of the country grew more and more level. We passed, at intervals of about seven miles apart, the two villages of Groveton and Centreville; and seven miles from thence brought us to the larger town of Fairfax, where the County Courts are held. A numerous assemblage of people from the neighbouring country were now in attendance here. Besides the parties having actual business at these Courts, very many of the country residents come into town on those public days, in the hope of meeting their friends, and thus a sort of Social Exchange is established, where, for two or three days in succession, the principal farmers of the county and their families have a reunion several times a year, which maintains their friendly relations, and keeps up a kind feeling among them all.

We dined at the public table about two o'clock, and proceeding onward to Alexandria, a distance of fourteen miles from hence, we reached it at six. The entrance into this place presents a striking contrast with the towns of America generally; these being almost all in a rising and progressively increasing condition, but this is in a falling and gradually decaying state, from the removal or transfer of all its maritime trade to Baltimore, in consequence of the railroads from the

Residence and Tomb of Washington, Mount Vernon, on the Potomac

interior communicating with that city. In the suburbs of Alexandria the houses are almost wholly untenanted, and many are in ruins. Within the city itself, which is large, and planned with great regularity, there are many houses without occupants, and in some of the less frequented streets the grass has grown up so as almost to obscure the pavement; while, in even the most public thoroughfares, there is nothing of the stir and bustle so characteristic of American towns.

We slept at Alexandria, and on the following morning, September 17, paid a visit to Mount Vernon, the estate of General Washington, where he had resided after the stirring scenes of the Revolution, and where he ended his days in retirement and peace. The distance from Alexandria to Mount Vernon is only seven miles, and the road is very agreeable all the way. Nothing can be more beautiful than the site chosen for the mansion and grounds of this delightful residence, which stands on a bold and rounded promontory overhanging the broad Potomac. The river is here about a mile and a half across, and goes on expanding its width gradually, till it exceeds ten miles, before it empties itself into the great bay of the Chesapeake. The mansion itself is not remarkable for size or elegance, but it is well arranged for domestic comfort; it has a broad portico in front, with open colonnades connecting the wings in the rear, and a fine old turret on the centre.

On entering the hall, there is seen suspended within a glass frame, made for the purpose, the old and rusty key of the French Bastille, which was sent to General Washington, by his friend and fellow soldier, Lafayette. Beneath it is an engraving representing the demolition of that scene of suffering and oppression, by the infuriated populace of Paris.

In one of the sitting rooms is a portrait of Lawrence Washington, the brother of the General, dressed in the old English costume of the reign of Queen Anne, with a scarlet coat without collar, small tight cravat, and well coiffed hair. It was the brother to whom the estate originally belonged; and he, being an officer in the British Navy, had served under Admiral Vernon, and named the estate, in honour of that distinguished navigator, Mount Vernon. In the same room were busts of Neckar and Lafayette, and a bust of General Washington, by Houdon, the French sculptor, who executed the full length figure taken from the life, now in the Capitol at Richmond. Among the engravings around the walls were four battle pieces, two by sea, and two by land; the former were the Siege and Relief of Gibraltar, and the latter were the Battle of Bunker Hill, and the Death of General Montgomery. In another of the sitting rooms was a good picture of the present Washington family, a lady and three children, by an American artist; and in the same room, a beautiful marble chimney piece, with exquisite sculpture of Italian workmanship, representing rural subjects. This was presented to the General soon after the signing of the American

Declaration of Independence, by an English gentleman in London, who was a great admirer of his character.

The apartment in which he breathed his last is not shown to visitors, as it is now used as a private bedroom of the family in occupation. In the garden, which is nearly in the same state as when the General took his morning and evening walks through it, we were permitted to take a slip from an orange tree planted by Washington's own hand; and we learnt from the old negro gardener, who had lived here since he was a child, that the cultivation of fruits and flowers was a recreation in which his former master both delighted and excelled.

After examining the dwelling and garden, we visited the tomb. The body of Washington was originally deposited in the old family vault, near the bank of the river, and that of his wife, who died soon after him, was laid in the same spot. But the number of persons belonging to collateral branches of the family, interred in the same place since their death, so crowded the space allotted for the vault, that a new place of burial was determined on. The spot chosen for this purpose, was one in which General Washington had been known to express a wish to be laid, though why that wish was not complied with earlier, does not appear. In 1831, however, the removal of the bodies took place; and in 1837, the body of General Washington was taken up, for the purpose of being transferred from its first coffin, to a fine marble sarcophagus prepared for that purpose, in which it now lies, above the ground.

The sarcophagus is of the ancient Roman shape, of white marble, with a flat cover, and has in its upper part, sculptured in relief, an eagle, with the national escutcheon of America, the stars and stripes of her Union, and the word "Washington" only, beneath it. At the foot of the sarcophagus, on the perpendicular end, is an inscription, recording the gift of it, by T. Struthers, a marblemason of Philadelphia, in 1837. Close beside this sarcophagus of the General, is another, of similar form and material, containing the ashes of his wife, and on it the only inscription that we could perceive was—

Martha, Consort of Washington.

Both of these are above ground, in an open space in front of the family vault, and are seen through a lofty iron gate, over which is an arch of plain brick work, and on its front, an inscription, indicating this to be the burial place of the Washington Family. There is about the whole, however, an air of so much simplicity, that it is difficult for those who have been accustomed to see the splendid mausoleum erected to the memory of rulers, statesmen, and heroes, in the old world reconcile themselves to such a monument as this, for such a man as Washington. But the fame of this deliverer of his country is happily independent of monumental marble, or the pomp and pageantry of sepulchral grandeur; for in the language of Pericles, in his funeral oration over the Greeks who fell at Marathon, "the whole earth is the sepulchre of illustrious men; nor is the epitaph engraved on tombstones in their native land, the sole guardian of their fame; but the memories of their actions in *other countries*, forms a more faithful record in the heart, than any that human hands can fabricate."

From all I have witnessed in this country, I fear the name of Washington is oftener in the mouths, than a veneration for his virtues is in the hearts of his countrymen; and I feel persuaded, that the people of England would go far beyond those of America, in devoting their labour and money towards the erection of a suitable monument to his memory, on the spot that contains his mortal remains.

The whole estate ought to be purchased by the National Government of America, and the residence and the tomb of this Father of his Country ought to be kept up, at the national cost, in a becoming state of repair and preservation. But as it is, with a total neglect on the part of the Government, and a very inadequate attention on the part of the surviving family, it seems likely, in less than a century, to be as completely dilapidated, as the first settlement of the British, at James-Town; though the name of Washington will be honoured in all countries, and to the latest period of time, as long as the history of America shall endure.

On our return to Alexandria, we visited the Museum of that city, where many curious objects of Nature and Art are collected together, and especially relics of Washington, contributed by his family and personal friends. Among these, is the silk robe in which he was baptised when an infant; and a pen knife, which he received from his mother when a boy, and preserved carefully to the end of his life. The anecdote connected with this gift is remarkable. When Admiral Vernon's ship was in the Chesapeake, and Washington was yet a boy, he is said to have gone on board to visit his brother Lawrence, then an officer under the British flag; and to have been so pleased with the ship and a sea life, from the little he had seen of it there, that he assented to Admiral Vernon's proposition to join the ship as a midshipman or volunteer. On communicating this fact to his mother, she expressed great sorrow at his taking such a step without consulting her, but hoped he would recall his engagement. This he consented to do immediately, as he had never disobeyed his parents in any thing; and as a token of her approbation, the penknife was given to him, which he valued so highly, that he then declared his resolution never to part with it, and kept his word.

A masonic apron, and a pair of gloves, the former worked in embroidery by the hands of Madame Lafayette, and presented to Washington by her husband, are also in this Museum; and lastly, the bier on which the coffin of the General rested, at the door of his mansion, before it was taken to the place of his interment. It was said that this bier had been in the family for a century; and that during the General's life, the corpse of every one of his slaves and servants dying on his estate, was laid on it in a coffin at the door, in the same manner as his own, before they were conveyed to the burial ground.

The *first* flag captured by Washington in the Revolutionary war, of beautiful white satin, embroidered with gold, and worked by one of the German princesses for the Hessian regiment from which it was taken, is displayed in this Museum, and is called "Alpha" while, close by it, is the *last* flag captured by Washington in the same war, an English red silk ensign, with the regimental badge and decorations, and this is called "Omega." All these were sent to the Museum by members of the Washington family; their identity is certified by such authorities as are well known on the spot, and leave no doubt of their being genuine.

Among the other curiosities of this collection may be mentioned, the largest piece of brain coral yet known, being upwards of three feet in diameter, brought from the rocks of Bermuda, the skeleton of a horse with three heads, one of a horse, one of a sheep, and one of a dog, the latter less perfect than the two former. There are also several large live eagles, and a beautiful scarlet winged flamingo in the aviary. The key of the Castle of Tripoli, delivered up to Captain Decatur of the American Navy, and a beautiful Roman sword, of undoubted antiquity, found there also, enriches the collection. There is also a model of the French Bastille, and of the guillotines used in the French Revolution; a most curious Greek cross, about seven feet high, and one foot broad, made of more than ten thousand separate pieces of wood united without nails, having the appearance of a hollow network, and being extremely light and elastic, so that it can be bent and made to wave to and fro without breaking. It had been taken from Greece to Smyrna in the Greek revolution, and purchased there by an American gentleman, who presented it to the Museum. A superb Mameluke saddle, of crimson velvet, thickly worked over with gold; several fine Malay creases, some wavy and some poisoned; a collection of Indian weapons generally, including bows, arrows, and scalping knives and many curiosities of art, made up a catalogue of interesting objects, in the examination of which, a visitor might spend several days.

CHAPTER LVI

We left Alexandria at two in the afternoon for Washington, by an extra stage engaged for the purpose. The road lying along the south bank of the Potomac, the prospect all the way was extremely beautiful. The river was covered with small craft, with white sails, and the water being nearly calm, their forms were reflected as in the brightest mirror. When we crossed the river by the long bridge, a mile in length, the view up and down the stream was extremely fine; Fort Washington, the Navy Yard, and the Capitol, being on the right, and Georgetown, and the President's Mansion on the left. But the city itself, when we entered it, seemed like a deserted town, as in reality it is during all the summer and autumn, when the Congress is not in session.

At Washington we took the railroad cars for Baltimore, and went thirty-five miles in about an hour and a half, with great comfort, and at a cheap rate, the fare being only two dollars each. We found excellent accommodations at Barnum's City Hotel, and passed the evening in visiting a few of the families, whose kindness we had experienced on our former stay, and by whom we were most cordially received.

On the following morning, the 18th of September, we left Baltimore, by the railroad, for Philadelphia, in a tremendous storm of rain and hail, which began to fall just as we set out at nine o'clock. As the road continued for some way along the western bank of the Chesapeake, with frequent openings into the bay, and fine sheets of water running up into the land, the ride was full of interest. Two spots that we passed, called Gunpowder Creek, and Bush River, were studded with beautiful villas and cottages, for the summer residences of Baltimore families. Strange juxtaposition of names is as common here, however, as elsewhere in America, for in the short space of a couple of hours, we passed by Gotham, Joppa, and Havre-de-Grace. It was at this last place that we crossed the Susquehannah, a beautiful river, which flows for 570 miles through Pennsylvania before it reaches this spot, and has more lovely valleys in its course than almost any other stream in America. There are already more than 500 miles of navigable canal along its banks, for inland traffic; and the railroads and canals executed by the State of Pennsylvania, to communicate with this stream and its tributaries, already extend over 1,576 miles! The trade in iron, coal, timber, wheat, flour, potash, and various other kinds of produce, on these great highways, is always considerable, and is increasing every month in the year.

After crossing the Susquehannah in an immense steamboat, which took all the baggage-cars on the roof, and might be considered a floating-bridge, we resumed the railroad conveyance to Wilmington, in Delaware, and from thence embarked on the beautiful river of that name for Philadelphia. Our passage up this stream was threatened with some interruption, by the gathering of one of the darkest storms I ever remember to have seen. The sky in the south was as black as pitch, varied only by the deep smoky tinge of the rolling masses of gathering cloud, accumulating in successive ridges or billows one over the other. There were, perhaps, fifty sail of vessels, of different rig and sizes, beating down the bay, and some few coming up before the wind, under full sail at this time; and their white sails, contrasted with the inky background of the picture, looked like pearl or alabaster. At length, the more prudent began to shorten sail, and come to an anchor; but the bolder continuing to carry on, were punished for their temerity, for when the storm burst, it rent their canvass into ribbons, and carried away the masts of several by the board. As the storm swept onward towards our steam vessel, it assumed the appearance of a whirlwind, or water spout, drawing up the water in spiral circles, and covering all the surface of its track with a thick mist or spray. Fortunately it passed about a mile to the eastward of us, for if it had taken our boat, it would have unroofed the light upper deck and awnings; and if any terror had occasioned the passengers, of which there were about 300, to crowd to one side of the deck, rather than the other, we might have been upset. Such, indeed, was the strength of the current of wind, which passed about a mile from us, that it took two small houses in its course, whirled them into the air, and threw around the bricks, beams, windows, doors, and movables, as if they were so many straws, or as if there had been an explosion of gunpowder, and where the two houses stood, nothing remained but their foundations! As these were on one of the small low islands in the Delaware, they were probably not inhabited at the time; if they had been, the inmates could hardly have escaped without injury. For ourselves, we had only a heavy fall of rain, and hail as large as cherries, with sufficient wind to alarm the great mass of the passengers, but not to do any injury. The sound of the thunder was louder than the report of a thousand cannon, and seemed sometimes like the crashing fall of a hundred hills above our heads; while the forked lightning was so vivid, as to produce a momentary sense of blindness after the flash had passed.

When we reached Philadelphia we had more than an hour's drive around to the principal hotels of the city before we could find a bed, every public place of lodging or accommodation being filled with the great number of Southerners waiting here on their way home, to hear of the abatement of the sickness before they proceeded farther, and of merchants and traders from the West, to lay in their winterstocks of goods for sale; so that every house was crowded.

I remained at Philadelphia on the following day, September 1st, to perform the painful duty of attending to the grave the remains of the late venerable and excellent Matthew Carey, one of the most prominent philanthropists of his age. I had enjoyed the pleasure of Mr. Carey's friendship and society on my two former visits to Philadelphia, and heard of his death with deep regret, though he had filled up the measure of his useful and honourable life to the age of eighty, and done more deeds of kindness and charity in that period than most men of the same means. He was a native of Ireland, and came to this country at an early age, but without any other means of acquiring wealth than his own industry. From a journeyman printer, like Franklin, he became the publisher of a newspaper, then its editor and proprietor, and lastly a publishing bookseller, in which capacity, he realized a handsome fortune, and retired from active life, leaving his business to his sons. He was, however, never idle; but, with his pen, and purse, as well as with his personal efforts, he advocated and assisted every benevolent measure presented to him, and originated and supported a great number himself. His latter days indeed were one uninterrupted course of benevolence and charity, and he may fairly be numbered among the Howards of the Western world.

Mr. Carey being a Roman Catholic, his funeral was conducted according to the ritual of that church; and his interment took place in the burial ground of St. Mary's. I attended, with my son, among the personal friends assembled at his residence, and we walked together in the melancholy procession which followed the hearse from his house to the grave, the number of persons joining in this, being upwards of a thousand, and the empty carriages of his friends and acquaintance filling the streets for nearly the whole of the way. The church was crowded, when we reached it with an auditory of more than 2,000 persons; and about 500 found admission with the corpse into the aisles below. The service was very simple, consisting merely of a funeral anthem by the choir, a most feeling and appropriate address by the Catholic priest, to the congregation, over the bier, and a second funeral anthem at its close. The solemn dirge for the dead, played by the full-toned organ, and the mingling of rich and sweet voices in the lamentations and rejoicings which were alternately expressed in the anthem sung, were full of the most touching pathos; and few, I think, could have been present, whether Catholic or Protestant, without having had their hearts penetrated with the solemnity of the scene; and being induced to utter the emphatic prayer, "Lord let me die the death of the righteous; and let my last end be like his."

We left Philadelphia on the morning of the 20th, at seven o'clock, by a steamer for New York, and were as much pleased as ever with the beautiful banks of the Delaware, which present a succession of fertile fields, graceful woods, and pleasant mansions and gardens, all the way up to the pretty little towns of Burlington and Bristol, and thence to Bordentown. Here we landed, to take the railroad cars; and from thence, going across New Jersey, we reached the port of Perth Amboy, and there again embarked in the steam-boat for New York.

The passage through the narrow strait of Staten Island was romantically beautiful; and the fine villas and cottages, seen all the way from the entrance of the strait, up to its opening into the bay, by New Brighton, the fine hotels and-boarding houses there, and the general fertility and verdure of the land on both sides formed a constant succession of exquisite pictures. As we opened the bay of New York, the prospect expanded and became grander, the numerous ships at the Quarantine anchorage, the sight of the Atlantic sea through the Narrows and the distant spires of the city of New York rising in the northern horizon with the numerous vessels, of all sizes and forms under sail, coming and going and the great ocean-steamer, the British Queen, ploughing her way up the harbour, freighted with 200 passengers, and bringing intelligence for which thousands were waiting with anxiety in every part of America all gave great and varied interest to the view.

As we drew nearer to the town, we passed a French brig of war at anchor, from Vera Cruz, and, landing at the wharf in the Hudson river, we proceeded in search of quarters. Here, however, the hotels and boarding-houses were even more crowded than at Philadelphia, from the same causes; and we were three hours employed in making applications to every place known to us in the city, before we could obtain even a single room; and only secured this at last by the conversion of a private parlour, at the Athenæum, into a sitting-room, so thronged was New York in every quarter of the city.

During our stay at New York, we renewed our intercourse with most of our former friends here and were received with all the cordiality we could desire. We found the city gayer, as we thought, than ever; and expensiveness in furniture, dress, and equipages, seemed to be carried much farther than when we were here before. From all that we could learn, however, the prosperity of the city was not so great as usual. There had been more failures, and more winding up of insolvent accounts, than in the preceding year; and many were thought to be even now tottering on the brink of a precipice. But amidst all this, the theatres were never more crowded, the hotels more thronged, or the expenditure in every way more lavish, than at present. Some attributed this to the natural recklessness of desperation; and others accounted for it by the growing laxity of principle, which, every year, according to their view, is getting worse and worse; so that all distinctions in society, between a man who lives prudently and pays all his debts, and one who lives extravagantly and defrauds his creditors, seems fast disappearing. We heard of men living at the rate of 20,000 dollars a year, who were a year or two ago known to be without any capital at all; and of ladies laying out, in a single morning's shopping, 400 dollars in worked cambric pocket handkerchiefs; while the fullness of all the dress and jewellery stores bespoke the large demand made for these materials. According to the testimony of the storekeepers themselves, however, the largest portion of their business was done on credit; and in one house we learnt, that though the city was never before so full of people, nor the people ever more in a spending humour than at present, they had not received more than five per cent in cash, of their whole sales for the last three months; the other ninety-five per cent being entered on the books to the credit of the purchasing parties. The prices of everything, therefore, kept up to the highest standard, to make up for the loss by bad debts which was sure to accrue. Merchants were said to be so embarrassed for want of immediate funds to meet their engagements, that they were raising money by large sacrifices of property, and by paying interest at the rate of two per cent per month, and in some instances at the rate of twenty-five per cent per annum. Nearly all parties, therefore, were losing ground, except the few great capitalists who could advance money at these extravagant rates; and thus increase their wealth from the high interest paid amidst the general distress.

Such was the state of things, as represented to us in almost every circle in which we visited; and yet, amidst it all, the external aspect of the streets, shops, and houses, would lead a stranger to imagine, that every one was basking in the full sunshine of prosperity. The public promenade of Broadway exhibited a greater number of expensively dressed ladies than could be seen in the same space in either London or Paris; and it must be added, much more of feminine beauty. Indeed it may be doubted whether any city in the world contains so many handsome women, in proportion to its population, as New York.

POSTSCRIPT

At the close of the First Series of my Work on the *Northern* Free States of America, (vol. iii. p.582) a Second Series was promised on the *Southern* Slave States, which are less known to the British public. I have accordingly redeemed my pledge, by presenting these Volumes—as the Second Series adverted to—confining them exclusively, as originally intended and announced, to my Travels in the SOUTHERN or Slave States of America.

It remains to be seen, whether this New Series, which goes over so large a portion of un-travelled ground, will enjoy the same flattering reception as the First; and upon that issue will depend whether the remainder of my unpublished Journals, of Travels in the EASTERN States, and in the rich and fertile territories of the WEST, shall follow at some future and convenient period.

There may have been some few, perhaps, who would have preferred a Brief Sketch or Outline of the whole Tour of nearly four years, in a single Series, as they desire only to be *amused*, and therefore they like to "get rapidly over the ground" without waiting to gather much by the way. For such readers there are no lack of Travels, from Captain Head's "Rough Ride over the Pampas" to Colonel Maxwell's "Run through the United States" and "Captain Barclay's Tour of Four Months through America and the Canadas". Those who gallop over a country, or traverse it by railroad and steamboat, may bring their contributions to the stock of public information within a very narrow compass; and, where the object is chiefly to entertain, the labour is light and easy.

My own impression, however, has always been, that, without disparaging the taste or talents of those who supply the public demand with a commodity suited to the literary market of the day, there is abundant room for a more comprehensive Work on America, at least than any that has yet appeared; and it has been an object of ambition with me to present such a Work to the world. To the collector of the facts necessary for such a publication, I believe I may say with truth, that I have devoted more time, and expended more labour, than any who have preceded me in the same path; and it is because the facts collected are more numerous, and the scenes and objects visited more varied than usual, that therefore its limits are unavoidably more extensive.

If the great Republican Union were a country like Spain, or Portugal, or Italy, or Greece, or Palestine, or Egypt, or Belgium, or Holland, or Denmark, or Sweden, it would be easy to examine it in a Summer Trip, and present a full and faithful description of it in a few volumes. But it should be considered, that the Twenty-six States, and Three Territories, now composing the Federal Union, cover as large an extent of area, and embrace as wide a zone of climate and productions, as all the countries I have named, put together. In the various cities, districts, and provinces of the whole, there are continually springing up, from year to year, new developments, new combinations, and new undertakings, of the greatest interest to other countries, because of their probable effects on the commerce of the world. To all which it may be added, that there is more of political, commercial, manufacturing, mining, and agricultural competition, and far more of invention, enterprise, and intellectual activity, in continual exercise among the eighteen millions of people spread over this vast surface than in all the countries I have enumerated, united into one.

For these reasons, more time is required for a careful examination of such an extensive area; and more space is requisite for a full and faithful description of it, than readers are generally aware. And as the rank now enjoyed by the United States as one of the great Powers, whose influence, being cast into the balance, may determine the fate of nations—is such as to make everything connected with its institutions, resources, and prospects, of great interest and importance to the civilized world, I am not without a hope, that my humble endeavours to present as full and faithful an account of all that I examined and observed, during the three years and a half that I passed in traversing every portion of that extensive and beautiful region, may be crowned with present success, and honoured with future respect and commendation.